West's Law School Advisory Board

JESSE H. CHOPER
Professor of Law and Dean Emeritus,
University of California, Berkeley

JOSHUA DRESSLER
Professor of Law, Michael E. Moritz College of Law,
The Ohio State University

YALE KAMISAR
Professor of Law, University of San Diego
Professor of Law Emeritus, University of Michigan

MARY KAY KANE
Professor of Law, Chancellor and Dean Emeritus,
University of California,
Hastings College of the Law

LARRY D. KRAMER
Dean and Professor of Law, Stanford Law School

JONATHAN R. MACEY
Professor of Law, Yale Law School

ARTHUR R. MILLER
University Professor, New York University
Professor of Law Emeritus, Harvard University

GRANT S. NELSON
Professor of Law, Pepperdine University
Professor of Law Emeritus, University of California, Los Angeles

A. BENJAMIN SPENCER
Associate Professor of Law,
Washington & Lee University School of Law

JAMES J. WHITE
Professor of Law, University of Michigan

2010
STUDENTS' GUIDE TO ARTICLE 9
AND RELATED STATUTES

Annotated by

Grace Chiang, Shital Desai, Frank Fogelbach, Kimberly Ann Gertner,
Ilan Hornstein, P. Beth Lloyd, Loren Lowe, Holly N. Mancl,
Gina Najolia, Travis Norton, James Olmsted, Daniel Paisley,
James Parker, Trevor Reid, Eleanor Richmond, Florencia Rueda,
Christopher Rutledge Smith, Shaileen Stillmank, Andrew Thau

Faculty Editors

Larry Bates, David G. Epstein, David Frisch, Ingrid Michelsen
Hillinger, Elizabeth H. McCullough, Douglas K. Moll,
Thomas E. Plank, Mark Wessman

WEST
A Thomson Reuters business

Mat #40889215

Thomson Reuters created this publication to provide you with accurate and authoritative information concerning the subject matter covered. However, this publication was not necessarily prepared by persons licensed to practice law in a particular jurisdiction. Thomson Reuters does not render legal or other professional advice, and this publication is not a substitute for the advice of an attorney. If you require legal or other expert advice, you should seek the services of a competent attorney or other professional.

© West, a Thomson business, 2008
© 2009, Thomson Reuters
    610 Opperman Drive
    Eagan, MN 55123
    Phone Toll Free 1–800–313–9378
Printed in the United States of America

ISBN: 978–0–314–20811–8

First Unofficial Comments for Students

The title of this book, Students' Guide to Article 9 and Related Statutes is appropriate because the book was written in substantial part by law students from Baylor, Boston College, Charleston, Harvard, Houston, New York University, Richmond, Tennessee, and Tulane. Most of the listed authors are law students; most of the work on the original text in this book was done by these student authors and reviewed and edited by professors.

More important, this title is appropriate because we have written this book for you. Drawing on our different experiences in both taking and teaching courses on Article 9 at various law schools, we have tried to make Article 9 easier for you to use and understand.

Article 9 used to be easy. The initial drafts of the original Article 9 were written primarily by Grant Gilmore, a guy with a Ph.D in French Literature who, in his own words did not have even the slightest practical experience in the field.[1] Both students and commercial law professors use the words clear, elegant, graceful and lucid to describe Gilmore and the original Article 9.

No one uses these words to describe the Revised Article 9 which is now the law of the land, and the law of law schools, and the law of bar exams. Revised Article 9 is the product of committees dominated by partners from big firms with big clients whose professional lives are devoted to these big clients and their big, complicated deals. That does not make them bad people.[2] That did make Revised Article 9 a bad statute for law students.

Again, our goal in this book is to make Article 9 better for you. Although some of us speak French and some of us have read literature[3], none of us can claim to be Grant Gilmore. While we can not claim we have made Revised Article 9 clear, elegant, graceful, or lucid, we have made it easier for you to use and understand it by (1) alerting you to important statutory words and phrases with Non–Obvious Definitions and (2) identifying Other UCC Sections to Look to When You Look at Section _____ and (3) explaining what to look for when reading important sections in our Unofficial Comments and more extended commentaries.

David G. Epstein, Editor

*

1. Grant Gilmore, Dedication to Professor Homer Kripke, 56 NYU L. Rev. 9, 10 (1981).
2. Your authors are somewhat divided on this point.
3. And, of course, some of us have stayed at a Holiday Inn Express.

Table of Contents

		Page
Unit 1.	Uniform Commercial Code	1
Unit 2.	Uniform Commercial Code	10
Unit 3.	Uniform Commercial Code	26
Unit 4.	Uniform Commercial Code	35
Unit 5.	More Extended Student Article 9 Comments	364
	More on 9–109 and the sale of receivables	364
	More on 9–203 and attachment	365
	More on 9–204 and floating lien	369
	More on 9–309 and the sale of receivables	370
	More on 9–315 and "authorized"	371
	More on 9–316 and change in location	372
	More on 9–317 and priority	373
	More on 9–320 and sale of collateral	374
	More on 9–322 and sp v. sp priority	375
	More on 9–334 and fixtures	377
	More on 9–335 and accessions	380
	More on 9–601 and rights on default	381
	More on 9–607 and what secured party can do on default	386
	More on 9–608 and default proceeds	393
	More on 9–620 and secured party's keeping collateral	396
	More on 9–621 default notification	403
	More on 9–622 and secured party's keeping collateral	408
	More on consignments	409
	More on leases	411
	More on sales of receivables	413
Unit 6.	Bankruptcy Code	417
Unit 7.	Federal Tax Lien Act (Title 28)	441
Unit 8.	Uniform Fraudulent Transfer Act	448
Unit 9.	Uniform Certificate of Title Act	457

2010
STUDENTS' GUIDE TO ARTICLE 9
AND RELATED STATUTES

*

Unit 1

UNIFORM COMMERCIAL CODE

Article 1
Selected Sections

(Original Version)

PART 1. SHORT TITLE, CONSTRUCTION, APPLICATION AND SUBJECT MATTER OF THE ACT

Sec.
1–102. Purposes; Rules of Construction; Variation by Agreement
1–103. Supplementary General Principles of Law Applicable

PART 2. GENERAL DEFINITIONS AND PRINCIPLES OF INTERPRETATION

1–201. General Definitions
1–203. Obligation of Good Faith
1–204. Time; Reasonable Time; "Seasonably"
1–205. Course of Dealing and Usage of Trade
1–208. Option to Accelerate at Will

PART 1. SHORT TITLE, CONSTRUCTION, APPLICATION AND SUBJECT MATTER OF THE ACT

§ 1–102. Purposes; Rules of Construction; Variation by Agreement

(1) This Act shall be liberally construed and applied to promote its underlying purposes and policies.

(2) Underlying purposes and policies of this Act are

(a) to simplify, clarify and modernize the law governing commercial transactions;

(b) to permit the continued expansion of commercial practices through custom, usage and agreement of the parties;

(c) to make uniform the law among the various jurisdictions.

(3) The effect of provisions of this Act may be varied by agreement, except as otherwise provided in this Act and except that the obligations

of good faith, diligence, reasonableness and care prescribed by this Act may not be disclaimed by agreement but the parties may by agreement determine the standards by which the performance of such obligations is to be measured if such standards are not manifestly unreasonable.

(4) The presence in certain provisions of this Act of the words "unless otherwise agreed" or words of similar import does not imply that the effect of other provisions may not be varied by agreement under subsection (3).

(5) In this Act unless the context otherwise requires

(a) words in the singular number include the plural, and in the plural include the singular;

(b) words of the masculine gender include the feminine and the neuter, and when the sense so indicates words of the neuter gender may refer to any gender.

§ 1–103. Supplementary General Principles of Law Applicable

Unless displaced by the particular provisions of this Act, the principles of law and equity, including the law merchant and the law relative to capacity to contract, principal and agent, estoppel, fraud, misrepresentation, duress, coercion, mistake, bankruptcy, or other validating or invalidating cause shall supplement its provisions.

PART 2. GENERAL DEFINITIONS AND PRINCIPLES OF INTERPRETATION

§ 1–201. General Definitions

Subject to additional definitions contained in the subsequent Articles of this Act which are applicable to specific Articles or Parts thereof, and unless the context otherwise requires, in this Act:

* * *

(3) "Agreement" means the bargain of the parties in fact as found in their language or by implication from other circumstances including course of dealing or usage of trade or course of performance as provided in this Act (Sections 1–205, 2–208, and 2A–207). Whether an agreement has legal consequences is determined by the provisions of this Act, if applicable; otherwise by the law of contracts (Section 1–103). (Compare "Contract".)

* * *

(5) "Bearer" means the person in possession of an instrument, document of title, or certificated security payable to bearer or indorsed in blank.

(6) "Bill of lading" means a document evidencing the receipt of goods for shipment issued by a person engaged in the business of transporting or forwarding goods, and includes an airbill. "Airbill" means a document serving for air transportation as a bill of lading does for marine or rail transportation, and includes an air consignment note or air waybill.

* * *

(9) "Buyer in ordinary course of business" means a person that buys goods in good faith, without knowledge that the sale violates the rights of another person in the goods, and in the ordinary course from a person, other than a pawnbroker, in the business of selling goods of that kind. A person buys goods in the ordinary course if the sale to the person comports with the usual or customary practices in the kind of business in which the seller is engaged or with the seller's own usual or customary practices. * * * A buyer in ordinary course of business may buy for cash, by exchange of other property, or on secured or unsecured credit, and may acquire goods or documents of title under a pre-existing contract for sale. Only a buyer that takes possession of the goods or has a right to recover the goods from the seller under Article 2 may be a buyer in ordinary course of business. A person that acquires goods in a transfer in bulk or as security for or in total or partial satisfaction of a money debt is not a buyer in ordinary course of business.

* * *

(12) "Creditor" includes a general creditor, a secured creditor, a lien creditor and any representative of creditors, including an assignee for the benefit of creditors, a trustee in bankruptcy, a receiver in equity and an executor or administrator of an insolvent debtor's or assignor's estate.

* * *

(15) "Document of title" includes bill of lading, dock warrant, dock receipt, warehouse receipt or order for the delivery of goods, and also any other document which in the regular course of business or financing is treated as adequately evidencing that the person in possession of it is entitled to receive, hold and dispose of the document and the goods it covers. To be a document of title a document must purport to be issued by or addressed to a bailee and purport to cover goods in the bailee's possession which are either identified or are fungible portions of an identified mass.

* * *

(17) "Fungible" with respect to goods or securities means goods or securities of which any unit is, by nature or usage of trade, the equivalent of any other like unit. Goods which are not fungible shall be deemed fungible for the purposes of this Act to the extent that under a particular agreement or document unlike units are treated as equivalents.

* * *

(19) "Good faith" means honesty in fact in the conduct or transaction concerned.

(20) "Holder," with respect to a negotiable instrument, means the person in possession if the instrument is payable to bearer or, in the case of an instrument payable to an identified person, if the identified person is in possession. "Holder" with respect to a document of title means the person in possession if the goods are deliverable to bearer or to the order of the person in possession.

* * *

(23) A person is "insolvent" who either has ceased to pay his debts in the ordinary course of business or cannot pay his debts as they become due or is insolvent within the meaning of the federal bankruptcy law.

(24) "Money" means a medium of exchange authorized or adopted by a domestic or foreign government and includes a monetary unit of account established by an intergovernmental organization or by agreement between two or more nations.

(25) A person has "notice" of a fact when

    (a) he has actual knowledge of it; or

    (b) he has received a notice or notification of it; or

    (c) from all the facts and circumstances known to him at the time in question he has reason to know that it exists.

A person "knows" or has "knowledge" of a fact when he has actual knowledge of it. "Discover" or "learn" or a word or phrase of similar import refers to knowledge rather than to reason to know. The time and circumstances under which a notice or notification may cease to be effective are not determined by this Act.

(26) A person "notifies" or "gives" a notice or notification to another by taking such steps as may be reasonably required to inform the other in ordinary course whether or not such other actually comes to know of it. A person "receives" a notice or notification when

    (a) it comes to his attention; or

    (b) it is duly delivered at the place of business through which the contract was made or at any other place held out by him as the place for receipt of such communications.

(27) Notice, knowledge or a notice or notification received by an organization is effective for a particular transaction from the time when it is brought to the attention of the individual conducting that transaction, and in any event from the time when it would have been brought to his attention if the organization had exercised due diligence. An organization exercises due diligence if it maintains reasonable routines for communicating significant information to the person conducting the transaction and there is reasonable compliance with the routines. Due diligence does not require an individual acting for the organization to communicate information unless such communication is part of his regular duties or unless he has reason to know of the transaction and that the transaction would be materially affected by the information.

(28) "Organization" includes a corporation, government or governmental subdivision or agency, business trust, estate, trust, partnership or association, two or more persons having a joint or common interest, or any other legal or commercial entity.

* * *

(32) "Purchase" includes taking by sale, discount, negotiation, mortgage, pledge, lien, security interest, issue or re-issue, gift, or any other voluntary transaction creating an interest in property.

(33) "Purchaser" means a person who takes by purchase.

(34) "Remedy" means any remedial right to which an aggrieved party is entitled with or without resort to a tribunal.

(35) "Representative" includes an agent, an officer of a corporation or association, and a trustee, executor or administrator of an estate, or any other person empowered to act for another.

(36) "Rights" includes remedies.

(37) "Security interest" means an interest in personal property or fixtures which secures payment or performance of an obligation.

The term also includes any interest of a consignor and a buyer of accounts, chattel paper, a payment intangible, or a promissory note in a transaction that is subject to Article 9. The special property interest of a buyer of goods on identification of those goods to a contract for sale under Section 2–401 is not a "security interest", but a buyer may also acquire a "security interest" by complying with Article 9. Except as otherwise provided in Section 2–505, the right of a seller or lessor of goods under Article 2 or 2A to retain or acquire possession of the goods is not a "security interest", but a seller or lessor may also acquire a "security interest" by complying with Article 9. The retention or reservation of title by a seller of goods notwithstanding shipment or delivery to the buyer (Section 2–401) is limited in effect to a reservation of a "security interest".

Whether a transaction creates a lease or security interest is determined by the facts of each case; however, a transaction creates a security interest if the consideration the lessee is to pay the lessor for the right to possession and use of the goods is an obligation for the term of the lease not subject to termination by the lessee, and

> **(a)** the original term of the lease is equal to or greater than the remaining economic life of the goods,
>
> **(b)** the lessee is bound to renew the lease for the remaining economic life of the goods or is bound to become the owner of the goods,
>
> **(c)** the lessee has an option to renew the lease for the remaining economic life of the goods for no additional consideration or nominal additional consideration upon compliance with the lease agreement, or
>
> **(d)** the lessee has an option to become the owner of the goods for no additional consideration or nominal additional consideration upon compliance with the lease agreement.

A transaction does not create a security interest merely because it provides that

> **(a)** the present value of the consideration the lessee is obligated to pay the lessor for the right to possession and use of the goods is substantially equal to or is greater than the fair market value of the goods at the time the lease is entered into,
>
> **(b)** the lessee assumes risk of loss of the goods, or agrees to pay taxes, insurance, filing, recording, or registration fees, or service or maintenance costs with respect to the goods,

(c) the lessee has an option to renew the lease or to become the owner of the goods,

(d) the lessee has an option to renew the lease for a fixed rent that is equal to or greater than the reasonably predictable fair market rent for the use of the goods for the term of the renewal at the time the option is to be performed, or

(e) the lessee has an option to become the owner of the goods for a fixed price that is equal to or greater than the reasonably predictable fair market value of the goods at the time the option is to be performed.

For purposes of this subsection (37):

(x) Additional consideration is not nominal if (i) when the option to renew the lease is granted to the lessee the rent is stated to be the fair market rent for the use of the goods for the term of the renewal determined at the time the option is to be performed, or (ii) when the option to become the owner of the goods is granted to the lessee the price is stated to be the fair market value of the goods determined at the time the option is to be performed. Additional consideration is nominal if it is less than the lessee's reasonably predictable cost of performing under the lease agreement if the option is not exercised;

(y) "Reasonably predictable" and "remaining economic life of the goods" are to be determined with reference to the facts and circumstances at the time the transaction is entered into; and

(z) "Present value" means the amount as of a date certain of one or more sums payable in the future, discounted to the date certain. The discount is determined by the interest rate specified by the parties if the rate is not manifestly unreasonable at the time the transaction is entered into; otherwise, the discount is determined by a commercially reasonable rate that takes into account the facts and circumstances of each case at the time the transaction was entered into.

(38) "Send" in connection with any writing or notice means to deposit in the mail or deliver for transmission by any other usual means of communication with postage or cost of transmission provided for and properly addressed and in the case of an instrument to an address specified thereon or otherwise agreed, or if there be none to any address reasonable under the circumstances. The receipt of any writing or notice within the time at which it would have arrived if properly sent has the effect of a proper sending.

(39) "Signed" includes any symbol executed or adopted by a party with present intention to authenticate a writing.

* * *

(44) "Value". Except as otherwise provided with respect to negotiable instruments and bank collections (Sections 3–303, 4–210, and 4–211) a person gives "value" for rights if he acquires them

(a) in return for a binding commitment to extend credit or for the extension of immediately available credit whether or not drawn upon and whether or not a chargeback is provided for in the event of difficulties in collection; or

(b) as security for or in total or partial satisfaction of a pre-existing claim; or

(c) by accepting delivery pursuant to a pre-existing contract for purchase; or

(d) generally, in return for any consideration sufficient to support a simple contract.

(45) "Warehouse receipt" means a receipt issued by a person engaged in the business of storing goods for hire.

(46) "Written" or "writing" includes printing, typewriting or any other intentional reduction to tangible form.

§ 1–203. Obligation of Good Faith

Every contract or duty within this Act imposes an obligation of good faith in its performance or enforcement.

§ 1–204. Time; Reasonable Time; "Seasonably"

(1) Whenever this Act requires any action to be taken within a reasonable time, any time which is not manifestly unreasonable may be fixed by agreement.

(2) What is a reasonable time for taking any action depends on the nature, purpose and circumstances of such action.

(3) An action is taken "seasonably" when it is taken at or within the time agreed or if no time is agreed at or within a reasonable time.

§ 1–205. Course of Dealing and Usage of Trade

(1) A course of dealing is a sequence of previous conduct between the parties to a particular transaction which is fairly to be regarded as

establishing a common basis of understanding for interpreting their expressions and other conduct.

(2) A usage of trade is any practice or method of dealing having such regularity of observance in a place, vocation or trade as to justify an expectation that it will be observed with respect to the transaction in question. The existence and scope of such a usage are to be proved as facts. If it is established that such a usage is embodied in a written trade code or similar writing the interpretation of the writing is for the court.

(3) A course of dealing between parties and any usage of trade in the vocation or trade in which they are engaged or of which they are or should be aware give particular meaning to and supplement or qualify terms of an agreement.

(4) The express terms of an agreement and an applicable course of dealing or usage of trade shall be construed wherever reasonable as consistent with each other; but when such construction is unreasonable express terms control both course of dealing and usage of trade and course of dealing controls usage of trade.

(5) An applicable usage of trade in the place where any part of performance is to occur shall be used in interpreting the agreement as to that part of the performance.

(6) Evidence of a relevant usage of trade offered by one party is not admissible unless and until he has given the other party such notice as the court finds sufficient to prevent unfair surprise to the latter.

§ 1–208. Option to Accelerate at Will

A term providing that one party or his successor in interest may accelerate payment or performance or require collateral or additional collateral "at will" or "when he deems himself insecure" or in words of similar import shall be construed to mean that he shall have power to do so only if he in good faith believes that the prospect of payment or performance is impaired. The burden of establishing lack of good faith is on the party against whom the power has been exercised.

Unit 2

UNIFORM COMMERCIAL CODE

Article 1
Selected Sections

(Revised Version)

PART 1. GENERAL PROVISIONS

Sec.
1–102. Scope of Article
1–103. Construction of [Uniform Commercial Code] to Promote Its Purposes and Policies; Applicability of Supplemental Principles of Law

PART 2. GENERAL DEFINITIONS AND PRINCIPLES OF INTERPRETATION

1–201. General Definitions
1–202. Notice; Knowledge
1–203. Lease Distinguished From Security Interest
1–204. Value
1–205. Reasonable Time; Seasonableness

PART 3. TERRITORIAL APPLICABILITY AND GENERAL RULES

1–302. Variation by Agreement
1–303. Course of Performance, Course of Dealing, and Usage of Trade
1–304. Obligation of Good Faith
1–309. Option to Accelerate at Will
1–310. Subordinated Obligations

PART 1. GENERAL PROVISIONS

§ 1–102. Scope of Article

This article applies to a transaction to the extent that it is governed by another article of [the Uniform Commercial Code].

§ 1–103. Construction of [Uniform Commercial Code] to Promote Its Purposes and Policies; Applicability of Supplemental Principles of Law

(a) [The Uniform Commercial Code] must be liberally construed and applied to promote its underlying purposes and policies, which are:

(1) to simplify, clarify, and modernize the law governing commercial transactions;

(2) to permit the continued expansion of commercial practices through custom, usage, and agreement of the parties; and

(3) to make uniform the law among the various jurisdictions.

(b) Unless displaced by the particular provisions of [the Uniform Commercial Code], the principles of law and equity, including the law merchant and the law relative to capacity to contract, principal and agent, estoppel, fraud, misrepresentation, duress, coercion, mistake, bankruptcy, and other validating or invalidating cause supplement its provisions.

PART 2. GENERAL DEFINITIONS AND PRINCIPLES OF INTERPRETATION

§ 1–201. General Definitions

(a) Unless the context otherwise requires, words or phrases defined in this section, or in the additional definitions contained in other articles of [the Uniform Commercial Code] that apply to particular articles or parts thereof, have the meanings stated.

(b) Subject to definitions contained in other articles of [the Uniform Commercial Code] that apply to particular articles or parts thereof:

* * *

(3) "Agreement", as distinguished from "contract", means the bargain of the parties in fact, as found in their language or inferred from other circumstances, including course of performance, course of dealing, or usage of trade as provided in Section 1–303.

(4) "Bank" means a person engaged in the business of banking and includes a savings bank, savings and loan association, credit union, and trust company.

(5) "Bearer" means a person in control of a negotiable electronic document of title or a person in possession of a negotiable instrument, negotiable tangible document of title, or certificated security that is payable to bearer or indorsed in blank.

(6) "Bill of lading" means a document of title evidencing the receipt of goods for shipment issued by a person engaged in the business of directly or indirectly transporting or forwarding goods. The term does not include a warehouse receipt.

* * *

(9) "Buyer in ordinary course of business" means a person that buys goods in good faith, without knowledge that the sale violates the rights of another person in the goods, and in the ordinary course from a person, other than a pawnbroker, in the business of selling goods of that kind. A person buys goods in the ordinary course if the sale to the person comports with the usual or customary practices in the kind of business in which the seller is engaged or with the seller's own usual or customary practices. A person that sells oil, gas, or other minerals at the wellhead or minehead is a person in the business of selling goods of that kind. A buyer in ordinary course of business may buy for cash, by exchange of other property, or on secured or unsecured credit, and may acquire goods or documents of title under a preexisting contract for sale. Only a buyer that takes possession of the goods or has a right to recover the goods from the seller under Article 2 may be a buyer in ordinary course of business. "Buyer in ordinary course of business" does not include a person that acquires goods in a transfer in bulk or as security for or in total or partial satisfaction of a money debt.

* * *

(11) "Consumer" means an individual who enters into a transaction primarily for personal, family, or household purposes.

* * *

(13) "Creditor" includes a general creditor, a secured creditor, a lien creditor, and any representative of creditors, including an assignee for the benefit of creditors, a trustee in bankruptcy, a receiver in equity, and an executor or administrator of an insolvent debtor's or assignor's estate.

* * *

(15) "Delivery", with respect to an electronic document of title means voluntary transfer of control and with respect to an instrument, a tangible document of title, or chattel paper, means voluntary transfer of possession.

(16) "Document of title" means a record (i) that in the regular course of business or financing is treated as adequately evidencing that the person in possession or control of the record is entitled to receive, control, hold, and dispose of the record and the goods the record covers and (ii) that purports to be issued by or addressed to a bailee and to cover goods in the bailee's possession which are either identified or are fungible portions of an identified mass. The term includes a bill of lading, transport document, dock warrant, dock receipt, warehouse receipt, and order for delivery of goods. An electronic document of title means a document of title evidenced by a record consisting of information stored in an electronic medium. A tangible document of title means a document of title evidenced by a record consisting of information that is inscribed on a tangible medium.

* * *

(20) "Good faith," except as otherwise provided in Article 5, means honesty in fact and the observance of reasonable commercial standards of fair dealing.

(21) "Holder" means:

(A) the person in possession of a negotiable instrument that is payable either to bearer or to an identified person that is the person in possession;

(B) the person in possession of a negotiable tangible document of title if the goods are deliverable either to bearer or to the order of the person in possession; or

(C) the person in control of a negotiable electronic document of title.

(22) "Insolvency proceeding" includes an assignment for the benefit of creditors or other proceeding intended to liquidate or rehabilitate the estate of the person involved.

(23) "Insolvent" means:

(A) having generally ceased to pay debts in the ordinary course of business other than as a result of bona fide dispute;

(B) being unable to pay debts as they become due; or

(C) being insolvent within the meaning of federal bankruptcy law.

(24) "Money" means a medium of exchange currently authorized or adopted by a domestic or foreign government. The term includes a monetary unit of account established by an intergovernmental organization or by agreement between two or more countries.

(25) "Organization" means a person other than an individual.

(26) "Party", as distinguished from "third party", means a person that has engaged in a transaction or made an agreement subject to [the Uniform Commercial Code].

(27) "Person" means an individual, corporation, business trust, estate, trust, partnership, limited liability company, association, joint venture, government, governmental subdivision, agency, or instrumentality, public corporation, or any other legal or commercial entity.

(28) "Present value" means the amount as of a date certain of one or more sums payable in the future, discounted to the date certain by use of either an interest rate specified by the parties if that rate is not manifestly unreasonable at the time the transaction is entered into or, if an interest rate is not so specified, a commercially reasonable rate that takes into account the facts and circumstances at the time the transaction is entered into.

(29) "Purchase" means taking by sale, lease, discount, negotiation, mortgage, pledge, lien, security interest, issue or reissue, gift, or any other voluntary transaction creating an interest in property.

(30) "Purchaser" means a person that takes by purchase.

(31) "Record" means information that is inscribed on a tangible medium or that is stored in an electronic or other medium and is retrievable in perceivable form.

(32) "Remedy" means any remedial right to which an aggrieved party is entitled with or without resort to a tribunal.

(33) "Representative" means a person empowered to act for another, including an agent, an officer of a corporation or association, and a trustee, executor, or administrator of an estate.

(34) "Right" includes remedy.

(35) "Security interest" means an interest in personal property or fixtures which secures payment or performance of an obligation. "Security interest" includes any interest of a consignor and a buyer of accounts, chattel paper, a payment intangible, or a promissory note in a transaction that is subject to Article 9. "Security interest" does not include the special property interest of a buyer of goods on identification of those goods to a contract for sale under Section 2–401, but a buyer may also acquire a "security interest" by complying with Article 9. Except as otherwise provided in Section 2–505, the right of a seller or lessor of goods under Article 2 or 2A to retain or acquire possession of the goods is not a "security interest", but a seller or lessor may also acquire a "security interest" by complying with Article 9. The retention or reservation of title by a seller of goods notwithstanding shipment or delivery to the buyer under Section 2–401 is limited in effect to a reservation of a "security interest."

Whether a transaction in the form of a lease creates a "security interest" is determined pursuant to Section 1–203.

(36) "Send" in connection with a writing, record, or notice means:

(A) to deposit in the mail or deliver for transmission by any other usual means of communication with postage or cost of transmission provided for and properly addressed and, in the case of an instrument, to an address specified thereon or otherwise agreed, or if there be none to any address reasonable under the circumstances; or

(B) in any other way to cause to be received any record or notice within the time it would have arrived if properly sent.

(37) "Signed" includes using any symbol executed or adopted with present intention to adopt or accept a writing.

* * *

(39) "Surety" includes a guarantor or other secondary obligor.

* * *

(42) "Warehouse receipt" means a document of title issued by a person engaged in the business of storing goods for hire.

(43) "Writing" includes printing, typewriting, or any other intentional reduction to tangible form. "Written" has a corresponding meaning.

OFFICIAL COMMENT

* * *

9. "Buyer in ordinary course of business." Except for minor stylistic changes, identical to former Section 1–201 (as amended in conjunction with the 1999 revisions to Article 9). The major significance of the phrase lies in Section 2–403 and in the Article on Secured Transactions (Article 9).

The first sentence of paragraph (9) makes clear that a buyer from a pawnbroker cannot be a buyer in ordinary course of business. The second sentence explains what it means to buy "in the ordinary course." The penultimate sentence prevents a buyer that does not have the right to possession as against the seller from being a buyer in ordinary course of business. Concerning when a buyer obtains possessory rights, see Sections 2–502 and 2–716. However, the penultimate sentence is not intended to affect a buyer's status as a buyer in ordinary course of business in cases (such as a "drop shipment") involving delivery by the seller to a person buying from the buyer or a donee from the buyer. The requirement relates to whether *as against the seller* the buyer or one taking through the buyer has possessory rights.

* * *

20. "Good faith." Former Section 1–201(19) defined "good faith" simply as honesty in fact; the definition contained no element of commercial reasonableness. Initially, that definition applied throughout the Code with only one exception. Former Section 2–103(1)(b) provided that

"*in that Article* ... good faith in the case of a merchant means honesty in fact and the observance of reasonable commercial standards of fair dealing in the trade." This alternative definition was limited in applicability though, because it applied only to transactions within the scope of Article 2 and it applied only to merchants.

Over time, however, amendments to the Uniform Commercial Code brought the Article 2 merchant concept of good faith (subjective honesty and objective commercial reasonableness) into other Articles. First, Article 2A explicitly incorporated the Article 2 standard. See Section 2A–103(7). Then, other Articles broadened the applicability of that standard by adopting it for all parties rather than just for merchants. *See, e.g.*, Sections 3–103(a)(4), 4A–105(a)(6), 7–102(a)(6), 8–102(a)(10), and 9–102(a)(43). Finally, Articles 2 and 2A were amended so as to apply the standard to non-merchants as well as merchants. See Sections 2–103(1)(j), 2A–103(1)(m). All of these definitions are comprised of two elements–honesty in fact *and* the observance of reasonable commercial standards of fair dealing. Only revised Article 5 defines "good faith" solely in terms of subjective honesty, and only Article 6 (in the few states that have not chosen to delete the Article) is without definition of good faith. (It should be noted that, while revised Article 6 did not define good faith, Comment 2 to revised Section 6–102 states that "this Article adopts the definition of 'good faith' in Article 1 in all cases, even when the buyer is a merchant.")

Thus, the definition of "good faith" in this section merely confirms what has been the case for a number of years as Articles of the UCC have been amended or revised–the obligation of "good faith," applicable in each Article, is to be interpreted in the context of all Articles except for Article 5 as including both the subjective element of honesty in fact and the objective element of the observance of reasonable commercial standards of fair dealing. As a result, both the subjective and objective elements are part of the standard of "good faith," whether that obligation is specifically referenced in another Article of the Code (other than Article 5) or is provided by this Article.

Of course, as noted in the statutory text, the definition of "good faith" in this section does not apply when the narrower definition of "good faith" in revised Article 5 is applicable.

As noted above, the definition of "good faith" in this section requires not only honesty in fact but also "observance of reasonable commercial standards of fair dealing." Although "fair dealing" is a broad term that must be defined in context, it is clear that it is concerned with the fairness of conduct rather than the care with which an act is performed. This is an entirely different concept than whether a party exercised ordinary care in conducting a transaction. Both concepts are to be determined in the light of reasonable commercial standards, but those standards in each case are directed to different aspects of commercial conduct. See e.g., Sections 3–103(a)(9) and 4–104(c) and Comment 4 to Section 3–103.

* * *

23. "Insolvent." Derived from former Section 1–201. The three tests of insolvency–"generally ceased to pay debts in the ordinary course of business other than as a result of a bona fide dispute as to them," "unable to pay debts as they become due," and "insolvent within the meaning of the federal bankruptcy law"–are expressly set up as alternative tests and must be approached from a commercial standpoint.

* * *

35. "Security Interest." The definition is the first paragraph of the definition of "security interest" in former Section 1–201, with minor stylistic changes. The remaining portion of that definition has been moved to Section 1–203. Note that, because of the scope of Article 9, the term includes the interest of certain outright buyers of certain kinds of property.

* * *

§ 1-202. Notice; Knowledge

(a) Subject to subsection (f), a person has "notice" of a fact if the person:

(1) has actual knowledge of it;

(2) has received a notice or notification of it; or

(3) from all the facts and circumstances known to the person at the time in question, has reason to know that it exists.

(b) "Knowledge" means actual knowledge. "Knows" has a corresponding meaning.

(c) "Discover", "learn", or words of similar import refer to knowledge rather than to reason to know.

(d) A person "notifies" or "gives" a notice or notification to another person by taking such steps as may be reasonably required to inform the other person in ordinary course, whether or not the other person actually comes to know of it.

(e) Subject to subsection (f), a person "receives" a notice or notification when:

(1) it comes to that person's attention; or

(2) it is duly delivered in a form reasonable under the circumstances at the place of business through which the contract was made or at another location held out by that person as the place for receipt of such communications.

(f) Notice, knowledge, or a notice or notification received by an organization is effective for a particular transaction from the time it is brought to the attention of the individual conducting that transaction and, in any event, from the time it would have been brought to the individual's attention if the organization had exercised due diligence. An organization exercises due diligence if it maintains reasonable routines for communicating significant information to the person conducting the transaction and there is reasonable compliance with the routines. Due diligence does not require an individual acting for the organization to communicate information unless the communication is part of the individual's regular duties or the individual has reason to know of the transaction and that the transaction would be materially affected by the information.

§ 1-203. Lease Distinguished From Security Interest

(a) Whether a transaction in the form of a lease creates a lease or security interest is determined by the facts of each case.

(b) A transaction in the form of a lease creates a security interest if the consideration that the lessee is to pay the lessor for the right to possession and use of the goods is an obligation for the term of the lease and is not subject to termination by the lessee, and:

(1) the original term of the lease is equal to or greater than the remaining economic life of the goods;

(2) the lessee is bound to renew the lease for the remaining economic life of the goods or is bound to become the owner of the goods;

(3) the lessee has an option to renew the lease for the remaining economic life of the goods for no additional consideration or for nominal additional consideration upon compliance with the lease agreement; or

(4) the lessee has an option to become the owner of the goods for no additional consideration or for nominal additional consideration upon compliance with the lease agreement.

(c) A transaction in the form of a lease does not create a security interest merely because:

(1) the present value of the consideration the lessee is obligated to pay the lessor for the right to possession and use of the goods is substantially equal to or is greater than the fair market value of the goods at the time the lease is entered into;

(2) the lessee assumes risk of loss of the goods;

(3) the lessee agrees to pay, with respect to the goods, taxes, insurance, filing, recording, or registration fees, or service or maintenance costs;

(4) the lessee has an option to renew the lease or to become the owner of the goods;

(5) the lessee has an option to renew the lease for a fixed rent that is equal to or greater than the reasonably predictable fair market rent for the use of the goods for the term of the renewal at the time the option is to be performed; or

(6) the lessee has an option to become the owner of the goods for a fixed price that is equal to or greater than the reasonably predictable fair market value of the goods at the time the option is to be performed.

(d) Additional consideration is nominal if it is less than the lessee's reasonably predictable cost of performing under the lease agreement if the option is not exercised. Additional consideration is not nominal if:

(1) when the option to renew the lease is granted to the lessee, the rent is stated to be the fair market rent for the use of the goods for the term of the renewal determined at the time the option is to be performed; or

(2) when the option to become the owner of the goods is granted to the lessee, the price is stated to be the fair market value of the goods determined at the time the option is to be performed.

(e) The "remaining economic life of the goods" and "reasonably predictable" fair market rent, fair market value, or cost of performing under the lease agreement must be determined with reference to the facts and circumstances at the time the transaction is entered into.

OFFICIAL COMMENT

Source: Former Section 1–201(37).

Changes from former law: This section is substantively identical to those portions of former Section 1–201(37) that distinguished "true" leases from security interests, except that the definition of "present value" formerly embedded in Section 1–201(37) has been placed in Section 1–201(28).

1. An interest in personal property or fixtures which secures payment or performance of an obligation is a "security interest." See Section 1–201(37). Security interests are sometimes created by transactions in the form of leases. Because it can be difficult to distinguish leases that create security interests from those that do not, this section provides rules that govern the determination of whether a transaction in the form of a lease creates a security interest.

2. One of the reasons it was decided to codify the law with respect to leases was to resolve an issue that created considerable confusion in the courts: what is a lease? The confusion existed, in part, due to the last two sentences of the definition of security interest in the 1978 Official Text of the Act, Section 1–201(37). The confusion was compounded by the rather considerable change in the federal, state and local tax laws and accounting rules as they relate to leases of goods. The answer is important because the definition of lease determines not only the rights and remedies of the parties to the lease but also those of third parties. If a transaction creates a lease and not a security interest, the lessee's interest in the goods is limited to its leasehold estate; the residual interest in the goods belongs to the lessor. This has significant implications to the lessee's creditors. "On common law theory, the lessor, since he has not parted with title, is entitled to full protection against the lessee's creditors and trustee in bankruptcy...." 1 G. Gilmore, *Security Interests in Personal Property* Section 3.6, at 76 (1965).

Under pre-UCC chattel security law there was generally no requirement that the lessor file the lease, a financing statement, or the like, to enforce the lease agreement against the lessee or any third party; the Article on Secured Transactions (Article 9) did not change the common law in that respect. Coogan, Leasing and the Uniform Commercial Code, in *Equipment Leasing—Leveraged Leasing* 681, 700 n.25, 729 n.80 (2d ed.1980). The Article on Leases (Article 2A) did not change the law in that respect, except for leases of fixtures. Section 2A–309. An examination of the common law will not provide an adequate answer to the question of what is a lease. The definition of security interest in Section 1–201(37) of the 1978 Official Text of the Act provided that the Article on Secured Transactions (Article 9) governs security interests disguised as leases, *i.e.*, leases intended as security; however, the definition became vague and outmoded.

Lease is defined in Article 2A as a transfer of the right to possession and use of goods for a term, in return for consideration. Section 2A–103(1)(j). The definition continues by stating that the retention or creation of a security interest is not a lease. Thus, the task of sharpening the line between true leases and security interests disguised as leases continues to be a function of this Article.

This section begins where Section 1–201(35) leaves off. It draws a sharper line between leases and security interests disguised as leases to create greater certainty in commercial transactions.

Prior to enactment of the rules now codified in this section, the 1978 Official Text of Section 1–201(37) provided that whether a lease was intended as security (*i.e.*, a security interest disguised as a lease) was to be determined from the facts of each case; however, (a) the inclusion of an option to purchase did not itself make the lease one intended for security, and (b) an agreement that upon compliance with the terms of the lease the lessee would become, or had the option to become, the owner of the property for no additional consideration, or for a nominal consideration, did make the lease one intended for security.

Reference to the intent of the parties to create a lease or security interest led to unfortunate results. In discovering intent, courts relied upon factors that were thought to be more consistent with sales or loans than leases. Most of these criteria, however, were as applicable to true leases as to security interests. Examples include the typical net lease provisions, a purported lessor's lack of storage facilities or its character as a financing party rather than a dealer in goods. Accordingly, this section contains no reference to the parties' intent.

Subsections (a) and (b) were originally taken from Section 1(2) of the Uniform Conditional Sales Act (act withdrawn 1943), modified to reflect current leasing practice. Thus, reference to the case law prior to the incorporation of those concepts in this article will provide a useful source of precedent. Gilmore, *Security Law, Formalism and Article 9*, 47 Neb. L.Rev. 659, 671 (1968). Whether a transaction creates a lease or a security interest continues to be determined by the facts of each case. Subsection (b) further provides that a transaction creates a security interest if the lessee has an obligation to continue paying consideration for the term of the lease, if the obligation is not terminable by the lessee (thus correcting early statutory gloss, *e.g., In re Royer's Bakery, Inc.*, 1 U.C.C. Rep.Serv. (Callaghan) 342 (Bankr.E.D.Pa.1963)) and if one of four additional tests is met. The first of these four tests, subparagraph (1), is that the original lease term is equal to or greater than the remaining economic life of the goods. The second of these tests, subparagraph (2), is that the lessee is either bound to renew the lease for the remaining economic life of the goods or to become the owner of the goods. *In re Gehrke Enters.*, 1 Bankr. 647, 651–52 (Bankr.W.D.Wis.1979). The third of these tests, subparagraph (3), is whether the lessee has an option to renew the lease for the remaining economic life of the goods for no additional consideration or for nominal additional consideration, which is defined later in this section. *In re Celeryvale Transp.*, 44 Bankr. 1007, 1014–15 (Bankr.E.D.Tenn.1984). The fourth of these tests, subparagraph (4), is whether the lessee has an option to become the owner of the goods for no additional consideration or for nominal additional consideration. All of these tests focus on economics, not the intent of the parties. *In re Berge*, 32 Bankr. 370, 371–73 (Bankr.W.D.Wis.1983).

The focus on economics is reinforced by subsection (c). It states that a transaction does not create a security interest merely because the transaction has certain characteristics listed therein. Subparagraph (1) has no statutory derivative; it states that a full payout lease does not *per se* create a security interest. *Rushton v. Shea*, 419 F.Supp. 1349, 1365 (D.Del. 1976). Subparagraphs (2) and (3) provide the same regarding the provisions of the typical net lease. *Compare All–States Leasing Co. v. Ochs*, 42 Or.App. 319, 600 P.2d 899 (Ct.App.1979), *with In re Tillery*, 571 F.2d 1361 (5th Cir.1978). Subparagraph (4) restates and expands the provisions of the 1978 Official Text of

Section 1–201(37) to make clear that the option can be to buy or renew. Subparagraphs (5) and (6) treat fixed price options and provide that fair market value must be determined at the time the transaction is entered into. *Compare Arnold Mach. Co. v. Balls*, 624 P.2d 678 (Utah 1981), *with Aoki v. Shepherd Mach. Co.*, 665 F.2d 941 (9th Cir.1982).

The relationship of subsection (b) to subsection (c) deserves to be explored. The fixed price purchase option provides a useful example. A fixed price purchase option in a lease does not of itself create a security interest. This is particularly true if the fixed price is equal to or greater than the reasonably predictable fair market value of the goods at the time the option is to be performed. A security interest is created only if the option price is nominal and the conditions stated in the introduction to the second paragraph of this subsection are met. There is a set of purchase options whose fixed price is less than fair market value but greater than nominal that must be determined on the facts of each case to ascertain whether the transaction in which the option is included creates a lease or a security interest.

It was possible to provide for various other permutations and combinations with respect to options to purchase and renew. For example, this section could have stated a rule to govern the facts of *In re Marhoefer Packing Co.*, 674 F.2d 1139 (7th Cir.1982). This was not done because it would unnecessarily complicate the definition. Further development of this rule is left to the courts.

Subsections (d) and (e) provide definitions and rules of construction.

§ 1–204. Value

Except as otherwise provided in Articles 3, 4, [and] 5, [and 6], a person gives value for rights if the person acquires them:

(1) in return for a binding commitment to extend credit or for the extension of immediately available credit, whether or not drawn upon and whether or not a charge-back is provided for in the event of difficulties in collection;

(2) as security for, or in total or partial satisfaction of, a preexisting claim;

(3) by accepting delivery under a preexisting contract for purchase; or

(4) in return for any consideration sufficient to support a simple contract.

§ 1–205. Reasonable Time; Seasonableness

(a) Whether a time for taking an action required by [the Uniform Commercial Code] is reasonable depends on the nature, purpose, and circumstances of the action.

(b) An action is taken seasonably if it is taken at or within the time agreed or, if no time is agreed, at or within a reasonable time.

PART 3. TERRITORIAL APPLICABILITY AND GENERAL RULES

§ 1–302. Variation by Agreement

(a) Except as otherwise provided in subsection (b) or elsewhere in [the Uniform Commercial Code], the effect of provisions of [the Uniform Commercial Code] may be varied by agreement.

(b) The obligations of good faith, diligence, reasonableness, and care prescribed by [the Uniform Commercial Code] may not be disclaimed by agreement. The parties, by agreement, may determine the standards by which the performance of those obligations is to be measured if those standards are not manifestly unreasonable. Whenever [the Uniform Commercial Code] requires an action to be taken within a reasonable time, a time that is not manifestly unreasonable may be fixed by agreement.

(c) The presence in certain provisions of [the Uniform Commercial Code] of the phrase "unless otherwise agreed", or words of similar import, does not imply that the effect of other provisions may not be varied by agreement under this section.

* * *

§ 1–303. Course of Performance, Course of Dealing, and Usage of Trade

(a) A "course of performance" is a sequence of conduct between the parties to a particular transaction that exists if:

  (1) the agreement of the parties with respect to the transaction involves repeated occasions for performance by a party; and

  (2) the other party, with knowledge of the nature of the performance and opportunity for objection to it, accepts the performance or acquiesces in it without objection.

(b) A "course of dealing" is a sequence of conduct concerning previous transactions between the parties to a particular transaction that is fairly to be regarded as establishing a common basis of understanding for interpreting their expressions and other conduct.

(c) A "usage of trade" is any practice or method of dealing having such regularity of observance in a place, vocation, or trade as to justify an expectation that it will be observed with respect to the transaction in question. The existence and scope of such a usage must be proved as facts. If it is established that such a usage is embodied in a trade code or similar record, the interpretation of the record is a question of law.

(d) A course of performance or course of dealing between the parties or usage of trade in the vocation or trade in which they are engaged or of which they are or should be aware is relevant in ascertaining the meaning of the parties' agreement, may give particular meaning to specific terms of the agreement, and may supplement or qualify the terms of the agreement. A usage of trade applicable in the place in which part of the performance under the agreement is to occur may be so utilized as to that part of the performance.

(e) Except as otherwise provided in subsection (f), the express terms of an agreement and any applicable course of performance, course of dealing, or usage of trade must be construed whenever reasonable as consistent with each other. If such a construction is unreasonable:

(1) express terms prevail over course of performance, course of dealing, and usage of trade;

(2) course of performance prevails over course of dealing and usage of trade; and

(3) course of dealing prevails over usage of trade.

(f) Subject to Section 2–209, a course of performance is relevant to show a waiver or modification of any term inconsistent with the course of performance.

(g) Evidence of a relevant usage of trade offered by one party is not admissible unless that party has given the other party notice that the court finds sufficient to prevent unfair surprise to the other party.

§ 1–304. Obligation of Good Faith

Every contract or duty within [the Uniform Commercial Code] imposes an obligation of good faith in its performance and enforcement.

§ 1–309. Option to Accelerate at Will

A term providing that one party or that party's successor in interest may accelerate payment or performance or require collateral or additional collateral "at will" or when the party "deems itself insecure," or words of similar import, means that the party has power to do so only if that party in good faith believes that the prospect of payment or performance is impaired. The burden of establishing lack of good faith is on the party against which the power has been exercised.

OFFICIAL COMMENT

Source: Former Section 1–208.

Changes from former law: Except for minor stylistic changes, this section is identical to former Section 1–208.

1. The common use of acceleration clauses in many transactions governed by the Uniform Commercial Code, including sales of goods on credit, notes payable at a definite time, and secured transactions, raises an issue as to the effect to be given to a clause that seemingly grants the power to accelerate at the whim and caprice of one party. This section is intended to make clear that despite language that might be so construed and which further might be held to make the agreement void as against public policy or to make the contract illusory or too indefinite for enforcement, the option is to be exercised only in the good faith belief that the prospect of payment or performance is impaired.

Obviously this section has no application to demand instruments or obligations whose very nature permits call at any time with or without reason. This section applies only to an obligation of payment or performance which in the first instance is due at a future date.

§ 1–310. Subordinated Obligations

An obligation may be issued as subordinated to performance of another obligation of the person obligated, or a creditor may subordinate its right to performance of an obligation by agreement with either the person obligated or another creditor of the person obligated. Subordination does not create a security interest as against either the common debtor or a subordinated creditor.

OFFICIAL COMMENT

Source: Former Section 1–209.

Changes from former law: This section is substantively identical to former Section 1–209. The language in that section stating that it "shall be construed as declaring the law as it existed prior to the enactment of this section and not as modifying it" has been deleted.

1. Billions of dollars of subordinated debt are held by the public and by institutional investors. Commonly, the subordinated debt is subordinated on issue or acquisition and is evidenced by an investment security or by a negotiable or nonnegotiable note. Debt is also sometimes subordinated after it arises, either by agreement between the subordinating creditor and the debtor, by agreement between two creditors of the same debtor, or by agreement of all three parties. The subordinated creditor may be a stockholder or other "insider" interested in the common debtor; the subordinated debt may consist of accounts or other rights to payment not evidenced by any instrument. All such cases are included in the terms "subordinated obligation," "subordination," and "subordinated creditor."

2. Subordination agreements are enforceable between the parties as contracts; and in the bankruptcy of the common debtor dividends otherwise payable to the subordinated creditor are turned over to the superior creditor. This "turnover" practice has on occasion been explained in terms of "equitable lien," "equitable assignment," or "constructive trust," but whatever the label the practice is essentially an equitable remedy and does not mean that there is a transaction "that creates a security interest in personal property ... by contract" or a "sale of accounts, chattel paper, payment intangibles, or promissory notes" within the meaning of Section 9–109. On the other hand, nothing in this section prevents one creditor from assigning his rights to another creditor of the same debtor in such a way as to create a security interest within Article 9, where the parties so intend.

3. The enforcement of subordination agreements is largely left to supplementa-

ry principles under Section 1–103. If the subordinated debt is evidenced by a certificated security, Section 8–202(a) authorizes enforcement against purchasers on terms stated or referred to on the security certificate. If the fact of subordination is noted on a negotiable instrument, a holder under Sections 3–302 and 3–306 is subject to the term because notice precludes him from taking free of the subordination. Sections 3–302(3)(a), 3–306, and 8–317 severely limit the rights of levying creditors of a subordinated creditor in such cases.

Unit 3

UNIFORM COMMERCIAL CODE

Article 2

Selected Sections

(Original Version)

PART 1. SHORT TITLE, GENERAL CONSTRUCTION AND SUBJECT MATTER

Sec.
2–102. Scope; Certain Security and Other Transactions Excluded from this Article
2–105. Definitions: Transferability; "Goods"; "Future" Goods; "Lot"; "Commercial Unit"
2–106. Definitions: "Contract"; "Agreement"; "Contract for Sale"; "Sale"; "Present Sale"; "Conforming" to Contract; "Termination"; "Cancellation"

PART 4. TITLE, CREDITORS, AND GOOD–FAITH PURCHASERS

2–401. Passing of Title; Reservation for Security; Limited Application of This Section
2–402. Rights of Seller's Creditors Against Sold Goods
2–403. Power to Transfer; Good Faith Purchase of Goods; "Entrusting"

PART 5. PERFORMANCE

2–501. Insurable Interest in Goods; Manner of Identification of Goods
2–503. Manner of Seller's Tender of Delivery
2–507. Effect of Seller's Tender; Delivery on Condition
2–511. Tender of Payment by Buyer; Payment by Check

PART 7. REMEDIES

2–702. Seller's Remedies on Discovery of Buyer's Insolvency
2–705. Seller's Stoppage of Delivery in Transit or Otherwise

PART 1. SHORT TITLE, GENERAL CONSTRUCTION AND SUBJECT MATTER

§ 2–102. Scope; Certain Security and Other Transactions Excluded From This Article

Unless the context otherwise requires, this Article applies to transactions in goods; it does not apply to any transaction which although in the form of an unconditional contract to sell or present sale is intended to operate only as a security transaction nor does this Article impair or repeal any statute regulating sales to consumers, farmers or other specified classes of buyers.

§ 2–105. Definitions: Transferability; "Goods"; "Future" Goods; "Lot"; "Commercial Unit"

(1) "Goods" means all things (including specially manufactured goods) which are movable at the time of identification to the contract for sale other than the money in which the price is to be paid, investment securities (Article 8) and things in action. "Goods" also includes the unborn young of animals and growing crops and other identified things attached to realty as described in the section on goods to be severed from realty (Section 2–107).

(2) Goods must be both existing and identified before any interest in them can pass. Goods which are not both existing and identified are "future" goods. A purported present sale of future goods or of any interest therein operates as a contract to sell.

(3) There may be a sale of a part interest in existing identified goods.

(4) An undivided share in an identified bulk of fungible goods is sufficiently identified to be sold although the quantity of the bulk is not determined. Any agreed proportion of such a bulk or any quantity thereof agreed upon by number, weight or other measure may to the extent of the seller's interest in the bulk be sold to the buyer who then becomes an owner in common.

(5) "Lot" means a parcel or a single article which is the subject matter of a separate sale or delivery, whether or not it is sufficient to perform the contract.

(6) "Commercial unit" means such a unit of goods as by commercial usage is a single whole for purposes of sale and division of which materially impairs its character or value on the market or in use. A commercial unit may be a single article (as a machine) or a set of articles (as a suite of furniture or an assortment of sizes) or a quantity (as a bale, gross, or carload) or any other unit treated in use or in the relevant market as a single whole.

§ 2–106. Definitions: "Contract"; "Agreement"; "Contract for Sale"; "Sale"; "Present Sale"; "Conforming" to Contract; "Termination"; "Cancellation"

(1) In this Article unless the context otherwise requires "contract" and "agreement" are limited to those relating to the present or future sale of goods. "Contract for sale" includes both a present sale of goods and a contract to sell goods at a future time. A "sale" consists in the passing of title from the seller to the buyer for a price (Section 2–401). A "present sale" means a sale which is accomplished by the making of the contract.

(2) Goods or conduct including any part of a performance are "conforming" or conform to the contract when they are in accordance with the obligations under the contract.

(3) "Termination" occurs when either party pursuant to a power created by agreement or law puts an end to the contract otherwise than for its breach. On "termination" all obligations which are still executory on both sides are discharged but any right based on prior breach or performance survives.

(4) "Cancellation" occurs when either party puts an end to the contract for breach by the other and its effect is the same as that of "termination" except that the cancelling party also retains any remedy for breach of the whole contract or any unperformed balance.

PART 4. TITLE, CREDITORS, AND GOOD–FAITH PURCHASERS

§ 2–401. Passing of Title; Reservation for Security; Limited Application of This Section

Each provision of this Article with regard to the rights, obligations, and remedies of the seller, the buyer, purchasers, or other third parties applies irrespective of title to the goods except where the provision refers to such title. Insofar as situations are not covered by the other provisions of this Article and matters concerning title become material, the following rules apply:

(1) Title to goods cannot pass under a contract for sale prior to their identification to the contract (Section 2–501), and unless otherwise explicitly agreed, the buyer acquires by their identification a special property as limited by this Act. Any retention or reservation by the seller of the title (property) in goods shipped or delivered to

the buyer is limited in effect to a reservation of a security interest. Subject to these provisions and to Article 9, title to goods passes from the seller to the buyer in any manner and on any conditions explicitly agreed on by the parties.

(2) Unless otherwise explicitly agreed title passes to the buyer at the time and place at which the seller completes performance with reference to the delivery of the goods, despite any reservation of a security interest and even if a document of title is to be delivered at a different time or place; and in particular and despite any reservation of a security interest by the bill of lading:

(a) if the contract requires or authorizes the seller to send the goods to the buyer but does not require the seller to deliver them at destination, title passes to the buyer at the time and place of shipment; but

(b) if the contract requires delivery at destination, title passes on tender there.

(3) Unless otherwise explicitly agreed, if delivery is to be made without moving the goods,

(a) if the seller is to deliver a tangible document of title, title passes at the time when and the place where the seller delivers the document, and if the seller is to deliver an electronic document of title, title passes when the seller delivers the document; or

(b) if the goods are at the time of contracting already identified and no documents of title are to be delivered, title passes at the time and place of contracting.

(4) A rejection or other refusal by the buyer to receive or retain the goods, whether or not justified, or a justified revocation of acceptance revests title to the goods in the seller. Such revesting occurs by operation of law and is not a "sale".

§ 2–402. Rights of Seller's Creditors Against Sold Goods

(1) Except as provided in subsections (2) and (3), rights of unsecured creditors of the seller with respect to goods which have been identified to a contract for sale are subject to the buyer's rights to recover the goods under this Article (Sections 2–502 and 2–716).

(2) A creditor of the seller may treat a sale or an identification of goods to a contract for sale as void if as against him a retention of possession by the seller is fraudulent under any rule of law of the state where the goods are situated, except that retention of possession in good faith and current course of trade by a merchant-seller for a commercially reasonable time after a sale or identification is not fraudulent.

(3) Nothing in this Article shall be deemed to impair the rights of creditors of the seller

(a) under the provisions of the Article on Secured Transactions (Article 9); or

(b) where identification to the contract or delivery is made not in current course of trade but in satisfaction of or as security for a pre-existing claim for money, security or the like and is made under circumstances which under any rule of law of the state where the goods are situated would apart from this Article constitute the transaction a fraudulent transfer or voidable preference.

§ 2–403. Power to Transfer; Good Faith Purchase of Goods; "Entrusting"

(1) A purchaser of goods acquires all title which his transferor had or had power to transfer except that a purchaser of a limited interest acquires rights only to the extent of the interest purchased. A person with voidable title has power to transfer a good title to a good faith purchaser for value. When goods have been delivered under a transaction of purchase the purchaser has such power even though

(a) the transferor was deceived as to the identity of the purchaser, or

(b) the delivery was in exchange for a check which is later dishonored, or

(c) it was agreed that the transaction was to be a "cash sale", or

(d) the delivery was procured through fraud punishable as larcenous under the criminal law.

(2) Any entrusting of possession of goods to a merchant who deals in goods of that kind gives him power to transfer all rights of the entruster to a buyer in ordinary course of business.

(3) "Entrusting" includes any delivery and any acquiescence in retention of possession regardless of any condition expressed between the parties to the delivery or acquiescence and regardless of whether the procurement of the entrusting or the possessor's disposition of the goods have been such as to be larcenous under the criminal law.

[*Publisher's Editorial Note: If a state adopts the repealer of Article 6—Bulk Transfers (Alternative A), subsec. (4) should read as follows:*]

(4) The rights of other purchasers of goods and of lien creditors are governed by the Articles on Secured Transactions (Article 9) and Documents of Title (Article 7).

[*Publisher's Editorial Note: If a state adopts Revised Article 6—Bulk Sales (Alternative B), subsec. (4) should read as follows:*]

(4) The rights of other purchasers of goods and of lien creditors are governed by the Articles on Secured Transactions (Article 9), Bulk Sales (Article 6) and Documents of Title (Article 7).

OFFICIAL COMMENT

* * *

4. Except as provided in subsection (1), the rights of purchasers other than buyers in ordinary course are left to the Articles on Secured Transactions, Documents of Title, and Bulk Sales.

PART 5. PERFORMANCE

§ 2–501. Insurable Interest in Goods; Manner of Identification of Goods

(1) The buyer obtains a special property and an insurable interest in goods by identification of existing goods as goods to which the contract refers even though the goods so identified are non-conforming and he has an option to return or reject them. Such identification can be made at any time and in any manner explicitly agreed to by the parties. In the absence of explicit agreement identification occurs

(a) when the contract is made if it is for the sale of goods already existing and identified;

(b) if the contract is for the sale of future goods other than those described in paragraph (c), when goods are shipped, marked or otherwise designated by the seller as goods to which the contract refers;

(c) when the crops are planted or otherwise become growing crops or the young are conceived if the contract is for the sale of unborn young to be born within twelve months after contracting or for the sale of crops to be harvested within twelve months or the next normal harvest season after contracting whichever is longer.

(2) The seller retains an insurable interest in goods so long as title to or any security interest in the goods remains in him and where the identification is by the seller alone he may until default or insolvency or notification to the buyer that the identification is final substitute other goods for those identified.

(3) Nothing in this section impairs any insurable interest recognized under any other statute or rule of law.

§ 2–502. Buyer's Right to Goods on Seller's Insolvency.

(1) Subject to subsections (2) and (3) and even though the goods have not been shipped a buyer who has paid a part or all of the price of goods in which he has a special property under the provisions of the immediately preceding section may on making and keeping good a tender of any unpaid portion of their price recover them from the seller if:

  (a) in the case of goods bought for personal, family, or household purposes, the seller repudiates or fails to deliver as required by the contract; or

  (b) in all cases, the seller becomes insolvent within ten days after receipt of the first installment on their price.

(2) The buyer's right to recover the goods under subsection (1)(a) vests upon acquisition of a special property, even if the seller had not then repudiated or failed to deliver.

(3) If the identification creating his special property has been made by the buyer he acquires the right to recover the goods only if they conform to the contract for sale.

OFFICIAL COMMENT

* * *

2. The question of whether the buyer also acquires a security interest in identified goods and has rights to the goods when insolvency takes place after the ten-day period provided in this section depends upon compliance with the provisions of the Article on Secured Transactions (Article 9).

3. Under subsection (2), the buyer's right to recover consumer goods under subsection (1)(a) vests upon acquisition of a special property, which occurs upon identification of the goods to the contract. See Section 2–501. Inasmuch as a secured party normally acquires no greater rights in its collateral that its debtor had or had power to convey, see Section 2–403(1) (first sentence), a buyer who acquires a right to recover under this section will take free of a security interest created by the seller if it attaches to the goods after the goods have been identified to the contract. The buyer will take free, even if the buyer does not buy in ordinary course and even if the security interest is perfected. Of course, to the extent that the buyer pays the price after the security interest attaches, the payments will constitute proceeds of the security interest.

* * *

§ 2–507. Effect of Seller's Tender; Delivery on Condition

(1) Tender of delivery is a condition to the buyer's duty to accept the goods and, unless otherwise agreed, to his duty to pay for them.

Tender entitles the seller to acceptance of the goods and to payment according to the contract.

(2) Where payment is due and demanded on the delivery to the buyer of goods or documents of title, his right as against the seller to retain or dispose of them is conditional upon his making the payment due.

OFFICIAL COMMENT

* * *

3. Subsection (2) deals with the effect of a conditional delivery by the seller and in such a situation makes the buyer's "right as against the seller" conditional upon payment. These words are used as words of limitation to conform with the policy set forth in the bona fide purchase sections of this Article. Should the seller after making such a conditional delivery fail to follow up his rights, the condition is waived. This subsection (2) codifies the cash seller's right of reclamation which is in the nature of a lien. There is no specific time limit for a cash seller to exercise the right of reclamation. However, the right will be defeated by delay causing prejudice to the buyer, waiver, estoppel, or ratification of the buyer's right to retain possession. Common law rules and precedents governing such principles are applicable (Section 1–103). If third parties are involved, Section 2–403(1) protects good faith purchasers.

§ 2–511. Tender of Payment by Buyer; Payment by Check

(1) Unless otherwise agreed tender of payment is a condition to the seller's duty to tender and complete any delivery.

(2) Tender of payment is sufficient when made by any means or in any manner current in the ordinary course of business unless the seller demands payment in legal tender and gives any extension of time reasonably necessary to procure it.

(3) Subject to the provisions of this Act on the effect of an instrument on an obligation (Section 3–310), payment by check is conditional and is defeated as between the parties by dishonor of the check on due presentment.

PART 7. REMEDIES

§ 2–702. Seller's Remedies on Discovery of Buyer's Insolvency

(1) Where the seller discovers the buyer to be insolvent he may refuse delivery except for cash including payment for all goods theretofore delivered under the contract, and stop delivery under this Article (Section 2–705).

(2) Where the seller discovers that the buyer has received goods on credit while insolvent he may reclaim the goods upon demand made within ten days after the receipt, but if misrepresentation of solvency has been made to the particular seller in writing within three months before delivery the ten day limitation does not apply. Except as provided in this subsection the seller may not base a right to reclaim goods on the buyer's fraudulent or innocent misrepresentation of solvency or of intent to pay.

(3) The seller's right to reclaim under subsection (2) is subject to the rights of a buyer in ordinary course or other good faith purchaser under this Article (Section 2–403). Successful reclamation of goods excludes all other remedies with respect to them.

§ 2–705. Seller's Stoppage of Delivery in Transit or Otherwise

(1) A seller may stop delivery of goods in the possession of a carrier or other bailee if the seller discovers the buyer to be insolvent (Section 2–702) or if the buyer repudiates or fails to make a payment due before delivery or if for any other reason the seller has a right to withhold or reclaim the goods.

(2) As against such buyer the seller may stop delivery until:

(a) receipt of the goods by the buyer;

(b) acknowledgment to the buyer by any bailee of the goods, except a carrier, that the bailee holds the goods for the buyer;

(c) such acknowledgment to the buyer by a carrier by reshipment or as warehouse; or

(d) negotiation to the buyer of any negotiable document of title covering the goods.

(3)(a) To stop delivery the seller must so notify as to enable the bailee by reasonable diligence to prevent delivery of the goods.

(b) After such notification the bailee must hold and deliver the goods according to the directions of the seller but the seller is liable to the bailee for any ensuing charges or damages.

(c) If a negotiable document of title has been issued for goods, the bailee is not obliged to obey a notification to stop until surrender of possession or control of the document.

(d) A carrier that has issued a nonnegotiable bill of lading is not obliged to obey a notification to stop received from a person other than the consignor.

Unit 4

UNIFORM COMMERCIAL CODE
Article 9
Article 9 was revised in 1999.

PART 1. GENERAL PROVISIONS

[SUBPART 1. SHORT TITLE, DEFINITIONS, AND GENERAL CONCEPTS]

Sec.
9–101. Short Title
9–102. Definitions and Index of Definitions
9–103. Purchase-Money Security Interest; Application of Payments; Burden of Establishing
9–104. Control of Deposit Account
9–105. Control of Electronic Chattel Paper
9–106. Control of Investment Property
9–107. Control of Letter-of-Credit Right
9–108. Sufficiency of Description

[SUBPART 2. APPLICABILITY OF ARTICLE]

9–109. Scope
9–110. Security Interests Arising Under Article 2 or 2A

PART 2. EFFECTIVENESS OF SECURITY AGREEMENT; ATTACHMENT OF SECURITY INTEREST; RIGHTS OF PARTIES TO SECURITY AGREEMENT

[SUBPART 1. EFFECTIVENESS AND ATTACHMENT]

9–201. General Effectiveness of Security Agreement
9–202. Title to Collateral Immaterial
9–203. Attachment and Enforceability of Security Interest; Proceeds; Supporting Obligations; Formal Requisites
9–204. After-Acquired Property; Future Advances
9–205. Use or Disposition of Collateral Permissible
9–206. *Security Interest Arising in Purchase or Delivery of Financial Asset*

[SUBPART 2. RIGHTS AND DUTIES]

9–207. Rights and Duties of Secured Party Having Possession or Control of Collateral
9–208. *Additional Duties of Secured Party Having Control of Collateral**

---

* The few sections in italics have been omitted. These sections are largely ignored in law school classes and completely ignored on law school exams.

35

Sec.
9–209. Duties of Secured Party if Account Debtor Has Been Notified of Assignment
9–210. Request for Accounting; Request Regarding List of Collateral or Statement of Account

PART 3. PERFECTION AND PRIORITY

[SUBPART 1. LAW GOVERNING PERFECTION AND PRIORITY]

9–301. Law Governing Perfection and Priority of Security Interests
9–302. Law Governing Perfection and Priority of Agricultural Liens
9–303. Law Governing Perfection and Priority of Security Interests in Goods Covered by a Certificate of Title
9–304. Law Governing Perfection and Priority of Security Interests in Deposit Accounts
9–305. Law Governing Perfection and Priority of Security Interests in Investment Property
9–306. Law Governing Perfection and Priority of Security Interests in Letter-of-Credit Rights
9–307. Location of Debtor

[SUBPART 2. PERFECTION]

9–308. When Security Interest Is Perfected; Continuity of Perfection
9–309. Security Interest Perfected Upon Attachment
9–310. When Filing Required to Perfect Security Interest; Security Interests to Which Filing Provisions Do Not Apply
9–311. Perfection of Security Interests in Property Subject to Certain Statutes, Regulations, and Treaties
9–312. Perfection of Security Interests in Chattel Paper, Deposit Accounts, Documents, Goods Covered by Documents, Instruments, Investment Property, Letter-of-Credit Rights, and Money; Perfection by Permissive Filing; Temporary Perfection Without Filing or Transfer of Possession
9–313. When Possession by or Delivery to Secured Party Perfects Security Interest Without Filing
9–314. Perfection by Control
9–315. Secured Party's Rights on Disposition of Collateral and in Proceeds
9–316. Continued Perfection of Security Interest Following Change in Governing Law

[SUBPART 3. PRIORITY]

9–317. Interests That Take Priority Over or Take Free of Security Interest or Agricultural Lien
9–318. No Interest Retained in Right to Payment That Is Sold; Rights and Title of Seller of Account or Chattel Paper With Respect to Creditors and Purchasers
9–319. Rights and Title of Consignee With Respect to Creditors and Purchasers
9–320. Buyer of Goods
9–321. Licensee of General Intangible and Lessee of Goods in Ordinary Course of Business
9–322. Priorities Among Conflicting Security Interests in and Agricultural Lien Same Collateral

Sec.
9–323. Future Advances
9–324. Priority of Purchase-Money Security Interests
9–325. Priority of Security Interests in Transferred Collateral
9–326. Priority of Security Interests Created by New Debtor
9–327. Priority of Security Interests in Deposit Account
9–328. Priority of Security Interests in Investment Property
9–329. Priority of Security Interests in Letter-of-Credit Right
9–330. Priority of Purchaser of Chattel Paper or Instrument
9–331. Priority of Rights of Purchasers of Instruments, Documents, and Securities Under Other Articles; Priority of Interests in Financial Assets and Security Entitlements Under Article 8
9–332. Transfer of Money; Transfer of Funds From Deposit Account
9–333. Priority of Certain Liens Arising by Operation of Law
9–334. Priority of Security Interests in Fixtures and Crops
9–335. Accessions
9–336. Commingled Goods
9–337. Priority of Security Interests in Goods Covered by Certificate of Title
9–338. Priority of Security Interest or Agricultural Lien Perfected by Filed Financing Statement Providing Certain Incorrect Information
9–339. Priority Subject to Subordination

[SUBPART 4. RIGHTS OF BANK]

9–340. Effectiveness of Right of Recoupment or Set-Off Against Deposit Account
9–341. Bank's Rights and Duties With Respect to Deposit Account
9–342. Bank's Right to Refuse to Enter Into or Disclose Existence of Control Agreement

PART 4. RIGHTS OF THIRD PARTIES

9–401. Alienability of Debtor's Rights
9–402. Secured Party Not Obligated on Contract of Debtor or in Tort
9–403. Agreement Not to Assert Defenses Against Assignee
9–404. Rights Acquired by Assignee; Claims and Defenses Against Assignee
9–405. Modification of Assigned Contract
9–406. Discharge of Account Debtor; Notification of Assignment; Identification and Proof of Assignment; Restrictions on Assignment of Accounts, Chattel Paper, Payment Intangibles, and Promissory Notes Ineffective
9–407. Restrictions on Creation or Enforcement of Security Interest in Leasehold Interest or in Lessor's Residual Interest
9–408. Restrictions on Assignment of Promissory Notes, Health-Care-Insurance Receivables, and Certain General Intangibles Ineffective
9–409. Restrictions on Assignment of Letter-of-Credit Rights Ineffective

PART 5. FILING

[SUBPART 1. FILING OFFICE; CONTENTS AND EFFECTIVENESS OF FINANCING STATEMENT]

9–501. Filing Office
9–502. Contents of Financing Statement; Record of Mortgage as Financing Statement; Time of Filing Financing Statement
9–503. Name of Debtor and Secured Party

Sec.
9–504. Indication of Collateral
9–505. Filing and Compliance With Other Statutes and Treaties for Consignments, Leases, Other Bailments, and Other Transactions
9–506. Effect of Errors or Omissions
9–507. Effect of Certain Events on Effectiveness of Financing Statement
9–508. Effectiveness of Financing Statement if New Debtor Becomes Bound by Security Agreement
9–509. Persons Entitled to File a Record
9–510. Effectiveness of Filed Record
9–511. Secured Party of Record
9–512. Amendment of Financing Statement
9–513. Termination Statement
9–514. Assignment of Powers of Secured Party of Record
9–515. Duration and Effectiveness of Financing Statement; Effect of Lapsed Financing Statement
9–516. What Constitutes Filing; Effectiveness of Filing
9–517. Effect of Indexing Errors
9–518. Claim Concerning Inaccurate or Wrongfully Filed Record

[SUBPART 2. DUTIES AND OPERATION OF FILING OFFICE]

9–519. Numbering, Maintaining, and Indexing Records; Communicating Information Provided in Records
9–520. Acceptance and Refusal to Accept Record
9–521. Uniform Form of Written Financing Statement and Amendment
9–522. *Maintenance and Destruction of Records*
9–523. Information From Filing Office; Sale or License of Records
9–524. *Delay by Filing Office*
9–525. *Fees*
9–526. *Filing–Office Rules*
9–527. *Duty to Report*

PART 6. DEFAULT

[SUBPART 1. DEFAULT AND ENFORCEMENT OF SECURITY INTEREST]

9–601. Rights After Default; Judicial Enforcement; Consignor or Buyer of Accounts, Chattel Paper, Payment Intangibles, or Promissory Notes
9–602. Waiver and Variance of Rights and Duties
9–603. Agreement on Standards Concerning Rights and Duties
9–604. Procedure if Security Agreement Covers Real Property or Fixtures
9–605. Unknown Debtor or Secondary Obligor
9–606. *Time of Default for Agricultural Lien*
9–607. Collection and Enforcement by Secured Party
9–608. Application of Proceeds of Collection or Enforcement; Liability for Deficiency and Right to Surplus
9–609. Secured Party's Right to Take Possession After Default
9–610. Disposition of Collateral After Default
9–611. Notification Before Disposition of Collateral
9–612. Timeliness of Notification Before Disposition of Collateral
9–613. Contents and Form of Notification Before Disposition of Collateral: General

Sec.
9–614. Contents and Form of Notification Before Disposition of Collateral: Consumer-Goods Transaction
9–615. Application of Proceeds of Disposition; Liability for Deficiency and Right to Surplus
9–616. *Explanation of Calculation of Surplus or Deficiency*
9–617. Rights of Transferee of Collateral
9–618. *Rights and Duties of Certain Secondary Obligors*
9–619. *Transfer of Record or Legal Title*
9–620. Acceptance of Collateral in Full or Partial Satisfaction of Obligation; Compulsory Disposition of Collateral
9–621. Notification of Proposal to Accept Collateral
9–622. Effect of Acceptance of Collateral
9–623. Right to Redeem Collateral
9–624. Waiver

[SUBPART 2. NONCOMPLIANCE WITH ARTICLE]

9–625. Remedies for Secured Party's Failure to Comply With Article
9–626. Action in Which Deficiency or Surplus Is in Issue
9–627. Determination of Whether Conduct Was Commercially Reasonable
9–628. Nonliability and Limitation on Liability of Secured Party; Liability of Secondary Obligor

PART 7. TRANSITION

9–701. *Effective Date*
9–702. *Savings Clause*
9–703. *Security Interest Perfected Before Effective Date*
9–704. *Security Interest Unperfected Before Effective Date*
9–705. *Effectiveness of Action Taken Before Effective Date*
9–706. *When Initial Financing Statement Suffices to Continue Effectiveness of Financing Statement*
9–707. *Amendment of Pre-Effective-Date Financing Statement*
9–708. *Persons Entitled to File Initial Financing Statement or Continuation Statement*
9–709. *Priority*

PART 1. GENERAL PROVISIONS

[SUBPART 1. SHORT TITLE, DEFINITIONS, AND GENERAL CONCEPTS]

§ 9–101. Short Title.

This article may be cited as Uniform Commercial Code–Secured Transactions.

OFFICIAL COMMENT

1. **Source.** This Article supersedes former Uniform Commercial Code (UCC) Article 9. As did its predecessor, it provides a comprehensive scheme for the regulation of security interests in personal

property and fixtures. For the most part this Article follows the general approach and retains much of the terminology of former Article 9. In addition to describing many aspects of the operation and interpretation of this Article, these Comments explain the material changes that this Article makes to former Article 9. Former Article 9 superseded the wide variety of pre-UCC security devices. Unlike the Comments to former Article 9, however, these Comments dwell very little on the pre-UCC state of the law. For that reason, the Comments to former Article 9 will remain of substantial historical value and interest. They also will remain useful in understanding the background and general conceptual approach of this Article.

Citations to "Bankruptcy Code Section ____" in these Comments are to Title 11 of the United States Code as in effect on December 31, 1998.

* * *

3. **Reorganization and Renumbering; Captions; Style.** This Article reflects a substantial reorganization of former Article 9 and renumbering of most sections. New Part 4 deals with several aspects of third-party rights and duties that are unrelated to perfection and priority. Some of these were covered by Part 3 of former Article 9. Part 5 deals with filing (covered by former Part 4) and Part 6 deals with default and enforcement (covered by former Part 5). Appendix I contains conforming revisions to other articles of the UCC, and Appendix II contains model provisions for production-money priority.

This Article also includes headings for the subsections as an aid to readers. Unlike section captions, which are part of the UCC, see Section 1–109, subsection headings are not a part of the official text itself and have not been approved by the sponsors. Each jurisdiction in which this Article is introduced may consider whether to adopt the headings as a part of the statute and whether to adopt a provision clarifying the effect, if any, to be given to the headings. This Article also has been conformed to current style conventions.

4. **Summary of Revisions.** Following is a brief summary of some of the more significant revisions of Article 9 that are included in this Article.

a. **Scope of Article 9.** This Article expands the scope of Article 9 in several respects.

Deposit accounts. Section 9–109 includes within this Article's scope deposit accounts as original collateral, except in consumer transactions. Former Article 9 dealt with deposit accounts only as proceeds of other collateral.

Sales of payment intangibles and promissory notes. Section 9–109 also includes within the scope of this Article most sales of "payment intangibles" (defined in Section 9–102 as general intangibles under which an account debtor's principal obligation is monetary) and "promissory notes" (also defined in Section 9–102). Former Article 9 included sales of accounts and chattel paper, but not sales of payment intangibles or promissory notes. In its inclusion of sales of payment intangibles and promissory notes, this Article continues the drafting convention found in former Article 9; it provides that the sale of accounts, chattel paper, payment intangibles, or promissory notes creates a "security interest." The definition of "account" in Section 9–102 also has been expanded to include various rights to payment that were general intangibles under former Article 9.

Health-care-insurance receivables. Section 9–109 narrows Article 9's exclusion of transfers of interests in insurance policies by carving out of the exclusion "health-care-insurance receivables" (defined in Section 9–102). A health-care-insurance receivable is included within the definition of "account" in Section 9–102.

Nonpossessory statutory agricultural liens. Section 9–109 also brings nonpossessory statutory agricultural liens within the scope of Article 9.

Consignments. Section 9–109 provides that "true" consignments-bailments for the purpose of sale by the bailee are security interests covered by Article 9, with certain exceptions. See Section 9–102 (defining "consignment"). Currently, many consignments are subject to Article 9's filing requirements by operation of former Section 2–326.

Supporting obligations and property securing rights to payment. This Article also addresses explicitly (i) obligations, such as guaranties and letters of credit, that support payment or performance of collateral such as accounts, chattel paper, and payment intangibles, and (ii) any property (including real property) that secures a right to payment or performance that is subject to an Article 9 security interest. See Sections 9–203, 9–308.

Commercial tort claims. Section 9–109 expands the scope of Article 9 to include the assignment of commercial tort claims by narrowing the exclusion of tort claims generally. However, this Article continues to exclude tort claims for bodily injury and other non-business tort claims of a natural person. See Section 9–102 (defining "commercial tort claim").

Transfers by States and governmental units of States. Section 9–109 narrows the exclusion of transfers by States and their governmental units. It excludes only transfers covered by another statute (other than a statute generally applicable to security interests) to the extent the statute governs the creation, perfection, priority, or enforcement of security interests.

Nonassignable general intangibles, promissory notes, health-care-insurance receivables, and letter-of-credit rights. This Article enables a security interest to attach to letter-of-credit rights, health-care-insurance receivables, promissory notes, and general intangibles, including contracts, permits, licenses, and franchises, notwithstanding a contractual or statutory prohibition against or limitation on assignment. This Article explicitly protects third parties against any adverse effect of the creation or attempted enforcement of the security interest. See Sections 9–408, 9–409.

Subject to Sections 9–408 and 9–409 and two other exceptions (Sections 9406, concerning accounts, chattel paper, and payment intangibles, and 9407, concerning interests in leased goods), Section 9–401 establishes a baseline rule that the inclusion of transactions and collateral within the scope of Article 9 has no effect on non-Article 9 law dealing with the alienability or inalienability of property. For example, if a commercial tort claim is nonassignable under other applicable law, the fact that a security interest in the claim is within the scope of Article 9 does not override the other applicable law's effective prohibition of assignment.

b. **Duties of Secured Party.** This Article provides for expanded duties of secured parties.

Release of control. Section 9–208 imposes upon a secured party having control of a deposit account, investment property, or a letter-of-credit right the duty to release control when there is no secured obligation and no commitment to give value. Section 9–209 contains analogous provisions when an account debtor has been notified to pay a secured party.

Information. Section 9–210 expands a secured party's duties to provide the debtor with information concerning collateral and the obligations that it secures.

Default and enforcement. Part 6 also includes some additional duties of secured parties in connection with default and enforcement. See, e.g., Section 9–616 (duty to explain calculation of deficiency or surplus in a consumer-goods transaction).

c. **Choice of Law.** The choice-of-law rules for the law governing perfection, the effect of perfection or nonperfection, and priority are found in Part 3, Subpart 1 (Sections 9–301 through 9–307). See also Section 9–316.

Where to file: Location of debtor. This Article changes the choice-of-law rule governing perfection (i.e., where to file) for most collateral to the law of the jurisdiction where the debtor is located. See Section 9–301. Under former Article 9, the jurisdiction of the debtor's location governed only perfection and priority of a security interest in accounts, general intangibles, mobile goods, and, for purposes of perfection by filing, chattel paper and investment property.

Determining debtor's location. As a baseline rule, Section 9–307 follows former Section 9–103, under which the location of the debtor is the debtor's place of business (or chief executive office, if the debtor has more than one place of business). Section 9–307 contains three major exceptions. First, a "registered organization," such as a corporation or limited liability company, is located in the State under whose law the debtor is organized, e.g., a corporate debtor's State of incorporation. Second, an individual debtor is located at his or her principal residence. Third, there are special rules for determining the location of the United States and registered organizations organized under the law of the United States.

Location of non-U.S. debtors. If, applying the foregoing rules, a debtor is located in a jurisdiction whose law does not require public notice as a condition of perfection of a nonpossessory security interest, the entity is deemed located in the District of Columbia. See Section 9307. Thus, to the extent that this Article applies to non-U.S. debtors, perfection could be accomplished in many cases by a domestic filing.

Priority. For tangible collateral such as goods and instruments, Section 9–301 provides that the law applicable to priority and the effect of perfection or nonperfection will remain the law of the jurisdiction where the collateral is located, as under former Section 9–103 (but without the confusing "last event" test). For intangible collateral, such as accounts, the applicable law for priority will be that of the jurisdiction in which the debtor is located.

Possessory security interests; agricultural liens. Perfection, the effect of perfection or nonperfection, and priority of a possessory security interest or an agricultural lien are governed by the law of the jurisdiction where the collateral subject to the security interest or lien is located. See Sections 9–301, 9302.

Goods covered by certificates of title; deposit accounts; letter-of-credit rights; investment property. This Article includes several refinements to the treatment of choice-of-law matters for goods covered by certificates of title. See Section 9–303. It also provides special choice-of-law rules, similar to those for investment property under current Articles 8 and 9, for deposit accounts (Section 9–304), investment property (Section 9–305), and letter-of-credit rights (Section 9306).

Change in applicable law. Section 9–316 addresses perfection following a change in applicable law.

d. **Perfection.** The rules governing perfection of security interests and agricultural liens are found in Part 3, Subpart 2 (Sections 9–308 through 9–316).

Deposit accounts; letter-of-credit rights. With certain exceptions, this Article provides that a security interest in a deposit account or a letter-of-credit right may be perfected *only* by the secured party's acquiring "control" of the deposit account or letter-of-credit right. See Sections 9–312, 9–314. Under Section 9–104, a secured party has "control" of a deposit account when, with the consent of the debtor, the secured party obtains the depositary bank's agreement to act on the secured party's instructions (including when the secured party becomes the account holder) or when the secured party is itself the depositary bank. The control requirements are patterned on Section 8106, which specifies the requirements for control of investment property. Under Section 9–107, "control" of a letter-of-credit right occurs when the issuer or nominated person consents to an assignment of proceeds under Section 5114.

Electronic chattel paper. Section 9–102 includes a new defined term: "electronic chattel paper." Electronic chattel paper is a record or records consisting of information stored in an electronic medium (i.e., it is not written). Perfection of a security interest in electronic chattel paper may be by control or filing. See Sections 9–105 (*sui generis* definition of control of electronic chattel paper), 9312 (perfection by filing), 9314 (perfection by control).

Investment property. The perfection requirements for "investment property" (defined in Section 9–102), including perfection by control under Section 9–106, remain substantially unchanged. However, a new provision in Section 9–314 is designed to ensure that a secured party retains control in "repledge" transactions that are typical in the securities markets.

Instruments, agricultural liens, and commercial tort claims. This Article expands the types of collateral in which a security interest may be perfected by filing to include instruments. See Section 9–312. Agricultural liens and security interests in commercial tort claims also are perfected by filing, under this Article. See Sections 9–308, 9–310.

Sales of payment intangibles and promissory notes. Although former Article 9 covered the outright sale of accounts and chattel paper, sales of most other types of receivables also are financing transactions to which Article 9 should apply. Accordingly, Section 9–102 expands the definition of "account" to include many types of receivables (including "health-care-insurance receivables," defined in Section 9–102) that former Article 9 classified as "general intangibles." It thereby subjects to Article 9's filing system sales of more types of receivables than did former Article 9. Certain sales of payment intangibles-primarily bank loan participation transactions–should not be subject to the Article 9 filing rules. These transactions fall in a residual category of collateral, "payment intangibles" (general intangibles under which the account debtor's principal obligation is monetary), the sale of which is exempt from the filing requirements of Article 9. See Sections 9–102, 9–109, 9–309 (perfection upon attachment). The perfection rules for sales of promissory notes are the same as those for sales of payment intangibles.

Possessory security interests. Several provisions of this Article address aspects of security interests involving a secured party or a third party who is in possession of the collateral. In particular, Section 9–313 resolves a number of uncertainties under former Section 9–305. It provides that a security interest in collateral in the possession of a third party is perfected when the third party acknowledges in an authenticated record that it holds for the secured party's benefit. Section 9–313 also provides that a third party need not so acknowledge and that its acknowledgment does not impose any duties on it, unless it otherwise agrees. A special rule in Section 9–313 provides that if a secured party already is in possession of collateral, its security interest remains perfected by possession if it delivers the collateral to a third party and the collateral is accompanied by instructions to hold it for the secured party or to redeliver it to the secured party. Section 9–313 also clarifies the limited circumstances under which a security interest in goods covered by a certificate of title may be perfected by the secured party's taking possession.

Automatic perfection. Section 9–309 lists various types of security interests as to which no public-notice step is required for perfection (e.g., purchase-money security interests in consumer goods other than automobiles). This automatic perfection also extends to a transfer of a health-care-insurance receivable *to* a health-care provider. Those transfers normally will be made by natural persons who receive health-care services; there is little value in requiring filing for perfection in that context. Automatic perfection also applies to security interests created by sales of payment intangibles and promissory notes. Section 9–308 provides that a perfected security interest in collateral supported by a "supporting obligation" (such as an account supported by a guaranty) also is a perfected security interest in the supporting obligation, and that a perfected security interest in an obligation secured by a security interest or lien on property (e.g., a real-property mortgage) also is a perfected security interest in the security interest or lien.

e. **Priority; Special Rules for Banks and Deposit Accounts.** The rules governing priority of security interests and agricultural liens are found in Part 3, Subpart 3 (Sections 9–317 through 9–342). This Article includes several new priority rules and some special rules relating to banks and deposit accounts (Sections 9–340 through 9–342).

Purchase-money security interests: General; consumer-goods transactions; inventory. Section 9–103 substantially rewrites the definition of purchase-money security interest (PMSI) (although the term is not formally "defined"). The substantive changes, however, apply only to non-consumer-goods transactions. (Consumer transactions and consumer-goods transactions are discussed below in Comment 4.j.) For non-consumer-goods transactions, Section 9–103 makes clear that a security interest in collateral may be (to some extent) both a PMSI as well as a non-PMSI, in accord with the "dual status" rule applied by some courts under former Article 9 (thereby rejecting the "transformation" rule). The definition provides an even broader conception of a PMSI in inventory, yielding a result that accords with private agreements entered into in response to the uncertainty under former Article 9. It also treats consignments as purchase-money security interests in inventory. Section 9–324 revises the PMSI priority rules, but for the most part without material change in substance. Section 9–324 also clarifies the priority rules for competing PMSIs in the same collateral.

Purchase-money security interests in livestock; agricultural liens. Section 9–324 provides a special PMSI priority, similar to the inventory PMSI priority rule, for livestock. Section 9–322 (which contains the baseline first-to-file-or-perfect priority rule) also recognizes special non-Article 9 priority rules for agricultural liens, which can override the baseline first-in-time rule.

Purchase-money security interests in software. Section 9–324 contains a new priority rule for a software purchase-money security interest. (Section 9–102 includes a definition of "software.") Under Section 9–103, a software PMSI includes a PMSI in software that is used in goods that are also subject to a PMSI. (Note also that the definition of "chattel paper" has been expanded to include records that evidence a monetary obligation and a security interest in specific goods and software used in the goods.)

Investment property. The priority rules for investment property are substantially similar to the priority rules found in former Section 9–115, which was added in conjunction with the 1994 revisions to UCC Article 8. Under Section 9–328, if a secured party has control of investment property (Sections 8106, 9106), its security interest is senior to a security interest perfected in another manner (e.g., by filing). Also under Section 9328, security interests perfected by control generally rank according to the time that control is obtained or, in the case of a security entitlement or a commodity contract carried in a commodity account, the time when the control arrangement is entered into. This is a change from former Section 9–115, under which the security interests ranked equally. However, as between a securities intermediary's security interest in a security entitlement that it maintains for the debtor and a security interest held by another secured party, the securities intermediary's security interest is senior.

Deposit accounts. This Article's priority rules applicable to deposit accounts are found in Section 9–327. They are patterned on and are similar to those for investment property in former Section 9–115 and Section 9–328 of this Article. Under Section 9–327, if a secured party has control of a deposit account, its security interest is senior to a security interest perfected in another manner (i.e., as cash proceeds). Also under Section 9327, security interests perfected by control rank according to the time that control is obtained, but as between a depositary bank's security interest and one held by another secured party, the depositary bank's security interest is senior. A corresponding rule in Section 9–340 makes a depositary bank's right of set-off generally senior to a security interest held by another secured party. However, if the other secured party becomes the depositary bank's customer with respect to the deposit account, then its security interest is senior to the depositary bank's security interest and right of set-off. Sections 9–327, 9–340.

Letter-of-credit rights. The priority rules for security interests in letter-of-credit rights are found in Section 9–329. They are somewhat analogous to those for deposit accounts. A security interest perfected by control has priority over one perfected in another manner (i.e., as a supporting obligation for the collateral in which a security interest is perfected). Security interests in a letter-of-credit right perfected by control rank according to the time that control is obtained. However, the rights of a transferee beneficiary or a nominated person are independent and superior to the extent provided in Section 5–114. See Section 9–109(c)(4).

Chattel paper and instruments. Section 9–330 is the successor to former Section 9–308. As under former Section 9–308, differing priority rules apply to purchasers of chattel paper who give new value and take possession (or, in the case of electronic chattel paper, obtain control) of the collateral depending on whether a conflicting security interest in the collateral is claimed merely as proceeds. The principal change relates to the role of knowledge and the effect of an indication of a previous assignment of the collateral. Section 9–330 also affords priority to purchasers of instruments who take possession in good faith and without knowledge that the purchase violates the rights of the competing secured party. In addition, to qualify for priority, purchasers of chattel paper, but not of instruments, must purchase in the ordinary course of business.

Proceeds. Section 9–322 contains new priority rules that clarify when a special priority of a security interest in collateral continues or does not continue with respect to proceeds of the collateral. Other refinements to the priority rules for proceeds are included in Sections 9–324 (purchase-money security interest priority) and 9–330 (priority of certain purchasers of chattel paper and instruments).

Miscellaneous priority provisions. This Article also includes (i) clarifications of selected good-faith-purchase and similar issues (Sections 9–317, 9–331); (ii) new priority rules to deal with the "double debtor" problem arising when a debtor creates a security interest in collateral acquired by the debtor subject to a security interest created by another person (Section 9–325); (iii) new priority rules to deal with the problems created when a change in corporate structure or the like results in a new entity that has become bound by the original debtor's after-acquired property agreement (Section 9–326); (iv) a provision enabling most transferees of funds from a deposit account or money to take free of a security interest (Section 9–332); (v) substantially rewritten and refined priority rules dealing with accessions and commingled goods (Sections 9–335, 9–336); (vi) revised priority rules for security interests in goods covered by a certificate of title (Section 9–337); and (vii) provisions designed to ensure that security interests in deposit accounts will not extend to most transferees of funds on deposit or payees from deposit accounts and will not otherwise "clog" the payments system (Sections 9–341, 9–342).

Model provisions relating to production-money security interests. Appendix II to this Article contains model definitions and priority rules relating to "production-money security interests" held by secured parties who give new value used in the production of crops. Because no consensus emerged on the wisdom of these provisions during the drafting process, the sponsors make no recommendation on whether these model provisions should be enacted.

f. **Proceeds.** Section 9–102 contains an expanded definition of "proceeds" of collateral which includes additional rights and property that arise out of collateral, such as distributions on account of collateral and claims arising out of the loss or nonconformity of, defects in, or damage to collateral. The term also includes collections on account of "supporting obligations," such as guarantees.

g. **Part 4: Additional Provisions Relating to Third–Party Rights.** New Part 4 contains several provisions relating to the relationships between certain third parties and the parties to secured transactions. It contains new Sections 9–

401 (replacing former Section 9–311) (alienability of debtor's rights), 9–402 (replacing former Section 9–317) (secured party not obligated on debtor's contracts), 9–403 (replacing former Section 9–206) (agreement not to assert defenses against assignee), 9–404, 9–405, and 9–406 (replacing former Section 9–318) (rights acquired by assignee, modification of assigned contract, discharge of account debtor, restrictions on assignment of account, chattel paper, promissory note, or payment intangible ineffective), 9–407 (replacing some provisions of former Section 2A–303) (restrictions on creation or enforcement of security interest in leasehold interest or lessor's residual interest ineffective). It also contains new Sections 9–408 (restrictions on assignment of promissory notes, health-care-insurance receivables ineffective, and certain general intangibles ineffective) and 9–409 (restrictions on assignment of letter-of-credit rights ineffective), which are discussed above.

h. **Filing.** Part 5 (formerly Part 4) of Article 9 has been substantially rewritten to simplify the statutory text and to deal with numerous problems of interpretation and implementation that have arisen over the years.

Medium-neutrality. This Article is "medium-neutral"; that is, it makes clear that parties may file and otherwise communicate with a filing office by means of records communicated and stored in media other than on paper.

Identity of person who files a record; authorization. Part 5 is largely indifferent as to the person who effects a filing. Instead, it addresses whose authorization is necessary for a person to file a record with a filing office. The filing scheme does not contemplate that the identity of a "filer" will be a part of the searchable records. This approach is consistent with, and a necessary aspect of, eliminating signatures or other evidence of authorization from the system (except to the extent that filing offices may choose to employ authentication procedures in connection with electronic communications). As long as the appropriate person authorizes the filing, or, in the case of a termination statement, the debtor is entitled to the termination, it is largely insignificant whether the secured party or another person files any given record.

Section 9–509 collects in one place most of the rules that determine when a record may be filed. In general, the debtor's authorization is required for the filing of an initial financing statement or an amendment that adds collateral. With one further exception, a secured party of record's authorization is required for the filing of other amendments. The exception arises if a secured party has failed to provide a termination statement that is required because there is no outstanding secured obligation or commitment to give value. In that situation, a debtor is authorized to file a termination statement indicating that it has been filed by the debtor.

Financing statement formal requisites. The formal requisites for a financing statement are set out in Section 9–502. A financing statement must provide the name of the debtor and the secured party and an indication of the collateral that it covers. Sections 9–503 and 9–506 address the sufficiency of a name provided on a financing statement and clarify when a debtor's name is correct and when an incorrect name is insufficient. Section 9–504 addresses the indication of collateral covered. Under Section 9–504, a super-generic description (e.g.,"all assets" or "all personal property") in a financing statement is a sufficient indication of the collateral. (Note, however, that a super-generic description is inadequate for purposes of a security agreement. See Sections 9–108, 9–203.) To facilitate electronic filing, this Article does not require that the debtor's signature or other authorization appear on a financing statement. Instead, it prohibits the filing of unauthorized financing statements and imposes liability upon those who violate the prohibition. See Sections 9–509, 9–626.

Filing-office operations. Part 5 contains several provisions governing filing operations. First, it prohibits the filing office from rejecting an initial financing statement or other record for a reason other than one of the few that are specified. See

Sections 9–520, 9–516. Second, the filing office is obliged to link all subsequent records (e.g., assignments, continuation statements, etc.) to the initial financing statement to which they relate. See Section 9–519. Third, the filing office may delete a financing statement and related records from the files no earlier than one year after lapse (lapse normally is five years after the filing date), and then only if a continuation statement has not been filed. See Sections 9–515, 9–519, 9–522. Thus, a financing statement and related records would be discovered by a search of the files even after the filing of a termination statement. This approach helps eliminate filing-office discretion and also eases problems associated with multiple secured parties and multiple partial assignments. Fourth, Part 5 mandates performance standards for filing offices. See Sections 9–519, 9–520, 9–523. Fifth, it provides for the promulgation of filing-office rules to deal with details best left out of the statute and requires the filing office to submit periodic reports. See Sections 9–526, 9–527.

Correction of records: Defaulting or missing secured parties and fraudulent filings. In some areas of the country, serious problems have arisen from fraudulent financing statements that are filed against public officials and other persons. This Article addresses the fraud problem by providing the opportunity for a debtor to file a termination statement when a secured party wrongfully refuses or fails to provide a termination statement. See Section 9–509. This opportunity also addresses the problem of secured parties that simply disappear through mergers or liquidations. In addition, Section 9–518 affords a statutory method by which a debtor who believes that a filed record is inaccurate or was wrongfully filed may indicate that fact in the files by filing a correction statement, albeit without affecting the efficacy, if any, of the challenged record.

Extended period of effectiveness for certain financing statements. Section 9–515 contains an exception to the usual rule that financing statements are effective for five years unless a continuation statement is filed to continue the effectiveness for another five years. Under that section, an initial financing statement filed in connection with a "public-finance transaction" or a "manufactured-home transaction" (terms defined in Section 9–102) is effective for 30 years.

National form of financing statement and related forms. Section 9–521 provides for uniform, national written forms of financing statements and related written records that must be accepted by a filing office that accepts written records.

i. **Default and Enforcement.** Part 6 of Article 9 extensively revises former Part 5. Provisions relating to enforcement of consumer-goods transactions and consumer transactions are discussed in Comment 4.j.

Debtor, secondary obligor; waiver. Section 9–602 clarifies the identity of persons who have rights and persons to whom a secured party owes specified duties under Part 6. Under that section, the rights and duties are enjoyed by and run to the "debtor," defined in Section 9–102 to mean any person with a non-lien property interest in collateral, and to any "obligor." However, with one exception (Section 9–616, as it relates to a consumer obligor), the rights and duties concerned affect non-debtor obligors only if they are "secondary obligors." "Secondary obligor" is defined in Section 9–102 to include one who is secondarily obligated on the secured obligation, e.g., a guarantor, or one who has a right of recourse against the debtor or another obligor with respect to an obligation secured by collateral. However, under Section 9–628, the secured party is relieved from any duty or liability to any person unless the secured party knows that the person is a debtor or obligor. Resolving an issue on which courts disagreed under former Article 9, this Article generally prohibits waiver by a secondary obligor of its rights and a secured party's duties under Part 6. See Section 9–602. However, Section 9–624 permits a secondary obligor or debtor to waive the right to notification of disposition of collateral and, in a non-consumer transaction, the right to redeem collateral, if the secondary obligor or debtor agrees to do so after default.

Rights of collection and enforcement of collateral. Section 9–607 explains in greater detail than former 9–502 the rights of a secured party who seeks to collect or enforce collateral, including accounts, chattel paper, and payment intangibles. It also sets forth the enforcement rights of a depositary bank holding a security interest in a deposit account maintained with the depositary bank. Section 9–607 relates solely to the rights of a secured party vis-a-vis a debtor with respect to collections and enforcement. It does not affect the rights or duties of third parties, such as account debtors on collateral, which are addressed elsewhere (e.g., Section 9–406). Section 9–608 clarifies the manner in which proceeds of collection or enforcement are to be applied.

Disposition of collateral: Warranties of title. Section 9–610 imposes on a secured party who disposes of collateral the warranties of title, quiet possession, and the like that are otherwise applicable under other law. It also provides rules for the exclusion or modification of those warranties.

Disposition of collateral: Notification, application of proceeds, surplus and deficiency, other effects. Section 9–611 requires a secured party to give notification of a disposition of collateral to other secured parties and lienholders who have filed financing statements against the debtor covering the collateral. (That duty was eliminated by the 1972 revisions to Article 9.) However, that section relieves the secured party from that duty when the secured party undertakes a search of the records and a report of the results is unreasonably delayed. Section 9–613, which applies only to non-consumer transactions, specifies the contents of a sufficient notification of disposition and provides that a notification sent 10 days or more before the earliest time for disposition is sent within a reasonable time. Section 9–615 addresses the application of proceeds of disposition, the entitlement of a debtor to any surplus, and the liability of an obligor for any deficiency. Section 9–619 clarifies the effects of a disposition by a secured party, including the rights of transferees of the collateral.

Rights and duties of secondary obligor. Section 9–618 provides that a secondary obligor obtains the rights and assumes the duties of a secured party if the secondary obligor receives an assignment of a secured obligation, agrees to assume the secured party's rights and duties upon a transfer to it of collateral, or becomes subrogated to the rights of the secured party with respect to the collateral. The assumption, transfer, or subrogation is not a disposition of collateral under Section 9–610, but it does relieve the former secured party of further duties. Former Section 9–504(5) did not address whether a secured party was relieved of its duties in this situation.

Transfer of record or legal title. Section 9–619 contains a new provision making clear that a transfer of record or legal title to a secured party is not of itself a disposition under Part 6. This rule applies regardless of the circumstances under which the transfer of title occurs.

Strict foreclosure. Section 9–620, unlike former Section 9–505, permits a secured party to accept collateral in partial satisfaction, as well as full satisfaction, of the obligations secured. This right of strict foreclosure extends to intangible as well as tangible property. Section 9–622 clarifies the effects of an acceptance of collateral on the rights of junior claimants. It rejects the approach taken by some courts–deeming a secured party to have constructively retained collateral in satisfaction of the secured obligations–in the case of a secured party's unreasonable delay in the disposition of collateral. Instead, unreasonable delay is relevant when determining whether a disposition under Section 9–610 is commercially reasonable.

Effect of noncompliance: "Rebuttable presumption" test. Section 9–626 adopts the "rebuttable presumption" test for the failure of a secured party to proceed in accordance with certain provisions of Part 6. (As discussed in Comment 4.j., the test does not necessarily apply to consumer transactions.) Under this approach, the deficiency claim of a noncomplying secured party is calculated by crediting the obligor with the greater of the actual net proceeds of a disposition and the amount of net proceeds that would have been realized if the disposition had been conducted in accordance with Part 6 (e.g., in a commercially reasonable manner). For non-consumer transactions, Section 9–626 rejects the "absolute bar" test that some courts have imposed; that approach bars a noncomplying secured party from recovering any deficiency, regardless of the loss (if any) the debtor suffered as a consequence of the noncompliance.

"Low-price" dispositions: Calculation of deficiency and surplus. Section 9–615(f) addresses the problem of procedurally regular dispositions that fetch a low price. Subsection (f) provides a special method for calculating a deficiency if the proceeds of a disposition of collateral to a secured party, a person related to the secured party, or a secondary obligor are "significantly below the range of proceeds that a complying disposition to a person other than the secured party, a person related to the secured party, or a secondary obligor would have brought." ("Person related to" is defined in Section 9–102.) In these situations there is reason to suspect that there may be inadequate incentives to obtain a better price. Consequently, instead of calculating a deficiency (or surplus) based on the actual net proceeds, the deficiency (or surplus) would be calculated based on the proceeds that would have been received in a disposition to a person other than the secured party, a person related to the secured party, or a secondary obligor.

j. Consumer Goods, Consumer-Goods Transactions, and Consumer Transactions. This Article (including the accompanying conforming revisions (see Appendix I)) includes several special rules for "consumer goods," "consumer transactions," and "consumer-goods transactions." Each term is defined in Section 9–102.

(i) Revised Sections 2–502 and 2–716 provide a buyer of consumer goods with enhanced rights to possession of the goods, thereby accelerating the opportunity to achieve "buyer in ordinary course of business" status under Section 1–201.

(ii) Section 9–103(e) (allocation of payments for determining extent of purchase-money status), (f) (purchase-money status not affected by cross-collateralization, refinancing, restructuring, or the like), and (g) (secured party has burden of establishing extent of purchase-money status) do not apply to consumer-goods transactions. Sections 9–103 also provides that the limitation of those provisions to transactions other than consumer-goods transactions leaves to the courts the proper rules for consumer-goods transactions and prohibits the courts from drawing inferences from that limitation.

(iii) Section 9–108 provides that in a consumer transaction a description of consumer goods, a security entitlement, securities account, or commodity account "only by [UCC-defined] type of collateral" is not a sufficient collateral description in a security agreement.

(iv) Sections 9–403 and 9–404 make effective the Federal Trade Commission's anti-holder-in-due-course rule (when applicable), 16 C.F.R. Part 433, even in the absence of the required legend.

(v) The 10-day safe-harbor for notification of a disposition provided by Section 9–612 does not apply in a consumer transaction.

(vi) Section 9–613 (contents and form of notice of disposition) does not apply to a consumer-goods transaction.

(vii) Section 9–614 contains special requirements for the contents of a notification of disposition and a safe-harbor, "plain English" form of notification, for consumer-goods transactions.

(viii) Section 9–616 requires a secured party in a consumer-goods transaction to provide a debtor with a notification of how it calculated a deficiency at the time it first undertakes to collect a deficiency.

(ix) Section 9–620 prohibits partial strict foreclosure with respect to consumer goods collateral and, unless the debtor agrees to waive the requirement in an authenticated record after default, in certain cases requires the secured party to dispose of consumer goods collateral which has been repossessed.

(x) Section 9–626 ("rebuttable presumption" rule) does not apply to a consumer transaction. Section 9–626 also provides that its limitation to transactions other than consumer transactions leaves to the courts the proper rules for consumer transactions and prohibits the courts from drawing inferences from that limitation.

k. **Good Faith.** Section 9–102 contains a new definition of "good faith" that includes not only "honesty in fact" but also "the observance of reasonable commercial standards of fair dealing." The definition is similar to the ones adopted in connection with other, recently completed revisions of the UCC.

* * *

§ 9–102. Definitions and Index of Definitions

(a) **[Article 9 definitions.]** In this article:

(1) "Accession" means goods that are physically united with other goods in such a manner that the identity of the original goods is not lost.

(2) "Account", except as used in "account for", means a right to payment of a monetary obligation, whether or not earned by performance, (i) for property that has been or is to be sold, leased, licensed, assigned, or otherwise disposed of, (ii) for services rendered or to be rendered, (iii) for a policy of insurance issued or to be issued, (iv) for a secondary obligation incurred or to be incurred, * * * arising out of the use of a credit or charge card or information contained on or for use with the card, or * * *. The term includes health-care-insurance receivables. The term does not include (i) rights to payment evidenced by chattel paper or an instrument, (ii) commercial tort claims, (iii) deposit accounts, (iv) investment property, (v) letter-of-credit rights or letters of credit, or (vi) rights to payment for money or funds advanced or sold, other than rights arising out of the use of a credit or charge card or information contained on or for use with the card.

(3) "Account debtor" means a person obligated on an account, chattel paper, or general intangible. The term does not include persons obligated to pay a negotiable instrument, even if the instrument constitutes part of chattel paper.

(4) "Accounting", except as used in "accounting for", means a record:

(A) authenticated by a secured party;

(B) indicating the aggregate unpaid secured obligations as of a date not more than 35 days earlier or 35 days later than the date of the record; and

(C) identifying the components of the obligations in reasonable detail.

(5) "Agricultural lien" means an interest in farm products:

(A) which secures payment or performance of an obligation for:

(i) goods or services furnished in connection with a debtor's farming operation; or

(ii) rent on real property leased by a debtor in connection with its farming operation;

(B) which is created by statute in favor of a person that:

(i) in the ordinary course of its business furnished goods or services to a debtor in connection with a debtor's farming operation; or

(ii) leased real property to a debtor in connection with the debtor's farming operation; and

(C) whose effectiveness does not depend on the person's possession of the personal property.

(6) "As-extracted collateral" means:

(A) oil, gas, or other minerals that are subject to a security interest that:

(i) is created by a debtor having an interest in the minerals before extraction; and

(ii) attaches to the minerals as extracted; or

(B) accounts arising out of the sale at the wellhead or minehead of oil, gas, or other minerals in which the debtor had an interest before extraction.

(7) "Authenticate" means:

(A) to sign; or

(B) to execute or otherwise adopt a symbol, or encrypt or similarly process a record in whole or in part, with the present intent of the authenticating person to identify the person and adopt or accept a record.

(8) "Bank" means an organization that is engaged in the business of banking. The term includes savings banks, savings and loan associations, credit unions, and trust companies.

(9) "Cash proceeds" means proceeds that are money, checks, deposit accounts, or the like.

(10) "Certificate of title" means a certificate of title with respect to which a statute provides for the security interest in question to be indicated on the certificate as a condition or result of the security interest's obtaining priority over the rights of a lien creditor with respect to the collateral.

(11) "Chattel paper" means a record or records that evidence both a monetary obligation and a security interest in specific goods, a security interest in specific goods and software used in the goods, a security interest in specific goods and license of software used in the goods, a lease of specific goods, or a lease of specific goods and license of software used in the goods. In this paragraph, "monetary obligation" means a monetary obligation secured by the goods or owed under a lease of the goods and includes a monetary obligation with respect to software used in the goods. The term does not include (i) charters or other contracts involving the use or hire of a vessel or (ii) records that evidence a right to payment arising out of the use of a credit or charge card or information contained on or for use with the card. If a transaction is evidenced by records that include an instrument or series of instruments, the group of records taken together constitutes chattel paper.

(12) "Collateral" means the property subject to a security interest or agricultural lien. The term includes:

(A) proceeds to which a security interest attaches;

(B) accounts, chattel paper, payment intangibles, and promissory notes that have been sold; and

(C) goods that are the subject of a consignment.

(13) "Commercial tort claim" means a claim arising in tort with respect to which:

(A) the claimant is an organization; or

(B) the claimant is an individual and the claim:

(i) arose in the course of the claimant's business or profession; and

(ii) does not include damages arising out of personal injury to or the death of an individual.

(14) "Commodity account" means an account maintained by a commodity intermediary in which a commodity contract is carried for a commodity customer.

(15) "Commodity contract" means a commodity futures contract, an option on a commodity futures contract, a commodity option, or another contract if the contract or option is:
  (A) traded on or subject to the rules of a board of trade that has been designated as a contract market for such a contract pursuant to federal commodities laws; or
  (B) traded on a foreign commodity board of trade, exchange, or market, and is carried on the books of a commodity intermediary for a commodity customer.

* * *

(18) "Communicate" means:
  (A) to send a written or other tangible record;
  (B) to transmit a record by any means agreed upon by the persons sending and receiving the record; or
  (C) in the case of transmission of a record to or by a filing office, to transmit a record by any means prescribed by filing-office rule.

(19) "Consignee" means a merchant to which goods are delivered in a consignment.

(20) "Consignment" means a transaction, regardless of its form, in which a person delivers goods to a merchant for the purpose of sale and:
  (A) the merchant:
    (i) deals in goods of that kind under a name other than the name of the person making delivery;
    (ii) is not an auctioneer; and
    (iii) is not generally known by its creditors to be substantially engaged in selling the goods of others;
  (B) with respect to each delivery, the aggregate value of the goods is $1,000 or more at the time of delivery;
  (C) the goods are not consumer goods immediately before delivery; and
  (D) the transaction does not create a security interest that secures an obligation.

(21) "Consignor" means a person that delivers goods to a consignee in a consignment.

(22) "Consumer debtor" means a debtor in a consumer transaction.

(23) "Consumer goods" means goods that are used or bought for use primarily for personal, family, or household purposes.

(24) "Consumer-goods transaction" means a consumer transaction in which:

  (A) an individual incurs an obligation primarily for personal, family, or household purposes; and

  (B) a security interest in consumer goods secures the obligation.

(25) "Consumer obligor" means an obligor who is an individual and who incurred the obligation as part of a transaction entered into primarily for personal, family, or household purposes.

(26) "Consumer transaction" means a transaction in which (i) an individual incurs an obligation primarily for personal, family, or household purposes, (ii) a security interest secures the obligation, and (iii) the collateral is held or acquired primarily for personal, family, or household purposes. The term includes consumer-goods transactions.

(27) "Continuation statement" means an amendment of a financing statement which:

  (A) identifies, by its file number, the initial financing statement to which it relates; and

  (B) indicates that it is a continuation statement for, or that it is filed to continue the effectiveness of, the identified financing statement.

(28) "Debtor" means:

  (A) a person having an interest, other than a security interest or other lien, in the collateral, whether or not the person is an obligor;

  (B) a seller of accounts, chattel paper, payment intangibles, or promissory notes; or

  (C) a consignee.

(29) "Deposit account" means a demand, time, savings, passbook, or similar account maintained with a bank. The term does not include investment property or accounts evidenced by an instrument.

(30) "Document" means a document of title or a receipt of the type described in Section 7–201(b).

(31) "Electronic chattel paper" means chattel paper evidenced by a record or records consisting of information stored in an electronic medium.

(32) "Encumbrance" means a right, other than an ownership interest, in real property. The term includes mortgages and other liens on real property.

(33) "Equipment" means goods other than inventory, farm products, or consumer goods.

(34) "Farm products" means goods, other than standing timber, with respect to which the debtor is engaged in a farming operation and which are:

    (A) crops grown, growing, or to be grown, including:

        (i) crops produced on trees, vines, and bushes; and

        (ii) aquatic goods produced in aquacultural operations;

    (B) livestock, born or unborn, including aquatic goods produced in aquacultural operations;

    (C) supplies used or produced in a farming operation; or

    (D) products of crops or livestock in their unmanufactured states.

(35) "Farming operation" means raising, cultivating, propagating, fattening, grazing, or any other farming, livestock, or aquacultural operation.

(36) "File number" means the number assigned to an initial financing statement pursuant to Section 9–519(a).

(37) "Filing office" means an office designated in Section 9–501 as the place to file a financing statement.

(38) "Filing-office rule" means a rule adopted pursuant to Section 9–526.

(39) "Financing statement" means a record or records composed of an initial financing statement and any filed record relating to the initial financing statement.

(40) "Fixture filing" means the filing of a financing statement covering goods that are or are to become fixtures and satisfying Section 9–502(a) and (b). The term includes the filing of a financing statement covering goods of a transmitting utility which are or are to become fixtures.

(41) "Fixtures" means goods that have become so related to particular real property that an interest in them arises under real property law.

(42) "General intangible" means any personal property, including things in action, other than accounts, chattel paper, commercial tort claims, deposit accounts, documents, goods, instruments, investment property, letter-of-credit rights, letters of credit, money, and oil, gas, or other minerals before extraction. The term includes payment intangibles and software.

(43) [reserved] ["Good faith" means honesty in fact and the observance of reasonable commercial standards of fair dealing.] *Deleted by Revised Art. 1 (2001).*

(44) "Goods" means all things that are movable when a security interest attaches. The term includes (i) fixtures, (ii) standing timber that is to be cut and removed under a conveyance or contract for sale, (iii) the unborn young of animals, (iv) crops grown, growing, or to be grown, even if the crops are produced on trees, vines, or bushes, and (v) manufactured homes. The term also includes a computer program embedded in goods and any supporting information provided in connection with a transaction relating to the program if (i) the program is associated with the goods in such a manner that it customarily is considered part of the goods, or (ii) by becoming the owner of the goods, a person acquires a right to use the program in connection with the goods. The term does not include a computer program embedded in goods that consist solely of the medium in which the program is embedded. The term also does not include accounts, chattel paper, commercial tort claims, deposit accounts, documents, general intangibles, instruments, investment property, letter-of-credit rights, letters of credit, money, or oil, gas, or other minerals before extraction.

(45) "Governmental unit" means a subdivision, agency, department, county, parish, municipality, or other unit of the government of the United States, a State, or a foreign country. The term includes an organization having a separate corporate existence if the organization is eligible to issue debt on which interest is exempt from income taxation under the laws of the United States.

(46) "Health-care-insurance receivable" means an interest in or claim under a policy of insurance which is a right to payment of

a monetary obligation for health-care goods or services provided or to be provided.

(47) "Instrument" means a negotiable instrument or any other writing that evidences a right to the payment of a monetary obligation, is not itself a security agreement or lease, and is of a type that in ordinary course of business is transferred by delivery with any necessary indorsement or assignment. The term does not include (i) investment property, (ii) letters of credit, or (iii) writings that evidence a right to payment arising out of the use of a credit or charge card or information contained on or for use with the card.

(48) "Inventory" means goods, other than farm products, which:

    (A) are leased by a person as lessor;

    (B) are held by a person for sale or lease or to be furnished under a contract of service;

    (C) are furnished by a person under a contract of service; or

    (D) consist of raw materials, work in process, or materials used or consumed in a business.

(49) "Investment property" means a security, whether certificated or uncertificated, security entitlement, securities account, commodity contract, or commodity account.

(50) "Jurisdiction of organization", with respect to a registered organization, means the jurisdiction under whose law the organization is organized.

(51) "Letter-of-credit right" means a right to payment or performance under a letter of credit, whether or not the beneficiary has demanded or is at the time entitled to demand payment or performance. The term does not include the right of a beneficiary to demand payment or performance under a letter of credit.

(52) "Lien creditor" means:

    (A) a creditor that has acquired a lien on the property involved by attachment, levy, or the like;

    (B) an assignee for benefit of creditors from the time of assignment;

    (C) a trustee in bankruptcy from the date of the filing of the petition; or

(D) a receiver in equity from the time of appointment.

* * *

(55) "Mortgage" means a consensual interest in real property, including fixtures, which secures payment or performance of an obligation.

(56) "New debtor" means a person that becomes bound as debtor under Section 9–203(d) by a security agreement previously entered into by another person.

(57) "New value" means (i) money, (ii) money's worth in property, services, or new credit, or (iii) release by a transferee of an interest in property previously transferred to the transferee. The term does not include an obligation substituted for another obligation.

(58) "Noncash proceeds" means proceeds other than cash proceeds.

(59) "Obligor" means a person that, with respect to an obligation secured by a security interest in or an agricultural lien on the collateral, (i) owes payment or other performance of the obligation, (ii) has provided property other than the collateral to secure payment or other performance of the obligation, or (iii) is otherwise accountable in whole or in part for payment or other performance of the obligation. The term does not include issuers or nominated persons under a letter of credit.

(60) "Original debtor", except as used in Section 9–310(c), means a person that, as debtor, entered into a security agreement to which a new debtor has become bound under Section 9–203(d).

(61) "Payment intangible" means a general intangible under which the account debtor's principal obligation is a monetary obligation.

(62) "Person related to", with respect to an individual, means:

    (A) the spouse of the individual;

    (B) a brother, brother-in-law, sister, or sister-in-law of the individual;

    (C) an ancestor or lineal descendant of the individual or the individual's spouse; or

(D) any other relative, by blood or marriage, of the individual or the individual's spouse who shares the same home with the individual.

(63) "Person related to", with respect to an organization, means:

(A) a person directly or indirectly controlling, controlled by, or under common control with the organization;

(B) an officer or director of, or a person performing similar functions with respect to, the organization;

(C) an officer or director of, or a person performing similar functions with respect to, a person described in subparagraph (A);

(D) the spouse of an individual described in subparagraph (A), (B), or (C); or

(E) an individual who is related by blood or marriage to an individual described in subparagraph (A), (B), (C), or (D) and shares the same home with the individual.

(64) "Proceeds", except as used in Section 9–609(b), means the following property:

(A) whatever is acquired upon the sale, lease, license, exchange, or other disposition of collateral;

(B) whatever is collected on, or distributed on account of, collateral;

(C) rights arising out of collateral;

(D) to the extent of the value of collateral, claims arising out of the loss, nonconformity, or interference with the use of, defects or infringement of rights in, or damage to, the collateral; or

(E) to the extent of the value of collateral and to the extent payable to the debtor or the secured party, insurance payable by reason of the loss or nonconformity of, defects or infringement of rights in, or damage to, the collateral.

(65) "Promissory note" means an instrument that evidences a promise to pay a monetary obligation, does not evidence an order to pay, and does not contain an acknowledgment by a bank that the bank has received for deposit a sum of money or funds.

(66) "Proposal" means a record authenticated by a secured party which includes the terms on which the secured party is willing

to accept collateral in full or partial satisfaction of the obligation it secures pursuant to Sections 9–620, 9–621, and 9–622.

* * *

(68) "Pursuant to commitment", with respect to an advance made or other value given by a secured party, means pursuant to the secured party's obligation, whether or not a subsequent event of default or other event not within the secured party's control has relieved or may relieve the secured party from its obligation.

(69) "Record", except as used in "for record", "of record", "record or legal title", and "record owner", means information that is inscribed on a tangible medium or which is stored in an electronic or other medium and is retrievable in perceivable form.

(70) "Registered organization" means an organization organized solely under the law of a single State or the United States and as to which the State or the United States must maintain a public record showing the organization to have been organized.

(71) "Secondary obligor" means an obligor to the extent that:

(A) the obligor's obligation is secondary; or

(B) the obligor has a right of recourse with respect to an obligation secured by collateral against the debtor, another obligor, or property of either.

(72) "Secured party" means:

(A) a person in whose favor a security interest is created or provided for under a security agreement, whether or not any obligation to be secured is outstanding;

(B) a person that holds an agricultural lien;

(C) a consignor;

(D) a person to which accounts, chattel paper, payment intangibles, or promissory notes have been sold;

(E) a trustee, indenture trustee, agent, collateral agent, or other representative in whose favor a security interest or agricultural lien is created or provided for; or

(F) a person that holds a security interest arising under Section 2–401, 2–505, 2–711(3), 2A–508(5), 4–210, or 5–118.

(73) "Security agreement" means an agreement that creates or provides for a security interest.

(74) "Send", in connection with a record or notification, means:
  (A) to deposit in the mail, deliver for transmission, or transmit by any other usual means of communication, with postage or cost of transmission provided for, addressed to any address reasonable under the circumstances; or
  (B) to cause the record or notification to be received within the time that it would have been received if properly sent under subparagraph (A).

(75) "Software" means a computer program and any supporting information provided in connection with a transaction relating to the program. The term does not include a computer program that is included in the definition of goods.

(76) "State" means a State of the United States, the District of Columbia, Puerto Rico, the United States Virgin Islands, or any territory or insular possession subject to the jurisdiction of the United States.

(77) "Supporting obligation" means a letter-of-credit right or secondary obligation that supports the payment or performance of an account, chattel paper, a document, a general intangible, an instrument, or investment property.

(78) "Tangible chattel paper" means chattel paper evidenced by a record or records consisting of information that is inscribed on a tangible medium.

(79) "Termination statement" means an amendment of a financing statement which:
  (A) identifies, by its file number, the initial financing statement to which it relates; and
  (B) indicates either that it is a termination statement or that the identified financing statement is no longer effective.

* * *

(b) [Definitions in other articles.] "Control" as provided in Section 7–106 and the following definitions in other articles apply to this article:

"Applicant". Section 5–102.

"Beneficiary". Section 5–102.

"Broker". Section 8–102.

"Certificated security". Section 8–102.

"Check". Section 3–104.

"Clearing corporation". Section 8–102.

"Contract for sale". Section 2–106.

"Customer". Section 4–104.

"Entitlement holder". Section 8–102.

"Financial asset". Section 8–102.

"Holder in due course". Section 3–302.

"Issuer" (with respect to a letter of credit or letter-of-credit right). Section 5–102.

"Issuer" (with respect to a security). Section 8–201.

"Issuer" (with respect to documents of title). Section 7–102.

"Lease". Section 2A–103.

"Lease agreement". Section 2A–103.

"Lease contract". Section 2A–103.

"Leasehold interest". Section 2A–103.

"Lessee". Section 2A–103.

"Lessee in ordinary course of business". Section 2A–103.

"Lessor". Section 2A–103.

"Lessor's residual interest". Section 2A–103.

"Letter of credit". Section 5–102.

"Merchant". Section 2–104.

"Negotiable instrument". Section 3–104.

"Nominated person". Section 5–102.

"Note". Section 3–104.

"Proceeds of a letter of credit". Section 5–114.

"Prove". Section 3–103.

"Sale". Section 2–106.

"Securities account". Section 8–501.

"Securities intermediary". Section 8–102.

"Security". Section 8–102.

"Security certificate". Section 8–102.

"Security entitlement". Section 8–102.

"Uncertificated security". Section 8–102.

(c) [Article 1 definitions and principles.] Article 1 contains general definitions and principles of construction and interpretation applicable throughout this article.

UNOFFICIAL COMMENTS

Definitions are incredibly important. Most but not all of the important definitions are in section 9–102.

You need to keep coming back to this section to check for definitions. Here is our exam prep check list of the most important section 9–102 definitions:

accession

account (and how account is different from "chattel paper" and different from a "deposit account")

cash proceeds

certificate of title

chattel paper

collateral

consumer goods

continuation statement

debtor

deposit account

encumbrance

equipment

financing statement

fixture filing

fixtures

general intangibles

goods (and how to recognize goods as "consumer goods", "equipment", "farm products" or "inventory" depending on how the debtor uses the goods)

inventory

lien creditor

new debtor

obligor

original debtor

proceeds

secured party

security agreement

termination statement

Some of the important definitions are new terms like "chattel paper." While "chattel paper" may be a new term to you, it has some history. What we now call "goods" lawyers used to call "chattels." What we now call "security agreements" and "security interests", lawyers used to call "chattel mortgages."

If, for example, X buys equipment on credit from Y and executes a security agreement granting Y a security interest in the equipment, old lawyers would say Y has a chattel mortgage on X's chattel.

Lawyers today use the term "chattel paper" in connection with a "second generation" secured transaction in which someone who was the secured party in an earlier transaction, uses its rights from that first transaction as collateral for the second transaction. For example, Y later borrows from Z and grants Z a security interest in its rights against X from the transaction in the prior paragraph, i.e. in its "chattel paper."

The term "consignment" may also be new to some of you. Regardless, there is new stuff in the section 9–102 definition of consignment that you need to know. You need to know about section 9–102's definition of consignments because section 9–109(a)(4) provides that Article 9 applies to consignments as defined in section 9–102. **For a more extended discussion of consignments, see pages 409–411.**

Other important definitions are familiar terms that, for Article 9 purposes, have unfamiliar definitions. Look, for example at the definition of "debtor." In the example in the preceding paragraph, Y would be a "debtor" if it sold the chattel paper to Z. No debt from Y to Z but Y is still an Article 9 "debtor." **For a more extended discussion of sales of chattel paper (and other receivables–accounts, payment intangibles and promissory notes), see pages 413–416.**

Here is another example of the section 9–102(a)(28) definition of debtor that you are more likely to see on your exam: S makes a loan to O which O promises to repay. D's, O's dad, puts up his car as collateral for S's loan to O. Under these facts, O, the person who is indebted, is not the "debtor." D is the "debtor."

OFFICIAL COMMENT

1. **Source.** All terms that are defined in Article 9 and used in more than one section are consolidated in this section. Note that the definition of "security interest" is found in Section 1–201, not in this Article, and has been revised. See Appendix I. Many of the definitions in this section are new; many others derive from those in former Section 9–105. The following Comments also indicate other sections of former Article 9 that defined (or explained) terms.

2. **Parties to Secured Transactions.**

a. **"Debtor"; "Obligor"; "Secondary Obligor."** Determining whether a person was a "debtor" under former Section 9–105(1)(d) required a close examination of the context in which the term was used. To reduce the need for this examination, this Article redefines "debtor" and adds new defined terms, "secondary obligor" and "obligor." In the context of Part 6 (default and enforcement), these definitions distinguish among three classes of persons: (i) those persons who may have a stake in the proper enforcement of a security interest by virtue of their non-lien property interest (typically, an ownership interest) in the collateral, (ii) those persons who may have a stake in the proper enforcement of the security interest because of their obligation to pay the secured debt, and (iii) those persons who have an obligation to pay the secured debt but have no stake in the proper enforcement of the security interest. Persons in the first class are debtors. Persons in the second class are secondary obligors if any portion of the obligation is secondary or if the obligor has a right of recourse against the debtor or another obligor with respect to an obligation secured by collateral. One must consult the law of suretyship to determine whether an obligation is secondary. The Restatement (3d), Suretyship and Guaranty § 1 (1996), contains a useful explanation of the concept. Obligors in the third class are neither debtors nor secondary obligors. With one exception (Section 9–616, as it relates to a consumer obligor), the rights and duties provided by Part 6 affect non-debtor obligors only if they are "secondary obligors."

By including in the definition of "debtor" all persons with a property interest (other than a security interest in or other lien on collateral), the definition includes transferees of collateral, whether or not the secured party knows of the transfer or the transferee's identity. Exculpatory provisions in Part 6 protect the secured party in that circumstance. See Sections 9–605 and 9–628. The definition renders unnecessary former Section 9–112, which governed situations in which collateral was not owned by the debtor. The definition also includes a "consignee," as defined in this section, as well as a seller of accounts, chattel paper, payment intangibles, or promissory notes.

Secured parties and other lienholders are excluded from the definition of "debtor" because the interests of those parties normally derive from and encumber a debtor's interest. However, if in a *separate* secured transaction a secured party grants, *as debtor*, a security interest in its own interest (i.e., its security interest and any obligation that it secures), the secured party is a debtor *in that transaction*. This typically occurs when a secured party with a security interest in specific goods assigns chattel paper.

Consider the following examples:

Example 1: Behnfeldt borrows money and grants a security interest in her Miata to secure the debt. Behnfeldt is a debtor and an obligor.

Example 2: Behnfeldt borrows money and grants a security interest in her Miata to secure the debt. Bruno co-signs a negotiable note as maker. As before, Behnfeldt is the debtor and an obligor. As an accommodation party (see Section 3–419), Bruno is a secondary obligor. Bruno has this status even if the note states that her obligation is a primary obligation and that she waives all suretyship defenses.

Example 3: Behnfeldt borrows money on an unsecured basis. Bruno co-signs the note and grants a security interest in her Honda to secure her obligation. Inasmuch as Behnfeldt does not have a property interest in the Honda, Behnfeldt is not a debtor. Having granted the security interest, Bruno is the debtor. Because Behnfeldt is a principal obligor, she is not a secondary obligor. Whatever the outcome of enforcement of the security interest against the Honda or Bruno's secondary obligation, Bruno will look to Behnfeldt for her losses. The enforcement will not affect Behnfeldt's aggregate obligations.

When the principal obligor (borrower) and the secondary obligor (surety) each has granted a security interest in different collateral, the status of each is determined by the collateral involved.

Example 4: Behnfeldt borrows money and grants a security interest in her Miata to secure the debt. Bruno co-signs the note and grants a security interest in her Honda to secure her obligation. When the secured party enforces the security interest in Behnfeldt's Miata, Behnfeldt is the debtor, and Bruno is a secondary obligor. When the secured party enforces the security interest in the Honda, Bruno is the "debtor." As in Example 3, Behnfeldt is an obligor, but not a secondary obligor.

b. **"Secured Party."** The secured party is the person in whose favor the security interest has been created, as determined by reference to the security agreement. This definition controls, among other things, which person has the duties and potential liability that Part 6 imposes upon a secured party. The definition of "secured party" also includes a "consignor," a person to which accounts, chattel paper, payment intangibles, or promissory notes have been sold, and the holder of an agricultural lien.

The definition of "secured party" clarifies the status of various types of representatives. Consider, for example, a multi-bank facility under which Bank A, Bank B, and Bank C are lenders and Bank A serves as the collateral agent. If the security interest is granted to the banks, then they are the secured parties. If the security interest is granted to Bank A as collateral agent, then Bank A is the secured party.

c. **Other Parties.** A "consumer obligor" is defined as the obligor in a consumer transaction. Definitions of "new debtor" and "original debtor" are used in the special rules found in Sections 9–326 and 9–508.

3. **Definitions Relating to Creation of a Security Interest.**

a. **"Collateral."** As under former Section 9–105, "collateral" is the property subject to a security interest and includes accounts and chattel paper that have been sold. It has been expanded in this Article. The term now explicitly includes proceeds subject to a security interest. It also reflects the broadened scope of the Article. It includes property subject to an agricultural lien as well as payment intangibles and promissory notes that have been sold.

b. **"Security Agreement."** The definition of "security agreement" is substantially the same as under former Section 9–105—an agreement that creates or provides for a security interest. However, the term frequently was used colloquially in former Article 9 to refer to the document or writing that contained a debtor's security agreement. This Article eliminates that usage, reserving the term for the more precise meaning specified in the definition.

Whether an agreement creates a security interest depends not on whether the parties intend that the law *characterize* the transaction as a security interest but rather on whether the transaction falls within the definition of "security interest" in Section 1–201. Thus, an agreement that the parties characterize as a "lease" of goods may be a "security agreement," notwithstanding the parties' stated intention that the law treat the transaction as a lease and not as a secured transaction. See Section 1–203.

4. **Goods-Related Definitions.**

a. **"Goods"; "Consumer Goods"; "Equipment"; "Farm Products"; "Farming Operation"; "Inventory."**

The definition of "goods" is substantially the same as the definition in former Section 9–105. This Article also retains the four mutually-exclusive "types" of collateral that consist of goods: "consumer goods," "equipment," "farm products," and "inventory." The revisions are primarily for clarification.

The classes of goods are mutually exclusive. For example, the same property cannot simultaneously be both equipment and inventory. In borderline cases—a physician's car or a farmer's truck that might be either consumer goods or equipment—the principal use to which the property is put is determinative. Goods can fall into different classes at different times. For example, a radio may be inventory in the hands of a dealer and consumer goods in the hands of a consumer. As under former Article 9, goods are "equipment" if they do not fall into another category.

The definition of "consumer goods" follows former Section 9–109. The classification turns on whether the debtor uses or bought the goods for use "primarily for personal, family, or household purposes."

Goods are inventory if they are leased by a lessor or held by a person for sale or lease. The revised definition of "inventory" makes clear that the term includes goods leased by the debtor to others as well as goods held for lease. (The same result should have obtained under the former definition.) Goods to be furnished or furnished under a service contract, raw materials, and work in process also are inventory. Implicit in the definition is the criterion that the sales or leases are or will be in the ordinary course of business. For example, machinery used in manufacturing is equipment, not inventory, even though it is the policy of the debtor to sell machinery when it becomes obsolete or worn. Inventory also includes goods that are consumed in a business (e.g., fuel used in operations). In general, goods used in a business are equipment if they are fixed assets or have, as identifiable units, a relatively long period of use, but are inventory, even though not held for sale or lease, if they are used up or consumed in a short period of time in producing a product or providing a service.

Goods are "farm products" if the debtor is engaged in farming operations with respect to the goods. Animals in a herd of livestock are covered whether the debtor acquires them by purchase or as a result of natural increase. Products of crops or livestock remain farm products as long as they have not been subjected to a manufacturing process. The terms "crops" and "livestock" are not defined. The new definition of "farming operations" is for clarification only.

Crops, livestock, and their products cease to be "farm products" when the debtor ceases to be engaged in farming operations with respect to them. If, for example, they come into the possession of a marketing agency for sale or distribution or of a manufacturer or processor as raw materials, they become inventory. Products of crops or livestock, even though they remain in the possession of a person engaged in farming operations, lose their status as farm products if they are subjected to a manufacturing process. What is and what is not a manufacturing operation is not specified in this Article. At one end of the spectrum, some processes are so closely connected with farming—such as pasteurizing milk or boiling sap to produce maple syrup or sugar—that they would not constitute manufacturing. On the other hand an extensive canning operation would be manufacturing. Once farm products have been subjected to a manufacturing operation, they normally become inventory.

The revised definition of "farm products" clarifies the distinction between crops and standing timber and makes clear that aquatic goods produced in aquacultural operations may be either crops or livestock. Although aquatic goods that are vegetable in nature often would be crops and those that are animal would be livestock, this Article leaves the courts free to classify the goods on a case-by-case basis. See Section 9–324, Comment 11.

The definitions of "goods" and "software" are also mutually exclusive. Computer programs usually constitute "software," and, as such, are not "goods" as this Article uses the terms. However, under the circumstances specified in the definition of "goods," computer programs embedded in goods are part of the "goods" and are not "software."

* * *

5. **Receivables-related Definitions.**

a. **"Account"; "Health–Care–Insurance Receivable"; "As–Extracted Collateral."** The definition of "account" has been expanded and reformulated. It is no longer limited to rights to payment relating to goods or services. Many categories of rights to payment that were classified as general intangibles under former Article 9 are accounts under this Article. Thus, if they are sold, a financing statement must be filed to perfect the buyer's interest in them. Among the types of property that are expressly excluded from the definition is "a right to payment for money or funds advanced or sold." As defined in Section 1–201, "money" is limited essentially to currency. As used in the exclusion from the definition of "account," however, "funds" is a broader concept (although the term is not defined). For example, when a bank-lender credits a borrower's deposit account for the amount of a loan, the bank's advance of funds is not a transaction giving rise to an account.

The definition of "health-care-insurance receivable" is new. It is a subset of the definition of "account." However, the rules generally applicable to account debtors on accounts do not apply to insurers obligated on health-care-insurance receivables. See Sections 9–404(e), 9–405(d), 9–406(i).

Note that certain accounts also are "as-extracted collateral." See Comment 4.c., Examples 6 and 7.

b. **"Chattel Paper"; "Electronic Chattel Paper"; "Tangible Chattel Paper."** "Chattel paper" consists of a monetary obligation together with a security interest in or a lease of specific goods if the obligation and security interest or lease are evidenced by "a record or records." The definition has been expanded from that found in former Article 9 to include records that evidence a monetary obligation and a security interest in specific goods and software used in the goods, *a security interest in specific goods and license of software used in the goods, or a lease of specific goods and license of software used in the goods. The expanded definition covers transactions in which the debtor's or lessee's monetary obligation includes amounts owed with respect to software used in the goods. The monetary obligation with respect to the software need not be owed under a license from the secured party or lessor, and the secured party or lessor need not be a party to the license transaction itself. Among the types of monetary obligations that are included in "chattel paper" are amounts that have been advanced by the secured party or lessor to enable the debtor or lessee to acquire or obtain financing for a license of the software used in the goods.** The definition also makes clear that rights to payment arising out of credit-card transactions are not chattel paper.

Charters of vessels are expressly excluded from the definition of chattel paper; they are accounts. The term "charter" as used in this section includes bareboat charters, time charters, successive voyage charters, contracts of affreightment, contracts of carriage, and all other arrangements for the use of vessels. Under former Section 9–105, only if the evidence of an obligation consisted of "a writing or writings" could an obligation qualify as chattel paper. In this Article, traditional, written chattel paper is included in the definition of "tangible chattel paper." "Electronic chattel paper" is chattel paper that is stored in an electronic medium instead of in tangible form. The concept of an electronic medium should be construed liberally to include electrical, digital,

---

* Amendments in italics approved by the Permanent Editorial Board for Uniform Commercial Code October 20, 1999.

magnetic, optical, electromagnetic, or any other current or similar emerging technologies.

The definition of electronic chattel paper does not dictate that it be created in any particular fashion. For example, a record consisting of a tangible writing may be converted to electronic form (e.g., by creating electronic images of a signed writing). Or, records may be initially created and executed in electronic form (e.g., a lessee might authenticate an electronic record of a lease that is then stored in electronic form). In either case the resulting records are electronic chattel paper.

c. **"Instrument"; "Promissory Note."** The definition of "instrument" includes a negotiable instrument. As under former Section 9–105, it also includes any other right to payment of a monetary obligation that is evidenced by a writing of a type that in ordinary course of business is transferred by delivery (and, if necessary, an indorsement or assignment). Except in the case of chattel paper, the fact that an instrument is secured by a security interest or encumbrance on property does not change the character of the instrument as such or convert the combination of the instrument and collateral into a separate classification of personal property. The definition makes clear that rights to payment arising out of credit-card transactions are not instruments. The definition of "promissory note" is new, necessitated by the inclusion of sales of promissory notes within the scope of Article 9. It explicitly excludes obligations arising out of "orders" to pay (e.g., checks) as opposed to "promises" to pay. See Section 3–104.

d. **"General Intangible"; "Payment Intangible."** "General intangible" is the residual category of personal property, including things in action, that is not included in the other defined types of collateral. Examples are various categories of intellectual property and the right to payment of a loan of funds that is not evidenced by chattel paper or an instrument. As used in the definition of "general intangible," "things in action" includes rights that arise under a license of intellectual property, including the right to exploit the intellectual property without liability for infringement. The definition has been revised to exclude commercial tort claims, deposit accounts, and letter-of-credit rights. Each of the three is a separate type of collateral. One important consequence of this exclusion is that tortfeasors (commercial tort claims), banks (deposit accounts), and persons obligated on letters of credit (letter-of-credit rights) are not "account debtors" having the rights and obligations set forth in Sections 9–404, 9–405, and 9–406. In particular, tortfeasors, banks, and persons obligated on letters of credit are not obligated to pay an assignee (secured party) upon receipt of the notification described in Section 9–404(a). See Comment 5.h. Another important consequence relates to the adequacy of the description in the security agreement. See Section 9–108.

"Payment intangible" is a subset of the definition of "general intangible." The sale of a payment intangible is subject to this Article. See Section 9–109(a)(3). Virtually any intangible right could give rise to a right to payment of money once one hypothesizes, for example, that the account debtor is in breach of its obligation. The term "payment intangible," however, embraces only those general intangibles "under which the account debtor's *principal* obligation is a monetary obligation." (Emphasis added.)

In classifying intangible collateral, a court should begin by identifying the particular rights that have been assigned. The account debtor (promisor) under a particular contract may owe several types of monetary obligations as well as other, nonmonetary obligations. If the promisee's right to payment of money is assigned separately, the right is an account or payment intangible, depending on how the account debtor's obligation arose. When all the promisee's rights are assigned together, an account, a payment intangible, and a general intangible all may be involved, depending on the nature of the rights.

A right to the payment of money is frequently buttressed by ancillary covenants, such as covenants in a purchase agreement, note, or mortgage requiring insurance on the collateral or forbidding removal of the collateral, or covenants to preserve the creditworthiness of the promisor, such as covenants restricting dividends and the like. This Article does not treat these ancillary rights separately from the rights to payment to which they relate. For example, attachment and perfection of an assignment of a right to payment of a monetary obligation, whether it be an account or payment intangible, also carries these ancillary rights.

Every "payment intangible" is also a "general intangible." Likewise, "software" is a "general intangible" for purposes of this Article. See Comment 25. Accordingly, except as otherwise provided, statutory provisions applicable to general intangibles apply to payment intangibles and software.

e. **"Letter-of-Credit Right."** The term "letter-of-credit right" embraces the rights to payment and performance under a letter of credit (defined in Section 5–102). However, it does not include a beneficiary's right to demand payment or performance. Transfer of those rights to a transferee beneficiary is governed by Article 5. See Sections 9–107, Comment 4, and 9–329, Comments 3 and 4.

f. **"Supporting Obligation."** This new term covers the most common types of credit enhancements—suretyship obligations (including guarantees) and letter-of-credit rights that support one of the types of collateral specified in the definition. As explained in Comment 2.a., suretyship law determines whether an obligation is "secondary" for purposes of this definition. Section 9–109 generally excludes from this Article transfers of interests in insurance policies. However, the regulation of a secondary obligation as an insurance product does not necessarily mean that it is a "policy of insurance" for purposes of the exclusion in Section 9–109. Thus, this Article may cover a secondary obligation (as a supporting obligation), even if the obligation is issued by a regulated insurance company and the obligation is subject to regulation as an "insurance" product.

This Article contains rules explicitly governing attachment, perfection, and priority of security interests in supporting obligations. See Sections 9–203, 9–308, 9–310, and 9–322. These provisions reflect the principle that a supporting obligation is an incident of the collateral it supports.

Collections of or other distributions under a supporting obligation are "proceeds" of the supported collateral as well as "proceeds" of the supporting obligation itself. See Section 9–102 (defining "proceeds") and Comment 13.b. As such, the collections and distributions are subject to the priority rules applicable to proceeds generally. See Section 9–322. However, under the special rule governing security interests in a letter-of-credit right, a secured party's failure to obtain control (Section 9–107) of a letter-of-credit right supporting collateral may leave its security interest exposed to a priming interest of a party who does take control. See Section 9–329 (security interest in a letter-of-credit right perfected by control has priority over a conflicting security interest).

g. **"Commercial Tort Claim."** This term is new. A tort claim may serve as original collateral under this Article only if it is a "commercial tort claim." See Section 9–109(d). Although security interests in commercial tort claims are within its scope, this Article does not override other applicable law restricting the assignability of a tort claim. See Section 9–401. A security interest in a tort claim also may exist under this Article if the claim is proceeds of other collateral.

h. **"Account Debtor."** An "account debtor" is a person obligated on an account, chattel paper, or general intangible. The account debtor's obligation often is a monetary obligation; however, this is not always the case. For example, if a franchisee uses its rights under a franchise agreement (a general intangible) as collateral, then the franchisor is an "account debtor." As a general matter, Article 3, and not Article 9, governs obligations on negotiable instruments. Accordingly, the definition of "account debtor" excludes obligors on negotiable instruments constituting part of chattel paper. The principal effect of this change from the definition in former Article 9 is that the rules in Sections 9–403, 9–404, 9–405, and 9–406, dealing with the rights of an assignee and duties of an account debtor, do not apply to an assignment of chattel paper in which the obligation to pay is evidenced by a negotiable instrument. (Section 9–406(d), however, does apply to promissory notes, including negotiable promissory notes.) Rather, the assignee's rights are governed by Article 3. Similarly, the duties of an obligor on a nonnegotiable instrument are governed by non-Article 9 law unless the nonnegotiable instrument is a part of chattel paper, in which case the obligor is an account debtor.

i. **Receivables Under Government Entitlement Programs**. This Article does not contain a defined term that encompasses specifically rights to payment or performance under the many and varied government entitlement programs. Depending on the nature of a right under a program, it could be an account, a payment intangible, a general intangible other than a payment intangible, or another type of collateral. The right also might be proceeds of collateral (e.g., crops).

6. **Investment–Property–Related Definitions: "Commodity Account"; "Commodity Contract"; "Commodity Customer"; "Commodity Intermediary"; "Investment Property."** These definitions are substantially the same as the corresponding definitions in former Section 9–115. "Investment property" includes securities, both certificated and uncertificated, securities accounts, security entitlements, commodity accounts, and commodity contracts. The term investment property includes a "securities account" in order to facilitate transactions in which a debtor wishes to create a security interest in all of the investment positions held through a particular account rather than in particular positions carried in the account. Former Section 9–115 was added in conjunction with Revised Article 8 and contained a variety of rules applicable to security interests in investment property. These rules have been relocated to the appropriate sections of Article 9. See, e.g., Sections 9–203 (attachment), 9–314 (perfection by control), 9–328 (priority).

The terms "security," "security entitlement," and related terms are defined in Section 8–102, and the term "securities account" is defined in Section 8–501. The terms "commodity account," "commodity contract," "commodity customer," and "commodity intermediary" are defined in this section. Commodity contracts are not "securities" or "financial assets" under Article 8. See Section 8–103(f). Thus, the relationship between commodity intermediaries and commodity customers is not governed by the indirect-holding-system rules of Part 5 of Article 8. For securities, Article 9 contains rules on security interests, and Article 8 contains rules on the rights of transferees, including secured parties, on such matters as the rights of a transferee if the transfer was itself wrongful and gives rise to an adverse claim. For commodity contracts, Article 9 establishes rules on security interests, but questions of the sort dealt with in Article 8 for securities are left to other law.

The indirect-holding-system rules of Article 8 are sufficiently flexible to be applied to new developments in the securities and financial markets, where that is appropriate. Accordingly, the definition of "commodity contract" is narrowly drafted to ensure that it does not operate as an obstacle to the application of the Article 8 indirect-holding-system rules to new products. The term "commodity contract" covers those contracts that are traded on or subject to the rules of a designated contract market and foreign commodity contracts that are carried on the books of American commodity intermediaries. The effect of this definition is that the category of commodity contracts that are excluded from Article 8 but governed by Article 9 is essentially the same as the category of contracts that fall within the exclusive regulatory jurisdiction of the federal Commodity Futures Trading Commission.

Commodity contracts are different from securities or other financial assets. A person who enters into a commodity futures contract is not buying an asset having a certain value and holding it in anticipation of increase in value. Rather the person is entering into a contract to buy or sell a commodity at set price for delivery at a future time. That contract may become advantageous or disadvantageous as the price of the commodity fluctuates during the term of the contract. The rules of the commodity exchanges require that the contracts be marked to market on a daily basis; that is, the customer pays or receives any increment attributable to that day's price change. Because commodity customers may incur obligations on their contracts, they are required to provide collateral at the outset, known as "original margin," and may be required to provide additional amounts, known as "variation margin," during the term of the contract.

The most likely setting in which a person would want to take a security interest in a commodity contract is where a lender who is advancing funds to finance an inventory of a physical commodity requires the borrower to enter into a commodity contract as a hedge against the risk of decline in the value of the commodity. The lender will want to take a security interest in both the commodity itself and the hedging commodity contract. Typically, such arrangements are structured as security interests in the entire commodity account in which the borrower carries the hedging contracts, rather than in individual contracts.

One important effect of including commodity contracts and commodity accounts in Article 9 is to provide a clearer legal structure for the analysis of the rights of commodity clearing organizations against their participants and futures commission merchants against their customers. The rules and agreements of commodity clearing organizations generally provide that the clearing organization has the right to liquidate any participant's positions in order to satisfy obligations of the participant to the clearing corporation. Similarly, agreements between futures commission merchants and their customers generally provide that the futures commission merchant has the right to liquidate a customer's positions in order to satisfy obligations of the customer to the futures commission merchant.

The main property that a commodity intermediary holds as collateral for the obligations that the commodity customer may incur under its commodity contracts is not other commodity contracts carried by the customer but the other property that the customer has posted as margin. Typically, this property will be securities. The commodity intermediary's security interest in such securities is governed by the rules of this Article on security interests in securities, not the rules on security interests in commodity contracts or commodity accounts.

Although there are significant analytic and regulatory differences between commodities and securities, the development of commodity contracts on financial products in the past few decades has resulted in a system in which the commodity markets and securities markets are closely linked. The rules on security interests in commodity contracts and commodity accounts provide a structure that may be essential in times of stress in the financial markets. Suppose, for example that a firm has a position in a securities market that is hedged by a position in a commodity market, so that payments that the firm is obligated to make with respect to the securities position will be covered by the receipt of funds from the commodity position. Depending upon the settlement cycles of the different markets, it is possible that the firm could find itself in a position where it is obligated to make the payment with respect to the securities position before it receives the matching funds from the commodity position. If cross-margining arrangements have not been developed between the two markets, the firm may need to borrow funds temporarily to make the earlier payment. The rules on security interests in investment property would facilitate the use of positions in one market as collateral for loans needed to cover obligations in the other market.

7. Consumer-Related Definitions: "Consumer Debtor"; "Consumer Goods"; "Consumer-goods transac-

tion''; ''**Consumer Obligor**''; ''**Consumer Transaction.**'' The definition of ''consumer goods'' (discussed above) is substantially the same as the definition in former Section 9–109. The definitions of ''consumer debtor,'' ''consumer obligor,'' ''consumer-goods transaction,'' and ''consumer transaction'' have been added in connection with various new (and old) consumer-related provisions and to designate certain provisions that are inapplicable in consumer transactions.

''Consumer-goods transaction'' is a subset of ''consumer transaction.'' Under each definition, both the obligation secured and the collateral must have a personal, family, or household purpose. However, ''mixed'' business and personal transactions also may be characterized as a consumer-goods transaction or consumer transaction. Subparagraph (A) of the definition of consumer-goods transactions and clause (i) of the definition of consumer transaction are primary purposes tests. Under these tests, it is necessary to determine the primary purpose of the obligation or obligations secured. Subparagraph (B) and clause (iii) of these definitions are satisfied if any of the collateral is consumer goods, in the case of a consumer-goods transaction, or ''is held or acquired primarily for personal, family, or household purposes,'' in the case of a consumer transaction. The fact that some of the obligations secured or some of the collateral for the obligation does not satisfy the tests (e.g., some of the collateral is acquired for a business purpose) does not prevent a transaction from being a ''consumer transaction'' or ''consumer-goods transaction.''

8. **Filing-Related Definitions: ''Continuation Statement''; ''File Number''; ''Filing Office''; ''Filing-office Rule''; ''Financing Statement''; ''Fixture Filing''; ''Manufactured-Home Transaction''; ''New Debtor''; ''Original Debtor''; ''Public–Finance Transaction''; ''Termination Statement''; ''Transmitting Utility.''** These definitions are used exclusively or primarily in the filing-related provisions in Part 5. Most are self-explanatory and are discussed in the Comments to Part 5. A financing statement filed in a manufactured-home transaction or a public-finance transaction may remain effective for 30 years instead of the 5 years applicable to other financing statements. See Section 9–515(b). The definitions relating to medium neutrality also are significant for the filing provisions. See Comment 9.

The definition of ''transmitting utility'' has been revised to embrace the business of transmitting communications generally to take account of new and future types of communications technology. The term designates a special class of debtors for whom separate filing rules are provided in Part 5, thereby obviating the many local fixture filings that would be necessary under the rules of Section 9–501 for a far-flung public-utility debtor. A transmitting utility will not necessarily be regulated by or operating as such in a jurisdiction where fixtures are located. For example, a utility might own transmission lines in a jurisdiction, although the utility generates no power and has no customers in the jurisdiction.

9. **Definitions Relating to Medium Neutrality.**

a. **''Record.''** In many, but not all, instances, the term ''record'' replaces the term ''writing'' and ''written.'' A ''record'' includes information that is in intangible form (e.g., electronically stored) as well as tangible form (e.g., written on paper). Given the rapid development and commercial adoption of modern communication and storage technologies, requirements that documents or communications be ''written,'' ''in writing,'' or otherwise in tangible form do not necessarily reflect or aid commercial practices.

A ''record'' need not be permanent or indestructible, but the term does not include any oral or other communication that is not stored or preserved by any means. The information must be stored on paper or in some other medium. Information that has not been retained other than through human memory does not qualify as a record. Examples of current technologies commercially used to communicate or store information include, but are not limited to, magnetic media, optical discs, digital voice messaging systems, electronic mail, audio tapes, and photographic media, as well as paper. "Record" is an inclusive term that includes all of these methods of storing or communicating information. Any "writing" is a record. A record may be authenticated. See Comment 9.b. A record may be created without the knowledge or intent of a particular person.

Like the terms "written" or "in writing," the term "record" does not establish the purposes, permitted uses, or legal effect that a record may have under any particular provision of law. Whatever is filed in the Article 9 filing system, including financing statements, continuation statements, and termination statements, whether transmitted in tangible or intangible form, would fall within the definition. However, in some instances, statutes or filing-office rules may require that a paper record be filed. In such cases, even if this Article permits the filing of an electronic record, compliance with those statutes or rules is necessary. Similarly, a filer must comply with a statute or rule that requires a particular type of encoding or formatting for an electronic record.

This Article sometimes uses the terms "for record," "of record," "record or legal title," and "record owner." Some of these are terms traditionally used in real-property law. The definition of "record" in this Article now explicitly excepts these usages from the defined term. Also, this Article refers to a record that is filed or recorded in real-property recording systems to record a mortgage as a "record of a mortgage." This usage recognizes that the defined term "mortgage" means an interest in real property; it does not mean the record that evidences, or is filed or recorded with respect to, the mortgage.

b. **"Authenticate"; "Communicate"; "Send."** The terms "authenticate" and "authenticated" generally replace "sign" and "signed." "Authenticated" replaces and broadens the definition of "signed," in Section 1–201, to encompass authentication of all records, not just writings. (References to authentication of, e.g., an agreement, demand, or notification mean, of course, authentication of a record containing an agreement, demand, or notification.) The terms "communicate" and "send" also contemplate the possibility of communication by nonwritten media. These definitions include the act of transmitting both tangible and intangible records. The definition of "send" replaces, for purposes of this Article, the corresponding term in Section 1–201. The reference to "usual means of communication" in that definition contemplates an inquiry into the appropriateness of the method of transmission used in the particular circumstances involved.

10. **Scope-Related Definitions.**

a. **Expanded Scope of Article: "Agricultural Lien"; "Consignment"; "Payment Intangible"; "Promissory Note."** These new definitions reflect the expanded scope of Article 9, as provided in Section 9–109(a).

b. **Reduced Scope of Exclusions: "Governmental Unit"; "Health–Care–Insurance Receivable"; "Commercial Tort Claims."** These new definitions reflect the reduced scope of the exclusions, provided in Section 9–109(c) and (d), of transfers by governmental debtors and assignments of interests in insurance policies and commercial tort claims.

11. **Choice-of-Law–Related Definitions: "Certificate of Title"; "Governmental Unit"; "Jurisdiction of Organization"; "Registered Organization"; "State."** These new definitions reflect the changes in the law governing perfection and priority of security interests and agricultural liens provided in Part 3, Subpart 1.

Not every organization that may provide information about itself in the public records is a "registered organization." For example, a general partnership is not a "registered organization," even if it files a statement of partnership authority under Section 303 of the Uniform Partnership Act (1994) or an assumed name ("dba") certificate. This is because the State under whose law the partnership is organized is not required to maintain a public record showing that the partnership has been organized. In contrast, corporations, limited liability companies, and limited partnerships are "registered organizations."

12. **Deposit–Account–Related Definitions: "Deposit Account"; "Bank."** The revised definition of "deposit account" incorporates the definition of "bank," which is new. The definition derives from the definitions of "bank" in Sections 4–105(1) and 4A–105(a)(2), which focus on whether the organization is "engaged in the business of banking."

Deposit accounts evidenced by Article 9 "instruments" are excluded from the term "deposit account." In contrast, former Section 9–105 excluded from the former definition "an account evidenced by a certificate of deposit." The revised definition clarifies the proper treatment of nonnegotiable or uncertificated certificates of deposit. Under the definition, an uncertificated certificate of deposit would be a deposit account (assuming there is no writing evidencing the bank's obligation to pay) whereas a nonnegotiable certificate of deposit would be a deposit account only if it is not an "instrument" as defined in this section (a question that turns on whether the nonnegotiable certificate of deposit is "of a type that in ordinary course of business is transferred by delivery with any necessary indorsement or assignment.")

A deposit account evidenced by an instrument is subject to the rules applicable to instruments generally. As a consequence, a security interest in such an instrument cannot be perfected by "control" (see Section 9–104), and the special priority rules applicable to deposit accounts (see Sections 9–327 and 9–340) do not apply.

The term "deposit account" does not include "investment property," such as securities and security entitlements. Thus, the term also does not include shares in a money-market mutual fund, even if the shares are redeemable by check.

13. **Proceeds-Related Definitions: "Cash Proceeds"; "Noncash Proceeds"; "Proceeds."** The revised definition of "proceeds" expands the definition beyond that contained in former Section 9–306 and resolves ambiguities in the former section.

a. **Distributions on Account of Collateral.** The phrase "whatever is collected on, or distributed on account of, collateral," in subparagraph (B), is broad enough to cover cash or stock dividends distributed on account of securities or other investment property that is original collateral. Compare former Section 9–306 ("Any payments or distributions made with respect to investment property collateral are proceeds."). This section rejects the holding of *FDIC v. Hastie*, 2 F.3d 1042 (10th Cir. 1993) (postpetition cash dividends on stock subject to a prepetition pledge are not "proceeds" under Bankruptcy Code Section 552(b)), to the extent the holding relies on the Article 9 definition of "proceeds."

b. **Distributions on Account of Supporting Obligations.** Under subparagraph (B), collections on and distributions on account of collateral consisting of various credit-support arrangements ("supporting obligations," as defined in Section 9–102) also are proceeds. Consequently, they are afforded treatment identical to proceeds collected from or distributed by the obligor on the underlying (supported) right to payment or other collateral. Proceeds of supporting obligations also are proceeds of the underlying rights to payment or other collateral.

c. **Proceeds of Proceeds.** The definition of "proceeds" no longer provides that proceeds of proceeds are themselves proceeds. That idea is expressed in the revised definition of "collateral" in Section 9–102. No change in meaning is intended.

d. **Proceeds Received by Person Who Did Not Create Security Interest.** When collateral is sold subject to a security interest and the buyer then resells the collateral, a question arose under former Article 9 concerning whether the "debtor" had "received" what the buyer received on resale and, therefore, whether those receipts were "proceeds" under former Section 9–306(2). This Article contains no requirement that property be "received" by the debtor for the property to qualify as proceeds. It is necessary only that the property be traceable, directly or indirectly, to the original collateral.

e. **Cash Proceeds and Noncash Proceeds.** The definition of "cash proceeds" is substantially the same as the corresponding definition in former Section 9–306. The phrase "and the like" covers property that is functionally equivalent to "money, checks, or deposit accounts," such as some money-market accounts that are securities or part of securities entitlements. Proceeds other than cash proceeds are noncash proceeds.

14. **Consignment-Related Definitions: "Consignee"; "Consignment"; "Consignor."** The definition of "consignment" excludes, in subparagraphs (B) and (C), transactions for which filing would be inappropriate or of insufficient benefit to justify the costs. A consignment excluded from the application of this Article by one of those subparagraphs may still be a true consignment; however, it is governed by non-Article 9 law. The definition also excludes, in subparagraph (D), what have been called "consignments intended for security." These "consignments" are not bailments but secured transactions. Accordingly, all of Article 9 applies to them. See Sections 1–201(b)(35), 9–109(a)(1). The "consignor" is the person who delivers goods to the "consignee" in a consignment.

The definition of "consignment" requires that the goods be delivered "to a merchant for the purpose of sale." If the goods are delivered for another purpose as well, such as milling or processing, the transaction is a consignment nonetheless because a purpose of the delivery is "sale." On the other hand, if a merchant-processor-bailee will not be selling the goods itself but will be delivering to buyers to which the owner-bailor agreed to sell the goods, the transaction would not be a consignment.

15. **"Accounting."** This definition describes the record and information that a debtor is entitled to request under Section 9–210.

16. **"Document."** The definition of "document" incorporates both tangible and electronic documents of title. See Section 1–201(15)[1–201(b)16] and Comment 15 [16].

Legislative Note: Former Article 1 defined document of title in section 1–201(15) and accompanying comment 15. Revised Article 1 defines document of title in Section 1–201(b)(16) and accompanying comment 16. Cross references should be adapted depending upon which version of Article 1 is in force in the jurisdiction.

18. **"Fixtures."** This definition is unchanged in substance from the corresponding definition in former Section 9–313. See Section 9–334 (priority of security interests in fixtures and crops).

19. **"Good Faith."** This Article expands the definition of "good faith" to include "the observance of reasonable commercial standards of fair dealing." The definition in this section applies when the term is used in this Article, and the same concept applies in the context of this Article for purposes of the obligation of good faith imposed by Section 1–203. See subsection (c).

20. **"Lien Creditor"** This definition is unchanged in substance from the corresponding definition in former Section 9–301.

21. **"New Value."** This Article deletes former Section 9–108. Its broad formulation of new value, which embraced the taking of after-acquired collateral for a pre-existing claim, was unnecessary, counterintuitive, and ineffective for its original purpose of sheltering after-acquired collateral from attack as a voidable preference in bankruptcy. The new definition derives from Bankruptcy Code Section 547(a). The term is used with respect to temporary perfection of security interests in instruments, certificated securities, or negotiable documents under Section 9–312(e) and with respect to chattel paper priority in Section 9–330.

22. **"Person Related To."** Section 9–615 provides a special method for calculating a deficiency or surplus when "the secured party, a person related to the secured party, or a secondary obligor" acquires the collateral at a foreclosure disposition. Separate definitions of the term are provided with respect to an individual secured party and with respect to a secured party that is an organization. The definitions are patterned on the corresponding definition in Section 1.301(32) of the Uniform Consumer Credit Code (1974).

23. **"Proposal."** This definition describes a record that is sufficient to propose to retain collateral in full or partial satisfaction of a secured obligation. See Sections 9–620, 9–621, 9–622.

24. **"Pursuant to Commitment."** This definition is unchanged in substance from the corresponding definition in former Section 9–105. It is used in connection with special priority rules applicable to future advances. See Section 9–323.

25. **"Software."** The definition of "software" is used in connection with the priority rules applicable to purchase-money security interests. See Sections 9–103, 9–324. Software, like a payment intangible, is a type of general intangible for purposes of this Article. See Comment 4.a., above, regarding the distinction between "goods" and "software."

26. **Terminology: "Assignment" and "Transfer."** In numerous provisions, this Article refers to the "assignment" or the "transfer" of property interests. These terms and their derivatives are not defined. This Article generally follows common usage by using the terms "assignment" and "assign" to refer to transfers of rights to payment, claims, and liens and other security interests. It generally uses the term "transfer" to refer to other transfers of interests in property. Except when used in connection with a letter-of-credit transaction (see Section 9–107, Comment 4), no significance should be placed on the use of one term or the other. Depending on the context, each term may refer to the assignment or transfer of an outright ownership interest or to the assignment or transfer of a limited interest, such as a security interest.

§ 9–103. Purchase-Money Security Interest; Application of Payments; Burden of Establishing

(a) [Definitions.] In this section:

(1) "purchase-money collateral" means goods or software that secures a purchase-money obligation incurred with respect to that collateral; and

(2) "purchase-money obligation" means an obligation of an obligor incurred as all or part of the price of the collateral or for value given to enable the debtor to acquire rights in or the use of the collateral if the value is in fact so used.

(b) [Purchase-money security interest in goods.] A security interest in goods is a purchase-money security interest:

(1) to the extent that the goods are purchase-money collateral with respect to that security interest;

(2) if the security interest is in inventory that is or was purchase-money collateral, also to the extent that the security interest secures a purchase-money obligation incurred with respect

to other inventory in which the secured party holds or held a purchase-money security interest; and

(3) also to the extent that the security interest secures a purchase-money obligation incurred with respect to software in which the secured party holds or held a purchase-money security interest.

(c) [Purchase-money security interest in software.] A security interest in software is a purchase-money security interest to the extent that the security interest also secures a purchase-money obligation incurred with respect to goods in which the secured party holds or held a purchase-money security interest if:

(1) the debtor acquired its interest in the software in an integrated transaction in which it acquired an interest in the goods; and

(2) the debtor acquired its interest in the software for the principal purpose of using the software in the goods.

(d) [Consignor's inventory purchase-money security interest.] The security interest of a consignor in goods that are the subject of a consignment is a purchase-money security interest in inventory.

(e) [Application of payment in non-consumer-goods transaction.] In a transaction other than a consumer-goods transaction, if the extent to which a security interest is a purchase-money security interest depends on the application of a payment to a particular obligation, the payment must be applied:

(1) in accordance with any reasonable method of application to which the parties agree;

(2) in the absence of the parties' agreement to a reasonable method, in accordance with any intention of the obligor manifested at or before the time of payment; or

(3) in the absence of an agreement to a reasonable method and a timely manifestation of the obligor's intention, in the following order:

(A) to obligations that are not secured; and

(B) if more than one obligation is secured, to obligations secured by purchase-money security interests in the order in which those obligations were incurred.

(f) [No loss of status of purchase-money security interest in non-consumer-goods transaction.] In a transaction other than a consumer-goods transaction, a purchase-money security interest does not lose its status as such, even if:

(1) the purchase-money collateral also secures an obligation that is not a purchase-money obligation;

(2) collateral that is not purchase-money collateral also secures the purchase-money obligation; or

(3) the purchase-money obligation has been renewed, refinanced, consolidated, or restructured.

(g) [Burden of proof in non-consumer-goods transaction.] In a transaction other than a consumer-goods transaction, a secured party claiming a purchase-money security interest has the burden of establishing the extent to which the security interest is a purchase-money security interest.

(h) [Non-consumer-goods transactions; no inference.] The limitation of the rules in subsections (e), (f), and (g) to transactions other than consumer-goods transactions is intended to leave to the court the determination of the proper rules in consumer-goods transactions. The court may not infer from that limitation the nature of the proper rule in consumer-goods transactions and may continue to apply established approaches.

UNOFFICIAL COMMENTS

The concept of purchase-money security interest is important primarily in dealing with commercial transactions with secured party v. secured party priority problems, i.e., problems in which two or more secured parties have security interests in the same equipment or inventory and the value of the collateral is not enough to satisfy the amounts owed to all of the secured parties

You also might encounter the purchase-money security interest concept in questions involving consumer transactions in which the issue is whether (i) the security interest is automatically perfected under section 9–309 or (ii) the debtor in a bankruptcy case can avoid the security interest under the Bankruptcy Code section 522(f) or (iii) the debtor in a bankruptcy case can strip down the amount of a car lender's secured claim under section 1325(a)

OFFICIAL COMMENT

* * *

2. **Scope of This Section.** Under Section 9–309(1), a purchase-money security interest in consumer goods is perfected when it attaches. Sections 9–317 and 9–324 provide special priority rules for purchase-money security interests in a variety of contexts. This section explains when a security interest enjoys purchase-money status.

3. **"Purchase-Money Collateral"; "Purchase–Money Obligation"; "Purchase-Money Security Interest."** Subsection (a) defines "purchase-money collateral" and "purchase-money obligation." These terms are essential to the description of what constitutes a purchase-money security interest under subsection (b). As used in subsection (a)(2), the definition of "purchase-money obligation," the "price" of collateral or the "value given to enable" includes obligations for expenses incurred in connection with acquiring rights in the collateral, sales taxes, duties, finance charges, interest, freight charges, costs of storage in transit, demurrage, administrative charges, expenses of collection and enforcement, attorney's fees, and other similar obligations.

The concept of "purchase-money security interest" requires a close nexus between the acquisition of collateral and the secured obligation. Thus, a security interest does not qualify as a purchase-money security interest if a debtor acquires property on unsecured credit and subsequently creates the security interest to secure the purchase price.

4. **Cross-Collateralization of Purchase-Money Security Interests in Inventory.** Subsection (b)(2) deals with the problem of cross-collateralized purchase-money security interests in inventory. Consider a simple example:

> **Example:** Seller (S) sells an item of inventory (Item–1) to Debtor (D), retaining a security interest in Item–1 to secure Item–1's price and all other obligations, existing and future, of D to S. S then sells another item of inventory to D (Item–2), again retaining a security interest in Item–2 to secure Item–2's price as well as all other obligations of D to S. D then pays to S Item–1's price. D then sells Item–2 to a buyer in ordinary course of business, who takes Item–2 free of S's security interest.

Under subsection (b)(2), S's security interest in *Item–1* securing *Item–2's unpaid price* would be a purchase-money security interest. This is so because S has a purchase-money security interest in Item–1, Item–1 secures the price of (a "purchase-money obligation incurred with respect to") Item–2 ("other inventory"), and Item–2 itself was subject to a purchase-money security interest. Note that, to the extent Item–1 secures the price of Item–2, S's security interest in Item–1 would not be a purchase-money security interest under subsection (b)(1). The security interest in Item–1 is a purchase-money security interest under subsection (b)(1) only to the extent that Item–1 is "purchase-money collateral," i.e., only to the extent that Item–1 "secures a purchase-money obligation incurred with respect to that collateral" (i.e., Item–1). See subsection (a)(1).

5. **Purchase-Money Security Interests in Goods and Software.** Subsections (b) and (c) limit purchase-money security interests to security interests in goods, including fixtures, and software. Otherwise, no change in meaning from former Section 9–107 is intended. The second sentence of former Section 9–115(5)(f) made the purchase-money priority rule (former Section 9–312(4)) inapplicable to investment property. This section's limitation makes that provision unnecessary.

Subsection (c) describes the limited circumstances under which a security interest in goods may be accompanied by a purchase-money security interest in software. The software must be acquired by the debtor in a transaction integrated with the transaction in which the debtor acquired the goods, and the debtor must acquire the software for the principal purpose of using the software in the goods. "Software" is defined in Section 9–102.

6. **Consignments.** Under former Section 9–114, the priority of the consignor's interest is similar to that of a purchase-money security interest. Subsection (d) achieves this result more directly, by defining the interest of a "consignor," defined in Section 9–102, to be a purchase-money security interest in inventory for purposes of this Article. This drafting convention obviates any need to set forth special priority rules applicable to the interest of a consignor. Rather, the priority of the consignor's interest as against the

rights of lien creditors of the consignee, competing secured parties, and purchasers of the goods from the consignee can be determined by reference to the priority rules generally applicable to inventory, such as Sections 9–317, 9–320, 9–322, and 9–324. For other purposes, including the rights and duties of the consignor and consignee as between themselves, the consignor would remain the owner of goods under a bailment arrangement with the consignee. See Section 9–319.

7. **Provisions Applicable Only to Non–Consumer–Goods Transactions.**

a. **"Dual-Status" Rule.** For transactions other than consumer-goods transactions, this Article approves what some cases have called the "dual-status" rule, under which a security interest may be a purchase-money security interest to some extent and a non-purchase-money security interest to some extent. (Concerning consumer-goods transactions, see subsection (h) and Comment 8.) Some courts have found this rule to be explicit or implicit in the words "to the extent," found in former Section 9–107 and continued in subsections (b)(1) and (b)(2). The rule is made explicit in subsection (e). For non-consumer-goods transactions, this Article rejects the "transformation" rule adopted by some cases, under which any cross-collateralization, refinancing, or the like destroys the purchase-money status entirely.

Consider, for example, what happens when a $10,000 loan secured by a purchase-money security interest is refinanced by the original lender, and, as part of the transaction, the debtor borrows an additional $2,000 secured by the collateral. Subsection (f) resolves any doubt that the security interest remains a purchase-money security interest. Under subsection (b), however, it enjoys purchase-money status only to the extent of $10,000.

b. **Allocation of Payments.** Continuing with the example, if the debtor makes a $1,000 payment on the $12,000 obligation, then one must determine the extent to which the security interest remains a purchase-money security interest—$9,000 or $10,000. Subsection (e)(1) expresses the overriding principle, applicable in cases other than consumer-goods transactions, for determining the extent to which a security interest is a purchase-money security interest under these circumstances: freedom of contract, as limited by principle of reasonableness. An unconscionable method of application, for example, is not a reasonable one and so would not be given effect under subsection (e)(1). In the absence of agreement, subsection (e)(2) permits the obligor to determine how payments should be allocated. If the obligor fails to manifest its intention, obligations that are not secured will be paid first. (As used in this Article, the concept of "obligations that are not secured" means obligations for which the debtor has not created a security interest. This concept is different from and should not be confused with the concept of an "unsecured claim" as it appears in Bankruptcy Code Section 506(a).) The obligor may prefer this approach, because unsecured debt is likely to carry a higher interest rate than secured debt. A creditor who would prefer to be secured rather than unsecured also would prefer this approach.

After the unsecured debt is paid, payments are to be applied first toward the obligations secured by purchase-money security interests. In the event that there is more than one such obligation, payments first received are to be applied to obligations first incurred. See subsection (e)(3). Once these obligations are paid, there are no purchase-money security interests and no additional allocation rules are needed.

Subsection (f) buttresses the dual-status rule by making it clear that (in a transaction other than a consumer-goods transaction) cross-collateralization and renewals, refinancings, and restructurings do not cause a purchase-money security interest to lose its status as such. The statutory terms "renewed," "refinanced," and "restructured" are not defined. Whether the terms encompass a particular transaction depends upon whether, under the particular facts, the purchase-money character of the security interest fairly can be said to survive. Each term contemplates that an identifiable portion of the purchase-money obligation could be traced to the new obligation resulting from a renewal, refinancing, or restructuring.

c. **Burden of Proof.** As is the case when the extent of a security interest is in issue, under subsection (g) the secured party claiming a purchase-money security interest in a transaction other than a consumer-goods transaction has the burden of establishing whether the security interest retains its purchase-money status. This is so whether the determination is to be made following a renewal, refinancing, or restructuring or otherwise.

8. **Consumer-Goods Transactions; Characterization Under Other Law.** Under subsection (h), the limitation of subsections (e), (f), and (g) to transactions other than consumer-goods transactions leaves to the court the determination of the proper rules in consumer-goods transactions. Subsection (h) also instructs the court not to draw any inference from this limitation as to the proper rules for consumer-goods transactions and leaves the court free to continue to apply established approaches to those transactions.

This section addresses only whether a security interest is a "purchase-money security interest" under this Article, primarily for purposes of perfection and priority. See, e.g., Sections 9–317, 9–324. In particular, its adoption of the dual-status rule, allocation of payments rules, and burden of proof standards for non-consumer-goods transactions is not intended to affect or influence characterizations under other statutes. Whether a security interest is a "purchase-money security interest" under other law is determined by that law. For example, decisions under Bankruptcy Code Section 522(f) have applied both the dual-status and the transformation rules. The Bankruptcy Code does not expressly adopt the state law definition of "purchase-money security interest." Where federal law does not defer to this Article, this Article does not, and could not, determine a question of federal law.

§ 9–104. Control of Deposit Account

(a) [Requirements for control.] A secured party has control of a deposit account if:

(1) the secured party is the bank with which the deposit account is maintained;

(2) the debtor, secured party, and bank have agreed in an authenticated record that the bank will comply with instructions originated by the secured party directing disposition of the funds in the deposit account without further consent by the debtor; or

(3) the secured party becomes the bank's customer with respect to the deposit account.

(b) [Debtor's right to direct disposition.] A secured party that has satisfied subsection (a) has control, even if the debtor retains the right to direct the disposition of funds from the deposit account.

UNOFFICIAL COMMENTS

You can't perfect a security interest in a deposit account by filing a financing statement. Control is the only way to perfect a security interest in a deposit account. This section lists the 3 different ways to perfect a deposit account by control:

First, in (a)(1), if the bank at which the account is maintained is the secured party, then the bank has control and therefore is perfected. This is a form of automatic perfection. Other creditors are always on notice that the bank holding the deposit account may have an interest in the deposit account.

Second, in (a)(2), the bank is not the secured party, but the bank still maintains the deposit account. The debtor, the bank, and the secured party must sign an agreement whereby the debtor authorizes the bank to comply with the secured party's instructions regarding the deposit account. The secured party's control of the account is separate from the debtor's ability to access the funds in the account. A debtor is not prohibited from accessing the account. However, the secured party can deny the debtor access to the deposit account.

Third, in (a)(3), a secured party can obtain control by arranging to become the customer of the deposit account instead of, or in addition to, the debtor. Accordingly, the secured party has the ability to withdraw funds or close the account. Look to sections 4–104(a)(5), 4–401(a), and 4–403(a) [in some more complete version of the Uniform Commercial Code] for a detailed description of "customer" and other requirements associated with being a customer.

NON–OBVIOUS DEFINITIONS

"Deposit account" is defined in section 9–102; key part of the definition is the phrase "with a bank."

OFFICIAL COMMENT

1. **Source.** New; derived from Section 8–106.

2. **Why "Control" Matters.** This section explains the concept of "control" of a deposit account. "Control" under this section may serve two functions. First, "control ... pursuant to the debtor's agreement" may substitute for an authenticated security agreement as an element of attachment. See Section 9–203(b)(3)(D). Second, when a deposit account is taken as original collateral, the only method of perfection is obtaining control under this section. See Section 9–312(b)(1).

3. **Requirements for "Control."** This section derives from Section 8–106 of Revised Article 8, which defines "control" of securities and certain other investment property. Under subsection (a)(1), the bank with which the deposit account is maintained has control. The effect of this provision is to afford the bank automatic perfection. No other form of public notice is necessary; all actual and potential creditors of the debtor are always on notice that the bank with which the debtor's deposit account is maintained may assert a claim against the deposit account.

Under subsection (a)(2), a secured party may obtain control by obtaining the bank's authenticated agreement that it will comply with the secured party's instructions without further consent by the debtor. The analogous provision in Section 8–106 does not require that the agreement be authenticated. An agreement to comply with the secured party's instructions suffices for "control" of a deposit account under this section even if the bank's agreement is subject to specified conditions, e.g., that the secured party's instructions are accompanied by a certification that the debtor is in default. (Of course, if the condition is the *debtor's* further consent, the statute explicitly provides that the agreement would *not* confer control.) See revised Section 8–106, Comment 7.

Under subsection (a)(3), a secured party may obtain control by becoming the bank's "customer," as defined in Section 4–104. As the customer, the secured party would enjoy the right (but not necessarily the exclusive right) to withdraw funds from, or close, the deposit account. See Sections 4–401(a), 4–403(a).

Although the arrangements giving rise to control may themselves prevent, or may enable the secured party at its discretion to prevent, the debtor from reaching the funds on deposit, subsection (b) makes clear that the debtor's ability to reach the funds is not inconsistent with "control."

Perfection by control is not available for bank accounts evidenced by an instrument (e.g., certain certificates of deposit), which by definition are "instruments" and not "deposit accounts." See Section 9–102 (defining "deposit account" and "instrument").

§ 9–105. Control of Electronic Chattel Paper

A secured party has control of electronic chattel paper if the record or records comprising the chattel paper are created, stored, and assigned in such a manner that:

(1) a single authoritative copy of the record or records exists which is unique, identifiable and, except as otherwise provided in paragraphs (4), (5), and (6), unalterable;

(2) the authoritative copy identifies the secured party as the assignee of the record or records;

(3) the authoritative copy is communicated to and maintained by the secured party or its designated custodian;

(4) copies or revisions that add or change an identified assignee of the authoritative copy can be made only with the participation of the secured party;

(5) each copy of the authoritative copy and any copy of a copy is readily identifiable as a copy that is not the authoritative copy; and

(6) any revision of the authoritative copy is readily identifiable as an authorized or unauthorized revision.

OFFICIAL COMMENT

1. **Source.** New.

2. **"Control" of Electronic Chattel Paper.** This Article covers security interests in "electronic chattel paper," a new term defined in Section 9–102. This section governs how "control" of electronic chattel paper may be obtained. A secured party's control of electronic chattel paper (i) may substitute for an authenticated security agreement for purposes of attachment under Section 9–203, (ii) is a method of perfection under Section 9–

314, and (iii) is a condition for obtaining special, non-temporal priority under Section 9–330. Because electronic chattel paper cannot be transferred, assigned, or possessed in the same manner as tangible chattel paper, a special definition of control is necessary. In descriptive terms, this section provides that control of electronic chattel paper is the functional equivalent of possession of "tangible chattel paper" (a term also defined in Section 9–102).

3. **"Authoritative Copy" of Electronic Chattel Paper.** One requirement for establishing control is that a particular copy be an "authoritative copy." Although other copies may exist, they must be distinguished from the authoritative copy. This may be achieved, for example, through the methods of authentication that are used or by business practices involving the marking of any additional copies. When tangible chattel paper is converted to electronic chattel paper, in order to establish that a copy of the electronic chattel paper is the authoritative copy it may be necessary to show that the tangible chattel paper no longer exists or has been permanently marked to indicate that it is not the authoritative copy.

4. **Development of Control Systems.** This Article leaves to the marketplace the development of systems and procedures, through a combination of suitable technologies and business practices, for dealing with control of electronic chattel paper in a commercial context. However, achieving control under this section requires more than the agreement of interested persons that the elements of control are satisfied. For example, paragraph (4) contemplates that control requires that it be a physical impossibility (or sufficiently unlikely or implausible so as to approach practical impossibility) to add or change an identified assignee without the participation of the secured party (or its authorized representative). It would not be enough for the assignor merely to agree that it will not change the identified assignee without the assignee-secured party's consent. However, the standards applied to determine whether a party is in control of electronic chattel paper should not be more stringent than the standards now applied to determine whether a party is in possession of tangible chattel paper. Control of electronic chattel paper contemplates systems or procedures such that the secured party must take some action (either directly or through its designated custodian) to effect a change or addition to the authoritative copy. But just as a secured party does not lose possession of tangible chattel paper merely by virtue of the possibility that a person acting on its behalf *could* wrongfully redeliver the chattel paper to the debtor, so control of electronic chattel paper would not be defeated by the possibility that the secured party's interest *could* be subverted by the wrongful conduct of a person (such as a custodian) acting on its behalf.

Systems that evolve for control of electronic chattel paper may or may not involve a third party custodian of the relevant records. However, this section and the concept of control of electronic chattel paper are not based on the same concepts as are control of deposit accounts (Section 9–104), security entitlements, a type of investment property (Section 9–106), and letter-of-credit rights (Section 9–107). The rules for control of that collateral are based on existing market practices and legal and regulatory regimes for institutions such as banks and securities intermediaries. Analogous practices for electronic chattel paper are developing nonetheless. The flexible approach adopted by this section, moreover, should not impede the development of these practices and, eventually, legal and regulatory regimes, which may become analogous to those for, e.g., investment property.

§ 9–106. Control of Investment Property

(a) [Control under Section 8–106.] A person has control of a certificated security, uncertificated security, or security entitlement as provided in Section 8–106.

(b) [Control of commodity contract.] A secured party has control of a commodity contract if:

(1) the secured party is the commodity intermediary with which the commodity contract is carried; or

(2) the commodity customer, secured party, and commodity intermediary have agreed that the commodity intermediary will apply any value distributed on account of the commodity contract as directed by the secured party without further consent by the commodity customer.

(c) [Effect of control of securities account or commodity account.] A secured party having control of all security entitlements or commodity contracts carried in a securities account or commodity account has control over the securities account or commodity account.

OFFICIAL COMMENT

1. **Source.** Former Section 9–115(e).

2. **"Control" Under Article 8.** For an explanation of "control" of securities and certain other investment property, see Section 8–106, Comments 4 and 7.

3. **"Control" of Commodity Contracts.** This section, as did former Section 9–115(1)(e), contains provisions relating to control of commodity contracts which are analogous to those in Section 8–106 for other types of investment property.

4. **Securities Accounts and Commodity Accounts.** For drafting convenience, control with respect to a securities account or commodity account is defined in terms of obtaining control over the security entitlements or commodity contracts. Of course, an agreement that provides that (without further consent of the debtor) the securities intermediary or commodity intermediary will honor instructions from the secured party concerning a securities account or commodity account described as such is sufficient. Such an agreement necessarily implies that the intermediary will honor instructions concerning all security entitlements or commodity contracts carried in the account and thus affords the secured party control of all the security entitlements or commodity contracts.

§ 9–107. Control of Letter-of-Credit Right

A secured party has control of a letter-of-credit right to the extent of any right to payment or performance by the issuer or any nominated person if the issuer or nominated person has consented to an assignment of proceeds of the letter of credit under Section 5–114(c) or otherwise applicable law or practice.

OFFICIAL COMMENT

1. **Source.** New.

2. **"Control" of Letter-of-Credit Right.** Whether a secured party has control of a letter-of-credit right may determine the secured party's priority as against competing secured parties. See Section 9–329. This section provides that a secured party acquires control of a letter-of-credit right by receiving an assignment if the secured party obtains the consent of the issuer or any nominated person, such as a confirmer or negotiating bank, under Section 5–114 or other applicable law or practice. Because both issuers and nominated persons may give or

be obligated to give value under a letter of credit, this section contemplates that a secured party obtains control of a letter-of-credit right with respect to the issuer or a particular nominated person only to the extent that the issuer or that nominated person consents to the assignment. For example, if a secured party obtains control to the extent of an issuer's obligation but fails to obtain the consent of a nominated person, the secured party does not have control to the extent that the nominated person gives value. In many cases the person or persons who will give value under a letter of credit will be clear from its terms. In other cases, prudence may suggest obtaining consent from more than one person. The details of the consenting issuer's or nominated person's duties to pay or otherwise render performance to the secured party are left to the agreement of the parties.

3. **"Proceeds of a Letter of Credit."** Section 5–114 follows traditional banking terminology by referring to a letter of credit beneficiary's assignment of its right to receive payment thereunder as an assignment of the "proceeds of a letter of credit." However, as the seller of goods can assign its right to receive payment (an "account") before it has been earned by delivering the goods to the buyer, so the beneficiary of a letter of credit can assign its contingent right to payment before the letter of credit has been honored. See Section 5–114(b). If the assignment creates a security interest, the security interest can be perfected at the time it is created. An assignment of, including the creation of a security interest in, a letter-of-credit right is an assignment of a present interest.

4. **"Transfer" vs. "Assignment."** Letter-of-credit law and practice distinguish the "transfer" of a letter of credit from an "assignment." Under a transfer, the transferee itself becomes the beneficiary and acquires the right to draw. Whether a new, substitute credit is issued or the issuer advises the transferee of its status as such, the transfer constitutes a novation under which the transferee is the new, substituted beneficiary (but only to the extent of the transfer, in the case of a partial transfer).

Section 5–114(e) provides that the rights of a transferee beneficiary or nominated person are independent of the beneficiary's assignment of the proceeds of a letter of credit and are superior to the assignee's right to the proceeds. For this reason, transfer does not appear in this Article as a means of control or perfection. Section 9–109(c)(4) recognizes the independent and superior rights of a transferee beneficiary under Section 5–114(e); this Article does not apply to the rights of a transferee beneficiary or nominated person to the extent that those rights are independent and superior under Section 5–114.

5. **Supporting Obligation: Automatic Attachment and Perfection.** A letter-of-credit right is a type of "supporting obligation," as defined in Section 9–102. Under Sections 9–203 and 9–308, a security interest in a letter-of-credit right automatically attaches and is automatically perfected if the security interest in the supported obligation is a perfected security interest. However, unless the secured party has control of the letter-of-credit right or itself becomes a transferee beneficiary, it cannot obtain any rights against the issuer or a nominated person under Article 5. Consequently, as a practical matter, the secured party's rights would be limited to its ability to locate and identify proceeds distributed by the issuer or nominated person under the letter of credit.

§ 9–108. Sufficiency of Description

(a) [Sufficiency of description.] Except as otherwise provided in subsections (c), (d), and (e), a description of personal or real property is sufficient, whether or not it is specific, if it reasonably identifies what is described.

(b) [Examples of reasonable identification.] Except as otherwise provided in subsection (d), a description of collateral reasonably identifies the collateral if it identifies the collateral by:

(1) specific listing;

(2) category;

(3) except as otherwise provided in subsection (e), a type of collateral defined in [the Uniform Commercial Code];

(4) quantity;

(5) computational or allocational formula or procedure; or

(6) except as otherwise provided in subsection (c), any other method, if the identity of the collateral is objectively determinable.

(c) [Supergeneric description not sufficient.] A description of collateral as "all the debtor's assets" or "all the debtor's personal property" or using words of similar import does not reasonably identify the collateral.

(d) [Investment property.] Except as otherwise provided in subsection (e), a description of a security entitlement, securities account, or commodity account is sufficient if it describes:

(1) the collateral by those terms or as investment property; or

(2) the underlying financial asset or commodity contract.

(e) [When description by type insufficient.] A description only by type of collateral defined in [the Uniform Commercial Code] is an insufficient description of:

(1) a commercial tort claim; or

(2) in a consumer transaction, consumer goods, a security entitlement, a securities account, or a commodity account.

UNOFFICIAL COMMENTS

The title to section 9–108(e)—"[When description by type insufficient"] suggests that description by "type" is generally sufficient. The section 9–108(e) phrase "type of collateral" is not defined in the Uniform Commercial Code. In using the term, lawyers and judges look to the definitions in section 9–102.

You will probably be asked to look at one or more of the following four section 9–102 definitions of types of "goods": (1) consumer goods, (2) equipment, (3) inventory and least important (4) farm products. These four types are mutually exclusive and depend on the debtor's use of the collateral.

For example, a high definition television set is

— consumer goods if the debtor uses it in her home;

— equipment if the debtor uses it in its business;

— inventory if the debtor sells or leases it in its business.

Accordingly, if the security agreement describes the collateral as "equipment" that meets the 9–203 requirement of a "description of the collateral" and the 9–108(a) requirement of "reasonably identifies" and that security agreement includes the television sets that a debtor sports bar uses in the sports bar but not the television sets that an appliance store debtor has for lease or sale.

Don't confuse description of collateral in security agreements with indication of the collateral in financing statements. Security agreements and financing statements are different documents that serve different purposes and are subject to different statutory requirements.

OTHER UCC SECTIONS TO LOOK TO WHEN YOU LOOK AT SECTION 9–108

If the secured party is in possession of the collateral at the time of the security agreement, look to section 9–203(b)(3)(B): If the secured party is in possession of the collateral, there will not be any need to look at section 9–108, nor any issue as to what the collateral is—the collateral is the stuff that the secured party has in its possession.

OFFICIAL COMMENT

* * *

2. **General Rules.** * * * Subsection (b) expands upon subsection (a) by indicating a variety of ways in which a description might reasonably identify collateral. * * * Subsection (b) is subject to subsection (c), which follows prevailing case law and adopts the view that an "all assets" or "all personal property" description for purposes of a *security agreement* is *not* sufficient. Note, however, that under Section 9–504, a *financing statement* sufficiently indicates the collateral if it "covers all assets or all personal property."

The purpose of requiring a description of collateral in a security agreement under Section 9–203 is evidentiary. The test of sufficiency of a description under this section, as under former Section 9–110, is that the description do the job assigned to it: make possible the identification of the collateral described. This section rejects any requirement that a description is insufficient unless it is exact and detailed (the so-called "serial number" test).

3. **After-Acquired Collateral.** Much litigation has arisen over whether a description in a security agreement is sufficient to include after-acquired collateral if the agreement does not explicitly so provide. This question is one of contract interpretation and is not susceptible to a statutory rule (other than a rule to the effect that it is a question of contract interpretation). Accordingly, this section contains no reference to descriptions of after-acquired collateral.

4. **Investment Property.** Under subsection (d), the use of the wrong Article 8 terminology does not render a description invalid (e.g., a security agreement intended to cover a debtor's "security entitlements" is sufficient if it refers to the debtor's "securities"). Note also that given the broad definition of "securities account" in Section 8–501, a security interest in a securities account also includes all other rights of the debtor against the securities intermediary arising out of the securities account. For example, a security interest in a securities account would include credit balances due to the debtor from the securities intermediary, whether or not they are proceeds of a security entitlement. Moreover, describing collateral as a securities account is a simple way of describing all of the security entitlements carried in the account.

5. **Consumer Investment Property; Commercial Tort Claims.** Subsection (e) requires greater specificity of description in order to prevent debtors from inadvertently encumbering certain property. Subsection (e) requires that a description by defined "type" of collateral alone of a commercial tort claim or, in a consumer transaction, of a security entitlement, securities account, or commodity account, is not sufficient. For example, "all existing and after-acquired investment property" or "all existing and after-acquired security entitlements," without more, would be insufficient in a consumer transaction to describe a security entitlement, securities account, or commodity account. The reference to "*only* by type" in subsection (e) means that a description is sufficient if it satisfies subsection (a) and contains a descriptive component beyond the "type" alone. Moreover, if the collateral consists of a securities account or commodity account, a description of the account is sufficient to cover all existing and future security entitlements or commodity contracts carried in the account. See Section 9–203(h), (i).

Under Section 9–204, an after-acquired collateral clause in a security agreement will not reach future commercial tort claims. It follows that when an effective security agreement covering a commercial tort claim is entered into the claim already will exist. Subsection (e) does not require a description to be specific. For example, a description such as "all tort claims arising out of the explosion of debtor's factory" would suffice, even if the exact amount of the claim, the theory on which it may be based, and the identity of the tortfeasor(s) are not described. (Indeed, those facts may not be known at the time.)

[SUBPART 2. APPLICABILITY OF ARTICLE]

§ 9–109. Scope

(a) [General scope of article.] Except as otherwise provided in subsections (c) and (d), this article applies to:

(1) a transaction, regardless of its form, that creates a security interest in personal property or fixtures by contract;

(2) an agricultural lien;

(3) a sale of accounts, chattel paper, payment intangibles, or promissory notes;

(4) a consignment;

(5) a security interest arising under Section 2–401, 2–505, 2–711(3), or 2A–508(5), as provided in Section 9–110; and

(6) a security interest arising under Section 4–210 or 5–118.

(b) [Security interest in secured obligation.] The application of this article to a security interest in a secured obligation is not affected by the fact that the obligation is itself secured by a transaction or interest to which this article does not apply.

(c) [Extent to which article does not apply.] This article does not apply to the extent that:

(1) a statute, regulation, or treaty of the United States preempts this article;

(2) another statute of this State expressly governs the creation, perfection, priority, or enforcement of a security interest created by this State or a governmental unit of this State;

(3) a statute of another State, a foreign country, or a governmental unit of another State or a foreign country, other than a statute generally applicable to security interests, expressly governs creation, perfection, priority, or enforcement of a security interest created by the State, country, or governmental unit; or

(4) the rights of a transferee beneficiary or nominated person under a letter of credit are independent and superior under Section 5–114.

(d) [Inapplicability of article.] This article does not apply to:

(1) a landlord's lien, other than an agricultural lien;

(2) a lien, other than an agricultural lien, given by statute or other rule of law for services or materials, but Section 9–333 applies with respect to priority of the lien;

(3) an assignment of a claim for wages, salary, or other compensation of an employee;

(4) a sale of accounts, chattel paper, payment intangibles, or promissory notes as part of a sale of the business out of which they arose;

(5) an assignment of accounts, chattel paper, payment intangibles, or promissory notes which is for the purpose of collection only;

(6) an assignment of a right to payment under a contract to an assignee that is also obligated to perform under the contract;

(7) an assignment of a single account, payment intangible, or promissory note to an assignee in full or partial satisfaction of a preexisting indebtedness;

(8) a transfer of an interest in or an assignment of a claim under a policy of insurance, other than an assignment by or to a health-care provider of a health-care-insurance receivable and any subsequent assignment of the right to payment, but Sections 9–315 and 9–322 apply with respect to proceeds and priorities in proceeds;

(9) an assignment of a right represented by a judgment, other than a judgment taken on a right to payment that was collateral;

(10) a right of recoupment or set-off, but:

   (A) Section 9–340 applies with respect to the effectiveness of rights of recoupment or set-off against deposit accounts; and

   (B) Section 9–404 applies with respect to defenses or claims of an account debtor;

(11) the creation or transfer of an interest in or lien on real property, including a lease or rents thereunder, except to the extent that provision is made for:

   (A) liens on real property in Sections 9–203 and 9–308;

   (B) fixtures in Section 9–334;

   (C) fixture filings in Sections 9–501, 9–502, 9–512, 9–516, and 9–519; and

   (D) security agreements covering personal and real property in Section 9–604;

(12) an assignment of a claim arising in tort, other than a commercial tort claim, but Sections 9–315 and 9–322 apply with respect to proceeds and priorities in proceeds; or

(13) an assignment of a deposit account in a consumer transaction, but Sections 9–315 and 9–322 apply with respect to proceeds and priorities in proceeds.

UNOFFICIAL COMMENTS

Most transactions within the scope of Article 9 involve either a sale of goods on credit with the seller or some third-party financing entity providing credit and obtaining a security interest in the goods or a loan with the lender obtaining a security interest in something other than real property such as the debtor's equipment, inventory or rights to payment.

In determining whether a transaction is within the scope of Article 9, look at the substance of the transaction, rather than the form. **More**

specifically, if a transaction is in the form of a lease of goods, look to section 1–203 (revised) and our discussion on pages 411–413 infra.

Some transactions that are not sales of goods on credit or loans secured by goods are still within the scope of Article 9. Consignments and sales of receivables can also be Article 9 transactions, and so can also be exam questions. **If your prof covered consignments and sales of receivables in class, you might want to read our extended comments about consignments on pages 409–411 and receivables on 413–416.**

OFFICIAL COMMENT

* * *

2. **Basic Scope Provision.** Subsection (a)(1) derives from former Section 9–102(1) and (2). These subsections have been combined and shortened. No change in meaning is intended. Under subsection (a)(1), all consensual security interests in personal property and fixtures are covered by this Article, except for transactions excluded by subsections (c) and (d). As to which transactions give rise to a "security interest," the definition of that term in Section 1–201 must be consulted. When a security interest is created, this Article applies regardless of the form of the transaction or the name that parties have given to it.

3. **Agricultural Liens.** Subsection (a)(2) is new. It expands the scope of this Article to cover agricultural liens, as defined in Section 9–102.

4. **Sales of Accounts, Chattel Paper, Payment Intangibles, Promissory Notes, and Other Receivables.** Under subsection (a)(3), as under former Section 9–102, this Article applies to sales of accounts and chattel paper. This approach generally has been successful in avoiding difficult problems of distinguishing between transactions in which a receivable secures an obligation and those in which the receivable has been sold outright. In many commercial financing transactions the distinction is blurred.

Subsection (a)(3) expands the scope of this Article by including the sale of a "payment intangible" (defined in Section 9–102 as "a general intangible under which the account debtor's principal obligation is a monetary obligation") and a "promissory note" (also defined in Section 9–102). To a considerable extent, this Article affords these transactions treatment identical to that given sales of accounts and chattel paper. In some respects, however, sales of payment intangibles and promissory notes are treated differently from sales of other receivables. See, e.g., Sections 9–309 (automatic perfection upon attachment), 9–408 (effect of restrictions on assignment). By virtue of the expanded definition of "account" (defined in Section 9–102), this Article now covers sales of (and other security interests in) "health-care-insurance receivables" (also defined in Section 9–102). Although this Article occasionally distinguishes between outright sales of receivables and sales that secure an obligation, neither this Article nor the definition of "security interest" (Section 1–201(37)) delineates how a particular transaction is to be classified. That issue is left to the courts.

5. **Transfer of Ownership in Sales of Receivables.** A "sale" of an account, chattel paper, a promissory note, or a payment intangible includes a sale of a right in the receivable, such as a sale of a participation interest. The term also includes the sale of an enforcement right. For example, a "[p]erson entitled to enforce" a negotiable promissory note (Section 3–301) may sell its ownership rights in the instrument. See Section 3–203, Comment 1 ("Ownership rights in instruments may be determined by principles of the law of property, independent of Article 3, which do not depend upon whether the instrument was transferred under Section 3–203."). Also, the right under Section 3–309 to enforce a lost, destroyed, or stolen negotiable promissory note may

be sold to a purchaser who could enforce that right by causing the seller to provide the proof required under that section. This Article rejects decisions reaching a contrary result, e.g., *Dennis Joslin Co. v. Robinson Broadcasting*, 977 F. Supp. 491 (D.D.C. 1997).

Nothing in this section or any other provision of Article 9 prevents the transfer of full and complete ownership of an account, chattel paper, an instrument, or a payment intangible in a transaction of sale. However, as mentioned in Comment 4, neither this Article nor the definition of "security interest" in Section 1–201 provides rules for distinguishing sales transactions from those that create a security interest securing an obligation. This Article applies to both types of transactions. The principal effect of this coverage is to apply this Article's perfection and priority rules to these sales transactions. Use of terminology such as "security interest," "debtor," and "collateral" is merely a drafting convention adopted to reach this end, and its use has no relevance to distinguishing sales from other transactions. See PEB Commentary No. 14.

Following a debtor's outright sale and transfer of ownership of a receivable, the debtor-seller retains no legal or equitable rights in the receivable that has been sold. See Section 9–318(a). This is so whether or not the buyer's security interest is perfected. (A security interest arising from the sale of a promissory note or payment intangible is perfected upon attachment without further action. See Section 9–309.) However, if the buyer's interest in accounts or chattel paper is unperfected, a subsequent lien creditor, perfected secured party, or qualified buyer can reach the sold receivable and achieve priority over (or take free of) the buyer's unperfected security interest under Section 9–317. This is so not because the seller of a receivable retains rights in the property sold; it does not. Nor is this so because the seller of a receivable is a "debtor" and the buyer of a receivable is a "secured party" under this Article (they are). It is so for the simple reason that Sections 9–318(b), 9–317, and 9–322 make it so, as did former Sections 9–301 and 9–312. Because the buyer's security interest is unperfected, for purposes of determining the rights of creditors of and purchasers for value from the debtor-seller, under Section 9–318(b) the debtor-seller is deemed to have the rights and title it sold. Section 9–317 subjects the buyer's unperfected interest in accounts and chattel paper to that of the debtor-seller's lien creditor and other persons who qualify under that section.

6. **Consignments.** Subsection (a)(4) is new. This Article applies to every "consignment." The term, defined in Section 9–102, includes many but not all "true" consignments (i.e., bailments for the purpose of sale). If a transaction is a "sale or return," as defined in revised Section 2–326, it is not a "consignment." In a "sale or return" transaction, the buyer becomes the owner of the goods, and the seller may obtain an enforceable security interest in the goods only by satisfying the requirements of Section 9–203.

Under common law, creditors of a bailee were unable to reach the interest of the bailor (in the case of a consignment, the consignor-owner). Like former Section 2–326 and former Article 9, this Article changes the common-law result; however, it does so in a different manner. For purposes of determining the rights and interests of third-party creditors of, and purchasers of the goods from, the consignee, but not for other purposes, such as remedies of the consignor, the consignee is deemed to acquire under this Article whatever rights and title the consignor had or had power to transfer. See Section 9–319. The interest of a consignor is defined to be a security interest under revised Section 1–201(37), more specifically, a purchase-money security interest in the consignee's inventory. See Section 9–103(d). Thus, the rules pertaining to lien creditors, buyers, and attachment, perfection, and priority of competing security interests apply to consigned goods. The relationship between the consignor and consignee is left to other law. Consignors also have no duties under Part 6. See Section 9–601(g).

Sometimes parties characterize transactions that secure an obligation (other than the bailee's obligation to returned bailed goods) as "consignments." These transactions are not "consignments" as contemplated by Section 9–109(a)(4). See Section 9–102. This Article applies also to these transactions, by virtue of Section 9–109(a)(1). They create a security interest within the meaning of the first sentence of Section 1–201(37).

This Article does not apply to bailments for sale that fall outside the definition of "consignment" in Section 9–102 and that do not create a security interest that secures an obligation.

7. **Security Interest in Obligation Secured by Non–Article 9 Transaction.** Subsection (b) is unchanged in substance from former Section 9–102(3). The following example provides an illustration.

Example 1: O borrows $10,000 from M and secures its repayment obligation, evidenced by a promissory note, by granting to M a mortgage on O's land. This Article does not apply to the creation of the real-property mortgage. However, if M sells the promissory note to X or gives a security interest in the note to secure M's own obligation to X, this Article applies to the security interest thereby created in favor of X. The security interest in the promissory note is covered by this Article even though the note is secured by a real-property mortgage. Also, X's security interest in the note gives X an attached security interest in the mortgage lien that secures the note and, if the security interest in the note is perfected, the security interest in the mortgage lien likewise is perfected. See Sections 9–203, 9–308.

It also follows from subsection (b) that an attempt to obtain or perfect a security interest in a secured obligation by complying with non-Article 9 law, as by an assignment of record of a real-property mortgage, would be ineffective. Finally, it is implicit from subsection (b) that one cannot obtain a security interest in a lien, such as a mortgage on real property, that is not also coupled with an equally effective security interest in the secured obligation. This Article rejects cases such as In re *Maryville Savings & Loan Corp.*, 743 F.2d 413 (6th Cir. 1984), clarified on reconsideration, 760 F.2d 119 (1985).

8. **Federal Preemption.** Former Section 9–104(a) excluded from Article 9 "a security interest subject to any statute of the United States, to the extent that such statute governs the rights of parties to and third parties affected by transactions in particular types of property." Some (erroneously) read the former section to suggest that Article 9 sometimes deferred to federal law even when federal law did not preempt Article 9. Subsection (c)(1) recognizes explicitly that this Article defers to federal law only when and to the extent that it must—i.e., when federal law preempts it.

9. **Governmental Debtors.** Former Section 9–104(e) excluded transfers by governmental debtors. It has been revised and replaced by the exclusions in new paragraphs (2) and (3) of subsection (c). These paragraphs reflect the view that Article 9 should apply to security interests created by a State, foreign country, or a "governmental unit" (defined in Section 9–102) of either except to the extent that another statute governs the issue in question. Under paragraph (2), this Article defers to all statutes of the forum State. (A forum cannot determine whether it should consult the choice-of-law rules in the forum's UCC unless it first determines that its UCC applies to the transaction before it.) Paragraph (3) defers to statutes of another State or a foreign country only to the extent that those statutes contain rules applicable specifically to security interests created by the governmental unit in question.

Example 2: A New Jersey state commission creates a security interest in favor of a New York bank. The validity of the security interest is litigated in New York. The relevant security agreement provides that it is governed by New York law. To the extent that a New Jersey statute contains rules peculiar to creation of security interests by governmental units generally, to creation of security interests by state commissions, or to creation of security interests by this particular state commission, then that law will govern. On the other hand, to the extent that New Jersey law provides that security interests created by governmental units, state commissions, or this state commission are governed by the law generally applicable to secured transactions (i.e., New Jersey's Article 9), then New York's Article 9 will govern.

Example 3: An airline that is an instrumentality of a foreign country creates a security interest in favor of a New York bank. The analysis used in the previous example would apply here. That is, if the matter is litigated in New York, New York law would govern except to the extent that the foreign country enacted a statute applicable to security interests created by governmental units generally or by the airline specifically.

The fact that New York law applies does not necessarily mean that perfection is accomplished by filing in New York. Rather, it means that the court should apply New York's Article 9, including its choice-of-law provisions. Under New York's Section 9–301, perfection is governed by the law of the jurisdiction in which the debtor is located. Section 9–307 determines the debtor's location for choice-of-law purposes.

If a transaction does not bear an appropriate relation to the forum State, then that State's Article 9 will not apply, regardless of whether the transaction would be excluded by paragraph (3).

Example 4: A Belgian governmental unit grants a security interest in its equipment to a Swiss secured party. The equipment is located in Belgium. A dispute arises and, for some reason, an action is brought in a New Mexico state court. Inasmuch as the transaction bears no "appropriate relation" to New Mexico, New Mexico's UCC, including its Article 9, is inapplicable. See Section 1–105(1). New Mexico's Section 9–109(c) on excluded transactions should not come into play. Even if the parties agreed that New Mexico law would govern, the parties' agreement would not be effective because the transaction does not bear a "reasonable relation" to New Mexico. See Section 1–105(1).

Conversely, Article 9 will come into play only if the litigation arises in a UCC jurisdiction or if a foreign choice-of-law rule leads a foreign court to apply the law of a UCC jurisdiction. For example, if issues concerning a security interest granted by a foreign airline to a New York bank are litigated overseas, the court may be bound to apply the law of the debtor's jurisdiction and not New York's Article 9.

10. **Certain Statutory and Common–Law Liens; Interests in Real Property.** With few exceptions (nonconsensual agricultural liens being one), this Article applies only to consensual security interests in personal property. Following former Section 9–104(b) and (j), paragraphs (1) and (11) of subsection (d) exclude landlord's liens and leases and most other interests in or liens on real property. These exclusions generally reiterate the limitations on coverage (i.e., "by contract," "in personal property and fixtures") made explicit in subsection (a)(1). Similarly, most jurisdictions provide special liens to suppliers of many types of services and materials, either by statute or by common law. With the exception of agricultural liens, it is not necessary for this Article to provide general codification of this lien structure, which is determined in large part by local conditions and which is far removed from ordinary commercial financing. As under former Section 9–104(c), subsection (d)(2) excludes these suppliers' liens (other than agricultural liens) from this Article. However, Section 9–333 provides a rule for determining priorities between certain possessory suppliers' liens and security interests covered by this Article.

11. **Wage and Similar Claims.** As under former Section 9–104(d), subsection (d)(3) excludes assignments of claims for wages and the like from this Article. These assignments present important social issues that other law addresses. The Federal Trade Commission has ruled

that, with some exceptions, the taking of an assignment of wages or other earnings is an unfair act or practice under the Federal Trade Commission Act. See 16 C.F.R. Part 444. State statutes also may regulate such assignments.

12. **Certain Sales and Assignments of Receivables; Judgments.** In general this Article covers security interests in (including sales of) accounts, chattel paper, payment intangibles, and promissory notes. Paragraphs (4), (5), (6), and (7) of subsection (d) exclude from the Article certain sales and assignments of receivables that, by their nature, do not concern commercial financing transactions. These paragraphs add to the exclusions in former Section 9–104(f) analogous sales and assignments of payment intangibles and promissory notes. For similar reasons, subsection (d)(9) retains the exclusion of assignments of judgments under former Section 9–104(h) (other than judgments taken on a right to payment that itself was collateral under this Article).

13. **Insurance.** Subsection (d)(8) narrows somewhat the broad exclusion of interests in insurance policies under former Section 9–104(g). This Article now covers assignments by or to a health-care provider of "health-care-insurance receivables" (defined in Section 9–102).

14. **Set-Off.** Subsection (d)(10) adds two exceptions to the general exclusion of set-off rights from Article 9 under former Section 9–104(i). The first takes account of new Section 9–340, which regulates the effectiveness of a set-off against a deposit account that stands as collateral. The second recognizes Section 9–404, which affords the obligor on an account, chattel paper, or general intangible the right to raise claims and defenses against an assignee (secured party).

15. **Tort Claims.** Subsection (d)(12) narrows somewhat the broad exclusion of transfers of tort claims under former Section 9–104(k). This Article now applies to assignments of "commercial tort claims" (defined in Section 9–102) as well as to security interests in tort claims that constitute proceeds of other collateral (e.g., a right to payment for negligent destruction of the debtor's inventory). Note that once a claim arising in tort has been settled and reduced to a contractual obligation to pay, the right to payment becomes a payment intangible and ceases to be a claim arising in tort.

This Article contains two special rules governing creation of a security interest in tort claims. First, a description of collateral in a security agreement as "all tort claims" is insufficient to meet the requirement for attachment. See Section 9–108(e). Second, no security interest attaches under an after-acquired property clause to a tort claim. See Section 9–204(b). In addition, this Article does not determine whom the tortfeasor must pay to discharge its obligation. Inasmuch as a tortfeasor is not an "account debtor," the rules governing waiver of defenses and discharge of an obligation by an obligor (Sections 9–403, 9–404, 9–405, and 9–406) are inapplicable to tort-claim collateral.

16. **Deposit Accounts.** Except in consumer transactions, deposit accounts may be taken as original collateral under this Article. Under former Section 9–104(*l*), deposit accounts were excluded as original collateral, leaving security interests in deposit accounts to be governed by the common law. The common law is nonuniform, often difficult to discover and comprehend, and frequently costly to implement. As a consequence, debtors who wished to use deposit accounts as collateral sometimes were precluded from doing so as a practical matter. By excluding deposit accounts from the Article's scope as original collateral in consumer transactions, subsection (d)(13) leaves those transactions to law other than this Article. However, in both consumer and non-consumer transactions, sections 9–315 and 9–322 apply to deposit accounts as proceeds and with respect to priorities in proceeds.

This Article contains several safeguards to protect debtors against inadvertently encumbering deposit accounts and to reduce the likelihood that a secured party will realize a windfall from a debtor's deposit accounts. For example, because "deposit account" is a separate type of collateral, a security agreement covering general intangibles will not adequately describe deposit accounts. Rather, a security agreement must reasonably identify the deposit accounts that are the subject of a security interest, e.g., by using the term "deposit accounts." See Section 9–108. To perfect a security interest in a deposit account as original collateral, a secured party (other than the bank with which the deposit account is maintained) must obtain "control" of the account either by obtaining the bank's authenticated agreement or by becoming the bank's customer with respect to the deposit account. See Sections 9–312(b)(1), 9–104. Either of these steps requires the debtor's consent.

This Article also contains new rules that determine which State's law governs perfection and priority of a security interest in a deposit account (Section 9–304), priority of conflicting security interests in and set-off rights against a deposit account (Sections 9–327, 9–340), the rights of transferees of funds from an encumbered deposit account (Section 9–332), the obligations of the bank (Section 9–341), enforcement of security interests in a deposit account (Section 9–607(c)), and the duty of a secured party to terminate control of a deposit account (Section 9–208(b)).

§ 9–110. Security Interests Arising Under Article 2 or 2A

A security interest arising under Section 2–401, 2–505, 2–711(3), or 2A–508(5) is subject to this article. However, until the debtor obtains possession of the goods:

(1) the security interest is enforceable, even if Section 9–203(b)(3) has not been satisfied;

(2) filing is not required to perfect the security interest;

(3) the rights of the secured party after default by the debtor are governed by Article 2 or 2A; and

(4) the security interest has priority over a conflicting security interest created by the debtor.

OFFICIAL COMMENTS

* * *

2. **Background.** Former Section 9–113, from which this section derives, referred generally to security interests "arising solely under the Article on Sales (Article 2) or the Article on Leases (Article 2A)." Views differed as to the precise scope of that section. In contrast, Section 9–110 specifies the security interests to which it applies.

3. **Security Interests Under Articles 2 and 2A.** Section 2–505 explains how a seller of goods may reserve a security interest in them. Section 2–401 indicates that a reservation of title by the seller of goods, despite delivery to the buyer, is limited to reservation of a security interest. As did former Article 9, this Article governs a security interest arising solely under one of those sections; however, until the buyer obtains possession of the goods, the security interest is enforceable even in the absence of a security agreement, filing is not necessary to perfect the security interest, and the seller-secured party's rights on the buyer's default are governed by Article 2.

Sections 2–711(3) and 2A–508(5) create a security interest in favor of a buyer or lessee in possession of goods that were rightfully rejected or as to which acceptance was justifiably revoked. As did former Article 9, this Article governs a security interest arising solely under one of those sections; however, until the seller or lessor obtains possession of the goods, the security interest is enforceable even in the absence of a security agreement, filing is not necessary to perfect the security interest, and the secured party's (buyer's or lessee's) rights on the debtor's (seller's or lessor's) default are governed by Article 2 or 2A, as the case may be.

4. **Priority.** This section adds to former Section 9–113 a priority rule. Until the debtor obtains possession of the goods, a security interest arising under one of the specified sections of Article 2 or 2A has priority over conflicting security interests created by the debtor. Thus, a security interest arising under Section 2–401 or 2–505 has priority over a conflicting security interest in the buyer's after-acquired goods, even if the goods in question are inventory. Arguably, the same result would obtain under Section 9–322, but even if it would not, a purchase-money-like priority is appropriate. Similarly, a security interest under Section 2–711(3) or 2A–508(5) has priority over security interests claimed by the seller's or lessor's secured lender. This result is appropriate, inasmuch as the payments giving rise to the debt secured by the Article 2 or 2A security interest are likely to be included among the lender's proceeds.

Example: Seller owns equipment subject to a security interest created by Seller in favor of Lender. Buyer pays for the equipment, accepts the goods, and then justifiably revokes acceptance. As long as Seller does not recover possession of the equipment, Buyer's security interest under Section 2–711(3) is senior to that of Lender.

In the event that a security interest referred to in this section conflicts with a security interest that is created by a person other than the debtor, Section 9–325 applies. Thus, if Lender's security interest in the example was created not by Seller but by the person from whom Seller acquired the goods, Section 9–325 would govern.

5. **Relationship to Other Rights and Remedies Under Articles 2 and 2A.** This Article does not specifically address the conflict between (i) a security interest created by a buyer or lessee and (ii) the seller's or lessor's right to withhold delivery under Section 2–702(1), 2–703(a), or 2A–525, the seller's or lessor's right to stop delivery under Section 2–705 or 2A–526, or the seller's right to reclaim under Section 2–507(2) or 2–702(2). These conflicts are governed by the first sentence of Section 2–403(1), under which the buyer's secured party obtains no greater rights in the goods than the buyer had or had power to convey, or Section 2A–307(1), under which creditors of the lessee take subject to the lease contract.

PART 2. EFFECTIVENESS OF SECURITY AGREEMENT; ATTACHMENT OF SECURITY INTEREST; RIGHTS OF PARTIES TO SECURITY AGREEMENT

[SUBPART 1. EFFECTIVENESS AND ATTACHMENT]

§ 9–201. General Effectiveness of Security Agreement

(a) [General effectiveness.] Except as otherwise provided in [the Uniform Commercial Code], a security agreement is effective according to its terms between the parties, against purchasers of the collateral, and against creditors.

(b) [Applicable consumer laws and other law.] A transaction subject to this article is subject to any applicable rule of law which establishes a different rule for consumers and [insert reference to (i) any other statute or regulation that regulates the rates, charges, agreements, and practices for loans, credit sales, or other extensions of credit and (ii) any consumer-protection statute or regulation].

(c) [Other applicable law controls.] In case of conflict between this article and a rule of law, statute, or regulation described in subsection (b), the rule of law, statute, or regulation controls. Failure to comply with a statute or regulation described in subsection (b) has only the effect the statute or regulation specifies.

(d) [Further deference to other applicable law.] This article does not:

(1) validate any rate, charge, agreement, or practice that violates a rule of law, statute, or regulation described in subsection (b); or

(2) extend the application of the rule of law, statute, or regulation to a transaction not otherwise subject to it.

NON–OBVIOUS UCC DEFINITIONS

Most people use the term "purchaser" and "buyer" interchangeably. The guys that wrote Article 9 did not and so you can not when you are doing Article 9 stuff. Under the definitions of "purchaser" and "purchase" in section 1–201, a "purchaser" includes a secured party as well as a buyer. In other words (or more importantly in the words of Article 9), some creditors are "purchasers."

OTHER UCC SECTIONS TO LOOK TO WHEN YOU LOOK AT SECTION 9–201

When you think about the phrase "except as otherwise provided" in section 9–201(a), you need to think about

— section 9–315 and its exception for authorized sales

— section 9–317(b) and its exception for unperfected security interests

— section 9–320 and its exceptions for ordinary course transactions and for sales between consumers

— section 9–330 and its exceptions for purchasers of chattel paper and instruments who take possession.

If the secured party makes advances after some third party becomes a "lien creditor" or a "buyer" look to section 9–323.

UNOFFICIAL COMMENTS

You need to think of section 9–201 as the general priority rule. More specifically you need to think of section 9–201 when you are thinking about a law school exam question in which a secured party and some "purchaser" both claim rights in the collateral. By saying "the security agreement is effective according to its terms ... against purchasers of the collateral", section 9–201 is saying that the claim of the secured party is superior to the claim of the purchaser, i.e., has priority. Sections 9–315(a)(1) 9–317(b), 9–320 and 9–330 mentioned above set out the important exceptions to this general priority rule.

OFFICIAL COMMENT

* * *

2. **Effectiveness of Security Agreement.** Subsection (a) provides that a security agreement is generally effective. With certain exceptions, a security agreement is effective between the debtor and secured party and is likewise effective against third parties. Note that "security agreement" is used here (and elsewhere in this Article) as it is defined in Section 9–102: "an agreement that creates or provides for a security interest." It follows that subsection (a) does not provide that every term or provision contained in a record that contains a security agreement or that is so labeled is effective. Properly read, former Section 9–201 was to the same effect. Exceptions to the general rule of subsection (a) arise where there is an overriding provision in this Article or any other Article of the UCC. For example, Section 9–317 subordinates unperfected security interests to lien creditors and certain buyers, and several provisions in Part 3 subordinate some security interests to other security interests and interests of purchasers.

3. **Law, Statutes, and Regulations Applicable to Certain Transactions.** Subsection (b) makes clear that certain transactions, although subject to this Article, also are subject to other applicable laws relating to consumers or specified in that subsection. Subsection (c) provides that the other law is controlling in the event of a conflict, and that a violation of other law does not *ipso facto* constitute a violation of this Article. Subsection (d) provides that this Article does not validate violations under or extend the application of the other applicable laws.

§ 9–202. Title to Collateral Immaterial

Except as otherwise provided with respect to consignments or sales of accounts, chattel paper, payment intangibles, or promissory notes, the provisions of this article with regard to rights and obligations apply whether title to collateral is in the secured party or the debtor.

OFFICIAL COMMENT

2. **Title Immaterial.** The rights and duties of parties to a secured transaction and affected third parties are provided in this Article without reference to the location of "title" to the collateral. For example, the characteristics of a security interest that secures the purchase price of goods are the same whether the secured party appears to have retained title or the debtor appears to have obtained title and then conveyed title or a lien to the secured party.

3. **When Title Matters.**

a. **Under This Article.** This section explicitly acknowledges two circumstances in which the effect of certain

Article 9 provisions turns on ownership (title). First, in some respects sales of accounts, chattel paper, payment intangibles, and promissory notes receive special treatment. See, e.g., Sections 9–207(a), 9–210(b), 9–615(e). Buyers of receivables under former Article 9 were treated specially, as well. See, e.g., former Section 9–502(2). Second, the remedies of a consignor under a true consignment and, for the most part, the remedies of a buyer of accounts, chattel paper, payment intangibles, or promissory notes are determined by other law and not by Part 6. See Section 9–601(g).

b. **Under Other Law.** This Article does not determine which line of interpretation (e.g., title theory or lien theory, retained title or conveyed title) should be followed in cases in which the applicability of another rule of law depends upon who has title. If, for example, a revenue law imposes a tax on the "legal" owner of goods or if a corporation law makes a vote of the stockholders prerequisite to a corporation "giving" a security interest but not if it acquires property "subject" to a security interest, this Article does not attempt to define whether the secured party is a "legal" owner or whether the transaction "gives" a security interest for the purpose of such laws. Other rules of law or the agreement of the parties determines the location and source of title for those purposes.

§ 9–203. Attachment and Enforceability of Security Interest; Proceeds; Supporting Obligations; Formal Requisites

(a) **[Attachment.]** A security interest attaches to collateral when it becomes enforceable against the debtor with respect to the collateral, unless an agreement expressly postpones the time of attachment.

(b) **[Enforceability.]** Except as otherwise provided in subsections (c) through (i), a security interest is enforceable against the debtor and third parties with respect to the collateral only if :

(1) value has been given;

(2) the debtor has rights in the collateral or the power to transfer rights in the collateral to a secured party; and

(3) one of the following conditions is met:

(A) the debtor has authenticated a security agreement that provides a description of the collateral and, if the security interest covers timber to be cut, a description of the land concerned;

(B) the collateral is not a certificated security and is in the possession of the secured party under Section 9–313 pursuant to the debtor's security agreement;

(C) the collateral is a certificated security in registered form and the security certificate has been delivered to the secured party under Section 8–301 pursuant to the debtor's security agreement; or

(D) the collateral is deposit accounts, electronic chattel paper, investment property, letter-of-credit rights, or electronic documents, and the secured party has control under Section 7–106, 9–104, 9–105, 9–106, or 9–107 pursuant to the debtor's security agreement.

* * *

(d) [When person becomes bound by another person's security agreement.] A person becomes bound as debtor by a security agreement entered into by another person if, by operation of law other than this article or by contract:

(1) the security agreement becomes effective to create a security interest in the person's property; or

(2) the person becomes generally obligated for the obligations of the other person, including the obligation secured under the security agreement, and acquires or succeeds to all or substantially all of the assets of the other person.

(e) [Effect of new debtor becoming bound.] If a new debtor becomes bound as debtor by a security agreement entered into by another person:

(1) the agreement satisfies subsection (b)(3) with respect to existing or after-acquired property of the new debtor to the extent the property is described in the agreement; and

(2) another agreement is not necessary to make a security interest in the property enforceable.

(f) [Proceeds and supporting obligations.] The attachment of a security interest in collateral gives the secured party the rights to proceeds provided by Section 9–315 and is also attachment of a security interest in a supporting obligation for the collateral.

(g) [Lien securing right to payment.] The attachment of a security interest in a right to payment or performance secured by a security interest or other lien on personal or real property is also attachment of a security interest in the security interest, mortgage, or other lien.

(h) [Security entitlement carried in securities account.] The attachment of a security interest in a securities account is also attachment of a security interest in the security entitlements carried in the securities account.

(i) [Commodity contracts carried in commodity account.] The attachment of a security interest in a commodity account is also attachment of a security interest in the commodity contracts carried in the commodity account.

UNOFFICIAL COMMENTS

When you think "attachment," think creation, think existence. Attachment creates a security interest. A security interest does not exist until the attachment requirements of section 9–203 are satisfied.

And, when you think Article 9, remember section 9–203's requirement of a security agreement. There must be an agreement between the debtor and the secured party that creates a security interest. In a sense then, a course in Article 9 is an advanced contracts course.

There are three 9–203 concepts that you need to watch for on your exam.

— First, the "debtor" may not be the person indebted. Take another look at the definition of "debtor." If B Bank makes a loan to Bubba secured by Bubba's bass boat, then Bubba is both the "debtor" and the "obligor". If, however, C Credit Union makes a loan to Bubba and the collateral for the loan is Momma's collection of pick-up trucks, then Momma and only Momma is the "debtor" as that term is used throughout Article 9 and Bubba is only the "obligor," a term defined in section 9–102(59).

— Second, 9–203 requires that "value has been given" before there can be a security interest but it does not require that the value be given to the debtor. Note that neither section 9–203 nor section 1–201(44) specify the person to whom value must be given. Accordingly, it would seem that if C Credit Union makes a loan to Bubba and the collateral for the loan is Momma's collection of pick-up trucks, then C Credit Union has satisfied the value requirement of section 9–203(b)(1).

— Third, there can be an authenticated security agreement without a security interest. If the debtor has authenticated a security agreement before either value has been given or before the debtor has rights in the collateral, then the requirements of attachment have not yet been satisfied and there is not yet a security interest.

Understanding attachment is so important that we have a more complete explanation of section 9–203 on pages 365–368, infra.

OTHER UCC SECTIONS TO LOOK TO WHEN YOU LOOK AT SECTION 9–203

§ 9–108: Sufficiency of Description

In the typical situation involving a written security agreement, the security agreement must contain "a description of the collateral." § 9–203(b)(3)(A). The sufficiency of the description is governed by § 9–108.

§ 9–204: After–Acquired Property; Future Advances

A security agreement may cover "after-acquired property"—essentially collateral acquired by the debtor after the attachment of the security interest. If the secured creditor wants to have a security interest in after-acquired property, it usually needs to include an after-acquired property clause in the security agreement (*e.g.*, "Debtor grants a security interest to Creditor in Debtor's equipment, *now owned or later acquired* . . . "). In addition, a security agreement may provide that the described collateral secures not only the initial loan at issue, but also any subsequent loans that the creditor may make. This is known as a "future advance" clause. Both after-acquired property clauses and future advance clauses are governed by § 9–204.

§ 9–315: Secured Party's Rights on Disposition of Collateral and in Proceeds

Section 9–203(f) indicates that the attachment of a security interest in collateral gives the secured creditor the right to proceeds provided by § 9–315. Section 9–315(a)(2) makes it clear that a security interest attaches only to *identifiable* proceeds. "Identifiable" essentially means that the secured creditor can prove that the proceeds came from its collateral. Issues related to perfection in proceeds are governed by § 9–315(c)-(e).

NON–OBVIOUS DEFINITIONS

Debtor, 9–102(a)(28): People generally think about a "debtor" as being the person who is "indebted." Under Article 9 talk, the "obligor," defined in 9–102(a)(59) is the person who is indebted and, while that person is usually also the "debtor," not always.

New debtor, 9–102(a)(56): Every "new debtor" is a "debtor" but not every "debtor" is a "new debtor." Look for "new debtor" if there has been a change in business structure (e.g., partnership becomes a corporation) or merger.

Value, 1–201(44) or revised 1–204: Different from first year contracts concept of consideration. "Past consideration" such as antecedent debt is "value."

OFFICIAL COMMENT	2. **Creation, Attachment, and Enforceability.** Subsection (a) states the general rule that a security interest attaches to collateral only when it becomes
* * *	

enforceable against the debtor. Subsection (b) specifies the circumstances under which a security interest becomes enforceable. Subsection (b) states three basic prerequisites to the existence of a security interest: value (paragraph (1)), rights or power to transfer rights in collateral (paragraph (2)), and agreement plus satisfaction of an evidentiary requirement (paragraph (3)). When all of these elements exist, a security interest becomes enforceable between the parties and attaches under subsection (a). Subsection (c) identifies certain exceptions to the general rule of subsection (b).

3. **Security Agreement; Authentication.** Under subsection (b)(3), enforceability requires the debtor's security agreement and compliance with an evidentiary requirement in the nature of a Statute of Frauds. Paragraph (3)(A) represents the most basic of the evidentiary alternatives, under which the debtor must authenticate a security agreement that provides a description of the collateral. Under Section 9–102, a "security agreement" is "an agreement that creates or provides for a security interest." Neither that definition nor the requirement of paragraph (3)(A) rejects the deeply rooted doctrine that a bill of sale, although absolute in form, may be shown in fact to have been given as security. Under this Article, as under prior law, a debtor may show by parol evidence that a transfer purporting to be absolute was in fact for security. Similarly, a self-styled "lease" may serve as a security agreement if the agreement creates a security interest. See Section 1–201(37) (distinguishing security interest from lease).

4. **Possession, Delivery, or Control Pursuant to Security Agreement.** The other alternatives in subsection (b)(3) dispense with the requirement of an authenticated security agreement and provide alternative evidentiary tests. Under paragraph (3)(B), the secured party's possession substitutes for the debtor's authentication under paragraph (3)(A) if the secured party's possession is "pursuant to the debtor's security agreement." That phrase refers to the debtor's agreement to the secured party's possession for the purpose of creating a security interest. The phrase should not be confused with the phrase "debtor has authenticated a security agreement," used in paragraph (3)(A), which contemplates the debtor's authentication of a record. In the unlikely event that possession is obtained without the debtor's agreement, possession would not suffice as a substitute for an authenticated security agreement. However, once the security interest has become enforceable and has attached, it is not impaired by the fact that the secured party's possession is maintained without the agreement of a subsequent debtor (e.g., a transferee). Possession as contemplated by Section 9–313 is possession for purposes of subsection (b)(3)(B), even though it may not constitute possession "pursuant to the debtor's agreement" and consequently might not serve as a substitute for an authenticated security agreement under subsection (b)(3)(A). Subsection (b)(3)(C) provides that delivery of a certificated security to the secured party under Section 8–301 pursuant to the debtor's security agreement is sufficient as a substitute for an authenticated security agreement. Similarly, under subsection (b)(3)(D), control of investment property, a deposit account, electronic chattel paper, a letter-of-credit right, or electronic documents satisfies the evidentiary test if control is pursuant to the debtor's security agreement.

5. **Collateral Covered by Other Statute or Treaty.** * * *

6. **Debtor's Rights; Debtor's Power to Transfer Rights.** Subsection (b)(2) conditions attachment on the debtor's having "rights in the collateral or the power to transfer rights in the collateral to a secured party." A debtor's limited rights in collateral, short of full ownership, are sufficient for a security interest to attach. However, in accordance with basic personal property conveyancing principles, the baseline rule is that a security interest attaches only to whatever rights a debtor may have, broad or limited as those rights may be.

Certain exceptions to the baseline rule enable a debtor to transfer, and a security interest to attach to, greater rights than the debtor has. See Part 3, Subpart 3 (priority rules). The phrase, "or the power to transfer rights in the collateral to a secured party," accommodates those exceptions. In some cases, a debtor may have power to transfer another person's rights only to a class of transferees that excludes secured parties. See, e.g., Section 2–403(2) (giving certain merchants power to transfer an entruster's rights to a buyer in ordinary course of business). Under those circumstances, the debtor would not have the power to create a security interest in the other person's rights, and the condition in subsection (b)(2) would not be satisfied.

7. **New Debtors.** Subsection (e) makes clear that the enforceability requirements of subsection (b)(3) are met when a new debtor becomes bound under an original debtor's security agreement. If a new debtor becomes bound as debtor by a security agreement entered into by another person, the security agreement satisfies the requirement of subsection (b)(3) as to the existing and after-acquired property of the new debtor to the extent the property is described in the agreement.

Subsection (d) explains when a new debtor becomes bound. Persons who become bound under paragraph (2) are limited to those who both become primarily liable for the original debtor's obligations and succeed to (or acquire) its assets. Thus, the paragraph excludes sureties and other secondary obligors as well as persons who become obligated through veil piercing and other non-successorship doctrines. In many cases, paragraph (2) will exclude successors to the assets and liabilities of a division of a debtor. See also Section 9–508, Comment 3.

8. **Supporting Obligations.** Under subsection (f), a security interest in a "supporting obligation" (defined in Section 9–102) automatically follows from a security interest in the underlying, supported collateral. * * * Implicit in subsection (f) is the principle that the secured party's interest in a supporting obligation extends to the supporting obligation only to the extent that it supports the collateral in which the secured party has a security interest. * * *

9. **Collateral Follows Right to Payment or Performance.** Subsection (g) codifies the common-law rule that a transfer of an obligation secured by a security interest or other lien on personal or real property also transfers the security interest or lien. See Restatement (3d), Property (Mortgages) § 5.4(a) (1997). See also Section 9–308(e) (analogous rule for perfection).

10. **Investment Property.** Subsections (h) and (i) make clear that attachment of a security interest in a securities account or commodity account is also attachment in security entitlements or commodity contracts carried in the accounts.

§ 9–204. After-Acquired Property; Future Advances

(a) [After-acquired collateral.] Except as otherwise provided in subsection (b), a security agreement may create or provide for a security interest in after-acquired collateral.

(b) [When after-acquired property clause not effective.] A security interest does not attach under a term constituting an after-acquired property clause to:

    (1) consumer goods, other than an accession when given as additional security, unless the debtor acquires rights in them within 10 days after the secured party gives value; or

    (2) a commercial tort claim.

(c) [Future advances and other value.] A security agreement may provide that collateral secures, or that accounts, chattel paper, payment intangibles, or promissory notes are sold in connection with, future advances or other value, whether or not the advances or value are given pursuant to commitment.

UNOFFICIAL COMMENTS

Again, you have to know this stuff. A big part of every Article 9 final exam is at least one question with multiple secured parties with security interests in the same collateral.

Your teacher will have to "flag" the 9–204 issue for you because section 9–204 requires security agreement language to trigger section 9–204; note the phrase "security agreement may provide" in 9–204(a) and (c).

Two related issues to watch for on your exam. First, including after-acquired property or future advance clauses in financing statements is both unnecessary and ineffective. Have to have language in the security agreement. Second, regardless of language in the security agreement, after-acquired property clauses are effective in consumer goods transactions only if the debtor acquires rights in the new stuff within ten days after the secured party gives value. See section 9–204(b).

Understanding floating liens is so important that we have a more complete explanation of 9–204 on pages 369–370.

NON–OBVIOUS DEFINITIONS

The definitions of "after-acquired property" and "future advances" are especially non-obvious. These terms are not defined in your UCC anywhere. And, the definitions of "after-acquired property" and "future advances" are especially important. Sure to be in your exam somewhere.

"After-acquired property" describes property that the debtor acquired after the security interest attached. For example, if SP's security interest in all of D's inventory attached on January 15, after-acquired property would be the inventory that D acquired after January 15. Similarly, "future advances" describes money or other value provided by the secured party after the security interest attached. For example, if SP's security interest attached on January 15 and the security agreement covered future advances, then SP's April 5 loan to D would be a "future advance."

The term "floating lien" does not appear in the UCC but appears in all Article 9 casebooks. A security interest that includes after-acquired property is a "floating lien" because collateral subject to the security interest can change, i.e, float.

Similarly, a security interest that includes future advances is a "floating lien" because the amount secured can float.

OTHER UCC SECTIONS TO LOOK TO WHEN YOU LOOK AT SECTION 9–204

After-acquired property or future advances are especially important in priority contests. See section 9–322, Official Comment 5; sections 9–323, 9–324.

You will also run into after-acquired property issues if your teacher is a bankruptcy maven and covers Bankruptcy Code sections 547(c)(5) and/or 552.

OFFICIAL COMMENT

* * *

2. **After-Acquired Property; Continuing General Lien.** Subsection (a) makes clear that a security interest arising by virtue of an after-acquired property clause is no less valid than a security interest in collateral in which the debtor has rights at the time value is given. A security interest in after-acquired property is not merely an "equitable" interest; no further action by the secured party—such as a supplemental agreement covering the new collateral—is required. This section adopts the principle of a "continuing general lien" or "floating lien." It validates a security interest in the debtor's existing and (upon acquisition) future assets, even though the debtor has liberty to use or dispose of collateral without being required to account for proceeds or substitute new collateral. See Section 9–205. Subsection (a), together with subsection (c), also validates "cross-collateral" clauses under which collateral acquired at any time secures advances whenever made.

3. **After-Acquired Consumer Goods.** Subsection (b)(1) makes ineffective an after-acquired property clause covering consumer goods (defined in Section 9–109), except as accessions (see Section 9–335), acquired more than 10 days after the secured party gives value. Subsection (b)(1) is unchanged in substance from the corresponding provision in former Section 9–204(2).

4. **Commercial Tort Claims.** Subsection (b)(2) provides that an after-acquired property clause in a security agreement does not reach future commercial tort claims. In order for a security interest in a tort claim to attach, the claim must be in existence when the security agreement is authenticated. In addition, the security agreement must describe the tort claim with greater specificity than simply "all tort claims." See Section 9–108(e).

5. **Future Advances; Obligations Secured.** Under subsection (c) collateral may secure future as well as past or present advances if the security agreement so provides. This is in line with the policy of this Article toward security interests in after-acquired property under subsection (a). Indeed, the parties are free to agree that a security interest secures any obligation whatsoever. Determining the obligations secured by collateral is solely a matter of construing the parties' agreement under applicable law. This Article rejects the holdings of cases decided under former Article 9 that applied other tests, such as whether a future advance or other subsequently incurred obligation was of the same or a similar type or class as earlier advances and obligations secured by the collateral.

6. **Sales of Receivables.** Subsections (a) and (c) expressly validate after-acquired property and future advance clauses not only when the transaction is for security purposes but also when the transaction is the sale of accounts, chattel paper, payment intangibles, or promisso-

ry notes .. This result was implicit under former Article 9.

7. **Financing Statements.** The effect of after-acquired property and future advance clauses as components of a security agreement should not be confused with the requirements applicable to financing statements under this Article's system of perfection by notice filing. The references to after-acquired property clauses and future advance clauses in this section are limited to security agreements. There is no need to refer to after-acquired property or future advances or other obligations secured in a financing statement. See Section 9–502, Comment 2.

§ 9–205. Use or Disposition of Collateral Permissible

(a) [When security interest not invalid or fraudulent.] A security interest is not invalid or fraudulent against creditors solely because:

(1) the debtor has the right or ability to:

(A) use, commingle, or dispose of all or part of the collateral, including returned or repossessed goods;

(B) collect, compromise, enforce, or otherwise deal with collateral;

(C) accept the return of collateral or make repossessions; or

(D) use, commingle, or dispose of proceeds; or

(2) the secured party fails to require the debtor to account for proceeds or replace collateral.

(b) [Requirements of possession not relaxed.] This section does not relax the requirements of possession if attachment, perfection, or enforcement of a security interest depends upon possession of the collateral by the secured party.

OFFICIAL COMMENT

* * *

2. **Validity of Unrestricted "Floating Lien."** This Article expressly validates the "floating lien" on shifting collateral. See Sections 9–201, 9–204 and Comment 2. This section provides that a security interest is not invalid or fraudulent by reason of the debtor's liberty to dispose of the collateral without being required to account to the secured party for proceeds or substitute new collateral. As did former Section 9–205, this section repeals the rule of *Benedict v. Ratner*, 268 U.S. 353 (1925), and other cases which held such arrangements void as a matter of law because the debtor was given unfettered dominion or control over collateral. The *Benedict* rule did not effectively discourage or eliminate security transactions in inventory and receivables. Instead, it forced financing arrangements to be self-liquidating. Although this section repeals *Benedict*, the filing and other perfection requirements (see Part 3, Subpart 2, and Part 5) provide for public notice that overcomes any potential misleading effects of a debtor's use and control of collateral. Moreover, nothing in this section prevents the debtor and secured party from agreeing to procedures by which the secured party polices or monitors collateral or to restrictions on the debtor's dominion. However, this Article leaves these matters to agreement based on business considerations, not on legal requirements.

3. **Possessory Security Interests.** Subsection (b) makes clear that this section does not relax the requirements for perfection by possession under Section 9–313. If a secured party allows the debtor access to and control over collateral its security interest may be or become unperfected.

4. **Permissible Freedom for Debtor to Enforce Collateral.** Former Section 9–205 referred to a debtor's "liberty. .to collect or compromise accounts or chattel paper." This section recognizes the broader rights of a debtor to "enforce," as well as to "collect" and "compromise" collateral. This section's reference to collecting, compromising, and enforcing "collateral" instead of "accounts or chattel paper" contemplates the many other types of collateral that a debtor may wish to "collect, compromise, or enforce": e.g., deposit accounts, documents, general intangibles, instruments, investment property, and letter-of-credit rights.

§ 9–206. Security Interest Arising in Purchase or Delivery of Financial Asset

(a) **[Security interest when person buys through securities intermediary.]** A security interest in favor of a securities intermediary attaches to a person's security entitlement if:

(1) the person buys a financial asset through the securities intermediary in a transaction in which the person is obligated to pay the purchase price to the securities intermediary at the time of the purchase; and

(2) the securities intermediary credits the financial asset to the buyer's securities account before the buyer pays the securities intermediary.

(b) **[Security interest secures obligation to pay for financial asset.]** The security interest described in subsection (a) secures the person's obligation to pay for the financial asset.

(c) **[Security interest in payment against delivery transaction.]** A security interest in favor of a person that delivers a certificated security or other financial asset represented by a writing attaches to the security or other financial asset if:

(1) the security or other financial asset:

(A) in the ordinary course of business is transferred by delivery with any necessary indorsement or assignment; and

(B) is delivered under an agreement between persons in the business of dealing with such securities or financial assets; and

(2) the agreement calls for delivery against payment.

(d) [Security interest secures obligation to pay for delivery.] The security interest described in subsection (c) secures the obligation to make payment for the delivery.

[SUBPART 2. RIGHTS AND DUTIES]

§ 9–207. Rights and Duties of Secured Party Having Possession or Control of Collateral

(a) [Duty of care when secured party in possession.] Except as otherwise provided in subsection (d), a secured party shall use reasonable care in the custody and preservation of collateral in the secured party's possession. In the case of chattel paper or an instrument, reasonable care includes taking necessary steps to preserve rights against prior parties unless otherwise agreed.

(b) [Expenses, risks, duties, and rights when secured party in possession.] Except as otherwise provided in subsection (d), if a secured party has possession of collateral:

- **(1)** reasonable expenses, including the cost of insurance and payment of taxes or other charges, incurred in the custody, preservation, use, or operation of the collateral are chargeable to the debtor and are secured by the collateral;

- **(2)** the risk of accidental loss or damage is on the debtor to the extent of a deficiency in any effective insurance coverage;

- **(3)** the secured party shall keep the collateral identifiable, but fungible collateral may be commingled; and

- **(4)** the secured party may use or operate the collateral:

  - **(A)** for the purpose of preserving the collateral or its value;

  - **(B)** as permitted by an order of a court having competent jurisdiction; or

  - **(C)** except in the case of consumer goods, in the manner and to the extent agreed by the debtor.

(c) [Duties and rights when secured party in possession or control.] Except as otherwise provided in subsection (d), a secured party having possession of collateral or control of collateral under Section 7–106, 9–104, 9–105, 9–106, or 9–107:

- **(1)** may hold as additional security any proceeds, except money or funds, received from the collateral;

(2) shall apply money or funds received from the collateral to reduce the secured obligation, unless remitted to the debtor; and

(3) may create a security interest in the collateral.

(d) [Buyer of certain rights to payment.] If the secured party is a buyer of accounts, chattel paper, payment intangibles, or promissory notes or a consignor:

(1) subsection (a) does not apply unless the secured party is entitled under an agreement:

(A) to charge back uncollected collateral; or

(B) otherwise to full or limited recourse against the debtor or a secondary obligor based on the nonpayment or other default of an account debtor or other obligor on the collateral; and

(2) subsections (b) and (c) do not apply.

UNOFFICIAL COMMENTS

There are two very different exam fact patterns that might raise 9–207 issues: (1) secured party has repossessed collateral on debtor's default, or (2) secured party has perfected its security interest by possession.

OFFICIAL COMMENT

* * *

2. **Duty of Care for Collateral in Secured Party's Possession.** * * * Subsection (a) imposes a duty of care, similar to that imposed on a pledgee at common law, on a secured party in possession of collateral. See Restatement, Security §§ 17, 18. In many cases a secured party in possession of collateral may satisfy this duty by notifying the debtor of action that should be taken and allowing the debtor to take the action itself. If the secured party itself takes action, its reasonable expenses may be added to the secured obligation. The revised definitions of "collateral," "debtor," and "secured party" in Section 9–102 make this section applicable to collateral subject to an agricultural lien if the collateral is in the lienholder's possession. Under Section 1–102 the duty to exercise reasonable care may not be disclaimed by agreement, although under that section the parties remain free to determine by agreement standards that are not manifestly unreasonable as to what constitutes reasonable care. Unless otherwise agreed, for a secured party in possession of chattel paper or an instrument, reasonable care includes the preservation of rights against prior parties. The secured party's right to have instruments or documents indorsed or transferred to it or its order is dealt with in the relevant sections of Articles 3, 7, and 8. See Sections 3–201, 7–506, 8–304(d).

3. **Specific Rules When Secured Party in Possession or Control of Collateral.** Subsections (b) and (c) provide rules following common-law precedents which apply unless the parties otherwise agree. The rules in subsection (b) apply to typical issues that may arise while a secured party is in possession of collateral, including expenses, insurance, and taxes, risk of loss or damage, identifiable and fungible collateral, and use or operation of collateral. Subsection (c) con-

tains rules that apply in certain circumstances that may arise when a secured party is in either possession or control of collateral. These circumstances include the secured party's receiving proceeds from the collateral and the secured party's creation of a security interest in the collateral.

4. **Applicability Following Default.** This section applies when the secured party has possession of collateral either before or after default. See Sections 9–601(b), 9–609. Subsection (b)(4)(C) limits agreements concerning the use or operation of collateral other than consumer goods. Under Section 9–602(1), a debtor cannot waive or vary that limitation.

* * *

7. **Buyers of Chattel Paper and Other Receivables; Consignors.** This section has been revised to reflect the fact that a seller of accounts, chattel paper, payment intangibles, or promissory notes retains no interest in the collateral and so is not disadvantaged by the secured party's noncompliance with the requirements of this section. Accordingly, subsection (d) provides that subsection (a) applies only to security interests that secure an obligation and to sales of receivables in which the buyer has recourse against the debtor. (Of course, a buyer of accounts or payment intangibles could not have "possession" of original collateral, but might have possession of proceeds, such as promissory notes or checks.) The meaning of "recourse" in this respect is limited to recourse arising out of the account debtor's failure to pay or other default.

Subsection (d) makes subsections (b) and (c) inapplicable to buyers of accounts, chattel paper, payment intangibles, or promissory notes and consignors. Of course, there is no reason to believe that a buyer of receivables or a consignor could not, for example, create a security interest or otherwise transfer an interest in the collateral, regardless of who has possession of the collateral. However, this section leaves the rights of those owners to law other than Article 9.

§ 9–209. Duties of Secured Party if Account Debtor Has Been Notified of Assignment

(a) [Applicability of section.] Except as otherwise provided in subsection (c), this section applies if:

(1) there is no outstanding secured obligation; and

(2) the secured party is not committed to make advances, incur obligations, or otherwise give value.

(b) [Duties of secured party after receiving demand from debtor.] Within 10 days after receiving an authenticated demand by the debtor, a secured party shall send to an account debtor that has received notification of an assignment to the secured party as assignee under Section 9–406(a) an authenticated record that releases the account debtor from any further obligation to the secured party.

(c) [Inapplicability to sales.] This section does not apply to an assignment constituting the sale of an account, chattel paper, or payment intangible.

§ 9–210. Request for Accounting; Request Regarding List of Collateral or Statement of Account

(a) [Definitions.] In this section:

(1) "Request" means a record of a type described in paragraph (2), (3), or (4).

(2) "Request for an accounting" means a record authenticated by a debtor requesting that the recipient provide an accounting of the unpaid obligations secured by collateral and reasonably identifying the transaction or relationship that is the subject of the request.

(3) "Request regarding a list of collateral" means a record authenticated by a debtor requesting that the recipient approve or correct a list of what the debtor believes to be the collateral securing an obligation and reasonably identifying the transaction or relationship that is the subject of the request.

(4) "Request regarding a statement of account" means a record authenticated by a debtor requesting that the recipient approve or correct a statement indicating what the debtor believes to be the aggregate amount of unpaid obligations secured by collateral as of a specified date and reasonably identifying the transaction or relationship that is the subject of the request.

(b) [Duty to respond to requests.] Subject to subsections (c), (d), (e), and (f), a secured party, other than a buyer of accounts, chattel paper, payment intangibles, or promissory notes or a consignor, shall comply with a request within 14 days after receipt:

(1) in the case of a request for an accounting, by authenticating and sending to the debtor an accounting; and

(2) in the case of a request regarding a list of collateral or a request regarding a statement of account, by authenticating and sending to the debtor an approval or correction.

(c) [Request regarding list of collateral; statement concerning type of collateral.] A secured party that claims a security interest in all of a particular type of collateral owned by the debtor may comply with a request regarding a list of collateral by sending to the debtor an authenticated record including a statement to that effect within 14 days after receipt.

(d) [Request regarding list of collateral; no interest claimed.] A person that receives a request regarding a list of collateral, claims no interest in the collateral when it receives the request, and claimed an interest in the collateral at an earlier time shall comply with the request within 14 days after receipt by sending to the debtor an authenticated record:

(1) disclaiming any interest in the collateral; and

(2) if known to the recipient, providing the name and mailing address of any assignee of or successor to the recipient's interest in the collateral.

(e) [Request for accounting or regarding statement of account; no interest in obligation claimed.] A person that receives a request for an accounting or a request regarding a statement of account, claims no interest in the obligations when it receives the request, and claimed an interest in the obligations at an earlier time shall comply with the request within 14 days after receipt by sending to the debtor an authenticated record:

(1) disclaiming any interest in the obligations; and

(2) if known to the recipient, providing the name and mailing address of any assignee of or successor to the recipient's interest in the obligations.

(f) [Charges for responses.] A debtor is entitled without charge to one response to a request under this section during any six-month period. The secured party may require payment of a charge not exceeding $25 for each additional response.

OTHER UCC SECTIONS TO LOOK TO WHEN YOU LOOK AT SECTION 9–210

Need to read sections 9–502 and 9–210 together to understand what information you get from the section 9–502 filing: notice filing and what additional information you can get with section 9–210 request.

OFFICIAL COMMENT

* * *

2. **Scope and Purpose.** This section provides a procedure whereby a debtor may obtain from a secured party information about the secured obligation and the collateral in which the secured party may claim a security interest. It clarifies and resolves some of the issues that arose under former Section 9–208 and makes information concerning the secured indebtedness readily available to debtors, both before and after default. It applies to agricultural lien transactions (see the definitions of "debtor," "secured party," and "collateral" in Section 9–102), but generally not to sales of receivables. See subsection (b).

3. **Requests by Debtors Only.** A financing statement filed under Part 5 may disclose only that a secured party may have a security interest in specified types of collateral. In most cases the financing statement will contain no indication of the obligation (if any) secured, whether any security interest actually exists, or the particular property subject to a security interest. Because creditors of and prospective purchasers from a debtor may have legitimate needs for more detailed information, it is necessary to provide a

procedure under which the secured party will be required to provide information. On the other hand, the secured party should not be under a duty to disclose any details of the debtor's financial affairs to any casual inquirer or competitor who may inquire. For this reason, this section gives the right to request information to the debtor only. The debtor may submit a request in connection with negotiations with subsequent creditors and purchasers, as well as for the purpose of determining the status of its credit relationship or demonstrating which of its assets are free of a security interest.

4. **Permitted Types of Requests for Information.** Subsection (a) contemplates that a debtor may request three types of information by submitting three types of "requests" to the secured party. First, the debtor may request the secured party to prepare and send an "accounting" (defined in Section 9–102). Second, the debtor may submit to the secured party a list of collateral for the secured party's approval or correction. Third, the debtor may submit to the secured party for its approval or correction a statement of the aggregate amount of unpaid secured obligations. Inasmuch as a secured party may have numerous transactions and relationships with a debtor, each request must identify the relevant transactions or relationships. Subsections (b) and (c) require the secured party to respond to a request within 14 days following receipt of the request.

5. **Recipients Claiming No Interest in the Transaction.** A debtor may be unaware that a creditor with whom it has dealt has assigned its security interest or the secured obligation. Subsections (d) and (e) impose upon recipients of requests under this section the duty to inform the debtor that they claim no interest in the collateral or secured obligation, respectively, and to inform the debtor of the name and mailing address of any known assignee or successor. As under subsections (b) and (c), a response to a request under subsection (d) or (e) is due 14 days following receipt.

6. **Waiver; Remedy for Failure to Comply.** The debtor's rights under this section may not be waived or varied. See Section 9–602(2). Section 9–625 sets forth the remedies for noncompliance with the requirements of this section.

7. **Limitation on Free Responses to Requests.** Under subsection (f), during a six-month period a debtor is entitled to receive from the secured party one free response to a request. The debtor is not entitled to a free response to *each* type of request (i.e., three free responses) during a six-month period.

PART 3. PERFECTION AND PRIORITY
[SUBPART 1. LAW GOVERNING PERFECTION AND PRIORITY]

§ 9–301. Law Governing Perfection and Priority of Security Interests

Except as otherwise provided in Sections 9–303 through 9–306, the following rules determine the law governing perfection, the effect of perfection or nonperfection, and the priority of a security interest in collateral:

(1) Except as otherwise provided in this section, while a debtor is located in a jurisdiction, the local law of that jurisdiction governs perfection, the effect of perfection or nonperfection, and the priority of a security interest in collateral.

(2) While collateral is located in a jurisdiction, the local law of that jurisdiction governs perfection, the effect of perfection or nonperfection, and the priority of a possessory security interest in that collateral.

(3) Except as otherwise provided in paragraph (4), while tangible negotiable documents, goods, instruments, money, or tangible chattel paper is located in a jurisdiction, the local law of that jurisdiction governs:

> **(A)** perfection of a security interest in the goods by filing a fixture filing;
>
> **(B)** perfection of a security interest in timber to be cut; and
>
> **(C)** the effect of perfection or nonperfection and the priority of a nonpossessory security interest in the collateral.

(4) The local law of the jurisdiction in which the wellhead or minehead is located governs perfection, the effect of perfection or nonperfection, and the priority of a security interest in as-extracted collateral.

UNOFFICIAL COMMENTS

The most important law school use of this section is to figure out in which state a financing statement should be filed. General rule is that financing statement needs to be filed in the state in which the debtor is located, as determined by section 9–307. Sections 9–303 to 9–306 contain special rules for special forms of collateral.

OTHER UCC SECTIONS TO LOOK TO WHEN YOU LOOK AT SECTION 9–301

Key phrase in section 9–301 is "debtor is located", and section 9–307 tells you how to tell where the debtor is located.

OFFICIAL COMMENT

* * *

2. Scope of This Subpart. Part 3, Subpart 1 (Sections 9–301 through 9–307) contains choice-of-law rules similar to those of former Section 9–103. Former Section 9–103 generally addresses which State's law governs "perfection and the effect of perfection or non-perfection of" security interests. See, e.g., former Section 9–103(1)(b). This Article follows the broader and more precise formulation in former Section 9–103(6)(b), which was revised in connection with the promulgation of Revised Article 8 in 1994: "perfection, the effect of perfection or non-perfection, and the priority of" security interests. Priority, in this context, subsumes all of the rules in Part 3, including "cut off" or "take free" rules such as Sections 9–317(b), (c), and (d), 9–320(a), (b), and (d), and 9–332. This subpart does not address choice of law for other purposes. For example, the law applicable to issues such as attachment, validity, characterization (e.g., true lease or security interest), and enforcement is governed by the rules in Section 1–105; that governing law typically is specified in the same agreement that contains the security agreement. And, another jurisdiction's law may govern other third-party matters addressed in this Article. See Section 9–401, Comment 3.

3. **Scope of Referral.** In designating the jurisdiction whose law governs, this Article directs the court to apply only the substantive ("local") law of a particular jurisdiction and not its choice-of-law rules.

Example 1: Litigation over the priority of a security interest in accounts arises in State X. State X has adopted the official text of this Article, which provides that priority is determined by the local law of the jurisdiction in which the debtor is located. See Section 9–301(1). The debtor is located in State Y. Even if State Y has retained former Article 9 or enacted a nonuniform choice-of-law rule (e.g., one that provides that perfection is governed by the law of State Z), a State X court should look only to the substantive law of State Y and disregard State Y's choice-of-law rule. State Y's substantive law (e.g., its Section 9–501) provides that financing statements should be filed in a filing office in State Y. Note, however, that if the identical perfection issue were to be litigated in State Y, the court would look to State Y's former Section 9–103 or nonuniform 9–301 and conclude that a filing in State Y is ineffective.

Example 2: In the preceding Example, assume that State X has adopted the official text of this Article, and State Y has adopted a nonuniform Section 9–301(1) under which perfection is governed by the whole law of State X, including its choice-of-law rules. If litigation occurs in State X, the court should look to the substantive law of State Y, which provides that financing statements are to be filed in a filing office in State Y. If litigation occurs in State Y, the court should look to the law of State X, whose choice-of-law rule requires that the court apply the substantive law of State Y. Thus, regardless of the jurisdiction in which the litigation arises, the financing statement should be filed in State Y.

4. **Law Governing Perfection: General Rule.** Paragraph (1) contains the general rule: the law governing perfection of security interests in both tangible and intangible collateral, whether perfected by filing or automatically, is the law of the jurisdiction of the debtor's location, as determined under Section 9–307.

Paragraph (1) substantially simplifies the choice-of-law rules. Former Section 9–103 contained different choice-of-law rules for different types of collateral. Under Section 9–301(1), the law of a single jurisdiction governs perfection with respect to most types of collateral, both tangible and intangible. Paragraph (1) eliminates the need for former Section 9–103(1)(c), which concerned purchase-money security interests in tangible collateral that is intended to move from one jurisdiction to the other. It is likely to reduce the frequency of cases in which the governing law changes after a financing statement is properly filed. (Presumably, debtors change their own location less frequently than they change the location of their collateral.) The approach taken in paragraph (1) also eliminates some difficult priority issues and the need to distinguish between "mobile" and "ordinary" goods, and it reduces the number of filing offices in which secured parties must file or search when collateral is located in several jurisdictions.

5. **Law Governing Perfection: Exceptions.** The general rule is subject to several exceptions. It does not apply to goods covered by a certificate of title (see Section 9–303), deposit accounts (see Section 9–304), investment property (see Section 9–305), or letter-of-credit rights (see Section 9–306). Nor does it apply to possessory security interests, i.e., security interests that the secured party has perfected by taking possession of the collateral (see paragraph (2)), security interests perfected by filing a fixture filing (see subparagraph (3)(A)), security interests in timber to be cut (subparagraph (3)(B)), or security interests in as-extracted collateral (see paragraph (4)).

a. **Possessory Security Interests.** Paragraph (2) applies to possessory security interests and provides that perfection is governed by the local law of the jurisdiction in which the collateral is located. This is the rule of former Section 9–103(1)(b), except paragraph (2) eliminates the troublesome "last event" test of former law.

The distinction between nonpossessory and possessory security interests creates the potential for the same jurisdiction to apply two different choice-of-law rules to determine perfection in the same collateral. For example, were a secured party in possession of an instrument or a tangible document to relinquish possession in reliance on temporary perfection, the applicable law immediately would change from that of the location of the collateral to that of the location of the debtor. The applicability of two different choice-of-law rules for perfection is unlikely to lead to any material practical problems. The perfection rules of one Article 9 jurisdiction are likely to be identical to those of another. Moreover, under paragraph (3), the relative priority of competing security interests in tangible collateral is resolved by reference to the law of the jurisdiction in which the collateral is located, regardless of how the security interests are perfected.

b. **Fixtures.** Application of the general rule in paragraph (1) to perfection of a security interest in fixtures would yield strange results. For example, perfection of a security interest in fixtures located in Arizona and owned by a Delaware corporation would be governed by the law of Delaware. Although Delaware law would send one to a filing office in Arizona for the place to file a financing statement as a fixture filing, see Section 9–501, Delaware law would not take account of local, nonuniform, real-property filing and recording requirements that Arizona law might impose. For this reason, paragraph (3)(A) contains a special rule for security interests perfected by a fixture filing; the law of the jurisdiction in which the fixtures are located governs perfection, including the formal requisites of a fixture filing. Under paragraph (3)(C), the same law governs priority. Fixtures are "goods" as defined in Section 9–102.

* * *

d. **As–Extracted Collateral.** Paragraph (4) adopts the rule of former Section 9–103(5) with respect to certain security interests in minerals and related accounts. Like security interests in fixtures perfected by filing a fixture filing, security interests in minerals that are as-extracted collateral are perfected by filing in the office designated for the filing or recording of a mortgage on the real property. For the same reasons, the law governing perfection and priority is the law of the jurisdiction in which the wellhead or minehead is located.

6. **Change in Law Governing Perfection.** When the debtor changes its location to another jurisdiction, the jurisdiction whose law governs perfection under paragraph (1) changes, as well. Similarly, the law governing perfection of a possessory security interest in collateral under paragraph (2) changes when the collateral is removed to another jurisdiction. Nevertheless, these changes will not result in an immediate loss of perfection. See Section 9–316(a), (b).

7. **Law Governing Effect of Perfection and Priority: Goods, Documents, Instruments, Money, Negotiable Documents, and Tangible Chattel Paper.** Under former Section 9–103, the law of a single jurisdiction governed both questions of perfection and those of priority. This Article generally adopts that approach. See paragraph (1). But the approach may create problems if the debtor and collateral are located in different jurisdictions. For example, assume a security interest in equipment located in Pennsylvania is perfected by filing in Illinois, where the debtor is located. If the law of the jurisdiction in which the debtor is located were to govern priority, then the priority of an execution lien on goods located in Pennsylvania would be governed by rules enacted by the Illinois legislature.

To address this problem, paragraph (3)(C) divorces questions of perfection from questions of "the effect of perfection or nonperfection and the priority of a security interest." Under paragraph (3)(C), the rights of competing claimants to tangible collateral are resolved by reference to the law of the jurisdiction in which the collateral is located. A similar bifurcation applied to security interests in investment property under former Section 9–103(6). See Section 9–305.

Paragraph (3)(C) applies the law of the situs to determine priority only with respect to goods (including fixtures), instruments, money, tangible negotiable documents, and tangible chattel paper. Compare former Section 9–103(1), which applied the law of the location of the collateral to documents, instruments, and "ordinary" (as opposed to "mobile") goods. This Article does not distinguish among types of goods. The ordinary/mobile goods distinction appears to address concerns about where to file and search, rather than concerns about priority. There is no reason to preserve this distinction under the bifurcated approach.

Particularly serious confusion may arise when the choice-of-law rules of a given jurisdiction result in each of two competing security interests in the same collateral being governed by a different priority rule. The potential for this confusion existed under former Section 9–103(4) with respect to chattel paper: Perfection by possession was governed by the law of the location of the paper, whereas perfection by filing was governed by the law of the location of the debtor. Consider the mess that would have been created if the language or interpretation of former Section 9–308 were to differ in the two relevant States, or if one of the relevant jurisdictions (e.g., a foreign country) had not adopted Article 9. The potential for confusion could have been exacerbated when a secured party perfected both by taking possession in the State where the collateral is located (State A) and by filing in the State where the debtor is located (State B)—a common practice for some chattel paper financers. By providing that the law of the jurisdiction in which the collateral is located governs priority, paragraph (3) substantially diminishes this problem.

8. **Non–U.S. Debtors.** This Article applies the same choice-of-law rules to all debtors, foreign and domestic. For example, it adopts the bifurcated approach for determining the law applicable to security interests in goods and other tangible collateral. See Comment 5.a., above. The Article contains a new rule specifying the location of non-U.S. debtors for purposes of this Part. The rule appears in Section 9–307 and is explained in the Comments to that section. Former Section 9–103(3)(c), which contained a special choice-of-law rule governing security interests created by debtors located in a non-U.S. jurisdiction, proved unsatisfactory and was deleted.

§ 9–302. Law Governing Perfection and Priority of Agricultural Liens

While farm products are located in a jurisdiction, the local law of that jurisdiction governs perfection, the effect of perfection or nonperfection, and the priority of an agricultural lien on the farm products.

OFFICIAL COMMENT

* * *

2. **Agricultural Liens.** This section provides choice-of-law rules for agricultural liens on farm products. Perfection, the effect of perfection or nonperfection, and priority all are governed by the law of the jurisdiction in which the farm products are located. Other choice-of-law rules, including Section 1–105, determine which jurisdiction's law governs other matters, such as the secured party's rights on default. See Section 9–301, Comment 2. Inasmuch as no agricultural lien on proceeds arises under this Article,

this section does not expressly apply to proceeds of agricultural liens. However, if another statute creates an agricultural lien on proceeds, it may be appropriate for courts to apply the choice-of-law rule in this section to determine priority in the proceeds.

§ 9–303. Law Governing Perfection and Priority of Security Interests in Goods Covered by a Certificate of Title

(a) [Applicability of section.] This section applies to goods covered by a certificate of title, even if there is no other relationship between the jurisdiction under whose certificate of title the goods are covered and the goods or the debtor.

(b) [When goods covered by certificate of title.] Goods become covered by a certificate of title when a valid application for the certificate of title and the applicable fee are delivered to the appropriate authority. Goods cease to be covered by a certificate of title at the earlier of the time the certificate of title ceases to be effective under the law of the issuing jurisdiction or the time the goods become covered subsequently by a certificate of title issued by another jurisdiction.

(c) [Applicable law.] The local law of the jurisdiction under whose certificate of title the goods are covered governs perfection, the effect of perfection or nonperfection, and the priority of a security interest in goods covered by a certificate of title from the time the goods become covered by the certificate of title until the goods cease to be covered by the certificate of title.

UNOFFICIAL COMMENTS

Look for an exam problem in which two different states issue certificates of title on the same motor vehicle. Look to the last sentence of section 9–303(b) for the answer.

OTHER UCC SECTIONS TO LOOK TO WHEN YOU LOOK AT SECTION 9–303

Section 9–311(a) provides for perfection of security interests in motor vehicles by indicating the security interest on the certificate of title.

If your prof really got into this stuff, then you probably need to get into the Uniform Motor Vehicle Certificate of Title Act, infra at pages 457–483.

OFFICIAL COMMENT

* * *

2. **Scope of This Section.** This section applies to "goods covered by a certificate of title." The new definition of "certificate of title" in Section 9–102 makes clear that this section applies not only to certificate-of-title statutes under which perfection occurs upon notation of the

security interest on the certificate but also to those that contemplate notation but provide that perfection is achieved by another method, e.g., delivery of designated documents to an official. Subsection (a), which is new, makes clear that this section applies to certificates of a jurisdiction having no other contacts with the goods or the debtor. This result comports with most of the reported cases on the subject and with contemporary business practices in the trucking industry.

3. **Law Governing Perfection and Priority.** Subsection (c) is the basic choice-of-law rule for goods covered by a certificate of title. Perfection and priority of a security interest are governed by the law of the jurisdiction under whose certificate of title the goods are covered from the time the goods become covered by the certificate of title until the goods cease to be covered by the certificate of title.

Normally, under the law of the relevant jurisdiction, the perfection step would consist of compliance with that jurisdiction's certificate-of-title statute and a resulting notation of the security interest on the certificate of title. See Section 9–311(b). In the typical case of an automobile or over-the-road truck, a person who wishes to take a security interest in the vehicle can ascertain whether it is subject to any security interests by looking at the certificate of title. But certificates of title cover certain types of goods in some States but not in others. A secured party who does not realize this may extend credit and attempt to perfect by filing in the jurisdiction in which the debtor is located. If the goods had been titled in another jurisdiction, the lender would be unperfected.

Subsection (b) explains when goods become covered by a certificate of title and when they cease to be covered. Goods may become covered by a certificate of title, even though no certificate of title has issued. Former Section 9–103(2)(b) provided that the law of the jurisdiction issuing the certificate ceases to apply upon "surrender" of the certificate. This Article eliminates the concept of "surrender." However, if the certificate is surrendered in conjunction with an appropriate application for a certificate to be issued by another jurisdiction, the law of the original jurisdiction ceases to apply because the goods became covered subsequently by a certificate of title from another jurisdiction. Alternatively, the law of the original jurisdiction ceases to apply when the certificate "ceases to be effective" under the law of that jurisdiction. Given the diversity in certificate-of-title statutes, the term "effective" is not defined.

4. **Continued Perfection.** The fact that the law of one State ceases to apply under subsection (b) does not mean that a security interest perfected under that law becomes unperfected automatically. In most cases, the security interest will remain perfected. See Section 9–316(d), (e). Moreover, a perfected security interest may be subject to defeat by certain buyers and secured parties. See Section 9–337.

5. **Inventory.** Compliance with a certificate-of-title statute generally is *not* the method of perfecting security interests in inventory. Section 9–311(d) provides that a security interest created in inventory held by a person in the business of selling goods of that kind is subject to the normal filing rules; compliance with a certificate-of-title statute is not necessary or effective to perfect the security interest. Most certificate-of-title statutes are in accord.

The following example explains the subtle relationship between this rule and the choice-of-law rules in Section 9–303 and former Section 9–103(2):

Example: Goods are located in State A and covered by a certificate of title issued under the law of State A. The State A certificate of title is "clean"; it does not reflect a security interest. Owner takes the goods to State B and sells (trades in) the goods to Dealer, who is in the business of selling goods of that kind and is located (within the meaning of Section 9–307) in State B. As is customary, Dealer retains the duly assigned State A certificate of title pending resale of the goods. Dealer's inventory financer, SP, obtains a security interest in the goods under its after-acquired property clause.

Under Section 9–311(d) of both State A and State B, Dealer's inventory financer, SP, must perfect by filing instead of complying with a certificate-of-title statute. If Section 9–303 were read to provide that the law applicable to perfection of SP's security interest is that of State A, because the goods are covered by a State A certificate, then SP would be required to file in State A under State A's Section 9–501. That result would be anomalous, to say the least, since the principle underlying Section 9–311(d) is that the inventory should be treated as ordinary goods.

Section 9–303 (and former Section 9–103(2)) should be read as providing that the law of State B, not State A, applies. A court looking to the forum's Section 9–303(a) would find that Section 9–303 applies only if two conditions are met: (i) the goods are covered by the certificate as explained in Section 9–303(b), i.e., application had been made for a State (here, State A) to issue a certificate of title covering the goods and (ii) the certificate is a "certificate of title" as defined in Section 9–102, i.e., "a statute provides for the security interest in question to be indicated on the certificate as a condition or result of the security interest's obtaining priority over the rights of a lien creditor." Stated otherwise, Section 9–303 applies only when compliance with a certificate-of-title statute, and not filing, is the appropriate method of perfection. Under the law of State A, *for purposes of perfecting SP's security interest in the dealer's inventory*, the proper method of perfection is filing—not compliance with State A's certificate-of-title statute. For that reason, the goods are not covered by a "certificate of title," and the second condition is not met. Thus, Section 9–303 does not apply to the goods. Instead, Section 9–301 applies, and the applicable law is that of State B, where the debtor (dealer) is located.

6. **External Constraints on This Section.** The need to coordinate Article 9 with a variety of nonuniform certificate-of-title statutes, the need to provide rules to take account of situations in which multiple certificates of title are outstanding with respect to particular goods, and the need to govern the transition from perfection by filing in one jurisdiction to perfection by notation in another all create pressure for a detailed and complex set of rules. In an effort to minimize complexity, this Article does not attempt to coordinate Article 9 with the entire array of certificate-of-title statutes. In particular, Sections 9–303, 9–311, and 9–316(d) and (e) assume that the certificate-of-title statutes to which they apply do not have relation-back provisions (i.e., provisions under which perfection is deemed to occur at a time earlier than when the perfection steps actually are taken). A Legislative Note to Section 9–311 recommends the elimination of relation-back provisions in certificate-of-title statutes affecting perfection of security interests.

Ideally, at any given time, only one certificate of title is outstanding with respect to particular goods. In fact, however, sometimes more than one jurisdiction issues more than one certificate of title with respect to the same goods. This situation results from defects in certificate-of-title laws and the interstate coordination of those laws, not from deficiencies in this Article. As long as the possibility of multiple certificates of title remains, the potential for innocent parties to suffer losses will continue. At best, this Article can identify clearly which innocent parties will bear the losses in familiar fact patterns.

§ 9–307. Location of Debtor

(a) ["Place of business."] In this section, "place of business" means a place where a debtor conducts its affairs.

(b) [Debtor's location: general rules.] Except as otherwise provided in this section, the following rules determine a debtor's location:

(1) A debtor who is an individual is located at the individual's principal residence.

(2) A debtor that is an organization and has only one place of business is located at its place of business.

(3) A debtor that is an organization and has more than one place of business is located at its chief executive office.

(c) [Limitation of applicability of subsection (b).] Subsection (b) applies only if a debtor's residence, place of business, or chief executive office, as applicable, is located in a jurisdiction whose law generally requires information concerning the existence of a nonpossessory security interest to be made generally available in a filing, recording, or registration system as a condition or result of the security interest's obtaining priority over the rights of a lien creditor with respect to the collateral. If subsection (b) does not apply, the debtor is located in the District of Columbia.

(d) [Continuation of location: cessation of existence, etc.] A person that ceases to exist, have a residence, or have a place of business continues to be located in the jurisdiction specified by subsections (b) and (c).

(e) [Location of registered organization organized under State law.] A registered organization that is organized under the law of a State is located in that State.

(f) [Location of registered organization organized under federal law; bank branches and agencies.] Except as otherwise provided in subsection (i), a registered organization that is organized under the law of the United States and a branch or agency of a bank that is not organized under the law of the United States or a State are located:

(1) in the State that the law of the United States designates, if the law designates a State of location;

(2) in the State that the registered organization, branch, or agency designates, if the law of the United States authorizes the registered organization, branch, or agency to designate its State of location; or

(3) in the District of Columbia, if neither paragraph (1) nor paragraph (2) applies.

(g) [Continuation of location: change in status of registered organization.] A registered organization continues to be located in the jurisdiction specified by subsection (e) or (f) notwithstanding:

(1) the suspension, revocation, forfeiture, or lapse of the registered organization's status as such in its jurisdiction of organization; or

(2) the dissolution, winding up, or cancellation of the existence of the registered organization.

* * *

(k) [Section applies only to this part.] This section applies only for purposes of this part.

OFFICIAL COMMENT

1. **Source.** Former Section 9-103(3)(d), substantially revised.

2. **General Rules.** As a general matter, the location of the debtor determines the jurisdiction whose law governs perfection of a security interest. See Sections 9-301(1), 9-305(c). It also governs priority of a security interest in certain types of intangible collateral, such as accounts, electronic chattel paper, and general intangibles. This section determines the location of the debtor for choice-of-law purposes, but not for other purposes. See subsection (k).

Subsection (b) states the general rules: An individual debtor is deemed to be located at the individual's principal residence with respect to both personal and business assets. Any other debtor is deemed to be located at its place of business if it has only one, or at its chief executive office if it has more than one place of business.

As used in this section, a "place of business" means a place where the debtor conducts its affairs. See subsection (a). Thus, every organization, even eleemosynary institutions and other organizations that do not conduct "for profit" business activities, has a "place of business." Under subsection (d), a person who ceases to exist, have a residence, or have a place of business continues to be located in the jurisdiction determined by subsection (b).

The term "chief executive office" is not defined in this Section or elsewhere in the Uniform Commercial Code. "Chief executive office" means the place from which the debtor manages the main part of its business operations or other affairs. This is the place where persons dealing with the debtor would normally look for credit information, and is the appropriate place for filing. With respect to most multi-state debtors, it will be simple to determine which of the debtor's offices is the "chief executive office." Even when a doubt arises, it would be rare that there could be more than two possibilities. A secured party in such a case may protect itself by perfecting under the law of each possible jurisdiction.

Similarly, the term "principal residence" is not defined. If the security interest in question is a purchase-money security interest in consumer goods which is perfected upon attachment, see Section 9-309(1), the choice of law may make no difference. In other cases, when a doubt arises, prudence may dictate perfecting under the law of each jurisdiction that might be the debtor's "principal residence."

The general rule is subject to several exceptions, each of which is discussed below.

3. **Non-U.S. Debtors.** Under the general rules of this section, a non-U.S. debtor normally would be located in a foreign jurisdiction and, as a consequence, foreign law would govern perfection. When foreign law affords no public notice of security interests, the general rule yields unacceptable results.

Accordingly, subsection (c) provides that the normal rules for determining the location of a debtor (i.e., the rules in subsection (b)) apply only if they yield a location that is "a jurisdiction whose law generally requires information concerning the existence of a nonpossessory security interest to be made generally available in a filing, recording, or registration system as a condition or result of the security interest's obtaining priority over the rights of a lien creditor with respect to the collateral." The phrase "generally requires" is meant to include legal regimes that generally require notice in a filing or recording system as a condition of perfecting nonpossessory security interests, but which permit perfection by another method (e.g., control, automatic perfection, temporary perfection) in limited circumstances. A jurisdiction that has adopted this Article or an earlier version of this Article is such a jurisdiction. If the rules in subsection (b) yield a jurisdiction whose law does not generally require notice in a filing or registration system, the debtor is located in the District of Columbia.

Example 1: Debtor is an English corporation with 7 offices in the United States and its chief executive office in London, England. Debtor creates a security interest in its accounts. Under subsection (b)(3), Debtor would be located in England. However, subsection (c) provides that subsection (b) applies only if English law generally conditions perfection on giving public notice in a filing, recording, or registration system. Otherwise, Debtor is located in the District of Columbia. Under Section 9–301(1), perfection, the effect of perfection, and priority are governed by the law of the jurisdiction of the debtor's location—here, England or the District of Columbia (depending on the content of English law).

Example 2: Debtor is an English corporation with 7 offices in the United States and its chief executive office in London, England. Debtor creates a security interest in equipment located in London. Under subsection (b)(3) Debtor would be located in England. However, subsection (c) provides that subsection (b) applies only if English law generally conditions perfection on giving public notice in a filing, recording, or registration system. Otherwise, Debtor is located in the District of Columbia. Under Section 9–301(1), perfection is governed by the law of the jurisdiction of the debtor's location, whereas, under Section 9–301(3), the law of the jurisdiction in which the collateral is located—here, England—governs priority.

The foregoing discussion assumes that each transaction bears an appropriate relation to the forum State. In the absence of an appropriate relation, the forum State's entire UCC, including the choice-of-law provisions in Article 9 (Sections 9–301 through 9–307), will not apply. See Section 9–109, Comment 9.

4. **Registered Organizations Organized Under Law of a State.** Under subsection (e), a registered organization (e.g., a corporation or limited partnership) organized under the law of a "State" (defined in Section 9–102) is located in its State of organization. Subsection (g) makes clear that events affecting the status of a registered organization, such as the dissolution of a corporation or revocation of its charter, do not affect its location for purposes of subsection (e). However, certain of these events may result in, or be accompanied by, a transfer of collateral from the registered organization to another debtor. This section does not determine whether a transfer occurs, nor does it determine the legal consequences of any transfer.

Determining the registered organization-debtor's location by reference to the jurisdiction of organization could provide some important side benefits for the filing systems. A jurisdiction could structure its filing system so that it would be impossible to make a mistake in a registered organization-debtor's name on a financing statement. For example, a filer would be informed if a filed record designated an incorrect corporate name for the debtor. Linking filing to the jurisdiction of organization also could reduce pressure on the system imposed by transactions in which registered organizations cease to exist—as a consequence of merger or consolidation, for example. The jurisdiction of organization might prohibit such transactions unless steps were taken to ensure that existing filings were refiled against a successor or terminated by the secured party.

* * *

[SUBPART 2. PERFECTION]

§ 9–308. When Security Interest Is Perfected; Continuity of Perfection

(a) [Perfection of security interest.] Except as otherwise provided in this section and Section 9–309, a security interest is perfected if it has attached and all of the applicable requirements for perfection in Sections 9–310 through 9–316 have been satisfied. A security interest is perfected when it attaches if the applicable requirements are satisfied before the security interest attaches.

* * *

(c) [Continuous perfection; perfection by different methods.] A security interest * * * is perfected continuously if it is originally perfected by one method under this article and is later perfected by another method under this article, without an intermediate period when it was unperfected.

* * *

UNOFFICIAL COMMENTS

Not much important here that is not obvious. 9–308(a) tells you that you can't have a perfected security interest until you have a security interest.

OFFICIAL COMMENT

* * *

2. **General Rule.** This Article uses the term "attach" to describe the point at which property becomes subject to a security interest. The requisites for attachment are stated in Section 9–203. When it attaches, a security interest may be either perfected or unperfected. "Perfected" means that the security interest has attached and the secured party has taken all the steps required by this Article as specified in Sections 9–310 through 9–316. A perfected security interest may still be or become subordinate to other interests. See, e.g., Sections 9–320, 9–322. However, in general, after perfection the secured party is protected against creditors and transferees of the debtor and, in particular, against any representative of creditors in insolvency proceedings instituted by or against the debtor. See, e.g., Section 9–317.

Subsection (a) explains that the time of perfection is when the security interest has attached and any necessary steps for perfection, such as taking possession or filing, have been taken. The "except" clause refers to the perfection-upon-attachment rules appearing in Section 9–309. It also reflects that other subsections of this section, e.g., subsection (d), contain automatic-perfection rules. If the steps for perfection have been taken in advance, as when the secured party files a financing statement before giving value or before the debtor acquires rights in the collateral, then the security interest is perfected when it attaches.

* * *

4. **Continuous Perfection.** The following example illustrates the operation of subsection (c):

> **Example 1:** Debtor, an importer, creates a security interest in goods that it imports and the documents of title that cover the goods. The secured party, Bank, takes possession of a tangible negotiable bill of lading covering certain imported goods and thereby perfects its security interest in the bill of lading and the goods. See Sections 9–313(a), 9–312(c)(1). Bank releases the bill of lading to the debtor for the purpose of procuring the goods from the carrier and selling them. Under Section 9–312(f), Bank continues to have a perfected security interest in the document and goods for 20 days. Bank files a financing statement covering the collateral before the expiration of the 20–day period. Its security interest now continues perfected for as long as the filing is good.
>
> If the successive stages of Bank's security interest succeed each other without an intervening gap, the security interest is "perfected continuously," and the date of perfection is when the security interest first became perfected (i.e., when Bank received possession of the tangible bill of lading). If, however, there is a gap between stages—for example, if Bank does not file until after the expiration of the 20–day period specified in Section 9–312(f) and leaves the collateral in the debtor's possession—then, the chain being broken, the perfection is no longer continuous. The date of perfection would now be the date of filing (after expiration of the 20–day period). Bank's security interest would be vulnerable to any interests arising during the gap period which under Section 9–317 take priority over an unperfected security interest.

* * *

§ 9–309. Security Interest Perfected Upon Attachment

The following security interests are perfected when they attach:

(1) a purchase-money security interest in consumer goods, except as otherwise provided in Section 9–311(b) with respect to consumer goods that are subject to a statute or treaty described in Section 9–311(a);

(2) an assignment of accounts or payment intangibles which does not by itself or in conjunction with other assignments to the same assignee transfer a significant part of the assignor's outstanding accounts or payment intangibles;

(3) a sale of a payment intangible;

(4) a sale of a promissory note;

(5) a security interest created by the assignment of a health-care-insurance receivable to the provider of the health-care goods or services;

* * *

UNOFFICIAL COMMENTS

While the section itself does not use the phrase "automatic perfection", Official Comment 2 does (and more important, your professor does) and so should you. Far and away the most important law school example of automatic perfection is 9–309(1): purchase-money security interests in consumer goods.

Also, watch for sales of "payment intangibles" and promissory notes. Remember that sales of payment intangibles and promissory notes are Article 9 transactions under section 9–109. <u>If your teacher spent time on this, then you probably need to spend some time reading our extended comments relating to automatic perfection and the sale of receivables on pages 413–416.</u>

OTHER UCC SECTIONS TO LOOK TO WHEN YOU LOOK AT SECTION 9–309

Look to section 9–103 for explanation of "purchase-money security interest."

OFFICIAL COMMENT

* * *

2. **Automatic Perfection.** This section contains the perfection-upon-attachment rules previously located in former Sections 9–302(1), 9–115(4)(c), (d), and 9–116. Rather than continue to state the rule by indirection, this section explicitly provides for perfection upon attachment.

3. **Purchase-Money Security Interest in Consumer Goods.** Former Section 9–302(1)(d) has been revised and appears here as paragraph (1). No filing or other step is required to perfect a purchase-money security interest in consumer goods, other than goods, such as automobiles, that are subject to a statute or treaty described in Section 9–311(a). However, filing is required to perfect a non-purchase-money security interest in consumer goods and is necessary to prevent a buyer of consumer goods from taking free of a security interest under Section 9–320(b). A fixture filing is required for priority over conflicting interests in fixtures to the extent provided in Section 9–334.

4. **Rights to Payment.** Paragraph (2) expands upon former Section 9–302(1)(e) by affording automatic perfection to certain assignments of payment intangibles as well as accounts. The purpose of paragraph (2) is to save from *ex post facto* invalidation casual or isolated assignments—assignments which no one would think of filing. Any person who regularly takes assignments of any debtor's accounts or payment intangibles should file. In this connection Section 9–109(d)(4) through (7), which excludes certain transfers of accounts, chattel paper, payment intangibles, and promissory notes from this Article, should be consulted.

Paragraphs (3) and (4), which are new, afford automatic perfection to sales of payment intangibles and promissory notes, respectively. * * * To the extent that the exception in paragraph (2) covers outright sales of payment intangibles, which automatically are perfected under paragraph (3), the exception is redundant.

Paragraph (14), which is new, affords automatic perfection to sales by individuals of an "account" (as defined in Section 9–102) consisting of the right to winnings in a lottery or other game of chance. Payments on these accounts typically extend for periods of twenty years or more.

It would be unduly burdensome for the secured party, who would have no other reason to maintain contact with the seller, to monitor the the seller's whereabouts for such a length of time. This paragraph was added in 2001. It applies to a sale of an account described in it, even if the sale was entered into before the effective date of the paragraph. However, if the relative priorities of conflicting claims to the account were established before the paragraph took effect, Article 9 as in effect immediately prior to the date the paragraph took effect determines priority.

5. **Health-Care-Insurance Receivables.** Paragraph (5) extends automatic perfection to assignments of health-care-insurance receivables if the assignment is made to the health-care provider that provided the health-care goods or services. The primary effect is that, when an individual assigns a right to payment under an insurance policy to the person who provided health-care goods or services, the provider has no need to file a financing statement against the individual. The normal filing requirements apply to other assignments of health-care-insurance receivables covered by this Article, e.g., assignments from the health-care provider to a financer.

* * *

§ 9–310. When Filing Required to Perfect Security Interest; Security Interests to Which Filing Provisions Do Not Apply

(a) [General rule: perfection by filing.] Except as otherwise provided in subsection (b) and Section 9–312(b), a financing statement must be filed to perfect all security interests * * *.

(b) [Exceptions: filing not necessary.] The filing of a financing statement is not necessary to perfect a security interest:

(1) that is perfected under Section 9–308(d), (e), (f), or (g);

(2) that is perfected under Section 9–309 when it attaches;

(3) in property subject to a statute, regulation, or treaty described in Section 9–311(a);

(4) in goods in possession of a bailee which is perfected under Section 9–312(d)(1) or (2);

(5) in certificated securities, documents, goods, or instruments which is perfected without filing, control, or possession under Section 9–312(e), (f), or (g);

(6) in collateral in the secured party's possession under Section 9–313;

(7) in a certificated security which is perfected by delivery of the security certificate to the secured party under Section 9–313;

(8) in deposit accounts, electronic chattel paper, electronic documents, investment property, or letter-of-credit rights which is perfected by control under Section 9–314;

(9) in proceeds which is perfected under Section 9–315; or

(10) that is perfected under Section 9–316.

(c) [Assignment of perfected security interest.] If a secured party assigns a perfected security interest * * *, a filing under this article is not required to continue the perfected status of the security interest against creditors of and transferees from the original debtor.

UNOFFICIAL COMMENTS

The titles to subsections (a) and (b) tell it all. Almost. As noted below, be sure and read section 9–310 together with sections 9–312(b) and 9–313.

OTHER UCC SECTIONS TO LOOK TO WHEN YOU LOOK AT SECTION 9–310

If you look closely at section 9–310(a), you will see the reference to section 9–312(b). And, if you want to make a good grade in this course, you will look to section 9–312(b) [and section 9–314] and learn when the only method of perfection is control.

Even more important to a good grade in this course (although apparently not to the guys that wrote section 9–310) is your looking at section 9–313 which recognizes possession as another method of perfection.

OFFICIAL COMMENT

* * *

2. **General Rule.** Subsection (a) establishes a central Article 9 principle: Filing a financing statement is necessary for perfection of security interests and agricultural liens. However, filing is not necessary to perfect a security interest that is perfected by another permissible method, see subsection (b), nor does filing ordinarily perfect a security interest in a deposit account, letter-of-credit right, or money. See Section 9–312(b). Part 5 of the Article deals with the office in which to file, mechanics of filing, and operations of the filing office.

3. **Exemptions from Filing.** Subsection (b) lists the security interests for which filing is not required as a condition of perfection, because they are perfected automatically upon attachment (subsections (b)(2) and (b)(9)) or upon the occurrence of another event (subsections (b)(1), (b)(5), and (b)(9)), because they are perfected under the law of another jurisdiction (subsection (b)(10)), or because they are perfected by another method, such as by the secured party's taking possession or control (subsections (b)(3), (b)(4), (b)(5), (b)(6), (b)(7), and (b)(8)).

4. **Assignments of Perfected Security Interests.** Subsection (c) concerns assignment of a perfected security interest or agricultural lien. It provides that no filing is necessary in connection with an assignment by a secured party to an assignee in order to maintain perfection as against creditors of and transferees from the original debtor.

Example 1: Buyer buys goods from Seller, who retains a security interest in them. After Seller perfects the security interest by filing, Seller assigns the perfected security interest to X. The security interest, in X's hands and without further steps on X's part, continues perfected against *Buyer's* transferees and creditors.

Example 2: Dealer creates a security interest in specific equipment in favor of Lender. After Lender perfects the security interest in the equipment by filing, Lender assigns the chattel paper (which includes the perfected security interest in Dealer's equipment) to X. The security interest in the equipment, in X's hands and without further steps on X's part, continues perfected against *Dealer's* transferees and creditors. However, regardless of whether Lender made the assignment to secure Lender's obligation to X or whether the assignment was an outright sale of the chattel paper, the assignment creates a security interest in the chattel paper in favor of X. Accordingly, X must take whatever steps may be required for perfection in order to be protected against *Lender's* transferees and creditors with respect to the chattel paper.

Subsection (c) applies not only to an assignment of a security interest perfected by filing but also to an assignment of a security interest perfected by a method other than by filing, such as by control or by possession. Although subsection (c) addresses explicitly only the absence of an additional filing requirement, the same result normally will follow in the case of an assignment of a security interest perfected by a method other than by filing. For example, as long as possession of collateral is maintained by an assignee or by the assignor or another person on behalf of the assignee, no further perfection steps need be taken on account of the assignment to continue perfection as against creditors and transferees of the original debtor. Of course, additional action may be required for perfection of the assignee's interest as against creditors and transferees of the *assignor*.

Similarly, subsection (c) applies to the assignment of a security interest perfected by compliance with a statute, regulation, or treaty under Section 9–311(b), such as a certificate-of-title statute. Unless the statute expressly provides to the contrary, the security interest will remain perfected against creditors of and transferees from the original debtor, even if the assignee takes no action to cause the certificate of title to reflect the assignment or to cause its name to appear on the certificate of title. See PEB Commentary No. 12, which discusses this issue under former Section 9–302(3). Compliance with the statute is "equivalent to filing" under Section 9–311(b).

§ 9–311. Perfection of Security Interests in Property Subject to Certain Statutes, Regulations, and Treaties

(a) [Security interest subject to other law.] Except as otherwise provided in subsection (d), the filing of a financing statement is not necessary or effective to perfect a security interest in property subject to:

(1) a statute, regulation, or treaty of the United States whose requirements for a security interest's obtaining priority over the rights of a lien creditor with respect to the property preempt Section 9–310(a);

(2) [list any certificate-of-title statute covering automobiles, trailers, mobile homes, boats, farm tractors, or the like, which provides for a security interest to be indicated on the certificate as a condition or result of perfection, and any non-Uniform Commercial Code central filing statute]; or

(3) a certificate-of-title statute of another jurisdiction which provides for a security interest to be indicated on the certificate as a condition or result of the security interest's obtaining

priority over the rights of a lien creditor with respect to the property.

(b) [Compliance with other law.] Compliance with the requirements of a statute, regulation, or treaty described in subsection (a) for obtaining priority over the rights of a lien creditor is equivalent to the filing of a financing statement under this article. Except as otherwise provided in subsection (d) and Sections 9–313 and 9–316(d) and (e) for goods covered by a certificate of title, a security interest in property subject to a statute, regulation, or treaty described in subsection (a) may be perfected only by compliance with those requirements, and a security interest so perfected remains perfected notwithstanding a change in the use or transfer of possession of the collateral.

(c) [Duration and renewal of perfection.] Except as otherwise provided in subsection (d) and Section 9–316(d) and (e), duration and renewal of perfection of a security interest perfected by compliance with the requirements prescribed by a statute, regulation, or treaty described in subsection (a) are governed by the statute, regulation, or treaty. In other respects, the security interest is subject to this article.

(d) [Inapplicability to certain inventory.] During any period in which collateral subject to a statute specified in subsection (a)(2) is inventory held for sale or lease by a person or leased by that person as lessor and that person is in the business of selling goods of that kind, this section does not apply to a security interest in that collateral created by that person.

Legislative Note: This Article contemplates that perfection of a security interest in goods covered by a certificate of title occurs upon receipt by appropriate State officials of a properly tendered application for a certificate of title on which the security interest is to be indicated, without a relation back to an earlier time. States whose certificate-of-title statutes provide for perfection at a different time or contain a relation-back provision should amend the statutes accordingly.

UNOFFICIAL COMMENTS

Most professors use airplane parts (recording in Oklahoma City with the FAA) and copyrighted software (recording with the federal copyright office in DC) as examples of section 9–311(a).

Be sure that you understand section 9–311(d). Perfect by UCC filing, not certificate of lien notation, if (i) collateral is inventory of motor vehicles held for sale or lease and (ii) debtor is in business of selling motor vehicles.

OFFICIAL COMMENT

* * *

2. **Federal Statutes, Regulations, and Treaties.** Subsection (a)(1) exempts from the filing provisions of this Article transactions as to which a system of filing—state or federal—has been established under federal law. Subsection (b) makes clear that when such a system exists, perfection of a relevant security interest can be achieved only through compliance with that system (i.e., filing under this Article is not a permissible alternative).

An example of the type of federal statute referred to in subsection (a)(1) is 49 U.S.C. §§ 44107–11, for civil aircraft of the United States. The Assignment of Claims Act of 1940, as amended, provides for notice to contracting and disbursing officers and to sureties on bonds but does not establish a national filing system and therefore is not within the scope of subsection (a)(1). An assignee of a claim against the United States may benefit from compliance with the Assignment of Claims Act. But regardless of whether the assignee complies with that Act, the assignee must file under this Article in order to perfect its security interest against creditors and transferees of its assignor.

Subsection (a)(1) provides explicitly that the filing requirement of this Article defers only to federal statutes, regulations, or treaties whose requirements for a security interest's obtaining priority over the rights of a lien creditor preempt Section 9–310(a). The provision eschews reference to the term "perfection," inasmuch as Section 9–308 specifies the meaning of that term and a preemptive rule may use other terminology.

3. **State Statutes.** Subsections (a)(2) and (3) exempt from the filing requirements of this Article transactions covered by State certificate-of-title statutes covering motor vehicles and the like. The description of certificate-of-title statutes in subsections (a)(2) and (a)(3) tracks the language of the definition of "certificate of title" in Section 9–102. For a discussion of the operation of state certificate-of-title statutes in interstate contexts, see the Comments to Section 9–303.

Some states have enacted central filing statutes with respect to secured transactions in kinds of property that are of special importance in the local economy. Subsection (a)(2) defers to these statutes with respect to filing for that property.

4. **Inventory Covered by Certificate of Title.** Under subsection (d), perfection of a security interest in the inventory of a person in the business of selling goods of that kind is governed by the normal perfection rules, even if the inventory is subject to a certificate-of-title statute. Compliance with a certificate-of-title statute is both unnecessary and ineffective to perfect a security interest in inventory to which this subsection applies. Thus, a secured party who finances an automobile dealer that is in the business of selling and leasing its inventory of automobiles can perfect a security interest in all the automobiles by filing a financing statement but not by compliance with a certificate-of-title statute.

Subsection (d), and thus the filing and other perfection provisions of this Article, does not apply to inventory that is subject to a certificate-of-title statute and is of a kind that the debtor is not in the business of selling. For example, if goods are subject to a certificate-of-title statute and the debtor is in the business of leasing but not of selling, goods of that kind, the other subsections of this section govern perfection of a security interest in the goods. The fact that the debtor eventually sells the goods does not, of itself, mean that the debtor "is in the business of selling goods of that kind."

The filing and other perfection provisions of this Article apply to goods subject to a certificate-of-title statute only "during any period in which collateral is inventory held for sale or lease or leased." If the debtor takes goods of this kind out of inventory and uses them, say, as equipment, a filed financing statement would not remain effective to perfect a security interest.

5. **Compliance with Perfection Requirements of Other Statute.** Subsection (b) makes clear that compliance with the perfection requirements (i.e., the requirements for obtaining priority over a lien creditor), but not other requirements, of a statute, regulation, or treaty described in subsection (a) is sufficient for perfection under this Article. Perfection of a security interest under such a statute, regulation, or treaty has all the consequences of perfection under this Article.

The interplay of this section with certain certificate-of-title statutes may create confusion and uncertainty. For example, statutes under which perfection does not occur until a certificate of title is issued will create a gap between the time that the goods are covered by the certificate under Section 9–303 and the time of perfection. If the gap is long enough, it may result in turning some unobjectionable transactions into avoidable preferences under Bankruptcy Code Section 547. (The preference risk arises if more than 10 days (or 20 days, in the case of a purchase-money security interest) passes between the time a security interest attaches (or the debtor receives possession of the collateral, in the case of a purchase-money security interest) and the time it is perfected.) Accordingly, the Legislative Note to this section instructs the legislature to amend the applicable certificate-of-title statute to provide that perfection occurs upon receipt by the appropriate State official of a properly tendered application for a certificate of title on which the security interest is to be indicated.

Under some certificate-of-title statutes, including the Uniform Motor Vehicle Certificate of Title and Anti–Theft Act, perfection generally occurs upon delivery of specified documents to a state official but may, under certain circumstances, relate back to the time of attachment. This relation-back feature can create great difficulties for the application of the rules in Sections 9–303 and 9–311(b). Accordingly, the Legislative Note also recommends to legislatures that they remove any relation-back provisions from certificate-of-title statutes affecting security interests.

6. **Compliance with Perfection Requirements of Other Statute as Equivalent to Filing.** Under Subsection (b), compliance with the perfection requirements (i.e., the requirements for obtaining priority over a lien creditor) of a statute, regulation, or treaty described in subsection (a) "is equivalent to the filing of a financing statement."

The quoted phrase appeared in former Section 9–302(3). Its meaning was unclear, and many questions arose concerning the extent to which and manner in which Article 9 rules referring to "filing" were applicable to perfection by compliance with a certificate-of-title statute. This Article takes a variety of approaches for applying Article 9's filing rules to compliance with other statutes and treaties. First, as discussed above in Comment 5, it leaves the determination of some rules, such as the rule establishing time of perfection (Section 9–516(a)), to the other statutes themselves. Second, this Article explicitly applies some Article 9 filing rules to perfection under other statutes or treaties. See, e.g., Section 9–505. Third, this Article makes other Article 9 rules applicable to security interests perfected by compliance with another statute through the "equivalent to ... filing" provision in the first sentence of Section 9–311(b). The third approach is reflected for the most part in occasional Comments explaining how particular rules apply when perfection is accomplished under Section 9–311(b). See, e.g., Section 9–310, Comment 4; Section 9–315, Comment 6; Section 9–317, Comment 8. The absence of a Comment indicating that a particular filing provision applies to perfection pursuant to Section 9–311(b) does not mean the provision is inapplicable.

7. **Perfection by Possession of Goods Covered by Certificate-of-Title Statute.** A secured party who holds a security interest perfected under the law of State A in goods that subsequently are covered by a State B certificate of title may face a predicament. Ordinarily, the secured party will have four months under State B's Section 9–316(c) and (d) in which to (re)perfect as against a purchas-

er of the goods by having its security interest noted on a State B certificate. This procedure is likely to require the cooperation of the debtor and any competing secured party whose security interest has been noted on the certificate. Comment 4(e) to former Section 9–103 observed that "that cooperation is not likely to be forthcoming from an owner who wrongfully procured the issuance of a new certificate not showing the out-of-state security interest, or from a local secured party finding himself in a priority contest with the out-of-state secured party." According to that Comment, "[t]he only solution for the out-of-state secured party under present certificate of title statutes seems to be to reperfect by possession, i.e., by repossessing the goods." But the "solution" may not have worked:

Former Section 9–302(4) provided that a security interest in property subject to a certificate-of-title statute "can be perfected only by compliance therewith."

Sections 9–316(d) and (e), 9–311(c), and 9–313(b) of this Article resolve the conflict by providing that a security interest that remains perfected solely by virtue of Section 9–316(e) can be (re)perfected by the secured party's taking possession of the collateral. These sections contemplate only that taking possession of goods covered by a certificate of title will work as a method of perfection. None of these sections creates a right to take possession. Section 9–609 and the agreement of the parties define the secured party's right to take possession.

§ 9–312. Perfection of Security Interests in Chattel Paper, Deposit Accounts, Documents, Goods Covered by Documents, Instruments, Investment Property, Letter-of-Credit Rights, and Money; Perfection by Permissive Filing; Temporary Perfection Without Filing or Transfer of Possession

(a) [Perfection by filing permitted.] A security interest in chattel paper, negotiable documents, instruments, or investment property may be perfected by filing.

(b) [Control or possession of certain collateral.] Except as otherwise provided in Section 9–315(c) and (d) for proceeds:

 (1) a security interest in a deposit account may be perfected only by control under Section 9–314;

 (2) and except as otherwise provided in Section 9–308(d), a security interest in a letter-of-credit right may be perfected only by control under Section 9–314; and

 (3) a security interest in money may be perfected only by the secured party's taking possession under Section 9–313.

(c) [Goods covered by negotiable document.] While goods are in the possession of a bailee that has issued a negotiable document covering the goods:

 (1) a security interest in the goods may be perfected by perfecting a security interest in the document; and

(2) a security interest perfected in the document has priority over any security interest that becomes perfected in the goods by another method during that time.

(d) [Goods covered by nonnegotiable document.] While goods are in the possession of a bailee that has issued a nonnegotiable document covering the goods, a security interest in the goods may be perfected by:

(1) issuance of a document in the name of the secured party;

(2) the bailee's receipt of notification of the secured party's interest; or

(3) filing as to the goods.

(e) [Temporary perfection: new value.] A security interest in certificated securities, negotiable documents, or instruments is perfected without filing or the taking of possession or control for a period of 20 days from the time it attaches to the extent that it arises for new value given under an authenticated security agreement.

(f) [Temporary perfection: goods or documents made available to debtor.] A perfected security interest in a negotiable document or goods in possession of a bailee, other than one that has issued a negotiable document for the goods, remains perfected for 20 days without filing if the secured party makes available to the debtor the goods or documents representing the goods for the purpose of:

(1) ultimate sale or exchange; or

(2) loading, unloading, storing, shipping, transshipping, manufacturing, processing, or otherwise dealing with them in a manner preliminary to their sale or exchange.

(g) [Temporary perfection: delivery of security certificate or instrument to debtor.] A perfected security interest in a certificated security or instrument remains perfected for 20 days without filing if the secured party delivers the security certificate or instrument to the debtor for the purpose of:

(1) ultimate sale or exchange; or

(2) presentation, collection, enforcement, renewal, or registration of transfer.

(h) [Expiration of temporary perfection.] After the 20-day period specified in subsection (e), (f), or (g) expires, perfection depends upon compliance with this article.

OTHER UCC SECTIONS TO LOOK TO WHEN YOU LOOK AT SECTION 9–312

Look at section 9–310(a) to see that section 9–312(a) simply states some of the situations in which perfection by filing is permitted.

If you are doing a perfection by control problem, you also need to look at section 9–314.

OFFICIAL COMMENT

* * *

2. **Instruments.** Under subsection (a), a security interest in instruments may be perfected by filing. This rule represents an important change from former Article 9, under which the secured party's taking possession of an instrument was the only method of achieving long-term perfection. The rule is likely to be particularly useful in transactions involving a large number of notes that a debtor uses as collateral but continues to collect from the makers. A security interest perfected by filing is subject to defeat by certain subsequent purchasers (including secured parties). Under Section 9–330(d), purchasers for value who take possession of an instrument without knowledge that the purchase violates the rights of the secured party generally would achieve priority over a security interest in the instrument perfected by filing. In addition, Section 9–331 provides that filing a financing statement does not constitute notice that would preclude a subsequent purchaser from becoming a holder in due course and taking free of all claims under Section 3–306.

3. **Chattel Paper; Negotiable Documents.** Subsection (a) further provides that filing is available as a method of perfection for security interests in chattel paper and negotiable documents. Tangible chattel paper is sometimes delivered to the assignee, and sometimes left in the hands of the assignor for collection. Subsection (a) allows the assignee to perfect its security interest by filing in the latter case. Alternatively, the assignee may perfect by taking possession. See Section 9–313(a). An assignee of electronic chattel paper may perfect by taking control. See Sections 9–314(a), 9–105. The security interest of an assignee who takes possession or control may qualify for priority over a competing security interest perfected by filing. See Section 9–330.

Negotiable documents may be, and usually are, delivered to the secured party. See Article 1, Section 1–201 (definition of "delivery"). The secured party's taking possession of a tangible document or control of an electronic document will suffice as a perfection step. See Sections 9–313(a), 9–314 and 7–106. However, as is the case with chattel paper, a security interest in a negotiable document may be perfected by filing.

4. **Investment Property.** A security interest in investment property, including certificated securities, uncertificated securities, security entitlements, and securities accounts, may be perfected by filing. However, security interests created by brokers, securities intermediaries, or commodity intermediaries are automatically perfected; filing is of no effect. See Section 9–309(10), (11). A security interest in all kinds of investment property also may be perfected by control, see Sections 9–314, 9–106, and a security interest in a certificated security also may be perfected by the secured party's taking delivery under Section 8–301. See Section 9–313(a). A security interest perfected only by filing is subordinate to a conflicting security interest perfected by control or delivery. See Section 9–328(1), (5). Thus, although filing is a permissible method of perfection, a secured party who perfects by filing takes the risk that the debtor has granted or will grant a security interest in the same collateral to another party who obtains control. Also, perfection by filing would not give the secured party protection against other types of adverse claims, since the Article 8 adverse claim

cut-off rules require control. See Section 8–510.

5. **Deposit Accounts**. Under new subsection (b)(1), the only method of perfecting a security interest in a deposit account as original collateral is by control. Filing is ineffective, except as provided in Section 9–315 with respect to proceeds. As explained in Section 9–104, "control" can arise as a result of an agreement among the secured party, debtor, and bank, whereby the bank agrees to comply with instructions of the secured party with respect to disposition of the funds on deposit, even though the debtor retains the right to direct disposition of the funds. Thus, subsection (b)(1) takes an intermediate position between certain non-UCC law, which conditions the effectiveness of a security interest on the secured party's enjoyment of such dominion and control over the deposit account that the debtor is unable to dispose of the funds, and the approach this Article takes to securities accounts, under which a secured party who is unable to reach the collateral without resort to judicial process may perfect by filing. By conditioning perfection on "control," rather than requiring the secured party to enjoy absolute dominion to the exclusion of the debtor, subsection (b)(1) permits perfection in a wide variety of transactions, including those in which the secured party actually relies on the deposit account in extending credit and maintains some meaningful dominion over it, but does not wish to deprive the debtor of access to the funds altogether.

6. **Letter-of-Credit Rights.** Letter-of-credit rights commonly are "supporting obligations," as defined in Section 9–102. Perfection as to the related account, chattel paper, document, general intangible, instrument, or investment property will perfect as to the letter-of-credit rights. See Section 9–308(d). Subsection (b)(2) provides that, in other cases, a security interest in a letter-of-credit right may be perfected only by control. "Control," for these purposes, is explained in Section 9–107.

7. **Goods Covered by Document of Title.** Subsection (c) applies to goods in the possession of a bailee who has issued a negotiable document covering the goods. Subsection (d) applies to goods in the possession of a bailee who has issued a nonnegotiable document of title, including a document of title that is "nonnegotiable" under Section 7–104. Section 9–313 governs perfection of a security interest in goods in the possession of a bailee who has not issued a document of title.

Subsection (c) clarifies the perfection and priority rules in former Section 9–304(2). Consistently with the provisions of Article 7, subsection (c) takes the position that, as long as a negotiable document covering goods is outstanding, title to the goods is, so to say, locked up in the document. Accordingly, a security interest in goods covered by a negotiable document may be perfected by perfecting a security interest in the document. The security interest also may be perfected by another method, e.g., by filing. The priority rule in subsection (c) governs only priority between (i) a security interest in goods which is perfected by perfecting in the document and (ii) a security interest in the goods which becomes perfected by another method while the goods are covered by the document.

Example 1: While wheat is in a grain elevator and covered by a negotiable warehouse receipt, Debtor creates a security interest in the wheat in favor of SP–1 and SP–2. SP–1 perfects by filing a financing statement covering "wheat." Thereafter, SP–2 perfects by filing a financing statement describing the warehouse receipt. Subsection (c)(1) provides that SP–2's security interest is perfected. Subsection (c)(2) provides that SP–2's security interest is senior to SP–1's.

Example 2: The facts are as in Example 1, but SP–1's security interest attached and was perfected before the goods were delivered to the grain elevator. Subsection (c)(2) does not apply, because SP–1's security interest did not become perfected during the time that the wheat was in the possession of a bailee. Rather, the first-to-file-or-perfect priority rule applies. See Sections 9–322 and 7–503.

A secured party may become "a holder to whom a negotiable document of title has been duly negotiated" under Section 7–501. If so, the secured party acquires the rights specified by Article 7. Article 9 does not limit those rights, which may include the right to priority over an earlier-perfected security interest. See Section 9–331(a).

Subsection (d) takes a different approach to the problem of goods covered by a nonnegotiable document. Here, title to the goods is not looked on as being locked up in the document, and the secured party may perfect its security interest directly in the goods by filing as to them. The subsection provides two other methods of perfection: issuance of the document in the secured party's name (as consignee of a straight bill of lading or the person to whom delivery would be made under a non-negotiable warehouse receipt) and receipt of notification of the secured party's interest by the bailee. Perfection under subsection (d) occurs when the bailee receives notification of the secured party's interest in the goods, regardless of who sends the notification. Receipt of notification is effective to perfect, regardless of whether the bailee responds. Unlike former Section 9–304(3), from which it derives, subsection (d) does not apply to goods in the possession of a bailee who has not issued a document of title. Section 9–313(c) covers that case and provides that perfection by possession as to goods not covered by a document requires the bailee's acknowledgment.

8. **Temporary Perfection Without Having First Otherwise Perfected.** Subsection (e) follows former Section 9–304(4) in giving perfected status to security interests in certificated securities, instruments, and negotiable documents for a short period (reduced from 21 to 20 days, which is the time period generally applicable in this Article), although there has been no filing and the collateral is in the debtor's possession or control. The 20–day temporary perfection runs from the date of attachment. There is no limitation on the purpose for which the debtor is in possession, but the secured party must have given "new value" (defined in Section 9–102) under an authenticated security agreement.

9. **Maintaining Perfection After Surrendering Possession.** There are a variety of legitimate reasons—many of them are described in subsections (f) and (g)—why certain types of collateral must be released temporarily to a debtor. No useful purpose would be served by cluttering the files with records of such exceedingly short term transactions.

Subsection (f) affords the possibility of 20–day perfection in negotiable documents and goods in the possession of a bailee but not covered by a negotiable document. Subsection (g) provides for 20–day perfection in certificated securities and instruments. These subsections derive from former Section 9–305(5). However, the period of temporary perfection has been reduced from 21 to 20 days, which is the time period generally applicable in this Article, and "enforcement" has been added in subsection (g) as one of the special and limited purposes for which a secured party can release an instrument or certificated security to the debtor and still remain perfected. The period of temporary perfection runs from the date a secured party who already has a perfected security interest turns over the collateral to the debtor. There is no new value requirement, but the turnover must be for one or more of the purposes stated in subsection (f) or (g). The 20–day period may be extended by perfecting as to the collateral by another method before the period expires. However, if the security interest is not perfected by another method until after the 20–day period expires, there will be a gap during which the security interest is unperfected.

Temporary perfection extends only to the negotiable document or goods under subsection (f) and only to the certificated security or instrument under subsection (g). It does not extend to proceeds. If the collateral is sold, the security interest will continue in the proceeds for the period specified in Section 9–315.

141

Subsections (f) and (g) deal only with perfection. Other sections of this Article govern the priority of a security interest in goods after surrender of possession or control of the document covering them. In the case of a purchase-money security interest in inventory, priority may be conditioned upon giving notification to a prior inventory financer. See Section 9–324.

§ 9–313. When Possession by or Delivery to Secured Party Perfects Security Interest Without Filing

(a) [Perfection by possession or delivery.] Except as otherwise provided in subsection (b), a secured party may perfect a security interest in tangible negotiable documents, goods, instruments, money, or tangible chattel paper by taking possession of the collateral. A secured party may perfect a security interest in certificated securities by taking delivery of the certificated securities under Section 8–301.

(b) [Goods covered by certificate of title.] With respect to goods covered by a certificate of title issued by this State, a secured party may perfect a security interest in the goods by taking possession of the goods only in the circumstances described in Section 9–316(d).

(c) [Collateral in possession of person other than debtor.] With respect to collateral other than certificated securities and goods covered by a document, a secured party takes possession of collateral in the possession of a person other than the debtor, the secured party, or a lessee of the collateral from the debtor in the ordinary course of the debtor's business, when:

> **(1)** the person in possession authenticates a record acknowledging that it holds possession of the collateral for the secured party's benefit; or
>
> **(2)** the person takes possession of the collateral after having authenticated a record acknowledging that it will hold possession of collateral for the secured party's benefit.

(d) [Time of perfection by possession; continuation of perfection.] If perfection of a security interest depends upon possession of the collateral by a secured party, perfection occurs no earlier than the time the secured party takes possession and continues only while the secured party retains possession.

(e) [Time of perfection by delivery; continuation of perfection.] A security interest in a certificated security in registered form is perfected by delivery when delivery of the certificated security occurs under Section 8–301 and remains perfected by delivery until the debtor obtains possession of the security certificate.

(f) [Acknowledgment not required.] A person in possession of collateral is not required to acknowledge that it holds possession for a secured party's benefit.

(g) [Effectiveness of acknowledgment; no duties or confirmation.] If a person acknowledges that it holds possession for the secured party's benefit:

> **(1)** the acknowledgment is effective under subsection (c) or Section 8–301(a), even if the acknowledgment violates the rights of a debtor; and
>
> **(2)** unless the person otherwise agrees or law other than this article otherwise provides, the person does not owe any duty to the secured party and is not required to confirm the acknowledgment to another person.

(h) [Secured party's delivery to person other than debtor.] A secured party having possession of collateral does not relinquish possession by delivering the collateral to a person other than the debtor or a lessee of the collateral from the debtor in the ordinary course of the debtor's business if the person was instructed before the delivery or is instructed contemporaneously with the delivery:

> **(1)** to hold possession of the collateral for the secured party's benefit; or
>
> **(2)** to redeliver the collateral to the secured party.

(i) [Effect of delivery under subsection (h); no duties or confirmation.] A secured party does not relinquish possession, even if a delivery under subsection (h) violates the rights of a debtor. A person to which collateral is delivered under subsection (h) does not owe any duty to the secured party and is not required to confirm the delivery to another person unless the person otherwise agrees or law other than this article otherwise provides.

OTHER UCC SECTIONS TO LOOK TO WHEN YOU LOOK AT SECTION 9–313

Look at section 9–207 for rights and duties of secured party in possession of the collateral.

OFFICIAL COMMENT

* * *

2. Perfection by Possession. As under the common law of pledge, no filing is required by this Article to perfect a security interest if the secured party takes possession of the collateral. See Section 9–310(b)(6).

This section permits a security interest to be perfected by the taking of possession only when the collateral is goods, instruments, tangible negotiable documents, money, or tangible chattel paper. Accounts, commercial tort claims, deposit accounts, investment property, letter-of-credit rights, letters of credit, and oil, gas, or other minerals before extraction are excluded. (But see Comment 6, below, regarding certificated securities.) A security interest in accounts and payment intangibles—property not ordinarily represented by any writing whose delivery operates to transfer the right to payment—may under this Article be perfected only by filing. This rule would not be affected by the fact that a security agreement or other record described the assignment of such collateral as a "pledge." Section 9–309(2) exempts from filing certain assignments of accounts or payment intangibles which are out of the ordinary course of financing. These exempted assignments are perfected when they attach. Similarly, under Section 9–309(3), sales of payment intangibles are automatically perfected.

3. **"Possession."** This section does not define "possession." It adopts the general concept as it developed under former Article 9. As under former Article 9, in determining whether a particular person has possession, the principles of agency apply. For example, if the collateral is in possession of an agent of the secured party for the purposes of possessing on behalf of the secured party, and if the agent is not also an agent of the debtor, the secured party has taken actual possession, and subsection (c) does not apply. Sometimes a person holds collateral both as an agent of the secured party and as an agent of the debtor. The fact of dual agency is not of itself inconsistent with the secured party's having taken possession (and thereby having rendered subsection (c) inapplicable). The debtor cannot qualify as an agent for the secured party for purposes of the secured party's taking possession. And, under appropriate circumstances, a court may determine that a person in possession is so closely connected to or controlled by the debtor that the debtor has retained effective possession, even though the person may have agreed to take possession on behalf of the secured party. If so, the person's taking possession would not constitute the secured party's taking possession and would not be sufficient for perfection. See also Section 9–205(b). In a typical escrow arrangement, where the escrowee has possession of collateral as agent for both the secured party and the debtor, the debtor's relationship to the escrowee is not such as to constitute retention of possession by the debtor.

4. **Goods in Possession of Third Party: Perfection.** Former Section 9–305 permitted perfection of a security interest by notification to a bailee in possession of collateral. This Article distinguishes between goods in the possession of a bailee who has issued a document of title covering the goods and goods in the possession of a third party who has not issued a document. Section 9–312(c) or (d) applies to the former, depending on whether the document is negotiable. Section 9–313(c) applies to the latter. It provides a method of perfection by possession when the collateral is possessed by a third person who is not the secured party's agent.

Notification of a third person does not suffice to perfect under Section 9–313(c). Rather, perfection does not occur unless the third person authenticates an acknowledgment that it holds possession of the collateral for the secured party's benefit. Compare Section 9–312(d), under which receipt of notification of the security party's interest by a bailee holding goods covered by a nonnegotiable document is sufficient to perfect, even if the bailee does not acknowledge receipt of the notification. A third person may acknowledge that it will hold for the secured party's benefit goods to be received in the future. Under these circumstances, perfection by possession occurs when the third person obtains possession of the goods.

Under subsection (c), acknowledgment of notification by a "lessee ... in ... ordinary course of ... business" (defined in Section 2A–103) does not suffice for possession. The section thus rejects the reasoning of *In re Atlantic Systems, Inc.*, 135 B.R. 463 (Bankr. S.D.N.Y. 1992) (holding that notification to debtor-lessor's lessee sufficed to perfect security interest in leased goods). See Steven O. Weise, *Perfection by Possession: The Need for an Objective Test*, 29 Idaho Law Rev. 705 (1992–93) (arguing that lessee's possession in ordinary course of debtor-lessor's business does not provide adequate public notice of possible security interest in leased goods). Inclusion of a per se rule concerning lessees is not meant to preclude a court, under appropriate circumstances, from determining that a third person is so closely connected to or controlled by the debtor that the debtor has retained effective possession. If so, the third person's acknowledgment would not be sufficient for perfection.

In some cases, it may be uncertain whether a person who has possession of collateral is an agent of the secured party or a non-agent bailee. Under those circumstances, prudence might suggest that the secured party obtain the person's acknowledgment to avoid litigation and ensure perfection by possession regardless of how the relationship between the secured party and the person is characterized.

5. **No Relation Back.** Former Section 9–305 provided that a security interest is perfected by possession from the time possession is taken "without a relation back." As the Comment to former Section 9–305 observed, the relation-back theory, under which the taking of possession was deemed to relate back to the date of the original security agreement, has had little vitality since the 1938 revision of the Federal Bankruptcy Act. The theory is inconsistent with former Article 9 and with this Article. See Section 9–313(d). Accordingly, this Article deletes the quoted phrase as unnecessary. Where a pledge transaction is contemplated, perfection dates only from the time possession is taken, although a security interest may attach, unperfected. The only exceptions to this rule are the short, 20–day periods of perfection provided in Section 9–312(e), (f), and (g), during which a debtor may have possession of specified collateral in which there is a perfected security interest.

6. **Certificated Securities.** The second sentence of subsection (a) reflects the traditional rule for perfection of a security interest in certificated securities. Compare Section 9–115(6) (1994 Official Text); Sections 8–321, 8–313(1)(a) (1978 Official Text); Section 9–305 (1972 Official Text). It has been modified to refer to "delivery" under Section 8–301. Corresponding changes appear in Section 9–203(b).

Subsection (e), which is new, applies to a secured party in possession of security certificates or another person who has taken delivery of security certificates and holds them for the secured party's benefit under Section 8–301. See Comment 8.

Under subsection (e), a possessory security interest in a certificated security remains perfected until the debtor obtains possession of the security certificate. This rule is analogous to that of Section 9–314(c), which deals with perfection of security interests in investment property by control. See Section 9–314, Comment 3.

7. **Goods Covered by Certificate of Title.** Subsection (b) is necessary to effect changes to the choice-of-law rules governing goods covered by a certificate of title. These changes are described in the Comments to Section 9–311. Subsection (b), like subsection (a), does not create a right to take possession. Rather, it indicates the circumstances under which the secured party's taking possession of goods covered by a certificate of title is effective to perfect a security interest in the goods: the goods become covered by a certificate of title issued by this State at a time when the security interest is perfected by any method under the law of another jurisdiction.

8. **Goods in Possession of Third Party: No Duty to Acknowledge; Consequences of Acknowledgment.** Subsections (f) and (g) are new and address matters as to which former Article 9 was silent. They derive in part from Section 8–106(g). Subsection (f) provides that a person in possession of collateral is not required to acknowledge that it holds for a secured party. Subsection (g)(1) provides that an acknowledgment is effective

even if wrongful as to the debtor. Subsection (g)(2) makes clear that an acknowledgment does not give rise to any duties or responsibilities under this Article. Arrangements involving the possession of goods are hardly standardized. They include bailments for services to be performed on the goods (such as repair or processing), for use (leases), as security (pledges), for carriage, and for storage. This Article leaves to the agreement of the parties and to any other applicable law the imposition of duties and responsibilities upon a person who acknowledges under subsection (c). For example, by acknowledging, a third party does not become obliged to act on the secured party's direction or to remain in possession of the collateral unless it agrees to do so or other law so provides.

9. **Delivery to Third Party by Secured Party.** New subsections (h) and (i) address the practice of mortgage warehouse lenders. These lenders typically send mortgage notes to prospective purchasers under cover of letters advising the prospective purchasers that the lenders hold security interests in the notes. These lenders relied on notification to maintain perfection under former 9–305. Requiring them to obtain authenticated acknowledgments from each prospective purchaser under subsection (c) could be unduly burdensome and disruptive of established practices. Under subsection (h), when a secured party in possession itself delivers the collateral to a third party, instructions to the third party would be sufficient to maintain perfection by possession; an acknowledgment would not be necessary. Under subsection (i), the secured party does not relinquish possession by making a delivery under subsection (h), even if the delivery violates the rights of the debtor. That subsection also makes clear that a person to whom collateral is delivered under subsection (h) does not owe any duty to the secured party and is not required to confirm the delivery to another person unless the person otherwise agrees or law other than this Article provides otherwise.

§ 9–314. Perfection by Control

(a) **[Perfection by control.]** A security interest in investment property, deposit accounts, letter-of-credit rights, electronic chattel paper, or electronic documents may be perfected by control of the collateral under Section 7–106, 9–104, 9–105, 9–106, or 9–107.

(b) **[Specified collateral: time of perfection by control; continuation of perfection.]** A security interest in deposit accounts, electronic chattel paper, letter-of-credit rights, or electronic documents is perfected by control under Section 7–106, 9–104, 9–105, or 9–107 when the secured party obtains control and remains perfected by control only while the secured party retains control.

(c) **[Investment property: time of perfection by control; continuation of perfection.]** A security interest in investment property is perfected by control under Section 9–106 from the time the secured party obtains control and remains perfected by control until:

(1) the secured party does not have control; and

(2) one of the following occurs:

(A) if the collateral is a certificated security, the debtor has or acquires possession of the security certificate;

(B) if the collateral is an uncertificated security, the issuer has registered or registers the debtor as the registered owner; or

(C) if the collateral is a security entitlement, the debtor is or becomes the entitlement holder.

NON–OBVIOUS DEFINITIONS

The term "control" does not have a single definition. As Official Comment 2 points out, control has different meanings for different types of collateral.

OFFICIAL COMMENT

* * *

2. **Control.** This section provides for perfection by control with respect to investment property, deposit accounts, letter-of-credit rights, electronic chattel paper, and electronic documents. For explanations of how a secured party takes control of these types of collateral, see Sections 9–104 through 9–107 and Section 7–106. Subsection (b) explains when a security interest is perfected by control and how long a security interest remains perfected by control. Like Section 9–313(d) and for the same reasons, subsection (b) makes no reference to the doctrine of "relation back." See Section 9–313, Comment 5. As to an electronic document that is reissued in a tangible medium, Section 7–105, a secured party that is perfected by control in the electronic document should file as to the document before relinquishing control in order to maintain continuous perfection in the document. See Section 9–308.

3. **Investment Property.** Subsection (c) provides a special rule for investment property. Once a secured party has control, its security interest remains perfected by control until the secured party ceases to have control and the debtor receives possession of collateral that is a certificated security, becomes the registered owner of collateral that is an uncertificated security, or becomes the entitlement holder of collateral that is a security entitlement. The result is particularly important in the "repledge" context. See Section 9–207, Comment 5.

In a transaction in which a secured party who has control grants a security interest in investment property or sells outright the investment property, by virtue of the debtor's consent or applicable legal rules, a purchaser from the secured party typically will cut off the debtor's rights in the investment property or be immune from the debtor's claims. See Section 9–207, Comments 5 and 6. If the investment property is a security, the debtor normally would retain no interest in the security following the purchase from the secured party, and a claim of the debtor against the secured party for redemption (Section 9–623) or otherwise with respect to the security would be a purely personal claim. If the investment property transferred by the secured party is a financial asset in which the debtor had a security entitlement credited to a securities account maintained with the secured party as a securities intermediary, the debtor's claim against the secured party could arise as a part of its securities account notwithstanding its personal nature. (This claim would be analogous to a "credit balance" in the securities account, which is a component of the securities account even though it is a personal claim against the intermediary.) In the case in which the debtor may retain an interest in investment property notwithstanding a repledge or sale by the secured party, subsection (c) makes clear that the security interest will remain perfected by control.

§ 9–315. Secured Party's Rights on Disposition of Collateral and in Proceeds

(a) [Disposition of collateral: continuation of security interest or agricultural lien; proceeds.] Except as otherwise provided in this article and in Section 2–403(2):

> **(1)** a security interest or agricultural lien continues in collateral notwithstanding sale, lease, license, exchange, or other disposition thereof unless the secured party authorized the disposition free of the security interest or agricultural lien; and
>
> **(2)** a security interest attaches to any identifiable proceeds of collateral.

(b) [When commingled proceeds identifiable.] Proceeds that are commingled with other property are identifiable proceeds:

> **(1)** if the proceeds are goods, to the extent provided by Section 9–336; and
>
> **(2)** if the proceeds are not goods, to the extent that the secured party identifies the proceeds by a method of tracing, including application of equitable principles, that is permitted under law other than this article with respect to commingled property of the type involved.

(c) [Perfection of security interest in proceeds.] A security interest in proceeds is a perfected security interest if the security interest in the original collateral was perfected.

(d) [Continuation of perfection.] A perfected security interest in proceeds becomes unperfected on the 21st day after the security interest attaches to the proceeds unless:

> **(1)** the following conditions are satisfied:
>
>> **(A)** a filed financing statement covers the original collateral;
>>
>> **(B)** the proceeds are collateral in which a security interest may be perfected by filing in the office in which the financing statement has been filed; and
>>
>> **(C)** the proceeds are not acquired with cash proceeds;
>
> **(2)** the proceeds are identifiable cash proceeds; or
>
> **(3)** the security interest in the proceeds is perfected other than under subsection (c) when the security interest attaches to the proceeds or within 20 days thereafter.

(e) [When perfected security interest in proceeds becomes unperfected.] If a filed financing statement covers the original collateral, a security interest in proceeds which remains perfected under subsection (d)(1) becomes unperfected at the later of:

(1) when the effectiveness of the filed financing statement lapses under Section 9–515 or is terminated under Section 9–513; or

(2) the 21st day after the security interest attaches to the proceeds.

UNOFFICIAL COMMENTS

You will to look to this section when the debtor sells or otherwise disposes of collateral. Most of the section deals with the secured party's rights in what the debtor receives, i.e., proceeds.

This section answers two proceeds questions: (1) when a secured party has a security interest in proceeds and (2) whether that security interest is perfected. Sort of.

The answer to the question of when does a secured party have a security interest in proceeds leaves you with the question of when are proceeds "identifiable." If your professor covered the "lowest intermediate balance" rule referred to in Official Comment 4, then you probably should practice addition and subtraction.

The section also sets out the general rule that a security interest sticks with the original collateral even if it is sold, leased, licensed, exchanged, or otherwise disposed of. There are important exceptions to this rule. The following are situations in which disposition ends the security interest in the original collateral:

- The secured party authorizes the disposition of the collateral free of the security interest *(9–315(a))*
- The collateral is entrusted to a merchant who is in the business of selling that collateral where merchant ends up selling that collateral to a customer in the ordinary course of business (2–403(2))
- Certain buyers of goods in the ordinary course of business (9–320(a))
- Certain consumer buyers of *consumer* goods (9–320(b))
- Certain transfers of collateral subject to an unperfected security interest (9–317)
- Certain licensees of general intangibles in the ordinary course of business (9–321)

- Certain buyers of chattel paper (9–330)
- Buyers of instruments, documents and securities (9–331)
- Transfers of money or transfer of funds from a deposit account (9–332)

For more extended comments on "authorized", see pages 371–372.

NON–OBVIOUS DEFINITIONS

Read the definition of proceeds in 9–102(a)(64). Carefully

Even less obvious but really important is a UCC "non-definition": "identifiable proceeds." Cf. Official Comment 3 to section 9–315.

OTHER UCC SECTIONS TO LOOK TO WHEN YOU LOOK AT SECTION 9–315

Look to section 9–322 to see the priority rules for security interests in proceeds.

If your teacher taught you bankruptcy as well as article 9, then you need to look at section 552(b) of the Bankruptcy Code to see that the Bankruptcy Code leaves a holder of a secured claim with its Article 9 proceeds rights.

OFFICIAL COMMENT

* * *

2. **Continuation of Security Interest or Agricultural Lien Following Disposition of Collateral.** Subsection (a)(1), which derives from former Section 9–306(2), contains the general rule that a security interest survives disposition of the collateral. In these cases, the secured party may repossess the collateral from the transferee or, in an appropriate case, maintain an action for conversion. The secured party may claim both any proceeds and the original collateral but, of course, may have only one satisfaction.

In many cases, a purchaser or other transferee of collateral will take free of a security interest, and the secured party's only right will be to proceeds. For example, the general rule does not apply, and a security interest does not continue in collateral, if the secured party authorized the disposition, in the agreement that contains the security agreement or otherwise. Subsection (a)(1) adopts the view of PEB Commentary No. 3 and makes explicit that the authorized disposition to which it refers is an authorized disposition "free of" the security interest or agricultural lien. The secured party's right to proceeds under this section or under the express terms of an agreement does not in itself constitute an authorization of disposition. The change in language from former Section 9–306(2) is not intended to address the frequently litigated situation in which the effectiveness of the secured party's consent to a disposition is conditioned upon the secured party's receipt of the proceeds. In that situation, subsection (a) leaves the determination of authorization to the courts, as under former Article 9.

This Article contains several provisions under which a transferee takes free of a security interest or agricultural lien. For example, Section 9–317 states when transferees take free of unperfected security interests; Sections 9–320 and 9–321 on goods, 9–321 on general intangibles, 9–330 on chattel paper and instruments, and 9–331 on negotiable instruments, negotiable documents, and securities state when purchasers of such collateral take free of a security interest, even though perfected and even though the disposition was not authorized. Section 9–332 enables most transferees (including non-purchasers) of funds from a deposit account and most transferees of money to take free of a perfected security interest in the deposit account or money.

Likewise, the general rule that a security interest survives disposition does not apply if the secured party entrusts goods collateral to a merchant who deals in goods of that kind and the merchant sells the collateral to a buyer in ordinary course of business. Section 2–403(2) gives the merchant the power to transfer all the secured party's rights to the buyer, even if the sale is wrongful as against the secured party. Thus, under subsection (a)(1), an entrusting secured party runs the same risk as any other entruster.

3. **Secured Party's Right to Identifiable Proceeds.** Under subsection (a)(2), which derives from former Section 9–306(2), a security interest attaches to any identifiable "proceeds," as defined in Section 9–102. See also Section 9–203(f). Subsection (b) is new. It indicates when proceeds commingled with other property are identifiable proceeds and permits the use of whatever methods of tracing other law permits with respect to the type of property involved. Among the "equitable principles" whose use other law may permit is the "lowest intermediate balance rule." See Restatement (2d), Trusts § 202.

4. **Automatic Perfection in Proceeds: General Rule.** Under subsection (c), a security interest in proceeds is a perfected security interest if the security interest in the original collateral was perfected. This Article extends the period of automatic perfection in proceeds from 10 days to 20 days. Generally, a security interest in proceeds becomes unperfected on the 21st day after the security interest attaches to the proceeds. See subsection (d). The loss of perfected status under subsection (d) is prospective only. Compare, e.g., Section 9–515(c) (deeming security interest unperfected retroactively).

5. **Automatic Perfection in Proceeds: Proceeds Acquired with Cash Proceeds.** Subsection (d)(1) derives from former Section 9–306(3)(a). It carries forward the basic rule that a security interest in proceeds remains perfected beyond the period of automatic perfection if a filed financing statement covers the original collateral (e.g., inventory) and the proceeds are collateral in which a security interest may be perfected by filing in the office where the financing statement has been filed (e.g., equipment). A different rule applies if the proceeds are acquired with cash proceeds, as is the case if the original collateral (inventory) is sold for cash (cash proceeds) that is used to purchase equipment (proceeds). Under these circumstances, the security interest in the equipment proceeds remains perfected only if the description in the filed financing indicates the type of property constituting the proceeds (e.g., "equipment").

This section reaches the same result but takes a different approach. It recognizes that the treatment of proceeds acquired with cash proceeds under former Section 9–306(3)(a) essentially was superfluous. In the example, had the filing covered "equipment" as well as "inventory," the security interest in the proceeds would have been perfected under the usual rules governing after-acquired equipment (see former Sections 9–302, 9–303); paragraph (3)(a) added only an exception to the general rule. Subsection (d)(1)(C) of this section takes a more direct approach. It makes the general rule of continued perfection inapplicable to proceeds acquired with cash proceeds, leaving perfection of a security interest in those proceeds to the generally applicable perfection rules under subsection (d)(3).

Example 1: Lender perfects a security interest in Debtor's inventory by filing a financing statement covering "inventory." Debtor sells the inventory and deposits the buyer's check into a deposit account. Debtor draws a check on the deposit account and uses it to pay for equipment. Under the "lowest intermediate balance rule," which is a permitted method of tracing in the relevant jurisdiction, see Comment 3, the funds used to pay for the equipment were identifiable proceeds of the inventory. Because the proceeds (equipment) were acquired with cash proceeds (deposit account), subsection (d)(1) does not extend perfection beyond the 20-day automatic period.

Example 2: Lender perfects a security interest in Debtor's inventory by filing a financing statement covering "all debtor's property." As in Example 1, Debtor sells the inventory, deposits the buyer's check into a deposit account, draws a check on the deposit account, and uses the check to pay for equipment. Under the "lowest intermediate balance rule," which is a permitted method of tracing in the relevant jurisdiction, see Comment 3, the funds used to pay for the equipment were identifiable proceeds of the inventory. Because the proceeds (equipment) were acquired with cash proceeds (deposit account), subsection (d)(1) does not extend perfection beyond the 20-day automatic period. However, because the financing statement is sufficient to perfect a security interest in debtor's equipment, under subsection (d)(3) the security interest in the equipment proceeds remains perfected beyond the 20-day period.

6. **Automatic Perfection in Proceeds: Lapse or Termination of Financing Statement During 20-Day Period; Perfection Under Other Statute or Treaty.** Subsection (e) provides that a security interest in proceeds perfected under subsection (d)(1) ceases to be perfected when the financing statement covering the original collateral lapses or is terminated. If the lapse or termination occurs before the 21st day after the security interest attaches, however, the security interest in the proceeds remains perfected until the 21st day. Section 9–311(b) provides that compliance with the perfection requirements of a statute or treaty described in Section 9–311(a) "is equivalent to the filing of a financing statement." It follows that collateral subject to a security interest perfected by such compliance under Section 9–311(b) is covered by a "filed financing statement" within the meaning of Section 9–315(d) and (e).

7. **Automatic Perfection in Proceeds: Continuation of Perfection in Cash Proceeds.** Former Section 9–306(3)(b) provided that if a filed financing statement covered original collateral, a security interest in identifiable cash proceeds of the collateral remained perfected beyond the ten-day period of automatic perfection. Former Section 9–306(3)(c) contained a similar rule with respect to identifiable cash proceeds of investment property. Subsection (d)(2) extends the benefits of former Sections 9–306(3)(b) and (3)(c) to identifiable cash proceeds of all types of original collateral in which a security interest is perfected by any method. Under subsection (d)(2), if the security interest in the original collateral was perfected, a security interest in identifiable cash proceeds will remain perfected indefinitely, regardless of whether the security interest in the original collateral remains perfected. In many cases, however, a purchaser or other transferee of the cash proceeds will take free of the perfected security interest. See, e.g., Sections 9–330(d) (purchaser of check), 9–331 (holder in due course of check), 9–332 (transferee of money or funds from a deposit account).

* * *

9. **Proceeds of Collateral Subject to Agricultural Lien.** This Article does not determine whether a lien extends to proceeds of farm products encumbered by an agricultural lien. If, however, the proceeds are themselves farm products on which an "agricultural lien" (defined in Section 9–102) arises under other law, then the agricultural-lien provisions of this Article apply to the agricultural lien on the proceeds in the same way in which they would apply had the farm products not been proceeds.

§ 9–316. Continued Perfection of Security Interest Following Change in Governing Law

(a) **[General rule: effect on perfection of change in governing law.]** A security interest perfected pursuant to the law of the jurisdiction designated in Section 9–301(1) or 9–305(c) remains perfected until the earliest of:

> (1) the time perfection would have ceased under the law of that jurisdiction;
>
> (2) the expiration of four months after a change of the debtor's location to another jurisdiction; or
>
> (3) the expiration of one year after a transfer of collateral to a person that thereby becomes a debtor and is located in another jurisdiction.

(b) **[Security interest perfected or unperfected under law of new jurisdiction.]** If a security interest described in subsection (a) becomes perfected under the law of the other jurisdiction before the earliest time or event described in that subsection, it remains perfected thereafter. If the security interest does not become perfected under the law of the other jurisdiction before the earliest time or event, it becomes unperfected and is deemed never to have been perfected as against a purchaser of the collateral for value.

(c) **[Possessory security interest in collateral moved to new jurisdiction.]** A possessory security interest in collateral, other than goods covered by a certificate of title and as-extracted collateral consisting of goods, remains continuously perfected if:

> (1) the collateral is located in one jurisdiction and subject to a security interest perfected under the law of that jurisdiction;
>
> (2) thereafter the collateral is brought into another jurisdiction; and
>
> (3) upon entry into the other jurisdiction, the security interest is perfected under the law of the other jurisdiction.

(d) **[Goods covered by certificate of title from this state.]** Except as otherwise provided in subsection (e), a security interest in goods covered by a certificate of title which is perfected by any method under the law of another jurisdiction when the goods become covered by a certificate of title from this State remains perfected until the security interest would have become unperfected under the law of the other jurisdiction had the goods not become so covered.

(e) [When subsection (d) security interest becomes unperfected against purchasers.] A security interest described in subsection (d) becomes unperfected as against a purchaser of the goods for value and is deemed never to have been perfected as against a purchaser of the goods for value if the applicable requirements for perfection under Section 9–311(b) or 9–313 are not satisfied before the earlier of:

- (1) the time the security interest would have become unperfected under the law of the other jurisdiction had the goods not become covered by a certificate of title from this State; or
- (2) the expiration of four months after the goods had become so covered.

(f) [Change in jurisdiction of bank, issuer, nominated person, securities intermediary, or commodity intermediary.] A security interest in deposit accounts, letter-of-credit rights, or investment property which is perfected under the law of the bank's jurisdiction, the issuer's jurisdiction, a nominated person's jurisdiction, the securities intermediary's jurisdiction, or the commodity intermediary's jurisdiction, as applicable, remains perfected until the earlier of:

- (1) the time the security interest would have become unperfected under the law of that jurisdiction; or
- (2) the expiration of four months after a change of the applicable jurisdiction to another jurisdiction.

(g) [Subsection (f) security interest perfected or unperfected under law of new jurisdiction.] If a security interest described in subsection (f) becomes perfected under the law of the other jurisdiction before the earlier of the time or the end of the period described in that subsection, it remains perfected thereafter. If the security interest does not become perfected under the law of the other jurisdiction before the earlier of that time or the end of that period, it becomes unperfected and is deemed never to have been perfected as against a purchaser of the collateral for value.

UNOFFICIAL COMMENT

The title to this section is somewhat confusing. The section is not about some state changing its laws. Rather, look to this section when there are changes in the debtor, location of the debtor or location of the collateral that would affect application of section 9–301. Example 1 in Official Comment 2 is (not surprisingly) another example. **For a more complete explanation of section 9–316, see pages 372–373 infra.**

OFFICIAL COMMENT

* * *

2. **Continued Perfection.** This section deals with continued perfection of security interests that have been perfected under the law of another jurisdiction. The fact that the law of a particular jurisdiction ceases to govern perfection under Sections 9–301 through 9–307 does not necessarily mean that a security interest perfected under that law automatically becomes unperfected. To the contrary: This section generally provides that a security interest perfected under the law of one jurisdiction remains perfected for a fixed period of time (four months or one year, depending on the circumstances), even though the jurisdiction whose law governs perfection changes. However, cessation of perfection under the law of the original jurisdiction cuts short the fixed period. The four-month and one-year periods are long enough for a secured party to discover in most cases that the law of a different jurisdiction governs perfection and to reperfect (typically by filing) under the law of that jurisdiction. If a secured party properly reperfects a security interest before it becomes unperfected under subsection (a), then the security interest remains perfected continuously thereafter. See subsection (b).

Example 1: Debtor is a general partnership whose chief executive office is in Pennsylvania. Lender perfects a security interest in Debtor's equipment by filing in Pennsylvania on May 15, 2002. On April 1, 2005, without Lender's knowledge, Debtor moves its chief executive office to New Jersey. Lender's security interest remains perfected for four months after the move. See subsection (a)(2).

Example 2: Debtor is a general partnership whose chief executive office is in Pennsylvania. Lender perfects a security interest in Debtor's equipment by filing in Pennsylvania on May 15, 2002. On April 1, 2007, without Lender's knowledge, Debtor moves its chief executive office to New Jersey. Lender's security interest remains perfected only through May 14, 2007, when the effectiveness of the filed financing statement lapses. See subsection (a)(1). Although, under these facts, Lender would have only a short period of time to discover that Debtor had relocated and to reperfect under New Jersey law, Lender could have protected itself by filing a continuation statement in Pennsylvania before Debtor relocated. By doing so, Lender would have prevented lapse and allowed itself the full four months to discover Debtor's new location and refile there or, if Debtor is in default, to perfect by taking possession of the equipment.

Example 3: Under the facts of Example 2, Lender files a financing statement in New Jersey before the effectiveness of the Pennsylvania financing statement lapses. Under subsection (b), Lender's security interest is continuously perfected beyond May 14, 2007, for a period determined by New Jersey's Article 9.

Subsection (a)(3) allows a one-year period in which to reperfect. The longer period is necessary, because, even with the exercise of due diligence, the secured party may be unable to discover that the collateral has been transferred to a person located in another jurisdiction.

Example 4: Debtor is a Pennsylvania corporation. Lender perfects a security interest in Debtor's equipment by filing in Pennsylvania. Debtor's shareholders decide to "reincorporate" in Delaware. They form a Delaware corporation (Newcorp) into which they merge Debtor. The merger effectuates a transfer of the collateral from Debtor to Newcorp, which thereby becomes a debtor and is located in another jurisdiction. Under subsection (a)(3), the security interest remains perfected for one year after the merger. If a financing statement is filed in Delaware against Newcorp within the year following the merger, then the security interest remains perfected thereafter for a period determined by Delaware's Article 9.

Note that although Newcorp is a "new debtor" as defined in Section 9–102, the application of subsection (a)(3) is not limited to transferees who are new debtors. Note also that, under Section 9–507, the financing statement naming Debtor remains effective even though Newcorp has become the debtor.

This section addresses security interests that are perfected (i.e., that have attached and as to which any required perfection step has been taken) before the debtor changes its location. As the following example explains, this section does not apply to security interests that have not attached before the location changes.

Example 5: Debtor is a Pennsylvania corporation. Debtor grants to Lender a security interest in Debtor's existing and after-acquired inventory. Lender perfects by filing in Pennsylvania. Debtor's shareholders decide to "reincorporate" in Delaware. They form a Delaware corporation (Newcorp) into which they merge Debtor. By virtue of the merger, Newcorp becomes bound by Debtor's security agreement. See Section 9–203. After the merger, Newcorp acquires inventory to which Lender's security interest attaches. Because Newcorp is located in Delaware, Delaware law governs perfection of a security interest in Newcorp's inventory. See Sections 9–301, 9–307. Having failed to perfect under Delaware law, Lender holds an unperfected security interest in the inventory acquired by Newcorp after the merger. The same result follows regardless of the name of the Delaware corporation (i.e., even if the Delaware corporation and Debtor have the same name). A different result would occur if Debtor and Newcorp were incorporated in the same state. See Section 9–508, Comment 4.

3. **Retroactive Unperfection.** Subsection (b) sets forth the consequences of the failure to reperfect before perfection ceases under subsection (a): the security interest becomes unperfected prospectively and, as against purchasers for value, including buyers and secured parties, but not as against donees or lien creditors, retroactively. The rule applies to agricultural liens, as well. See also Section 9–515 (taking the same approach with respect to lapse). Although this approach creates the potential for circular priorities, the alternative—retroactive unperfection against lien creditors—would create substantial and unjustifiable preference risks.

Example 6: Under the facts of Example 4, six months after the merger, Buyer bought from Newcorp some equipment formerly owned by Debtor. At the time of the purchase, Buyer took subject to Lender's perfected security interest, of which Buyer was unaware. See Section 9–315(a)(1). However, subsection (b) provides that if Lender fails to reperfect in Delaware within a year after the merger, its security interest becomes unperfected and is deemed never to have been perfected against Buyer. Having given value and received delivery of the equipment without knowledge of the security interest and before it was perfected, Buyer would take free of the security interest. See Section 9–317(b).

Example 7: Under the facts of Example 4, one month before the merger, Debtor created a security interest in certain equipment in favor of Financer, who perfected by filing in Pennsylvania. At that time, Financer's security interest is subordinate to Lender's. See Section 9–322(a)(1). Financer reperfects by filing in Delaware within a year after the merger, but Lender fails to do so. Under subsection (b), Lender's security interest is deemed never to have been perfected against Financer, a purchaser for value. Consequently, under Section 9–322(a)(2), Financer's security interest is now senior.

Of course, the expiration of the time period specified in subsection (a) does not of itself prevent the secured party from later reperfecting under the law of the new jurisdiction. If the secured party does so, however, there will be a gap in perfection, and the secured party may lose priority as a result. Thus, in Example 7, if Lender perfects by filing in Delaware more than one year under the merger, it will have a new date of filing and perfection for purposes of Section 9–322(a)(1). Financer's security interest, whose perfection dates back to the filing in Pennsylvania under subsection (b), will remain senior.

4. **Possessory Security Interests.** Subsection (c) deals with continued perfection of possessory security interests. It applies not only to security interests perfected solely by the secured party's having taken possession of the collateral. It also applies to security interests perfected by a method that includes as an element of perfection the secured party's having taken possession, such as perfection by taking delivery of a certificated security in registered form, see Section 9–313(a), and perfection by obtaining control over a certificated security. See Section 9–314(a).

5. **Goods Covered by Certificate of Title.** Subsections (d) and (e) address continued perfection of a security interest in goods covered by a certificate of title. The following examples explain the operation of those subsections.

Example 8: Debtor's automobile is covered by a certificate of title issued by Illinois. Lender perfects a security interest in the automobile by complying with Illinois' certificate-of-title statute. Thereafter, Debtor applies for a certificate of title in Indiana. Six months thereafter, Creditor acquires a judicial lien on the automobile. Under Section 9–303(b), Illinois law ceases to govern perfection; rather, once Debtor delivers the application and applicable fee to the appropriate Indiana authority, Indiana law governs. Nevertheless, under Indiana's Section 9–316(d), Lender's security interest remains perfected until it would become unperfected under Illinois law had no certificate of title been issued by Indiana. (For example, Illinois' certificate-of-title statute may provide that the surrender of an Illinois certificate of title in connection with the issuance of a certificate of title by another jurisdiction causes a security interest noted thereon to become unperfected.) If Lender's security interest remains perfected, it is senior to Creditor's judicial lien.

Example 9: Under the facts in Example 8, five months after Debtor applies for an Indiana certificate of title, Debtor sells the automobile to Buyer. Under subsection (e)(2), because Lender did not reperfect within the four months after the goods became covered by the Indiana certificate of title, Lender's security interest is deemed never to have been perfected against Buyer. Under Section 9–317(b), Buyer is likely to take free of the security interest. Lender could have protected itself by perfecting its security interest either under Indiana's certificate-of-title statute, see Section 9–311, or, if it had a right to do so under an agreement or Section 9–609, by taking possession of the automobile. See Section 9–313(b).

The results in Examples 8 and 9 do not depend on the fact that the original perfection was achieved by notation on a certificate of title. Subsection (d) applies regardless of the method by which a security interest is perfected under the law of another jurisdiction when the goods became covered by a certificate of title from this State.

Section 9–337 affords protection to a limited class of persons buying or acquiring a security interest in the goods while a security interest is perfected under the law of another jurisdiction but after this State has issued a clean certificate of title.

6. **Deposit Accounts, Letter-of-Credit Rights, and Investment Property.** Subsections (f) and (g) address changes in the jurisdiction of a bank, issuer of an uncertificated security, issuer of or nominated person under a letter of credit, securities intermediary, and commodity intermediary. The provisions are analogous to those of subsections (a) and (b).

* * *

[SUBPART 3. PRIORITY]

§ 9–317. Interests That Take Priority Over or Take Free of Security Interest or Agricultural Lien

(a) [Conflicting security interests and rights of lien creditors.] A security interest or agricultural lien * * * is subordinate to the rights of:

    (1) a person entitled to priority under Section 9–322; and

    (2) except as otherwise provided in subsection (e), a person that becomes a lien creditor before the earlier of the time:

        (A) the security interest or agricultural lien is perfected; or

        (B) one of the conditions specified in Section 9–203(b)(3) is met and a financing statement covering the collateral is filed.

(b) [Buyers that receive delivery.] Except as otherwise provided in subsection (e), a buyer, other than a secured party, of tangible chattel paper, tangible documents, goods, instruments, or a security certificate takes free of a security interest or agricultural lien if the buyer gives value and receives delivery of the collateral without knowledge of the security interest or agricultural lien and before it is perfected.

(c) [Lessees that receive delivery.] Except as otherwise provided in subsection (e), a lessee of goods takes free of a security interest or agricultural lien if the lessee gives value and receives delivery of the collateral without knowledge of the security interest or agricultural lien and before it is perfected.

(d) [Licensees and buyers of certain collateral.] A licensee of a general intangible or a buyer, other than a secured party, of accounts, electronic chattel paper, electronic documents, general intangibles, or investment property other than a certificated security takes free of a security interest if the licensee or buyer gives value without knowledge of the security interest and before it is perfected.

(e) [Purchase-money security interest.] Except as otherwise provided in Sections 9–320 and 9–321, if a person files a financing statement with respect to a purchase-money security interest before or within 20 days after the debtor receives delivery of the collateral, the security interest takes priority over the rights of a buyer, lessee, or lien creditor which arise between the time the security interest attaches and the time of filing.

UNOFFICIAL COMMENTS

Would have been helpful if the word "unperfected" was in the section title. Will be very helpful to read section 9–317(a)(2) carefully. Real carefully.

Notice the phrase "without notice" in section 9–317(b), (c), and (d). Now, notice that the phrase "without notice" is not in section 9–317(a).

Somewhere on your exam, you are going to have to understand what section 9–317(a)(2)(B) adds to section 9–317(a)(2)(A)–i.e. why a secured party wants to file a financing statement even before the security agreement attaches. See section 9–502(d) and section 9–309.

If your professor covered Bankruptcy Code section 544(a), you need to understand that an unperfected security interest can be avoided by the bankruptcy trustee because of section 9–317. And, if your professor covered the Federal Tax Lien Act, you need to understand that a federal tax lien takes priority over an earlier-in-time unperfected security interest because of section 9–317.

Because section 9–317 is so important to success on your exam, we have also done a subsection by subsection summary on pages 373–374 infra.

NON–OBVIOUS DEFINITIONS

You would think that a "lien creditor" would be a creditor with a lien. Not exactly. Look at the definition in section 9–102(a)(52). Not every creditor with a lien is a "lien creditor": only creditors with liens obtained by the judicial process, "attachment, levy and the like." The IRS with a federal tax lien is not a "lien creditor."

And not every lien creditor even has a lien. A bankruptcy trustee is a "lien creditor." That is real important if your professor covered Bankruptcy Code section 544.

OTHER UCC SECTIONS TO LOOK TO WHEN YOU LOOK AT SECTION 9–317

Under section 9–401(b), agreements between the debtor and secured party can not prevent transfers of rights in the collateral to third parties.

Section 9–201 establishes the general rule that security interests have priority over claims of other third parties ("effective . . . against").

Since this section creates exceptions if a person becomes a "lien creditor" or buyer or lessee or licensee before the security interest is perfected, section 9–308 on when a security interest is perfected is important.

And, since there is grace period for purchase-money security interests in section 9–317(e), look at section 9–103 on the requirements for a purchase money security interest.

Section 9–317(a)(2)(B) is understandable only if you understand sections 9–502(d) and 9–309.

If the secured party makes advances after some third party becomes a "lien creditor" or a "buyer", look to section 9–323.

OFFICIAL COMMENT

* * *

2. **Scope of This Section.** As did former Section 9–301, this section lists the classes of persons who take priority over, or take free of, an unperfected security interest. Section 9–308 explains when a security interest * * * is "perfected." A security interest that has attached (see Section 9–203) but as to which a required perfection step has not been taken is "unperfected." Certain provisions have been moved from former Section 9–301. The definition of "lien creditor" now appears in Section 9–102, and the rules governing priority in future advances are found in Section 9–323.

3. **Competing Security Interests.** Section 9–322 states general rules for determining priority among conflicting security interests and refers to other sections that state special rules of priority in a variety of situations. The security interests given priority under Section 9–322 and the other sections to which it refers take priority in general even over a perfected security interest. *A fortiori* they take priority over an unperfected security interest. ~~Paragraph (a)(1) of this section so states.~~*

4. **Filed but Unattached Security Interest vs. Lien Creditor.** Under former Section 9–301(1)(b), a lien creditor's rights had priority over an unperfected security interest. Perfection required attachment (former Section 9–303), and attachment required the giving of value (former Section 9–203). It followed that, if a secured party had filed a financing statement, but the debtor had not entered into a security agreement and value had not yet been given, an intervening lien creditor whose lien arose after filing but before attachment of the security interest acquired rights that are senior to those of the secured party who later gives value. This result comported with the *nemo dat* concept: When the security interest attached, the collateral was already subject to the judicial lien.

On the other hand, this approach treated the first secured advance differently from all other advances, even in circumstances in which a security agreement covering the collateral had been entered into before the judicial lien attached. The special rule for future advances in former Section 9–301(4) (substantially reproduced in Section 9–323(b)) afforded priority to a discretionary advance made by a secured party within 45 days after the lien creditor's rights arose as long as the secured party was "perfected" when the lien creditor's lien arose–i.e., as long as the advance was not the first one and an earlier advance had been made.

Subsection (a)(2) revises former Section 9–301(1)(b) and, in appropriate cases, treats the first advance the same as subsequent advances. More specifically, a judicial lien that arises after the security-agreement condition of Section 9–203(b)(3) is satisfied and a financing statement is filed, but before the security interest attaches and becomes perfected, is subordinate to all advances secured by the security interest, even the first advance, except as otherwise provided in

* Amendments in italics approved by the Permanent Editorial Board for Uniform Commercial Code Oct. 20, 1999.

Section 9–323(b). However, if the security interest becomes unperfected (e.g., because the effectiveness of the filed financing statement lapses) before the judicial lien arises, the security interest is subordinate. If a financing statement is filed but a security interest does not attach, then no priority contest arises. The lien creditor has the only enforceable claim to the property.

5. **Security Interest of Consignor or Receivables Buyer vs. Lien Creditor.** Section 1–201(37) defines "security interest" to include the interest of most true consignors of goods and the interest of most buyers of certain receivables (accounts, chattel paper, payment intangibles, and promissory notes). A consignee of goods or a seller of accounts or chattel paper each is deemed to have rights in the collateral which a lien creditor may reach, as long as the competing security interest of the consignor or buyer is unperfected. This is so even though, as between the consignor and the debtor-consignee, the latter has only limited rights, and, as between the buyer and debtor-seller, the latter does not have any rights in the collateral. See Sections 9–318 (seller), 9–319 (consignee). Security interests arising from sales of payment intangibles and promissory notes are automatically perfected. See Section 9–309. Accordingly, a subsequent judicial lien always would be subordinate to the rights of a buyer of those types of receivables.

6. **Purchasers Other Than Secured Parties.** Subsections (b), (c), and (d) afford priority over an unperfected security interest to certain purchasers (other than secured parties) of collateral. They derive from former Sections 9–301(1)(c), 2A–307(2), and 9–301(d). Former Section 9–301(1)(c) and (1)(d) provided that unperfected security interests are "subordinate" to the rights of certain purchasers. But, as former Comment 9 suggested, the practical effect of subordination in this context is that the purchaser takes free of the security interest. To avoid any possible misinterpretation, subsections (b) and (d) of this section use the phrase "takes free."

Subsection (b) governs goods, as well as intangibles of the type whose transfer is effected by physical delivery of the representative piece of paper (tangible chattel paper, tangible documents, instruments, and security certificates). To obtain priority, a buyer must both give value and receive delivery of the collateral without knowledge of the existing security interest and before perfection. Even if the buyer gave value without knowledge and before perfection, the buyer would take subject to the security interest if perfection occurred before physical delivery of the collateral to the buyer. Subsection (c) contains a similar rule with respect to lessees of goods. Note that a lessee of goods in ordinary course of business takes free of all security interests created by the lessor, even if perfected. See Section 9–321.

Normally, there will be no question when a buyer of tangible chattel paper, tangible documents, instruments, or security certificates "receives delivery" of the property. See Section 1–201 (defining "delivery"). However, sometimes a buyer or lessee of goods, such as complex machinery, takes delivery of the goods in stages and completes assembly at its own location. Under those circumstances, the buyer or lessee "receives delivery" within the meaning of subsections (b) and (c) when, after an inspection of the portion of the goods remaining with the seller or lessor, it would be apparent to a potential lender to the seller or lessor that another person might have an interest in the goods.

The rule of subsection (b) obviously is not appropriate where the collateral consists of intangibles and there is no representative piece of paper whose physical delivery is the only or the customary method of transfer. Therefore, with respect to such intangibles (accounts, electronic chattel paper, electronic documents, general intangibles, and investment property other than certificated securities), subsection (d) gives priority to any buyer who gives value without knowledge, and before perfection, of the security interest. A licensee of a general intangible takes free of an unperfected security interest in the general intangible under the same circumstances. Note that a licensee of a general intangible in ordinary course of business takes rights under a nonexclusive license free of security interests created by the licensor, even if perfected. See Section 9–321.

Unless Section 9–109 excludes the transaction from this Article, a buyer of accounts, chattel paper, payment intangibles, or promissory notes is a "secured party" (defined in Section 9–102), and subsections (b) and (d) do not determine priority of the security interest created by the sale. Rather, the priority rules generally applicable to competing security interests apply. See Section 9–322.

7. **Agricultural Liens.** Subsections (a), (b), and (c) subordinate unperfected agricultural liens in the same manner in which they subordinate unperfected security interests.

8. **Purchase-Money Security Interests.** Subsection (e) derives from former Section 9–301(2). It provides that, if a purchase-money security interest is perfected by filing no later than 20 days after the debtor receives delivery of the collateral, the security interest takes priority over the rights of buyers, lessees, or lien creditors which arise between the time the security interest attaches and the time of filing. Subsection (e) differs from former Section 9–301(2) in two significant respects. First, subsection (e) protects a purchase-money security interest against all buyers and lessees, not just against transferees in bulk. Second, subsection (e) conditions this protection on filing within 20, as opposed to ten, days after delivery.

Section 9–311(b) provides that compliance with the perfection requirements of a statute or treaty described in Section 9–311(a) "is equivalent to the filing of a financing statement." It follows that a person who perfects a security interest in goods covered by a certificate of title by complying with the perfection requirements of an applicable certificate-of-title statute "files a financing statement" within the meaning of subsection (e).

§ 9–318. No Interest Retained in Right to Payment That Is Sold; Rights and Title of Seller of Account or Chattel Paper With Respect to Creditors and Purchasers

(a) [Seller retains no interest.] A debtor that has sold an account, chattel paper, payment intangible, or promissory note does not retain a legal or equitable interest in the collateral sold.

(b) [Deemed rights of debtor if buyer's security interest unperfected.] For purposes of determining the rights of creditors of, and purchasers for value of an account or chattel paper from, a debtor that has sold an account or chattel paper, while the buyer's security interest is unperfected, the debtor is deemed to have rights and title to the account or chattel paper identical to those the debtor sold.

OFFICIAL COMMENT

* * *

2. **Sellers of Accounts, Chattel Paper, Payment Intangibles, and Promissory Notes.** Section 1–201(37) defines "security interest" to include the interest of a buyer of accounts, chattel paper, payment intangibles, or promissory notes. See also Section 9–109(a) and Comment 5. Subsection (a) makes explicit what was implicit, but perfectly obvious, under former Article 9: The fact that a sale of an account or chattel paper gives rise to a "security interest" does not imply that the seller retains an interest in the prop-

erty that has been sold. To the contrary, a seller of an account or chattel paper retains no interest whatsoever in the property to the extent that it has been sold. Subsection (a) also applies to sales of payment intangibles and promissory notes, transactions that were not covered by former Article 9. Neither this Article nor the definition of "security interest" in Section 1–201 provides rules for distinguishing sales transactions from those that create a security interest securing an obligation.

3. **Buyers of Accounts and Chattel Paper.** Another aspect of sales of accounts and chattel paper also was implicit, and equally obvious, under former Article 9: If the buyer's security interest is unperfected, then for purposes of determining the rights of certain third parties, the seller (debtor) is deemed to have all rights and title that the seller sold. The seller is deemed to have these rights even though, as between the parties, it has sold all its rights to the buyer. Subsection (b) makes this explicit. As a consequence of subsection (b), if the buyer's security interest is unperfected, the seller can transfer, and the creditors of the seller can reach, the account or chattel paper as if it had not been sold.

Example: Debtor sells accounts or chattel paper to Buyer–1 and retains no interest in them. Buyer–1 does not file a financing statement. Debtor then sells the same receivables to Buyer–2.

Buyer–2 files a proper financing statement. Having sold the receivables to Buyer–1, Debtor would not have any rights in the collateral so as to permit Buyer–2's security (ownership) interest to attach. Nevertheless, under this section, for purposes of determining the rights of purchasers for value from Debtor, Debtor is deemed to have the rights that Debtor sold. Accordingly, Buyer–2's security interest attaches, is perfected by the filing, and, under Section 9–322, is senior to Buyer–1's interest.

4. **Effect of Perfection.** If the security interest of a buyer of accounts or chattel paper is perfected the usual result would take effect: transferees from and creditors of the seller could not acquire an interest in the sold accounts or chattel paper. The same result generally would occur if payment intangibles or promissory notes were sold, inasmuch as the buyer's security interest is automatically perfected under Section 9–309. However, in certain circumstances a purchaser who takes possession of a promissory note will achieve priority, under Sections 9–330 or 9–331, over the security interest of an earlier buyer of the promissory note. It necessarily follows that the seller in those circumstances retains the power to transfer the promissory note, as if it had not been sold, to a purchaser who obtains priority under either of those sections. See Section 9–203(b)(3), Comment 6.

§ 9–319. Rights and Title of Consignee With Respect to Creditors and Purchasers

(a) [Consignee has consignor's rights.] Except as otherwise provided in subsection (b), for purposes of determining the rights of creditors of, and purchasers for value of goods from, a consignee, while the goods are in the possession of the consignee, the consignee is deemed to have rights and title to the goods identical to those the consignor had or had power to transfer.

(b) [Applicability of other law.] For purposes of determining the rights of a creditor of a consignee, law other than this article determines the rights and title of a consignee while goods are in the consignee's possession if, under this part, a perfected security interest held by the consignor would have priority over the rights of the creditor.

OFFICIAL COMMENT

* * *

2. **Consignments.** This section takes an approach to consignments similar to that taken by Section 9–318 with respect to buyers of accounts and chattel paper. Revised Section 1–201(37) defines "security interest" to include the interest of a consignor of goods under many true consignments. Section 9–319(a) provides that, for purposes of determining the rights of certain third parties, the consignee is deemed to acquire all rights and title that the consignor had, if the consignor's security interest is unperfected. The consignee acquires these rights even though, as between the parties, it purchases a limited interest in the goods (as would be the case in a true consignment, under which the consignee acquires only the interest of a bailee). As a consequence of this section, creditors of the consignee can acquire judicial liens and security interests in the goods.

* * *

The priority rules for purchase-money security interests in inventory apply to assignments. See Section 9–103(d). Section 9–317 determines whether the rights of a judicial lien creditor are senior to the interest of the consignor, Sections 9–322 and 9–324 govern competing security interests in consigned goods, and Sections 9–317, 9–315, and 9–320 determine whether a buyer takes free of the consignor's interest.

The following example explains the operation of this section:

Example 1: SP–1 delivers goods to Debtor in a transaction constituting a "consignment" as defined in Section 9–102. SP–1 does not file a financing statement. Debtor then grants a security interest in the goods to SP–2. SP–2 files a proper financing statement. Assuming Debtor is a mere bailee, as in a "true" consignment, Debtor would not have any rights in the collateral (beyond those of a bailee) so as to permit SP–2's security interest to attach to any greater rights. Nevertheless, under this section, for purposes of determining the rights of Debtor's creditors, Debtor is deemed to acquire SP–1's rights. Accordingly, SP–2's security interest attaches, is perfected by the filing, and, under Section 9–322, is senior to SP–1's interest.

3. **Effect of Perfection.** Subsection (b) contains a special rule with respect to consignments that are perfected. If application of this Article would result in the consignor having priority over a competing creditor, then other law determines the rights and title of the consignee.

Example 2: SP–1 delivers goods to Debtor in a transaction constituting a "consignment" as defined in Section 9–102. SP–1 files a proper financing statement. Debtor then grants a security interest in the goods to SP–2. Under Section 9–322, SP–1's security interest is senior to SP–2's. Subsection (b) indicates that, for purposes of determining SP–2's rights, other law determines the rights and title of the consignee. If, for example, a consignee obtains only the special property of a bailee, then SP–2's security interest would attach only to that special property.

Example 3: SP–1 obtains a security interest in all Debtor's existing and after-acquired inventory. SP–1 perfects its security interest with a proper filing. Then SP–2 delivers goods to Debtor in a transaction constituting a "consignment" as defined in Section 9–102. SP–2 files a proper financing statement but does not send notification to SP–1 under Section 9–324(b). Accordingly, SP–2's security interest is junior to SP–1's under Section 9–322(a). Under Section 9–319(a), Debtor is deemed to have the consignor's rights and title, so that SP–1's security interest attaches to SP–2's ownership interest in the goods. Thereafter, Debtor grants a security interest in the goods to SP–3, and SP–3 perfects by filing. Because SP–2's perfected security interest is senior to SP–3's under Section 9–322(a), Section 9–319(b) applies: Other law determines Debtor's rights and title to the goods insofar as SP–3 is concerned, and SP–

3's security interest attaches to those rights.

§ 9–320. Buyer of Goods

(a) [Buyer in ordinary course of business.] Except as otherwise provided in subsection (e), a buyer in ordinary course of business, other than a person buying farm products from a person engaged in farming operations, takes free of a security interest created by the buyer's seller, even if the security interest is perfected and the buyer knows of its existence.

(b) [Buyer of consumer goods.] Except as otherwise provided in subsection (e), a buyer of goods from a person who used or bought the goods for use primarily for personal, family, or household purposes takes free of a security interest, even if perfected, if the buyer buys:

(1) without knowledge of the security interest;

(2) for value;

(3) primarily for the buyer's personal, family, or household purposes; and

(4) before the filing of a financing statement covering the goods.

(c) [Effectiveness of filing for subsection (b).] To the extent that it affects the priority of a security interest over a buyer of goods under subsection (b), the period of effectiveness of a filing made in the jurisdiction in which the seller is located is governed by Section 9–316(a) and (b).

* * *

(e) [Possessory security interest not affected.] Subsections (a) and (b) do not affect a security interest in goods in the possession of the secured party under Section 9–313.

UNOFFICIAL COMMENTS

This section applies when there is both a (1) secured party with a perfected security interest in goods and (2) a buyer of the goods who is either (a) a buyer in the ordinary course of business or (b) a buyer of consumer goods from another consumer. Notice that "knowledge" is disqualifying under section 9–320(b), but not section 9–320(a). Also, in section 9–320(b) the seller must be another consumer ("from a person who used or bought . . .") but in section 9–320(a), the seller must be in business ("kind of business in which the seller", section 1–201(b)(9)).

NON–OBVIOUS DEFINITIONS

The definition of buyer in the ordinary course of business in section 1–201(b)(9) is long, complicated and important. Another certain exam issue.

OTHER UCC SECTIONS TO LOOK TO WHEN YOU LOOK AT SECTION 9–320

Under section 9–401(b), agreements between the debtor and secured party can not affect the effectiveness of the debtor's later sale of encumbered property.

This section, section 9–320, has two priority rules for situations involving secured parties with perfected security interests and certain buyers. Look to section 9–317, not section 9–320, if the security interest is not perfected. Look to section 9–201, not section 9–320, if the security interest is perfected but the buyer is different from the buyers described in section 9–320(a) or (b).

For more complete comments on section 9–320, see pages 374–375 infra.

OFFICIAL COMMENT

* * *

2. **Scope of This Section.** This section states when buyers of goods take free of a security interest even though perfected. Of course, a buyer who takes free of a perfected security interest takes free of an unperfected one. Section 9–317 should be consulted to determine what purchasers, in addition to the buyers covered in this section, take free of an unperfected security interest. Article 2 states general rules on purchase of goods from a seller with defective or voidable title (Section 2–403).

3. **Buyers in Ordinary Course.** Subsection (a) derives from former Section 9–307(1). The definition of "buyer in ordinary course of business" in Section 1–201 restricts its application to buyers "from a person, other than a pawnbroker, in the business of selling goods of that kind." Thus subsection (a) applies primarily to inventory collateral. The subsection further excludes from its operation buyers of "farm products"(defined in Section 9–102) from a person engaged in farming operations. The buyer in ordinary course of business is defined as one who buys goods "in good faith, without knowledge that the sale violates the rights of another person and in the ordinary course." Subsection (a) provides that such a buyer takes free of a security interest, even though perfected, and even though the buyer knows the security interest exists. Reading the definition together with the rule of law results in the buyer's taking free if the buyer merely knows that a security interest covers the goods but taking subject if the buyer knows, in addition, that the sale violates a term in an agreement with the secured party.

As did former Section 9–307(1), subsection (a) applies only to security interests created by the seller of the goods to the buyer in ordinary course. However, under certain circumstances a buyer in ordinary course who buys goods that were encumbered with a security interest created by a person other than the seller may take free of the security interest, as Example 2 explains. See also Comment 6, below.

Example 1: Manufacturer, who is in the business of manufacturing appliances, owns manufacturing equipment subject to a perfected security interest in favor of Lender. Manufacturer sells the equipment to Dealer, who is in the business of buying and selling used equipment. Buyer buys the equipment from Dealer. Even if Buyer qualifies as a buyer in the ordinary course of business, Buyer does not take free of Lender's security interest under subsection (a), because Dealer did not create the security interest; Manufacturer did.

Example 2: Manufacturer, who is in the business of manufacturing appliances, owns manufacturing equipment subject to a perfected security interest in favor of Lender. Manufacturer sells the equipment to Dealer, who is in the business of buying and selling used equipment. Lender learns of the sale but does nothing to assert its security interest. Buyer buys the equipment from Dealer. Inasmuch as Lender's acquiescence constitutes an "entrusting" of the goods to Dealer within the meaning of Section 2–403(3) Buyer takes free of Lender's security interest under Section 2–403(2) if Buyer qualifies as a buyer in ordinary course of business.

4. **Buyers of Farm Products.** This section does not enable a buyer of farm products to take free of a security interest created by the seller, even if the buyer is a buyer in ordinary course of business. However, a buyer of farm products may take free of a security interest under Section 1324 of the Food Security Act of 1985, 7 U.S.C. § 1631.

5. **Buyers of Consumer Goods.** Subsection (b), which derives from former Section 9–307(2), deals with buyers of collateral that the debtor-seller holds as "consumer goods" (defined in Section 9–102). Under Section 9–309(1), a purchase-money interest in consumer goods, except goods that are subject to a statute or treaty described in Section 9–311(a) (such as automobiles that are subject to a certificate-of-title statute), is perfected automatically upon attachment. There is no need to file to perfect. Under subsection (b) a buyer of consumer goods takes free of a security interest, even though perfected, if the buyer buys (1) without knowledge of the security interest, (2) for value, (3) primarily for the buyer's own personal, family, or household purposes, and (4) before a financing statement is filed.

As to purchase-money-security interests which are perfected without filing under Section 9–309(1): A secured party may file a financing statement, although filing is not required for perfection. If the secured party does file, all buyers take subject to the security interest. If the secured party does not file, a buyer who meets the qualifications stated in the preceding paragraph takes free of the security interest.

As to security interests for which a perfection step is required: This category includes all non-purchase-money security interests, and all security interests, whether or not purchase-money, in goods subject to a statute or treaty described in Section 9–311(a), such as automobiles covered by a certificate-of-title statute. As long as the required perfection step has not been taken and the security interest remains unperfected, not only the buyers described in subsection (b) but also the purchasers described in Section 9–317 will take free of the security interest. After a financing statement has been filed or the perfection requirements of the applicable certificate-of-title statute have been complied with (compliance is the equivalent of filing a financing statement; see Section 9–311(b)), all subsequent buyers, under the rule of subsection (b), are subject to the security interest.

The rights of a buyer under subsection (b) turn on whether a financing statement has been filed against consumer goods. Occasionally, a debtor changes his or her location after a filing is made. Subsection (c), which derives from former Section 9–103(1)(d)(iii), deals with the continued effectiveness of the filing under those circumstances. It adopts the rules of Sections 9–316(a) and (b). These rules are explained in the Comments to that section.

6. **Authorized Dispositions.** The limitations that subsections (a) and (b) impose on the persons who may take free of a security interest apply of course only to unauthorized sales by the debtor. If the secured party authorized the sale in an

express agreement or otherwise, the buyer takes free under Section 9–315(a) without regard to the limitations of this section. (That section also states the right of a secured party to the proceeds of a sale, authorized or unauthorized.) Moreover, the buyer also takes free if the secured party waived or otherwise is precluded from asserting its security interest against the buyer. See Section 1–103.

* * *

8. **Possessory Security Interests.** Subsection (e) is new. It rejects the holding of *Tanbro Fabrics Corp. v. Deering Milliken, Inc.*, 350 N.E.2d 590 (N.Y. 1976) and, together with Section 9–317(b), prevents a buyer of goods collateral from taking free of a security interest if the collateral is in the possession of the secured party. "The secured party" referred in subsection (e) is the holder of the security interest referred to in subsection (a) or (b). Section 9–313 determines whether a secured party is in possession for purposes of this section. Under some circumstances, Section 9–313 provides that a secured party is in possession of collateral even if the collateral is in the physical possession of a third party.

§ 9–321. Licensee of General Intangible and Lessee of Goods in Ordinary Course of Business

(a) **["Licensee in ordinary course of business."]** In this section, "licensee in ordinary course of business" means a person that becomes a licensee of a general intangible in good faith, without knowledge that the license violates the rights of another person in the general intangible, and in the ordinary course from a person in the business of licensing general intangibles of that kind. A person becomes a licensee in the ordinary course if the license to the person comports with the usual or customary practices in the kind of business in which the licensor is engaged or with the licensor's own usual or customary practices.

(b) **[Rights of licensee in ordinary course of business.]** A licensee in ordinary course of business takes its rights under a nonexclusive license free of a security interest in the general intangible created by the licensor, even if the security interest is perfected and the licensee knows of its existence.

(c) **[Rights of lessee in ordinary course of business.]** A lessee in ordinary course of business takes its leasehold interest free of a security interest in the goods created by the lessor, even if the security interest is perfected and the lessee knows of its existence.

OFFICIAL COMMENT

* * *

2. **Licensee in Ordinary Course.** Like the analogous rules in Section 9–320(a) with respect to buyers in ordinary course and subsection (c) with respect to lessees in ordinary course, the new rule in subsection (b) reflects the expectations of the parties and the marketplace: a licensee under a nonexclusive license takes subject to a security interest unless the secured party authorizes the license free of the security interest or other, controlling law such as that of this section (protecting ordinary-course licensees) dictates a contrary result. See Sections 9–201, 9–315. The definition of "licensee in ordinary course of business" in subsection (a)

is modeled upon that of "buyer in ordinary course of business."

3. **Lessee in Ordinary Course.** Subsection (c) contains the rule formerly found in Section 2A–307(3). The rule works in the same way as that of Section 9–320(a).

§ 9–322. Priorities Among Conflicting Security Interests in and Agricultural Lien Same Collateral

(a) [General priority rules.] Except as otherwise provided in this section, priority among conflicting security interests and agricultural liens in the same collateral is determined according to the following rules:

(1) Conflicting perfected security interests and agricultural lien rank according to priority in time of filing or perfection. Priority dates from the earlier of the time a filing covering the collateral is first made or the security interest or agricultural lien is first perfected, if there is no period thereafter when there is neither filing nor perfection.

(2) A perfected security interest or agricultural lien has priority over a conflicting unperfected security interest or agricultural lien.

(3) The first security interest or agricultural lien attach or become effective has priority if conflicting security interests and agricultural lien are unperfected.

(b) [Time of perfection: proceeds and supporting obligations.] For the purposes of subsection (a)(1):

(1) the time of filing or perfection as to a security interest in collateral is also the time of filing or perfection as to a security interest in proceeds; and

(2) the time of filing or perfection as to a security interest in collateral supported by a supporting obligation is also the time of filing or perfection as to a security interest in the supporting obligation.

(c) [Special priority rules: proceeds and supporting obligations.] Except as otherwise provided in subsection (f), a security interest in collateral which qualifies for priority over a conflicting security interest under Section 9–327, 9–328, 9–329, 9–330, or 9–331 also has priority over a conflicting security interest in:

(1) any supporting obligation for the collateral; and

(2) proceeds of the collateral if:

(A) the security interest in proceeds is perfected;

(B) the proceeds are cash proceeds or of the same type as the collateral; and

(C) in the case of proceeds that are proceeds of proceeds, all intervening proceeds are cash proceeds, proceeds of the same type as the collateral, or an account relating to the collateral.

(d) [First-to-file priority rule for certain collateral.] Subject to subsection (e) and except as otherwise provided in subsection (f), if a security interest in chattel paper, deposit accounts, negotiable documents, instruments, investment property, or letter-of-credit rights is perfected by a method other than filing, conflicting perfected security interests in proceeds of the collateral rank according to priority in time of filing.

(e) [Applicability of subsection (d).] Subsection (d) applies only if the proceeds of the collateral are not cash proceeds, chattel paper, negotiable documents, instruments, investment property, or letter-of-credit rights.

* * *

UNOFFICIAL COMMENTS

The basic priority rule is first to file or perfect, whichever first occurred, section 9–322(a)(1). You must understand this rule. Sure to be on the exam. Be sure you understand Example 1 in Official Comment 4.

Watch out for an exam question that tells you that one of the secured parties knows of the other security interest. You need to know that what the various secured parties know is irrelevant. In first year property talk, section 9–322 is a "pure race" statute.

The secured party who was the first file or perfect generally has priority as to proceeds. That is the general rule; exam important exceptions are set out in subsections (b) and (c) and explained in Official Comments 6–9. **For a more complete subsection by subsection summary of section 9–322, see pages 375–377.**

As Official Comment 4 to section 9–322 explains , section 9–322(a)(1)'s first to file or perfect, whichever first occurred, rule also applies as to future advances. Example 1 in Official Comment 3 to section 9–323 is helpful.

And, section 9–322(a)(1)'s first to file or perfect, whichever first occurred, rule extends to after-acquired property, unless there is a purchase-money security interest. If there is a purchase-money security interest, look to section 9–324.

OTHER SECTIONS TO LOOK TO WHEN YOU LOOK AT SECTION 9–322

Under section 9–401(b), agreements between the debtor and the secured party prohibiting the debtor from granting security interests to others are not effective.

To understand the section 9–322(a)(1) test of "time of filing or perfection", it is necessary to understand that a financing statement can be filed before a security interest attaches, before perfection. See sections 9–309, 9–502(d).

There are a number of "exam-important" exceptions to the general rule of section 9–322(a)(1). If one or more of the security interests is a "purchase money security interest" under section 9–103, look to section 9–324. If there is a sale of encumbered property to someone who has encumbered its property, look to section 9–325. And, if the collateral is chattel paper, look to section 9–330.

OFFICIAL COMMENT

* * *

2. **Scope of This Section.** In a variety of situations, two or more people may claim a security interest in the same collateral. This section states general rules of priority among conflicting security interests. As subsection (f) provides, the general rules in subsections (a) through (e) are subject to the rule in subsection (g) governing perfected agricultural liens and to the other rules in this Part of this Article. Rules that override this section include those applicable to purchase-money security interests (Section 9–324) and those qualifying for special priority in particular types of collateral. See, e.g., Section 9–327 (deposit accounts); Section 9–328 (investment property); Section 9–329 (letter-of-credit rights); Section 9–330 (chattel paper and instruments); Section 9–334 (fixtures). In addition, the general rules of sections (a) through (e) are subject to priority rules governing security interests arising under Articles 2, 2A, 4, and 5.

3. **General Rules.** Subsection (a) contains three general rules. Subsection (a)(1) governs the priority of competing perfected security interests. Subsection (a)(2) governs the priority of competing security interests if one is perfected and the other is not. Subsection (a)(3) governs the priority of competing unperfected security interests. The rules may be regarded as adaptations of the idea, deeply rooted at common law, of a race of diligence among creditors. The first two rules are based on precedence in the time as of which the competing secured parties either filed their financing statements or obtained perfected security interests. Under subsection (a)(1), the first secured party who files or perfects has priority. Under subsection (a)(2), which is new, a perfected security interest has priority over an unperfected one. Under subsection (a)(3), if both security interests are unperfected, the first to attach has priority. Note that Section 9–709(b) may affect the application of subsection (a) to a filing that occurred before the effective date of this Article and which would be ineffective to perfect a security interest under former Article 9 but effective under this Article.

4. **Competing Perfected Security Interests.** When there is more than one perfected security interest, the security interests rank according to priority in time of filing or perfection. "Filing," of course, refers to the filing of an effective financing statement. "Perfection" refers to the acquisition of a perfected security interest, i.e., one that has attached and as

to which any required perfection step has been taken. See Sections 9–308 and 9–309.

Example 1: On February 1, A files a financing statement covering a certain item of Debtor's equipment. On March 1, B files a financing statement covering the same equipment. On April 1, B makes a loan to Debtor and obtains a security interest in the equipment. On May 1, A makes a loan to Debtor and obtains a security interest in the same collateral. A has priority even though B's loan was made earlier and was perfected when made. It makes no difference whether A knew of B's security interest when A made its advance.

The problem stated in Example 1 is peculiar to a notice-filing system under which filing may occur before the security interest attaches (see Section 9–502). The justification for determining priority by order of filing lies in the necessity of protecting the filing system—that is, of allowing the first secured party who has filed to make subsequent advances without each time having to check for subsequent filings as a condition of protection. Note, however, that this first-to-file protection is not absolute. For example, Section 9–324 affords priority to certain purchase-money security interests, even if a competing secured party was the first to file or perfect.

Example 2: A and B make non-purchase-money advances secured by the same collateral. The collateral is in Debtor's possession, and neither security interest is perfected when the second advance is made. Whichever secured party first perfects its security interest (by taking possession of the collateral or by filing) takes priority. It makes no difference whether that secured party knows of the other security interest at the time it perfects its own.

The rule of subsection (a)(1), affording priority to the first to file or perfect, applies to security interests that are perfected by any method, including temporarily (Section 9–312) or upon attachment (Section 9–309), even though there may be no notice to creditors or subsequent purchasers and notwithstanding any common-law rule to the contrary. The form of the claim to priority, i.e., filing or perfection, may shift from time to time, and the rank will be based on the first filing or perfection as long as there is no intervening period without filing or perfection. See Section 9–308(c).

Example 3: On October 1, A acquires a temporarily perfected (20–day) security interest, unfiled, in a tangible negotiable document in the debtor's possession under Section 9–312(e). On October 5, B files and thereby perfects a security interest that previously had attached to the same document. On October 10, A files. A has priority, even after the 20–day period expires, regardless of whether A knows of B's security interest when A files. A was the first to perfect and maintained continuous perfection or filing since the start of the 20–day period. However, the perfection of A's security interest extends only "to the extent it arises for new value given." To the extent A's security interest secures advances made by A beyond the 20–day period, its security interest would be subordinate to B's, inasmuch as B was the first to file.

In general, the rule in subsection (a)(1) does not distinguish among various advances made by a secured party. The priority of every advance dates from the earlier of filing or perfection. However, in rare instances, the priority of an advance dates from the time the advance is made. See Example 3 and Section 9–323.

5. **Priority in After-Acquired Property.** The application of the priority rules to after-acquired property must be considered separately for each item of collateral. Priority does not depend only on time of perfection but may also be based on priority in filing before perfection.

Example 4: On February 1, A makes advances to Debtor under a security agreement covering "all Debtor's machinery, both existing and after-acquired." A promptly files a financing statement. On April 1, B takes a security interest in all Debtor's machinery, existing and after-acquired, to secure an outstanding loan. The following day, B files a financing statement. On May 1, Debtor acquires a new machine. When Debtor acquires rights in the new machine, both A and B acquire security interests in the machine simultaneously. Both security interests are perfected simultaneously. However, A has priority because A filed before B.

When after-acquired collateral is encumbered by more than one security interest, one of the security interests often is a purchase-money security interest that is entitled to special priority under Section 9–324.

6. **Priority in Proceeds: General Rule.** Subsection (b)(1) follows former Section 9–312(6). It provides that the baseline rules of subsection (a) apply generally to priority conflicts in proceeds except where otherwise provided (e.g., as in subsections (c) through (e)). Under Section 9–203, attachment cannot occur (and therefore, under Section 9–308, perfection cannot occur) as to particular collateral until the collateral itself comes into existence and the debtor has rights in it. Thus, a security interest in proceeds of original collateral does not attach and is not perfected until the proceeds come into existence and the debtor acquires rights in them.

Example 5: On April 1, Debtor authenticates a security agreement granting to A a security interest in all Debtor's existing and after-acquired inventory. The same day, A files a financing statement covering inventory. On May 1, Debtor authenticates a security agreement granting B a security interest in all Debtor's existing and future accounts. On June 1, Debtor sells inventory to a customer on 30–day unsecured credit. When Debtor acquires the account, B's security interest attaches to it and is perfected by B's financing statement. At the very same time, A's security interest attaches to the account as proceeds of the inventory and is automatically perfected. See Section 9–315. Under subsection (b) of this section, for purposes of determining A's priority in the account, the time of filing as to the original collateral (April 1, as to inventory) is also the time of filing as to proceeds (account). Accordingly, A's security interest in the account has priority over B's. Of course, had B filed its financing statement before A filed (e.g., on March 1), then B would have priority in the accounts.

Section 9–324 governs the extent to which a special purchase-money priority in goods or software carries over into the proceeds of the original collateral.

7. **Priority in Proceeds: Special Rules.** Subsections (c), (d), and (e), which are new, provide additional priority rules for proceeds of collateral in situations where the temporal (first-in-time) rules of subsection (a)(1) are not appropriate. These new provisions distinguish what these Comments refer to as "non-filing collateral" from what they call "filing collateral." As used in these Comments, non-filing collateral is collateral of a type for which perfection may be achieved by a method other than filing (possession or control, mainly) and for which secured parties who so perfect generally do not expect or need to conduct a filing search. More specifically, non-filing collateral is chattel paper, deposit accounts, negotiable documents, instruments, investment property, and letter-of-credit rights. Other collateral—accounts, commercial tort claims, general intangibles, goods, nonnegotiable documents, and payment intangibles–is filing collateral.

8. **Proceeds of Non-Filing Collateral: Non–Temporal Priority.** Subsection (c)(2) provides a baseline priority rule for proceeds of non-filing collateral which applies if the secured party has taken the steps required for non-temporal priority over a conflicting security interest in non-filing collateral (e.g., control, in the case of deposit accounts, letter-of-credit rights, investment property, and in some cases, electronic negotiable documents, section 9–331). This rule determines priority in proceeds of non-filing collateral whether or not there exists an actual conflicting security interest in the original non-filing collateral. Under sub-

section (c)(2), the priority in the original collateral continues in proceeds if the security interest in proceeds is perfected and the proceeds are cash proceeds or non-filing proceeds "of the same type" as the original collateral. As used in subsection (c)(2), "type" means a type of collateral defined in the Uniform Commercial Code and should be read broadly. For example, a security is "of the same type" as a security entitlement (i.e., investment property), and a promissory note is "of the same type" as a draft (i.e., an instrument).

> **Example 6:** SP–1 perfects its security interest in investment property by filing. SP–2 perfects subsequently by taking control of a certificated security. Debtor receives cash proceeds of the security (e.g., dividends deposited into Debtor's deposit account). If the first-to-file-or-perfect rule of subsection (a)(1) were applied, SP–1's security interest in the cash proceeds would be senior, although SP–2's security interest continues perfected under Section 9–315 beyond the 20–day period of automatic perfection. This was the result under former Article 9. Under subsection (c), however, SP–2's security interest is senior.

Note that a different result would obtain in Example 6 (i.e., SP–1's security interest would be senior) if SP–1 were to obtain control of the deposit-account proceeds. This is so because subsection (c) is subject to subsection (f), which in turn provides that the priority rules under subsections (a) through (e) are subject to "the other provisions of this part." One of those "other provisions" is Section 9–327, which affords priority to a security interest perfected by control. See Section 9–327(1).

> **Example 7:** SP–1 perfects its security interest in investment property by filing. SP–2 perfects subsequently by taking control of a certificated security. Debtor receives proceeds of the security consisting of a new certificated security issued as a stock dividend on the original collateral. Although the new security is of the same type as the original collateral (i.e., investment property), once the 20–day period of automatic perfection expires (see Section 9–315(d)), SP–2's security interest is unperfected. (SP–2 has not filed or taken delivery or control, and no temporary-perfection rule applies.) Consequently, once the 20–day period expires, subsection (c) does not confer priority, and, under subsection (a)(2), SP–1's security interest in the security is senior. This was the result under former Article 9.

> **Example 8:** SP–1 perfects its security interest in investment property by filing. SP–2 perfects subsequently by taking control of a certificated security and also by filing against investment property. Debtor receives proceeds of the security consisting of a new certificated security issued as a stock dividend of the collateral. Because the new security is of the same type as the original collateral (i.e., investment property) and (unlike Example 7) SP–2's security interest is perfected by filing, SP–2's security interest is senior under subsection (c). If the new security were redeemed by the issuer upon surrender and yet another security were received by Debtor, SP–2's security interest would continue to enjoy priority under subsection (c). The new security would be proceeds of proceeds.

> **Example 9:** SP–1 perfects its security interest in investment property by filing. SP–2 subsequently perfects its security interest in investment property by taking control of a certificated security and also by filing against investment property. Debtor receives proceeds of the security consisting of a dividend check that it deposits to a deposit account. Because the check and the deposit account are cash proceeds, SP–1's and SP–2's security interests in the cash proceeds are perfected under Section 9–315 beyond the 20–day period of automatic perfection. However, SP–2's security interest is senior under subsection (c).

> **Example 10:** SP–1 perfects its security interest in investment property by filing. SP–2 perfects subsequently by taking control of a certificated security and

also by filing against investment property. Debtor receives an instrument as proceeds of the security. (Assume that the instrument is not cash proceeds.) Because the instrument is not of the same type as the original collateral (i.e., investment property), SP–2's security interest, although perfected by filing, does not achieve priority under subsection (c). Under the first-to-file-or-perfect rule of subsection (a)(1), SP–1's security interest in the proceeds is senior.

The proceeds of proceeds are themselves proceeds. See Section 9–102 (defining "proceeds" and "collateral"). Sometimes competing security interests arise in proceeds that are several generations removed from the original collateral. As the following example explains, the applicability of subsection (c) may turn on the nature of the intervening proceeds.

Example 11: SP–1 perfects its security interest in Debtor's deposit account by obtaining control. Thereafter, SP–2 files against inventory, (presumably) searches, finds no indication of a conflicting security interest, and advances against Debtor's existing and after-acquired inventory. Debtor uses funds from the deposit account to purchase inventory, which SP–1 can trace as identifiable proceeds of its security interest in Debtor's deposit account, and which SP–2 claims as original collateral. The inventory is sold and the proceeds deposited into *another* deposit account, as to which SP–1 has not obtained control. Subsection (c) does not govern priority in this other deposit account. This deposit account is cash proceeds and is also the same type of collateral as SP–1's original collateral, as required by subsections (c)(2)(A) and (B). However, SP–1's security interest does not satisfy subsection (c)(2)(C) because the inventory proceeds, which intervened between the original deposit account and the deposit account constituting the proceeds at issue, are not cash proceeds, proceeds of the same type as the collateral (original deposit account), or an account relating to the collateral. Stated otherwise, once proceeds other than cash proceeds, proceeds of the same type as the original collateral, or an account relating to the original collateral intervene in the chain of proceeds, priority under subsection (c) is thereafter unavailable. The special priority rule in subsection (d) also is inapplicable to this case. See Comment 9, Example 13, below. Instead, the general first-to-file-or-perfect rule of subsections (a) and (b) apply. Under that rule, SP–1 has priority unless its security interest in the inventory proceeds became unperfected under Section 9–315(d). Had SP–2 filed against inventory before SP–1 obtained control of the original deposit account, the SP–2 would have had priority even if SP–1's security interest in the inventory proceeds remained perfected.

9. **Proceeds of Non–Filing Collateral: Special Temporal Priority.** Under subsections (d) and (e), if a security interest in non-filing collateral is perfected by a method other than filing (e.g., control or possession), it does not retain its priority over a conflicting security interest in proceeds that are filing collateral. Moreover, it is not entitled to priority in proceeds under the first-to file-or-perfect rule of subsections (a)(1) and (b). Instead, under subsection (d), priority is determined by a new first-to-file rule.

Example 12: SP–1 perfects its security interest in Debtor's deposit account by obtaining control. Thereafter, SP–2 files against equipment, (presumably) searches, finds no indication of a conflicting security interest, and advances against Debtor's equipment. SP–1 then files against Debtor's equipment. Debtor uses funds from the deposit account to purchase equipment, which SP–1 can trace as proceeds of its security interest in Debtor's deposit account. If the first-to-file-or-perfect rule were applied, SP–1's security interest would be senior under subsections (a)(1) and (b), because it was the first to perfect in the original collateral and there was no period during which its security interest was unperfected. Under subsection (d), however, SP–2's security interest would be senior because it filed first. This corresponds with the likely expectations of the parties.

Note that under subsection (e), the first-to-file rule of subsection (d) applies only if the proceeds in question are other than non-filing collateral (i.e., if the proceeds are filing collateral). If the proceeds are non-filing collateral, either the first-to-file-or-perfect rule under subsections (a) and (b) or the non-temporal priority rule in subsection (c) would apply, depending on the facts.

Example 13: SP–1 perfects its security interest in Debtor's deposit account by obtaining control. Thereafter, SP–2 files against inventory, (presumably) searches, finds no indication of a conflicting security interest, and advances against Debtor's existing and after-acquired inventory. Debtor uses funds from the deposit account to purchase inventory, which SP–1 can trace as identifiable proceeds of its security interest in Debtor's deposit account, and which SP–2 claims as original collateral. The inventory is sold and the proceeds deposited into *another* deposit account, as to which SP–1 has not obtained control. As discussed above in Comment 8, Example 11, subsection (c) does not govern priority in this deposit account. Subsection (d) also does not govern, because the proceeds at issue (the deposit account) are cash proceeds. See subsection (e). Rather, the general rules of subsections (a) and (b) govern.

10. **Priority in Supporting Obligations.** Under subsections (b)(2) and (c)(1), a security interest having priority in collateral also has priority in a supporting obligation for that collateral. However, the rules in these subsections are subject to the special rule in Section 9–329 governing the priority of security interests in a letter-of-credit right. See subsection (f). Under Section 9–329, a secured party's failure to obtain control (Section 9–107) of a letter-of-credit right that serves as supporting collateral leaves its security interest exposed to a priming interest of a party who does take control.

11. **Unperfected Security Interests.** Under subsection (a)(3), if conflicting security interests are unperfected, the first to attach has priority. This rule may be of merely theoretical interest, inasmuch as it is hard to imagine a situation where the case would come into litigation without either secured party's having perfected its security interest. If neither security interest had been perfected at the time of the filing of a petition in bankruptcy, ordinarily neither would be good against the trustee in bankruptcy under the Bankruptcy Code.

12. **Agricultural Liens.** Statutes other than this Article may purport to grant priority to an agricultural lien as against a conflicting security interest or agricultural lien. Under subsection (g), if another statute grants priority to an agricultural lien, the agricultural lien has priority only if the same statute creates the agricultural lien and the agricultural lien is perfected. Otherwise, subsection (a) applies the same priority rules to an agricultural lien as to a security interest, regardless of whether the agricultural lien conflicts with another agricultural lien or with a security interest.

Inasmuch as no agricultural lien on proceeds arises under this Article, subsections (b) through (e) do not apply to proceeds of agricultural liens. However, if an agricultural lien has priority under subsection (g) and the statute creating the agricultural lien gives the secured party a lien on proceeds of the collateral subject to the lien, a court should apply the principle of subsection (g) and award priority in the proceeds to the holder of the perfected agricultural lien.

§ 9–323. Future Advances

(a) [When priority based on time of advance.] Except as otherwise provided in subsection (c), for purposes of determining the priority of a perfected security interest under Section 9–322(a)(1), perfection of the security interest dates from the time an advance is made to the extent that the security interest secures an advance that:

    (1) is made while the security interest is perfected only:

        (A) under Section 9–309 when it attaches; or

        (B) temporarily under Section 9–312(e), (f), or (g); and

    (2) is not made pursuant to a commitment entered into before or while the security interest is perfected by a method other than under Section 9–309 or 9–312(e), (f), or (g).

(b) [Lien creditor.] Except as otherwise provided in subsection (c), a security interest is subordinate to the rights of a person that becomes a lien creditor to the extent that the security interest secures an advance made more than 45 days after the person becomes a lien creditor unless the advance is made:

    (1) without knowledge of the lien; or

    (2) pursuant to a commitment entered into without knowledge of the lien.

(c) [Buyer of receivables.] Subsections (a) and (b) do not apply to a security interest held by a secured party that is a buyer of accounts, chattel paper, payment intangibles, or promissory notes or a consignor.

(d) [Buyer of goods.] Except as otherwise provided in subsection (e), a buyer of goods other than a buyer in ordinary course of business takes free of a security interest to the extent that it secures advances made after the earlier of:

    (1) the time the secured party acquires knowledge of the buyer's purchase; or

    (2) 45 days after the purchase.

(e) [Advances made pursuant to commitment: priority of buyer of goods.] Subsection (d) does not apply if the advance is made pursuant to a commitment entered into without knowledge of the buyer's purchase and before the expiration of the 45–day period.

(f) [Lessee of goods.] Except as otherwise provided in subsection (g), a lessee of goods, other than a lessee in ordinary course of business, takes the leasehold interest free of a security interest to the extent that it secures advances made after the earlier of:

    (1) the time the secured party acquires knowledge of the lease; or

    (2) 45 days after the lease contract becomes enforceable.

(g) [Advances made pursuant to commitment: priority of lessee of goods.] Subsection (f) does not apply if the advance is made pursuant to a commitment entered into without knowledge of the lease and before the expiration of the 45-day period.

UNOFFICIAL COMMENTS

Seems like this section is in the wrong place. It goes with section 9-317 more than with section 9-322. Be sure that you go with section 9-322, not section 9-323, in answering priority questions involving multiple secured parties and future advances. See Official Comment 3 to section 9-323.

OFFICIAL COMMENT

* * *

2. **Scope of This Section.** A security agreement may provide that collateral secures future advances. See Section 9-204(c). This section collects all of the special rules dealing with the priority of advances made by a secured party after a third party acquires an interest in the collateral. Subsection (a) applies when the third party is a competing secured party. It replaces and clarifies former Section 9-312(7). Subsection (b) deals with lien creditors and replaces former Section 9-301(4). Subsections (d) and (e) deal with buyers and replace former Section 9-307(3). Subsections (f) and (g) deal with lessees and replace former Section 2A-307(4).

3. **Competing Security Interests.** Under a proper reading of the first-to-file-or-perfect rule of Section 9-322(a)(1) (and former Section 9-312(5)), it is abundantly clear that the time when an advance is made plays no role in determining priorities among conflicting security interests except when a financing statement was not filed and the advance is the giving of value as the last step for attachment and perfection. Thus, a secured party takes subject to all advances secured by a competing security interest having priority under Section 9-322(a)(1). This result generally obtains regardless of how the competing security interest is perfected and regardless of whether the advances are made "pursuant to commitment" (Section 9-102). Subsection (a) of this section states the only other instance when the time of an advance figures in the priority scheme in Section 9-322: when the security interest is perfected only automatically under Section 9-309 or temporarily under Section 9-312(e), (f), or (g), and the advance is not made pursuant to a commitment entered into while the security interest was perfected by another method. Thus, an advance has priority from the date it is made only in the rare case in which it is made without commitment and while the security interest is perfected only temporarily under Section 9-312.

The new formulation in subsection (a) clarifies the result when the initial advance is paid and a new ("future") advance is made subsequently. Under former Section 9-312(7), the priority of the new advance turned on whether it was "made while a security interest is perfected." This section resolves any ambiguity by omitting the quoted phrase.

Example 1: On February 1, A makes an advance secured by machinery in the debtor's possession and files a financing statement. On March 1, B makes an advance secured by the same machinery and files a financing statement. On April 1, A makes a further advance, under the original security agreement, against the same machinery. A was the first to file and so, under the first-to-file-or-perfect rule of Section 9-322(a)(1), A's security interest has priority over B's, both as to the February 1 and as to the April 1 advance. It makes no difference whether

A knows of B's intervening advance when A makes the second advance. Note that, as long as A was the first to file or perfect, A would have priority with respect to both advances if either A or B had perfected by taking possession of the collateral. Likewise, A would have priority if A's April 1 advance was not made under the original agreement with the debtor, but was under a new agreement.

Example 2: On October 1, A acquires a temporarily perfected (20–day) security interest, unfiled, in a tangible negotiable document in the debtor's possession under Section 9–312(e) or (f). The security interest secures an advance made on that day as well as future advances. On October 5, B files and thereby perfects a security interest that previously had attached to the same document. On October 8, A makes an additional advance. On October 10, A files. Under Section 9–322(a)(1), because A was the first to perfect and maintained continuous perfection or filing since the start of the 20–day period, A has priority, even after the 20–day period expires. See Section 9–322, Comment 4, Example 3. However, under this section, for purposes of Section 9–322(a)(1), to the extent A's security interest secures the October 8 advance, the security interest was perfected on October 8. Inasmuch as B perfected on October 5, B has priority over the October 8 advance.

The rule in subsection (a) is more liberal toward the priority of future advances than the corresponding rules applicable to intervening lien creditors (subsection (b)), buyers (subsections (d) and (e)), and lessees (subsections (f) and (g)).

4. **Competing Lien Creditors.** * * * Under Section 9–317(a)(2), a * * * security interest is senior to the rights of * * * a person who becomes a lien creditor, unless the person becomes a lien creditor before the security interest is perfected and before a financing statement covering the collateral is filed and Section 9–203(b)(3) is satisfied. Subsection (b) of this section * * * provides that a security interest is subordinate * * * to those rights to the extent that the specified circumstances occur. Subsection (b) does not elevate the priority of a security interest that is subordinate to the rights of a lien creditor under Section 9–317(a)(2); it only subordinates.*

As under former Section 9–301(4), a secured party's knowledge does not cut short the 45–day period during which future advances can achieve priority over an intervening lien creditor's interest. Rather, because of the impact of the rule in subsection (b) on the question whether the security interest for future advances is "protected" under Section 6323(c)(2) and (d) of the Internal Revenue Code as amended by the Federal Tax Lien Act of 1966, the priority of the security interest for future advances over a lien creditor is made absolute for 45 days regardless of knowledge of the secured party concerning the lien. If, however, the advance is made after the 45 days, the advance will not have priority unless it was made or committed without knowledge of the lien.

5. **Sales of Receivables; Consignments.** Subsections (a) and (b) do not apply to outright sales of accounts, chattel paper, payment intangibles, or promissory notes, nor do they apply to consignments.

6. **Competing Buyers and Lessees.** Under subsections (d) and (e), a buyer will not take subject to a security interest to the extent it secures advances made after the secured party has knowledge that the buyer has purchased the collateral or more than 45 days after the purchase unless the advances were made pursuant to a commitment entered into before the expiration of the 45–day period and without knowledge of the purchase. Subsections (f) and (g) provide an analogous rule for lessees. Of course, a buyer in ordinary course who takes free of the

---

* Amendments in italics approved by the Permanent Editorial Board for Uniform Commercial Code Oct. 20, 1999.

security interest under Section 9–320 and a lessee in ordinary course who takes free under Section 9–321 are not subject to any future advances. Subsections (d) and (e) replace former Section 9–307(3), and subsections (f) and (g) replace former Section 2A–307(4). No change in meaning is intended.

§ 9–324. Priority of Purchase-Money Security Interests

(a) [General rule: purchase-money priority.] Except as otherwise provided in subsection (g), a perfected purchase-money security interest in goods other than inventory or livestock has priority over a conflicting security interest in the same goods, and, except as otherwise provided in Section 9–327, a perfected security interest in its identifiable proceeds also has priority, if the purchase-money security interest is perfected when the debtor receives possession of the collateral or within 20 days thereafter.

(b) [Inventory purchase-money priority.] Subject to subsection (c) and except as otherwise provided in subsection (g), a perfected purchase-money security interest in inventory has priority over a conflicting security interest in the same inventory, has priority over a conflicting security interest in chattel paper or an instrument constituting proceeds of the inventory and in proceeds of the chattel paper, if so provided in Section 9–330, and, except as otherwise provided in Section 9–327, also has priority in identifiable cash proceeds of the inventory to the extent the identifiable cash proceeds are received on or before the delivery of the inventory to a buyer, if:

(1) the purchase-money security interest is perfected when the debtor receives possession of the inventory;

(2) the purchase-money secured party sends an authenticated notification to the holder of the conflicting security interest;

(3) the holder of the conflicting security interest receives the notification within five years before the debtor receives possession of the inventory; and

(4) the notification states that the person sending the notification has or expects to acquire a purchase-money security interest in inventory of the debtor and describes the inventory.

(c) [Holders of conflicting inventory security interests to be notified.] Subsections (b)(2) through (4) apply only if the holder of the conflicting security interest had filed a financing statement covering the same types of inventory:

(1) if the purchase-money security interest is perfected by filing, before the date of the filing; or

(2) if the purchase-money security interest is temporarily perfected without filing or possession under Section 9–312(f), before the beginning of the 20–day period thereunder.

(d) [Livestock purchase-money priority.] Subject to subsection (e) and except as otherwise provided in subsection (g), a perfected purchase-money security interest in livestock that are farm products has priority over a conflicting security interest in the same livestock, and, except as otherwise provided in Section 9–327, a perfected security interest in their identifiable proceeds and identifiable products in their unmanufactured states also has priority, if:

(1) the purchase-money security interest is perfected when the debtor receives possession of the livestock;

(2) the purchase-money secured party sends an authenticated notification to the holder of the conflicting security interest;

(3) the holder of the conflicting security interest receives the notification within six months before the debtor receives possession of the livestock; and

(4) the notification states that the person sending the notification has or expects to acquire a purchase-money security interest in livestock of the debtor and describes the livestock.

(e) [Holders of conflicting livestock security interests to be notified.] Subsections (d)(2) through (4) apply only if the holder of the conflicting security interest had filed a financing statement covering the same types of livestock:

(1) if the purchase-money security interest is perfected by filing, before the date of the filing; or

(2) if the purchase-money security interest is temporarily perfected without filing or possession under Section 9–312(f), before the beginning of the 20–day period thereunder.

(f) [Software purchase-money priority.] Except as otherwise provided in subsection (g), a perfected purchase-money security interest in software has priority over a conflicting security interest in the same collateral, and, except as otherwise provided in Section 9–327, a perfected security interest in its identifiable proceeds also has priority, to the extent that the purchase-money security interest in the goods in which the software was acquired for use has priority in the goods and proceeds of the goods under this section.

(g) [Conflicting purchase-money security interests.] If more than one security interest qualifies for priority in the same collateral under subsection (a), (b), (d), or (f):

- **(1)** a security interest securing an obligation incurred as all or part of the price of the collateral has priority over a security interest securing an obligation incurred for value given to enable the debtor to acquire rights in or the use of collateral; and

- **(2)** in all other cases, Section 9–322(a) applies to the qualifying security interests.

UNOFFICIAL COMMENTS

Section 9–324 works as an exception to the priority rules in sections 9–322 and 9–201. By complying with this section, a purchase-money security interest may have priority over other security interests, even though the other secured party filed or perfected first.

Remember that section 9–324(a) provides an exception to the first to file or perfect rule. If the purchase-money secured party does not comply with the requirements of section 9–324(a), then fall back on the general priority rule—i.e., the first to file or perfect rule.

Also, do not forget that section 9–324 is only a priority section. This section only determines priority and not whether there is a valid security interest. The loser in a priority dispute may be second in line, but will still have a security interest.

Section 9–324(a) applies to "goods other than inventory or livestock." Recall that a purchase-money security interest in consumer goods is automatically perfected. See section 9–309(1). Therefore, this subsection will normally apply where the collateral is equipment.

A purchase-money security interest in equipment has priority over another security interest in the same equipment if the purchase-money security interest is perfected when the debtor receives possession of the collateral or within 20 days thereafter. Note that there is no notice requirement for this sub-section.

If the purchase-money secured party qualifies for priority under this section 9–324(a) that priority will extend to identifiable proceeds.

Section 9–324(b) provides that a purchase-money security interest in inventory has priority over another security interest in the same inventory or proceeds of the inventory if the purchase-money security interest is (1) perfected when the debtor receives possession of the inventory, (2) the purchase-money secured party gives notice that states that the sender has or will have a purchase-money security interest in the inventory of the debtor, and (3) the holder receives the notice before the debtor receives possession of the purchase-money inventory.

Unlike priority under subsection (a), priority under subsection (b) does not extend to all identifiable proceeds but only to cash proceeds paid to the debtor by the buyer at or before delivery of the goods to the buyer. If, however, the collateral in question is not cash proceeds, the purchase-money secured party may still be able to attain priority under section 9–330 if the collateral in question is an instrument or chattel paper.

Collateral may be subject to more than one purchase-money security interest. In this situation, multiple security interests would qualify for priority under subsection (a) or (b). Subsection (g) resolves this conflict. The first provision, (g)(1), gives a seller's purchase-money security interest priority over a lender or bank's purchase-money security interest. If the conflicting purchase-money security interests do not include a seller, look to section 9–324(g)(2), which refers you to section 9–322(a). For example, if two banks have purchase-money security interests in the same collateral, and both qualify for priority under section 9–324(a) or (b), then the first bank to file or perfect would have priority under section 9–324(g)(2) and section 9–322(a)(1).

OTHER UCC SECTIONS TO LOOK TO WHEN YOU LOOK AT SECTION 9–324

Section 9–201 states the general rule: once a security interest has attached, it is effective against the debtor and against purchasers of the collateral. A secured party is one type of purchaser. Thus, a security interest that attached later in time will be subordinate to a security interest that attached earlier—unless some exception applies. Section 9–322 is one such exception.

Section 9–322, the basic rule of priority between two secured parties, is an important exception to the nemo dat principle of section 9–201. The result under section 9–322 will depend on which, if any, of the conflicting security interests are perfected. If both security interests are perfected, then the "first to file or perfect" rule, 9–322(a)(1), applies.

OFFICIAL COMMENT

* * *

2. **Priority of Purchase-Money Security Interests.** This section contains the priority rules applicable to purchase-money security interests, as defined in Section 9–103. It affords a special, non-temporal priority to those purchase-money security interests that satisfy the statutory conditions. In most cases, priority will be over a security interest asserted under an after-acquired property clause. See Section 9–204 on the extent to which security interests in after-acquired property are validated.

A purchase-money security interest can be created only in goods and software. See Section 9–103. Section 9–324(a), which follows former Section 9–312(4), contains the general rule for purchase-money security interests in goods. It is subject to subsections (b) and (c), which derive from former Section 9–312(3) and apply to purchase-money security interests in inventory, and subsections (d) and (e), which apply to purchase-money security interests in livestock that are farm products. Subsection (f) applies to purchase-money security interests in software. Subsection (g) deals with the relatively unusual case in which a debtor creates two purchase-money security interests in the same collateral and both security interests qualify for special priority under one of the other subsections.

Former Section 9–312(2) contained a rule affording special priority to those who provided secured credit that enabled a debtor to produce crops. This rule proved unworkable and has been eliminated from this Article. Instead, model Section 9–324A contains a revised production-money priority rule. That section is a model, not uniform, provision. The sponsors of the UCC have taken no position as to whether it should be enacted, instead leaving the matter for state legislatures to consider if they are so inclined.

3. **Purchase-Money Priority in Goods Other Than Inventory and Livestock.** Subsection (a) states a general rule applicable to all types of goods except inventory and farm-products livestock: the purchase-money interest takes priority if it is perfected when the debtor receives possession of the collateral or within 20 days thereafter. (As to the 20-day "grace period," compare Section 9–317(e). Former Sections 9–312(4) and 9–301(2) contained a 10-day grace period.) The perfection requirement means that the purchase-money secured party either has filed a financing statement before that time or has a temporarily perfected security interest in goods covered by documents under Section 9–312(e) and (f) which is continued in a perfected status by filing before the expiration of the 20-day period specified in that section. A purchase-money security interest qualifies for priority under subsection (a), even if the purchase-money secured party knows that a conflicting security interest has been created and/or that the holder of the conflicting interest has filed a financing statement covering the collateral.

Normally, there will be no question when "the debtor receives possession of the collateral" for purposes of subsection (a). However, sometimes a debtor buys goods and takes possession of them in stages, and then assembly and testing are completed (by the seller or debtor-buyer) at the debtor's location. Under those circumstances, the buyer "takes possession" within the meaning of subsection (a) when, after an inspection of the portion of the goods in the debtor's possession, it would be apparent to a potential lender to the debtor that the debtor has acquired an interest in the goods taken as a whole.

A similar issue concerning the time when "the debtor receives possession" arises when a person acquires possession of goods under a transaction that is not governed by this Article and then later agrees to buy the goods on secured credit. For example, a person may take possession of goods as lessee under a lease contract and then exercise an option to purchase the goods from the lessor on secured credit. Under Section 2A–307(1), creditors of the lessee generally take subject to the lease contract; filing a financing statement against the lessee is unnecessary to protect the lessor's leasehold or residual interest. Once the lease is converted to a security interest, filing a financing statement is necessary to protect the seller's (former lessor's) security interest. Accordingly, the 20–day period in subsection (a) does not commence until the goods become "collateral" (defined in Section 9–102), i.e., until they are subject to a security interest.

4. **Purchase-Money Security Interests in Inventory.** Subsections (b) and (c) afford a means by which a purchase-money security interest in inventory can achieve priority over an earlier-filed security interest in the same collateral. To achieve priority, the purchase-money security interest must be perfected when

the debtor receives possession of the inventory. For a discussion of when "the debtor receives possession," see Comment 3, above. The 20–day grace period of subsection (a) does not apply.

The arrangement between an inventory secured party and its debtor typically requires the secured party to make periodic advances against incoming inventory or periodic releases of old inventory as new inventory is received. A fraudulent debtor may apply to the secured party for advances even though it has already given a purchase-money security interest in the inventory to another secured party. For this reason, subsections (b)(2) through (4) and (c) impose a second condition for the purchase-money security interest's achieving priority: the purchase-money secured party must give notification to the holder of a conflicting security interest who filed against the same item or type of inventory before the purchase-money secured party filed or its security interest became perfected temporarily under Section 9–312(e) or (f). The notification requirement protects the non-purchase-money inventory secured party in such a situation: if the inventory secured party has received notification, it presumably will not make an advance; if it has not received notification (or if the other security interest does not qualify as purchase-money), any advance the inventory secured party may make ordinarily will have priority under Section 9–322. Inasmuch as an arrangement for periodic advances against incoming goods is unusual outside the inventory field, subsection (a) does not contain a notification requirement.

5. **Notification to Conflicting Inventory Secured Party: Timing.** Under subsection (b)(3), the perfected purchase-money security interest achieves priority over a conflicting security interest only if the holder of the conflicting security interest receives a notification within five years before the debtor receives possession of the purchase-money collateral. If the debtor never receives possession, the five-year period never begins, and the purchase-money security interest has priority, even if notification is not given. However, where the purchase-money inventory financing began by the purchase-money secured party's possession of a negotiable document of title, to retain priority the secured party must give the notification required by subsection (b) at or before the usual time, i.e., when the debtor gets possession of the inventory, even though the security interest remains perfected for 20 days under Section 9–312(e) or (f).

Some people have mistakenly read former Section 9–312(3)(b) to require, as a condition of purchase-money priority in inventory, that the purchase-money secured party give the notification before it files a financing statement. Read correctly, the "before" clauses compare (i) the time when the holder of the conflicting security interest filed a financing statement with (ii) the time when the purchase-money security interest becomes perfected by filing or automatically perfected temporarily. Only if (i) occurs before (ii) must notification be given to the holder of the conflicting security interest. Subsection (c) has been rewritten to clarify this point.

6. **Notification to Conflicting Inventory Secured Party: Address.** Inasmuch as the address provided as that of the secured party on a filed financing statement is an "address that is reasonable under the circumstances," the holder of a purchase-money security interest may satisfy the requirement to "send" notification to the holder of a conflicting security interest in inventory by sending a notification to that address, even if the address is or becomes incorrect. See Section 9–102 (definition of "send"). Similarly, because the address is "held out by [the holder of the conflicting security interest] as the place for receipt of such communications [i.e., communications relating to security interests]," the holder is deemed to have "received" a notification delivered to that address. See Section 1–201(26).

7. **Consignments.** Subsections (b) and (c) also determine the priority of a consignor's interest in consigned goods as against a security interest in the goods created by the consignee. Inasmuch as a

consignment subject to this Article is defined to be a purchase-money security interest, see Section 9–103(d), no inference concerning the nature of the transaction should be drawn from the fact that a consignor uses the term "security interest" in its notice under subsection (b)(4). Similarly, a notice stating that the consignor has delivered or expects to deliver goods, properly described, "on consignment" meets the requirements of subsection (b)(4), even if it does not contain the term "security interest," and even if the transaction subsequently is determined to be a security interest. Cf. Section 9–505 (use of "consignor" and "consignee" in financing statement).

8. **Priority in Proceeds: General.** When the purchase-money secured party has priority over another secured party, the question arises whether this priority extends to the proceeds of the original collateral. Subsections (a), (d), and (f) give an affirmative answer, but only as to proceeds in which the security interest is perfected (see Section 9–315). Although this qualification did not appear in former Section 9–312(4), it was implicit in that provision.

In the case of inventory collateral under subsection (b), where financing frequently is based on the resulting accounts, chattel paper, or other proceeds, the special priority of the purchase-money secured interest carries over into only certain types of proceeds. As under former Section 9–312(3), the purchase-money priority in inventory under subsection (b) carries over into identifiable cash proceeds (defined in Section 9–102) received on or before the delivery of the inventory to a buyer.

As a general matter, also like former Section 9–312(3), the purchase-money priority in inventory does *not* carry over into proceeds consisting of accounts or chattel paper. Many parties financing inventory are quite content to protect their first-priority security interest in the inventory itself. They realize that when the inventory is sold, someone else will be financing the resulting receivables (accounts or chattel paper), and the priority for inventory will not run forward to the receivables constituting the proceeds. Indeed, the cash supplied by the receivables financer often will be used to pay the inventory financing. In some situations, the party financing the inventory on a purchase-money basis makes contractual arrangements that the proceeds of receivables financing by another be devoted to paying off the inventory security interest.

However, the purchase-money priority in inventory *does* carry over to proceeds consisting of chattel paper and its proceeds (and also to instruments) to the extent provided in Section 9–330. Under Section 9–330(e), the holder of a purchase-money security interest in inventory is deemed to give new value for proceeds consisting of chattel paper. Taken together, Sections 9–324(b) and 9–330(e) enable a purchase-money inventory secured party to obtain priority in chattel paper constituting proceeds of the inventory, even if the secured party does not actually give new value for the chattel paper, provided the purchase-money secured party satisfies the other conditions for achieving priority.

When the proceeds of original collateral (goods or software) consist of a deposit account, Section 9–327 governs priority to the extent it conflicts with the priority rules of this section.

9. **Priority in Accounts Constituting Proceeds of Inventory.** The application of the priority rules in subsection (b) is shown by the following examples:

Example 1: Debtor creates a security interest in its existing and after-acquired inventory in favor of SP–1, who files a financing statement covering inventory. SP–2 subsequently takes a purchase-money security interest in certain inventory and, under subsection (b), achieves priority in this inventory over SP–1. This inventory is then sold, producing accounts. Accounts are not cash proceeds, and so the special purchase-money priority in the inventory does not control the priority in the accounts. Rather, the first-to-file-or-perfect rule of Section 9–322(a)(1) applies. The time of SP–1's filing as to the inventory is also the time of filing as to the accounts under Section 9–322(b). Assuming that each security interest in the accounts proceeds remains perfected under Section 9–315, SP–1 has priority as to the accounts.

Example 2: In Example 1, if SP–2 had filed directly against accounts, the date of that filing as to accounts would be compared with the date of SP–1's filing as to the inventory. The first filed would prevail under Section 9–322(a)(1).

Example 3: If SP–3 had filed against accounts in Example 1 before either SP–1 or SP–2 filed against inventory, SP–3's filing against accounts would have priority over the filings of SP–1 and SP–2. This result obtains even though the filings against inventory are effective to continue the perfected status of SP–1's and SP–2's security interest in the accounts beyond the 20–day period of automatic perfection. See Section 9–315. SP–1's and SP–2's position as to the inventory does not give them a claim to accounts (as proceeds of the inventory) which is senior to someone who has filed earlier against accounts. If, on the other hand, either SP–1's or SP–2's filing against the inventory preceded SP–3's filing against accounts, SP–1 or SP–2 would outrank SP–3 as to the accounts.

10. **Purchase-Money Security Interests in Livestock.** New subsections (d) and (e) provide a purchase-money priority rule for farm-products livestock. They are patterned on the purchase-money priority rule for inventory found in subsections (b) and (c) and include a requirement that the purchase-money secured party notify earlier-filed parties. Two differences between subsections (b) and (d) are noteworthy. First, unlike the purchase-money inventory lender, the purchase-money livestock lender enjoys priority in *all* proceeds of the collateral. Thus, under subsection (d), the purchase-money secured party takes priority in accounts over an earlier-filed accounts financer. Second, subsection (d) affords priority in certain products of the collateral as well as proceeds.

11. **Purchase-Money Security Interests in Aquatic Farm Products.** Aquatic goods produced in aquacultural operations (e.g., catfish raised on a catfish farm) are farm products. See Section 9–102 (definition of "farm products"). The definition does not indicate whether aquatic goods are "crops," as to which the model production money security interest priority in Section 9–324A applies, or "livestock," as to which the purchase-money priority in subsection (d) of this section applies. This Article leaves courts free to determine the classification of particular aquatic goods on a case-by-case basis, applying whichever priority rule makes more sense in the overall context of the debtor's business.

12. **Purchase-Money Security Interests in Software.** Subsection (f) governs the priority of purchase-money security interests in software. Under Section 9–103(c), a purchase-money security interest arises in software only if the debtor acquires its interest in the software for the principal purpose of using the software in goods subject to a purchase-money security interest. Under subsection (f), a purchase-money security interest in software has the same priority as the purchase-money security interest in the goods in which the software was acquired for use. This priority is determined under subsections (b) and (c) (for inventory) or (a) (for other goods).

13. **Multiple Purchase-Money Security Interests.** New subsection (g) governs priority among multiple purchase-money security interests in the same collateral. It grants priority to purchase-money security interests securing the price of collateral (i.e., created in favor of the seller) over purchase-money security interests that secure enabling loans. Section 7.2(c) of the Restatement (3d) of the Law of Property (Mortgages) (1997) adopts this rule with respect to real property mortgages. As Comment *d* to that section explains:

> the equities favor the vendor. Not only does the vendor part with specific real estate rather than money, but the vendor would never relinquish it at all except on the understanding that the

vendor will be able to use it to satisfy the obligation to pay the price. This is the case even though the vendor may know that the mortgagor is going to finance the transaction in part by borrowing from a third party and giving a mortgage to secure that obligation. In the final analysis, the law is more sympathetic to the vendor's hazard of losing real estate previously owned than to the third party lender's risk of being unable to collect from an interest in real estate that never previously belonged to it.

The first-to-file-or-perfect rule of Section 9–322 applies to multiple purchase-money security interests securing enabling loans.

§ 9–325. Priority of Security Interests in Transferred Collateral

(a) [Subordination of security interest in transferred collateral.] Except as otherwise provided in subsection (b), a security interest created by a debtor is subordinate to a security interest in the same collateral created by another person if:

> **(1)** the debtor acquired the collateral subject to the security interest created by the other person;
>
> **(2)** the security interest created by the other person was perfected when the debtor acquired the collateral; and
>
> **(3)** there is no period thereafter when the security interest is unperfected.

(b) [Limitation of subsection (a) subordination.] Subsection (a) subordinates a security interest only if the security interest:

> **(1)** otherwise would have priority solely under Section 9–322(a) or 9–324; or
>
> **(2)** arose solely under Section 2–711(3) or 2A–508(5).

UNOFFICIAL COMMENTS

As Official Comment 2 makes clear, this section deals with the "double debtor" problem. In essence, this section deals with a transfer of collateral from one debtor to another debtor, when each debtor's secured party claims an interest in that property.

The next section deals with the "new debtor" problem. Compare example 1 in the section 9–325 Official Comments with example 1 in the section 9–326 Official Comments for the difference between a "double debtor" problem and a "new debtor" problem.

NON–OBVIOUS DEFINITIONS

Official Comments to section 9–325, but not section 9–325 itself, use the term "double-debtor." That term is not defined.

"New debtor" is a defined term, section 9–102(a)(56). Whatever a "double-debtor" is, it is different from a "new debtor."

OFFICIAL COMMENT

* * *

2. **"Double Debtor Problem."** This section addresses the "double debtor" problem, which arises when a debtor acquires property that is subject to a security interest created by another debtor.

3. **Taking Subject to Perfected Security Interest.** Consider the following scenario:

Example 1: A owns an item of equipment subject to a perfected security interest in favor of SP–A. A sells the equipment to B, not in the ordinary course of business. B acquires its interest subject to SP–A's security interest. See Sections 9–201, 9–315(a)(1). Under this section, if B creates a security interest in the equipment in favor of SP–B, SP–B's security interest is subordinate to SP–A's security interest, even if SP–B filed against B before SP–A filed against A, and even if SP–B took a purchase-money security interest. Normally, SP–B could have investigated the source of the equipment and discovered SP–A's filing before making an advance against the equipment, whereas SP–A had no reason to search the filings against someone other than its debtor, A.

4. **Taking Subject to Unperfected Security Interest.** This section applies only if the security interest in the transferred collateral was perfected when the transferee acquired the collateral. See subsection (a)(2). If this condition is not met, then the normal priority rules apply.

Example 2: A owns an item of equipment subject to an unperfected security interest in favor of SP–A. A sells the equipment to B, who gives value and takes delivery of the equipment without knowledge of the security interest. B takes free of the security interest. See Section 9–317(b). If B then creates a security interest in favor of SP–B, no priority issue arises; SP–B has the only security interest in the equipment.

Example 3: The facts are as in Example 2, except that B knows of SP–A's security interest and therefore takes the equipment subject to it. If B creates a security interest in the equipment in favor of SP–B, this section does not determine the relative priority of the security interests. Rather, the normal priority rules govern. If SP–B perfects its security interest, then, under Section 9–322(a)(2), SP–A's unperfected security interest will be junior to SP–B's perfected security interest. The award of priority to SP–B is premised on the belief that SP–A's failure to file could have misled SP–B.

5. **Taking Subject to Perfected Security Interest that Becomes Unperfected.** This section applies only if the security interest in the transferred collateral did not become unperfected at any time after the transferee acquired the collateral. See subsection (a)(3). If this condition is not met, then the normal priority rules apply.

Example 4: As in Example 1, A owns an item of equipment subject to a perfected security interest in favor of SP–A. A sells the equipment to B, not in the ordinary course of business. B acquires its interest subject to SP–A's security interest. See Sections 9–201, 9–315(a)(1). B creates a security interest in favor of SP–B, and SP–B perfects its security interest. This section provides that SP–A's security interest is senior to SP–B's. However, if SP–A's financing statement lapses while SP–B's security interest is perfected, then the normal priority rules would apply, and SP–B's security interest would become senior to SP–A's security interest. See Sections 9–322(a)(2), 9–515(c).

6. **Unusual Situations.** The appropriateness of the rule of subsection (a) is most apparent when it works to subordinate security interests having priority under the basic priority rules of Section 9–322(a) or the purchase-money priority

rules of Section 9–324. The rule also works properly when applied to the security interest of a buyer under Section 2–711(3) or a lessee under Section 2A–508(5). However, subsection (a) may provide an inappropriate resolution of the "double debtor" problem in some of the wide variety of other contexts in which the problem may arise. Although subsection (b) limits the application of subsection (a) to those cases in which subordination is known to be appropriate, courts should apply the rule in other settings, if necessary to promote the underlying purposes and policies of the Uniform Commercial Code. See Section 1–103(a).

§ 9–326. Priority of Security Interests Created by New Debtor

(a) [Subordination of security interest created by new debtor.] Subject to subsection (b), a security interest created by a new debtor which is perfected by a filed financing statement that is effective solely under Section 9–508 in collateral in which a new debtor has or acquires rights is subordinate to a security interest in the same collateral which is perfected other than by a filed financing statement that is effective solely under Section 9–508.

(b) [Priority under other provisions; multiple original debtors.] The other provisions of this part determine the priority among conflicting security interests in the same collateral perfected by filed financing statements that are effective solely under Section 9–508. However, if the security agreements to which a new debtor became bound as debtor were not entered into by the same original debtor, the conflicting security interests rank according to priority in time of the new debtor's having become bound.

UNOFFICIAL COMMENTS

As the section title makes clear, this section deals with the "new debtor" problem. The prior section deals with the "double debtor" problem. Compare example 1 in the section 9–325 Official Comments with example 1 in the section 9–326 Official Comments for the difference between a "double debtor" problem and a "new debtor" problem.

OFFICIAL COMMENT

* * *

2. **Subordination of Security Interests Created by New Debtor.** This section addresses the priority contests that may arise when a new debtor becomes bound by the security agreement of an original debtor and each debtor has a secured creditor.

Subsection (a) subordinates the original debtor's secured party's security interest perfected against the new debtor solely under Section 9–508. The security interest is subordinated to security interests in the same collateral perfected by another method, e.g., by filing against the new debtor. As used in this section, "a filed financing statement that is effective solely under Section 9–508" refers to a financing statement filed against the *original debtor* that continues to be effective under Section 9–508. It does not encompass a new initial financing statement providing the name of the new debtor, even if the initial financing statement is filed to maintain the effectiveness of a financing statement under the circumstances described in Section 9–508(b). Nor does it encompass a financing statement filed against the original debtor which remains effective against collateral transferred by the original debtor to the new debtor. See Section 9–508(c). Concerning priority contests involving transferred collateral, see Sections 9–325 and 9–507.

Example 1: SP–X holds a perfected-by-filing security interest in X Corp's existing and after-acquired inventory, and SP–Z holds a perfected-by-possession security interest in an item of Z Corp's inventory. Z Corp becomes bound as debtor by X Corp's security agreement (e.g., Z Corp buys X Corp's assets and assumes its security agreement). See Section 9–203(d). Under Section 9–508, SP–X's financing statement is effective to perfect a security interest in the item of inventory in which Z Corp has rights. However, subsection (a) provides that SP–X's security interest is subordinate to SP–Z's, regardless of whether SP–X's financing statement was filed before SP–Z perfected its security interest.

Example 2: SP–X holds a perfected-by-filing security interest in X Corp's existing and after-acquired inventory, and SP–Z holds a perfected-by-filing security interest in Z Corp's existing and after-acquired inventory. Z Corp becomes bound as debtor by X Corp's security agreement. Subsequently, Z Corp acquires a new item of inventory. Under Section 9–508, SP–X's financing statement is effective to perfect a security interest in the new item of inventory in which Z Corp has rights. However, because SP–Z's security interest was perfected by another method, subsection (a) provides that SP–X's security interest is subordinate to SP–Z's, regardless of which financing statement was filed first. This would be the case even if SP–Z filed after Z Corp became bound by X Corp's security agreement.

3. **Other Priority Rules.** Subsection (b) addresses the priority among security interests created by the original debtor (X Corp). By invoking the other priority rules of this subpart, as applicable, subsection (b) preserves the relative priority of security interests created by the original debtor.

Example 3: Under the facts of Example 2, SP–Y also holds a perfected-by-filing security interest in X Corp's existing and after-acquired inventory. SP–Y filed after SP–X. Inasmuch as both SP–X's and SP–Y's security interests in inventory acquired by Z Corp after it became bound are perfected solely under Section 9–508, the normal priority rules determine their relative priorities. Under the "first-to-file-or-perfect" rule of Section 9–322(a)(1), SP–X has priority over SP–Y.

Example 4: Under the facts of Example 3, after Z Corp became bound by X Corp's security agreement, SP–Y promptly filed a new initial financing statement against Z Corp. At that time, SP–X's security interest was perfected only by virtue of its original filing against X Corp which was "effective solely under Section 9–508." Because SP–Y's security interest no longer is perfected by a financing statement that is "effective solely under Section 9–508," this section does not apply to the priority contest. Rather, the normal priority rules apply. Under Section 9–322, because SP–Y's financing statement was filed *against Z Corp*, the new debtor, before SP–X's, SP–Y's security interest is senior to that of SP–X. Similarly, the normal priority rules would govern priority between SP–Y and SP–Z.

The second sentence of subsection (b) effectively limits the applicability of the first sentence to situations in which a new debtor has become bound by more than one security agreement entered into by the *same* original debtor. When the new debtor has become bound by security agreements entered into by *different* original debtors, the second sentence provides that priority is based on priority in time of the new debtor's becoming bound.

Example 5: Under the facts of Example 2, SP–W holds a perfected-by-filing security interest in W Corp's existing and after-acquired inventory. After Z Corp became bound by X Corp's security agreement in favor of SP–X, Z Corp became bound by W Corp's security agreement. Under subsection (b), SP–W's security interest in inventory acquired by Z Corp is subordinate to that of SP–X, because Z Corp became bound under SP–X's security agreement before it became bound under SP–W's security agreement. This is the result regardless of which financing statement (SP–X's or SP–W's) was filed first.

The second sentence of subsection (b) reflects the generally accepted view that priority based on the first-to-file rule is inappropriate for resolving priority disputes when the filings were made against different debtors. Like subsection (a) and the first sentence of subsection (b), however, the second sentence of subsection (b) relates only to priority conflicts among security interests perfected by filed financing statements that are "effective solely under Section 9–508."

Example 6: Under the facts of Example 5, after Z Corp became bound by W Corp's security agreement, SP–W promptly filed a new initial financing statement against Z Corp. At that time, SP–X's security interest was perfected only pursuant to its original filing against X Corp which was "effective solely under Section 9–508." Because SP–W's security interest is not perfected by a financing statement that is "effective solely under Section 9–508," this section does not apply to the priority contest. Rather, the normal priority rules apply. Under Section 9–322, because SP–W's financing statement was the first to be filed *against Z Corp*, the new debtor, SP–W's security interest is senior to that of SP–X. Similarly, the normal priority rules would govern priority between SP–W and SP–Z.

§ 9–327. Priority of Security Interests in Deposit Account

The following rules govern priority among conflicting security interests in the same deposit account:

(1) A security interest held by a secured party having control of the deposit account under Section 9–104 has priority over a conflicting security interest held by a secured party that does not have control.

(2) Except as otherwise provided in paragraphs (3) and (4), security interests perfected by control under Section 9–314 rank according to priority in time of obtaining control.

(3) Except as otherwise provided in paragraph (4), a security interest held by the bank with which the deposit account is maintained has priority over a conflicting security interest held by another secured party.

(4) A security interest perfected by control under Section 9–104(a)(3) has priority over a security interest held by the bank with which the deposit account is maintained.

UNOFFICIAL COMMENTS

To understand this section, you need to understand the two different ways that a "deposit account" becomes collateral: (1) as initial collateral described in the security agreement and (2) as proceeds of initial collateral described in the security agreement.

When a deposit account is "initial" collateral, the only method of perfection is control pursuant to section 9–104. Recall that there are three ways in which a secured party might effect control, and, under this section, some are more effective than others.

First, there is secured party who has obtained control by "becoming the bank's customer." For example, X, a secured party, agrees with the debtor that the debtor will put X's name on the debtor's deposit account in Bank Y. *See section* 9–104(a)(3). Second, there is the control that arises simply by virtue of the fact that the secured party is the bank where the funds are on deposit—without taking any action to perfect, Bank Y has control of a deposit account at Bank Y. *See* section 9–104(a)(1). Under section 9–327(4), X (who "became the customer") has priority over Bank Y (whose control arose simply by operation of law). Finally, consider secured party Z, who has a written agreement with Bank Y, stating that Y will comply with Z's directions regarding the disposition of the funds in the account. This agreement gives Z control under section 9–104(a)(2). Unlike X, however, Z will not have priority over Bank Y. *See section* 9–327(3). Official Comment 4 explains the rationale for treating X and Z differently.

In the last example, Z can avoid being subordinate to the bank's security interest in two ways. He can do what X did—become the customer. Or, under section 9–339, Z can agree with Bank Y to change the normal priority rule via a subordination agreement. *See* Official Comment 4.

If more than one secured party has control (a "very rare" scenario in real life, according to Official Comment 3), and none of the above rules solve the conflict, the result is predictable: whoever obtained control first, has priority, section 9–327(2).

More commonly, in the real world and on exams, the priority dispute involves (1) a secured party who took a security interest in a deposit account as "initial collateral" and thereafter perfected by control and (2) a second secured party who has a perfected security interest in a deposit account because it is has identifiable proceeds from the sale of collateral. For example, S has a security interest in D's inventory, perfected by filing. When D sells inventory, it puts the cash proceeds in a deposit account in B bank that contains only proceeds from the sale of S's collateral. S has perfected security interest in the deposit account. If B Bank later makes a loan to D secured by the deposit account, B Bank will have perfection by control under section 9–104. And under section 9–327, B Bank's later in time security interest in the deposit account, perfected by control, will have priority over S's earlier in time perfected security interest.

NON–OBVIOUS DEFINITIONS

The definition of "deposit account" in section 9–102(a)(29) needs to become obvious to you. While the term "bank" is also defined, what is important is that you see the term "bank" in the definition of "deposit account."

OTHER UCC SECTIONS TO LOOK TO WHEN YOU LOOK AT SECTION 9–327

This section is in essence an exception to section 9–322 which establishes general rules for resolving priority disputes among secured parties. Critical to this section 9–327 exception to the section 9–322 rules is control of a deposit account under sections and 9–314 and 9–104.

OFFICIAL COMMENT

* * *

2. **Scope of This Section.** This section contains the rules governing the priority of conflicting security interests in deposit accounts. It overrides conflicting priority rules. See Sections 9–322(f)(1), 9–324(a), (b), (d), (f). This section does not apply to accounts evidenced by an instrument (e.g., certain certificates of deposit), which by definition are not "deposit accounts."

3. **Control.** Under paragraph (1), security interests perfected by control (Sections 9–314, 9–104) take priority over those perfected otherwise, e.g., as identifiable cash proceeds under Section 9–315. Secured parties for whom the deposit account is an integral part of the credit decision will, at a minimum, insist upon the right to immediate access to the deposit account upon the debtor's default (i.e., control). Those secured parties for whom the deposit account is less essential will not take control, thereby running the risk that the debtor will dispose of funds on deposit (either outright or for collateral purposes) after default but before the account can be frozen by court order or the secured party can obtain control.

Paragraph (2) governs the case (expected to be very rare) in which a bank enters into a Section 9–104(a)(2) control agreement with more than one secured party. It provides that the security interests rank according to time of obtaining control. If the bank is solvent and the control agreements are well drafted, the bank will be liable to each secured party, and the priority rule will have no practical effect.

4. **Priority of Bank.** Under paragraph (3), the security interest of the bank with which the deposit account is maintained normally takes priority over all other conflicting security interests in the deposit account, regardless of whether the deposit account constitutes the competing secured party's original collateral or its proceeds. A rule of this kind enables banks to extend credit to their depositors without the need to examine either the public record or their own records to determine whether another party might have a security interest in the deposit account.

A secured party who takes a security interest in the deposit account as original collateral can protect itself against the results of this rule in one of two ways. It can take control of the deposit account by becoming the bank's customer. Under paragraph (4), this arrangement operates to subordinate the bank's security interest. Alternatively, the secured party can obtain a subordination agreement from the bank. See Section 9–339.

A secured party who claims the deposit account as proceeds of other collateral can reduce the risk of becoming junior by obtaining the debtor's agreement to deposit proceeds into a specific cash-collateral account and obtaining the agreement of that bank to subordinate all its claims to those of the secured party. But if the debtor violates its agreement and deposits funds into a deposit account other than the cash-collateral account, the secured party risks being subordinated.

5. **Priority in Proceeds of, and Funds Transferred from, Deposit Account.** The priority afforded by this section does not extend to proceeds of a deposit account. Rather, Section 9–322(c) through (e) and the provisions referred to in Section 9–322(f) govern priorities in proceeds of a deposit account. Section 9–315(d) addresses continuation of perfection in proceeds of deposit accounts. As to funds transferred from a deposit account that serves as collateral, see Section 9–332.

§ 9–328. Priority of Security Interests in Investment Property

The following rules govern priority among conflicting security interests in the same investment property:

(1) A security interest held by a secured party having control of investment property under Section 9–106 has priority over a security interest held by a secured party that does not have control of the investment property.

(2) Except as otherwise provided in paragraphs (3) and (4), conflicting security interests held by secured parties each of which has control under Section 9–106 rank according to priority in time of:

(A) if the collateral is a security, obtaining control;

(B) if the collateral is a security entitlement carried in a securities account and:

(i) if the secured party obtained control under Section 8–106(d)(1), the secured party's becoming the person for which the securities account is maintained;

(ii) if the secured party obtained control under Section 8–106(d)(2), the securities intermediary's agreement to comply with the secured party's entitlement orders with respect to security entitlements carried or to be carried in the securities account; or

(iii) if the secured party obtained control through another person under Section 8–106(d)(3), the time on which priority would be based under this paragraph if the other person were the secured party; or

(C) if the collateral is a commodity contract carried with a commodity intermediary, the satisfaction of the requirement for control specified in Section 9–106(b)(2) with respect to commodity contracts carried or to be carried with the commodity intermediary.

(3) A security interest held by a securities intermediary in a security entitlement or a securities account maintained with the securities intermediary has priority over a conflicting security interest held by another secured party.

(4) A security interest held by a commodity intermediary in a commodity contract or a commodity account maintained with the commodity intermediary has priority over a conflicting security interest held by another secured party.

(5) A security interest in a certificated security in registered form which is perfected by taking delivery under Section 9–313(a) and not by control under Section 9–314 has priority over a conflicting security interest perfected by a method other than control.

(6) Conflicting security interests created by a broker, securities intermediary, or commodity intermediary which are perfected without control under Section 9–106 rank equally.

(7) In all other cases, priority among conflicting security interests in investment property is governed by Sections 9–322 and 9–323.

UNOFFICIAL COMMENTS

This section provides the priority rules for conflicting perfected security interests in investment property. Recall, there are three primary methods of perfection for investment property; control, delivery, and filing. Control perfection has priority over both delivery perfection and filing perfection or other methods of perfection. Delivery perfection has priority over filing perfection or other methods of perfection.

Determining which secured party has priority when both conflicting security interests rely on perfection by control is more complex. Under 9–328(2) priority is determined by the time of obtaining control, with different requirements for obtaining control depending on the type of investment property.

NON–OBVIOUS DEFINITIONS

Lots of unfamiliar terms used in this section and defined in other sections. In alphabetical order, bearer form, section 8–102(a)(2); certificated security, section 8–102(a)(4); commodity contract, section 9–102(a)(15); control of securities and securities entitlements, section 8–106; delivery of securities, 8–301(a); registered form, section 8–102(a)(13); securities account, 8–501(a); securities entitlement, section 8–102(a)(17); securities intermediary, 8–102(a)(14).

OTHER UCC SECTIONS TO LOOK TO WHEN YOU LOOK AT SECTION 9–328

Section 9:106, Control of Investment Property. Section 9–106(a) incorporates by reference the Article 8 definition of control of securities and security entitlements. Subsection (b) states similar principles applicable to commodity contracts. Finally, under subsection (c), a secured party is deemed to have control over a securities account if his control extends to *all* the securities entitlements in the account.

OFFICIAL COMMENT

* * *

2. **Scope of This Section.** This section contains the rules governing the priority of conflicting security interests in investment property. Paragraph (1) states the most important general rule—that a secured party who obtains control has priority over a secured party who does not obtain control. Paragraphs (2) through (4) deal with conflicting security interests each of which is perfected by control. Paragraph (5) addresses the priority of a security interest in a certificated security which is perfected by delivery but not control. Paragraph (6) deals with the relatively unusual circumstance in which a broker, securities intermediary, or commodity intermediary has created conflicting security interests none of which is perfected by control. Paragraph (7) provides that the general priority rules of Sections 9–322 and 9–323 apply to cases not covered by the specific rules in this section. The principal application of this residual rule is that the usual first in time of filing rule applies to conflicting security interests that are perfected only by filing. Because the control priority rule of paragraph (1) provides for the ordinary cases in which persons purchase securities on margin credit from their brokers, there is no need for special rules for purchase-money security interests. See also Section 9–103 (limiting purchase-money collateral to goods and software).

3. **General Rule: Priority of Security Interest Perfected by Control.** Under paragraph (1), a secured party who obtains control has priority over a secured party who does not obtain control. The control priority rule does not turn on either temporal sequence or awareness of conflicting security interests. Rather, it is a structural rule, based on the principle that a lender should be able to rely on the collateral without question if the lender has taken the necessary steps to assure itself that it is in a position where it can foreclose on the collateral without further action by the debtor. The control priority rule is necessary because the perfection rules provide considerable flexibility in structuring secured financing arrangements. For example, at the "retail" level, a secured lender to an investor who wants the full measure of protection can obtain control, but the creditor may be willing to accept the greater measure of risk that follows from perfection by filing. Similarly, at the "wholesale" level, a lender to securities firms can leave the collateral with the debtor and obtain a perfected security interest under the automatic perfection rule of Section 9–309(10), but a lender who wants to be entirely sure of its position will want to obtain control. The control priority rule of paragraph (1) is an essential part of this system of flexibility. It is feasible to provide more than one method of perfecting security interests only if the rules ensure that those who take the necessary steps to obtain the full measure of protection do not run the risk of subordination to those who have not taken such steps. A secured party who is unwilling to run the risk that the debtor has granted or will grant a conflicting control security interest should not make a loan without obtaining control of the collateral.

As applied to the retail level, the control priority rule means that a secured party who obtains control has priority over a conflicting security interest perfected by filing without regard to inquiry into whether the control secured party was aware of the filed security interest. Prior to the 1994 revisions to Articles 8 and 9, Article 9 did not permit perfection of security interests in securities by filing. Accordingly, parties who deal in securities never developed a practice of searching the UCC files before conducting securities transactions. Although filing is now a permissible method of perfection, in order to avoid disruption of existing practices in this business it is necessary to give perfection by filing a different and more limited effect for securities than for some other forms of collateral. The priority rules are not based on the assumption that parties who perfect by the usual method of obtaining control will search the files. Quite the contrary, the control priority rule is intended to ensure that, with respect to investment property, secured parties who do obtain control are entirely unaffected by filings. To state the point another way, perfection by filing is intended to affect only general creditors or other secured creditors who rely on filing. The rule that a security interest perfected by filing can be primed by a control security interest, without regard to awareness, is a consequence of the system of perfection and priority rules for investment property. These rules are designed to take account of the circumstances of the securities markets, where filing is not given the same effect as for some other forms of property. No implication is made about the effect of filing with respect to security interests in other forms of property, nor about other Article 9 rules, e.g., Section 9–330, which govern the circumstances in which security interests in other forms of property perfected by filing can be primed by subsequent perfected security interests.

The following examples illustrate the application of the priority rule in paragraph (1):

Example 1: Debtor borrows from Alpha and grants Alpha a security interest in a variety of collateral, including all of Debtor's investment property. At that time Debtor owns 1000 shares of XYZ Co. stock for which Debtor has a certificate. Alpha perfects by filing. Later, Debtor borrows from Beta and grants Beta a security interest in the 1000 shares of XYZ Co. stock. Debtor delivers the certificate, properly indorsed, to Beta. Alpha and Beta both have perfected security interests in the XYZ Co. stock. Beta has control, see Section 8–106(b)(1), and hence has priority over Alpha.

Example 2: Debtor borrows from Alpha and grants Alpha a security interest in a variety of collateral, including all of Debtor's investment property. At that time Debtor owns 1000 shares of XYZ Co. stock, held through a securities account with Able & Co. Alpha perfects by filing. Later, Debtor borrows from Beta and grants Beta a security interest in the 1000 shares of XYZ Co. stock. Debtor instructs Able to have the 1000 shares transferred through the clearing corporation to Custodian Bank, to be credited to Beta's account with Custodian Bank. Alpha and Beta both have perfected security interests in the XYZ Co. stock. Beta has control, see Section 8–106(d)(1), and hence priority over Alpha.

Example 3: Debtor borrows from Alpha and grants Alpha a security interest in a variety of collateral, including all of Debtor's investment property. At that time Debtor owns 1000 shares of XYZ Co. stock, which is held through a securities account with Able & Co. Alpha perfects by filing. Later, Debtor borrows from Beta and grants Beta a security interest in the 1000 shares of XYZ Co. stock. Debtor, Able, and Beta enter into an agreement under which Debtor will continue to receive dividends and distributions, and will continue to have the right to direct dispositions, but Beta will also have the right to direct dispositions and receive the proceeds. Alpha and Beta both have perfected security interests in the XYZ Co. stock (more precisely, in the Debtor's security entitlement to the financial asset consisting of the XYZ Co. stock). Beta has control, see Section 8–

106(d)(2), and hence has priority over Alpha.

Example 4: Debtor borrows from Alpha and grants Alpha a security interest in a variety of collateral, including all of Debtor's investment property. At that time Debtor owns 1000 shares of XYZ Co. stock, held through a securities account with Able & Co. Alpha perfects by filing. Debtor's agreement with Able & Co. provides that Able has a security interest in all securities carried in the account as security for any obligations of Debtor to Able. Debtor incurs obligations to Able and later defaults on the obligations to Alpha and Able. Able has control by virtue of the rule of Section 8–106(e) that if a customer grants a security interest to its own intermediary, the intermediary has control. Since Alpha does not have control, Able has priority over Alpha under the general control priority rule of paragraph (1).

4. **Conflicting Security Interests Perfected by Control: Priority of Securities Intermediary or Commodity Intermediary.** Paragraphs (2) through (4) govern the priority of conflicting security interests each of which is perfected by control. The following example explains the application of the rules in paragraphs (3) and (4):

Example 5: Debtor holds securities through a securities account with Able & Co. Debtor's agreement with Able & Co. provides that Able has a security interest in all securities carried in the account as security for any obligations of Debtor to Able. Debtor borrows from Beta and grants Beta a security interest in 1000 shares of XYZ Co. stock carried in the account. Debtor, Able, and Beta enter into an agreement under which Debtor will continue to receive dividends and distributions and will continue to have the right to direct dispositions, but Beta will also have the right to direct dispositions and receive the proceeds. Debtor incurs obligations to Able and later defaults on the obligations to Beta and Able. Both Beta and Able have control, so the general control priority rule of paragraph (1) does not apply. Compare Example 4. Paragraph (3) provides that a security interest held by a securities intermediary in positions of its own customer has priority over a conflicting security interest of an external lender, so Able has priority over Beta. (Paragraph (4) contains a parallel rule for commodity intermediaries.) The agreement among Able, Beta, and Debtor could, of course, determine the relative priority of the security interests of Able and Beta, see Section 9–339, but the fact that the intermediary has agreed to act on the instructions of a secured party such as Beta does not itself imply any agreement by the intermediary to subordinate.

5. **Conflicting Security Interests Perfected by Control: Temporal Priority.** Former Section 9–115 introduced into Article 9 the concept of conflicting security interests that rank equally. Paragraph (2) of this section governs priority in those circumstances in which more than one secured party (other than a broker, securities intermediary, or commodity intermediary) has control. It replaces the equal-priority rule for conflicting security interests in investment property with a temporal rule. For securities, both certificated and uncertificated, under paragraph (2)(A) priority is based on the time that control is obtained. For security entitlements carried in securities accounts, the treatment is more complex. Paragraph (2)(B) bases priority on the timing of the steps taken to achieve control. The following example illustrates the application of paragraph (2).

Example 6: Debtor borrows from Alpha and grants Alpha a security interest in a variety of collateral, including all of Debtor's investment property. At that time Debtor owns a security entitlement that includes 1000 shares of XYZ Co. stock that Debtor holds through a securities account with Able & Co. Debtor, Able, and Alpha enter into an agreement under which Debtor will continue to receive dividends and distributions, and will continue to have the right to direct dispositions, but Alpha will also have the right to direct dispositions and receive the proceeds. Later, Debtor borrows from Beta and grants Beta a security interest in all its investment property, existing and after-acquired. Debtor, Able, and Beta enter into an agreement under which Debtor will continue to receive dividends and distributions, and will continue to have the right to direct dispositions, but Beta will also have the right to direct dispositions and receive the proceeds. Alpha and Beta both have perfected-by-control security interests in the security entitlement to the XYZ Co. stock by virtue of their agreements with Able. See Sections 9–314(a), 9–106(a), 8–106(d)(2). Under paragraph (2)(B)(ii), the priority of each security interest dates from the time of the secured party's agreement with Able. Because Alpha's agreement was first in time, Alpha has priority. This priority applies equally to security entitlements to financial assets credited to the account after the agreement was entered into.

The priority rule is analogous to "first-to-file" priority under Section 9–322 with respect to after-acquired collateral. Paragraphs (2)(B)(i) and (2)(B)(iii) provide similar rules for security entitlements as to which control is obtained by other methods, and paragraph (2)(C) provides a similar rule for commodity contracts carried in a commodity account. Section 8–510 also has been revised to provide a temporal priority conforming to paragraph (2)(B).

6. **Certificated Securities.** A longstanding practice has developed whereby secured parties whose collateral consists of a security evidenced by a security certificate take possession of the security certificate. If the security certificate is in bearer form, the secured party's acquisition of possession constitutes "delivery" under Section 8–301(a)(1), and the delivery constitutes "control" under Section 8–106(a). Comment 5 discusses the priority of security interests perfected by control of investment property.

If the security certificate is in registered form, the secured party will not achieve control over the security unless the security certificate contains an appropriate indorsement or is (re)registered in the secured party's name. See Section 8–106(b). However, the secured party's acquisition of possession constitutes "delivery" of the security certificate under Section 8–301 and serves to perfect the security interest under Section 9–313(a), even if the security certificate has not been appropriately indorsed and has not been (re)registered in the secured party's name. A security interest perfected by this method has priority over a security interest perfected other than by control (e.g., by filing). See paragraph (5).

The priority rule stated in paragraph (5) may seem anomalous, in that it can afford less favorable treatment to purchasers who buy collateral outright that to those who take a security interest in it. For example, a buyer of a security certificate would cut off a security interest perfected by filing only if the buyer achieves the status of a protected purchaser under Section 8–303. The buyer would not be a protected purchaser, for example, if it does not obtain "control" under Section 8–106 (e.g., if it fails to obtain a proper indorsement of the certificate) or if it had notice of an adverse claim under Section 8–105. The apparent anomaly disappears, however, when one understands the priority rule not as one intended to protect careless or guilty parties, but as one that eliminates the need to conduct a search of the public records only insofar as necessary to serve the needs of the securities markets.

7. **Secured Financing of Securities Firms.** Priority questions concerning security interests granted by brokers and securities intermediaries are governed by the general control-beats-non-control priority rule of paragraph (1), as supplemented by the special rules set out in paragraphs (2) (temporal priority—first to control), (3) (special priority for securities intermediary), and (6) (equal priority for non-control). The following examples illustrate the priority rules as applied to this setting. (In all cases it is assumed that the debtor retains sufficient other securities to satisfy all customers' claims. This section deals with the relative rights of secured lenders to a securities firm.

Disputes between a secured lender and the firm's own customers are governed by Section 8–511.)

Example 7: Able & Co., a securities dealer, enters into financing arrangements with two lenders, Alpha Bank and Beta Bank. In each case the agreements provide that the lender will have a security interest in the securities identified on lists provided to the lender on a daily basis, that the debtor will deliver the securities to the lender on demand, and that the debtor will not list as collateral any securities which the debtor has pledged to any other lender. Upon Able's insolvency it is discovered that Able has listed the same securities on the collateral lists provided to both Alpha and Beta. Alpha and Beta both have perfected security interests under the automatic-perfection rule of Section 9–309(10). Neither Alpha nor Beta has control. Paragraph (6) provides that the security interests of Alpha and Beta rank equally, because each of them has a non-control security interest granted by a securities firm. They share pro-rata.

Example 8: Able enters into financing arrangements, with Alpha Bank and Beta Bank as in Example 7. At some point, however, Beta decides that it is unwilling to continue to provide financing on a non-control basis. Able directs the clearing corporation where it holds its principal inventory of securities to move specified securities into Beta's account. Upon Able's insolvency it is discovered that a list of collateral provided to Alpha includes securities that had been moved to Beta's account. Both Alpha and Beta have perfected security interests; Alpha under the automatic-perfection rule of Section 9–309(10), and Beta under that rule and also the perfection-by-control rule in Section 9–314(a). Beta has control but Alpha does not. Beta has priority over Alpha under paragraph (1).

Example 9: Able & Co. carries its principal inventory of securities through Clearing Corporation, which offers a "shared control" facility whereby a participant securities firm can enter into an arrangement with a lender under which the securities firm will retain the power to trade and otherwise direct dispositions of securities carried in its account, but Clearing Corporation agrees that, at any time the lender so directs, Clearing Corporation will transfer any securities from the firm's account to the lender's account or otherwise dispose of them as directed by the lender. Able enters into financing arrangements with two lenders, Alpha and Beta, each of which obtains such a control agreement from Clearing Corporation. The agreement with each lender provides that Able will designate specific securities as collateral on lists provided to the lender on a daily or other periodic basis, and that it will not pledge the same securities to different lenders. Upon Able's insolvency, it is discovered that Able has listed the same securities on the collateral lists provided to both Alpha and Beta. Both Alpha and Beta have control over the disputed securities. Paragraph (2) awards priority to whichever secured party first entered into the agreement with Clearing Corporation.

8. **Relation to Other Law.** Section 1–103 provides that "unless displaced by particular provisions of this Act, the principles of law and equity ... shall supplement its provisions." There may be circumstances in which a secured party's action in acquiring a security interest that has priority under this section constitutes conduct that is wrongful under other law. Though the possibility of such resort to other law may provide an appropriate "escape valve" for cases of egregious conduct, care must be taken to ensure that this does not impair the certainty and predictability of the priority rules. Whether a court may appropriately look to other law to impose liability upon or estop a secured party from asserting its Article 9 priority depends on an assessment of the secured party's conduct under the standards established by such other law as well as a determination of whether the particular application of such other law is displaced by the UCC.

Some circumstances in which other law is clearly displaced by the UCC rules are readily identifiable. Common law "first in time, first in right" principles, or correlative tort liability rules such as common law conversion principles under which a purchaser may incur liability to a person with a prior property interest without regard to awareness of that claim, are necessarily displaced by the priority rules set out in this section since these rules determine the relative ranking of security interests in investment property. So too, Article 8 provides protections against adverse claims to certain purchasers of interests in investment property. In circumstances where a secured party not only has priority under Section 9–328, but also qualifies for protection against adverse claims under Section 8–303, 8–502, or 8–510, resort to other law would be precluded.

In determining whether it is appropriate in a particular case to look to other law, account must also be taken of the policies that underlie the commercial law rules on securities markets and security interests in securities. A principal objective of the 1994 revision of Article 8 and the provisions of Article 9 governing investment property was to ensure that secured financing transactions can be implemented on a simple, timely, and certain basis. One of the circumstances that led to the revision was the concern that uncertainty in the application of the rules on secured transactions involving securities and other financial assets could contribute to systemic risk by impairing the ability of financial institutions to provide liquidity to the markets in times of stress. The control priority rule is designed to provide a clear and certain rule to ensure that lenders who have taken the necessary steps to establish control do not face a risk of subordination to other lenders who have not done so.

The control priority rule does not turn on an inquiry into the state of a secured party's awareness of potential conflicting claims because a rule under which a person's rights depended on that sort of after-the-fact inquiry could introduce an unacceptable measure of uncertainty. If an inquiry into awareness could provide a complete and satisfactory resolution of the problem in all cases, the priority rules of this section would have incorporated that test. The fact that they do not necessarily means that resort to other law based solely on that factor is precluded, though the question whether a control secured party induced or encouraged its financing arrangement with actual knowledge that the debtor would be violating the rights of another secured party may, in some circumstances, appropriately be treated as a factor in determining whether the control party's action is the kind of egregious conduct for which resort to other law is appropriate.

§ 9–329. Priority of Security Interests in Letter-of-Credit Right

The following rules govern priority among conflicting security interests in the same letter-of-credit right:

(1) A security interest held by a secured party having control of the letter-of-credit right under Section 9–107 has priority to the extent of its control over a conflicting security interest held by a secured party that does not have control.

(2) Security interests perfected by control under Section 9–314 rank according to priority in time of obtaining control.

OFFICIAL COMMENT

* * *

2. **General Rule.** Paragraph (1) awards priority to a secured party who perfects a security interest directly in letter-of-credit rights (i.e., one that takes an assignment of proceeds and obtains consent of the issuer or any nominated person under Section 5–114(c)) over another conflicting security interest (i.e., one that is perfected automatically in the letter-of-credit rights as supporting obligations under Section 9–308(d)). This is consistent with international letter-of-credit practice and provides finality to payments made to recognized assignees of letter-of-credit proceeds. If an issuer or nominated person recognizes multiple security interests in a letter-of-credit right, resulting in multiple parties having control (Section 9–107), under paragraph (2) the security interests rank according to the time of obtaining control.

3. **Drawing Rights; Transferee Beneficiaries.** Drawing under a letter of credit is personal to the beneficiary and requires the beneficiary to perform the conditions for drawing under the letter of credit. Accordingly, a beneficiary's grant of a security interest in a letter of credit includes the beneficiary's "letter-of-credit right" as defined in Section 9–102 and the right to "proceeds of [the] letter of credit" as defined in Section 5–114(a), but does not include the right to demand payment under the letter of credit.

Section 5–114(e) provides that the "[r]ights of a transferee beneficiary or nominated person are independent of the beneficiary's assignment of the proceeds of a letter of credit and are superior to the assignee's right to the proceeds." To the extent the rights of a transferee beneficiary or nominated person are independent and superior, this Article does not apply. See Section 9–109(c).

Under Article 5, there is in effect a novation upon the transfer with the issuer becoming bound on a new, independent obligation to the transferee. The rights of nominated persons and transferee beneficiaries under a letter of credit include the right to demand payment from the issuer. Under Section 5–114(e), their rights to payment are independent of their obligations to the beneficiary (or original beneficiary) and superior to the rights of assignees of letter-of-credit proceeds (Section 5–114(c)) and others claiming a security interest in the beneficiary's (or original beneficiary's) letter-of-credit rights.

A transfer of drawing rights under a transferable letter of credit establishes independent Article 5 rights in the transferee and does not create or perfect an Article 9 security interest in the transferred drawing rights. The definition of "letter-of-credit right" in Section 9–102 excludes a beneficiary's drawing rights. The exercise of drawing rights by a transferee beneficiary may breach a contractual obligation of the transferee to the original beneficiary concerning when and how much the transferee may draw or how it may use the funds received under the letter of credit. If, for example, drawing rights are transferred to support a sale or loan from the transferee to the original beneficiary, then the transferee would be obligated to the original beneficiary under the sale or loan agreement to account for any drawing and for the use of any funds received. The transferee's obligation would be governed by the applicable law of contracts or restitution.

4. **Secured Party-Transferee Beneficiaries.** As described in Comment 3, drawing rights under letters of credit are transferred in many commercial contexts in which the transferee is not a secured party claiming a security interest in an underlying receivable supported by the letter of credit. Consequently, a transfer of a letter of credit is not a method of "perfection" of a security interest. The transferee's independent right to draw under the letter of credit and to receive and retain the value thereunder (in effect, priority) is not based on Article 9 but on letter-of-credit law and the terms of the letter of credit. Assume, however, that a secured party does hold a security interest in a receivable that is owned by a beneficiary-debtor and supported by a

transferable letter of credit. Assume further that the beneficiary-debtor causes the letter of credit to be transferred to the secured party, the secured party draws under the letter of credit, and, upon the issuer's payment to the secured party-transferee, the underlying account debtor's obligation to the original beneficiary-debtor is satisfied. In this situation, the payment to the secured party-transferee is proceeds of the receivable collected by the secured party-transferee. Consequently, the secured party-transferee would have certain duties to the debtor and third parties under Article 9. For example, it would be obliged to collect under the letter of credit in a commercially reasonable manner and to remit any surplus pursuant to Sections 9–607 and 9–608.

This scenario is problematic under letter-of-credit law and practice, inasmuch as a transferee beneficiary collects in its own right arising from its own performance. Accordingly, under Section 5–114, the independent and superior rights of a transferee control over any inconsistent duties under Article 9. A transferee beneficiary may take a transfer of drawing rights to avoid reliance on the original beneficiary's credit and collateral, and it may consider any Article 9 rights superseded by its Article 5 rights. Moreover, it will not always be clear (i) whether a transferee beneficiary has a security interest in the underlying collateral, (ii) whether any security interest is senior to the rights of others, or (iii) whether the transferee beneficiary is aware that it holds a security interest. There will be clear cases in which the role of a transferee beneficiary as such is merely incidental to a conventional secured financing. There also will be cases in which the existence of a security interest may have little to do with the position of a transferee beneficiary as such. In dealing with these cases and less clear cases involving the possible application of Article 9 to a nominated person or a transferee beneficiary, the right to demand payment under a letter of credit should be distinguished from letter-of-credit rights. The courts also should give appropriate consideration to the policies and provisions of Article 5 and letter-of-credit practice as well as Article 9.

§ 9–330. Priority of Purchaser of Chattel Paper or Instrument

(a) [Purchaser's priority: security interest claimed merely as proceeds.] A purchaser of chattel paper has priority over a security interest in the chattel paper which is claimed merely as proceeds of inventory subject to a security interest if:

(1) in good faith and in the ordinary course of the purchaser's business, the purchaser gives new value and takes possession of the chattel paper or obtains control of the chattel paper under Section 9–105; and

(2) the chattel paper does not indicate that it has been assigned to an identified assignee other than the purchaser.

(b) [Purchaser's priority: other security interests.] A purchaser of chattel paper has priority over a security interest in the chattel paper which is claimed other than merely as proceeds of inventory subject to a security interest if the purchaser gives new value and takes possession of the chattel paper or obtains control of the chattel paper under Section 9–105 in good faith, in the ordinary course of the purchaser's business, and without knowledge that the purchase violates the rights of the secured party.

(c) [Chattel paper purchaser's priority in proceeds.] Except as otherwise provided in Section 9–327, a purchaser having priority in chattel paper under subsection (a) or (b) also has priority in proceeds of the chattel paper to the extent that:

(1) Section 9–322 provides for priority in the proceeds; or

(2) the proceeds consist of the specific goods covered by the chattel paper or cash proceeds of the specific goods, even if the purchaser's security interest in the proceeds is unperfected.

(d) [Instrument purchaser's priority.] Except as otherwise provided in Section 9–331(a), a purchaser of an instrument has priority over a security interest in the instrument perfected by a method other than possession if the purchaser gives value and takes possession of the instrument in good faith and without knowledge that the purchase violates the rights of the secured party.

(e) [Holder of purchase-money security interest gives new value.] For purposes of subsections (a) and (b), the holder of a purchase-money security interest in inventory gives new value for chattel paper constituting proceeds of the inventory.

(f) [Indication of assignment gives knowledge.] For purposes of subsections (b) and (d), if chattel paper or an instrument indicates that it has been assigned to an identified secured party other than the purchaser, a purchaser of the chattel paper or instrument has knowledge that the purchase violates the rights of the secured party.

UNOFFICIAL COMMENTS

This is another exception to the first to file or perfect priority rule of section 9–322.

A purchaser of chattel paper (which includes a secured party with a security interest in chattel paper) can take priority over an earlier in time perfected security interest by satisfying the requirements of either section 9–330(a) or (b).

Subsections (a) and (b) are very similar in their requirements. Both subsections require that the secured party (1) take the security interest in good faith and in the ordinary course of the secured party's business; (2) give new value for the chattel paper; and (3) that obtain possession (or, if electronic, obtain control) of the chattel paper.

In addition to these common requirements, subsection (a) requires that the chattel paper not have a legend indicating the existence of a security interest. *See* 9–330(a)(2).

Subsection (b), by contrast, requires that the secured party not have "knowledge that the purchase violates the rights of the secured party." Note subsection (e): if there is a legend of the type mentioned in subsection (a)(2), then, by definition, the secured party has knowledge.

Be careful to distinguish (a) from (b): if "merely as proceeds" do (a). And if you are doing (a), then the later secured party in possession will prevail unless there is a "legend." And if you are doing (b), the legend is simply one form of knowledge.

And, again, be careful to distinguish "new value," section 9–102(a)(57), from "value," section 1–204.

Section 9–330(d) provides a rule similar to subsections (a) and (b) for instruments. Note, however, that there is no "ordinary course of the purchaser's business" requirement. Note also that this subsection requires "value," whereas (a) and (b) require "new value." Therefore, for a secured party to take free of a prior perfected security interest under this subsection, it must (1) give value; (2) take possession of the instrument; and (3) take the instrument in good faith and without knowledge that its purchase violates the rights of the prior perfected secured party.

NON–OBVIOUS DEFINITIONS

The section 9–102 definition of "chattel paper" is not easy to understand but is important to understand. Again, a chattel paper transaction is a "second generation" or second stage transaction. The secured party from the first transaction is the debtor (or seller) in the second transaction. And the "paper" from the first transaction is the collateral (or what is sold) in the second transaction.

The terms "purchase" and "purchaser" as defined in section 1–201 do not always involve a sale or buyer. A secured party is a purchaser.

"Value" as defined in "1–204 is not always "new value" as defined by section 9–102(a)(57) and used in this section: while satisfying an antecedent debt is value, it is not "new value" as required by this section.

And notice is different from knowledge and knowledge as "defined" in section 9–330(p).

And the term "instrument" as defined in section 9–102(a)(47) never involves a guitar or piano.

While the word "proceeds" is defined in section 9–102(a)(6) , the important phrase "merely as proceeds" is defined only in case law.

OFFICIAL COMMENT

* * *

2. **Non-Temporal Priority.** This Article permits a security interest in chattel paper or instruments to be perfected either by filing or by the secured party's taking possession. This section enables secured parties and other purchasers of chattel paper (both electronic and tangible) and instruments to obtain priority over earlier-perfected security interests.

3. **Chattel Paper.** Subsections (a) and (b) follow former Section 9–308 in distinguishing between earlier-perfected security interests in chattel paper that is claimed merely as proceeds of inventory subject to a security interest and chattel paper that is claimed other than merely as proceeds. Like former Section 9–308, this section does not elaborate upon the phrase "merely as proceeds." For an elaboration, see PEB Commentary No. 8.

This section makes explicit the "good faith" requirement and retains the requirements of "the ordinary course of the purchaser's business" and the giving of "new value" as conditions for priority. Concerning the last, this Article deletes former Section 9–108 and adds to Section 9–102 a completely different definition of the term "new value." Under subsection (e), the holder of a purchase-money security interest in inventory is deemed to give "new value" for chattel paper constituting the proceeds of the inventory. Accordingly, the purchase-money secured party may qualify for priority in the chattel paper under subsection (a) or (b), whichever is applicable, even if it does not make an additional advance against the chattel paper.

If a possessory security interest in tangible chattel paper or a perfected-by-control security interest in electronic chattel paper does not qualify for priority under this section, it may be subordinate to a perfected-by-filing security interest under Section 9–322(a)(1).

4. **Possession.** The priority afforded by this section turns in part on whether a purchaser "takes possession" of tangible chattel paper. Similarly, the governing law provisions in Section 9–301 address both "possessory" and "nonpossessory" security interests. Two common practices have raised particular concerns. First, in some cases the parties create more than one copy or counterpart of chattel paper evidencing a single secured obligation or lease. This practice raises questions as to which counterpart is the "original" and whether it is necessary for a purchaser to take possession of all counterparts in order to "take possession" of the chattel paper. Second, parties sometimes enter into a single "master" agreement. The master agreement contemplates that the parties will enter into separate "schedules" from time to time, each evidencing chattel paper. Must a purchaser of an obligation or lease evidenced by a single schedule also take possession of the master agreement as well as the schedule in order to "take possession" of the chattel paper?

The problem raised by the first practice is easily solved. The parties may in the terms of their agreement and by designation on the chattel paper identify only one counterpart as the original chattel paper for purposes of taking possession of the chattel paper. Concerns about the second practice also are easily solved by careful drafting. Each schedule should provide that it incorporates the terms of the master agreement, not the other way around. This will make it clear that each schedule is a "stand alone" document.

5. **Chattel Paper Claimed Merely as Proceeds.** Subsection (a) revises the rule in former Section 9–308(b) to eliminate reference to what the purchaser knows. Instead, a purchaser who meets the possession or control, ordinary course, and new value requirements takes priority over a competing security interest unless the chattel paper itself indicates that it has been assigned to an identified assignee other than the purchaser. Thus subsection (a) recognizes the common practice of placing a "legend" on chattel paper to indicate that it has been assigned. This approach, under which the chattel paper purchaser who gives new

value in ordinary course can rely on possession of unlegended, tangible chattel paper without any concern for other facts that it may know, comports with the expectations of both inventory and chattel paper financers.

6. **Chattel Paper Claimed Other Than Merely as Proceeds.** Subsection (b) eliminates the requirement that the purchaser take without knowledge that the "specific paper" is subject to the security interest and substitutes for it the requirement that the purchaser take "without knowledge that the purchase violates the rights of the secured party." This standard derives from the definition of "buyer in ordinary course of business" in Section 1–201(9). The source of the purchaser's knowledge is irrelevant. Note, however, that "knowledge" means "actual knowledge." Section 1–201(25).

In contrast to a junior secured party in accounts, who may be required in some special circumstances to undertake a search under the "good faith" requirement, see Comment 5 to Section 9–331, a purchaser of chattel paper under this section is not required as a matter of good faith to make a search in order to determine the existence of prior security interests. There may be circumstances where the purchaser undertakes a search nevertheless, either on its own volition or because other considerations make it advisable to do so, e.g., where the purchaser also is purchasing accounts. Without more, a purchaser of chattel paper who has seen a financing statement covering the chattel paper or who knows that the chattel paper is encumbered with a security interest, does not have knowledge that its purchase violates the secured party's rights. However, if a purchaser sees a statement in a financing statement to the effect that a purchase of chattel paper from the debtor would violate the rights of the filed secured party, the purchaser would have such knowledge. Likewise, under new subsection (f), if the chattel paper itself indicates that it had been assigned to an identified secured party other than the purchaser, the purchaser would have wrongful knowledge for purposes of subsection (b), thereby preventing the purchaser from qualifying for priority under that subsection, even if the purchaser did not have actual knowledge. In the case of tangible chattel paper, the indication normally would consist of a written legend on the chattel paper. In the case of electronic chattel paper, this Article leaves to developing market and technological practices the manner in which the chattel paper would indicate an assignment.

7. **Instruments.** Subsection (d) contains a special priority rule for instruments. Under this subsection, a purchaser of an instrument has priority over a security interest perfected by a method other than possession (e.g., by filing, temporarily under Section 9–312(e) or (g), as proceeds under Section 9–315(d), or automatically upon attachment under Section 9–309(4) if the security interest arises out of a sale of the instrument) if the purchaser gives value and takes possession of the instrument in good faith and without knowledge that the purchase violates the rights of the secured party. Generally, to the extent subsection (d) conflicts with Section 3–306, subsection (d) governs. See Section 3–102(b). For example, notice of a conflicting security interest precludes a purchaser from becoming a holder in due course under Section 3–302 and thereby taking free of all claims to the instrument under Section 3–306. However, a purchaser who takes even with knowledge of the security interest qualifies for priority under subsection (d) if it takes without knowledge that the purchase violates the rights of the holder of the security interest. Likewise, a purchaser qualifies for priority under subsection (d) if it takes for "value" as defined in Section 1–201, even if it does not take for "value" as defined in Section 3–303.

Subsection (d) is subject to Section 9–331(a), which provides that Article 9 does not limit the rights of a holder in due course under Article 3. Thus, in the rare case in which the purchaser of an instrument qualifies for priority under subsection (d), but another person has the rights of a holder in due course of the instrument, the other person takes free of the purchaser's claim. See Section 3–306.

The rule in subsection (d) is similar to the rules in subsections (a) and (b), which govern priority in chattel paper. The observations in Comment 6 concerning the requirement of good faith and the phrase "without knowledge that the purchase violates the rights of the secured party" apply equally to purchasers of instruments. However, unlike a purchaser of chattel paper, to qualify for priority under this section a purchaser of an instrument need only give "value" as defined in Section 1–201; it need not give "new value." Also, the purchaser need not purchase the instrument in the ordinary course of its business.

Subsection (d) applies to checks as well as notes. For example, to collect and retain checks that are proceeds (collections) of accounts free of a senior secured party's claim to the same checks, a junior secured party must satisfy the good-faith requirement (honesty in fact and the observance of reasonable commercial standards of fair dealing) of this subsection. This is the same good-faith requirement applicable to holders in due course. See Section 9–331, Comment 5.

8. **Priority in Proceeds of Chattel Paper.** Subsection (c) sets forth the two circumstances under which the priority afforded to a purchaser of chattel paper under subsection (a) or (b) extends also to proceeds of the chattel paper. The first is if the purchaser would have priority under the normal priority rules applicable to proceeds. The second, which the following Comments discuss in greater detail, is if the proceeds consist of the specific goods covered by the chattel paper. Former Article 9 generally was silent as to the priority of a security interest in proceeds when a purchaser qualifies for priority under Section 9–308 (but see former Section 9–306(5)(b), concerning returned and repossessed goods).

9. **Priority in Returned and Repossessed Goods.** Returned and repossessed goods may constitute proceeds of chattel paper. The following Comments explain the treatment of returned and repossessed goods as proceeds of chattel paper. The analysis is consistent with that of PEB Commentary No. 5, which these Comments replace, and is based upon the following example:

Example: SP–1 has a security interest in all the inventory of a dealer in goods (Dealer); SP–1's security interest is perfected by filing. Dealer sells some of its inventory to a buyer in the ordinary course of business (BIOCOB) pursuant to a conditional sales contract (chattel paper) that does not indicate that it has been assigned to SP–1. SP–2 purchases the chattel paper from Dealer and takes possession of the paper in good faith, in the ordinary course of business, and without knowledge that the purchase violates the rights of SP–1. Subsequently, BIOCOB returns the goods to Dealer because they are defective. Alternatively, Dealer acquires possession of the goods following BIOCOB's default.

10. **Assignment of Non-Lease Chattel Paper.**

a. **Loan by SP–2 to Dealer Secured by Chattel Paper (or Functional Equivalent Pursuant to Recourse Arrangement).**

(1) **Returned Goods.** If BIOCOB returns the goods to Dealer for repairs, Dealer is merely a bailee and acquires thereby no meaningful rights in the goods to which SP–1's security interest could attach. (Although SP–1's security interest could attach to Dealer's interest as a bailee, that interest is not likely to be of any particular value to SP–1.) Dealer is the owner of the *chattel paper* (i.e., the owner of a right to payment secured by a security interest in the goods); SP–2 has a security interest in the chattel paper, as does SP–1 (as proceeds of the goods under Section 9–315). Under Section 9–330, SP–2's security interest in the chattel paper is senior to that of SP–1. SP–2 enjoys this priority regardless of whether, or when, SP–2 filed a financing statement covering the chattel paper. Because chattel paper and goods represent different types of collateral, Dealer does not have any meaningful interest in *goods* to which either SP–1's or SP–2's security interest could attach in order to secure Dealer's obligations to either creditor. See Section 9–

102 (defining "chattel paper" and "goods").

Now assume that BIOCOB returns the goods to Dealer under circumstances whereby Dealer once again becomes the owner of the goods. This would be the case, for example, if the goods were defective and BIOCOB was entitled to reject or revoke acceptance of the goods. See Sections 2–602 (rejection), 2–608 (revocation of acceptance). Unless BIOCOB has waived its defenses as against assignees of the chattel paper, SP–1's and SP–2's rights against BIOCOB would be subject to BIOCOB's claims and defenses. See Sections 9–403, 9–404. SP–1's security interest would attach again because the returned goods would be proceeds of the chattel paper. Dealer's acquisition of the goods easily can be characterized as "proceeds" consisting of an "in kind" collection on or distribution on account of the chattel paper. See Section 9–102 (definition of "proceeds"). Assuming that SP–1's security interest is perfected by filing against the goods and that the filing is made in the same office where a filing would be made against the chattel paper, SP–1's security interest in the goods would remain perfected beyond the 20–day period of automatic perfection. See Section 9–315(d).

Because Dealer's newly reacquired interest in the goods is proceeds of the chattel paper, SP–2's security interest also would attach in the goods as proceeds. If SP–2 had perfected its security interest in the chattel paper by filing (again, assuming that filing against the chattel paper was made in the same office where a filing would be made against the goods), SP–2's security interest in the reacquired goods would be perfected beyond 20 days. See Section 9–315(d). However, if SP–2 had relied only on its possession of the chattel paper for perfection and had not filed against the chattel paper or the goods, SP–2's security interest would be unperfected after the 20–day period. See Section 9–315(d). Nevertheless, SP–2's unperfected security interest in the goods would be senior to SP–1's security interest under Section 9–330(c). The result in this priority contest is not affected by SP–2's acquiescence or non-acquiescence in the return of the goods to Dealer.

(2) **Repossessed Goods.** As explained above, Dealer owns the chattel paper covering the goods, subject to security interests in favor of SP–1 and SP–2. In Article 9 parlance, Dealer has an interest in chattel paper, not goods. If Dealer, SP–1, or SP–2 repossesses the goods upon BIOCOB's default, whether the repossession is rightful or wrongful as among Dealer, SP–1, or SP–2, Dealer's interest will not change. The location of goods and the party who possesses them does not affect the fact that Dealer's interest is in chattel paper, not goods. The goods continue to be owned by BIOCOB. SP–1's security interest in the goods does not attach until such time as Dealer reacquires an interest (other than a bare possessory interest) in the goods. For example, Dealer might buy the goods at a foreclosure sale from SP–2 (whose security interest in the chattel paper is senior to that of SP–1); that disposition would cut off BIOCOB's rights in the goods. Section 9–617.

In many cases the matter would end upon sale of the goods to Dealer at a foreclosure sale and there would be no priority contest between SP–1 and SP–2; Dealer would be unlikely to buy the goods under circumstances whereby SP–2 would retain its security interest. There can be exceptions, however. For example, Dealer may be obliged to purchase the goods from SP–2 and SP–2 may be obliged to convey the goods to Dealer, but Dealer may fail to pay SP–2. Or, one could imagine that SP–2, like SP–1, has a general security interest in the inventory of Dealer. In the latter case, SP–2 should not receive the benefit of any special priority rule, since its interest in no way derives from priority under Section 9–330. In the former case, SP–2's security interest in the goods reacquired by Dealer is senior to SP–1's security interest under Section 9–330.

b. **Dealer's Outright Sale of Chattel Paper to SP–2.** Article 9 also applies to a transaction whereby SP–2 buys the chattel paper in an outright sale transaction without recourse against Dealer. Sections 1–201(37), 9–109(a). Although Dealer does not, in such a transaction, retain any residual ownership interest in the chattel paper, the chattel paper constitutes proceeds of the goods to which SP–1's security interest will attach and continue following the sale of the goods. Section 9–315(a). Even though Dealer has not retained any interest in the chattel paper, as discussed above BIOCOB subsequently may return the goods to Dealer under circumstances whereby Dealer reacquires an interest in the goods. The priority contest between SP–1 and SP–2 will be resolved as discussed above; Section 9–330 makes no distinction among purchasers of chattel paper on the basis of whether the purchaser is an outright buyer of chattel paper or one whose security interest secures an obligation of Dealer.

11. **Assignment of Lease Chattel Paper.** As defined in Section 9–102, "chattel paper" includes not only writings that evidence security interests in specific goods but also those that evidence true leases of goods.

The analysis with respect to lease chattel paper is similar to that set forth above with respect to non-lease chattel paper. It is complicated, however, by the fact that, unlike the case of chattel paper arising out of a sale, Dealer retains a residual interest in the *goods*. See Section 2A–103(1)(q) (defining "lessor's residual interest"); *In re Leasing Consultants, Inc.*, 486 F.2d 367 (2d Cir. 1973) (lessor's residual interest under true lease is an interest in goods and is a separate type of collateral from lessor's interest in the lease). If Dealer leases goods to a "lessee in ordinary course of business" (LIOCOB), then LIOCOB takes its interest under the lease (i.e., its "leasehold interest") free of the security interest of SP–1. See Sections 2A–307(3), 2A–103(1)(m) (defining "leasehold interest"), (1)(o) (defining "lessee in ordinary course of business"). SP–1 would, however, retain its security interest in the residual interest. In addition, SP–1 would acquire an interest in the lease chattel paper as proceeds. If Dealer then assigns the lease chattel paper to SP–2, Section 9–330 gives SP–2 priority over SP–1 with respect to the chattel paper, *but not* with respect to the residual interest in the *goods*. Consequently, assignees of lease chattel paper typically take a security interest in and file against the lessor's residual interest in goods, expecting their priority in the goods to be governed by the first-to-file-or-perfect rule of Section 9–322.

If the goods are returned to Dealer, other than upon expiration of the lease term, then the security interests of both SP–1 and SP–2 normally would attach to the goods as proceeds of the chattel paper. (If the goods are returned to Dealer at the expiration of the lease term and the lessee has made all payments due under the lease, however, then Dealer no longer has any rights under the chattel paper. Dealer's interest in the goods consists solely of its residual interest, as to which SP–2 has no claim.) This would be the case, for example, when the lessee rescinds the lease or when the lessor recovers possession in the exercise of its remedies under Article 2A. See, e.g., Section 2A–525. If SP–2 enjoyed priority in the chattel paper under Section 9–330, then SP–2 likewise would enjoy priority in the returned goods as proceeds. This does not mean that SP–2 necessarily is entitled to the entire value of the returned goods. The value of the goods represents the sum of the present value of (i) the value of their use for the term of the lease and (ii) the value of the residual interest. SP–2 has priority in the former, but SP–1 ordinarily would have priority in the latter. Thus, an allocation of a portion of the value of the goods to each component may be necessary. Where, as here, one secured party has a security interest in the lessor's residual interest and another has a priority security interest in the chattel paper, it may be advisable for the conflicting secured parties to establish a method for making such an allocation and otherwise to determine their relative rights in returned goods by agreement.

§ 9–331. Priority of Rights of Purchasers of Instruments, Documents, and Securities Under Other Articles; Priority of Interests in Financial Assets and Security Entitlements Under Article 8

(a) [Rights under Articles 3, 7, and 8 not limited.] This article does not limit the rights of a holder in due course of a negotiable instrument, a holder to which a negotiable document of title has been duly negotiated, or a protected purchaser of a security. These holders or purchasers take priority over an earlier security interest, even if perfected, to the extent provided in Articles 3, 7, and 8.

(b) [Protection under Article 8.] This article does not limit the rights of or impose liability on a person to the extent that the person is protected against the assertion of a claim under Article 8.

(c) [Filing not notice.] Filing under this article does not constitute notice of a claim or defense to the holders, or purchasers, or persons described in subsections (a) and (b).

UNOFFICIAL COMMENTS

Section 9–331 applies only to certain types of collateral that are treated extensively, and primarily, under other Articles of the UCC (and other law school courses): instruments, documents, securities, security entitlements, and financial assets. This section provides the general rule that Article 9 will not hinder rights established under Articles 3, 7, or 8 with respect to this collateral. Essentially what all this means is that the rules of negotiability carry over to Article 9.

OFFICIAL COMMENT

* * *

2. **"Priority."** In some provisions, this Article distinguishes between claimants that take collateral free of a security interest (in the sense that the security interest no longer encumbers the collateral) and those that take an interest in the collateral that is senior to a surviving security interest. See, e.g., Section 9–317. Whether a holder or purchaser referred to in this section takes free or is senior to a security interest depends on whether the purchaser is a buyer of the collateral or takes a security interest in it. The term "priority" is meant to encompass both scenarios, as it does in Section 9–330.

3. **Rights Acquired by Purchasers.** The rights to which this section refers are set forth in Sections 3–305 and 3–306 (holder in due course), 7–502 (holder to whom a negotiable document of title has been duly negotiated), and 8–303 (protected purchaser). The holders and purchasers referred to in this section do not always take priority over a security interest. See, e.g., Section 7–503 (affording paramount rights to certain owners and secured parties as against holder to whom a negotiable document of title has been duly negotiated). Accordingly, this section adds the clause, "to the extent provided in Articles 3, 7, and 8" to former Section 9–309.

4. **Financial Assets and Security Entitlements.** New subsection (b) provides explicit protection for those who deal with financial assets and security entitlements and who are immunized from liability under Article 8. See, e.g., Sections 8–502, 8–503(e), 8–510, 8–511. The new subsection makes explicit in Article 9 what is implicit in former Article 9 and explicit in several provisions of Article 8. It does not change the law.

5. **Collections by Junior Secured Party.** Under this section, a secured party with a junior security interest in receivables (accounts, chattel paper, promissory notes, or payment intangibles) may collect and retain the proceeds of those receivables free of the claim of a senior secured party to the same receivables, if the junior secured party is a holder in due course of the proceeds. In order to qualify as a holder in due course, the junior must satisfy the requirements of Section 3–302, which include taking in "good faith." This means that the junior not only must act "honestly" but also must observe "reasonable commercial standards of fair dealing" under the particular circumstances. See Section 9–102(a). Although "good faith" does not impose a general duty of inquiry, e.g., a search of the records in filing offices, there may be circumstances in which "reasonable commercial standards of fair dealing" would require such a search.

Consider, for example, a junior secured party in the business of financing or buying accounts who fails to undertake a search to determine the existence of prior security interests. Because a search, under the usages of trade of that business, would enable it to know or learn upon reasonable inquiry that collecting the accounts violated the rights of a senior secured party, the junior may fail to meet the good-faith standard. See Utility Contractors Financial Services, Inc. v. Amsouth Bank, NA, 985 F.2d 1554 (11th Cir. 1993). Likewise, a junior secured party who collects accounts when it knows or should know under the particular circumstances that doing so would violate the rights of a senior secured party, because the debtor had agreed not to grant a junior security interest in, or sell, the accounts, may not meet the good-faith test. Thus, if a junior secured party conducted or should have conducted a search and a financing statement filed on behalf of the senior secured party states such a restriction, the junior's collection would not meet the good-faith standard. On the other hand, if there was a course of performance between the senior secured party and the debtor which placed no such restrictions on the debtor and allowed the debtor to collect and use the proceeds without any restrictions, the junior secured party may then satisfy the requirements for being a holder in due course. This would be more likely in those circumstances where the junior secured party was providing additional financing to the debtor on an on-going basis by lending against or buying the accounts and had no notice of any restrictions against doing so. Generally, the senior secured party would not be prejudiced because the practical effect of such payment to the junior secured party is little different than if the debtor itself had made the collections and subsequently paid the secured party from the debtor's general funds. Absent collusion, the junior secured party would take the funds free of the senior security interests. See Section 9–332. In contrast, the senior secured party is likely to be prejudiced if the debtor is going out of business and the junior secured party collects the accounts by notifying the account debtors to make payments directly to the junior. Those collections may not be consistent with "reasonable commercial standards of fair dealing."

Whether the junior secured party qualifies as a holder in due course is fact-sensitive and should be decided on a case-by-case basis in the light of those circumstances. Decisions such as Financial Management Services, Inc. v. Familian, 905 P.2d 506 (Ariz. App. Div. 1995) (finding holder in due course status) could be determined differently under this application of the good-faith requirement.

The concepts addressed in this Comment are also applicable to junior secured parties as purchasers of instruments under Section 9–330(d). See Section 9–330, Comment 7.

§ 9–332. Transfer of Money; Transfer of Funds From Deposit Account

(a) [Transferee of money.] A transferee of money takes the money free of a security interest unless the transferee acts in collusion with the debtor in violating the rights of the secured party.

(b) [Transferee of funds from deposit account.] A transferee of funds from a deposit account takes the funds free of a security interest in the deposit account unless the transferee acts in collusion with the debtor in violating the rights of the secured party.

OFFICIAL COMMENT

* * *

2. **Scope of This Section.** This section affords broad protection to transferees who take funds from a deposit account and to those who take money. The term "transferee" is not defined; however, the debtor itself is not a transferee. Thus this section does not cover the case in which a debtor withdraws money (currency) from its deposit account or the case in which a bank debits an encumbered account and credits another account it maintains for the debtor.

A transfer of funds from a deposit account, to which subsection (b) applies, normally will be made by check, by funds transfer, or by debiting the debtor's deposit account and crediting another depositor's account.

Example 1: Debtor maintains a deposit account with Bank A. The deposit account is subject to a perfected security interest in favor of Lender. Debtor draws a check on the account, payable to Payee. Inasmuch as the check is not the proceeds of the deposit account (it is an order to pay funds from the deposit account), Lender's security interest in the deposit account does not give rise to a security interest in the check. Payee deposits the check into its own deposit account, and Bank A pays it. Unless Payee acted in collusion with Debtor in violating Lender's rights, Payee takes the funds (the credits running in favor of Payee) free of Lender's security interest. This is true regardless of whether Payee is a holder in due course of the check and even if Payee gave no value for the check.

Example 2: Debtor maintains a deposit account with Bank A. The deposit account is subject to a perfected security interest in favor of Lender. At Bank B's suggestion, Debtor moves the funds from the account at Bank A to Debtor's deposit account with Bank B. Unless Bank B acted in collusion with Debtor in violating Lender's rights, Bank B takes the funds (the credits running in favor of Bank B) free from Lender's security interest. See subsection (b). However, inasmuch as the deposit account maintained with Bank B constitutes the proceeds of the deposit account at Bank A, Lender's security interest would attach to that account as proceeds. See Section 9–315.

Subsection (b) also would apply if, in the example, Bank A debited Debtor's deposit account in exchange for the issuance of Bank A's cashier's check. Lender's security interest would attach to the cashier's check as proceeds of the deposit account, and the rules applicable to instruments would govern any competing claims to the cashier's check. See, e.g., Sections 3–306, 9–322, 9–330, 9–331.

If Debtor withdraws money (currency) from an encumbered deposit account and transfers the money to a third party, then subsection (a), to the extent not displaced by federal law relating to money, applies. It contains the same rule as subsection (b).

Subsection (b) applies to *transfers of funds from* a deposit account; it does not apply to *transfers of the deposit account* itself or of an interest therein. For example, this section does not apply to the creation of a security interest in a deposit account. Competing claims to the deposit account itself are dealt with by other Article 9 priority rules. See Sections 9–317(a), 9–327, 9–340, 9–341. Similarly, a corporate merger normally would not result in a transfer of funds from a deposit account. Rather, it might result in a transfer of the deposit account itself. If so, the normal rules applicable to transferred collateral would apply; this section would not.

3. **Policy.** Broad protection for transferees helps to ensure that security interests in deposit accounts do not impair the free flow of funds. It also minimizes the likelihood that a secured party will enjoy a claim to whatever the transferee purchases with the funds. Rules concerning recovery of payments traditionally have placed a high value on finality. The opportunity to upset a completed transaction, or even to place a completed transaction in jeopardy by bringing suit against the transferee of funds, should be severely limited. Although the giving of value usually is a prerequisite for receiving the ability to take free from third-party claims, where payments are concerned the law is even more protective. Thus, Section 3–418(c) provides that, even where the law of restitution otherwise would permit recovery of funds paid by mistake, no recovery may be had from a person "who in good faith changed position in reliance on the payment." Rather than adopt this standard, this section eliminates all reliance requirements whatsoever. Payments made by mistake are relatively rare, but payments of funds from encumbered deposit accounts (e.g., deposit accounts containing collections from accounts receivable) occur with great regularity. In most cases, unlike payment by mistake, no one would object to these payments. In the vast proportion of cases, the transferee probably would be able to show a change of position in reliance on the payment. This section does not put the transferee to the burden of having to make this proof.

4. **"Bad Actors."** To deal with the question of the "bad actor," this section borrows "collusion" language from Article 8. See, e.g., Sections 8–115, 8–503(e). This is the most protective (i.e., least stringent) of the various standards now found in the UCC. Compare, e.g., Section 1–201(9) ("without knowledge that the sale ... is in violation of the ... security interest"); Section 1–201(19) ("honesty in fact in the conduct or transaction concerned"); Section 3–302(a)(2)(v) ("without notice of any claim").

5. **Transferee Who Does Not Take Free.** This section sets forth the circumstances under which certain transferees of money or funds take free of security interests. It does not determine the rights of a transferee who does not take free of a security interest.

Example 3: The facts are as in Example 2, but, in wrongfully moving the funds from the deposit account at Bank A to Debtor's deposit account with Bank B, Debtor acts in collusion with Bank B. Bank B does not take the funds free of Lender's security interest under this section. If Debtor grants a security interest to Bank B, Section 9–327 governs the relative priorities of Lender and Bank B. Under Section 9–327(3), Bank B's security interest in the Bank B deposit account is senior to Lender's security interest in the deposit account as proceeds. However, Bank B's senior security interest does not protect Bank B against any liability to Lender that might arise from Bank B's wrongful conduct.

§ 9–333. Priority of Certain Liens Arising by Operation of Law

(a) ["Possessory lien."] In this section, "possessory lien" means an interest, other than a security interest or an agricultural lien:

> **(1)** which secures payment or performance of an obligation for services or materials furnished with respect to goods by a person in the ordinary course of the person's business;
>
> **(2)** which is created by statute or rule of law in favor of the person; and
>
> **(3)** whose effectiveness depends on the person's possession of the goods.

(b) [Priority of possessory lien.] A possessory lien on goods has priority over a security interest in the goods unless the lien is created by a statute that expressly provides otherwise.

OFFICIAL COMMENT

* * *

2. **"Possessory Liens."** This section governs the relative priority of security interests arising under this Article and "possessory liens," i.e., common-law and statutory liens whose effectiveness depends on the lienor's possession of goods with respect to which the lienor provided services or furnished materials in the ordinary course of its business. As under former Section 9–310, the possessory lien has priority over a security interest unless the possessory lien is created by a statute that expressly provides otherwise. If the statute creating the possessory lien is silent as to its priority relative to a security interest, this section provides a rule of interpretation that the possessory lien takes priority, even if the statute has been construed judicially to make the possessory lien subordinate.

§ 9–334. Priority of Security Interests in Fixtures and Crops

(a) [Security interest in fixtures under this article.] A security interest under this article may be created in goods that are fixtures or may continue in goods that become fixtures. A security interest does not exist under this article in ordinary building materials incorporated into an improvement on land.

(b) [Security interest in fixtures under real-property law.] This article does not prevent creation of an encumbrance upon fixtures under real property law.

(c) [General rule: subordination of security interest in fixtures.] In cases not governed by subsections (d) through (h), a security interest in fixtures is subordinate to a conflicting interest of an encumbrancer or owner of the related real property other than the debtor.

(d) [Fixtures purchase-money priority.] Except as otherwise provided in subsection (h), a perfected security interest in fixtures has priority over a conflicting interest of an encumbrancer or owner of the real property if the debtor has an interest of record in or is in possession of the real property and:

(1) the security interest is a purchase-money security interest;

(2) the interest of the encumbrancer or owner arises before the goods become fixtures; and

(3) the security interest is perfected by a fixture filing before the goods become fixtures or within 20 days thereafter.

(e) [Priority of security interest in fixtures over interests in real property.] A perfected security interest in fixtures has priority over a conflicting interest of an encumbrancer or owner of the real property if:

(1) the debtor has an interest of record in the real property or is in possession of the real property and the security interest:

(A) is perfected by a fixture filing before the interest of the encumbrancer or owner is of record; and

(B) has priority over any conflicting interest of a predecessor in title of the encumbrancer or owner;

(2) before the goods become fixtures, the security interest is perfected by any method permitted by this article and the fixtures are readily removable:

(A) factory or office machines;

(B) equipment that is not primarily used or leased for use in the operation of the real property; or

(C) replacements of domestic appliances that are consumer goods;

(3) the conflicting interest is a lien on the real property obtained by legal or equitable proceedings after the security interest was perfected by any method permitted by this article; or

(4) the security interest is:

(A) created in a manufactured home in a manufactured-home transaction; and

(B) perfected pursuant to a statute described in Section 9–311(a)(2).

(f) [Priority based on consent, disclaimer, or right to remove.] A security interest in fixtures, whether or not perfected, has priority over a conflicting interest of an encumbrancer or owner of the real property if:

(1) the encumbrancer or owner has, in an authenticated record, consented to the security interest or disclaimed an interest in the goods as fixtures; or

(2) the debtor has a right to remove the goods as against the encumbrancer or owner.

(g) [Continuation of paragraph (f)(2) priority.] The priority of the security interest under paragraph (f)(2) continues for a reasonable time if the debtor's right to remove the goods as against the encumbrancer or owner terminates.

(h) [Priority of construction mortgage.] A mortgage is a construction mortgage to the extent that it secures an obligation incurred for the construction of an improvement on land, including the acquisition cost of the land, if a recorded record of the mortgage so indicates. Except as otherwise provided in subsections (e) and (f), a security interest in fixtures is subordinate to a construction mortgage if a record of the mortgage is recorded before the goods become fixtures and the goods become fixtures before the completion of the construction. A mortgage has this priority to the same extent as a construction mortgage to the extent that it is given to refinance a construction mortgage.

(i) [Priority of security interest in crops.] A perfected security interest in crops growing on real property has priority over a conflicting interest of an encumbrancer or owner of the real property if the debtor has an interest of record in or is in possession of the real property.

(j) [Subsection (i) prevails.] Subsection (i) prevails over any inconsistent provisions of the following statutes:

UNOFFICIAL COMMENTS

Look to section 9–334 if (1) there is a fixture and (2) someone has security interest in the fixture and (3) someone else claims rights in that fixture because it either owns the real property to which the fixture is affixed or has a mortgage on that real property.

What you will see when you look at section 9–334 looks a lot like what you see when you look at sections 9–322 (first in time rule) and 9–324 (20 day grace period for purchase-money security interest), with special rules for "construction mortgages" and "readily removable fixtures."

Generally to prevail under section 9–334 a secured party must have perfected by a fixture filing. If, however, either (i) the fixtures are "readily removable" or (ii) the other party claiming rights in the fixture is a "lien creditor", then perfection by any means under Article 9 is sufficient.

We have a lot more stuff on fixtures on pages 377–380 infra.

NON–OBVIOUS DEFINITIONS

Section 9–102(a) defines "fixtures." We think our law professor's definition is more helpful: fixtures had a personal property past, have a real property present and have the possibility of a personal property future.

Section 9–102(a) also defines "fixture filing." What is more helpful than knowing what section 9–102 says is knowing what section 9–502(b) and (c) say about the additional information required for a fixture filing and what section 9–501(a)(1) says about where to make a fixture filing.

The term "encumbrance" as defined in section 9–102 includes mortgages and judgment liens on real property.

OTHER UCC SECTIONS TO LOOK TO WHEN YOU LOOK AT SECTION 9–334

Section 9–516(b)(3)(D) [read together with 9–520(a)] requires the clerk's office to refuse for filing a fixture filing that does not provide a sufficient description of the real property to which it relates. Section 9–519(d) requires the clerk's office to index a fixture filing under the names of the debtor and each owner of the real property shown on the fixture filing.

Section 9–604(b) provides a secured party with a security interest in fixtures the option of enforcing its security interest under the provisions of Article 9 or using the enforcement procedures available under generally applicable real property law. Electing to proceed under real property law makes the security interest enforcement provisions of Part 6 of Article 9 inapplicable.

Section 9–604 underscores the importance of the section 9–334 priority provisions. Sections 9–604(c) and (d) provide that a secured party with priority over competing interests in a fixture may remove its collateral from the real property. If someone other than the debtor owns the real property or has a lien on the real property, section 9–604 requires the secured party to reimburse all owners and encumbrancers of the real property for the cost of repairing any physical damage to the real property caused by removing the fixtures. A person entitled to reimbursement can prevent removal of the fixtures unless the secured party provides adequate assurance of reimbursement for any such damage done.

OFFICIAL COMMENT

* * *

2. **Scope of This Section.** This section contains rules governing the priority of security interests in fixtures and crops as against persons who claim an interest in real property. Priority contests with other Article 9 security interests are governed by the other priority rules of this Article. The provisions with respect to fixtures follow those of former Section 9–

313. However, they have been rewritten to conform to Section 2A–309 and to prevailing style conventions. Subsections (i) and (j), which apply to crops, are new.

3. **Security Interests in Fixtures.** Certain goods that are the subject of personal-property (chattel) financing become so affixed or otherwise so related to real property that they become part of the real property. These goods are called "fixtures." See Section 9–102 (definition of "fixtures"). Some fixtures retain their personal-property nature: a security interest under this Article may be created in fixtures and may continue in goods that become fixtures. See subsection (a). However, if the goods are ordinary building materials incorporated into an improvement on land, no security interest in them exists. Rather, the priority of claims to the building materials are determined by the law governing claims to real property. (Of course, the fact that no security interest exists in ordinary building materials incorporated into an improvement on land does not prejudice any rights the secured party may have against the debtor or any other person who violated the secured party's rights by wrongfully incorporating the goods into real property.)

Thus, this section recognizes three categories of goods: (1) those that retain their chattel character entirely and are not part of the real property; (2) ordinary building materials that have become an integral part of the real property and cannot retain their chattel character for purposes of finance; and (3) an intermediate class that has become real property for certain purposes, but as to which chattel financing may be preserved.

To achieve priority under certain provisions of this section, a security interest must be perfected by making a "fixture filing" (defined in Section 9–102) in the real-property records. Because the question whether goods have become fixtures often is a difficult one under applicable real-property law, a secured party may make a fixture filing as a precaution. Courts should not infer from a fixture filing that the secured party concedes that the goods are or will become fixtures.

4. **Priority in Fixtures: General.** In considering priority problems under this section, one must first determine whether real-property claimants per se have an interest in the crops or fixtures as part of real property. If not, it is immaterial, so far as concerns real property parties as such, whether a security interest arising under this Article is perfected or unperfected. In no event does a real-property claimant (e.g., owner or mortgagee) acquire an interest in a "pure" chattel just because a security interest therein is unperfected. If on the other hand real-property law gives real-property parties an interest in the goods, a conflict arises and this section states the priorities.

5. **Priority in Fixtures: Residual Rule.** Subsection (c) states the residual priority rule, which applies only if one of the other rules does not: A security interest in fixtures is subordinate to a conflicting interest of an encumbrancer or owner of the related real property other than the debtor.

6. **Priority in Fixtures: First to File or Record.** Subsection (e)(1), which follows former Section 9–313(4)(b), contains the usual priority rule of conveyancing, that is, the first to file or record prevails. In order to achieve priority under this rule, however, the security interest must be perfected by a "fixture filing" (defined in Section 9–102), i.e., a filing for record in the real property records and indexed therein, so that it will be found in a real-property search .. The condition in subsection (e)(1)(B), that the security interest must have had priority over any conflicting interest of a predecessor in title of the conflicting encumbrancer or owner, appears to limit to the first-in-time principle. However, this apparent limitation is nothing other than an expression of the usual rule that a person must be entitled to transfer what he has. Thus, if the fixture security interest is subordinate to a mortgage, it is subordinate to an interest of an assignee of the mortgage, even though the assignment is a later recorded instrument. Similarly if the fixture security interest is subordinate to the rights of an owner, it is subordinate to a subsequent grantee of

the owner and likewise subordinate to a subsequent mortgagee of the owner.

7. **Priority in Fixtures: Purchase-Money Security Interests.** Subsection (d), which follows former Section 9–313(4)(a), contains the principal exception to the first-to-file-or-record rule of subsection (e)(1). It affords priority to purchase-money security interests in fixtures as against *prior* recorded real-property interests, provided that the purchase-money security interest is filed as a fixture filing in the real-property records before the goods become fixtures or within 20 days thereafter. This priority corresponds to the purchase-money priority under Section 9–324(a). (Like other 10–day periods in former Article 9, the 10–day period in this section has been changed to 20 days.)

It should be emphasized that this purchase-money priority with the 20–day grace period for filing is limited to rights against real-property interests that arise *before* the goods become fixtures. There is no such priority with the 20–day grace period as against real-property interests that arise subsequently. The fixture security interest can defeat subsequent real-property interests only if it is filed first and prevails under the usual conveyancing rule in subsection (e)(1) or one of the other rules in this section.

8. **Priority in Fixtures: Readily Removable Goods.** Subsection (e)(2), which derives from Section 2A–309 and former Section 9–313(4)(d), contains another exception to the usual first-to-file-or-perfect rule. It affords priority to the holders of security interests in certain types of readily removable goods—factory and office machines, equipment that is not primarily used or leased for use in the operation of the real property, and (as discussed below) certain replacements of domestic appliances. This rule is made necessary by the confusion in the law as to whether certain machinery, equipment, and appliances become fixtures. It protects a secured party who, perhaps in the mistaken belief that the readily removable goods will not become fixtures, makes a UCC filing (or otherwise perfects under this Article) rather than making a fixture filing.

Frequently, under applicable law, goods of the type described in subsection (e)(2) will not be considered to have become part of the real property. In those cases, the fixture security interest does not conflict with a real-property interest, and resort to this section is unnecessary. However, if the goods have become part of the real property, subsection (e)(2) enables a fixture secured party to take priority over a conflicting real-property interest if the fixture security interest is perfected by a fixture filing or by any other method permitted by this Article. If perfection is by fixture filing, the fixture security interest would have priority over subsequently recorded real-property interests under subsection (e)(1) and, if the fixture security interest is a purchase-money security interest (a likely scenario), it would also have priority over most real property interests under the purchase-money priority of subsection (d). Note, however, that unlike the purchase-money priority rule in subsection (d), the priority rules in subsection (e) override the priority given to a construction mortgage under subsection (h).

The rule in subsection (e)(2) is limited to readily removable replacements of domestic appliances. It does not apply to original installations. Moreover, it is limited to appliances that are "consumer goods" (defined in Section 9–102) in the hands of the debtor. The principal effect of the rule is to make clear that a secured party financing occasional replacements of domestic appliances in noncommercial, owner-occupied contexts need not concern itself with real-property descriptions or records; indeed, for a purchase-money replacement of consumer goods, perfection without any filing will be possible. See Section 9–309(1).

9. **Priority in Fixtures: Judicial Liens.** Subsection (e)(3), which follows former Section 9–313(4)(d), adopts a first-in-time rule applicable to conflicts between a fixture security interest and a lien on the real property obtained by legal or equitable proceedings. Such a lien is subordinate to an earlier-perfected security interest, regardless of the method by

which the security interest was perfected. Judgment creditors generally are not reliance creditors who search real-property records. Accordingly, a perfected fixture security interest takes priority over a subsequent judgment lien or other lien obtained by legal or equitable proceedings, even if no evidence of the security interest appears in the relevant real-property records. Subsection (e)(3) thus protects a perfected fixture security interest from avoidance by a trustee in bankruptcy under Bankruptcy Code Section 544(a), regardless of the method of perfection.

10. **Priority in Fixtures: Manufactured Homes.** A manufactured home may become a fixture. New subsection (e)(4) contains a special rule granting priority to certain security interests created in a "manufactured home" as part of a "manufactured-home transaction" (both defined in Section 9–102). Under this rule, a security interest in a manufactured home that becomes a fixture has priority over a conflicting interest of an encumbrancer or owner of the real property if the security interest is perfected under a certificate-of-title statute (see Section 9–311). Subsection (e)(4) is only one of the priority rules applicable to security interests in a manufactured home that becomes a fixture. Thus, a security interest in a manufactured home which does not qualify for priority under this subsection may qualify under another.

11. **Priority in Fixtures: Construction Mortgages.** The purchase-money priority presents a difficult problem in relation to construction mortgages. The latter ordinarily will have been recorded even before the commencement of delivery of materials to the job, and therefore would take priority over fixture security interests were it not for the purchase-money priority. However, having recorded first, the holder of a construction mortgage reasonably expects to have first priority in the improvement built using the mortgagee's advances. Subsection (g) expressly gives priority to the construction mortgage recorded before the filing of the purchase-money security interest in fixtures. A refinancing of a construction mortgage has the same priority as the construction mortgage itself. The phrase "an obligation incurred for the construction of an improvement" covers both optional advances and advances pursuant to commitment. Both types of advances have the same priority under subsection (g).

The priority under this subsection applies only to goods that become fixtures during the construction period leading to the completion of the improvement. The construction priority will not apply to additions to the building made long after completion of the improvement, even if the additions are financed by the real-property mortgagee under an open-end clause of the construction mortgage. In such case, subsections (d), (e), and (f) govern.

Although this subsection affords a construction mortgage priority over a purchase-money security interest that otherwise would have priority under subsection (d), the subsection is subject to the priority rules in subsections (e) and (f). Thus, a construction mortgage may be junior to a fixture security interest perfected by a fixture filing before the construction mortgage was recorded. See subsection (e)(1).

12. **Crops.** Growing crops are "goods" in which a security interest may be created and perfected under this Article. In some jurisdictions, a mortgage of real property may cover crops, as well. In the event that crops are encumbered by both a mortgage and an Article 9 security interest, subsection (i) provides that the security interest has priority. States whose real-property law provides otherwise should either amend that law directly or override it by enacting subsection (j).

§ 9–335. Accessions

(a) [Creation of security interest in accession.] A security interest may be created in an accession and continues in collateral that becomes an accession.

(b) [Perfection of security interest.] If a security interest is perfected when the collateral becomes an accession, the security interest remains perfected in the collateral.

(c) [Priority of security interest.] Except as otherwise provided in subsection (d), the other provisions of this part determine the priority of a security interest in an accession.

(d) [Compliance with certificate-of-title statute.] A security interest in an accession is subordinate to a security interest in the whole which is perfected by compliance with the requirements of a certificate-of-title statute under Section 9–311(b).

(e) [Removal of accession after default.] After default, subject to Part 6, a secured party may remove an accession from other goods if the security interest in the accession has priority over the claims of every person having an interest in the whole.

(f) [Reimbursement following removal.] A secured party that removes an accession from other goods under subsection (e) shall promptly reimburse any holder of a security interest or other lien on, or owner of, the whole or of the other goods, other than the debtor, for the cost of repair of any physical injury to the whole or the other goods. The secured party need not reimburse the holder or owner for any diminution in value of the whole or the other goods caused by the absence of the accession removed or by any necessity for replacing it. A person entitled to reimbursement may refuse permission to remove until the secured party gives adequate assurance for the performance of the obligation to reimburse.

UNOFFICIAL COMMENTS

The most important thing about the law of accessions under section 9–335 is how unimportant it is. A new engine installed in a car is the usual law school example of an accession. If you understand Official Comments 2 and 3, you will understand that, from the perspective of the secured party with a security interest in the car, the car is the accession and the engine is the "other goods".

If your prof spent time on accessions, you might want to spend some time on our extended discussion of section 9–335 at pages 380–381 infra.

NON–OBVIOUS DEFINITIONS

"Accession" is defined in section 9–102. Official Comments 2 and 3 to section 9–335 do a better job of explaining not only the term "accession" but also the other statutory terms "whole" and "other goods."

OFFICIAL COMMENT

* * *

2. **"Accession."** This section applies to an "accession," as defined in Section 9–102, regardless of the cost or difficulty of removing the accession from the other goods, and regardless of whether the original goods have come to form an integral part of the other goods. This section does not apply to goods whose identity has been lost. Goods of that kind are "commingled goods" governed by Section 9–336. Neither this section nor the following one addresses the case of collateral that changes form without the addition of other goods.

3. **"Accession" vs. "Other Goods."** This section distinguishes among the "accession," the "other goods," and the "whole." The last term refers to the combination of the "accession" and the "other goods." If one person's collateral becomes physically united with another person's collateral, each is an "accession."

Example 1: SP–1 holds a security interest in the debtor's tractors (which are not subject to a certificate-of-title statute), and SP–2 holds a security interest in a particular tractor engine. The engine is installed in a tractor. From the perspective of SP–1, the tractor becomes an "accession" and the engine is the "other goods." From the perspective of SP–2, the engine is the "accession" and the tractor is the "other goods." The completed tractor—tractor cum engine—constitutes the "whole."

4. **Scope.** This section governs only a few issues concerning accessions. Subsection (a) contains rules governing continuation of a security interest in an accession. Subsection (b) contains a rule governing continued perfection of a security interest in goods that become an accession. Subsection (d) contains a special priority rule governing accessions that become part of a whole covered by a certificate of title. Subsections (e) and (f) govern enforcement of a security interest in an accession.

5. **Matters Left to Other Provisions of This Article: Attachment and Perfection.** Other provisions of this Article often govern accession-related issues. For example, this section does not address whether a secured party acquires a security interest in the whole if its collateral becomes an accession. Normally this will turn on the description of the collateral in the security agreement.

Example 2: Debtor owns a computer subject to a perfected security interest in favor of SP–1. Debtor acquires memory and installs it in the computer. Whether SP–1's security interest attaches to the memory depends on whether the security agreement covers it.

Similarly, this section does not determine whether perfection against collateral that becomes an accession is effective to perfect a security interest in the whole. Other provisions of this Article, including the requirements for indicating the collateral covered by a financing statement, resolve that question.

6. **Matters Left to Other Provisions of This Article: Priority.** With one exception, concerning goods covered by a certificate of title (see subsection (d)), the other provisions of this Part, including the rules governing purchase-money security interests, determine the priority of most security interests in an accession, including the relative priority of a security interest in an accession and a security interest in the whole. See subsection (c).

Example 3: Debtor owns an office computer subject to a security interest in favor of SP–1. Debtor acquires memory and grants a perfected security interest in the memory to SP–2. Debtor installs the memory in the computer, at which time (one assumes) SP–1's security interest attaches to the memory. The first-to-file-or-perfect rule of Section 9–322 governs priority in the memory. If, however, SP–2's security interest is a purchase-money security interest, Section 9–324(a) would afford priority in the memory to SP–2, regardless of which security interest was perfected first.

7. **Goods Covered by Certificate of Title.** This section does govern the priority of a security interest in an accession that is or becomes part of a whole that is subject to a security interest perfected by compliance with a certificate-of-title statute. Subsection (d) provides that a security interest in the whole, perfected by compliance with a certificate-of-title statute, takes priority over a security interest in the accession. It enables a secured party to rely upon a certificate of title without having to check the UCC files to determine whether any components of the collateral may be encumbered. The subsection imposes a corresponding risk upon those who finance goods that may become part of goods covered by a certificate of title. In doing so, it reverses the priority that appeared reasonable to most pre-UCC courts.

Example 4: Debtor owns an automobile subject to a security interest in favor of SP-1. The security interest is perfected by notation on the certificate of title. Debtor buys tires subject to a perfected-by-filing purchase-money security interest in favor of SP-2 and mounts the tires on the automobile's wheels. If the security interest in the automobile attaches to the tires, then SP-1 acquires priority over SP-2. The same result would obtain if SP-1's security interest attached to the automobile and was perfected after the tires had been mounted on the wheels.

§ 9–336. Commingled Goods

(a) ["Commingled goods."] In this section, "commingled goods" means goods that are physically united with other goods in such a manner that their identity is lost in a product or mass.

(b) [No security interest in commingled goods as such.] A security interest does not exist in commingled goods as such. However, a security interest may attach to a product or mass that results when goods become commingled goods.

(c) [Attachment of security interest to product or mass.] If collateral becomes commingled goods, a security interest attaches to the product or mass.

(d) [Perfection of security interest.] If a security interest in collateral is perfected before the collateral becomes commingled goods, the security interest that attaches to the product or mass under subsection (c) is perfected.

(e) [Priority of security interest.] Except as otherwise provided in subsection (f), the other provisions of this part determine the priority of a security interest that attaches to the product or mass under subsection (c).

(f) [Conflicting security interests in product or mass] If more than one security interest attaches to the product or mass under subsection (c), the following rules determine priority:

> **(1)** A security interest that is perfected under subsection (d) has priority over a security interest that is unperfected at the time the collateral becomes commingled goods.

(2) If more than one security interest is perfected under subsection (d), the security interests rank equally in proportion to the value of the collateral at the time it became commingled goods.

UNOFFICIAL COMMENTS

Under section 9–336(d), once a secured party's collateral is commingled with other goods and the original collateral is no longer independently identifiable, the security interest transfers and attaches to the resulting product. Additionally, if the security interest was originally perfected, the resulting security interest is likewise perfected in the new product. The perfection in the new product is automatic, and requires no further action by the secured party if the prior interest was properly perfected at the time of commingling. In the above example, a secured party who properly perfected an interest in the cup of flour, would automatically have a perfected security interest in the cake, so long as the original security interest in the cup of flour was properly perfected at the time the cake was baked. And, if there was another secured party with a perfected security interest in the eggs used in baking the cake, look to section 9–336(f)(2).

NON–OBVIOUS DEFINITIONS

If the definition of "commingled goods" is not obvious, then obviously you have not read section 9–336(a). The difference between "commingled goods" governed by section 9–336 and "accessions" governed by section 9–335 also needs to be obvious.

While an accession continues to retain its original identity despite its connection to other personal property, a commingled good is no longer identifiable after it is combined with other goods or materials. For example, while a computer hard drive is still independently identifiable after installation, a cup of flour mixed into a baked cake is not. Therefore the hard drive is an accession and the computer with the hard drive is the "whole" while the cup of flour is a commingled good and the cake is the "product.".

OTHER UCC SECTIONS TO LOOK TO WHEN YOU LOOK AT SECTION 9–336

A security interest automatically attaches to any proceeds of a secured party's original collateral as long as the proceeds are "identifiable". When proceeds are commingled with other property, section 9–315(b) provides that the proceeds remain identifiable, if the proceeds are goods, to the extent allowed under section 9–336. If the commingled proceeds, are cash proceeds, then 9–315(b) allows the secured party to use equitable tracing principles to identify the proceeds of its original collateral.

OFFICIAL COMMENT

* * *

2. **"Commingled Goods."** Subsection (a) defines "commingled goods." It is meant to include not only goods whose identity is lost through manufacturing or production (e.g., flour that has become part of baked goods) but also goods whose identity is lost by commingling with other goods from which they cannot be distinguished (e.g., ball bearings).

3. **Consequences of Becoming "Commingled Goods."** By definition, the identity of the original collateral cannot be determined once the original collateral becomes commingled goods. Consequently, the security interest in the specific original collateral alone is lost once the collateral becomes commingled goods, and no security interest in the original collateral can be created thereafter except as a part of the resulting product or mass. See subsection (b).

Once collateral becomes commingled goods, the secured party's security interest is transferred from the original collateral to the product or mass. See subsection (c). If the security interest in the original collateral was perfected, the security interest in the product or mass is a perfected security interest. See subsection (d). This perfection continues until lapse.

4. **Priority of Perfected Security Interests That Attach Under This Section.** This section governs the priority of competing security interests in a product or mass only when both security interests arise under this section. In that case, if both security interests are perfected by operation of this section (see subsections (c) and (d)), then the security interests rank equally, in proportion to the value of the collateral at the time it became commingled goods. See subsection (f)(2).

Example 1: SP–1 has a perfected security interest in Debtor's eggs, which have a value of $300 and secure a debt of $400, and SP–2 has a perfected security interest in Debtor's flour, which has a value of $500 and secures a debt of $700. Debtor uses the flour and eggs to make cakes, which have a value of $1000. The two security interests rank equally and share in the ratio of 3:5. Applying this ratio to the entire value of the product, SP–1 would be entitled to $375 (i.e., 3/8 x $1000), and SP–2 would be entitled to $625 (i.e., 5/8 x $1000).

Example 2: Assume the facts of Example 1, except that SP–1's collateral, worth $300, secures a debt of $200. Recall that, if the cake is worth $1000, then applying the ratio of 3:5 would entitle SP–1 to $375 and SP–2 to $625. However, SP–1 is not entitled to collect from the product more than it is owed. Accordingly, SP–1's share would be only $200, SP–2 would receive the remaining value, up to the amount it is owed ($700).

Example 3: Assume that the cakes in the previous examples have a value of only $600. Again, the parties share in the ratio of 3:5. If, as in Example 1, SP–1 is owed $400, then SP–1 is entitled to $225 (i.e., 3/8 x $600), and SP–2 is entitled to $375 (i.e., 5/8 x $600). Debtor receives nothing. If, however, as in Example 2, SP–1 is owed only $200, then SP–2 receives $400.

The results in the foregoing examples remain the same, regardless of whether SP–1 or SP–2 (or each) has a purchase-money security interest.

5. **Perfection: Unperfected Security Interests.** The rule explained in the preceding Comment applies only when both security interests in original collateral are perfected when the goods become commingled goods. If a security interest in original collateral is unperfected at the time the collateral becomes commingled goods, subsection (f)(1) applies.

Example 4: SP–1 has a perfected security interest in the debtor's eggs, and SP–2 has an unperfected security interest in the debtor's flour. Debtor uses the flour and eggs to make cakes. Under subsection (c), both security interests attach to the cakes. But since SP–1's security interest was perfected at the time of commingling and SP–2's was not, only SP–1's security interest in the cakes is perfected. See subsection (d). Under subsection (f)(1) and Section 9–322(a)(2), SP–1's perfected security interest has priority over SP–2's unperfected security interest.

If both security interests are unperfected, the rule of Section 9–322(a)(3) would apply.

6. **Multiple Security Interests.** On occasion, a single input may be encumbered by more than one security interest. In those cases, the multiple secured parties should be treated like a single secured party for purposes of determining their collective share under subsection (f)(2). The normal priority rules would determine how that share would be allocated between them. Consider the following example, which is a variation on Example 1 above:

> **Example 5:** SP–1A has a perfected, first-priority security interest in Debtor's eggs. SP–1B has a perfected, second-priority security interest in the same collateral. The eggs have a value of $300. Debtor owes $200 to SP–1A and $200 to SP–1B. SP–2 has a perfected security interest in Debtor's flour, which has a value of $500 and secures a debt of $600. Debtor uses the flour and eggs to make cakes, which have a value of $1000.

For purposes of subsection (f)(2), SP–1A and SP–1B should be treated like a single secured party. The collective security interest would rank equally with that of SP–2. Thus, the secured parties would share in the ratio of 3 (for SP–1A and SP–1B combined) to 5 (for SP–2). Applying this ratio to the entire value of the product, SP–1A and SP–1B in the aggregate would be entitled to $375 (i.e., 3/8 x $1000), and SP–2 would be entitled to $625 (i.e., 5/8 x $1000).

SP–1A and SP–1B would share the $375 in accordance with their priority, as established under other rules. Inasmuch as SP–1A has first priority, it would receive $200, and SP–1B would receive $175.

7. **Priority of Security Interests That Attach Other Than by Operation of This Section.** Under subsection (e), the normal priority rules determine the priority of a security interest that attaches to the product or mass other than by operation of this section. For example, assume that SP–1 has a perfected security interest in Debtor's existing and after-acquired baked goods, and SP–2 has a perfected security interest in Debtor's flour. When the flour is processed into cakes, subsections (c) and (d) provide that SP–2 acquires a perfected security interest in the cakes. If SP–1 filed against the baked goods before SP–2 filed against the flour, then SP–1 will enjoy priority in the cakes. See Section 9–322 (first-to-file-or-perfect). But if SP–2 filed against the flour before SP–1 filed against the baked goods, then SP–2 will enjoy priority in the cakes to the extent of its security interest.

§ 9–337. Priority of Security Interests in Goods Covered by Certificate of Title

If, while a security interest in goods is perfected by any method under the law of another jurisdiction, this State issues a certificate of title that does not show that the goods are subject to the security interest or contain a statement that they may be subject to security interests not shown on the certificate:

(1) a buyer of the goods, other than a person in the business of selling goods of that kind, takes free of the security interest if the buyer gives value and receives delivery of the goods after issuance of the certificate and without knowledge of the security interest; and

(2) the security interest is subordinate to a conflicting security interest in the goods that attaches, and is perfected under Section 9–311(b), after issuance of the certificate and without the conflicting secured party's knowledge of the security interest.

OFFICIAL COMMENT

* * *

2. **Protection for Buyers and Secured Parties.** This section affords protection to certain good-faith purchasers for value who are likely to have relied on a "clean" certificate of title, i.e., one that neither shows that the goods are subject to a particular security interest nor contains a statement that they may be subject to security interests not shown on the certificate. Under this section, a buyer can take free of, and the holder of a conflicting security interest can acquire priority over, a security interest that is perfected by any method under the law of another jurisdiction. The fact that the security interest has been reperfected by possession under Section 9–313 does not of itself disqualify the holder of a conflicting security interest from protection under paragraph (2).

* * *

§ 9–338. Priority of Security Interest or Agricultural Lien Perfected by Filed Financing Statement Providing Certain Incorrect Information

If a security interest or agricultural lien is perfected by a filed financing statement providing information described in Section 9–516(b)(5) which is incorrect at the time the financing statement is filed:

(1) the security interest or agricultural lien is subordinate to a conflicting perfected security interest in the collateral to the extent that the holder of the conflicting security interest gives value in reasonable reliance upon the incorrect information; and

(2) a purchaser, other than a secured party, of the collateral takes free of the security interest or agricultural lien to the extent that, in reasonable reliance upon the incorrect information, the purchaser gives value and, in the case of tangible chattel paper, tangible documents, goods, instruments, or a security certificate, receives delivery of the collateral.

§ 9–339. Priority Subject to Subordination

This article does not preclude subordination by agreement by a person entitled to priority.

OFFICIAL COMMENT

* * *

2. **Subordination by Agreement.** The preceding sections deal elaborately with questions of priority. This section makes it entirely clear that a person entitled to priority may effectively agree to subordinate its claim. Only the person entitled to priority may make such an agreement: a person's rights cannot be adversely affected by an agreement to which the person is not a party.

[SUBPART 4. RIGHTS OF BANK]

§ 9–340. Effectiveness of Right of Recoupment or Set-Off Against Deposit Account

(a) [Exercise of recoupment or set-off.] Except as otherwise provided in subsection (c), a bank with which a deposit account is maintained may exercise any right of recoupment or set-off against a secured party that holds a security interest in the deposit account.

(b) [Recoupment or set-off not affected by security interest.] Except as otherwise provided in subsection (c), the application of this article to a security interest in a deposit account does not affect a right of recoupment or set-off of the secured party as to a deposit account maintained with the secured party.

(c) [When set-off ineffective.] The exercise by a bank of a set-off against a deposit account is ineffective against a secured party that holds a security interest in the deposit account which is perfected by control under Section 9–104(a)(3), if the set-off is based on a claim against the debtor.

UNOFFICIAL COMMENTS

Under section 9–340, the setoff rights of a depositary bank will generally have priority over a conflicting security interest in a deposit account. The exception is when the secured party has control over the deposit account under section 9–104(a)(3) by becoming the account holder of record.

OTHER SECTIONS TO LOOK TO WHEN YOU LOOK AT SECTION 9–340

If you look closely as section 9–109(d)(10)(A) and section 9–109(d)(13) you will see that you will not look at section 9–340 if there has been an assignment of a deposit account in a consumer transaction

OFFICIAL COMMENT

* * *

2. **Set-off vs. Security Interest.** This section resolves the conflict between a security interest in a deposit account

and the bank's rights of recoupment and set-off.

Subsection (a) states the general rule and provides that the bank may effectively exercise rights of recoupment and set-off against the secured party. Subsection (c) contains an exception: if the secured party has control under Section 9–104(a)(3) (i.e., if it has become the bank's customer), then any set-off exercised by the bank against a debt owed by the debtor (as opposed to a debt owed to the bank by the secured party) is ineffective. The bank may, however, exercise its recoupment rights effectively. This result is consistent with the priority rule in Section 9–327(4), under which the security interest of a bank in a deposit account is subordinate to that of a secured party who has control under Section 9–104(a)(3).

This section deals with rights of set-off and recoupment that a bank may have under other law. It does not create a right of set-off or recoupment, nor is it intended to override any limitations or restrictions that other law imposes on the exercise of those rights.

3. **Preservation of Set-Off Right.** Subsection (b) makes clear that a bank may hold both a right of set-off against, and an Article 9 security interest in, the same deposit account. By holding a security interest in a deposit account, a bank does not impair any right of set-off it would otherwise enjoy. This subsection does not pertain to accounts evidenced by an instrument (e.g., certain certificates of deposit), which are excluded from the definition of "deposit accounts."

§ 9–341. Bank's Rights and Duties With Respect to Deposit Account

Except as otherwise provided in Section 9–340(c), and unless the bank otherwise agrees in an authenticated record, a bank's rights and duties with respect to a deposit account maintained with the bank are not terminated, suspended, or modified by:

(1) the creation, attachment, or perfection of a security interest in the deposit account;

(2) the bank's knowledge of the security interest; or

(3) the bank's receipt of instructions from the secured party.

OFFICIAL COMMENT

* * *

2. **Free Flow of Funds.** This section is designed to prevent security interests in deposit accounts from impeding the free flow of funds through the payment system. Subject to two exceptions, it leaves the bank's rights and duties with respect to the deposit account and the funds on deposit unaffected by the creation or perfection of a security interest or by the bank's knowledge of the security interest. In addition, the section permits the bank to ignore the instructions of the secured party unless it had agreed to honor them or unless other law provides to the contrary. A secured party who wishes to deprive the debtor of access to funds on deposit or to appropriate those funds for itself needs to obtain the agreement of the bank, utilize the judicial process, or comply with procedures set forth in other law. Section 4–303(a), concerning the effect of notice on a bank's right and duty to pay items, is not to the contrary. That section addresses only whether an otherwise effective notice comes too late; it does not determine whether a timely notice is otherwise effective.

3. **Operation of Rule.** The general rule of this section is subject to Section 9–340(c), under which a bank's right of set-off may not be exercised against a deposit

account in the secured party's name if the right is based on a claim against the debtor. This result reflects current law in many jurisdictions and does not appear to have unduly disrupted banking practices or the payments system. The more important function of this section, which is not impaired by Section 9–340, is the bank's right to follow the debtor's (customer's) instructions (e.g., by honoring checks, permitting withdrawals, etc.) until such time as the depository institution is served with judicial process or receives instructions with respect to the funds on deposit from a secured party who has control over the deposit account.

4. **Liability of Bank.** This Article does not determine whether a bank that pays out funds from an encumbered deposit is liable to the holder of a security interest. Although the fact that a secured party has control over the deposit account and the manner by which control was achieved may be relevant to the imposition of liability, whatever rule applies generally when a bank pays out funds in which a third party has an interest would determine liability to a secured party. Often, this rule is found in a non-UCC adverse claim statute.

5. **Certificates of Deposit.** This section does not address the obligations of banks that issue instruments evidencing deposits (e.g., certain certificates of deposit).

§ 9–342. Bank's Right to Refuse to Enter Into or Disclose Existence of Control Agreement

This article does not require a bank to enter into an agreement of the kind described in Section 9–104(a)(2), even if its customer so requests or directs. A bank that has entered into such an agreement is not required to confirm the existence of the agreement to another person unless requested to do so by its customer.

OFFICIAL COMMENT

* * *

2. **Protection for Bank.** This section protects banks from the need to enter into agreements against their will and from the need to respond to inquiries from persons other than their customers.

PART 4. RIGHTS OF THIRD PARTIES

§ 9–401. Alienability of Debtor's Rights

(a) [Other law governs alienability; exceptions.] Except as otherwise provided in subsection (b) and Sections 9–406, 9–407, 9–408, and 9–409, whether a debtor's rights in collateral may be voluntarily or involuntarily transferred is governed by law other than this article.

(b) [Agreement does not prevent transfer.] An agreement between the debtor and secured party which prohibits a transfer of the debtor's rights in collateral or makes the transfer a default does not prevent the transfer from taking effect.

OFFICIAL COMMENT

* * *

2. **Scope of This Part.** This Part deals with several issues affecting third

parties (i.e., parties other than the debtor and the secured party). These issues are not addressed in Part 3, Subpart 3, which deals with priorities. This Part primarily addresses the rights and duties of account debtors and other persons obligated on collateral who are not, themselves, parties to a secured transaction.

3. **Governing Law.** There was some uncertainty under former Article 9 as to which jurisdiction's law (usually, which jurisdiction's version of Article 9) applied to the matters that this Part addresses. Part 3, Subpart 1, does not determine the law governing these matters because they do not relate to perfection, the effect of perfection or nonperfection, or priority. However, it might be inappropriate for a designation of applicable law by a debtor and secured party under Section 1–105 to control the law applicable to an independent transaction or relationship between the debtor and an account debtor.

Consider an example under Section 9–408.

Example 1: State X has adopted this Article; former Article 9 is the law of State Y. A general intangible (e.g., a franchise agreement) between a debtor-franchisee, D, and an account debtor-franchisor, AD, is governed by the law of State Y. D grants to SP a security interest in its rights under the franchise agreement. The franchise agreement contains a term prohibiting D's assignment of its rights under the agreement. D and SP agree that their secured transaction is governed by the law of State X. Under State X's Section 9–408, the restriction on D's assignment is ineffective to prevent the creation, attachment, or perfection of SP's security interest. State Y's former Section 9–318(4), however, does not address restrictions on the creation of security interests in general intangibles other than general intangibles for money due or to become due. Accordingly, it does not address restrictions on the assignment to SP of D's rights under the franchise agreement. The non-Article–9 law of State Y, which does address restrictions, provides that the prohibition on assignment is effective.

This Article does not provide a specific answer to the question of which State's law applies to the restriction on assignment in the example. However, assuming that under non-UCC choice-of-law principles the effectiveness of the restriction would be governed by the law of State Y, which governs the franchise agreement, the fact that State X's Article 9 governs the secured transaction between SP and D would not override the otherwise applicable law governing the agreement. Of course, to the extent that jurisdictions eventually adopt identical versions of this Article and courts interpret it consistently, the inability to identify the applicable law in circumstances such as those in the example may be inconsequential.

4. **Inalienability Under Other Law.** Subsection (a) addresses the question whether property necessarily is transferable by virtue of its inclusion (i.e., its eligibility as collateral) within the scope of Article 9. It gives a negative answer, subject to the identified exceptions. The substance of subsection (a) was implicit under former Article 9.

5. **Negative Pledge Covenant.** Subsection (b) is an exception to the general rule in subsection (a). It makes clear that in secured transactions under this Article the debtor has rights in collateral (whether legal title or equitable) which it can transfer and which its creditors can reach. It is best explained with an example.

Example 2: A debtor, D, grants to SP a security interest to secure a debt in excess of the value of the collateral. D agrees with SP that it will not create a subsequent security interest in the collateral and that any security interest purportedly granted in violation of the agreement will be void. Subsequently, in violation of its agreement with SP, D purports to grant a security interest in the same collateral to another secured party.

Subsection (b) validates D's creation of the subsequent (prohibited) security interest, which might even achieve priority over the earlier security interest. See

Comment 7. However, unlike some other provisions of this Part, such as Section 9–406, subsection (b) does not provide that the agreement restricting assignment itself is "ineffective." Consequently, the debtor's breach may create a default.

6. **Rights of Lien Creditors.** Difficult problems may arise with respect to attachment, levy, and other judicial procedures under which a debtor's creditors may reach collateral subject to a security interest. For example, an obligation may be secured by collateral worth many times the amount of the obligation. If a lien creditor has caused all or a portion of the collateral to be seized under judicial process, it may be difficult to determine the amount of the debtor's "equity" in the collateral that has been seized. The section leaves resolution of this problem to the courts. The doctrine of marshaling may be appropriate.

7. **Sale of Receivables.** If a debtor sells an account, chattel paper, payment intangible, or promissory note outright, as against the buyer the debtor has no remaining rights to transfer. If, however, the buyer fails to perfect its interest, then solely insofar as the rights of certain third parties are concerned, the debtor is deemed to retain its rights and title. See Section 9–318. The debtor has the power to convey these rights to a subsequent purchaser. If the subsequent purchaser (buyer or secured lender) perfects its interest, it will achieve priority over the earlier, unperfected purchaser. See Section 9–322(a)(1).

* * *

§ 9–403. Agreement Not to Assert Defenses Against Assignee

(a) ["Value."] In this section, "value" has the meaning provided in Section 3–303(a).

(b) [Agreement not to assert claim or defense.] Except as otherwise provided in this section, an agreement between an account debtor and an assignor not to assert against an assignee any claim or defense that the account debtor may have against the assignor is enforceable by an assignee that takes an assignment:

> **(1)** for value;
>
> **(2)** in good faith;
>
> **(3)** without notice of a claim of a property or possessory right to the property assigned; and
>
> **(4)** without notice of a defense or claim in recoupment of the type that may be asserted against a person entitled to enforce a negotiable instrument under Section 3–305(a).

(c) [When subsection (b) not applicable.] Subsection (b) does not apply to defenses of a type that may be asserted against a holder in due course of a negotiable instrument under Section 3–305(b).

(d) [Omission of required statement in consumer transaction.] In a consumer transaction, if a record evidences the account debtor's obligation, law other than this article requires that the record include a statement to the effect that the rights of an assignee are subject to claims or defenses that the account debtor could assert against the original obligee, and the record does not include such a statement:

(1) the record has the same effect as if the record included such a statement; and

(2) the account debtor may assert against an assignee those claims and defenses that would have been available if the record included such a statement.

(e) [Rule for individual under other law.] This section is subject to law other than this article which establishes a different rule for an account debtor who is an individual and who incurred the obligation primarily for personal, family, or household purposes.

(f) [Other law not displaced.] Except as otherwise provided in subsection (d), this section does not displace law other than this article which gives effect to an agreement by an account debtor not to assert a claim or defense against an assignee.

OFFICIAL COMMENT

* * *

2. **Scope and Purpose.** Subsection (b), * * * generally validates an agreement between an account debtor and an assignor that the account debtor will not assert against an assignee claims and defenses that it may have against the assignor. These agreements are typical in installment sale agreements and leases. * * * It is not limited to account debtors that have bought or leased goods. This section applies only to the obligations of an "account debtor," as defined in Section 9–102. Thus, it does not determine the circumstances under which and the extent to which a person who is obligated on a negotiable instrument is disabled from asserting claims and defenses. Rather, Article 3 must be consulted. See, e.g., Sections 3–305, 3–306. Article 3 governs even when the negotiable instrument constitutes part of chattel paper. See Section 9–102 (an obligor on a negotiable instrument constituting part of chattel paper is not an "account debtor").

3. **Conditions of Validation; Relationship to Article 3.** Subsection (b) validates an account debtor's agreement only if the assignee takes an assignment for value, in good faith, and without notice of conflicting claims to the property assigned or of certain claims or defenses of the account debtor. * * * This section is designed to put the assignee in a position that is no better and no worse than that of a holder in due course of a negotiable instrument under Article 3. * * * Subsection (a) * * * provides that "value" has the meaning specified in Section 3–303(a). Similarly, subsection (c) provides that subsection (b) does not validate an agreement with respect to defenses that could be asserted against a holder in due course under Section 3–305(b) (the so-called "real" defenses). In 1990, the definition of "holder in due course" (Section 3–302) and the articulation of the rights of a holder in due course (Sections 3–305 and 3–306) were revised substantially. This section tracks more closely the rules of Sections 3–302, 3–305, and 3–306.

4. **Relationship to Terms of Assigned Property.** * * * This Article does not regulate the terms of the account, chattel paper, or general intangible that is assigned, except insofar as the account, chattel paper, or general intangible itself creates a security interest (as often is the case with chattel paper). Thus, Article 2, and not this Article, determines whether a seller of goods makes or effectively disclaims warranties, even if the sale is secured. Similarly, other law,

and not this Article, determines the effectiveness of an account debtor's undertaking to pay notwithstanding, and not to assert, any defenses or claims against an assign*or*–e.g., a "hell-or-high-water" provision in the underlying agreement that is assigned. If other law gives effect to this undertaking, then, under principles of *nemo dat*, the undertaking would be enforceable by the assignee (secured party). If other law prevents the assignor from enforcing the undertaking, this section nevertheless might permit the assignee to do so. The right of the assignee to enforce would depend upon whether, under the particular facts, the account debtor's undertaking fairly could be construed as an agreement that falls within the scope of this section and whether the assignee meets the requirements of this section.

5. **Relationship to Federal Trade Commission Rule.** Subsection (d) is new. It applies to rights evidenced by a record that is required to contain, but does not contain, the notice set forth in Federal Trade Commission Rule 433, 16 C.F.R. Part 433 (the "Holder-in-Due-Course Regulations"). Under this subsection, an assignee of such a record takes subject to the consumer account debtor's claims and defenses to the same extent as it would have if the writing had contained the required notice. Thus, subsection (d) effectively renders waiver-of-defense clauses ineffective in the transactions with consumers to which it applies.

6. **Relationship to Other Law.** * * * This section takes no position on the enforceability of waivers of claims and defenses by consumer account debtors, leaving that question to other law. However, the reference to "law other than this article" in subsection (e) encompasses administrative rules and regulations; * * *

This section does not displace other law that gives effect to a non-consumer account debtor's agreement not to assert defenses against an assignee, even if the agreement would not qualify under subsection (b). See subsection (f). It validates, but does not invalidate, agreements made by a non-consumer account debtor. This section also does not displace other law to the extent that the other law permits an assignee, who takes an assignment with notice of a claim of a property or possessory right, a defense, or a claim in recoupment, to enforce an account debtor's agreement not to assert claims and defenses against the assign*or* (e.g., a "hell-or-high-water" agreement). See Comment 4. It also does not displace an assignee's right to assert that an account debtor is estopped from asserting a claim or defense. Nor does this section displace other law with respect to waivers of potential future claims and defenses that are the subject of an agreement between the account debtor and the assign*ee*. Finally, it does not displace Section 1–107, concerning waiver of a breach that allegedly already has occurred.

§ 9–404. Rights Acquired by Assignee; Claims and Defenses Against Assignee

(a) [Assignee's rights subject to terms, claims, and defenses; exceptions.] Unless an account debtor has made an enforceable agreement not to assert defenses or claims, and subject to subsections (b) through (e), the rights of an assignee are subject to:

(1) all terms of the agreement between the account debtor and assignor and any defense or claim in recoupment arising from the transaction that gave rise to the contract; and

(2) any other defense or claim of the account debtor against the assignor which accrues before the account debtor receives a notification of the assignment authenticated by the assignor or the assignee.

(b) [Account debtor's claim reduces amount owed to assignee.] Subject to subsection (c) and except as otherwise provided in subsection (d), the claim of an account debtor against an assignor may be asserted against an assignee under subsection (a) only to reduce the amount the account debtor owes.

(c) [Rule for individual under other law.] This section is subject to law other than this article which establishes a different rule for an account debtor who is an individual and who incurred the obligation primarily for personal, family, or household purposes.

(d) [Omission of required statement in consumer transaction.] In a consumer transaction, if a record evidences the account debtor's obligation, law other than this article requires that the record include a statement to the effect that the account debtor's recovery against an assignee with respect to claims and defenses against the assignor may not exceed amounts paid by the account debtor under the record, and the record does not include such a statement, the extent to which a claim of an account debtor against the assignor may be asserted against an assignee is determined as if the record included such a statement.

(e) [Inapplicability to health-care-insurance receivable.] This section does not apply to an assignment of a health-care-insurance receivable.

OFFICIAL COMMENT

* * *

2. **Purpose; Rights of Assignee in General.** Subsection (a), like former Section 9–318(1), provides that an assignee generally takes an assignment subject to defenses and claims of an account debtor. Under subsection (a)(1), if the account debtor's defenses on an assigned claim arise from the transaction that gave rise to the contract with the assignor, it makes no difference whether the defense or claim accrues before or after the account debtor is notified of the assignment. Under subsection (a)(2), the assignee takes subject to other defenses or claims only if they accrue before the account debtor has been notified of the assignment. Of course, an account debtor may waive its right to assert defenses or claims against an assignee under Section 9–403 or other applicable law. Subsection (a) tracks Section 3–305(a)(3) more closely than its predecessor.

3. **Limitation on Affirmative Claims.** Subsection (b) is new. It limits the claim that the account debtor may assert against an assignee. Borrowing from Section 3–305(a)(3) and cases construing former Section 9–318, subsection (b) generally does not afford the account debtor the right to an affirmative recovery from an assignee.

4. **Consumer Account Debtors; Relationship to Federal Trade Commission Rule.** Subsections (c) and (d) also are new. Subsection (c) makes clear that the rules of this section are subject to other law establishing special rules for consumer account debtors. An "account debtor who is an individual" as used in subsection (c) includes individuals who are jointly or jointly and severally obligated. Subsection (d) applies to rights evidenced by a record that is required to contain, but does not contain, the notice

set forth in Federal Trade Commission Rule 433, 16 C.F.R. Part 433 (the "Holder-in-Due-Course Regulations"). Under subsection (d), a consumer account debtor has the same right to an affirmative recovery from an assignee of such a record as the consumer would have had against the assignee had the record contained the required notice.

5. **Scope; Application to "Account Debtor."** This section deals only with the rights and duties of "account debtors"—and for the most part only with account debtors on accounts, chattel paper, and payment intangibles. Subsection (e) provides that the obligation of an insurer with respect to a health-care-insurance receivable is governed by other law. References in this section to an "account debtor" include account debtors on collateral that is proceeds. Neither this section nor any other provision of this Article, including Sections 9–408 and 9–409, provides analogous regulation of the rights and duties of other obligors on collateral, such as the maker of a negotiable instrument (governed by Article 3), the issuer of or nominated person under a letter of credit (governed by Article 5), or the issuer of a security (governed by Article 8). Article 9 leaves those rights and duties untouched; however, Section 9–409 deals with the special case of letters of credit. When chattel paper is composed in part of a negotiable instrument, the obligor on the instrument is not an "account debtor," and Article 3 governs the rights of the assignee of the chattel paper with respect to the issues that this section addresses. See, e.g., Section 3–601 (dealing with discharge of an obligation to pay a negotiable instrument).

§ 9–405. Modification of Assigned Contract

(a) [Effect of modification on assignee.] A modification of or substitution for an assigned contract is effective against an assignee if made in good faith. The assignee acquires corresponding rights under the modified or substituted contract. The assignment may provide that the modification or substitution is a breach of contract by the assignor. This subsection is subject to subsections (b) through (d).

(b) [Applicability of subsection (a).] Subsection (a) applies to the extent that:

(1) the right to payment or a part thereof under an assigned contract has not been fully earned by performance; or

(2) the right to payment or a part thereof has been fully earned by performance and the account debtor has not received notification of the assignment under Section 9–406(a).

(c) [Rule for individual under other law.] This section is subject to law other than this article which establishes a different rule for an account debtor who is an individual and who incurred the obligation primarily for personal, family, or household purposes.

(d) [Inapplicability to health-care-insurance receivable.] This section does not apply to an assignment of a health-care-insurance receivable.

OFFICIAL COMMENT

* * *

2. **Modification of Assigned Contract.** The ability of account debtors and assignors to modify assigned contracts can be important, especially in the case of government contracts and complex contractual arrangements (e.g., construction contracts) with respect to which modifications are customary. Subsections (a) and (b) provide that good-faith modifications of assigned contracts are binding against an assignee to the extent that (i) the right to payment has not been fully earned or (ii) the right to payment has been earned and notification of the assignment has not been given to the account debtor. Former Section 9–318(2) did not validate modifications of fully-performed contracts under any circumstances, whether or not notification of the assignment had been given to the account debtor. Subsection (a) protects the interests of assignees by (i) limiting the effectiveness of modifications to those made in good faith, (ii) affording the assignee with corresponding rights under the contract as modified, and (iii) recognizing that the modification may be a breach of the assignor's agreement with the assignee.

3. **Consumer Account Debtors.** Subsection (c) is new. It makes clear that the rules of this section are subject to other law establishing special rules for consumer account debtors.

4. **Account Debtors on Health-Care-Insurance Receivables.** Subsection (d) also is new. It provides that this section does not apply to an assignment of a health-care-insurance receivable. The obligation of an insurer with respect to a health-care-insurance receivable is governed by other law.

§ 9–406. Discharge of Account Debtor; Notification of Assignment; Identification and Proof of Assignment; Restrictions on Assignment of Accounts, Chattel Paper, Payment Intangibles, and Promissory Notes Ineffective

(a) [Discharge of account debtor; effect of notification.] Subject to subsections (b) through (i), an account debtor on an account, chattel paper, or a payment intangible may discharge its obligation by paying the assignor until, but not after, the account debtor receives a notification, authenticated by the assignor or the assignee, that the amount due or to become due has been assigned and that payment is to be made to the assignee. After receipt of the notification, the account debtor may discharge its obligation by paying the assignee and may not discharge the obligation by paying the assignor.

(b) [When notification ineffective.] Subject to subsection (h), notification is ineffective under subsection (a):

(1) if it does not reasonably identify the rights assigned;

(2) to the extent that an agreement between an account debtor and a seller of a payment intangible limits the account debtor's duty to pay a person other than the seller and the limitation is effective under law other than this article; or

(3) at the option of an account debtor, if the notification notifies the account debtor to make less than the full amount of any

installment or other periodic payment to the assignee, even if:

 (A) only a portion of the account, chattel paper, or payment intangible has been assigned to that assignee;

 (B) a portion has been assigned to another assignee; or

 (C) the account debtor knows that the assignment to that assignee is limited.

(c) [Proof of assignment.] Subject to subsection (h), if requested by the account debtor, an assignee shall seasonably furnish reasonable proof that the assignment has been made. Unless the assignee complies, the account debtor may discharge its obligation by paying the assignor, even if the account debtor has received a notification under subsection (a).

(d) [Term restricting assignment generally ineffective.] Except as otherwise provided in subsection (e) and Sections 2A–303 and 9–407, and subject to subsection (h), a term in an agreement between an account debtor and an assignor or in a promissory note is ineffective to the extent that it:

 (1) prohibits, restricts, or requires the consent of the account debtor or person obligated on the promissory note to the assignment or transfer of, or the creation, attachment, perfection, or enforcement of a security interest in, the account, chattel paper, payment intangible, or promissory note; or

 (2) provides that the assignment or transfer or the creation, attachment, perfection, or enforcement of the security interest may give rise to a default, breach, right of recoupment, claim, defense, termination, right of termination, or remedy under the account, chattel paper, payment intangible, or promissory note.

(e) [Inapplicability of subsection (d) to certain sales.] Subsection (d) does not apply to the sale of a payment intangible or promissory note.

(f) [Legal restrictions on assignment generally ineffective.] Except as otherwise provided in Sections 2A–303 and 9–407 and subject to subsections (h) and (i), a rule of law, statute, or regulation that prohibits, restricts, or requires the consent of a government, governmental body or official, or account debtor to the assignment or transfer of, or creation of a security interest in, an account or chattel paper is ineffective to the extent that the rule of law, statute, or regulation:

(1) prohibits, restricts, or requires the consent of the government, governmental body or official, or account debtor to the assignment or transfer of, or the creation, attachment, perfection, or enforcement of a security interest in the account or chattel paper; or

(2) provides that the assignment or transfer or the creation, attachment, perfection, or enforcement of the security interest may give rise to a default, breach, right of recoupment, claim, defense, termination, right of termination, or remedy under the account or chattel paper.

(g) [Subsection (b)(3) not waivable.] Subject to subsection (h), an account debtor may not waive or vary its option under subsection (b)(3).

(h) [Rule for individual under other law.] This section is subject to law other than this article which establishes a different rule for an account debtor who is an individual and who incurred the obligation primarily for personal, family, or household purposes.

(i) [Inapplicability to health-care-insurance receivable.] This section does not apply to an assignment of a health-care-insurance receivable.

(j) [Section prevails over specified inconsistent law.] This section prevails over any inconsistent provisions of the following statutes, rules, and regulations:

[List here any statutes, rules, and regulations containing provisions inconsistent with this section.]

Legislative Note: States that amend statutes, rules, and regulations to remove provisions inconsistent with this section need not enact subsection (j)

OFFICIAL COMMENT

* * *

2. **Account Debtor's Right to Pay Assignor Until Notification.** Subsection (a) provides the general rule concerning an account debtor's right to pay the assignor until the account debtor receives appropriate notification. The revision makes clear that once the account debtor receives the notification, the account debtor cannot discharge its obligation by paying the assignor. It also makes explicit that payment to the assignor before notification, or payment to the assignee after notification, discharges the obligation.

* * * Nothing in this section conditions the effectiveness of a notification on the identity of the person who gives it. An account debtor that doubts whether the right to payment has been assigned may avail itself of the procedures in subsection (c). See Comment 4.

An effective notification under subsection (a) must be authenticated. This requirement normally could be satisfied by sending notification on the notifying person's letterhead or on a form on which the notifying person's name appears. In each case the printed name would be a symbol adopted by the notifying person for the purpose of identifying the person and adopting the notification. See Section 9–102 (defining "authenticate").

Subsection (a) applies only to account debtors on accounts, chattel paper, and payment intangibles. (Section 9–102 defines the term "account debtor" more broadly, to include those obligated on all general intangibles.) * * *

3. **Limitations on Effectiveness of Notification.** Subsection (b) contains some special rules concerning the effectiveness of a notification under subsection (a).

Subsection (b)(1) [makes] * * * ineffective a notification that does not reasonably identify the rights assigned. A reasonable identification need not identify the right to payment with specificity, but what is reasonable also is not left to the arbitrary decision of the account debtor. If an account debtor has doubt as to the adequacy of a notification, it may not be safe in disregarding the notification unless it notifies the assignee with reasonable promptness as to the respects in which the account debtor considers the notification defective.

Subsection (b)(2), * * * applies only to sales of payment intangibles. It makes a notification ineffective to the extent that other law gives effect to an agreement between an account debtor and a seller of a payment intangible that limits the account debtor's duty to pay a person other than the seller. Payment intangibles are substantially less fungible than accounts and chattel paper. In some (e.g., commercial bank loans), account debtors customarily and legitimately expect that they will not be required to pay any person other than the financial institution that has advanced funds.

It has become common in financing transactions to assign interests in a single obligation to more than one assignee. Requiring an account debtor that owes a single obligation to make multiple payments to multiple assignees would be unnecessarily burdensome. Thus, under subsection (b)(3), an account debtor that is notified to pay an assignee less than the full amount of any installment or other periodic payment has the option to treat the notification as ineffective, ignore the notice, and discharge the assigned obligation by paying the assignor. Some account debtors may not realize that the law affords them the right to ignore certain notices of assignment with impunity. By making the notification ineffective at the account debtor's option, subsection (b)(3) permits an account debtor to pay the assignee in accordance with the notice and thereby to satisfy its obligation *pro tanto*. Under subsection (g), the rights and duties created by subsection (b)(3) cannot be waived or varied.

4. **Proof of Assignment.** Subsection (c) links payment with discharge, as in subsection (a). * * * referring to the right of the account debtor to pay the assignor if the requested proof of assignment is not seasonably forthcoming. Even if the proof is not forthcoming, the notification of assignment would remain effective, so that, in the absence of reasonable proof of the assignment, the account debtor could discharge the obligation by paying either the assignee or the assignor. Of course, if the assignee did not in fact receive an assignment, the account debtor cannot discharge its obligation by paying a putative assignee who is a stranger. The observations in Comment 3 concerning the reasonableness of an identification of a right to payment also apply here. An account debtor that questions the adequacy of proof submitted by an assignee would be well advised to promptly inform the assignee of the defects.

An account debtor may face another problem if its obligation becomes due while the account debtor is awaiting reasonable proof of the assignment that it has requested from the assignee. This section does not excuse the account debtor from timely compliance with its obligations. Consequently, an account debtor that has received a notification of assignment and who has requested reasonable proof of the assignment may discharge its obligation by paying the assignor at the time (or even earlier if reasonably necessary to avoid risk of default) when a payment is due, even if the account debtor has not yet received a response to its request for proof. On the other hand, after requesting reasonable proof of the assignment, an account debtor may not discharge its obligation by paying the assignor substantially in advance of the time that the payment is due unless the assignee has failed to provide the proof seasonably.

5. **Contractual Restrictions on Assignment.** Former Section 9–318(4) rendered ineffective an agreement between an account debtor and an assignor which prohibited assignment of an account (whether outright or to secure an obligation) or prohibited a security assignment of a general intangible for the payment of money due or to become due. Subsection (d) essentially follows former Section 9–318(4), but expands the rule of free assignability to chattel paper (subject to Sections 2A–303 and 9–407) and promissory notes and explicitly overrides both restrictions and prohibitions of assignment. The policies underlying the ineffectiveness of contractual restrictions under this section build on common-law developments that essentially have eliminated legal restrictions on assignments of rights to payment as security and other assignments of rights to payment such as accounts and chattel paper. Any that might linger for accounts and chattel paper are addressed by new subsection (f). See Comment 6.

Former Section 9–318(4) did not apply to a sale of a payment intangible (as described in the former provision, "a general intangible for money due or to become due") but did apply to an assignment of a payment intangible for security. Subsection (e) continues this approach and also makes subsection (d) inapplicable to sales of promissory notes. Section 9–408 addresses anti-assignment clauses with respect to sales of payment intangibles and promissory notes.

Like former Section 9–318(4), subsection (d) provides that anti-assignment clauses are "ineffective." The quoted term means that the clause is of no effect whatsoever; the clause does not prevent the assignment from taking effect between the parties and the prohibited assignment does not constitute a default under the agreement between the account debtor and assignor. However, subsection (d) does not override terms that do not directly prohibit, restrict, or require consent to an assignment but which might, nonetheless, present a practical impairment of the assignment. Properly read, however, subsection (d) reaches only covenants that prohibit, restrict, or require consents to assignments; it does not override all terms that might "impair" an assignment in fact.

Example: Buyer enters into an agreement with Seller to buy equipment that Seller is to manufacture according to Buyer's specifications. Buyer agrees to make a series of prepayments during the construction process. In return, Seller agrees to set aside the prepaid funds in a special account and to use the funds solely for the manufacture of the designated equipment. Seller also agrees that it will not assign any of its rights under the sale agreement with Buyer. Nevertheless, Seller grants to Secured Party a security interest in its accounts. Seller's anti-assignment agreement is ineffective under subsection (d); its agreement concerning the use of prepaid funds, which is not a restriction or prohibition on assignment, is not. However, if Secured Party notifies Buyer to make all future payments directly to Secured Party, Buyer will be obliged to do so under subsection (a) if it wishes the payments to discharge its obligation. Unless Secured Party releases the funds to Seller so that Seller can comply with its use-of-funds covenant, Seller will be in breach of that covenant.

In the example, there appears to be a plausible business purpose for the use-of-funds covenant. However, a court may conclude that a covenant with no business purpose other than imposing an impediment to an assignment actually is a direct restriction that is rendered ineffective by subsection (d).

6. **Legal Restrictions on Assignment.** Former Section 9–318(4), like subsection (d) of this section, addressed only contractual restrictions on assignment. The former section was grounded on the

reality that legal, as opposed to contractual, restrictions on assignments of rights to payment had largely disappeared. New subsection (f) codifies this principle of free assignability for accounts and chattel paper. For the most part the discussion of contractual restrictions in Comment 5 applies as well to legal restrictions rendered ineffective under subsection (f).

7. **Multiple Assignments.** This section, like former Section 9–318, is not a complete codification of the law of assignments of rights to payment. In particular, it is silent concerning many of the ramifications for an account debtor in cases of multiple assignments of the same right. For example, an assignor might assign the same receivable to multiple assignees (which assignments could be either inadvertent or wrongful). Or, the assignor could assign the receivable to assignee–1, which then might re-assign it to assignee–2, and so forth. The rights and duties of an account debtor in the face of multiple assignments and in other circumstances not resolved in the statutory text are left to the common-law rules. See, e.g., Restatement (2d), Contracts §§ 338(3), 339. The failure of former Article 9 to codify these rules does not appear to have caused problems.

8. **Consumer Account Debtors.** Subsection (h) is new. It makes clear that the rules of this section are subject to other law establishing special rules for consumer account debtors.

9. **Account Debtors on Health-Care–Insurance Receivables.** Subsection (i) also is new. The obligation of an insurer with respect to a health-care-insurance receivable is governed by other law. Section 9–408 addresses contractual and legal restrictions on the assignment of a health-care-insurance receivable.

§ 9–408. Restrictions on Assignment of Promissory Notes, Health-Care-Insurance Receivables, and Certain General Intangibles Ineffective

(a) [Term restricting assignment generally ineffective.] Except as otherwise provided in subsection (b), a term in a promissory note or in an agreement between an account debtor and a debtor which relates to a health-care-insurance receivable or a general intangible, including a contract, permit, license, or franchise, and which term prohibits, restricts, or requires the consent of the person obligated on the promissory note or the account debtor to, the assignment or transfer of, or creation, attachment, or perfection of a security interest in, the promissory note, health-care-insurance receivable, or general intangible, is ineffective to the extent that the term:

(1) would impair the creation, attachment, or perfection of a security interest; or

(2) provides that the assignment or transfer or the creation, attachment, or perfection of the security interest may give rise to a default, breach, right of recoupment, claim, defense, termination, right of termination, or remedy under the promissory note, health-care-insurance receivable, or general intangible.

(b) [Applicability of subsection (a) to sales of certain rights to payment.] Subsection (a) applies to a security interest in a payment intangible or promissory note only if the security interest arises out of a sale of the payment intangible or promissory note.

(c) [Legal restrictions on assignment generally ineffective.] A rule of law, statute, or regulation that prohibits, restricts, or requires the consent of a government, governmental body or official, person obligated on a promissory note, or account debtor to the assignment or transfer of, or creation of a security interest in, a promissory note, health-care-insurance receivable, or general intangible, including a contract, permit, license, or franchise between an account debtor and a debtor, is ineffective to the extent that the rule of law, statute, or regulation:

(1) would impair the creation, attachment, or perfection of a security interest; or

(2) provides that the assignment or transfer or the creation, attachment, or perfection of the security interest may give rise to a default, breach, right of recoupment, claim, defense, termination, right of termination, or remedy under the promissory note, health-care-insurance receivable, or general intangible.

(d) [Limitation on ineffectiveness under subsections (a) and (c).] To the extent that a term in a promissory note or in an agreement between an account debtor and a debtor which relates to a health-care-insurance receivable or general intangible or a rule of law, statute, or regulation described in subsection (c) would be effective under law other than this article but is ineffective under subsection (a) or (c), the creation, attachment, or perfection of a security interest in the promissory note, health-care-insurance receivable, or general intangible:

(1) is not enforceable against the person obligated on the promissory note or the account debtor;

(2) does not impose a duty or obligation on the person obligated on the promissory note or the account debtor;

(3) does not require the person obligated on the promissory note or the account debtor to recognize the security interest, pay or render performance to the secured party, or accept payment or performance from the secured party;

(4) does not entitle the secured party to use or assign the debtor's rights under the promissory note, health-care-insurance receivable, or general intangible, including any related information or materials furnished to the debtor in the transaction giving rise to the promissory note, health-care-insurance receivable, or general intangible;

(5) does not entitle the secured party to use, assign, possess, or have access to any trade secrets or confidential information of the person obligated on the promissory note or the account debtor; and

(6) does not entitle the secured party to enforce the security interest in the promissory note, health-care-insurance receivable, or general intangible.

(e) [Section prevails over specified inconsistent law.] This section prevails over any inconsistent provisions of the following statutes, rules, and regulations:

[List here any statutes, rules, and regulations containing provisions inconsistent with this section.]

Legislative Note: States that amend statutes, rules, and regulations to remove provisions inconsistent with this section need not enact subsection (e).

OFFICIAL COMMENT

* * *

2. **Free Assignability.** This section makes ineffective any attempt to restrict the assignment of a general intangible, health-care-insurance receivable, or promissory note, whether the restriction appears in the terms of a promissory note or the agreement between an account debtor and a debtor (subsection (a)) or in a rule of law, including a statute or governmental rule or regulation (subsection (c)). This result allows the creation, attachment, and perfection of a security interest in a general intangible, such as an agreement for the nonexclusive license of software, as well as sales of certain receivables, such as a health-care-insurance receivable (which is an "account"), payment intangible, or promissory note, without giving rise to a default or breach by the assignor or from triggering a remedy of the account debtor or person obligated on a promissory note. This enhances the ability of certain debtors to obtain credit. On the other hand, subsection (d) protects the other party—the "account debtor" on a general intangible or the person obligated on a promissory note—from adverse effects arising from the security interest. It leaves the account debtor's or obligated person's rights and obligations unaffected in all material respects if a restriction rendered ineffective by subsection (a) or (c) would be effective under law other than Article 9.

Example 1: A term of an agreement for the nonexclusive license of computer software prohibits the licensee from assigning any of its rights as licensee with respect to the software. The agreement also provides that an attempt to assign rights in violation of the restriction is a default entitling the licensor to terminate the license agreement. The licensee, as debtor, grants to a secured party a security interest in its rights under the license and in the computers in which it is installed. Under this section, the term prohibiting assignment and providing for a default upon an attempted assignment is ineffective to prevent the creation, attachment, or perfection of the security interest or entitle the licensor to terminate the license agreement. However, under subsection (d), the secured party (absent the licensor's agreement) is not entitled to enforce the license or to use, assign, or otherwise enjoy the benefits of the licensed software, and the licensor need not recognize (or pay any attention to) the secured party. Even if the secured party takes possession of the computers on the debtor's default, the debtor would remain free to remove the software from the computer, load it on another computer, and continue to use it, if the license so permits. If the debtor does not remove the software, other law may require the secured party to remove it before disposing of the computer. Disposition of the software with the computer could violate an effective prohibition on enforcement of the security interest. See subsection (d).

3. **Nature of Debtor's Interest.** Neither this section nor any other provision of this Article determines whether a debtor has a property interest. The definition of the term "security interest" provides that it is an "interest in personal property." See Section 1–201(37). Ordinarily, a debtor can create a security interest in collateral only if it has "rights in the collateral." See Section 9–203(b). Other law determines whether a debtor has a property interest ("rights in the collateral") and the nature of that interest. For example, the nonexclusive license addressed in Example 1 may not create any property interest whatsoever in the intellectual property (e.g., copyright) that underlies the license and that effectively enables the licensor to grant the license. The debtor's property interest may be confined solely to its interest in the promises made by the licensor in the license agreement (e.g., a promise not to sue the debtor for its use of the software).

4. **Scope: Sales of Payment Intangibles and Other General Intangibles; Assignments Unaffected by this Section.** Subsections (a) and (c) render ineffective restrictions on assignments only "to the extent" that the assignments restrict the "creation, attachment, or perfection of a security interest," including sales of payment intangibles and promissory notes. This section does not render ineffective a restriction on an assignment that does not create a security interest. For example, if the debtor in Comment 2, Example 1 purported to assign the license to another entity that would use the computer software itself, other law would govern the effectiveness of the anti-assignment provisions.

Subsection (a) applies to a security interest in payment intangibles only if the security interest arises out of sale of the payment intangibles. Contractual restrictions directed to security interests in payment intangibles which secure an obligation are subject to Section 9–406(d). Subsection (a) also deals with sales of promissory notes which also create security interests. See Section 9–109(a). Subsection (c) deals with all security interests in payment intangibles or promissory notes, whether or not arising out of a sale.

Subsection (a) does not render ineffective any term, and subsection (c) does not render ineffective any law, statute or regulation, that restricts outright sales of general intangibles other than payment intangibles. They deal only with restrictions on security interests. The only sales of general intangibles that create security interests are sales of payment intangibles.

5. **Terminology: "Account Debtor"; "Person Obligated on a Promissory Note."** This section uses the term "account debtor" as it is defined in Section 9–102. The term refers to the party, other than the debtor, to a general intangible, including a permit, license, franchise, or the like, and the person obligated on a health-care-insurance receivable, which is a type of account. The definition of "account debtor" does not limit the term to persons who are obligated to *pay* under a general intangible. Rather, the term includes all persons who are obligated on a general intangible, including those who are obligated to render performance in exchange for payment. In some cases, e.g., the creation of a security interest in a franchisee's rights under a franchise agreement, the principal payment obligation may be owed *by* the debtor (franchisee) *to* the account debtor (franchisor). This section also refers to a "person obligated on a promissory note," inasmuch as those persons do not fall within the definition of "account debtor."

Example 2: A licensor and licensee enter into an agreement for the nonexclusive license of computer software. The licensee's interest in the license agreement is a general intangible. If the licensee grants to a secured party a security interest in its rights under the license agreement, the licensee is the debtor and the licensor is the account debtor. On the other hand, if the licensor grants to a secured party a security interest in its right to payment (an account) under the license agreement, the licensor is the debtor and the licensee is the account debtor. (This section applies to the security interest in the general intangible but not to the security interest in the account, which is not a health-care-insurance receivable.)

6. **Effects on Account Debtors and Persons Obligated on Promissory Notes.** Subsections (a) and (c) affect two classes of persons. These subsections affect account debtors on general intangibles and health-care-insurance receivables and persons obligated on promissory notes. Subsection (c) also affects governmental entities that enact or determine rules of law. *However, subsection (d) ensures that these affected persons are not affected adversely.* That provision removes any burdens or adverse effects on these persons for which any rational basis could exist to restrict the effectiveness of an assignment or to exercise any remedies. For this reason, the effects of subsections (a) and (c) are immaterial insofar as those persons are concerned.

Subsection (a) does not override terms that do not directly prohibit, restrict, or require consent to an assignment but which might, nonetheless, present a practical impairment of the assignment. Properly read, however, this section, like Section 9–406(d), reaches only covenants that prohibit, restrict, or require consents to assignments; it does not override all terms that might "impair" an assignment in fact.

Example 3: A licensor and licensee enter into an agreement for the nonexclusive license of valuable business software. The license agreement includes terms (i) prohibiting the licensee from assigning its rights under the license, (ii) prohibiting the licensee from disclosing to anyone certain information relating to the software and the licensor, and (iii) deeming prohibited assignments and prohibited disclosures to be defaults. The licensee wishes to obtain financing and, in exchange, is willing to grant a security interest in its rights under the license agreement. The secured party, reasonably, refuses to extend credit unless the licensee discloses the information that it is prohibited from disclosing under the license agreement. The secured party cannot determine the value of the proposed collateral in the absence of this information. Under this section, the terms of the license prohibiting the assignment (grant of the security interest) and making the assignment a default are ineffective. However, the nondisclosure covenant is not a term that prohibits the assignment or creation of a security interest in the license. Consequently, the nondisclosure term is enforceable even though the *practical* effect is to restrict the licensee's ability to use its rights under the license agreement as collateral.

The nondisclosure term also would be effective in the factual setting of Comment 2, Example 1. If the secured party's possession of the computers loaded with software would put it in a position to discover confidential information that the debtor was prohibited from disclosing, the licensor should be entitled to enforce its rights against the secured party. Moreover, the licensor could have required the debtor to obtain the secured party's agreement that (i) it would immediately return all copies of software loaded on the computers and that (ii) it would not examine or otherwise acquire any information contained in the software. This section does not prevent an account debtor from protecting by agreement its independent interests that are unrelated to the "creation, attachment, or perfection" of a security interest. In Example 1, moreover, the secured party is not in possession of copies of software by virtue of its security interest or in connection with enforcing its security interest *in the debtor's license of the software*. Its possession is incidental to its possession of the computers, in which it has a security interest. Enforcing against the secured party a restriction relating to the software in no way interferes with its security interest in the computers.

7. **Effect in Assignor's Bankruptcy.** This section could have a substantial effect if the assignor enters bankruptcy. Roughly speaking, Bankruptcy Code Section 552 invalidates security interests in property acquired after a bankruptcy petition is filed, except to the extent that the postpetition property constitutes proceeds of prepetition collateral.

Example 4: A debtor is the owner of a cable television franchise that, under applicable law, cannot be assigned without the consent of the municipal franchisor. A lender wishes to extend credit to the debtor, provided that the credit is secured by the debtor's "going business" value. To secure the loan, the debtor grants a security interest in all its existing and after-acquired property. The franchise represents the principal value of the business. The municipality refuses to consent to any assignment for collateral purposes. If other law were given effect, the security interest in the franchise would not attach; and if the debtor were to enter bankruptcy and sell the business, the secured party would receive but a fraction of the business's value. Under this section, however, the security interest would attach to the franchise. As a result, the security interest would attach to the proceeds of any sale of the franchise while a bankruptcy is pending. However, this section would protect the interests of the municipality by preventing the secured party from enforcing its security interest to the detriment of the municipality.

8. **Effect Outside of Bankruptcy.** The principal effects of this section will take place outside of bankruptcy. Compared to the relatively few debtors that enter bankruptcy, there are many more that do not. By making available previously unavailable property as collateral, this section should enable debtors to obtain additional credit. For purposes of determining whether to extend credit, under some circumstances a secured party may ascribe value to the collateral to which its security interest has attached, even if this section precludes the secured party from enforcing the security interest without the agreement of the account debtor or person obligated on the promissory note. This may be the case where the secured party sees a likelihood of obtaining that agreement in the future. This may also be the case where the secured party anticipates that the collateral will give rise to a type of proceeds as to which this section would not apply.

Example 5: Under the facts of Example 4, the debtor does not enter bankruptcy. Perhaps in exchange for a fee, the municipality agrees that the debtor may transfer the franchise to a buyer. As consideration for the transfer, the debtor receives from the buyer its check for part of the purchase price and its promissory note for the balance. The security interest attaches to the check and promissory note as proceeds. See Section 9–315(a)(2). This section does not apply to the security interest in the check, which is not a promissory note, health-care-insurance receivable, or general intangible. Nor does it apply to the security interest in the promissory note, inasmuch as it was not sold to the secured party.

9. **Contrary Federal Law.** This section does not override federal law to the contrary. However, it does reflect an important policy judgment that should provide a template for future federal law reforms.

PART 5. FILING

[SUBPART 1. FILING OFFICE; CONTENTS AND EFFECTIVENESS OF FINANCING STATEMENT]

§ 9–501. Filing Office

(a) **[Filing offices.]** Except as otherwise provided in subsection (b), if the local law of this State governs perfection of a security interest or agricultural lien, the office in which to file a financing statement to perfect the security interest or agricultural lien is:

  (1) the office designated for the filing or recording of a record of a mortgage on the related real property, if:

   (A) the collateral is as-extracted collateral or timber to be cut; or

   (B) the financing statement is filed as a fixture filing and the collateral is goods that are or are to become fixtures; or

  (2) the office of [ ] [or any office duly authorized by [ ]], in all other cases, including a case in which the collateral is goods that are or are to become fixtures and the financing statement is not filed as a fixture filing.

(b) **[Filing office for transmitting utilities.]** * * *

Legislative Note: The State should designate the filing office where the brackets appear. The filing office may be that of a governmental official (e.g., the Secretary of State) or a private party that maintains the State's filing system.

UNOFFICIAL COMMENTS

Once you have determined the appropriate state in which to file, you then need to determine the appropriate public office in that state to file the financing statement. To make this determination, review that state's version of section 9–501. Happily, most states have the "standard", no-local variation, version of section 9–501.

Section 9–501 can be tricky. The general rule is found at the end of section 9–501(a), not at the beginning of the section. Most filings will be governed by section 9–501(a)(2), not Section 9–501(a)(1). More specifically, in most states, most financing statements are filed with the Secretary of State.

NON–OBVIOUS DEFINITIONS

"Filing office" means an office designated in section 9–501 as the place to file a financing statement, section 9–102(a)(37). That one is obvious.

And it is obvious that the section 9–102(a)(39) definition of "financing statement" which defines a "financing statement" as a "financing statement" is obviously of no help. What needs to be obvious to you from that definition and from this section is that a "financing statement" is not the same thing as a "financial statement." Don't confuse the two.

OTHER UCC SECTIONS TO LOOK AT WHEN YOU LOOK AT SECTION 9–501

A financing statement will not be effective unless it is filed in the right place. To determine the right place to file, you need to first find out what is the right state in which to file. That question is answered by reviewing section 9–301 through section 9–307.

OFFICIAL COMMENT

* * *

2. **Where to File.** Subsection (a) indicates where in a given State a financing statement is to be filed. Former Article 9 afforded each State three alternative approaches, depending on the extent to which the State desires central filing (usually with the Secretary of State), local filing (usually with a county office), or both. As Comment 1 to former Section 9–401 observed, "The principal advantage of state-wide filing is ease of access to the credit information which the files exist to provide. Consider for example the national distributor who wishes to have current information about the credit standing of the thousands of persons he sells to on credit. The more completely the files are centralized on a state-wide basis, the easier and cheaper it becomes to procure credit information; the more the files are scattered in local filing units, the more burdensome and costly." Local filing increases the net costs of secured transactions also by increasing uncertainty and the number of required filings. Any benefit that local filing may have had in the 1950's is now insubstantial. Accordingly, this Article dictates central filing for most situations, while retaining local filing for real-estate-related collateral and special filing provisions for transmitting utilities.

* * *

4. **Fixtures.** There are two ways in which a secured party may file a financing statement to perfect a security interest in goods that are or are to become fixtures. It may file in the Article 9 records, as with most other goods. See subsection (a)(2). Or it may file the financing statement as a "fixture filing," defined in Section 9–102, in the office in which a record of a mortgage on the related real property would be filed. See subsection(a)(1)(B).

* * *

§ 9–502. Contents of Financing Statement; Record of Mortgage as Financing Statement; Time of Filing Financing Statement

(a) [Sufficiency of financing statement.] Subject to subsection (b), a financing statement is sufficient only if it:

(1) provides the name of the debtor;

(2) provides the name of the secured party or a representative of the secured party; and

(3) indicates the collateral covered by the financing statement.

(b) [Real-property-related financing statements.] Except as otherwise provided in Section 9–501(b), to be sufficient, a financing statement that covers as-extracted collateral or timber to be cut, or which is filed as a fixture filing and covers goods that are or are to become fixtures, must satisfy subsection (a) and also:

(1) indicate that it covers this type of collateral;

(2) indicate that it is to be filed [for record] in the real property records;

(3) provide a description of the real property to which the collateral is related [sufficient to give constructive notice of a mortgage under the law of this State if the description were contained in a record of the mortgage of the real property]; and

(4) if the debtor does not have an interest of record in the real property, provide the name of a record owner.

(c) [Record of mortgage as financing statement.] A record of a mortgage is effective, from the date of recording, as a financing statement filed as a fixture filing or as a financing statement covering as-extracted collateral or timber to be cut only if:

(1) the record indicates the goods or accounts that it covers;

(2) the goods are or are to become fixtures related to the real property described in the record or the collateral is related to the real property described in the record and is as-extracted collateral or timber to be cut;

(3) the record satisfies the requirements for a financing statement in this section other than an indication that it is to be filed in the real property records; and

(4) the record is [duly] recorded.

(d) [Filing before security agreement or attachment.] A financing statement may be filed before a security agreement is made or a security interest otherwise attaches.

* * *

UNOFFICIAL COMMENTS

A party with a security interest wants to make sure that its interest is not only enforceable against the debtor but also is enforceable against third-parties that may assert claims against the same property.

Thus, the secured party must perfect its security interest in the property. Section 9–310(a) provides the general rule that to perfect a security interest a financing statement must be filed. There are exceptions to this general rule in section 9–310(b).

Section 9–502(a) sets out the essential information to be included in the financing statement. To be effective, a financing statement must include the name of the debtor and the name of the secured party or its representative and must indicate the collateral to be covered by the financing statement. If the financing statement covers real-property-related collateral or is to act as a fixture filing, it also must (1) indicate that it covers this type of collateral, (2) indicate that it is to be filed in the real property records, (3) provide a description of the related real property, and (4) provide the name of the owner of the real property if it is not the debtor. See Subsection (b).

Notice that there is nothing in the financing statement about the amount of the debt. That is "notice filing", as explained in Official Comment 2 to section 9–502.

Section 9–502(d) permits a party to file an initial financing statement before a security agreement is made or a security interest attaches. The time of filing the financing statement can be important in determining the relative priority of security interests under section 9–322.

It is important to remember, however, that a person may file the initial financing statement only if it is entitled to do so, which in most cases requires authorization by the debtor. See section 9–509. A filed record is effective only to the extent that it was filed by a person entitled to file it. See section 9–510.

NON–OBVIOUS DEFINITIONS

The most important information on a financing statement is the debtor's name. "Debtor's name" is not a defined term although "debtor's name" is explained in Official Comment 2 to section 9–503.

You need to remember that the "debtor's name" will not always be the name of the person who is obligated to pay the debt. One more time, compare the definitions of "debtor" and "obligor" in section 9–102.

OTHER UCC SECTIONS TO LOOK TO WHEN YOU LOOK AT SECTION 9–502

Lots of sections are helpful to your understanding section 9–502.

This section tells you about the contents of a financing statement. Section 9–521 shows you the contents of a financing statement: Sections 9–521(a) and (b) provide a sample initial financing statement form and an amendment form, respectively for you to look at.

Here are some other sections to look at.

Section 9–308(a): Perfection of security interest

Except as otherwise provided in this section and section 9–309, a security interest is perfected if it has attached and all of the applicable requirements for perfection as set forth in sections 9–310 through 9–316 have been satisfied. A security interest is perfected when it attaches if the applicable requirements are satisfied before the security interest attaches.

Section 9–210: More Information About the Collateral or Debt

A financing statement may be filed before or after a security interest attaches. If the financing statement is filed before the security interest attaches, the financing statement then provides notice that a person may have a security interest in the indicated collateral. The filed financing statement does not provide (a) whether attachment has occurred, (b) information concerning the underlying obligation owed the secured party or (c) a description of the specific property covered by the security agreement. Both creditors of and purchasers from the debtor may need this missing information. Section 9–210 provides a procedure that allows only the debtor to request this information from the secured party.

Section 9–509: Who Can File

Section 9–502 does not require any signatures for the filing to be effective. Instead of signatures, section 9–509 requires that the records filed in the filing office must be authorized to be effective.

Section 9–510: Effectiveness of Filing

Section 9–510 provides, in part, that a filed financing statement is only effective if it has been filed by a party who was authorized to file the financing statement pursuant to section 9–509.

Section 9–625: Remedies for Unauthorized Filing

Section 9–625 provides a list of remedies that are available for an unauthorized filing of a record. The remedies include (1) injunctive relief limiting the secured party's rights to collect, enforce or dispose of the collateral, (2) the recovery of actual damages, and (3) the recovery of statutory damages.

Section 9–516: What Makes For Effective Financing Statement

Section 9–502 in essence sets out the minimum requirements for an effective financing statement. Section 9–516 sets out some additional requirements. The filing officer is supposed to reject for filing a financing statement that does not meet these additional section 9–516(b) requirements. Filing officers, just like other people, do not always do what they are supposed to do. If the filing officer accepts for filing a financing statement that meets all of the requirements of section 9–502 but does not meet all of the additional requirements of section 9–516(b), then that filing will be effective nevertheless.

Section 9–503: Names in Financing Statement

Section 9–502 requires that the financing statement contain the debtor's name. Filed financing statements are indexed in the filing office according to the debtor's name. Searches for what has been filed are conducted according to the debtor's name. Therefore, it is critical that the financing statement reflect the correct name of the debtor. Section 9–503(a) provides the rules that must be followed in naming the debtor in the financing statement.

Section 9–502 also requires that the financing statement name the secured party. Section 9–503(d), however, provides that the sufficiency of the secured party's name in the financing statement is not as critical as the debtor's name.

Section 9–504: Financing Statement Information About Collateral

Section 9–502 also requires that the financing statement "indicate" the collateral. Section 9–504 provides that either describing the collateral pursuant to section 9–108 or merely indicating that the financing statement covers "all assets" or "all personal property" constitutes a sufficient indication of the collateral.

OFFICIAL COMMENT

* * *

2. **"Notice Filing."** This section adopts the system of "notice filing." What is required to be filed is not, as under pre-UCC chattel mortgage and conditional sales acts, the security agreement itself, but only a simple record providing a limited amount of information (financing statement). The financing statement may be filed before the security interest attaches or thereafter. See subsection (d). See also Section 9–308(a) (contemplating situations in which a financing statement is filed before a security interest attaches).

The notice itself indicates merely that a person may have a security interest in the collateral indicated. Further inquiry from the parties concerned will be necessary to disclose the complete state of affairs. Section 9–210 provides a statutory procedure under which the secured party, at the debtor's request, may be required to make disclosure. However, in many cases, information may be forthcoming without the need to resort to the formalities of that section.

Notice filing has proved to be of great use in financing transactions involving inventory, accounts, and chattel paper, because it obviates the necessity of refiling on each of a series of transactions in a continuing arrangement under which the collateral changes from day to day. However, even in the case of filings that do not necessarily involve a series of transactions (e.g., a loan secured by a single item of equipment), a financing statement is effective to encompass transactions under a security agreement not in existence and not contemplated at the time the notice was filed, if the indication of collateral in the financing statement is sufficient to cover the collateral concerned. Similarly, a financing statement is effective to cover after-acquired property of the type indicated and to perfect with respect to future advances under security agreements, regardless of whether after-acquired property or future advances are mentioned in the financing statement and even if not in the contemplation of the parties at the time the financing statement was authorized to be filed.

3. **Debtor's Signature; Required Authorization.** Subsection (a) sets forth the simple formal requirements for an effective financing statement. These requirements are: (1) the debtor's name; (2) the name of a secured party or representative of the secured party; and (3) an indication of the collateral.

Whereas former Section 9–402(1) required the debtor's signature to appear on a financing statement, this Article contains no signature requirement. The elimination of the signature requirement facilitates paperless filing. (However, as PEB Commentary No. 15 indicates, a paperless financing statement was sufficient under former Article 9.) Elimination of the signature requirement also makes the exceptions provided by former Section 9–402(2) unnecessary.

The fact that this Article does not require that an authenticating symbol be contained in the public record does not mean that all filings are authorized. Rather, Section 9–509(a) entitles a person to file an initial financing statement, an amendment that adds collateral, or an amendment that adds a debtor only if the debtor authorizes the filing, and Section 9–509(d) entitles a person other than the debtor to file a termination statement only if the secured party of record authorizes the filing. Of course, a filing has legal effect only to the extent it is authorized. See Section 9–510.

Law other than this Article, including the law with respect to ratification of past acts, generally determines whether a person has the requisite authority to file a record under this Article. See Sections 1–103 and 9–509, Comment 3. However, under Section 9–509(b), the debtor's authentication of (or becoming bound by) a security agreement *ipso facto* constitutes the debtor's authorization of the filing of a financing statement covering the collateral described in the security agreement. The secured party need not obtain a separate authorization.

Section 9–625 provides a remedy for unauthorized filings. Making an unauthorized filing also may give rise to civil or criminal liability under other law. In addition, this Article contains provisions that assist in the discovery of unauthorized filings and the amelioration of their practical effect. For example, Section 9–518 provides a procedure whereby a person may add to the public record a statement to the effect that a financing statement indexed under the person's name was wrongfully filed, and Section 9–509(d) entitles any person to file a termination statement if the secured party of record fails to comply with its obligation to file or send one to the debtor, the debtor authorizes the filing, and the termination statement so indicates. However, the filing office is neither obligated nor permitted to inquire into issues of authorization. See Section 9–520(a).

4. **Certain Other Requirements.** Subsection (a) deletes other provisions of former Section 9–402(1) because they

seems unwise (real-property description for financing statements covering crops), unnecessary (adequacy of copies of financing statements), or both (copy of security agreement as financing statement). In addition, the filing office must reject a financing statement lacking certain other information formerly required as a condition of perfection (e.g., an address for the debtor or secured party). See Sections 9–516(b), 9–520(a). However, if the filing office accepts the record, it is effective nevertheless. See Section 9–520(c).

5. **Real-Property-Related Filings.** Subsection (b) contains the requirements for financing statements filed as fixture filings and financing statements covering timber to be cut or minerals and minerals-related accounts constituting as-extracted collateral. A description of the related real property must be sufficient to reasonably identify it. See Section 9–108. This formulation rejects the view that the real property description must be by metes and bounds, or otherwise conforming to traditional real-property practice in conveyancing, but, of course, the incorporation of such a description by reference to the recording data of a deed, mortgage or other instrument containing the description should suffice under the most stringent standards. The proper test is that a description of real property must be sufficient so that the financing statement will fit into the real-property search system and be found by a real-property searcher. Under the optional language in subsection (b)(3), the test of adequacy of the description is whether it would be adequate in a record of a mortgage of the real property. As suggested in the Legislative Note, more detail may be required if there is a tract indexing system or a land registration system.

If the debtor does not have an interest of record in the real property, a real-property-related financing statement must show the name of a record owner, and Section 9–519(d) requires the financing statement to be indexed in the name of that owner. This requirement also enables financing statements covering as-extracted collateral or timber to be cut and financing statements filed as fixture filings to fit into the real-property search system.

6. **Record of Mortgage Effective as Financing Statement.** Subsection (c) explains when a record of a mortgage is effective as a financing statement filed as a fixture filing or to cover timber to be cut or as-extracted collateral. Use of the term "record of a mortgage" recognizes that in some systems the record actually filed is not the record pursuant to which a mortgage is created. Moreover, "mortgage" is defined in Section 9–102 as an "interest in real property," not as the record that creates or evidences the mortgage or the record that is filed in the public recording systems. A record creating a mortgage may also create a security interest with respect to fixtures (or other goods) in conformity with this Article. A single agreement creating a mortgage on real property and a security interest in chattels is common and useful for certain purposes. Under subsection (c), the recording of the record evidencing a mortgage (if it satisfies the requirements for a financing statement) constitutes the filing of a financing statement as to the fixtures (but not, of course, as to other goods). Section 9–515(g) makes the usual five-year maximum life for financing statements inapplicable to mortgages that operate as fixture filings under Section 9–502(c). Such mortgages are effective for the duration of the real-property recording.

Of course, if a combined mortgage covers chattels that are not fixtures, a regular financing statement filing is necessary with respect to the chattels, and subsection (c) is inapplicable. Likewise, a financing statement filed as a "fixture filing" is not effective to perfect a security interest in personal property other than fixtures.

In some cases it may be difficult to determine whether goods are or will become fixtures. Nothing in this Part prohibits the filing of a "precautionary" fixture filing, which would provide protection in the event goods are determined to be fixtures. The fact of filing should not be a factor in the determining whether goods are fixtures. Cf. Section 9–505(b).

§ 9–503. Name of Debtor and Secured Party

(a) **[Sufficiency of debtor's name.]** A financing statement sufficiently provides the name of the debtor:

- (1) if the debtor is a registered organization, only if the financing statement provides the name of the debtor indicated on the public record of the debtor's jurisdiction of organization which shows the debtor to have been organized;

- (2) if the debtor is a decedent's estate, only if the financing statement provides the name of the decedent and indicates that the debtor is an estate;

- (3) if the debtor is a trust or a trustee acting with respect to property held in trust, only if the financing statement:

    - (A) provides the name specified for the trust in its organic documents or, if no name is specified, provides the name of the settlor and additional information sufficient to distinguish the debtor from other trusts having one or more of the same settlors; and

    - (B) indicates, in the debtor's name or otherwise, that the debtor is a trust or is a trustee acting with respect to property held in trust; and

- (4) in other cases:

    - (A) if the debtor has a name, only if it provides the individual or organizational name of the debtor; and

    - (B) if the debtor does not have a name, only if it provides the names of the partners, members, associates, or other persons comprising the debtor.

(b) **[Additional debtor-related information.]** A financing statement that provides the name of the debtor in accordance with subsection (a) is not rendered ineffective by the absence of:

- (1) a trade name or other name of the debtor; or

- (2) unless required under subsection (a)(4)(B), names of partners, members, associates, or other persons comprising the debtor.

(c) **[Debtor's trade name insufficient.]** A financing statement that provides only the debtor's trade name does not sufficiently provide the name of the debtor.

(d) [Representative capacity.] Failure to indicate the representative capacity of a secured party or representative of a secured party does not affect the sufficiency of a financing statement.

(e) [Multiple debtors and secured parties.] A financing statement may provide the name of more than one debtor and the name of more than one secured party.

UNOFFICIAL COMMENTS

Read Official Comment 2 to section 9–503 to understand why it is important for the financing statement to provide the correct name of the debtor. Section 9–503(a) through (d) provides the rules to be followed to make sure the debtor's name is correct.

If the name of the debtor in a financing statement is insufficient under section 9–503(a), then according to section 9–506(b) and (c), the financing statement will be "seriously misleading" and ineffective unless a search under the debtor's correct name discloses the flawed financing statement. If the search discloses the flawed financing statement, it will be deemed not "seriously misleading" and will be effective to perfect the security interest, assuming the financing statement contains the other information required by section 9–502.

NON–OBVIOUS DEFINITIONS

"Debtor's name" is not a defined term although "debtor's name" is explained in this section and in Official Comment 2. You need to remember that the "debtor's name" will not always be the name of the person who is obligated to pay the debt. One more time compare the definitions of "debtor" and "obligor" in section 9–102.

OTHER UCC SECTIONS TO LOOK TO WHEN YOU LOOK AT SECTION 9–503

Section 9–502: What Must Be in the Financing Statement

Section 9–502(a) provides the information that must be included in the financing statement for it to be sufficient to perfect a security interest. In addition to including the name of the secured party or its representative and an indication of the collateral covered, the financing statement must provide the debtor's name in accordance with the rules provided in section 9–503.

Section 9–516: Whether Filing Effective

Section 9–502 in essence sets out the minimum requirements for an effective financing statement. Section 9–516 sets out some additional requirements. The filing officer is supposed to reject for filing a financing statement that does not meet these additional section 9–516 requirements.

Filing officers, just like other people, do not always do what they are supposed to do. If the filing officer accepts for filing a financing statement that meets all of the requirements of section 9–502 but does not meet all of the additional requirements of section 9–516(b), then that filing will be effective nevertheless.

Section 9–520: Filing Officer

Section 9–520 requires a filing office to reject stuff for filing that is insufficient for any of the reasons listed in section 9–516(b). Section 9–520 also provides, however, that the reasons given in section 9–516(b) for refusal of a record are the only reasons that a filing office may reject the record.

As noted previously, failure to provide a name for the debtor when filing an initial financing statement or failure to identify the last name of an individual debtor when filing an initial financing statement or an amendment providing the debtor's name for the first time will cause the filing office to reject the record. Section 9–520(c) provides that if a record communicated for filing provides names and information concerning multiple debtors, the record may be accepted or rejected separately as to each listed debtor.

Section 9–506(b): Seriously Misleading Errors in Financing Statements

Section 9–506(b) provides that if the debtor's name provided in the financing statement is insufficient in accordance with section 9–503(a), then the financing statement is seriously misleading as a matter of law causing it to be ineffective unless a search in the proper filing office using the debtor's correct name discloses the financing statement with the debtor's incorrect name. In that case, the financing statement with the debtor's incorrect name would not be seriously misleading as a matter of law and would be effective.

OFFICIAL COMMENT

* * *

2. **Debtor's Name.** The requirement that a financing statement provide the debtor's name is particularly important. Financing statements are indexed under the name of the debtor, and those who wish to find financing statements search for them under the debtor's name. Subsection (a) explains what the debtor's name is for purposes of a financing statement. If the debtor is a "registered organization" (defined in Section 9–102 so as to ordinarily include corporations, limited partnerships, and limited liability companies), then the debtor's name is the name shown on the public records of the debtor's "jurisdiction of organization" (also defined in Section 9–102). Subsections (a)(2) and (a)(3) contain special rules for decedent's estates and common-law trusts. (Subsection (a)(1) applies to business trusts that are registered organizations.)

Subsection (a)(4)(A) essentially follows the first sentence of former Section 9–402(7). Section 1–201(28) defines the term "organization," which appears in subsection (a)(4), very broadly, to include all legal and commercial entities as well as associations that lack the status of a legal entity. Thus, the term includes corporations, partnerships of all kinds, business trusts, limited liability companies, unincorporated associations, personal trusts, governments, and estates. If the organization has a name, that name is the correct name to put on a financing statement. If the organization does not have a name, then the financing statement should name the individuals or other entities who comprise the organization.

Together with subsections (b) and (c), subsection (a) reflects the view prevailing under former Article 9 that the actual individual or organizational name of the debtor on a financing statement is both necessary and sufficient, whether or not the financing statement provides trade or other names of the debtor and, if the debtor has a name, whether or not the financing statement provides the names of the partners, members, or associates who comprise the debtor.

Note that, even if the name provided in an initial financing statement is correct, the filing office nevertheless must reject the financing statement if it does not identify an individual debtor's last name (e.g., if it is not clear whether the debtor's name is Perry Mason or Mason Perry). See Section 9–516(b)(3)(C).

3. **Secured Party's Name.** New subsection (d) makes clear that when the secured party is a representative, a financing statement is sufficient if it names the secured party, whether or not it indicates any representative capacity. Similarly, a financing statement that names a representative of the secured party is sufficient, even if it does not indicate the representative capacity.

Example: Debtor creates a security interest in favor of Bank X, Bank Y, and Bank Z, but not to their representative, the collateral agent (Bank A). The collateral agent is not itself a secured party. See Section 9–102. Under Sections 9–502(a) and 9–503(d), however, a financing statement is effective if it names as secured party Bank A and not the actual secured parties, even if it omits Bank A's representative capacity.

Each person whose name is provided in an initial financing statement as the name of the secured party or representative of the secured party is a secured party of record. See Section 9–511.

4. **Multiple Names.** Subsection (e) makes explicit what is implicit under former Article 9: a financing statement may provide the name of more than one debtor and secured party. See Section 1–102(5)(a) (words in the singular include the plural). With respect to records relating to more than one debtor, see Section 9–520(d). With respect to financing statements providing the name of more than one secured party, see Sections 9–509(e) and 9–510(b).

§ 9–504. Indication of Collateral

A financing statement sufficiently indicates the collateral that it covers if the financing statement provides:

(1) a description of the collateral pursuant to Section 9–108; or

(2) an indication that the financing statement covers all assets or all personal property.

UNOFFICIAL COMMENTS

Section 9–502(a) provides, in part, that for a financing statement to be sufficient it must indicate the collateral covered by the financing statement. Section 9–504 sets out two methods a secured party may use to indicate the collateral in the financing statement. The first method is to describe the collateral in accordance with section 9–108. The second method is to use an all-encompassing phrase such as "all the debtor's assets" or "all the debtor's personal property."

This second method is easier and safer. No possibility of leaving stuff out. No possibility of not being perfected because of problems with the collateral description. If there are errors or omissions in a specific collateral description that cause the financing statement to be seriously misleading, then the financing statement will be ineffective under section 9–506(a).

It is important to note again that while a supergeneric description may be used to "indicate" collateral covered by a financing statement, it may not be used to "describe" the collateral covered by a security agreement. Remember the differences in the purpose of a financing statement and the purpose of a security agreement. The filed financing statement merely provides notice that a person may have a security interest in the indicated collateral. The security agreement, on the other hand, creates the security interest in the described collateral, and the description of the collateral, therefore, must reasonably identify the collateral pursuant to the rules in section 9–108.

OTHER SECTIONS TO LOOK TO WHEN YOU LOOK AT SECTION 9–504

Not Section 9–108: Sufficiency of Description

Be careful in looking at section 9–108. Section 9–108(a), (b) and (c) describe what constitutes a "sufficient description" of collateral . Sections 9–108(c) and (e), provide certain descriptions of collateral that are insufficient. For example, a description of collateral in a security agreement as "all the debtor's assets" or "all the debtor's personal property" is not sufficient. That's because a security agreement has to contain a description of collateral.

While the use of such supergeneric descriptions is insufficient in a security agreement, it is sufficient in a financing statement. See section 9–504(2). That's because a financing statement does not have to contain a description of collateral.

OFFICIAL COMMENT

* * *

2. **Indication of Collateral.** To comply with Section 9–502(a), a financing statement must "indicate" the collateral it covers. A financing statement sufficiently indicates collateral claimed to be covered by the financing statement if it satisfies the purpose of conditioning perfection on the filing of a financing statement, i.e., if it provides notice that a person may have a security interest in the collateral claimed. See Section 9–502, Comment 2. In particular, an indication of collateral that would have satisfied the requirements of former Section 9–402(1) (i.e., "a statement indicating the types, or

describing the items, of collateral") suffices under Section 9502(a). An indication may satisfy the requirements of Section 9–502(a), even if it would not have satisfied the requirements of former Section 9–402(1).

This section provides two safe harbors. Under paragraph (1), a "description" of the collateral (as the term is explained in Section 9–108) suffices as an indication for purposes of the sufficiency of a financing statement.

Debtors sometimes create a security interest in all, or substantially all, of their assets. To accommodate this practice, paragraph (2) expands the class of sufficient collateral references to embrace "an indication that the financing statement covers all assets or all personal property." If the property in question belongs to the debtor and is personal property, any searcher will know that the property is covered by the financing statement. Of course, regardless of its breadth, a financing statement has no effect with respect to property indicated but to which a security interest has not attached. Note that a broad statement of this kind (e.g., "all debtor's personal property") would not be a sufficient "description" for purposes of a security agreement. See Sections 9–203(b)(3)(A), 9–108. It follows that a somewhat narrower description than "all assets," e.g., "all assets other than automobiles," is sufficient for purposes of this section, even if it does not suffice for purposes of a security agreement.

§ 9–505. Filing and Compliance With Other Statutes and Treaties for Consignments, Leases, Other Bailments, and Other Transactions

(a) [Use of terms other than "debtor" and "secured party."] A consignor, lessor, or other bailor of goods, a licensor, or a buyer of a payment intangible or promissory note may file a financing statement, or may comply with a statute or treaty described in Section 9–311(a), using the terms "consignor", "consignee", "lessor", "lessee", "bailor", "bailee", "licensor", "licensee", "owner", "registered owner", "buyer", "seller", or words of similar import, instead of the terms "secured party" and "debtor".

(b) [Effect of financing statement under subsection (a).] This part applies to the filing of a financing statement under subsection (a) and, as appropriate, to compliance that is equivalent to filing a financing statement under Section 9–311(b), but the filing or compliance is not of itself a factor in determining whether the collateral secures an obligation. If it is determined for another reason that the collateral secures an obligation, a security interest held by the consignor, lessor, bailor, licensor, owner, or buyer which attaches to the collateral is perfected by the filing or compliance.

UNOFFICIAL COMMENTS

Sometimes it is difficult to determine whether a transaction between parties is an Article 9 transaction, especially when the transaction takes the form of a lease, sale, consignment, or bailment. Section 9–505 permits a lessor, buyer, consignor, bailor or licensor to make a precautionary financing statement filing. This filing under Article 9 or compliance with other law pursuant to section 9–311(a), however, is not determinative of whether the transaction is an Article 9 transaction.

This precautionary filing can be real important if (1) there is a later bankruptcy and (2) the court concludes that the transaction was an Article 9 transaction. Remember, unperfected Article 9 transactions can be avoided under Bankruptcy Code section 544 read together with section 9–317.

For a more complete discussion of Article 9 and consignments, see pages 409–411 infra. For a more complete discussion of Article 9 and leases, see pages 411–413 infra.

NON–OBVIOUS DEFINITIONS

The section 9–102(a)(20) definition of "consignment" is real long. And real important.

OTHER UCC SECTIONS TO LOOK TO WHEN YOU LOOK AT SECTION 9–505

Section 9–109: Scope of Article 9

While most Article 9 transactions are either loans or sales on credit, Article 9 is not limited to transactions in any particular form. Regardless of what the transaction is called, it is within the scope of Article 9 if it creates a security interest in personal property or fixtures. Article 9 also applies to consignments.

Section 1–203: Leases

Look to this section to determine whether a transaction structured as a lease creates a security interest in personal property or fixtures and, therefore, is within the scope of Article 9.

OFFICIAL COMMENT

* * *

2. **Precautionary Filing.** Occasionally, doubts arise concerning whether a transaction creates a relationship to which this Article or its filing provisions apply. For example, questions may arise over whether a "lease" of equipment in fact creates a security interest or whether the "sale" of payment intangibles in fact secures an obligation, thereby requiring action to perfect the security interest. This section * * * affords the option of filing of a financing statement with appropriate changes of terminology but without affecting the substantive question of classification of the transaction.

* * *

4. **Consignments.** Although a "true" consignment is a bailment, the filing and priority provisions of former Article 9 applied to "true" consignments. * * * A consignment "intended as security" created a security interest that was in all respects subject to former Article 9. This Article subsumes most true consignments under the rubric of "security interest." See Sections 9–102 (definition of "consignment"), 9–109(a)(4), 1–201(37) (definition of "security interest"). Nevertheless, it maintains the distinction between

a (true) "consignment," as to which only certain aspects of Article 9 apply, and a so-called consignment that actually "secures an obligation," to which Article 9 applies in full. The revisions to this section reflect the change in terminology.

§ 9–506. Effect of Errors or Omissions

(a) [Minor errors and omissions.] A financing statement substantially satisfying the requirements of this part is effective, even if it has minor errors or omissions, unless the errors or omissions make the financing statement seriously misleading.

(b) [Financing statement seriously misleading.] Except as otherwise provided in subsection (c), a financing statement that fails sufficiently to provide the name of the debtor in accordance with Section 9–503(a) is seriously misleading.

(c) [Financing statement not seriously misleading.] If a search of the records of the filing office under the debtor's correct name, using the filing office's standard search logic, if any, would disclose a financing statement that fails sufficiently to provide the name of the debtor in accordance with Section 9–503(a), the name provided does not make the financing statement seriously misleading.

(d) ["Debtor's correct name."] For purposes of Section 9–508(b), the "debtor's correct name" in subsection (c) means the correct name of the new debtor.

UNOFFICIAL COMMENTS

Again, the most important information in the financing statement is the debtor's name. It is important to remember that financing statements are filed according to the debtor's name. Searches of filed financing statements also are made according to the debtor's name.

Look to this section if the financing statement does not have the correct name of the debtor. Section 9–506(b) provides a "seriously misleading" test to determine the sufficiency of the debtor's name. Pursuant to section 9–506(b), an incorrect debtor's name pursuant to section 9–503(a) is deemed seriously misleading as a matter of law unless the section 9–506(c) search logic rule proves helpful. The first paragraph of Official Comment 2 is especially useful in understanding the section 9–506(b) "seriously misleading" test and the search logic rule.

Also, look to this section if there is now a "new debtor" who is not mentioned in the financing statement. Our explanation of section 9–508 set out above [supra, for you law review types] should be helpful in dealing with this "new debtor" problem.

NON–OBVIOUS DEFINITIONS

Since the debtor's name is the most important information in the financing statement (and the most likely error), be sure that you know when the "debtor" is different from the "obligor" and when the "debtor" is also a "new debtor" and not an "original debtor." See section 9–102.

OTHER SECTIONS TO LOOK AT WHEN YOU LOOK AT SECTION 9–506

Section 9–502: Contents of a Financing Statement

Section 9–502 sets out the minimum requirements for the contents of a financing statement (or a record of a mortgage filed as a financing statement.) A financing statement is sufficient if it provides the name of the debtor, the name of the secured party or its representative, and an indication of the covered collateral. If the financing statement covers real-property-related collateral or is filed as a fixture filing, then the financing statement, to be sufficient, also must include other real-property-related information designated in section 9–502(b).

If the record filed is a record of a mortgage rather than a financing statement, then it will be effective as a financing statement to cover the real-property-related collateral or fixtures if the record of mortgage contains the information in section 9–502(c).

Pursuant to section 9–506(a), financing statements that substantially comply with the section 9–502 requirements will be effective even if they have minor errors or omissions unless the errors or omissions make the financing statement seriously misleading. An exception to this rule, however, is a financing statement that fails to provide sufficiently the name of the debtor in accordance with section 9–503(a). That financing statement, as a matter of law, will be deemed seriously misleading unless a search using the filing office's standard search logic and using the correct debtor name discloses the record filed in the incorrect debtor name. If the search discloses the flawed financing statement, it will not be deemed seriously misleading and will be effective nevertheless.

Section 9–503: Names

Filed financing statements are indexed in the filing office according to the debtor's name. Searches by the filing office also are conducted according to the debtor's name. Therefore, it is critical that the debtor's name in the financing statement be sufficient. Section 9–503(a) provides the rules that must be followed when naming the debtor in the financing statement.

The sufficiency of the secured party's name in the financing statement is not as critical

Section 9–508: New Debtor

Section 9–508 addresses the effectiveness of a financing statement in situations in which another person, a "new debtor", by contract or operation of law, becomes subsequently bound as debtor by a security agreement previously authenticated by someone else, the "original debtor". See sections 9–102(a)(56) and 9–203(d)(1). Once the new debtor becomes bound by the security agreement, its property will be subject to the security interest to the extent the new debtor's property comes within the description of collateral in the security agreement.

Section 9–508(a) provides that the financing statement filed as to the original debtor will be effective to perfect a security interest in property of the new debtor to the extent the financing statement would have been effective had the original debtor acquired rights in the property. Section 9–508(b), however, provides that should the name of the original debtor and the correct name of the new debtor be so different as to be seriously misleading, then the filed financing statement in the original debtor's name will be effective only to perfect a security interest in property acquired by the new debtor before and within four months after the new debtor becomes bound unless the secured party files an initial financing statement in the name of the new debtor before the expiration of the four month grace period.

OFFICIAL COMMENT

* * *

2. **Errors.** Like former Section 9–402(8), subsection (a) is in line with the policy of this Article to simplify formal requisites and filing requirements. It is designed to discourage the fanatical and impossibly refined reading of statutory requirements in which courts occasionally have indulged themselves. Subsection (a) provides the standard applicable to indications of collateral. Subsections (b) and (c), which are new, concern the effectiveness of financing statements in which the debtor's name is incorrect. Subsection (b) contains the general rule: a financing statement that fails sufficiently to provide the debtor's name in accordance with Section 9–503(a) is seriously misleading as a matter of law. Subsection (c) provides an exception: If the financing statement nevertheless would be discovered in a search under the debtor's correct name, using the filing office's standard search logic, if any, then as a matter of law the incorrect name does not make the financing statement seriously misleading. A financing statement that is seriously misleading under this section is ineffective even if it is disclosed by (i) using a search logic other than that of the filing office to search the official records, or (ii) using the filing office's standard search logic to search a data base other than that of the filing office.

In addition to requiring the debtor's name and an indication of the collateral, Section 9–502(a) requires a financing statement to provide the name of the secured party or a representative of the secured party. Inasmuch as searches are not conducted under the secured party's name, and no filing is needed to continue the perfected status of security interest after it is assigned, an error in the name of the secured party or its representative will not be seriously misleading. However, in an appropriate case, an error of this kind may give rise to an estoppel in favor of a particular holder of a conflicting claim to the collateral. See Section 1–103.

3. **New Debtors.** Subsection (d) provides that, in determining the extent to which a financing statement naming an original debtor is effective against a new debtor, the sufficiency of the financing statement should be tested against the name of the new debtor.

§ 9–507. Effect of Certain Events on Effectiveness of Financing Statement

(a) [Disposition.] A filed financing statement remains effective with respect to collateral that is sold, exchanged, leased, licensed, or otherwise disposed of and in which a security interest or agricultural lien continues, even if the secured party knows of or consents to the disposition.

(b) [Information becoming seriously misleading.] Except as otherwise provided in subsection (c) and Section 9–508, a financing statement is not rendered ineffective if, after the financing statement is filed, the information provided in the financing statement becomes seriously misleading under Section 9–506.

(c) [Change in debtor's name.] If a debtor so changes its name that a filed financing statement becomes seriously misleading under Section 9–506:

(1) the financing statement is effective to perfect a security interest in collateral acquired by the debtor before, or within four months after, the change; and

(2) the financing statement is not effective to perfect a security interest in collateral acquired by the debtor more than four months after the change, unless an amendment to the financing statement which renders the financing statement not seriously misleading is filed within four months after the change.

UNOFFICIAL COMMENTS

This section probably should be two different sections. Section 9–507 deals with two different "certain events": (1) the debtor sells the collateral to someone else in a transaction that does not affect the existence of the security interest or (2) the debtor changes its name.

These two different events have the same effect but trigger different rules. If either of these "certain events" occurs, the name of the debtor indicated on the financing statement may be "seriously misleading", i.e., may not indicate the name of the person now in possession of the collateral.

If the "certain event" in your problem is the debtor's sale of collateral to a transferee in the same jurisdiction, no refiling is necessary. See section 9–507(a) and Official Comment 3. That is easy.

If the "certain event" is the debtor's change of name, the rules are more complicated. Refiling may be necessary in order to be perfected as to new collateral acquired more than four months after the name change. See section 9–507(c) and the last part of Official Comment 4. Be careful with this four month rule. The rule is not that perfection is completely ineffective four months after the name change. Rather, the only effect of not refiling within four months after the name change is that perfection is ineffective ONLY as to collateral acquired after that four month grace period.

OTHER UCC SECTIONS TO LOOK TO WHEN YOU LOOK AT SECTION 9–507

Section 9–508(b) is an exception to the general rule in s section 9–507(b) that a financing statement will not be rendered ineffective by post-filing differences or inaccuracies in the financing statement even if those differences or inaccuracies make it seriously misleading.

OFFICIAL COMMENT

* * *

2. **Scope of Section.** This section deals with situations in which the information in a proper financing statement becomes inaccurate after the financing statement is filed. Compare Section 9–338, which deals with situations in which a financing statement contains a particular kind of information concerning the debtor (i.e., the information described in Section 9–516(b)(5)) that is incorrect at the time it is filed.

3. **Post-Filing Disposition of Collateral.** Under subsection (a), a financing statement remains effective even if the collateral is sold or otherwise disposed of. This subsection clarifies the third sentence of former Section 9–402(7) by providing that a financing statement remains effective following the disposition of collateral only when the security interest or agricultural lien continues in that collateral. This result is consistent with the conclusion of PEB Commentary No. 3. Normally, a security interest does continue after disposition of the collateral. See Section 9–315(a). Law other than this Article determines whether an agricultural lien survives disposition of the collateral.

As a consequence of the disposition, the collateral may be owned by a person other than the debtor against whom the financing statement was filed. Under subsection (a), the secured party remains perfected even if it does not correct the public record. For this reason, any person seeking to determine whether a debtor owns collateral free of security interests must inquire as to the debtor's source of title and, if circumstances seem to require it, search in the name of a former owner. Subsection (a) addresses only the sufficiency of the information contained in the financing statement. A disposition of collateral may result in loss of perfection for other reasons. See Section 9–316.

Example: Dee Corp. is an Illinois corporation. It creates a security interest in its equipment in favor of Secured Party. Secured Party files a proper financing statement in Illinois. Dee Corp. sells an item of equipment to Bee Corp., a Pennsylvania corporation, subject to the security interest. The security interest continues, see Section 9–315(a), and remains perfected, see Section 9–507(a), notwithstanding that the financing statement is filed under "D" (for Dee Corp.) and not under "B." However, because Bee Corp. is located in Pennsylvania and not Illinois, see Section 9–307, unless Secured Party perfects under Pennsylvania law within one year after the transfer, its security interest will become unperfected and will be deemed to have been unperfected against purchasers of the collateral. See Section 9–316.

4. **Other Post–Filing Changes.** Subsection (b) provides that, as a general matter, post-filing changes that render a financing statement inaccurate and seriously misleading have no effect on a financing statement. The financing statement remains effective. It is subject to two exceptions: Section 9–508 and Section 9–507(c). Section 9–508 addresses the effectiveness of a financing statement filed against an original debtor when a new debtor becomes bound by the original debtor's security agreement. It is discussed in the Comments to that section.

Section 9–507(c) addresses a "pure" change of the debtor's name, i.e., a change that does not implicate a new debtor. It clarifies former Section 9–402(7). If a name change renders a filed financing statement seriously misleading, the financing statement, unless amended to provide the debtor's new correct name, is effective only to perfect a security interest in collateral acquired by the debtor before, or within four months after, the change. If an amendment that provides the new correct name is filed within four months after the change, the financing statement as amended would be effective also with respect to collateral acquired more than four months after the change. If an amendment that provides the new correct name is filed more than four months after the change, the financing statement as amended would be effective also with respect to collateral acquired more than four months after the change, but only from the time of the filing of the amendment.

§ 9–508. Effectiveness of Financing Statement if New Debtor Becomes Bound by Security Agreement

(a) [Financing statement naming original debtor.] Except as otherwise provided in this section, a filed financing statement naming an original debtor is effective to perfect a security interest in collateral in which a new debtor has or acquires rights to the extent that the financing statement would have been effective had the original debtor acquired rights in the collateral.

(b) [Financing statement becoming seriously misleading.] If the difference between the name of the original debtor and that of the new debtor causes a filed financing statement that is effective under subsection (a) to be seriously misleading under Section 9–506:

(1) the financing statement is effective to perfect a security interest in collateral acquired by the new debtor before, and within four months after, the new debtor becomes bound under Section 9–203(d); and

(2) the financing statement is not effective to perfect a security interest in collateral acquired by the new debtor more than four months after the new debtor becomes bound under Section 9–203(d) unless an initial financing statement pro-

viding the name of the new debtor is filed before the expiration of that time.

(c) [When section not applicable.] This section does not apply to collateral as to which a filed financing statement remains effective against the new debtor under Section 9–507(a).

UNOFFICIAL COMMENTS

Do this section only if there is a "new debtor" in the same jurisdiction. Three different possible such "new debtor" perfection problems.

First, if there is a new debtor and the question involves the collateral of the "original debtor" that is now the "new debtor's", look at sections 9–508(c) and 9–507(a).

Second, if there is a "new debtor" and the question involves stuff that the "new debtor" had before it became a "new debtor", look at section 9–508(a).

Third, if there is a "new debtor" and the question involves stuff that the "new debtor" acquires after becoming a "new debtor", look at section 9–508(b).

If the new debtor and the old debtor are located in different jurisdictions, this section does not apply. See section 9–316, Official Comment 2, example 5. That would really be a tacky exam question.

NON–OBVIOUS DEFINITIONS

Again, look at the definitions in section 9–102 and be sure that you understand the difference between being a "debtor" and being a "new debtor." And the difference between acquiring the collateral by becoming a new debtor as contrasted with acquiring the collateral by buying the collateral.

OTHER UCC SECTIONS TO LOOK TO WHEN YOU LOOK AT SECTION 9–508

Section 9–203(d) governs when a "new debtor" becomes bound by another person's security agreement.

OFFICIAL COMMENT

* * *

2. **The Problem.** Section 9–203(d) and (e) and this section deal with situations where one party (the "new debtor") becomes bound as debtor by a security agreement entered into by another person (the "original debtor"). These situations often arise as a consequence of changes in business structure. For example, the original debtor may be an individual debtor who operates a business as a sole proprietorship and then incorporates it. Or, the original debtor may be a corporation that is merged into another corporation. Under both former Article 9 and this Article,

collateral that is transferred in the course of the incorporation or merger normally would remain subject to a perfected security interest. See Sections 9–315(a), 9–507(a). Former Article 9 was less clear with respect to whether an after-acquired property clause in a security agreement signed by the original debtor would be effective to create a security interest in property acquired by the new corporation or the merger survivor and, if so, whether a financing statement filed against the original debtor would be effective to perfect the security interest. This section and Sections 9–203(d) and (e) are a clarification.

3. **How New Debtor Becomes Bound.** Normally, a security interest is unenforceable unless the debtor has authenticated a security agreement describing the collateral. See Section 9–203(b). New Section 9–203(e) creates an exception, under which a security agreement entered into by one person is effective with respect to the property of another. This exception comes into play if a "new debtor" becomes bound as debtor by a security agreement entered into by another person (the "original debtor"). (The quoted terms are defined in Section 9–102.) If a new debtor does become bound, then the security agreement entered into by the original debtor satisfies the security-agreement requirement of Section 9–203(b)(3) as to existing or after-acquired property of the new debtor to the extent the property is described in the security agreement. In that case, no other agreement is necessary to make a security interest enforceable in that property. See Section 9–203(e).

Section 9–203(d) explains when a new debtor becomes bound by an original debtor's security agreement. Under Section 9–203(d)(1), a new debtor becomes bound as debtor if, by contract or operation of other law, the security agreement becomes effective to create a security interest in the new debtor's property. For example, if the applicable corporate law of mergers provides that when A Corp merges into B Corp, B Corp becomes a debtor under A Corp's security agreement, then B Corp would become bound as debtor following such a merger. Similarly, B Corp would become bound as debtor if B Corp contractually assumes A's obligations under the security agreement.

Under certain circumstances, a new debtor becomes bound for purposes of this Article even though it would not be bound under other law. Under Section 9–203(d)(2), a new debtor becomes bound when, by contract or operation of other law, it (i) becomes obligated not only for the secured obligation but also generally for the obligations of the original debtor and (ii) acquires or succeeds to substantially all the assets of the original debtor. For example, some corporate laws provide that, when two corporations merge, the surviving corporation succeeds to the assets of its merger partner and "has all liabilities" of both corporations. In the case where, for example, A Corp merges into B Corp (and A Corp ceases to exist), some people have questioned whether A Corp's grant of a security interest in its existing and after-acquired property becomes a "liability" of B Corp, such that B Corp's existing and after-acquired property becomes subject to a security interest in favor of A Corp's lender. Even if corporate law were to give a negative answer, under Section 9–203(d)(2), B Corp would become bound for purposes of Section 9–203(e) and this section. The "substantially all of the assets" requirement of Section 9–203(d)(2) excludes sureties and other secondary obligors as well as persons who become obligated through veil piercing and other non-successorship doctrines. In most cases, it will exclude successors to the assets and liabilities of a division of a debtor.

4. **When Financing Statement Effective Against New Debtor.** Subsection (a) provides that a filing against the original debtor generally is effective to perfect a security interest in collateral that a new debtor has at the time it becomes bound by the original debtor's security agreement and collateral that it acquires after the new debtor becomes bound. Under subsection (b), however, if the filing against the original debtor is seriously misleading as to the new debtor's name, the filing is effective as to

collateral acquired by the new debtor more than four months after the new debtor becomes bound only if a person files during the four-month period an initial financing statement providing the name of the new debtor. Compare Section 9–507(c) (four-month period of effectiveness with respect to collateral acquired by a debtor after the debtor changes its name). Moreover, if the original debtor and the new debtor are located in different jurisdictions, a filing against the original debtor would not be effective to perfect a security interest in collateral that the new debtor acquires or has acquired from a person other than the original debtor. See Example 5, Section 9–316, Comment 2.

5. **Transferred Collateral.** This section does not apply to collateral transferred by the original debtor to a new debtor. See subsection (c). Under those circumstances, the filing against the original debtor continues to be effective until it lapses or perfection is lost for another reason. See sections 9–316, 9–507(a).

6. **Priority.** Section 9–326 governs the priority contest between a secured creditor of the original debtor and a secured creditor of the new debtor.

§ 9–509. Persons Entitled to File a Record

(a) [Person entitled to file record.] A person may file an initial financing statement, amendment that adds collateral covered by a financing statement, or amendment that adds a debtor to a financing statement only if:

> **(1)** the debtor authorizes the filing in an authenticated record or pursuant to subsection (b) or (c); or
>
> **(2)** the person holds an agricultural lien that has become effective at the time of filing and the financing statement covers only collateral in which the person holds an agricultural lien.

(b) [Security agreement as authorization.] By authenticating or becoming bound as debtor by a security agreement, a debtor or new debtor authorizes the filing of an initial financing statement, and an amendment, covering:

> **(1)** the collateral described in the security agreement; and
>
> **(2)** property that becomes collateral under Section 9–315(a)(2), whether or not the security agreement expressly covers proceeds.

(c) [Acquisition of collateral as authorization.] By acquiring collateral in which a security interest or agricultural lien continues under Section 9–315(a)(1), a debtor authorizes the filing of an initial financing statement, and an amendment, covering the collateral and property that becomes collateral under Section 9–315(a)(2).

(d) [Person entitled to file certain amendments.] A person may file an amendment other than an amendment that adds collateral covered by a financing statement or an amendment that adds a debtor to a financing statement only if:

(1) the secured party of record authorizes the filing; or

(2) the amendment is a termination statement for a financing statement as to which the secured party of record has failed to file or send a termination statement as required by Section 9–513(a) or (c), the debtor authorizes the filing, and the termination statement indicates that the debtor authorized it to be filed.

(e) [Multiple secured parties of record.] If there is more than one secured party of record for a financing statement, each secured party of record may authorize the filing of an amendment under subsection (d).

UNOFFICIAL COMMENTS

There are the four basic rules that you need to be familiar with concerning this section and the next section, section 9–510.

1. The filing of a financing statement is effective to perfect a security interest only if the filing was authorized by the debtor;
2. If the filing occurs after the debtor signs the security agreement, this authorization is generally implied from the execution of the security agreement;
3. Filing may occur before the debtor signs the security agreement, however, separate express authorization by the debtor will be necessary; and
4. Issues of whether the filing was authorized generally arise because the debtor is in bankruptcy or because some other secured party is claiming that its later in time security interest has priority because of a prior unauthorized filing.

NON–OBVIOUS DEFINITIONS

"Authenticate" is defined in section 9–102(a)(7). Even without looking at the definition, you know (1) a signing must be one way of authenticating and (2) there must be other ways of authenticating or Article 9 would have used the word "sign" instead of the word "authenticate". Not clear what these other ways are. Intent was to facilitate electronic transactions.

OTHER UCC SECTIONS TO LOOK TO WHEN YOU LOOK AT SECTION 9–509

Section 9–510(a): Filed record effective if authorized

A filed record is effective to the extent that it was filed by a person that is entitled to file it under Section 9–509.

Section 9–502(d): Filing before security agreement or attachment

Section 9–502(d) permits a prospective secured party to file a financing statement before a security agreement is executed or a security interest attaches. The filing of the financing statement, however, must be authorized to be effective. Generally, the secured party obtains this authority by having the debtor authenticate a record that specifically grants the secured party the authority to file the financing statement before the debtor authenticates the security agreement.

Section 9–518(a): Correction statement

A person may file in the filing office a correction statement with respect to a record indexed there under the person's name if the person believes that the record is inaccurate or was wrongfully filed.

Section 9–625: Remedies for Unauthorized Filing

Section 9–625 provides the specific remedies available to persons who have been injured by a secured party's failure to adhere to the rules set forth in Article 9. One rule in particular that may subject the secured party to damages for failure to comply is the rule that the secured party must be authorized to file a record pursuant to section 9–509(a). If a secured party violates section 9–509(a), it may be liable for both actual damages and statutory damages as provided in section 9–625(b) and (e), respectively.

OFFICIAL COMMENT

* * *

2. **Scope and Approach of This Section.** This section collects in one place most of the rules determining whether a record may be filed. Section 9–510 explains the extent to which a filed record is effective. Under these sections, the identity of the person who effects a filing is immaterial. The filing scheme contemplated by this Part does not contemplate that the identity of a "filer" will be a part of the searchable records. This is consistent with, and a necessary aspect of, eliminating signatures or other evidence of authorization from the system. (Note that the 1972 amendments to this Article eliminated the requirement that a financing statement contain the signature of the secured party.) As long as the appropriate person authorizes the filing, or, in the case of a termination statement, the debtor is entitled to the termination, it is insignificant whether the secured party or another person files any given record. The question of authorization is one for the court, not the filing office. However, a filing office may choose to employ authentication procedures in connection with electronic communications, e.g., to verify the identity of a filer who seeks to charge the filing fee.

3. **Unauthorized Filings.** Records filed in the filing office do not require signatures for their effectiveness. Subsection (a)(1) substitutes for the debtor's signature on a financing statement the requirement that the debtor authorize in an authenticated record the filing of an initial financing statement or an amendment that adds collateral. Also, under subsection (a)(1), if an amendment adds a debtor, the debtor who is added must authorize the amendment. A person who files an unauthorized record in violation of subsection (a)(1) is liable under Section 9–625(b) and (e) for actual and statutory damages. Of course, a filed financing statement is ineffective to perfect a security interest if the filing is not authorized. See Section 9–510(a). Law other than this Article, including the law with respect to ratification of past acts, generally determines whether a person has the requisite

authority to file a record under this section. See Sections 1–103, 9–502, Comment 3. This Article applies to other issues, such as the priority of a security interest perfected by the filing of a financing statement.

4. *Ipso Facto* **Authorization.** Under subsection (b), the authentication of a security agreement *ipso facto* constitutes the debtor's authorization of the filing of a financing statement covering the collateral described in the security agreement. The secured party need not obtain a separate authorization. Similarly, a new debtor's becoming bound by a security agreement *ipso facto* constitutes the new debtor's authorization of the filing of a financing statement covering the collateral described in the security agreement by which the new debtor has become bound. And, under subsection (c), the acquisition of collateral in which a security interest continues after disposition under Section 9–315(a)(1) *ipso facto* constitutes an authorization to file an initial financing statement against the person who acquired the collateral. The authorization to file an initial financing statement also constitutes an authorization to file a record covering actual proceeds of the original collateral, even if the security agreement is silent as to proceeds.

> **Example 1:** Debtor authenticates a security agreement creating a security interest in Debtor's inventory in favor of Secured Party. Secured Party files a financing statement covering inventory and accounts. The financing statement is authorized insofar as it covers inventory and unauthorized insofar as it covers accounts. (Note, however, that the financing statement will be effective to perfect a security interest in accounts constituting proceeds of the inventory to the same extent as a financing statement covering only inventory.)

> **Example 2:** Debtor authenticates a security agreement creating a security interest in Debtor's inventory in favor of Secured Party. Secured Party files a financing statement covering inventory. Debtor sells some inventory, deposits the buyer's payment into a deposit account, and withdraws the funds to purchase equipment. As long as the equipment can be traced to the inventory, the security interest continues in the equipment. See Section 9–315(a)(2). However, because the equipment was acquired with cash proceeds, the financing statement becomes ineffective to perfect the security interest in the equipment on the 21st day after the security interest attaches to the equipment unless Secured Party continues perfection beyond the 20–day period by filing a financing statement against the equipment or amending the filed financing statement to cover equipment. See Section 9–315(d). Debtor's authentication of the security agreement authorizes the filing of an initial financing statement or amendment covering the equipment, which is "property that becomes collateral under Section 9–315(a)(2)." See Section 9–509(b)(2).

5. **Agricultural Liens.** Under subsection (a)(2), the holder of an agricultural lien may file a financing statement covering collateral subject to the lien without obtaining the debtor's authorization. Because the lien arises as matter of law, the debtor's consent is not required. A person who files an unauthorized record in violation of this subsection is liable under Section 9–625(e) for a statutory penalty and damages.

6. **Amendments; Termination Statements Authorized by Debtor.** Most amendments may not be filed unless the secured party of record, as determined under Section 9–511, authorizes the filing. See subsection (d)(1). However, under subsection (d)(2), the authorization of the secured party of record is not required for the filing of a termination statement if the secured party of record failed to send or file a termination statement as required by Section 9–513, the debtor authorizes it to be filed, and the termination statement so indicates.

7. **Multiple Secured Parties of Record.** Subsection (e) deals with multiple secured parties of record. It permits each secured party of record to authorize the filing of amendments. However, Section 9–510(b) protects the rights and powers of one secured party of record from

the effects of filings made by another secured party of record. See Section 9–510, Comment 3.

8. **Successor to Secured Party of Record.** A person may succeed to the powers of the secured party of record by operation of other law, e.g., the law of corporate mergers. In that case, the successor has the power to authorize filings within the meaning of this section.

§ 9–510. Effectiveness of Filed Record

(a) [Filed record effective if authorized.] A filed record is effective only to the extent that it was filed by a person that may file it under Section 9–509.

* * *

(c) [Continuation statement not timely filed.] A continuation statement that is not filed within the six-month period prescribed by Section 9–515(d) is ineffective.

UNOFFICIAL COMMENTS

Section 9–510(a) provides that the filed financing statement or amendment will be effective only if it was filed by a person who had the authority to file, as provided by Section 9–509.

Section 9–515 provides that a filed financing statement is effective for a specifically defined period of time after the date of filing unless, before the lapse of its effectiveness period, a continuation statement is filed. A continuation statement is an amendment of the initial financing statement. Its purpose is to continue the effectiveness of a filed financing statement beyond its defined term of effectiveness. For a continuation statement to be effective, the secured party must make sure that it files it within six months of the original filed financing statement's prescribed lapse. If a filing officer accepts an untimely continuation statement, section 9–510(c) makes the filing ineffective.

OFFICIAL COMMENT

* * *

2. **Ineffectiveness of Unauthorized or Overbroad Filings.** Subsection (a) provides that a filed financing statement is effective only to the extent it was filed by a person entitled to file it.

Example 1: Debtor authorizes the filing of a financing statement covering inventory. Under Section 9–509, the secured party may file a financing statement covering only inventory; it may not file a financing statement covering other collateral. The secured party files a financing statement covering inventory and equipment. This section provides that the financing statement is effective only to the extent the secured party may file it. Thus, the financing statement is effective to perfect a security interest in inventory but ineffective to perfect a security interest in equipment.

* * *

4. **Continuation Statements.** A continuation statement may be filed only within the six months immediately before lapse. See Section 9–515(d). The filing

office is obligated to reject a continuation statement that is filed outside the six-month period. See Sections 9–520(a), 9–516(b)(7). Subsection (c) provides that if the filing office fails to reject a continuation statement that is not filed in a timely manner, the continuation statement is ineffective nevertheless.

§ 9–511. Secured Party of Record

(a) [Secured party of record.] A secured party of record with respect to a financing statement is a person whose name is provided as the name of the secured party or a representative of the secured party in an initial financing statement that has been filed. If an initial financing statement is filed under Section 9–514(a), the assignee named in the initial financing statement is the secured party of record with respect to the financing statement.

(b) [Amendment naming secured party of record.] If an amendment of a financing statement which provides the name of a person as a secured party or a representative of a secured party is filed, the person named in the amendment is a secured party of record. If an amendment is filed under Section 9–514(b), the assignee named in the amendment is a secured party of record.

(c) [Amendment deleting secured party of record.] A person remains a secured party of record until the filing of an amendment of the financing statement which deletes the person.

OFFICIAL COMMENT

* * *

2. **Secured Party of Record.** This new section explains how the secured party of record is to be determined. If SP–1 is named as the secured party in an initial financing statement, it is the secured party of record. Similarly, if an initial financing statement reflects a total assignment from SP–0 to SP–1, then SP–1 is the secured party of record. See subsection (a). If, subsequently, an amendment is filed assigning SP–1's status to SP–2, then SP–2 becomes the secured party of record in place of SP–1. The same result obtains if a subsequent amendment deletes the reference to SP–1 and substitutes therefor a reference to SP–2. If, however, a subsequent amendment adds SP–2 as a secured party but does not purport to remove SP–1 as a secured party, then SP–2 and SP–1 each is a secured party of record. See subsection (b). An amendment purporting to remove the only secured party of record without providing a successor is ineffective. See Section 9–512(e). At any point in time, all effective records that comprise a financing statement must be examined to determine the person or persons that have the status of secured party of record.

3. **Successor to Secured Party of Record.** Application of other law may result in a person succeeding to the powers of a secured party of record. For example, if the secured party of record (A) merges into another corporation (B) and the other corporation (B) survives, other law may provide that B has all of A's powers. In that case, B is authorized to take all actions under this Part that A would have been authorized to take. Similarly, acts taken by a person who is authorized under generally applicable principles of agency to act on behalf of the secured party of record are effective under this Part.

§ 9–512. Amendment of Financing Statement

[Alternative A]

(a) [Amendment of information in financing statement.] Subject to Section 9–509, a person may add or delete collateral covered by, continue or terminate the effectiveness of, or, subject to subsection (e), otherwise amend the information provided in, a financing statement by filing an amendment that:

(1) identifies, by its file number, the initial financing statement to which the amendment relates; and

(2) if the amendment relates to an initial financing statement filed [or recorded] in a filing office described in Section 9–501(a)(1), provides the information specified in Section 9–502(b).

[Alternative B]

(a) [Amendment of information in financing statement.] Subject to Section 9–509, a person may add or delete collateral covered by, continue or terminate the effectiveness of, or, subject to subsection (e), otherwise amend the information provided in, a financing statement by filing an amendment that:

(1) identifies, by its file number, the initial financing statement to which the amendment relates; and

(2) if the amendment relates to an initial financing statement filed [or recorded] in a filing office described in Section 9–501(a)(1), provides the date [and time] that the initial financing statement was filed [or recorded] and the information specified in Section 9–502(b).

[End of Alternatives]

(b) [Period of effectiveness not affected.] Except as otherwise provided in Section 9–515, the filing of an amendment does not extend the period of effectiveness of the financing statement.

(c) [Effectiveness of amendment adding collateral.] A financing statement that is amended by an amendment that adds collateral is effective as to the added collateral only from the date of the filing of the amendment.

(d) [Effectiveness of amendment adding debtor.] A financing statement that is amended by an amendment that adds a debtor is effective as to the added debtor only from the date of the filing of the amendment.

(e) [Certain amendments ineffective.] An amendment is ineffective to the extent it:

(1) purports to delete all debtors and fails to provide the name of a debtor to be covered by the financing statement; or

(2) purports to delete all secured parties of record and fails to provide the name of a new secured party of record.

OFFICIAL COMMENT

* * *

2. **Changes to Financing Statements.** This section addresses changes to financing statements, including addition and deletion of collateral. Although termination statements, assignments, and continuation statements are types of amendment, this Article follows former Article 9 and contains separate sections containing additional provisions applicable to particular types of amendments. See Section 9–513 (termination statements); 9–514 (assignments); 9–515 (continuation statements). One should not infer from this separate treatment that this Article requires a separate amendment to accomplish each change. Rather, a single amendment would be legally sufficient to, e.g., add collateral and continue the effectiveness of the financing statement.

3. **Amendments.** An amendment under this Article may identify only the information contained in a financing statement that is to be changed; alternatively, it may take the form of an amended and restated financing statement. The latter would state, for example, that the financing statement "is amended and restated to read as follows: ..." References in this Part to an "amended financing statement" are to a financing statement as amended by an amendment using either technique.

This section revises former Section 9–402(4) to permit secured parties of record to make changes in the public record without the need to obtain the debtor's signature. However, the filing of an amendment that adds collateral or adds a debtor must be authorized by the debtor or it will not be effective. See Sections 9–509(a), 9–510(a).

4. **Amendment Adding Debtor.** An amendment that adds a debtor is effective, provided that the added debtor authorizes the filing. See Section 9–509(a). However, filing an amendment adding a debtor to a previously filed financing statement affords no advantage over filing an initial financing statement against that debtor and may be disadvantageous. With respect to the added debtor, for purposes of determining the priority of the security interest, the time of filing is the time of the filing of the amendment, not the time of the filing of the initial financing statement. See subsection (d). However, the effectiveness of the financing statement lapses with respect to added debtor at the time it lapses with respect to the original debtor. See subsection (b).

5. **Deletion of All Debtors or Secured Parties of Record.** Subsection (e) assures that there will be a debtor and secured party of record for every financing statement.

Example: A filed financing statement names A and B as secured parties of record and covers inventory and equipment. An amendment deletes equipment and purports to delete A and B as secured parties of record without adding a substitute secured party. The amendment is ineffective to the extent it purports to delete the secured parties of record but effective with respect to the deletion of collateral. As a consequence, the financing statement, as amended, covers only inventory, but A and B remain as secured parties of record.

§ 9–513. Termination Statement

(a) [Consumer goods.] A secured party shall cause the secured party of record for a financing statement to file a termination statement for the financing statement if the financing statement covers consumer goods and:

(1) there is no obligation secured by the collateral covered by the financing statement and no commitment to make an advance, incur an obligation, or otherwise give value; or

(2) the debtor did not authorize the filing of the initial financing statement.

(b) [Time for compliance with subsection (a).] To comply with subsection (a), a secured party shall cause the secured party of record to file the termination statement:

(1) within one month after there is no obligation secured by the collateral covered by the financing statement and no commitment to make an advance, incur an obligation, or otherwise give value; or

(2) if earlier, within 20 days after the secured party receives an authenticated demand from a debtor.

(c) [Other collateral.] In cases not governed by subsection (a), within 20 days after a secured party receives an authenticated demand from a debtor, the secured party shall cause the secured party of record for a financing statement to send to the debtor a termination statement for the financing statement or file the termination statement in the filing office if:

(1) except in the case of a financing statement covering accounts or chattel paper that has been sold or goods that are the subject of a consignment, there is no obligation secured by the collateral covered by the financing statement and no commitment to make an advance, incur an obligation, or otherwise give value;

(2) the financing statement covers accounts or chattel paper that has been sold but as to which the account debtor or other person obligated has discharged its obligation;

(3) the financing statement covers goods that were the subject of a consignment to the debtor but are not in the debtor's possession; or

(4) the debtor did not authorize the filing of the initial financing statement.

(d) [Effect of filing termination statement.] Except as otherwise provided in Section 9–510, upon the filing of a termination statement with the filing office, the financing statement to which the termination statement relates ceases to be effective. Except as otherwise provided in Section 9–510, for purposes of Sections 9–519(g), 9–522(a), and 9–523(c), the filing with the filing office of a termination statement relating to a financing statement that indicates that the debtor is a transmitting utility also causes the effectiveness of the financing statement to lapse.

UNOFFICIAL COMMENTS

Official Comment 2 is helpful in understanding termination statement issues. The most important fact is whether the collateral is "consumer goods".

If the collateral is "consumer goods", section 9–513(a) requires the secured party to take the initiative to file the termination statement. If the collateral is anything other than consumer goods, section 9–513(c) generally requires the debtor to take the initiative to file the termination statement.

NON–OBVIOUS DEFINITIONS

The non-obvious part of the section 9–102(a)(79) definition of "termination statement" is the word "amendment." A termination statement is a form of "amendment" and subject to the UCC requirements for amendments of financing statement.

OTHER UCC SECTIONS TO LOOK TO WHEN YOU LOOK AT SECTION 9–513

Section 9–512 requires that an amendment (which we now know includes a termination statement) "must identify by its file number" the financing statement that is being terminated. While terminating the filing completely must comply with sections 9–512 and 9–513, releasing some of the collateral from the coverage of a filing is subject to section 9–512 only.

OFFICIAL COMMENT

* * *

2. **Duty to File or Send.** This section specifies when a secured party must cause the secured party of record to file or send to the debtor a termination statement for a financing statement. Because most financing statements expire in five years unless a continuation statement is filed (Section 9–515), no compulsion is placed on the secured party to file a termination statement unless demanded by the debtor, except in the case of consumer goods. Because many consumers will not realize the importance to them of clearing the public record, an affirmative duty is put on the secured party in that case. But many purchase-money security interests in consumer goods will not be filed, ex-

cept for motor vehicles. See Section 9–309(1). Under Section 9–311(b), compliance with a certificate-of-title statute is "equivalent to the filing of a financing statement under this article." Thus, this section applies to a certificate of title unless the section is superseded by a certificate-of-title statute that contains a specific rule addressing a secured party's duty to cause a notation of a security interest to be removed from a certificate of title. In the context of a certificate of title, however, the secured party could comply with this section by causing the removal itself or providing the debtor with documentation sufficient to enable the debtor to effect the removal.

Subsections (a) and (b) apply to a financing statement covering consumer goods. Subsection (c) applies to other financing statements. Subsection (a) and (c) each makes explicit what was implicit under former Article 9: If the debtor did not authorize the filing of a financing statement in the first place, the secured party of record should file or send a termination statement. The liability imposed upon a secured party that fails to comply with subsection (a) or (c) is identical to that imposed for the filing of an unauthorized financing statement or amendment. See Section 9–625(e).

3. **"Bogus" Filings.** A secured party's duty to send a termination statement arises when the secured party "receives" an authenticated demand from the debtor. In the case of an unauthorized financing statement, the person named as debtor in the financing statement may have no relationship with the named secured party and no reason to know the secured party's address. Inasmuch as the address in the financing statement is "held out by [the person named as secured party in the financing statement] as the place for receipt of such communications [i.e., communications relating to security interests]," the putative secured party is deemed to have "received" a notification delivered to that address. See Section 1–201(26). If a termination statement is not forthcoming, the person named as debtor itself may authorize the filing of a termination statement, which will be effective if it indicates that the person authorized it to be filed. See Sections 9–509(d)(2), 9–510(c).

4. **Buyers of Receivables.** Applied literally, former Section 9–404(1) would have required many buyers of receivables to file a termination statement immediately upon filing a financing statement because "there is no outstanding secured obligation and no commitment to make advances, incur obligations, or otherwise give value." Subsections (c)(1) and (2) remedy this problem. While the security interest of a buyer of accounts or chattel paper (B–1) is perfected, the debtor is not deemed to retain an interest in the sold receivables and thus could transfer no interest in them to another buyer (B–2) or to a lien creditor (LC). However, for purposes of determining the rights of the debtor's creditors and certain purchasers of accounts or chattel paper from the debtor, while B–1's security interest is unperfected, the debtor-seller is deemed to have rights in the sold receivables, and a competing security interest or judicial lien may attach to those rights. See Sections 9–318, 9–109, Comment 5. Suppose that B–1's security interest in certain accounts and chattel paper is perfected by filing, but the effectiveness of the financing statement lapses. Both before and after lapse, B–1 collects some of the receivables. After lapse, LC acquires a lien on the accounts and chattel paper. B–1's unperfected security interest in the accounts and chattel paper is subordinate to LC's rights. See Section 9–317(a)(2). But collections on accounts and chattel paper are not "accounts" or "chattel paper." Even if B–1's security interest in the accounts and chattel paper is or becomes unperfected, neither the debtor nor LC acquires rights to the collections that B–1 collects (and owns) before LC acquires a lien.

5. **Effect of Filing.** Subsection (d) states the effect of filing a termination statement: the related financing statement ceases to be effective. If one of several secured parties of record files a termination statement, subsection (d) applies only with respect to the rights of the person who authorized the filing of the termination statement. See Section 9–

510(b). The financing statement remains effective with respect to the rights of the others. However, even if a financing statement is *terminated* (and thus no longer is effective) with respect to all secured parties of record, the financing statement, including the termination statement, will remain of record until at least one year after it *lapses* with respect to all secured parties of record. See Section 9–519(g).

§ 9–514. Assignment of Powers of Secured Party of Record

(a) [Assignment reflected on initial financing statement.] Except as otherwise provided in subsection (c), an initial financing statement may reflect an assignment of all of the secured party's power to authorize an amendment to the financing statement by providing the name and mailing address of the assignee as the name and address of the secured party.

(b) [Assignment of filed financing statement.] Except as otherwise provided in subsection (c), a secured party of record may assign of record all or part of its power to authorize an amendment to a financing statement by filing in the filing office an amendment of the financing statement which:

> **(1)** identifies, by its file number, the initial financing statement to which it relates;
>
> **(2)** provides the name of the assignor; and
>
> **(3)** provides the name and mailing address of the assignee.

(c) [Assignment of record of mortgage.] An assignment of record of a security interest in a fixture covered by a record of a mortgage which is effective as a financing statement filed as a fixture filing under Section 9–502(c) may be made only by an assignment of record of the mortgage in the manner provided by law of this State other than [the Uniform Commercial Code].

OFFICIAL COMMENT

* * *

2. Assignments. This section provides a permissive device whereby a secured party of record may effectuate an assignment of its power to affect a financing statement. It may also be useful for a secured party who has assigned all or part of its security interest or agricultural lien and wishes to have the fact noted of record, so that inquiries concerning the transaction would be addressed to the assignee. See Section 9–502, Comment 2. Upon the filing of an assignment, the assignee becomes the "secured party of record" and may authorize the filing of a continuation statement, termination statement, or other amendment. Note that under Section 9–310(c) no filing of an assignment is required as a condition of continuing the perfected status of the security interest against creditors and transferees of the original debtor. However, if an assignment is not filed, the assignor remains the secured party of record, with the power (even if not the right) to authorize the filing of effective amendments. See Sections 9–511(c), 9–509(d).

Where a record of a mortgage is effective as a financing statement filed as a fixture filing (Section 9–502(c)), then an assignment of record of the security interest may be made only in the manner in which an assignment of record of the mortgage may be made under local real-property law.

3. **Comparison to Prior Law.** Most of the changes reflected in this section are for clarification or to embrace medium-neutral drafting. As a general matter, this section preserves the opportunity given by former Section 9–405 to assign a security interest of record in one of two different ways. Under subsection (a), a secured party may assign all of its power to affect a financing statement by naming an assignee in the initial financing statement. The secured party of record may accomplish the same result under subsection (b) by making a subsequent filing. Subsection (b) also may be used for an assignment of only some of the secured party of record's power to affect a financing statement, e.g., the power to affect the financing statement as it relates to particular items of collateral or as it relates to an undivided interest in a security interest in all the collateral. An initial financing statement may not be used to change the secured party of record under these circumstances. However, an amendment adding the assignee as a secured party of record may be used.

§ 9–515. Duration and Effectiveness of Financing Statement; Effect of Lapsed Financing Statement

(a) [Five-year effectiveness.] Except as otherwise provided in subsections (b), (e), (f), and (g), a filed financing statement is effective for a period of five years after the date of filing.

(b) [Public-finance or manufactured-home transaction.] Except as otherwise provided in subsections (e), (f), and (g), an initial financing statement filed in connection with a public-finance transaction or manufactured-home transaction is effective for a period of 30 years after the date of filing if it indicates that it is filed in connection with a public-finance transaction or manufactured-home transaction.

(c) [Lapse and continuation of financing statement.] The effectiveness of a filed financing statement lapses on the expiration of the period of its effectiveness unless before the lapse a continuation statement is filed pursuant to subsection (d). Upon lapse, a financing statement ceases to be effective and any security interest or agricultural lien that was perfected by the financing statement becomes unperfected, unless the security interest is perfected otherwise. If the security interest or agricultural lien becomes unperfected upon lapse, it is deemed never to have been perfected as against a purchaser of the collateral for value.

(d) [When continuation statement may be filed.] A continuation statement may be filed only within six months before the expiration of the five-year period specified in subsection (a) or the 30–year period specified in subsection (b), whichever is applicable.

(e) [Effect of filing continuation statement.] Except as otherwise provided in Section 9–510, upon timely filing of a continuation statement, the effectiveness of the initial financing statement continues for a period of five years commencing on the day on which the financing statement would have become ineffective in the absence of the filing. Upon the expiration of the five-year period, the financing statement lapses in the same manner as provided in subsection (c), unless, before the lapse, another continuation statement is filed pursuant to subsection (d). Succeeding continuation statements may be filed in the same manner to continue the effectiveness of the initial financing statement.

(f) [Transmitting utility financing statement.] If a debtor is a transmitting utility and a filed financing statement so indicates, the financing statement is effective until a termination statement is filed.

(g) [Record of mortgage as financing statement.] A record of a mortgage that is effective as a financing statement filed as a fixture filing under Section 9–502(c) remains effective as a financing statement filed as a fixture filing until the mortgage is released or satisfied of record or its effectiveness otherwise terminates as to the real property.

UNOFFICIAL COMMENTS

When considering how long a financing statement is effective and how soon you have to act to extend the perfection, remember (1) 5 years and (2) $4\frac{1}{2}$ years.

First, 5 years. A financing statement is generally effective for five years from the date of filing. Five years is generally long enough for an obligation to be paid; most debts are repaid within five years.

Second, $4\frac{1}{2}$ years. If the secured party wants to extend the term of effectiveness of its financing statement beyond five years, then it must file a continuation statement no earlier than four and a half years and no later than five years after the initial filing.

The following example shows you why the timely filing of a continuation statement may prove to be critical for a secured party. The rules set forth in Section 9–515 are often tested on your exam with a fact pattern such as

> On January 10, 2010, F makes a loan to D and properly obtains and perfects a security interest in D's equipment.

> On February 2, 2011, S makes a loan to D and properly obtains and perfects a security interest in the same equipment.

Under these facts, F's security interest has priority over S's by reason of section 9–322(a)(1).

Now, assume that is the end of 2012, and D has not fully repaid F or S.

If F timely files a continuation statement, its priority over S will continue. If F fails to file a continuation statement until after January 10, 2013, then S's security interest will have priority over F's security interest under section 9–322(a)(2).

OTHER UCC SECTIONS TO LOOK TO WHEN YOU LOOK AT SECTION 9–515

Section 9–510(c): Continuation Statement not timely filed.

A continuation statement that is not filed within the six-month period prescribed by section 9–515(d) is ineffective.

Section 9–516(b)(7): Refusal to accept record; filing does not occur.

A filing office must refuse to accept a continuation statement that is being filed outside of the six-month period prescribed by section 9–515(d).

OFFICIAL COMMENT

* * *

2. **Period of Financing Statement's Effectiveness.** Subsection (a) states the general rule: a financing statement is effective for a five-year period unless its effectiveness is continued under this section or terminated under Section 9–513. Subsection (b) provides that if the financing statement relates to a public-finance transaction or a manufactured-home transaction and so indicates, the financing statement is effective for 30 years. These financings typically extend well beyond the standard, five-year period. Under subsection (f), a financing statement filed against a transmitting utility remains effective indefinitely, until a termination statement is filed. Likewise, under subsection (g), a mortgage effective as a fixture filing remains effective until its effectiveness terminates under real-property law.

3. **Lapse.** When the period of effectiveness under subsection (a) or (b) expires, the effectiveness of the financing statement lapses. The last sentence of subsection (c) addresses the effect of lapse. The deemed retroactive unperfection applies only with respect to purchasers for value; unlike former Section 9–403(2), it does not apply with respect to lien creditors.

Example 1: SP–1 and SP–2 both hold security interests in the same collateral. Both security interests are perfected by filing. SP–1 filed first and has priority under Section 9–322(a)(1). The effectiveness of SP–1's filing lapses. As long as SP–2's security interest remains perfected thereafter, SP–2 is entitled to priority over SP–1's security interest, which is deemed never to have been perfected as against a purchaser for value (SP–2). See Section 9–322(a)(2).

Example 2: SP holds a security interest perfected by filing. On July 1, LC acquires a judicial lien on the collateral. Two weeks later, the effectiveness of the financing statement lapses. Although the security interest becomes unperfected upon lapse, it was perfected when LC acquired its lien. Accordingly, notwithstanding the lapse, the perfected security interest has priority over the rights of LC, who is not a purchaser. See Section 9–317(a)(2).

4. **Effect of Debtor's Bankruptcy.** Under former Section 9–403(2), lapse was tolled if the debtor entered bankruptcy or another insolvency proceeding. Nevertheless, being unaware that insolvency proceedings had been commenced, filing of-

fices routinely removed records from the files as if lapse had not been tolled. Subsection (c) deletes the former tolling provision and thereby imposes a new burden on the secured party: to be sure that a financing statement does not lapse during the debtor's bankruptcy. The secured party can prevent lapse by filing a continuation statement, even without first obtaining relief from the automatic stay. See Bankruptcy Code Section 362(b)(3). Of course, if the debtor enters bankruptcy before lapse, the provisions of this Article with respect to lapse would be of no effect to the extent that federal bankruptcy law dictates a contrary result (e.g., to the extent that the Bankruptcy Code determines rights as of the date of the filing of the bankruptcy petition).

5. **Continuation Statements.** Subsection (d) explains when a continuation statement may be filed. A continuation statement filed at a time other than that prescribed by subsection (d) is ineffective, see Section 9–510(c), and the filing office may not accept it. See Sections 9–520(a), 9–516(b). Subsection (e) specifies the effect of a continuation statement and provides for successive continuation statements.

§ 9–516. What Constitutes Filing; Effectiveness of Filing

(a) **[What constitutes filing.]** Except as otherwise provided in subsection (b), communication of a record to a filing office and tender of the filing fee or acceptance of the record by the filing office constitutes filing.

(b) **[Refusal to accept record; filing does not occur.]** Filing does not occur with respect to a record that a filing office refuses to accept because:

> (1) the record is not communicated by a method or medium of communication authorized by the filing office;
>
> (2) an amount equal to or greater than the applicable filing fee is not tendered;
>
> (3) the filing office is unable to index the record because:
>
>> (A) in the case of an initial financing statement, the record does not provide a name for the debtor;
>>
>> (B) in the case of an amendment or correction statement, the record:
>>
>>> (i) does not identify the initial financing statement as required by Section 9–512 or 9–518, as applicable; or
>>>
>>> (ii) identifies an initial financing statement whose effectiveness has lapsed under Section 9–515;
>>
>> (C) in the case of an initial financing statement that provides the name of a debtor identified as an individual or an amendment that provides a name of a debtor identified as an individual which was not previously provided in

the financing statement to which the record relates, the record does not identify the debtor's last name; or

(D) in the case of a record filed [or recorded] in the filing office described in Section 9–501(a)(1), the record does not provide a sufficient description of the real property to which it relates;

(4) in the case of an initial financing statement or an amendment that adds a secured party of record, the record does not provide a name and mailing address for the secured party of record;

(5) in the case of an initial financing statement or an amendment that provides a name of a debtor which was not previously provided in the financing statement to which the amendment relates, the record does not:

(A) provide a mailing address for the debtor;

(B) indicate whether the debtor is an individual or an organization; or

(C) if the financing statement indicates that the debtor is an organization, provide:

(i) a type of organization for the debtor;

(ii) a jurisdiction of organization for the debtor; or

(iii) an organizational identification number for the debtor or indicate that the debtor has none;

(6) in the case of an assignment reflected in an initial financing statement under Section 9–514(a) or an amendment filed under Section 9–514(b), the record does not provide a name and mailing address for the assignee; or

(7) in the case of a continuation statement, the record is not filed within the six-month period prescribed by Section 9–515(d).

(c) [Rules applicable to subsection (b).] For purposes of subsection (b):

(1) a record does not provide information if the filing office is unable to read or decipher the information; and

(2) a record that does not indicate that it is an amendment or identify an initial financing statement to which it relates, as required by Section 9–512, 9–514, or 9–518, is an initial financing statement.

(d) [Refusal to accept record; record effective as filed record.] A record that is communicated to the filing office with tender of the filing fee, but which the filing office refuses to accept for a reason other than one set forth in subsection (b), is effective as a filed record except as against a purchaser of the collateral which gives value in reasonable reliance upon the absence of the record from the files.

UNOFFICIAL COMMENTS

Always read section 9–520 together with section 9–502 and section 9–516. Usually you will be reading these three provisions when addressing the problem of whether the filing officer accepted a record that she should not have.

Recall that section 9–502, in essence, sets out the minimum requirements for an effective financing statement. Section 9–516 sets out some additional requirements. Under section 9–520(a), the filing officer is supposed to reject for filing a financing statement or other record that does not meet these additional section 9–516 requirements.

Filing officers, just like other people, do not always do what they are supposed to do. If the filing officer accepts for filing a financing statement that meets all of the requirements of section 9–502 but does not meet all of the additional requirements of section 9–516, then under section 9–520(c) that filing will be effective.

OTHER UCC SECTIONS TO LOOK TO WHEN YOU LOOK AT SECTION 9–516

Section 9–520(a): Mandatory refusal to accept record

Section 9–520(a) provides that a filing officer is supposed to reject a record if it has any of the shortcomings listed in section 9–516(b). Section 9–520(c) provides that if the filing officer does not do what she is supposed to do and accepts the filing, the filing is still effective so long as it meets the minimum requirements of section 9–502.

Section 9–512 Amendment of Financing Statement

One type of record that may be presented to the filing office for filing is an amendment to a financing statement. Section 9–512 provides that an amendment to a financing statement must identify, by file number, the initial financing statement to which the amendment relates, and for an amendment to a financing statement covering real-property-related collateral, it also must contain information specified in section 9–502(b). Section 9–516(b) provides that if the amendment fails to identify the initial financing statement, then the filing office may refuse to accept the amendment, and upon refusal, the filing does not occur. Section 9–512 also provides the rules governing the effectiveness of a filed amendment.

Section 9–515: Duration and Effectiveness of Financing Statement; Effect of Lapsed Financing Statement

Section 9–515 addresses, in part, the duration of the effectiveness of a financing statement. Specifically, Section 9–515 provides the various periods of effectiveness of a financing statement for different types of transactions. It also provides that a financing statement lapses at the end of its period of effectiveness unless the term of the financing statement is continued by the filing of a continuation statement within six months before the lapse. Pursuant to section 9–516(b)(3)(B)(ii), a filing office may refuse to accept a record for filing if it identifies an initial financing statement whose effectiveness period has lapsed under section 9–515.

Section 9–501: Filing Office

Section 9–501, provides, in part, where in a particular state a financing statement should be filed.

OFFICIAL COMMENT

* * *

2. **What Constitutes Filing.** Subsection (a) deals generically with what constitutes filing of a record, including an initial financing statement and amendments of all kinds (e.g., assignments, termination statements, and continuation statements). It follows former Section 9–403(1), under which either acceptance of a record by the filing office or presentation of the record and tender of the filing fee constitutes filing.

3. **Effectiveness of Rejected Record.** Subsection (b) provides an exclusive list of grounds upon which the filing office may reject a record. See Section 9–520(a). Although some of these grounds would also be grounds for rendering a filed record ineffective (e.g., an initial financing statement does not provide a name for the debtor), many others would not be (e.g., an initial financing statement does not provide a mailing address for the debtor or secured party of record). Neither this section nor Section 9–520 requires or authorizes the filing office to determine, or even consider, the accuracy of information provided in a record. For example, the State A filing office may not reject under subsection (b)(5)(C) an initial financing statement indicating that the debtor is a State A corporation and providing a three-digit organizational identification number, even if all State A organizational identification numbers contain at least five digits and two letters. Some organizations that are not registered organizations (such as foreign corporations) have a readily determinable jurisdiction of organization. When that is not the case, with respect to an organization that is not a registered organization, for purposes of this section, the debtor's jurisdiction of organization is any jurisdiction that bears a reasonable relation to the debtor, such as the jurisdiction stated in any organizational document or agreement for the debtor as the jurisdiction under whose law the organization is formed or as the jurisdiction whose law is the governing law, or the jurisdiction in which the debtor is located under Section 9–307(b) (i.e., its place of business or its chief executive office). Thus, for purposes of this section, more than one jurisdiction may qualify as the debtor's jurisdiction of organization. See Comment 9.

A financing statement or other record that is communicated to the filing office but which the filing office refuses to accept provides no public notice, regardless of the reason for the rejection. However, this section distinguishes between records that the filing office rightfully rejects and those that it wrongfully rejects. A filer is able to prevent a rightful rejection by complying with the requirements of subsection (b). No purpose is served by giving effect to records that justifiably never find their way into the system, and subsection (b) so provides.

Subsection (d) deals with the filing office's unjustified refusal to accept a record. Here, the filer is in no position to prevent the rejection and as a general matter should not be prejudiced by it. Although wrongfully rejected records generally are effective, subsection (d) contains a special rule to protect a third-party purchaser of the collateral (e.g., a buyer or competing secured party) who gives value in reliance upon the apparent absence of the record from the files. As against a person who searches the public record and reasonably relies on what the public record shows, subsection (d) imposes upon the filer the risk that a record failed to make its way into the filing system because of the filing office's wrongful rejection of it. (Compare Section 9–517, under which a mis-indexed financing statement is fully effective.) This risk is likely to be small, particularly when a record is presented electronically, and the filer can guard against this risk by conducting a post-filing search of the records. Moreover, Section 9–520(b) requires the filing office to give prompt notice of its refusal to accept a record for filing.

4. **Method or Medium of Communication.** Rejection pursuant to subsection (b)(1) for failure to communicate a record properly should be understood to mean noncompliance with procedures relating to security, authentication, or other communication-related requirements that the filing office may impose. Subsection (b)(1) does not authorize a filing office to impose additional substantive requirements. See Section 9–520, Comment 2.

5. **Address for Secured Party of Record.** Under subsection (b)(4) and Section 9–520(a), the lack of a mailing address for the secured party of record requires the filing office to reject an initial financing statement. The failure to include an address for the secured party of record no longer renders a financing statement ineffective. See Section 9–502(a). The function of the address is not to identify the secured party of record but rather to provide an address to which others can send required notifications, e.g., of a purchase-money security interest in inventory or of the disposition of collateral. Inasmuch as the address shown on a filed financing statement is an "address that is reasonable under the circumstances," a person required to send a notification to the secured party may satisfy the requirement by sending a notification to that address, even if the address is or becomes incorrect. See Section 9–102 (definition of "send"). Similarly, because the address is "held out by [the secured party] as the place for receipt of such communications [i.e., communications relating to security interests]," the secured party is deemed to have received a notification delivered to that address. See Section 1–201(26).

6. **Uncertainty Concerning Individual Debtor's Last Name.** Subsection (b)(3)(C) requires the filing office to reject an initial financing statement or amendment adding an individual debtor if the office cannot index the record because it does not identify the debtor's last name (e.g., it is unclear whether the debtor's name is Elton John or John Elton).

7. **Inability of Filing Office to Read or Decipher Information.** Under subsection (c)(1), if the filing office cannot read or decipher information, the information is not provided by a record for purposes of subsection (b).

8. **Classification of Records.** For purposes of subsection (b), a record that does not indicate it is an amendment or identify an initial financing statement to which it relates is deemed to be an initial financing statement. See subsection (c)(2).

9. **Effectiveness of Rejectable But Unrejected Record.** Section 9–520(a) requires the filing office to refuse to accept an initial financing statement for a

reason set forth in subsection (b). However, if the filing office accepts such a financing statement nevertheless, the financing statement generally is effective if it complies with the requirements of Section 9–502(a) and (b). See Section 9–520(c). Similarly, an otherwise effective financing statement generally remains so even though the information in the financing statement becomes incorrect. See Section 9–507(b). (Note that if the information required by subsection (b)(5) is incorrect when the financing statement is filed, Section 9–338 applies.)

§ 9–517. Effect of Indexing Errors

The failure of the filing office to index a record correctly does not affect the effectiveness of the filed record.

OFFICIAL COMMENT

* * *

2. **Effectiveness of Mis–Indexed Records.** This section provides that the filing office's error in mis-indexing a record does not render ineffective an otherwise effective record. As did former Section 9–401, this section imposes the risk of filing-office error on those who search the files rather than on those who file.

§ 9–518. Claim Concerning Inaccurate or Wrongfully Filed Record

(a) **[Correction statement.]** A person may file in the filing office a correction statement with respect to a record indexed there under the person's name if the person believes that the record is inaccurate or was wrongfully filed.

[Alternative A]

(b) **[Sufficiency of correction statement.]** A correction statement must:

(1) identify the record to which it relates by the file number assigned to the initial financing statement to which the record relates;

(2) indicate that it is a correction statement; and

(3) provide the basis for the person's belief that the record is inaccurate and indicate the manner in which the person believes the record should be amended to cure any inaccuracy or provide the basis for the person's belief that the record was wrongfully filed.

[Alternative B]

(b) **[Sufficiency of correction statement.]** A correction statement must:

(1) identify the record to which it relates by:

(A) the file number assigned to the initial financing statement to which the record relates; and

(B) if the correction statement relates to a record filed [or recorded] in a filing office described in Section 9–501(a)(1), the date [and time] that the initial financing statement was filed [or recorded] and the information specified in Section 9–502(b);

(2) indicate that it is a correction statement; and

(3) provide the basis for the person's belief that the record is inaccurate and indicate the manner in which the person believes the record should be amended to cure any inaccuracy or provide the basis for the person's belief that the record was wrongfully filed.

[End of Alternatives]

(c) [Record not affected by correction statement.] The filing of a correction statement does not affect the effectiveness of an initial financing statement or other filed record.

Legislative Note: States whose real-estate filing offices require additional information in amendments and cannot search their records by both the name of the debtor and the file number should enact Alternative B to Sections 9–512(a), 9–518(b), 9–519(f) and 9–522(a).

OFFICIAL COMMENT

* * *

2. Correction Statements. Former Article 9 did not afford a nonjudicial means for a debtor to correct a financing statement or other record that was inaccurate or wrongfully filed. Subsection (a) affords the debtor the right to file a correction statement. Among other requirements, the correction statement must provide the basis for the debtor's belief that the public record should be corrected. See subsection (b). These provisions, which resemble the analogous remedy in the Fair Credit Reporting Act, 15 U.S.C. § 1681i, afford an aggrieved person the opportunity to state its position on the public record. They do not permit an aggrieved person to change the legal effect of the public record. Thus, although a filed correction statement becomes part of the "financing statement," as defined in Section 9–102, the filing does not affect the effectiveness of the initial financing statement or any other filed record. See subsection (c).

This section does not displace other provisions of this Article that impose liability for making unauthorized filings or failing to file or send a termination statement (see Section 9–625(e)), nor does it displace any available judicial remedies.

3. Resort to Other Law. This Article cannot provide a satisfactory or complete solution to problems caused by misuse of the public records. The problem of "bogus" filings is not limited to the UCC filing system but extends to the real-property records, as well. A summary judicial procedure for correcting the public record and criminal penalties for those who misuse the filing and recording systems are likely to be more effective and put less strain on the filing system than provisions authorizing or requiring action by filing and recording offices.

[SUBPART 2. DUTIES AND OPERATION OF FILING OFFICE]

§ 9–519. Numbering, Maintaining, and Indexing Records; Communicating Information Provided in Records

(a) [Filing office duties.] For each record filed in a filing office, the filing office shall:

(1) assign a unique number to the filed record;

(2) create a record that bears the number assigned to the filed record and the date and time of filing;

(3) maintain the filed record for public inspection; and

(4) index the filed record in accordance with subsections (c), (d), and (e).

* * *

(c) [Indexing: general.] Except as otherwise provided in subsections (d) and (e), the filing office shall:

(1) index an initial financing statement according to the name of the debtor and index all filed records relating to the initial financing statement in a manner that associates with one another an initial financing statement and all filed records relating to the initial financing statement; and

(2) index a record that provides a name of a debtor which was not previously provided in the financing statement to which the record relates also according to the name that was not previously provided.

(d) [Indexing: real-property-related financing statement.] If a financing statement is filed as a fixture filing or covers as-extracted collateral or timber to be cut, [it must be filed for record and] the filing office shall index it:

(1) under the names of the debtor and of each owner of record shown on the financing statement as if they were the mortgagors under a mortgage of the real property described; and

(2) to the extent that the law of this State provides for indexing of records of mortgages under the name of the mortgagee,

under the name of the secured party as if the secured party were the mortgagee thereunder, or, if indexing is by description, as if the financing statement were a record of a mortgage of the real property described.

* * *

(h) [Timeliness of filing office performance.] The filing office shall perform the acts required by subsections (a) through (e) at the time and in the manner prescribed by filing-office rule, but not later than two business days after the filing office receives the record in question.

[(i) [Inapplicability to real-property-related filing office.] Subsection[s] [(b)] [and] [(h)] do[es] not apply to a filing office described in Section 9–501(a)(1).]

* * *

OFFICIAL COMMENT

* * *

2. **Filing Office's Duties.** Subsections (a) through (e) set forth the duties of the filing office with respect to filed records. Subsection (h), which is new, imposes a minimum standard of performance for those duties. Prompt indexing is crucial to the effectiveness of any filing system. An accepted but un-indexed record affords no public notice. Subsection (f) requires the filing office to maintain appropriate storage and retrieval facilities, and subsection (g) contains minimum requirements for the retention of records.

3. **File Number.** Subsection (a)(1) requires the filing office to assign a unique number to each filed record. That number is the "file number" only if the record is an initial financing statement. See Section 9–102.

4. **Time of Filing.** Subsection (a)(2) and Section 9–523 refer to the "date and time" of filing. The statutory text does not contain any instructions to a filing office as to how the time of filing is to be determined. The method of determining or assigning a time of filing is an appropriate matter for filing-office rules to address.

5. **Related Records.** Subsections (c) and (f) are designed to ensure that an initial financing statement and all filed records relating to it are associated with one another, indexed under the name of the debtor, and retrieved together. To comply with subsection (f), a filing office (other than a real-property recording office in a State that enacts subsection (f), Alternative B) must be capable of retrieving records in each of two ways: by the name of the debtor and by the file number of the initial financing statement to which the record relates.

6. **Prohibition on Deleting Names from Index.** This Article contemplates that the filing office will not delete the name of a debtor from the index until at least one year passes after the effectiveness of the financing statement lapses as to all secured parties of record. See subsection (g). This rule applies even if the filing office accepts an amendment purporting to delete or modify the name of a debtor or terminate the effectiveness of the financing statement. If an amendment provides a modified name for a debtor, the amended name should be added to the index, see subsection (c)(2), but the pre-amendment name should remain in the index.

Compared to former Article 9, the rule in subsection (g) increases the amount of information available to those who search the public records. The rule also contemplates that searchers—not the filing office—will determine the significance and effectiveness of filed records.

§ 9–520. Acceptance and Refusal to Accept Record

(a) [Mandatory refusal to accept record.] A filing office shall refuse to accept a record for filing for a reason set forth in Section 9–516(b) and may refuse to accept a record for filing only for a reason set forth in Section 9–516(b).

(b) [Communication concerning refusal.] If a filing office refuses to accept a record for filing, it shall communicate to the person that presented the record the fact of and reason for the refusal and the date and time the record would have been filed had the filing office accepted it. The communication must be made at the time and in the manner prescribed by filing-office rule but [, in the case of a filing office described in Section 9–501(a)(2),] in no event more than two business days after the filing office receives the record.

(c) [When filed financing statement effective.] A filed financing statement satisfying Section 9–502(a) and (b) is effective, even if the filing office is required to refuse to accept it for filing under subsection (a). However, Section 9–338 applies to a filed financing statement providing information described in Section 9–516(b)(5) which is incorrect at the time the financing statement is filed.

* * *

OFFICIAL COMMENT

* * *

2. **Refusal to Accept Record for Filing.** * * * Under this section, the filing office is not expected to make legal judgments and is not permitted to impose additional conditions or requirements.

Subsection (a) both prescribes and limits the bases upon which the filing office must and may reject records by reference to the reasons set forth in Section 9–516(b). For the most part, the bases for rejection are limited to those that prevent the filing office from dealing with a record that it receives—because some of the requisite information (e.g., the debtor's name) is missing or cannot be deciphered, because the record is not communicated by a method (e.g., it is MIME-rather than UU-encoded) or medium (e.g., it is written rather than electronic) that the filing office accepts, or because the filer fails to tender an amount equal to or greater than the filing fee.

3. **Consequences of Accepting Rejectable Record.** Section 9–516(b) includes among the reasons for rejecting an initial financing statement the failure to give certain information that is not required as a condition of effectiveness. In conjunction with Section 9–516(b)(5), this section requires the filing office to refuse to accept a financing statement that is legally sufficient to perfect a security interest under Section 9–502 but does not contain a mailing address for the debtor, does not disclose whether the debtor is an individual or an organization (e.g., a partnership or corporation) or, if the debtor is an organization, does not give certain specified information concerning the or-

ganization. The information required by Section 9–516(b)(5) assists searchers in weeding out "false positives," i.e., records that a search reveals but which do not pertain to the debtor in question. It assists filers by helping to ensure that the debtor's name is correct and that the financing statement is filed in the proper jurisdiction.

If the filing office accepts a financing statement that does not give this information at all, the filing is fully effective. Section 9–520(c). The financing statement also generally is effective if the information is given but is incorrect; however, Section 9–338 affords protection to buyers and holders of perfected security interests who gives value in reasonable reliance upon the incorrect information.

4. **Filing Office's Duties with Respect to Rejected Record.** Subsection (b) requires the filing office to communicate the fact of rejection and the reason therefor within a fixed period of time. Inasmuch as a rightfully rejected record is ineffective and a wrongfully rejected record is not fully effective, prompt communication concerning any rejection is important.

* * *

§ 9–521. Uniform Form of Written Financing Statement and Amendment

(a) [Initial financing statement form.] A filing office that accepts written records may not refuse to accept a written initial financing statement in the following form and format except for a reason set forth in Section 9–516(b):

UCC FINANCING STATEMENT

FOLLOW INSTRUCTIONS (front and back) CAREFULLY

A. NAME & PHONE OF CONTACT AT FILER [optional]

B. SEND ACKNOWLEDGMENT TO: (Name and Address)

THE ABOVE SPACE IS FOR FILING OFFICE USE ONLY

1. DEBTOR'S EXACT FULL LEGAL NAME - insert only one debtor name (1a or 1b) - do not abbreviate or combine names

1a. ORGANIZATION'S NAME			
OR 1b. INDIVIDUAL'S LAST NAME	FIRST NAME	MIDDLE NAME	SUFFIX
1c. MAILING ADDRESS	CITY	STATE POSTAL CODE	COUNTRY
1d. TAX ID #: SSN OR EIN	ADD'L INFO RE ORGANIZATION DEBTOR	1e. TYPE OF ORGANIZATION	1f. JURISDICTION OF ORGANIZATION	1g. ORGANIZATIONAL ID #, if any ☐ NONE

2. ADDITIONAL DEBTOR'S EXACT FULL LEGAL NAME - insert only one debtor name (2a or 2b) - do not abbreviate or combine names

2a. ORGANIZATION'S NAME			
OR 2b. INDIVIDUAL'S LAST NAME	FIRST NAME	MIDDLE NAME	SUFFIX
2c. MAILING ADDRESS	CITY	STATE POSTAL CODE	COUNTRY
2d. TAX ID #: SSN OR EIN	ADD'L INFO RE ORGANIZATION DEBTOR	2e. TYPE OF ORGANIZATION	2f. JURISDICTION OF ORGANIZATION	2g. ORGANIZATIONAL ID #, if any ☐ NONE

3. SECURED PARTY'S NAME (or NAME of TOTAL ASSIGNEE of ASSIGNOR S/P) - insert only one secured party name (3a or 3b)

3a. ORGANIZATION'S NAME			
OR 3b. INDIVIDUAL'S LAST NAME	FIRST NAME	MIDDLE NAME	SUFFIX
3c. MAILING ADDRESS	CITY	STATE POSTAL CODE	COUNTRY

4. This FINANCING STATEMENT covers the following collateral:

5. ALTERNATIVE DESIGNATION [if applicable]: ☐ LESSEE/LESSOR ☐ CONSIGNEE/CONSIGNOR ☐ BAILEE/BAILOR ☐ SELLER/BUYER ☐ AG. LIEN ☐ NON-UCC FILING

6. ☐ This FINANCING STATEMENT is to be filed [for record] (or recorded) in the REAL ESTATE RECORDS. Attach Addendum [if applicable] **7.** Check to REQUEST SEARCH REPORT(S) on Debtor(s) [ADDITIONAL FEE] [optional] ☐ All Debtors ☐ Debtor 1 ☐ Debtor 2

8. OPTIONAL FILER REFERENCE DATA

NATIONAL UCC FINANCING STATEMENT (FORM UCC1) (REV. 07/29/98)

UCC FINANCING STATEMENT ADDENDUM
FOLLOW INSTRUCTIONS (front and back) CAREFULLY

9. NAME OF FIRST DEBTOR (1a or 1b) ON RELATED FINANCING STATEMENT
   - 9a. ORGANIZATION'S NAME
   - OR
   - 9b. INDIVIDUAL'S LAST NAME | FIRST NAME | MIDDLE NAME, SUFFIX

10. MISCELLANEOUS:

THE ABOVE SPACE IS FOR FILING OFFICE USE ONLY

11. ADDITIONAL DEBTOR'S EXACT FULL LEGAL NAME - insert only one name (11a or 11b) - do not abbreviate or combine names
   - 11a. ORGANIZATION'S NAME
   - OR
   - 11b. INDIVIDUAL'S LAST NAME | FIRST NAME | MIDDLE NAME | SUFFIX
   - 11c. MAILING ADDRESS | CITY | STATE | POSTAL CODE | COUNTRY
   - 11d. TAX ID #: SSN OR EIN | ADD'L INFO RE ORGANIZATION DEBTOR | 11e. TYPE OF ORGANIZATION | 11f. JURISDICTION OF ORGANIZATION | 11g. ORGANIZATIONAL ID #, if any | ☐ NONE

12. ☐ ADDITIONAL SECURED PARTY'S or ☐ ASSIGNOR S/P'S NAME - insert only one name (12a or 12b)
   - 12a. ORGANIZATION'S NAME
   - OR
   - 12b. INDIVIDUAL'S LAST NAME | FIRST NAME | MIDDLE NAME | SUFFIX
   - 12c. MAILING ADDRESS | CITY | STATE | POSTAL CODE | COUNTRY

13. This FINANCING STATEMENT covers ☐ timber to be cut or ☐ as-extracted collateral, or is filed as a ☐ fixture filing.
14. Description of real estate:

16. Additional collateral description:

15. Name and address of a RECORD OWNER of above-described real estate (if Debtor does not have a record interest):

17. Check only if applicable and check only one box.
    Debtor is a ☐ Trust or ☐ Trustee acting with respect to property held in trust or ☐ Decedent's Estate
18. Check only if applicable and check only one box.
    ☐ Debtor is a TRANSMITTING UTILITY
    ☐ Filed in connection with a Manufactured-Home Transaction — effective 30 years
    ☐ Filed in connection with a Public-Finance Transaction — effective 30 years

NATIONAL UCC FINANCING STATEMENT ADDENDUM (FORM UCC1Ad) (REV. 07/29/98)

(b) [Amendment form.] A filing office that accepts written records may not refuse to accept a written record in the following form and format except for a reason set forth in Section 9–516(b):

§ 9–521　　　　　　　　ART. 9　　　　　　　　Unit 4

UCC FINANCING STATEMENT AMENDMENT

FOLLOW INSTRUCTIONS (front and back) CAREFULLY

A. NAME & PHONE OF CONTACT AT FILER [optional]

B. SEND ACKNOWLEDGMENT TO: (Name and Address)

THE ABOVE SPACE IS FOR FILING OFFICE USE ONLY

1a. INITIAL FINANCING STATEMENT FILE #

1b. This FINANCING STATEMENT AMENDMENT is to be filed [for record] (or recorded) in the REAL ESTATE RECORDS.

2. ☐ TERMINATION: Effectiveness of the Financing Statement identified above is terminated with respect to security interest(s) of the Secured Party authorizing this Termination Statement.

3. ☐ CONTINUATION: Effectiveness of the Financing Statement identified above with respect to security interest(s) of the Secured Party authorizing this Continuation Statement is continued for the additional period provided by applicable law.

4. ☐ ASSIGNMENT (full or partial): Give name of assignee in item 7a or 7b and address of assignee in item 7c; and also give name of assignor in item 9.

5. AMENDMENT (PARTY INFORMATION): This Amendment affects ☐ Debtor or ☐ Secured Party of record. Check only one of these two boxes.
Also check one of the following three boxes and provide appropriate information in items 6 and/or 7.
☐ CHANGE name and/or address: Give current record name in item 6a or 6b; also give new name (if name change) in item 7a or 7b and/or new address (if address change) in item 7c.
☐ DELETE name: Give record name to be deleted in item 6a or 6b.
☐ ADD name: Complete item 7a or 7b, and also item 7c; also complete items 7d-7g (if applicable).

6. CURRENT RECORD INFORMATION:
6a. ORGANIZATION'S NAME			
OR 6b. INDIVIDUAL'S LAST NAME	FIRST NAME	MIDDLE NAME	SUFFIX

7. CHANGED (NEW) OR ADDED INFORMATION:
7a. ORGANIZATION'S NAME			
OR 7b. INDIVIDUAL'S LAST NAME	FIRST NAME	MIDDLE NAME	SUFFIX
7c. MAILING ADDRESS	CITY	STATE POSTAL CODE	COUNTRY
7d. TAX ID #: SSN OR EIN	ADD'L INFO RE ORGANIZATION DEBTOR	7e. TYPE OF ORGANIZATION	7f. JURISDICTION OF ORGANIZATION	7g. ORGANIZATIONAL ID #, if any ☐ NONE

8. AMENDMENT (COLLATERAL CHANGE): check only one box.
Describe collateral ☐ deleted or ☐ added, or give entire ☐ restated collateral description, or describe collateral ☐ assigned.

9. NAME OF SECURED PARTY OF RECORD AUTHORIZING THIS AMENDMENT (name of assignor, if this is an Assignment). If this is an Amendment authorized by a Debtor which adds collateral or adds the authorizing Debtor, or if this is a Termination authorized by a Debtor, check here ☐ and enter name of DEBTOR authorizing this Amendment.
9a. ORGANIZATION'S NAME			
OR 9b. INDIVIDUAL'S LAST NAME	FIRST NAME	MIDDLE NAME	SUFFIX

10. OPTIONAL FILER REFERENCE DATA

NATIONAL UCC FINANCING STATEMENT AMENDMENT (FORM UCC3) (REV. 07/29/98)

UCC FINANCING STATEMENT AMENDMENT ADDENDUM
FOLLOW INSTRUCTIONS (front and back) CAREFULLY

11. INITIAL FINANCING STATEMENT FILE # (same as item 1a on Amendment form)

12. NAME OF PARTY AUTHORIZING THIS AMENDMENT (same as item 9 on Amendment form)
- 12a. ORGANIZATION'S NAME
- OR 12b. INDIVIDUAL'S LAST NAME | FIRST NAME | MIDDLE NAME, SUFFIX

13. Use this space for additional information

THE ABOVE SPACE IS FOR FILING OFFICE USE ONLY

NATIONAL UCC FINANCING STATEMENT AMENDMENT ADDENDUM (FORM UCC3Ad) (REV. 07/29/98)

OFFICIAL COMMENT

* * *

2. **"Safe Harbor" Written Forms.** Although Section 9–520 limits the bases upon which the filing office can refuse to accept records, this section provides sample written forms that must be accepted in every filing office in the country, as long as the filing office's rules permit it to accept written communications. By completing one of the forms in this section, a secured party can be certain that the filing office is obligated to accept it.

The forms in this section are based upon national financing statement forms that were in use under former Article 9. Those forms were developed over an extended period and reflect the comments and suggestions of filing officers, secured parties and their counsel, and service companies. The formatting of those forms and of the ones in this section has been designed to reduce error by both filers and filing offices.

A filing office that accepts written communications may not reject, on grounds of form or format, a filing using these forms. Although filers are not required to use the forms, they are encouraged and can be expected to do so, inasmuch as the forms are well designed and avoid the risk of rejection on the basis of form or format. As their use expands, the forms will rapidly become familiar to both filers and filing-office personnel. Filing offices may and should encourage the use of these forms by declaring them to be the "standard" (but not exclusive) forms for each jurisdiction, albeit without in any way suggesting that alternative forms are unacceptable.

The multi-purpose form in subsection (b) covers changes with respect to the debtor, the secured party, the collateral, and the status of the financing statement (termination and continuation). A single form may be used for several different types of amendments at once (e.g., both to change a debtor's name and continue the effectiveness of the financing statement).

* * *

§ 9–523. Information From Filing Office; Sale or License of Records

(a) [Acknowledgment of filing written record.] If a person that files a written record requests an acknowledgment of the filing, the filing office shall send to the person an image of the record showing the number assigned to the record pursuant to Section 9–519(a)(1) and the date and time of the filing of the record. However, if the person furnishes a copy of the record to the filing office, the filing office may instead:

> **(1)** note upon the copy the number assigned to the record pursuant to Section 9–519(a)(1) and the date and time of the filing of the record; and
>
> **(2)** send the copy to the person.

* * *

(c) [Communication of requested information.] The filing office shall communicate or otherwise make available in a record the following information to any person that requests it:

> **(1)** whether there is on file on a date and time specified by the filing office, but not a date earlier than three business days

before the filing office receives the request, any financing statement that:

    (A) designates a particular debtor [or, if the request so states, designates a particular debtor at the address specified in the request];

    (B) has not lapsed under Section 9–515 with respect to all secured parties of record; and

    (C) if the request so states, has lapsed under Section 9–515 and a record of which is maintained by the filing office under Section 9–522(a);

(2) the date and time of filing of each financing statement; and

(3) the information provided in each financing statement.

* * *

PART 6. DEFAULT

[SUBPART 1. DEFAULT AND ENFORCEMENT OF SECURITY INTEREST]

§ 9–601. Rights After Default; Judicial Enforcement; Consignor or Buyer of Accounts, Chattel Paper, Payment Intangibles, or Promissory Notes

(a) [Rights of secured party after default.] After default, a secured party has the rights provided in this part and, except as otherwise provided in Section 9–602, those provided by agreement of the parties. A secured party:

    (1) may reduce a claim to judgment, foreclose, or otherwise enforce the claim, security interest, or agricultural lien by any available judicial procedure; and

    (2) if the collateral is documents, may proceed either as to the documents or as to the goods they cover.

(b) [Rights and duties of secured party in possession or control.] A secured party in possession of collateral or control of collateral under Section 7–106, 9–104, 9–105, 9–106, or 9–107 has the rights and duties provided in Section 9–207.

(c) [Rights cumulative; simultaneous exercise.] The rights under subsections (a) and (b) are cumulative and may be exercised simultaneously.

(d) [Rights of debtor and obligor.] Except as otherwise provided in subsection (g) and Section 9–605, after default, a debtor and an obligor have the rights provided in this part and by agreement of the parties.

(e) [Lien of levy after judgment.] If a secured party has reduced its claim to judgment, the lien of any levy that may be made upon the collateral by virtue of an execution based upon the judgment relates back to the earliest of:

    (1) the date of perfection of the security interest * * * in the collateral;

    (2) the date of filing a financing statement covering the collateral;

* * *

(f) [Execution sale.] A sale pursuant to an execution is a foreclosure of the security interest * * * by judicial procedure within the meaning of this section. A secured party may purchase at the sale and thereafter hold the collateral free of any other requirements of this article.

(g) [Consignor or buyer of certain rights to payment.] Except as otherwise provided in Section 9–607(c), this part imposes no duties upon a secured party that is a consignor or is a buyer of accounts, chattel paper, payment intangibles, or promissory notes.

UNOFFICIAL COMMENTS

Lots of the law of default comes from the security agreement. A security agreement typically defines default, provides for acceleration of debt on default, and describes what constitutes a waiver of default.

And a lot of the law of default comes from state creditors' rights law and federal bankruptcy law. This section traces the state creditors' rights law process of (i) judgment, (ii) levy and (iii) execution sale.

For a more complete, general review of default under Article 9, see pages 381–409.

NON–OBVIOUS DEFINITIONS

"Default" is the title of Part 6 of Article 9. Only do Part 6 if there is a "default" The word "default" appears in the various sections of Part 6. A definition of the word "default nowhere appears in Article 9. "Default" is generally defined in the security agreement. See Official Comment 3 to 9–601.

OTHER UCC SECTIONS TO LOOK TO WHEN YOU LOOK AT SECTION 9–601

In essence, you need to look at all of Part 6 together. For example, section 9–601(d) looks to the security agreement. In looking to the security agreement, you need to look to section 9–602 and 9–603.

If your professor covered bankruptcy, you also need to look at the automatic stay of Bankruptcy Code section 362.

If your professor covered acceleration clauses, you need to look at section 1–208/revised 1–309.

OFFICIAL COMMENT

* * *

2. **Enforcement: In General.** The rights of a secured party to enforce its security interest in collateral after the debtor's default are an important feature of a secured transaction. (Note that the term "rights," as defined in Section 1–201, includes "remedies.") This Part provides those rights as well as certain limitations on their exercise for the protection of the defaulting debtor, other creditors, and other affected persons. However, subsections (a) and (d) make clear that the rights provided in this Part do not exclude other rights provided by agreement.

3. **When Remedies Arise.** Under subsection (a) the secured party's rights arise "[a]fter default." As did former Section 9–501, this Article leaves to the agreement of the parties the circumstances giving rise to a default. This Article does not determine whether a secured party's post-default conduct can constitute a waiver of default in the face of an agreement stating that such conduct shall not constitute a waiver. Rather, it continues to leave to the parties' agreement, as supplemented by law other than this Article, the determination whether a default has occurred or has been waived. See Section 1–103.

4. **Possession of Collateral; Section 9–207.** After a secured party takes possession of collateral following a default, there is no longer any distinction between a security interest that before default was nonpossessory and a security interest that was possessory before default, as under a common-law pledge. This Part generally does not distinguish between the rights of a secured party with a nonpossessory security interest and those of a secured party with a possessory security interest. However, Section 9–207 addresses rights and duties with respect to collateral in a secured party's possession. Under subsection (b) of this section, Section 9–207 applies not only to possession before default but also to possession after default. Subsection (b) also has been conformed to Section 9–207, which, unlike former Section 9–207, applies to secured parties having control of collateral.

5. **Cumulative Remedies.** Former Section 9–501(1) provided that the secured party's remedies were cumulative, but it did not explicitly provide whether the remedies could be exercised simultaneously. Subsection (c) permits the simultaneous exercise of remedies if the secured party acts in good faith. The liability scheme of Subpart 2 affords redress to an aggrieved debtor or obligor. Moreover, permitting the simultaneous exercise of remedies under subsection (c) does not override any non-UCC law, including the law of tort and statutes regulating collection of debts, under which the simultaneous exercise of remedies in a particular case constitutes abusive behavior or harassment giving rise to liability.

6. **Judicial Enforcement.** Under subsection (a) a secured party may reduce its claim to judgment or foreclose its interest by any available procedure outside

this Article under applicable law. Subsection (e) generally follows former Section 9–501(5). It makes clear that any judicial lien that the secured party may acquire against the collateral effectively is a continuation of the original security interest (if perfected) and not the acquisition of a new interest or a transfer of property on account of a preexisting obligation. Under former Section 9–501(5), the judicial lien was stated to relate back to the date of perfection of the security interest. Subsection (e), however, provides that the lien relates back to the earlier of the date of filing or the date of perfection. This provides a secured party who enforces a security interest by judicial process with the benefit of the "first-to-file-or-perfect" priority rule of Section 9–322(a)(1).

* * *

8. **Execution Sales.** Subsection (f) also follows former Section 9–501(5). It makes clear that an execution sale is an appropriate method of foreclosure contemplated by this Part. However, the sale is governed by other law and not by this Article, and the limitations under Section 9–610 on the right of a secured party to purchase collateral do not apply.

9. **Sales of Receivables; Consignments.** Subsection (g) provides that, except as provided in Section 9–607(c), the duties imposed on secured parties do not apply to buyers of accounts, chattel paper, payment intangibles, or promissory notes. Although denominated "secured parties," these buyers own the entire interest in the property sold and so may enforce their rights without regard to the seller ("debtor") or the seller's creditors. Likewise, a true consignor may enforce its ownership interest under other law without regard to the duties that this Part imposes on secured parties. Note, however, that Section 9–615 governs cases in which a consignee's secured party (other than a consignor) is enforcing a security interest that is senior to the security interest (i.e., ownership interest) of a true consignor.

§ 9–602. Waiver and Variance of Rights and Duties

Except as otherwise provided in Section 9–624, to the extent that they give rights to a debtor or obligor and impose duties on a secured party, the debtor or obligor may not waive or vary the rules stated in the following listed sections:

(1) Section 9–207(b)(4)(C), which deals with use and operation of the collateral by the secured party;

(2) Section 9–210, which deals with requests for an accounting and requests concerning a list of collateral and statement of account;

(3) Section 9–607(c), which deals with collection and enforcement of collateral;

(4) Sections 9–608(a) and 9–615(c) to the extent that they deal with application or payment of noncash proceeds of collection, enforcement, or disposition;

(5) Sections 9–608(a) and 9–615(d) to the extent that they require accounting for or payment of surplus proceeds of collateral;

(6) Section 9–609 to the extent that it imposes upon a secured party that takes possession of collateral without judicial process the duty to do so without breach of the peace;

(7) Sections 9–610(b), 9–611, 9–613, and 9–614, which deal with disposition of collateral;

(8) Section 9–615(f), which deals with calculation of a deficiency or surplus when a disposition is made to the secured party, a person related to the secured party, or a secondary obligor;

(9) Section 9–616, which deals with explanation of the calculation of a surplus or deficiency;

(10) Sections 9–620, 9–621, and 9–622, which deal with acceptance of collateral in satisfaction of obligation;

(11) Section 9–623, which deals with redemption of collateral;

(12) Section 9–624, which deals with permissible waivers; and

(13) Sections 9–625 and 9–626, which deal with the secured party's liability for failure to comply with this article.

OFFICIAL COMMENT

* * *

2. **Waiver: In General.** Section 1–102(3) addresses which provisions of the UCC are mandatory and which may be varied by agreement. With exceptions relating to good faith, diligence, reasonableness, and care, immediate parties, as between themselves, may vary its provisions by agreement. However, in the context of rights and duties after default, our legal system traditionally has looked with suspicion on agreements that limit the debtor's rights and free the secured party of its duties. As stated in former Section 9–501, Comment 4, "no mortgage clause has ever been allowed to clog the equity of redemption." The context of default offers great opportunity for overreaching. The suspicious attitudes of the courts have been grounded in common sense. This section, like former Section 9–501(3), codifies this long-standing and deeply rooted attitude. The specified rights of the debtor and duties of the secured party may not be waived or varied except as stated. Provisions that are not specified in this section are subject to the general rules in Section 1–102(3).

3. **Nonwaivable Rights and Duties.** This section revises former Section 9–501(3) by restricting the ability to waive or modify additional specified rights and duties: (i) duties under Section 9–207(b)(4)(C), which deals with the use and operation of consumer goods, (ii) the right to a response to a request for an accounting, concerning a list of collateral, or concerning a statement of account (Section 9–210), (iii) the duty to collect collateral in a commercially reasonable manner (Section 9–607), (iv) the implicit duty to refrain from a breach of the peace in taking possession of collateral under Section 9–609, (v) the duty to apply non-cash proceeds of collection or disposition in a commercially reasonable manner (Sections 9–608 and 9–615), (vi) the right to a special method of calculating a surplus or deficiency in certain dispositions to a secured party, a person related to secured party, or a secondary obligor (Section 9–615), (vii) the duty to give an explanation of the calculation of a surplus or deficiency (Section 9–616), (viii) the right to limitations on the effectiveness of certain waivers (Section 9–624), and (ix) the right to hold a secured party liable for failure to comply with this Article (Sections 9–625 and 9–626). For clarity and consistency, this Article uses the term "waive or vary" instead of "renounc[e] or modify[]," which appeared in former Section 9–504(3).

This section provides generally that the specified rights and duties "may not be waived or varied." However, it does not restrict the ability of parties to agree to settle, compromise, or renounce claims for past conduct that may have constituted a violation or breach of those rights and duties, even if the settlement involves an express "waiver."

4. **Waiver by Debtors and Obligors.** The restrictions on waiver contained in this section apply to obligors as well as debtors. This resolves a question under former Article 9 as to whether secondary obligors, assuming that they were "debtors" for purposes of former Part 5, were permitted to waive, under the law of suretyship, rights and duties under that Part.

5. **Certain Post–Default Waivers.** Section 9–624 permits post-default waivers in limited circumstances. These waivers must be made in agreements that are authenticated. Under Section 1–201, an " 'agreement' means the bargain of the parties in fact." In considering waivers under Section 9–624 and analogous agreements in other contexts, courts should carefully scrutinize putative agreements that appear in records that also address many additional or unrelated matters.

§ 9–603. Agreement on Standards Concerning Rights and Duties

(a) [Agreed standards.] The parties may determine by agreement the standards measuring the fulfillment of the rights of a debtor or obligor and the duties of a secured party under a rule stated in Section 9–602 if the standards are not manifestly unreasonable.

(b) [Agreed standards inapplicable to breach of peace.] Subsection (a) does not apply to the duty under Section 9–609 to refrain from breaching the peace.

OFFICIAL COMMENT

* * *

2. **Limitation on Ability to Set Standards.** Subsection (a), like former Section 9–501(3), permits the parties to set standards for compliance with the rights and duties under this Part if the standards are not "manifestly unreasonable." Under subsection (b), the parties are not permitted to set standards measuring fulfillment of the secured party's duty to take collateral without breaching the peace.

§ 9–604. Procedure if Security Agreement Covers Real Property or Fixtures

(a) [Enforcement: personal and real property.] If a security agreement covers both personal and real property, a secured party may proceed:

> (1) under this part as to the personal property without prejudicing any rights with respect to the real property; or
>
> (2) as to both the personal property and the real property in accordance with the rights with respect to the real property, in which case the other provisions of this part do not apply.

(b) [Enforcement: fixtures.] Subject to subsection (c), if a security agreement covers goods that are or become fixtures, a secured party may proceed:

(1) under this part; or

(2) in accordance with the rights with respect to real property, in which case the other provisions of this part do not apply.

(c) [Removal of fixtures.] Subject to the other provisions of this part, if a secured party holding a security interest in fixtures has priority over all owners and encumbrancers of the real property, the secured party, after default, may remove the collateral from the real property.

(d) [Injury caused by removal.] A secured party that removes collateral shall promptly reimburse any encumbrancer or owner of the real property, other than the debtor, for the cost of repair of any physical injury caused by the removal. The secured party need not reimburse the encumbrancer or owner for any diminution in value of the real property caused by the absence of the goods removed or by any necessity of replacing them. A person entitled to reimbursement may refuse permission to remove until the secured party gives adequate assurance for the performance of the obligation to reimburse.

UNOFFICIAL COMMENTS

Notice the limiting language in section 9–604(c) that a secured party must have priority over owners and encumbrancers if it wants to remove a fixture.

NON–OBVIOUS DEFINITIONS

"Fixture" is defined in section 9–102(41). We like our professor's definition: a fixture is something that had a personal property past, has a real property present, and the possible prospect of a personal property future.

"Encumbrancer" is not defined in section 9–102 but "encumbrance" is. Look for someone with a mortgage (or possibly, but less likely, a judgment lien) on the real property to which the fixture is affixed.

"Owner" is not defined in section 9–102. The term is useful only if someone other than the debtor owns the real property to which the fixture is affixed.

OTHER UCC SECTIONS TO LOOK TO WHEN YOU LOOK AT SECTION 9–604

Section 9–334 controls priority as between a secured party and a non-debtor owner or encumbrancer of the real estate.

OFFICIAL COMMENT

* * *

2. **Real–Property–Related Collateral.** The collateral in many transactions consists of both real and personal property. In the interest of simplicity, speed, and economy, subsection (a), like former Section 9–501(4), permits (but does not require) the secured party to proceed as to both real and personal property in accordance with its rights and remedies with respect to the real property. Subsection (a) also makes clear that a secured party who exercises rights under Part 6 with respect to personal property does not prejudice any rights under real-property law.

This Article does not address certain other real-property-related problems. In a number of States, the exercise of remedies by a creditor who is secured by both real property and non-real property collateral is governed by special legal rules. For example, under some anti-deficiency laws, creditors risk loss of rights against personal property collateral if they err in enforcing their rights against the real property. Under a "one-form-of-action" rule (or rule against splitting a cause of action), a creditor who judicially enforces a real property mortgage and does not proceed in the same action to enforce a security interest in personalty may (among other consequences) lose the right to proceed against the personalty. Although statutes of this kind create impediments to enforcement of security interests, this Article does not override these limitations under other law.

3. **Fixtures.** Subsection (b) is new. It makes clear that a security interest in fixtures may be enforced either under real-property law or under any of the applicable provisions of Part 6, including sale or other disposition either before or after removal of the fixtures (see subsection (c)). Subsection (b) also serves to overrule cases holding that a secured party's only remedy after default is the removal of the fixtures from the real property. * * *

Subsection (c) generally follows former Section 9–313(8). It gives the secured party the right to remove fixtures under certain circumstances. A secured party whose security interest in fixtures has priority over owners and encumbrancers of the real property may remove the collateral from the real property. However, subsection (d) requires the secured party to reimburse any owner (other than the debtor) or encumbrancer for the cost of repairing any physical injury caused by the removal. This right to reimbursement is implemented by the last sentence of subsection (d), which gives the owner or encumbrancer a right to security or indemnity as a condition for giving permission to remove.

§ 9–605. Unknown Debtor or Secondary Obligor

A secured party does not owe a duty based on its status as secured party:

(1) to a person that is a debtor or obligor, unless the secured party knows:

(A) that the person is a debtor or obligor;

(B) the identity of the person; and

(C) how to communicate with the person; or

(2) to a secured party or lienholder that has filed a financing statement against a person, unless the secured party knows:

(A) that the person is a debtor; and

(B) the identity of the person.

OFFICIAL COMMENT

* * *

2. Duties to Unknown Persons. This section relieves a secured party from duties owed to a debtor or obligor, if the secured party does not know about the debtor or obligor. Similarly, it relieves a secured party from duties owed to a secured party or lienholder who has filed a financing statement against the debtor, if the secured party does not know about the debtor. For example, a secured party may be unaware that the original debtor has sold the collateral subject to the security interest and that the new owner has become the debtor. If so, the secured party owes no duty to the new owner (debtor) or to a secured party who has filed a financing statement against the new owner. This section should be read in conjunction with the exculpatory provisions in Section 9–628. Note that it relieves a secured party not only from duties arising under this Article but also from duties arising under other law by virtue of the secured party's status as such under this Article, unless the other law otherwise provides.

* * *

§ 9–607. Collection and Enforcement by Secured Party

(a) [Collection and enforcement generally.] If so agreed, and in any event after default, a secured party:

(1) may notify an account debtor or other person obligated on collateral to make payment or otherwise render performance to or for the benefit of the secured party;

(2) may take any proceeds to which the secured party is entitled under Section 9–315;

(3) may enforce the obligations of an account debtor or other person obligated on collateral and exercise the rights of the debtor with respect to the obligation of the account debtor or other person obligated on collateral to make payment or otherwise render performance to the debtor, and with respect to any property that secures the obligations of the account debtor or other person obligated on the collateral;

(4) if it holds a security interest in a deposit account perfected by control under Section 9–104(a)(1), may apply the balance of the deposit account to the obligation secured by the deposit account; and

(5) if it holds a security interest in a deposit account perfected by control under Section 9–104(a)(2) or (3), may instruct the bank to pay the balance of the deposit account to or for the benefit of the secured party.

(b) [Nonjudicial enforcement of mortgage.] If necessary to enable a secured party to exercise under subsection (a)(3) the right of a debtor to enforce a mortgage nonjudicially, the secured party may record in the office in which a record of the mortgage is recorded:

> (1) a copy of the security agreement that creates or provides for a security interest in the obligation secured by the mortgage; and
>
> (2) the secured party's sworn affidavit in recordable form stating that:
>
>> (A) a default has occurred; and
>>
>> (B) the secured party is entitled to enforce the mortgage nonjudicially.

(c) [Commercially reasonable collection and enforcement.] A secured party shall proceed in a commercially reasonable manner if the secured party:

> (1) undertakes to collect from or enforce an obligation of an account debtor or other person obligated on collateral; and
>
> (2) is entitled to charge back uncollected collateral or otherwise to full or limited recourse against the debtor or a secondary obligor.

(d) [Expenses of collection and enforcement.] A secured party may deduct from the collections made pursuant to subsection (c) reasonable expenses of collection and enforcement, including reasonable attorney's fees and legal expenses incurred by the secured party.

(e) [Duties to secured party not affected.] This section does not determine whether an account debtor, bank, or other person obligated on collateral owes a duty to a secured party.

UNOFFICIAL COMMENTS

Look for a situation in which account debtor AD buys goods on credit from debtor D. D then uses his right to payment from AD as collateral for a secured loan from S. D later defaults on his debt owing to S's. This section addresses S rights as against AD.

Some Article 9 courses never address this situation. **Too many others address it in a "half-ass way" (not a term defined in Article 9), so we address sales of receivables and 9–607 in detail on pages 386–393.**

NON–OBVIOUS DEFINITIONS

What you or I would call an "account receivable", Article 9 calls an "account" and defines "account" in section 9–102(a)(2).

This section does not use the term "account." Instead it use the term "account debtor", which, under section 9–102(a)(3) includes not only a person obligated on an account but also a person obligated on "chattel paper" or "general intangible", terms defined in section 9–102.

OTHER UCC SECTIONS TO LOOK TO WHEN YOU LOOK AT SECTION 9–607

Look to section 9–406 if the account debtor pays the debtor.

Look to sections 9–403 and 9–404 if the account debtor asserts defenses against the secured party.

Look to section 9–608 to see what happens to money collected from account debtor under 9–607.

OFFICIAL COMMENT

* * *

2. **Collections: In General.** Collateral consisting of rights to payment is not only the most liquid asset of a typical debtor's business but also is property that may be collected without any interruption of the debtor's business This situation is far different from that in which collateral is inventory or equipment, whose removal may bring the business to a halt. Furthermore, problems of valuation and identification, present with collateral that is tangible personal property, frequently are not as serious in the case of rights to payment and other intangible collateral. Consequently, this section, like former Section 9–502, recognizes that financing through assignments of intangibles lacks many of the complexities that arise after default in other types of financing. This section allows the assignee to liquidate collateral by collecting whatever may become due on the collateral, whether or not the method of collection contemplated by the security arrangement before default was direct (i.e., payment by the account debtor to the assignee, "notification" financing) or indirect (i.e., payment by the account debtor to the assignor, "nonnotification" financing).

3. **Scope.** The scope of this section is broader than that of former Section 9–502. It applies not only to collections from account debtors and obligors on instruments but also to enforcement more generally against all persons obligated on collateral. It explicitly provides for the secured party's enforcement of the debtor's rights in respect of the account debtor's (and other third parties') obligations and for the secured party's enforcement of supporting obligations with respect to those obligations. (Supporting obligations are components of the collateral under Section 9–203(f).) The rights of a secured party under subsection (a) include the right to enforce claims that the debtor may enjoy against others. For example, the claims might include a breach-of-warranty claim arising out of a defect in equipment that is collateral or a secured party's action for an injunction against infringement of a patent that is collateral. Those claims typically would be proceeds of original collateral under Section 9–315.

4. **Collection and Enforcement Before Default.** Like Part 6 generally, this section deals with the rights and duties of secured parties following default. However, as did former Section 9–502 with respect to collection rights, this section also applies to the collection and enforcement rights of secured parties even if a default has not occurred, as long as the debtor has so agreed. It is not unusual for debtors to agree that secured parties are entitled to collect and enforce rights against account debtors prior to default.

5. **Collections by Junior Secured Party.** A secured party who holds a secu-

rity interest in a right to payment may exercise the right to collect and enforce under this section, even if the security interest is subordinate to a conflicting security interest in the same right to payment. Whether the junior secured party has priority in the collected proceeds depends on whether the junior secured party qualifies for priority as a purchaser of an instrument (e.g., the account debtor's check) under Section 9–330(d), as a holder in due course of an instrument under Sections 3–305 and 9–331(a), or as a transferee of money under Section 9–332(a). See Sections 9–330, Comment 7; 9–331, Comment 5; and 9–332.

6. **Relationship to Rights and Duties of Persons Obligated on Collateral.** This section permits a secured party to collect and enforce obligations included in collateral in its capacity as a secured party. It is not necessary for a secured party first to become the owner of the collateral pursuant to a disposition or acceptance. However, the secured party's rights, as between it and the debtor, to collect from and enforce collateral against account debtors and others obligated on collateral under subsection (a) are subject to Section 9–341, Part 4, and other applicable law. *Neither this section nor former Section 9–502 should be understood to regulate the duties of an account debtor or other person obligated on collateral.* Subsection (e) makes this explicit. For example, the secured party may be unable to exercise the debtor's rights under an instrument if the debtor is in possession of the instrument, or under a non-transferable letter of credit if the debtor is the beneficiary. Unless a secured party has control over a letter-of-credit right and is entitled to receive payment or performance from the issuer or a nominated person under Article 5, its remedies with respect to the letter-of-credit right may be limited to the recovery of any identifiable proceeds from the debtor. This section establishes only the baseline rights of the secured party *vis-a-vis the debtor*—the secured party is entitled to enforce and collect after default or earlier if so agreed.

7. **Deposit Account Collateral.** Subsections (a)(4) and (5) set forth the self-help remedy for a secured party whose collateral is a deposit account. Subsection (a)(4) addresses the rights of a secured party that is the bank with which the deposit account is maintained. That secured party automatically has control of the deposit account under Section 9–104(a)(1). After default, and otherwise if so agreed, the bank/secured party may apply the funds on deposit to the secured obligation.

If a security interest of a third party is perfected by control (Section 9–104(a)(2) or (a)(3)), then after default, and otherwise if so agreed, the secured party may instruct the bank to pay out the funds in the account. If the third party has control under Section 9–104(a)(3), the depositary institution is obliged to obey the instruction because the secured party is its customer. See Section 4–401. If the third party has control under Section 9–104(a)(2), the control agreement determines the depositary institution's obligation to obey.

If a security interest in a deposit account is unperfected, or is perfected by filing by virtue of the proceeds rules of Section 9–315, the depositary institution ordinarily owes no obligation to obey the secured party's instructions. See Section 9–341. To reach the funds without the debtor's cooperation, the secured party must use an available judicial procedure.

8. **Rights Against Mortgagor of Real Property.** Subsection (b) addresses the situation in which the collateral consists of a mortgage note (or other obligation secured by a mortgage on real property). After the debtor's (mortgagee's) default, the secured party (assignee) may wish to proceed with a nonjudicial foreclosure of the mortgage securing the note but may be unable to do so because it has not become the assignee of record. The assignee/secured party may not have taken a recordable assignment at the commencement of the transaction (perhaps the mortgage note in question was one of hundreds assigned to the secured party as collateral). Having defaulted, the mortgagee may be unwilling to sign a

recordable assignment. This section enables the secured party (assignee) to become the assignee of record by recording in the applicable real-property records the security agreement and an affidavit certifying default. Of course, the secured party's rights derive from those of its debtor. Subsection (b) would not entitle the secured party to proceed with a foreclosure unless the mortgagor also were in default or the debtor (mortgagee) otherwise enjoyed the right to foreclose.

9. **Commercial Reasonableness.** Subsection (c) provides that the secured party's collection and enforcement rights under subsection (a) must be exercised in a commercially reasonable manner. These rights include the right to settle and compromise claims against the account debtor. The secured party's failure to observe the standard of commercial reasonableness could render it liable to an aggrieved person under Section 9–625, and the secured party's recovery of a deficiency would be subject to Section 9–626. Subsection (c) does not apply if, as is characteristic of most sales of accounts, chattel paper, payment intangibles, and promissory notes, the secured party (buyer) has no right of recourse against the debtor (seller) or a secondary obligor. However, if the secured party does have a right of recourse, the commercial-reasonableness standard applies to collection and enforcement even though the assignment to the secured party was a "true" sale. The obligation to proceed in a commercially reasonable manner arises because the collection process affects the extent of the seller's recourse liability, not because the seller retains an interest in the sold collateral (the seller does not). Concerning classification of a transaction, see Section 9–109, Comment 4.

10. **Attorney's Fees and Legal Expenses.** The phrase "reasonable attorney's fees and legal expenses," which appears in subsection (d), includes only those fees and expenses incurred in proceeding against account debtors or other third parties. The secured party's right to recover these expenses from the collections arises automatically under this section. The secured party also may incur other attorney's fees and legal expenses in proceeding against the debtor or obligor. Whether the secured party has a right to recover those fees and expenses depends on whether the debtor or obligor has agreed to pay them, as is the case with respect to attorney's fees and legal expenses under Sections 9–608(a)(1)(A) and 9–615(a)(1). The parties also may agree to allocate a portion of the secured party's overhead to collection and enforcement under subsection (d) or Section 9–608(a).

§ 9–608. Application of Proceeds of Collection or Enforcement; Liability for Deficiency and Right to Surplus

(a) [Application of proceeds, surplus, and deficiency if obligation secured.] If a security interest or agricultural lien secures payment or performance of an obligation, the following rules apply:

(1) A secured party shall apply or pay over for application the cash proceeds of collection or enforcement under Section 9–607 in the following order to:

(A) the reasonable expenses of collection and enforcement and, to the extent provided for by agreement and not prohibited by law, reasonable attorney's fees and legal expenses incurred by the secured party;

(B) the satisfaction of obligations secured by the security interest or agricultural lien under which the collection or enforcement is made; and

(C) the satisfaction of obligations secured by any subordinate security interest in or other lien on the collateral subject to the security interest or agricultural lien under which the collection or enforcement is made if the secured party receives an authenticated demand for proceeds before distribution of the proceeds is completed.

(2) If requested by a secured party, a holder of a subordinate security interest or other lien shall furnish reasonable proof of the interest or lien within a reasonable time. Unless the holder complies, the secured party need not comply with the holder's demand under paragraph (1)(C).

(3) A secured party need not apply or pay over for application noncash proceeds of collection and enforcement under Section 9–607 unless the failure to do so would be commercially unreasonable. A secured party that applies or pays over for application noncash proceeds shall do so in a commercially reasonable manner.

(4) A secured party shall account to and pay a debtor for any surplus, and the obligor is liable for any deficiency.

(b) [No surplus or deficiency in sales of certain rights to payment.] If the underlying transaction is a sale of accounts, chattel paper, payment intangibles, or promissory notes, the debtor is not entitled to any surplus, and the obligor is not liable for any deficiency.

NON–OBVIOUS DEFINITIONS

The term "subordinate security interest" is not defined. If X's security interest has priority over Y's, then Y's security interest is the "subordinate security interest."

OTHER UCC SECTIONS TO LOOK TO WHEN YOU LOOK AT SECTION 9–608

Look at the priority rules in sections such as 9–322 and 9–324 to determine if there is a "subordinate security interest".

Application of proceeds questions are more likely to occur in connection with sale of goods under 9–610 rather than collection of payment rights under 9–607. Application of proceeds under section 9–608 is in most respects similar to application of proceeds under 9–615.

Application of section 9–608 to any surplus or deficiency is different if the Article 9 transaction is a sale of payment rights. See section 9–608(d). Remember, a sale of payment rights is an Article 9 transaction. **Please see section 9–109(a)(3) and Official Comments 4 and 5 to 9–109 and our extended discussion of sales of payment rights on pages 413–416.**

For an extended discussion of 9–608, see pages 393–396 infra.

OFFICIAL COMMENT

* * *

3. **Surplus and Deficiency.** * * * The parties are always free to agree that an obligor will not be liable for a deficiency, even if the collateral secures an obligation, and that an obligor is liable for a deficiency, even if the transaction is a sale of receivables. * * *

4. **Noncash Proceeds.** Subsection (a)(3) addresses the situation in which an enforcing secured party receives noncash proceeds.

Example: An enforcing secured party receives a promissory note from an account debtor who is unable to pay an account when it is due. The secured party accepts the note in exchange for extending the date on which the account debtor's obligation is due. The secured party may wish to credit its debtor (the assignor) with the principal amount of the note upon receipt of the note, but probably will prefer to credit the debtor only as and when the note is paid.

Under subsection (a)(3), the secured party is under no duty to apply the note or its value to the outstanding obligation unless its failure to do so would be commercially unreasonable. If the secured party does apply the note to the outstanding obligation, however, it must do so in a commercially reasonable manner. The parties may provide for the method of application of noncash proceeds by agreement, if the method is not manifestly unreasonable. See Section 9–603. This section does not explain when the failure to apply noncash proceeds would be commercially unreasonable; it leaves that determination to case-by-case adjudication. In the example, the secured party appears to have accepted the account debtor's note in order to increase the likelihood of payment and decrease the likelihood that the account debtor would dispute its obligation. Under these circumstances, it may well be commercially reasonable for the secured party to credit its debtor's obligations only as and when cash proceeds are collected from the account debtor, especially given the uncertainty that attends the account debtor's eventual payment. For an example of a secured party's receipt of noncash proceeds in which it may well be commercially unreasonable for the secured party to delay crediting its debtor's obligations with the value of noncash proceeds, see Section 9–615, Comment 3.

When the secured party is not required to "apply or pay over for application noncash proceeds," the proceeds nonetheless remain collateral subject to this Article. If the secured party were to dispose of them, for example, appropriate notification would be required (see Section 9–611), and the disposition would be subject to the standards provided in this Part (see Section 9–610). Moreover, a secured party in possession of the noncash proceeds would have the duties specified in Section 9–207.

5. **No Effect on Priority of Senior Security Interest.** The application of proceeds required by subsection (a) does not affect the priority of a security interest in collateral which is senior to the interest of the secured party who is collecting or enforcing collateral under Section 9–607. Although subsection (a) im-

poses a duty to apply proceeds to the enforcing secured party's expenses and to the satisfaction of the secured obligations owed to it and to subordinate secured parties, that duty applies only among the enforcing secured party and those persons. Concerning the priority of a junior secured party who collects and enforces collateral, see Section 9–607, Comment 5.

§ 9–609. Secured Party's Right to Take Possession After Default

(a) [Possession; rendering equipment unusable; disposition on debtor's premises.] After default, a secured party:

(1) may take possession of the collateral; and

(2) without removal, may render equipment unusable and dispose of collateral on a debtor's premises under Section 9–610.

(b) [Judicial and nonjudicial process.] A secured party may proceed under subsection (a):

(1) pursuant to judicial process; or

(2) without judicial process, if it proceeds without breach of the peace.

(c) [Assembly of collateral.] If so agreed, and in any event after default, a secured party may require the debtor to assemble the collateral and make it available to the secured party at a place to be designated by the secured party which is reasonably convenient to both parties.

UNOFFICIAL COMMENTS

Note the words "after default." Be sure that there has been a default and no waiver of default.

Note the section 9–609(a)(2) alternative to taking possession of the collateral. Comes up a lot on exams.

Finally, note what neither section 9–609(a)(1) nor section 9–609(a)(2) says. Nothing in 9–609 that limits its use to the secured party who has priority over other secured parties. If a junior secured party uses section 9–609, look to Comment 5 to section 9–110.

NON–OBVIOUS DEFINITIONS

"Breach of the peace" is not defined in Article 9. Look to the cases you studied this semester and to the security agreement.

OTHER UCC SECTIONS TO LOOK TO WHEN YOU LOOK AT SECTION 9–609

If the security agreement has language about breach of the peace, look to the language of sections 9–602(6) and 9–603.

Judicial foreclosure under sections 9–609(b)(1) and 9–601(f) is an alternative to section 9–609(b)(2)'s self-help repossession.

After repossession, resale under section 9–610 or retention under section 9–620 are the secured party's primary alternatives. The debtor (and any "secondary obligor" as defined in section 9–102(a)(71)) has the right to redeem its collateral under section 9–623. **If your professor covered default in detail, then you should "cover" our detailed discussion of default on pages 381–409.**

And, if your professor covered bankruptcy, be sure that you know that secured party's collection efforts under section 9–609 is covered by Bankruptcy Code section 362(a)(3), (4) , i.e., is stayed.

OFFICIAL COMMENT

* * *

2. **Secured Party's Right to Possession.** This section follows former Section 9–503 and earlier uniform legislation. It provides that the secured party is entitled to take possession of collateral after default.

3. **Judicial Process; Breach of Peace.** Subsection (b) permits a secured party to proceed under this section without judicial process if it does so "without breach of the peace." Although former Section 9–503 placed the same condition on a secured party's right to take possession of collateral, subsection (b) extends the condition to the right provided in subsection (a)(2) as well. Like former Section 9–503, this section does not define or explain the conduct that will constitute a breach of the peace, leaving that matter for continuing development by the courts. In considering whether a secured party has engaged in a breach of the peace, however, courts should hold the secured party responsible for the actions of others taken on the secured party's behalf, including independent contractors engaged by the secured party to take possession of collateral.

This section does not authorize a secured party who repossesses without judicial process to utilize the assistance of a law-enforcement officer. A number of cases have held that a repossessing secured party's use of a law-enforcement officer without benefit of judicial process constituted a failure to comply with former Section 9–503.

4. **Damages for Breach of Peace.** Concerning damages that may be recovered based on a secured party's breach of the peace in connection with taking possession of collateral, see Section 9–625, Comment 3.

5. **Multiple Secured Parties.** More than one secured party may be entitled to take possession of collateral under this section. Conflicting rights to possession among secured parties are resolved by the priority rules of this Article. Thus, a senior secured party is entitled to possession as against a junior claimant. Non-UCC law governs whether a junior secured party in possession of collateral is liable to the senior in conversion. Normally, a junior who refuses to relinquish possession of collateral upon the demand of a secured party having a superior possessory right to the collateral would be liable in conversion.

6. **Secured Party's Right to Disable and Dispose of Equipment on Debtor's Premises.** In the case of some collateral, such as heavy equipment, the physical removal from the debtor's plant and the storage of the collateral pending disposition may be impractical or unduly expensive. This section follows former Section 9–503 by providing that, in lieu of removal, the secured party may render equipment unusable or may dispose of collateral on the debtor's premises. Unlike former Section 9–503, however, this section explicitly conditions these rights

on the debtor's default. Of course, this section does not validate unreasonable action by a secured party. Under Section 9–610, all aspects of a disposition must be commercially reasonable.

7. **Debtor's Agreement to Assemble Collateral.** This section follows former Section 9–503 also by validating a debtor's agreement to assemble collateral and make it available to a secured party at a place that the secured party designates. Similar to the treatment of agreements to permit collection prior to default under Section 9–607 and former 9–502, however, this section validates these agreements whether or not they are conditioned on the debtor's default. For example, a debtor might agree to make available to a secured party, from time to time, any instruments or negotiable documents that the debtor receives on account of collateral. A court should not infer from this section's validation that a debtor's agreement to assemble and make available collateral would not be enforceable under other applicable law.

8. **Agreed Standards.** Subject to the limitation imposed by Section 9–603(b), this section's provisions concerning agreements to assemble and make available collateral and a secured party's right to disable equipment and dispose of collateral on a debtor's premises are likely topics for agreement on standards as contemplated by Section 9–603.

§ 9–610. Disposition of Collateral After Default

(a) [Disposition after default.] After default, a secured party may sell, lease, license, or otherwise dispose of any or all of the collateral in its present condition or following any commercially reasonable preparation or processing.

(b) [Commercially reasonable disposition.] Every aspect of a disposition of collateral, including the method, manner, time, place, and other terms, must be commercially reasonable. If commercially reasonable, a secured party may dispose of collateral by public or private proceedings, by one or more contracts, as a unit or in parcels, and at any time and place and on any terms.

(c) [Purchase by secured party.] A secured party may purchase collateral:

(1) at a public disposition; or

(2) at a private disposition only if the collateral is of a kind that is customarily sold on a recognized market or the subject of widely distributed standard price quotations.

(d) [Warranties on disposition.] A contract for sale, lease, license, or other disposition includes the warranties relating to title, possession, quiet enjoyment, and the like which by operation of law accompany a voluntary disposition of property of the kind subject to the contract.

(e) [Disclaimer of warranties.] A secured party may disclaim or modify warranties under subsection (d):

(1) in a manner that would be effective to disclaim or modify the warranties in a voluntary disposition of property of the kind subject to the contract of disposition; or

(2) by communicating to the purchaser a record evidencing the contract for disposition and including an express disclaimer or modification of the warranties.

(f) [Record sufficient to disclaim warranties.] A record is sufficient to disclaim warranties under subsection (e) if it indicates "There is no warranty relating to title, possession, quiet enjoyment, or the like in this disposition" or uses words of similar import.

UNOFFICIAL COMMENT

If you have an exam fact pattern involving a secured party's sale of collateral, watch for information about (1) the reasonableness of the price received ("not of itself sufficient" section 9–627(a)); (2) the identity of the buyer (secured party? section 9–610(c) or "person related to" the "secured party", section 9–615(f)) and (3) the notice preceding the sale (sections 9–611 to 9–614).

NON–OBVIOUS DEFINITIONS

Obviously, the term "commercially reasonable" is important. Not defined but discussed in section 9–627.

"Public disposition" and "private disposition" are also obviously important. And not defined or discussed by any UCC section. Cf. Official Comment 7 to section 9–610.

The most important thing about the undefined term "recognized market" is how unimportant (limited) the term is. See Official Comment 9 to section 9–610.

OTHER UCC SECTIONS TO LOOK TO WHEN YOU LOOK AT SECTION 9–610

Another reminder. The various sections of Part 6 of Article 9 need to be read together. For example, section 9–610 (b) mandates that "every aspect of a disposition of collateral" be "commercially reasonable". Sections 9–611 to 9–614 describe what makes the notice aspect "commercially reasonable" and section 9–627(b) deals with what makes the sale itself "commercially reasonable."

And, again, remember the debtor (and any "secondary obligor" as defined in section 9–102(a)(71)) has the right before any section 9–610 disposition to redeem its collateral under section 9–623.

And yet again, if you are asked to look at security agreement language regarding what is a commercially reasonable disposition, be sure that you also look at sections 9–602(7) and 9–603.

If your professor covered bankruptcy, be sure that you know that a section 9–610 disposition is covered by Bankruptcy Code section 362(a)(3), (4), i.e., is stayed.

OFFICIAL COMMENT

* * *

2. **Commercially Reasonable Dispositions.** * * * Although subsection (b) permits both public and private dispositions, "every aspect of a disposition ... must be commercially reasonable." This section encourages private dispositions on the assumption that they frequently will result in higher realization on collateral for the benefit of all concerned. Subsection (a) does not restrict dispositions to sales; collateral may be sold, leased, licensed, or otherwise disposed. Section 9–627 provides guidance for determining the circumstances under which a disposition is "commercially reasonable."

3. **Time of Disposition.** This Article does not specify a period within which a secured party must dispose of collateral. This is consistent with this Article's policy to encourage private dispositions through regular commercial channels. It may, for example, be prudent not to dispose of goods when the market has collapsed. Or, it might be more appropriate to sell a large inventory in parcels over a period of time instead of in bulk. Of course, under subsection (b) every aspect of a disposition of collateral must be commercially reasonable. This requirement explicitly includes the "method, manner, time, place and other terms." For example, if a secured party does not proceed under Section 9–620 and holds collateral for a long period of time without disposing of it, and if there is no good reason for not making a prompt disposition, the secured party may be determined not to have acted in a "commercially reasonable" manner. See also Section 1–203 (general obligation of good faith).

4. **Pre-Disposition Preparation and Processing.** * * * Although courts should not be quick to impose a duty of preparation or processing on the secured party, subsection (a) does not grant the secured party the right to dispose of the collateral "in its then condition" under *all* circumstances. A secured party may not dispose of collateral "in its then condition" when, taking into account the costs and probable benefits of preparation or processing and the fact that the secured party would be advancing the costs at its risk, it would be commercially unreasonable to dispose of the collateral in that condition.

5. **Disposition by Junior Secured Party.** Disposition rights under subsection (a) are not limited to first-priority security interests. Rather, any secured party as to whom there has been a default enjoys the right to dispose of collateral under this subsection. The exercise of this right by a secured party whose security interest is subordinate to that of another secured party does not of itself constitute a conversion or otherwise give rise to liability in favor of the holder of the senior security interest. Section 9–615 addresses application of the proceeds of a disposition by a junior secured party. Under Section 9–615(a), a junior secured party owes no obligation to apply the proceeds of disposition to the satisfaction of obligations secured by a senior security interest. Section 9–615(g) builds on this general rule by protecting certain juniors from claims of a senior concerning cash proceeds of the disposition. Even if a senior were to have a non-Article 9 claim to proceeds of a junior's disposition, Section 9–615(g) would protect a junior that acts in good faith and without knowledge that its actions violate the rights of a senior party. Because the disposition by a junior would not cut off a senior's security interest or other lien (see Section 9–617), in many (probably most) cases the junior's receipt of the cash proceeds would not violate the rights of the senior.

The holder of a senior security interest is entitled, by virtue of its priority, to take possession of collateral from the junior secured party and conduct its own disposition, provided that the senior enjoys the right to take possession of the collateral from the debtor. See Section 9–609. The holder of a junior security interest normally must notify the senior secured party of an impending disposition. See Section 9–611. Regardless of whether the senior receives a notification from the junior, the junior's disposition does not of itself discharge the senior's security interest. See Section 9–617. Unless the senior secured party has authorized the disposition free and clear of its security interest, the senior's security interest ordinarily will survive the disposition by the junior and continue under Section 9–315(a). If the senior enjoys the right to repossess the collateral from the debtor, the senior likewise may recover the collateral from the transferee.

When a secured party's collateral is encumbered by another security interest or other lien, one of the claimants may seek to invoke the equitable doctrine of marshaling. As explained by the Supreme Court, that doctrine "rests upon the principle that a creditor having two funds to satisfy his debt, may not by his application of them to his demand, defeat another creditor, who may resort to only one of the funds." *Meyer v. United States*, 375 U.S. 233, 236 (1963), quoting *Sowell v. Federal Reserve Bank*, 268 U.S. 449, 456–57 (1925). The purpose of the doctrine is "to prevent the arbitrary action of a senior lienor from destroying the rights of a junior lienor or a creditor having less security." Id. at 237. Because it is an equitable doctrine, marshaling "is applied only when it can be equitably fashioned as to all of the parties" having an interest in the property. Id. This Article leaves courts free to determine whether marshaling is appropriate in any given case. See Section 1–103.

6. **Security Interests of Equal Rank.** Sometimes two security interests enjoy the same priority. This situation may arise by contract, e.g., pursuant to "equal and ratable" provisions in indentures, or by operation of law. See Section 9–328(6). This Article treats a security interest having equal priority like a senior security interest in many respects. Assume, for example, that SP–X and SP–Y enjoy equal priority, SP–W is senior to them, and SP–Z is junior. If SP–X disposes of the collateral under this section, then (i) SP–W's and SP–Y's security interests survive the disposition but SP–Z's does not, see Section 9–617, and (ii) neither SP–W nor SP–Y is entitled to receive a distribution of proceeds, but SP–Z is. See Section 9–615(a)(3).

When one considers the ability to obtain possession of the collateral, a secured party with equal priority is unlike a senior secured party. As the senior secured party, SP–W should enjoy the right to possession as against SP–X. See Section 9–609, Comment 5. If SP–W takes possession and disposes of the collateral under this section, it is entitled to apply the proceeds to satisfy its secured claim. SP–Y, however, should not have such a right to take possession from SP–X; otherwise, once SP–Y took possession from SP–X, SP–X would have the right to get possession from SP–Y, which would be obligated to redeliver possession to SP–X, and so on. Resolution of this problem is left to the parties and, if necessary, the courts.

7. **Public vs. Private Dispositions.** This Part maintains two distinctions between "public" and other dispositions: (i) the secured party may buy at the former, but normally not at the latter (Section 9–610(c)), and (ii) the debtor is entitled to notification of "the time and place of a public disposition" and notification of "the time after which" a private disposition or other intended disposition is to be made (Section 9–613(1)(E)). It does not retain the distinction under former Section 9–504(4), under which transferees in a noncomplying public disposition could lose protection more easily than transferees in other noncomplying dispositions. Instead, Section 9–617(b) adopts a unitary standard. Although the term is not defined, as used in this Article, a "public disposition" is one at which the price is determined after the public has had a meaningful opportunity for competitive bidding. "Meaningful opportunity" is meant to imply that some form of advertisement or public notice must precede the sale (or other disposition) and that

the public must have access to the sale (disposition).

8. **Investment Property.** Dispositions of investment property may be regulated by the federal securities laws. Although a "public" disposition of securities under this Article may implicate the registration requirements of the Securities Act of 1933, it need not do so. A disposition that qualifies for a "private placement" exemption under the Securities Act of 1933 nevertheless may constitute a "public" disposition within the meaning of this section. Moreover, the "commercially reasonable" requirements of subsection (b) need not prevent a secured party from conducting a foreclosure sale without the issuer's compliance with federal registration requirements.

9. **"Recognized Market."** A "recognized market," as used in subsection (c) and Section 9–611(d), is one in which the items sold are fungible and prices are not subject to individual negotiation. For example, the New York Stock Exchange is a recognized market. A market in which prices are individually negotiated or the items are not fungible is not a recognized market, even if the items are the subject of widely disseminated price guides or are disposed of through dealer auctions.

10. **Relevance of Price.** While not itself sufficient to establish a violation of this Part, a low price suggests that a court should scrutinize carefully all aspects of a disposition to ensure that each aspect was commercially reasonable. Note also that even if the disposition is commercially reasonable, Section 9–615(f) provides a special method for calculating a deficiency or surplus if (i) the transferee in the disposition is the secured party, a person related to the secured party, or a secondary obligor, and (ii) the amount of proceeds of the disposition is significantly below the range of proceeds that a complying disposition to a person other than the secured party, a person related to the secured party, or a secondary obligor would have brought.

11. **Warranties.** Subsection (d) affords the transferee in a disposition under this section the benefit of any title, possession, quiet enjoyment, and similar warranties that would have accompanied the disposition by operation of non-Article 9 law had the disposition been conducted under other circumstances. For example, the Article 2 warranty of title would apply to a sale of goods, the analogous warranties of Article 2A would apply to a lease of goods, and any common-law warranties of title would apply to dispositions of other types of collateral. See, e.g., Restatement (2d), Contracts § 333 (warranties of assignor).

Subsection (e) explicitly provides that these warranties can be disclaimed either under other applicable law or by communicating a record containing an express disclaimer. The record need not be written, but an oral communication would not be sufficient. See Section 9–102 (definition of "record"). Subsection (f) provides a sample of wording that will effectively exclude the warranties in a disposition under this section, whether or not the exclusion would be effective under non-Article 9 law.

The warranties incorporated by subsection (d) are those relating to "title, possession, quiet enjoyment, and the like." Depending on the circumstances, a disposition under this section also may give rise to other statutory or implied warranties, e.g., warranties of quality or fitness for purpose. Law other than this Article determines whether such other warranties apply to a disposition under this section. Other law also determines issues relating to disclaimer of such warranties. For example, a foreclosure sale of a car by a car dealer could give rise to an implied warranty of merchantability (Section 2–314) unless effectively disclaimed or modified (Section 2–316).

This section's approach to these warranties conflicts with the former Comment to Section 2–312. This Article rejects the baseline assumption that commercially reasonable dispositions under this section are out of the ordinary commercial course or peculiar. The Comment to Section 2–312 has been revised accordingly.

§ 9-611. Notification Before Disposition of Collateral

(a) ["Notification date."] In this section, "notification date" means the earlier of the date on which:

(1) a secured party sends to the debtor and any secondary obligor an authenticated notification of disposition; or

(2) the debtor and any secondary obligor waive the right to notification.

(b) [Notification of disposition required.] Except as otherwise provided in subsection (d), a secured party that disposes of collateral under Section 9-610 shall send to the persons specified in subsection (c) a reasonable authenticated notification of disposition.

(c) [Persons to be notified.] To comply with subsection (b), the secured party shall send an authenticated notification of disposition to:

(1) the debtor;

(2) any secondary obligor; and

(3) if the collateral is other than consumer goods:

(A) any other person from which the secured party has received, before the notification date, an authenticated notification of a claim of an interest in the collateral;

(B) any other secured party or lienholder that, 10 days before the notification date, held a security interest in or other lien on the collateral perfected by the filing of a financing statement that:

(i) identified the collateral;

(ii) was indexed under the debtor's name as of that date; and

(iii) was filed in the office in which to file a financing statement against the debtor covering the collateral as of that date; and

(C) any other secured party that, 10 days before the notification date, held a security interest in the collateral perfected by compliance with a statute, regulation, or treaty described in Section 9-311(a).

(d) [Subsection (b) inapplicable: perishable collateral; recognized market.] Subsection (b) does not apply if the collateral is perishable or threatens to decline speedily in value or is of a type customarily sold on a recognized market.

(e) [Compliance with subsection (c)(3)(B).] A secured party complies with the requirement for notification prescribed by subsection (c)(3)(B) if:

  (1) not later than 20 days or earlier than 30 days before the notification date, the secured party requests, in a commercially reasonable manner, information concerning financing statements indexed under the debtor's name in the office indicated in subsection (c)(3)(B); and

  (2) before the notification date, the secured party:

   (A) did not receive a response to the request for information; or

   (B) received a response to the request for information and sent an authenticated notification of disposition to each secured party or other lienholder named in that response whose financing statement covered the collateral.

OTHER UCC SECTIONS TO LOOK TO WHEN YOU LOOK AT SECTION 9–611

Section 9–610 requires "reasonable authenticated notification of disposition." Section 9–611 answers the question, "who?" (to whom, notice must be sent), section 9–612 answer the question, "when?" (how long before the sale notice must be sent) and sections 9–613 and 9–614 answer the question, "what?" (contents of the notification).

OFFICIAL COMMENT

* * *

2. **Reasonable Notification.** This section requires a secured party who wishes to dispose of collateral under Section 9–610 to send "a reasonable authenticated notification of disposition" to specified interested persons, subject to certain exceptions. The notification must be reasonable as to the manner in which it is sent, its timeliness (i.e., a reasonable time before the disposition is to take place), and its content. See Sections 9–612 (timeliness of notification), 9–613 (contents of notification generally), 9–614 (contents of notification in consumer-goods transactions).

3. **Notification to Debtors and Secondary Obligors.** This section imposes a duty to send notification of a disposition not only to the debtor but also to any secondary obligor. Subsections (b) and (c) resolve an uncertainty under former Article 9 by providing that secondary obligors (sureties) are entitled to receive notification of an intended disposition of collateral, regardless of who created the security interest in the collateral. If the surety created the security interest, it would be the debtor. If it did not, it would be a secondary obligor. (This Article also resolves the question of the secondary obligor's ability to waive, pre-default, the right to notification—waiver generally is not permitted. See Section 9–602.) Section 9–605 relieves a secured party from any duty to send notification to a debtor or secondary obligor unknown to the secured party.

Under subsection (b), the principal obligor (borrower) is not always entitled to notification of disposition.

Example: Behnfeldt borrows on an unsecured basis, and Bruno grants a security interest in her car to secure the debt. Behnfeldt is a primary obligor, not a secondary obligor. As such, she is not entitled to notification of disposition under this section.

4. **Notification to Other Secured Parties.** Prior to the 1972 amendments to Article 9, former Section 9–504(3) required the enforcing secured party to send reasonable notification of the disposition:

> except in the case of consumer goods to any other person who has a security interest in the collateral and who has duly filed a financing statement indexed in the name of the debtor in this State or who is known by the secured party to have a security interest in the collateral.

The 1972 amendments eliminated the duty to give notice to secured parties other than those from whom the foreclosing secured party had received written notice of a claim of an interest in the collateral.

Many of the problems arising from dispositions of collateral encumbered by multiple security interests can be ameliorated or solved by informing all secured parties of an intended disposition and affording them the opportunity to work with one another. To this end, subsection (c)(3)(B) expands the duties of the foreclosing secured party to include the duty to notify (and the corresponding burden of searching the files to discover) certain competing secured parties. The subsection imposes a search burden that in some cases may be greater than the pre-1972 burden on foreclosing secured parties but certainly is more modest than that faced by a new secured lender.

To determine who is entitled to notification, the foreclosing secured party must determine the proper office for filing a financing statement as of a particular date, measured by reference to the "notification date," as defined in subsection (a). This determination requires reference to the choice-of-law provisions of Part 3. The secured party must ascertain whether any financing statements covering the collateral and indexed under the debtor's name, as the name existed as of that date, in fact were filed in that office. The foreclosing secured party generally need not notify secured parties whose effective financing statements have become more difficult to locate because of changes in the location of the debtor, proceeds rules, or changes in the debtor's name.

Under subsection (c)(3)(C), the secured party also must notify a secured party who has perfected a security interest by complying with a statute or treaty described in Section 9–311(a), such as a certificate-of-title statute.

Subsection (e) provides a "safe harbor" that takes into account the delays that may be attendant to receiving information from the public filing offices. It provides, generally, that the secured party will be deemed to have satisfied its notification duty under subsection (c)(3)(B) if it requests a search from the proper office at least 20 but not more than 30 days before sending notification to the debtor and if it also sends a notification to all secured parties (and other lienholders) reflected on the search report. The secured party's duty under subsection (c)(3)(B) also will be satisfied if the secured party requests but does not receive a search report before the notification is sent to the debtor. Thus, if subsection (e) applies, a secured party who is entitled to notification under subsection (c)(3)(B) has no remedy against a foreclosing secured party who does not send the notification. The foreclosing secured party has complied with the notification requirement. Subsection (e) has no effect on the requirements of the other paragraphs of subsection (c). For example, if the foreclosing secured party received a notification from the holder of a conflicting security interest in accordance with subsection (c)(3)(A) but failed to send to the holder a notification of the disposition, the holder of the conflicting security interest would have the right to recover any loss under Section 9–625(b).

5. **Authentication Requirement.** Subsections (b) and (c) explicitly provide that a notification of disposition must be "authenticated." Some cases read former Section 9–504(3) as validating oral notification.

6. **Second Try.** This Article leaves to judicial resolution, based upon the facts of each case, the question whether the requirement of "reasonable notification" requires a "second try," i.e., whether a secured party who sends notification and learns that the debtor did not receive it must attempt to locate the debtor and send another notification.

7. **Recognized Market; Perishable Collateral.** New subsection (d) makes it clear that there is no obligation to give notification of a disposition in the case of perishable collateral or collateral customarily sold on a recognized market (e.g., marketable securities). Former Section 9–504(3) might be read (incorrectly) to relieve the secured party from its duty to notify a debtor but not from its duty to notify other secured parties in connection with dispositions of such collateral.

8. **Failure to Conduct Notified Disposition.** Nothing in this Article prevents a secured party from electing not to conduct a disposition after sending a notification. Nor does this Article prevent a secured party from electing to send a revised notification if its plans for disposition change. This assumes, however, that the secured party acts in good faith, the revised notification is reasonable, and the revised plan for disposition and any attendant delay are commercially reasonable.

9. **Waiver.** A debtor or secondary obligor may waive the right to notification under this section only by a post-default authenticated agreement. See Section 9–624(a).

§ 9–612. Timeliness of Notification Before Disposition of Collateral

(a) [Reasonable time is question of fact.] Except as otherwise provided in subsection (b), whether a notification is sent within a reasonable time is a question of fact.

(b) [10-day period sufficient in non-consumer transaction.] In a transaction other than a consumer transaction, a notification of disposition sent after default and 10 days or more before the earliest time of disposition set forth in the notification is sent within a reasonable time before the disposition.

OTHER UCC SECTIONS TO LOOK TO WHEN YOU LOOK AT SECTION 9–612

Section 9–610 requires "reasonable authenticated notification of disposition." Section 9–611 answers the question, "who?" (to whom, notice must be sent). Section 9–612 answer the question, "when?" Sections 9–613 and 9–614 answer the question, "what?"(contents of the notification).

OFFICIAL COMMENT

* * *

2. **Reasonable Notification.** Section 9–611(b) requires the secured party to send a "reasonable authenticated notification." Under that section, as under former Section 9–504(3), one aspect of a reasonable notification is its timeliness. This generally means that the notification must be sent at a reasonable time in advance of the date of a public disposition

or the date after which a private disposition is to be made. A notification that is sent so near to the disposition date that a notified person could not be expected to act on or take account of the notification would be unreasonable.

3. **Timeliness of Notification: Safe Harbor.** The 10–day notice period in subsection (b) is intended to be a "safe harbor" and not a minimum requirement. To qualify for the "safe harbor" the notification must be sent after default. A notification also must be sent in a commercially reasonable manner. See Section 9–611(b) ("reasonable authenticated notification"). These requirements prevent a secured party from taking advantage of the "safe harbor" by, for example, giving the debtor a notification at the time of the original extension of credit or sending the notice by surface mail to a debtor overseas.

§ 9–613. Contents and Form of Notification Before Disposition of Collateral: General

Except in a consumer-goods transaction, the following rules apply:

(1) The contents of a notification of disposition are sufficient if the notification:

(A) describes the debtor and the secured party;

(B) describes the collateral that is the subject of the intended disposition;

(C) states the method of intended disposition;

(D) states that the debtor is entitled to an accounting of the unpaid indebtedness and states the charge, if any, for an accounting; and

(E) states the time and place of a public disposition or the time after which any other disposition is to be made.

(2) Whether the contents of a notification that lacks any of the information specified in paragraph (1) are nevertheless sufficient is a question of fact.

(3) The contents of a notification providing substantially the information specified in paragraph (1) are sufficient, even if the notification includes:

(A) information not specified by that paragraph; or

(B) minor errors that are not seriously misleading.

(4) A particular phrasing of the notification is not required.

(5) The following form of notification and the form appearing in Section 9–614(3), when completed, each provides sufficient information:

NOTIFICATION OF DISPOSITION OF COLLATERAL

To: [*Name of debtor, obligor, or other person to which the notification is sent*]

From: [*Name, address, and telephone number of secured party*]

Name of Debtor(s): [*Include only if debtor(s) are not an addressee*]

[*For a public disposition:*]

We will sell [or lease or license, *as applicable*] the [*describe collateral*] [to the highest qualified bidder] in public as follows:

Day and Date: _____

Time: _____

Place: _____

[*For a private disposition:*]

We will sell [or lease or license, *as applicable*] the [*describe collateral*] privately sometime after [*day and date*].

You are entitled to an accounting of the unpaid indebtedness secured by the property that we intend to sell [or lease or license, *as applicable*] [for a charge of $_____]. You may request an accounting by calling us at [*telephone number*]

[End of Form]

* * *

OTHER UCC SECTIONS TO LOOK TO WHEN YOU LOOK AT SECTION 9–613

Section 9–610 requires "reasonable authenticated notification of disposition." Section 9–611 answers the question, "who?" (to whom, notice must be sent), section 9–612 answer the question, "when?" and sections 9–613 and 9–614 answer the question, "what?"(contents of the notification).

OFFICIAL COMMENT

* * *

2. **Contents of Notification.** To comply with the "reasonable authenticated notification" requirement of Section 9–611(b), the contents of a notification must be reasonable. Except in a consumer-goods transaction, the contents of a notification that includes the information set forth in paragraph (1) are sufficient as a matter of law, unless the parties agree otherwise. (The reference to "time" of disposition means here, as it did in former Section 9–504(3), not only the hour of the day but also the date.) Although a secured party may choose to include additional information concerning the transaction or the debtor's rights and obligations, no additional information is required unless the parties agree otherwise. A notification that lacks some of the information set forth in paragraph (1) nevertheless may be sufficient if found to be reasonable by the trier of fact, under paragraph (2). A properly completed sample form of notification in paragraph (5) or in Section 9–614(a)(3) is an example of a notification that would contain the information set forth in paragraph (1). Under paragraph (4), however, no particular phrasing of the notification is required.

§ 9–614. Contents and Form of Notification Before Disposition of Collateral: Consumer-Goods Transaction

In a consumer-goods transaction, the following rules apply:

(1) A notification of disposition must provide the following information:

    (A) the information specified in Section 9–613(1);

    (B) a description of any liability for a deficiency of the person to which the notification is sent;

    (C) a telephone number from which the amount that must be paid to the secured party to redeem the collateral under Section 9–623 is available; and

    (D) a telephone number or mailing address from which additiosal information concerning the disposition and the obligation secured is available.

(2) A particular phrasing of the notification is not required.

(3) The following form of notification, when completed, provides sufficient information:

[*Name and address of secured party*]

[*Date*]

NOTICE OF OUR PLAN TO SELL PROPERTY

[*Name and address of any obligor who is also a debtor*]

Subject: [*Identification of Transaction*]

We have your [*describe collateral*], because you broke promises in our agreement.

[*For a public disposition:*]

We will sell [*describe collateral*] at public sale. A sale could include a lease or license. The sale will be held as follows:

    Date: _____

    Time: _____

    Place: _____

You may attend the sale and bring bidders if you want.

[*For a private disposition:*]

We will sell [*describe collateral*] at private sale sometime after [*date*]. A sale could include a lease or license.

The money that we get from the sale (after paying our costs) will reduce the amount you owe. If we get less money than you owe, you [*will or will not, as applicable*] still owe us the difference. If we get more money than you owe, you will get the extra money, unless we must pay it to someone else.

You can get the property back at any time before we sell it by paying us the full amount you owe (not just the past due payments), including our expenses. To learn the exact amount you must pay, call us at [*telephone number*].

If you want us to explain to you in writing how we have figured the amount that you owe us, you may call us at [*telephone number*] [or write us at [*secured party's address*]] and request a written explanation. [We will charge you $for the explanation if we sent you another written explanation of the amount you owe us within the last six months.]

If you need more information about the sale call us at [*telephone number*] [or write us at [*secured party's address*]].

We are sending this notice to the following other people who have an interest in [*describe collateral*] or who owe money under your agreement:

[*Names of all other debtors and obligors, if any*]

[End of Form]

(4) A notification in the form of paragraph (3) is sufficient, even if additional information appears at the end of the form.

(5) A notification in the form of paragraph (3) is sufficient, even if it includes errors in information not required by paragraph (1), unless the error is misleading with respect to rights arising under this article.

(6) If a notification under this section is not in the form of paragraph (3), law other than this article determines the effect of including information not required by paragraph (1).

OTHER UCC SECTIONS TO LOOK TO WHEN YOU LOOK AT SECTION 9–614

Section 9–610 requires "reasonable authenticated notification of disposition." Section 9–611 answers the question, "who?" (to whom, notice must be sent), section 9–612 answer the question, "when?" and sections 9–613 and 9–614 answer the question, "what?"(contents of the notification).

OFFICIAL COMMENT

* * *

2. **Notification in Consumer-Goods Transactions.** Paragraph (1) sets forth the information required for a reasonable notification in a consumer-goods transaction. A notification that lacks any of the information set forth in paragraph (1) is insufficient as a matter of law. Compare Section 9–613(2), under which the trier of fact may find a notification to be sufficient even if it lacks some information listed in paragraph (1) of that section.

3. **Safe-Harbor Form of Notification; Errors in Information.** Although paragraph (2) provides that a particular phrasing of a notification is not required, paragraph (3) specifies a safe-harbor form that, when properly completed, satisfies paragraph (1). Paragraphs (4), (5), and (6) contain special rules applicable to erroneous and additional information. Under paragraph (4), a notification in the safe-harbor form specified in paragraph (3) is not rendered insufficient if it contains additional information at the end of the form. Paragraph (5) provides that non-misleading errors in information contained in a notification are permitted if the safe-harbor form is used *and if the errors are in information not required by paragraph (1)*. Finally, if a notification is in a form other than the paragraph (3) safe-harbor form, other law determines the effect of including in the notification information other than that required by paragraph (1).

§ 9–615. Application of Proceeds of Disposition; Liability for Deficiency and Right to Surplus

(a) [Application of proceeds.] A secured party shall apply or pay over for application the cash proceeds of disposition under Section 9–610 in the following order to:

(1) the reasonable expenses of retaking, holding, preparing for disposition, processing, and disposing, and, to the extent provided for by agreement and not prohibited by law, reasonable attorney's fees and legal expenses incurred by the secured party;

(2) the satisfaction of obligations secured by the security interest or agricultural lien under which the disposition is made;

(3) the satisfaction of obligations secured by any subordinate security interest in or other subordinate lien on the collateral if:

(A) the secured party receives from the holder of the subordinate security interest or other lien an authenticated demand for proceeds before distribution of the proceeds is completed; and

(B) in a case in which a consignor has an interest in the collateral, the subordinate security interest or other lien is senior to the interest of the consignor; and

(4) a secured party that is a consignor of the collateral if the secured party receives from the consignor an authenticated

demand for proceeds before distribution of the proceeds is completed.

(b) [Proof of subordinate interest.] If requested by a secured party, a holder of a subordinate security interest or other lien shall furnish reasonable proof of the interest or lien within a reasonable time. Unless the holder does so, the secured party need not comply with the holder's demand under subsection (a)(3).

(c) [Application of noncash proceeds.] A secured party need not apply or pay over for application noncash proceeds of disposition under Section 9–610 unless the failure to do so would be commercially unreasonable. A secured party that applies or pays over for application noncash proceeds shall do so in a commercially reasonable manner.

(d) [Surplus or deficiency if obligation secured.] If the security interest under which a disposition is made secures payment or performance of an obligation, after making the payments and applications required by subsection (a) and permitted by subsection (c):

(1) unless subsection (a)(4) requires the secured party to apply or pay over cash proceeds to a consignor, the secured party shall account to and pay a debtor for any surplus; and

(2) the obligor is liable for any deficiency.

(e) [No surplus or deficiency in sales of certain rights to payment.] If the underlying transaction is a sale of accounts, chattel paper, payment intangibles, or promissory notes:

(1) the debtor is not entitled to any surplus; and

(2) the obligor is not liable for any deficiency.

(f) [Calculation of surplus or deficiency in disposition to person related to secured party.] The surplus or deficiency following a disposition is calculated based on the amount of proceeds that would have been realized in a disposition complying with this part to a transferee other than the secured party, a person related to the secured party, or a secondary obligor if:

(1) the transferee in the disposition is the secured party, a person related to the secured party, or a secondary obligor; and

(2) the amount of proceeds of the disposition is significantly below the range of proceeds that a complying disposition to a person other than the secured party, a person related to the secured party, or a secondary obligor would have brought.

(g) [Cash proceeds received by junior secured party.] A secured party that receives cash proceeds of a disposition in good faith and without knowledge that the receipt violates the rights of the holder of a security interest or other lien that is not subordinate to the security interest or agricultural lien under which the disposition is made:

- **(1)** takes the cash proceeds free of the security interest or other lien;
- **(2)** is not obligated to apply the proceeds of the disposition to the satisfaction of obligations secured by the security interest or other lien; and
- **(3)** is not obligated to account to or pay the holder of the security interest or other lien for any surplus.

UNOFFICIAL COMMENTS

Assume that (1) X, Y and Z all have security interests in the same goods, (2) X's security interest has priority over Y's and Z's and Y's security interest has priority over Z's, (3) D defaults and Y wants to repossess and sell. There is nothing in sections 9–609 or 9–610 that limits repossession or resale to the secured party with priority. If Y repossess and sells to B, then, under section 9–617(a), B takes free from Y and Z's security interest but subject to X's security interest.

Now re-read section 9–615(a)(3) and 9–615(g).

* * *

NON–OBVIOUS DEFINITIONS

Notice that section 9–615(d)(1) uses the term "debtor", and section 9–615(d)(2) uses the term "obligor." Recall that under the section 9–102 definitions of "debtor" and "obligor", it is possible for the "debtor" and the "obligor" to be different people.

Section 9–615(f) uses the phrase "person related to the secured party." Section 9–102(a)(62) and (63) define who is a "person related to."

OTHER SECTIONS TO LOOK TO WHEN YOU LOOK AT SECTION 9–615

If the problem involves the secured party's right to recover a deficiency from the obligor under section 9–615(d)(2), look to section 9–626 . (If it is a "consumer transaction" [which it probably will be], then you only have to look at section 9–626(b).)

If the problem involves a sale by a junior secured party, then you need to understand the following three sections: Section 9–617(a)(3), section 9–615(a)(3) and section 9–615(g). Not just read, understand.

OFFICIAL COMMENT

* * *

2. **Application of Proceeds.** This section contains the rules governing application of proceeds and the debtor's liability for a deficiency following a disposition of collateral. Subsection (a) sets forth the basic order of application. The proceeds are applied first to the expenses of disposition, second to the obligation secured by the security interest that is being enforced, and third, in the specified circumstances, to interests that are subordinate to that security interest.

Subsections (a) and (d) also address the right of a consignor to receive proceeds of a disposition by a secured party whose interest is senior to that of the consignor. Subsection (a) requires the enforcing secured party to pay excess proceeds first to subordinate secured parties or lienholders whose interests are senior to that of a consignor and, finally, to a consignor. Inasmuch as a consignor is the owner of the collateral, secured parties and lienholders whose interests are junior to the consignor's interest will not be entitled to any proceeds. In like fashion, under subsection (d)(1) the debtor is not entitled to a surplus when the enforcing secured party is required to pay over proceeds to a consignor.

3. **Noncash Proceeds.** Subsection (c) addresses the application of noncash proceeds of a disposition, such as a note or lease. The explanation in Section 9–608, Comment 4, generally applies to this subsection.

Example: A secured party in the business of selling or financing automobiles takes possession of collateral (an automobile) following its debtor's default. The secured party decides to sell the automobile in a private disposition under Section 9–610 and sends appropriate notification under Section 9–611. After undertaking its normal credit investigation and in accordance with its normal credit policies, the secured party sells the automobile on credit, on terms typical of the credit terms normally extended by the secured party in the ordinary course of its business. The automobile stands as collateral for the remaining balance of the price. The noncash proceeds received by the secured party are chattel paper. The secured party may wish to credit its debtor (the assignor) with the principal amount of the chattel paper or may wish to credit the debtor only as and when the payments are made on the chattel paper by the buyer.

Under subsection (c), the secured party is under no duty to apply the noncash proceeds (here, the chattel paper) or their value to the secured obligation unless its failure to do so would be commercially unreasonable. If a secured party elects to apply the chattel paper to the outstanding obligation, however, it must do so in a commercially reasonable manner. The facts in the example indicate that it would be commercially unreasonable for the secured party to fail to apply the value of the chattel paper to the original debtor's secured obligation. Unlike the example in Comment 4 to Section 9–608, the noncash proceeds received in this example are of the type that the secured party regularly generates in the ordinary course of its financing business in nonforeclosure transactions. The original debtor should not be exposed to delay or uncertainty in this situation. Of course, there will be many situations that fall between the examples presented in the Comment to Section 9–608 and in this Comment. This Article leaves their resolution to the court based on the facts of each case.

One would expect that where noncash proceeds are or may be material, the secured party and debtor would agree to more specific standards in an agreement entered into before or after default. The parties may agree to the method of application of noncash proceeds if the method is not manifestly unreasonable. See Section 9–603.

When the secured party is not required to "apply or pay over for application noncash proceeds," the proceeds nonetheless remain collateral subject to this Article. See Section 9–608, Comment 4.

4. **Surplus and Deficiency.** Subsection (d) deals with surplus and deficiency. It revises former Section 9–504(2) by imposing an explicit requirement that the secured party "pay" the debtor for any surplus, while retaining the secured party's duty to "account." Inasmuch as the debtor may not be an obligor, subsection (d) provides that the obligor (not the debtor) is liable for the deficiency. The special rule governing surplus and deficiency when receivables have been sold likewise takes into account the distinction between a debtor and an obligor. Subsection (d) also addresses the situation in which a consignor has an interest that is subordinate to the security interest being enforced.

5. **Collateral Under New Ownership.** When the debtor sells collateral subject to a security interest, the original debtor (creator of the security interest) is no longer a debtor inasmuch as it no longer has a property interest in the collateral; the buyer is the debtor. See Section 9–102. As between the debtor (buyer of the collateral) and the original debtor (seller of the collateral), the debtor (buyer) normally would be entitled to the surplus following a disposition. Subsection (d) therefore requires the secured party to pay the surplus to the debtor (buyer), not to the original debtor (seller) with which it has dealt. But, because this situation typically arises as a result of the debtor's wrongful act, this Article does not expose the secured party to the risk of determining ownership of the collateral. If the secured party does not know about the buyer and accordingly pays the surplus to the original debtor, the exculpatory provisions of this Article exonerate the secured party from liability to the buyer. See Sections 9–605, 9–628(a), (b). If a debtor sells collateral *free* of a security interest, as in a sale to a buyer in ordinary course of business (see Section 9–320(a)), the property is no longer collateral and the buyer is not a debtor.

6. **Certain "Low-Price" Dispositions.** Subsection (f) provides a special method for calculating a deficiency or surplus when the secured party, a person related to the secured party (defined in Section 9–102), or a secondary obligor acquires the collateral at a foreclosure disposition. It recognizes that when the foreclosing secured party or a related party is the transferee of the collateral, the secured party sometimes lacks the incentive to maximize the proceeds of disposition. As a consequence, the disposition may comply with the procedural requirements of this Article (e.g., it is conducted in a commercially reasonable manner following reasonable notice) but nevertheless fetch a low price.

Subsection (f) adjusts for this lack of incentive. If the proceeds of a disposition of collateral to a secured party, a person related to the secured party, or a secondary obligor are "significantly below the range of proceeds that a complying disposition to a person other than the secured party, a person related to the secured party, or a secondary obligor would have brought," then instead of calculating a deficiency (or surplus) based on the actual net proceeds, the calculation is based upon the amount that would have been received in a commercially reasonable disposition to a person other than the secured party, a person related to the secured party, or a secondary obligor. Subsection (f) thus rejects the view that the secured party's receipt of such a price necessarily constitutes noncompliance with Part 6. However, such a price may suggest the need for greater judicial scrutiny. See Section 9–610, Comment 10.

7. **"Person Related To."** Section 9–102 defines "person related to." That term is a key element of the system provided in subsection (f) for low-price dispositions. One part of the definition applies when the secured party is an individual, and the other applies when the secured party is an organization. The definition is patterned closely on the corresponding

definition in Section 1.301(32) of the Uniform Consumer Credit Code.

§ 9–616. Explanation of Calculation of Surplus or Deficiency

(a) **[Definitions.]** In this section:

(1) "Explanation" means a writing that:

(A) states the amount of the surplus or deficiency;

(B) provides an explanation in accordance with subsection (c) of how the secured party calculated the surplus or deficiency;

(C) states, if applicable, that future debits, credits, charges, including additional credit service charges or interest, rebates, and expenses may affect the amount of the surplus or deficiency; and

(D) provides a telephone number or mailing address from which additional information concerning the transaction is available.

(2) "Request" means a record:

(A) authenticated by a debtor or consumer obligor;

(B) requesting that the recipient provide an explanation; and

(C) sent after disposition of the collateral under Section 9–610.

(b) **[Explanation of calculation.]** In a consumer-goods transaction in which the debtor is entitled to a surplus or a consumer obligor is liable for a deficiency under Section 9–615, the secured party shall:

(1) send an explanation to the debtor or consumer obligor, as applicable, after the disposition and:

(A) before or when the secured party accounts to the debtor and pays any surplus or first makes written demand on the consumer obligor after the disposition for payment of the deficiency; and

(B) within 14 days after receipt of a request; or

(2) in the case of a consumer obligor who is liable for a deficiency, within 14 days after receipt of a request, send to the consumer obligor a record waiving the secured party's right to a deficiency.

(c) **[Required information.]** To comply with subsection (a)(1)(B), a writing must provide the following information in the following order:

(1) the aggregate amount of obligations secured by the security interest under which the disposition was made, and, if the amount reflects a rebate of unearned interest or credit service charge, an indication of that fact, calculated as of a specified date:

(A) if the secured party takes or receives possession of the collateral after default, not more than 35 days before the secured party takes or receives possession; or

(B) if the secured party takes or receives possession of the collateral before default or does not take possession of the collateral, not more than 35 days before the disposition;

(2) the amount of proceeds of the disposition;

(3) the aggregate amount of the obligations after deducting the amount of proceeds;

(4) the amount, in the aggregate or by type, and types of expenses, including expenses of retaking, holding, preparing for disposition, processing, and disposing of the collateral, and attorney's fees secured by the collateral which are known to the secured party and relate to the current disposition;

(5) the amount, in the aggregate or by type, and types of credits, including rebates of interest or credit service charges, to which the obligor is known to be entitled and which are not reflected in the amount in paragraph (1); and

(6) the amount of the surplus or deficiency.

(d) **[Substantial compliance.]** A particular phrasing of the explanation is not required. An explanation complying substantially with the requirements of subsection (a) is sufficient, even if it includes minor errors that are not seriously misleading.

(e) **[Charges for responses.]** A debtor or consumer obligor is entitled without charge to one response to a request under this section during any six-month period in which the secured party did not send to the debtor or consumer obligor an explanation pursuant to subsection (b)(1). The secured party may require payment of a charge not exceeding $25 for each additional response.

§ 9–617. Rights of Transferee of Collateral

(a) [Effects of disposition.] A secured party's disposition of collateral after default:

   (1) transfers to a transferee for value all of the debtor's rights in the collateral;

   (2) discharges the security interest under which the disposition is made; and

   (3) discharges any subordinate security interest or other subordinate lien [other than liens created under [cite acts or statutes providing for liens, if any, that are not to be discharged]].

(b) [Rights of good-faith transferee.] A transferee that acts in good faith takes free of the rights and interests described in subsection (a), even if the secured party fails to comply with this article or the requirements of any judicial proceeding.

(c) [Rights of other transferee.] If a transferee does not take free of the rights and interests described in subsection (a), the transferee takes the collateral subject to:

   (1) the debtor's rights in the collateral;

   (2) the security interest or agricultural lien under which the disposition is made; and

   (3) any other security interest or other lien.

UNOFFICIAL COMMENTS

You need to read section 9–617(b) before you read 9–617(a). As section 9–617(b) provides (and Official Comment 2 explains), section 9–617(a) only applies to "good faith transferees."

And even a good faith transferee who buys from a secured party buys subject to any security interests that have priority over the security interest of the selling secured party. Cf. section 9–617(a)(3).

* * *

NON–OBVIOUS DEFINITIONS

The term "subordinate security interest" is not defined. If X's security interest has priority over Y's, then Y's security interest is the "subordinate security interest."

OFFICIAL COMMENT

* * *

2. **Title Taken by Good-Faith Transferee.** Subsection (a) sets forth the rights acquired by persons who qualify under subsection (b)—transferees who act in good faith. Such a person is a "transferee," inasmuch as a buyer at a foreclosure sale does not meet the definition of "purchaser" in Section 1–201 (the transfer is not, vis-a-vis the debtor, "voluntary"). By virtue of the expanded definition of the term "debtor" in Section 9–102, subsection (a) makes clear that the ownership interest of a person who bought the collateral subject to the security interest is terminated by a subsequent disposition under this Part. Such a person is a debtor under this Article. Under former Article 9, the result arguably was the same, but the statute was less clear. Under subsection (a), a disposition normally discharges the security interest being foreclosed and any subordinate security interests and other liens.

A disposition has the effect specified in subsection (a), even if the secured party fails to comply with this Article. An aggrieved person (e.g., the holder of a subordinate security interest to whom a notification required by Section 9–611 was not sent) has a right to recover any loss under Section 9–625(b).

3. **Unitary Standard in Public and Private Dispositions.** Subsection (b) now contains a unitary standard that applies to transferees in both private and public dispositions—acting in good faith. However, this change from former Section 9–504(4) should not be interpreted to mean that a transferee acts in good faith even though it has knowledge of defects or buys in collusion, standards applicable to public dispositions under the former section. Properly understood, those standards were specific examples of the absence of good faith.

4. **Title Taken by Nonqualifying Transferee.** Subsection (c) specifies the consequences for a transferee who does not qualify for protection under subsections (a) and (b) (i.e., a transferee who does not act in good faith). The transferee takes subject to the rights of the debtor, the enforcing secured party, and other security interests or other liens.

§ 9–620. Acceptance of Collateral in Full or Partial Satisfaction of Obligation; Compulsory Disposition of Collateral

(a) [Conditions to acceptance in satisfaction.] Except as otherwise provided in subsection (g), a secured party may accept collateral in full or partial satisfaction of the obligation it secures only if:

(1) the debtor consents to the acceptance under subsection (c);

(2) the secured party does not receive, within the time set forth in subsection (d), a notification of objection to the proposal authenticated by:

(A) a person to which the secured party was required to send a proposal under Section 9–621; or

(B) any other person, other than the debtor, holding an interest in the collateral subordinate to the security interest that is the subject of the proposal;

(3) if the collateral is consumer goods, the collateral is not in the possession of the debtor when the debtor consents to the acceptance; and

(4) subsection (e) does not require the secured party to dispose of the collateral or the debtor waives the requirement pursuant to Section 9–624.

(b) [Purported acceptance ineffective.] A purported or apparent acceptance of collateral under this section is ineffective unless:

(1) the secured party consents to the acceptance in an authenticated record or sends a proposal to the debtor; and

(2) the conditions of subsection (a) are met.

(c) [Debtor's consent.] For purposes of this section:

(1) a debtor consents to an acceptance of collateral in partial satisfaction of the obligation it secures only if the debtor agrees to the terms of the acceptance in a record authenticated after default; and

(2) a debtor consents to an acceptance of collateral in full satisfaction of the obligation it secures only if the debtor agrees to the terms of the acceptance in a record authenticated after default or the secured party:

(A) sends to the debtor after default a proposal that is unconditional or subject only to a condition that collateral not in the possession of the secured party be preserved or maintained;

(B) in the proposal, proposes to accept collateral in full satisfaction of the obligation it secures; and

(C) does not receive a notification of objection authenticated by the debtor within 20 days after the proposal is sent.

(d) [Effectiveness of notification.] To be effective under subsection (a)(2), a notification of objection must be received by the secured party:

(1) in the case of a person to which the proposal was sent pursuant to Section 9–621, within 20 days after notification was sent to that person; and

(2) in other cases:

(A) within 20 days after the last notification was sent pursuant to Section 9–621; or

(B) if a notification was not sent, before the debtor consents to the acceptance under subsection (c).

(e) [Mandatory disposition of consumer goods.] A secured party that has taken possession of collateral shall dispose of the collateral pursuant to Section 9–610 within the time specified in subsection (f) if:

(1) 60 percent of the cash price has been paid in the case of a purchase-money security interest in consumer goods; or

(2) 60 percent of the principal amount of the obligation secured has been paid in the case of a non-purchase-money security interest in consumer goods.

(f) [Compliance with mandatory disposition requirement.] To comply with subsection (e), the secured party shall dispose of the collateral:

(1) within 90 days after taking possession; or

(2) within any longer period to which the debtor and all secondary obligors have agreed in an agreement to that effect entered into and authenticated after default.

(g) [No partial satisfaction in consumer transaction.] In a consumer transaction, a secured party may not accept collateral in partial satisfaction of the obligation it secures.

UNOFFICIAL COMMENTS

Section 9–620 generally answers the question when can a secured party "accept" collateral in satisfaction of the obligation. Note the importance of whether the goods are "consumer goods", section 9–620(a)(3); 9–620(e) and 9–620(g).

What section 9–620 does not answer is the common sense question of how often acceptance of collateral in <u>full</u> satisfaction actually happens. It would seem that the only time that the secured party would propose section 9–620 acceptance is when the collateral is worth more than the amount owed. And, it would seem that the only time that the debtor would object to section 9–620 acceptance is when the collateral is worth more than the amount owed.

Official Comment 2 to section 9–620 uses the term "strict foreclosure." Your professor, if she is old, might also use the term "retention."

For a more complete explanation of section 9–620, see pages 397–403 infra.

NON–OBVIOUS DEFINITIONS

"Proposal" is defined in section 9–201(a)(66) and governed by section 9–621.

This section uses the term "debtor" throughout. Not the term "obligor." Remember that under the section 9–102 definitions, the "debtor" can be a different person from the "obligor."

OTHER UCC SECTIONS TO LOOK TO WHEN YOU LOOK AT SECTION 9–620

There are four sections that govern the secured party's keeping repossessed collateral: sections 9–201, 9–620, 9–621, and 9–622. If there is a timely objection to the secured party's proposal to keep repossessed collateral, then you need to look to the resale alternative of section 9–610 et seq.

OFFICIAL COMMENT

* * *

2. **Overview.** This section and the two sections following deal with strict foreclosure, a procedure by which the secured party acquires the debtor's interest in the collateral without the need for a sale or other disposition under Section 9–610. Although these provisions derive from former Section 9–505, they have been entirely reorganized and substantially rewritten. The more straightforward approach taken in this Article eliminates the fiction that the secured party always will present a "proposal" for the retention of collateral and the debtor will have a fixed period to respond. By eliminating the need (but preserving the possibility) for proceeding in that fashion, this section eliminates much of the awkwardness of former Section 9–505. It reflects the belief that strict foreclosures should be encouraged and often will produce better results than a disposition for all concerned.

Subsection (a) sets forth the conditions necessary to an effective acceptance (formerly, retention) of collateral in full or partial satisfaction of the secured obligation. Section 9–621 requires in addition that a secured party who wishes to proceed under this section notify certain other persons who have or claim to have an interest in the collateral. Unlike the failure to meet the conditions in subsection (a), under Section 9–622(b) the failure to comply with the notification requirement of Section 9–621 does not render the acceptance of collateral ineffective. Rather, the acceptance can take effect notwithstanding the secured party's noncompliance. A person to whom the required notice was not sent has the right to recover damages under Section 9–625(b). Section 9–622(a) sets forth the effect of an acceptance of collateral.

3. **Conditions to Effective Acceptance.** Subsection (a) contains the conditions necessary to the effectiveness of an acceptance of collateral. Subsection (a)(1) requires the debtor's consent. Under subsections (c)(1) and (c)(2), the debtor may consent by agreeing to the acceptance in writing after default. Subsection (c)(2) contains an alternative method by which to satisfy the debtor's-consent condition in subsection (a)(1). It follows the proposal-and-objection model found in former Section 9–505: The debtor consents if the secured party sends a proposal to the debtor and does not receive an objection within 20 days. Under subsection (c)(1), however, that silence is not deemed to be consent with respect to acceptances in partial satisfaction. Thus, a secured party who wishes to conduct a "partial strict foreclosure" must obtain the debtor's agreement in a record authenticated after default. In all other respects, the conditions necessary to an effective partial strict foreclosure are the same as those governing acceptance of collateral in full satisfaction. (But see subsection (g), prohibiting partial strict foreclosure of a security interest in consumer transactions.)

The time when a debtor consents to a strict foreclosure is significant in several circumstances under this section and the following one. See Sections 9–620(a)(1), (d)(2), 9–621(a)(1), (a)(2), (a)(3). For purposes of determining the time of consent, a debtor's conditional consent constitutes consent.

Subsection (a)(2) contains the second condition to the effectiveness of an acceptance under this section—the absence of a timely objection from a person holding a junior interest in the collateral or from a secondary obligor. Any junior party—secured party or lienholder–is entitled to lodge an objection to a proposal, even if that person was not entitled to notification under Section 9–621. Subsection (d), discussed below, indicates when an objection is timely.

Subsections (a)(3) and (a)(4) contain special rules for transactions in which consumers are involved. See Comment 12.

4. **Proposals.** Section 9–102 defines the term "proposal." It is necessary to send a "proposal" to the debtor only if the debtor does not agree to an acceptance in an authenticated record as described in subsection (c)(1) or (c)(2). Section 9–621(a) determines whether it is necessary to send a proposal to third parties. A proposal need not take any particular form as long as it sets forth the terms under which the secured party is willing to accept collateral in satisfaction. A proposal to accept collateral should specify the amount (or a means of calculating the amount, such as by including a per diem accrual figure) of the secured obligations to be satisfied, state the conditions (if any) under which the proposal may be revoked, and describe any other applicable conditions. Note, however, that a conditional proposal generally requires the debtor's agreement in order to take effect. See subsection (c).

5. **Secured Party's Agreement; No "Constructive" Strict Foreclosure.** The conditions of subsection (a) relate to actual or implied consent by the debtor and any secondary obligor or holder of a junior security interest or lien. To ensure that the debtor cannot unilaterally cause an acceptance of collateral, subsection (b) provides that compliance with these conditions is necessary but not sufficient to cause an acceptance of collateral. Rather, under subsection (b), acceptance does not occur unless, in addition, the secured party consents to the acceptance in an authenticated record or sends to the debtor a proposal. For this reason, a mere delay in collection or disposition of collateral does not constitute a "constructive" strict foreclosure. Instead, delay is a factor relating to whether the secured party acted in a commercially reasonable manner for purposes of Section 9–607 or 9–610. A debtor's voluntary surrender of collateral to a secured party and the secured party's acceptance of possession of the collateral does not, of itself, necessarily raise an implication that the secured party intends or is proposing to accept the collateral in satisfaction of the secured obligation under this section.

6. **When Acceptance Occurs.** This section does not impose any formalities or identify any steps that a secured party must take in order to accept collateral once the conditions of subsections (a) and (b) have been met. Absent facts or circumstances indicating a contrary intention, the fact that the conditions have been met provides a sufficient indication that the secured party has accepted the collateral on the terms to which the secured party has consented or proposed and the debtor has consented or failed to object. Following a proposal, acceptance of the collateral normally is automatic upon the secured party's becoming bound and the time for objection passing. As a matter of good business practice, an enforcing secured party may wish to memorialize its acceptance following a proposal, such as by notifying the debtor that the strict foreclosure is effective or by placing a written record to that effect in its files. The secured party's agreement to accept collateral is self-executing and cannot be breached. The secured party is bound by its agreement to accept collateral and by any proposal to which the debtor consents.

7. **No Possession Requirement.** This section eliminates the requirement in former Section 9–505 that the secured party be "in possession" of collateral. It

clarifies that intangible collateral, which cannot be possessed, may be subject to a strict foreclosure under this section. However, under subsection (a)(3), if the collateral is consumer goods, acceptance does not occur unless the debtor is not in possession.

8. **When Objection Timely.** Subsection (d) explains when an objection is timely and thus prevents an acceptance of collateral from taking effect. An objection by a person to which notification was sent under Section 9–621 is effective if it is received by the secured party within 20 days from the date the notification was sent to that person. Other objecting parties (i.e., third parties who are not entitled to notification) may object at any time within 20 days after the last notification is sent under Section 9–621. If no such notification is sent, third parties must object before the debtor agrees to the acceptance in writing or is deemed to have consented by silence. The former may occur any time after default, and the latter requires a 20–day waiting period. See subsection (c).

9. **Applicability of Other Law.** This section does not purport to regulate all aspects of the transaction by which a secured party may become the owner of collateral previously owned by the debtor. For example, a secured party's acceptance of a motor vehicle in satisfaction of secured obligations may require compliance with the applicable motor vehicle certificate-of-title law. State legislatures should conform those laws so that they mesh well with this section and Section 9–610, and courts should construe those laws and this section harmoniously. A secured party's acceptance of collateral in the possession of the debtor also may implicate statutes dealing with a seller's retention of possession of goods sold.

10. **Accounts, Chattel Paper, Payment Intangibles, and Promissory Notes.** If the collateral is accounts, chattel paper, payment intangibles, or promissory notes, then a secured party's acceptance of the collateral in satisfaction of secured obligations would constitute a sale to the secured party. That sale normally would give rise to a new security interest (the ownership interest) under Sections 1–201(37) and 9–109. In the case of accounts and chattel paper, the new security interest would remain perfected by a filing that was effective to perfect the secured party's original security interest. In the case of payment intangibles or promissory notes, the security interest would be perfected when it attaches. See Section 9–309. However, the procedures for acceptance of collateral under this section satisfy all necessary formalities and a new security agreement authenticated by the debtor would not be necessary.

11. **Role of Good Faith.** Section 1–203 imposes an obligation of good faith on a secured party's enforcement under this Article. This obligation may not be disclaimed by agreement. See Section 1–102. Thus, a proposal and acceptance made under this section in bad faith would not be effective. For example, a secured party's proposal to accept marketable securities worth $1,000 in full satisfaction of indebtedness in the amount of $100, made in the hopes that the debtor might inadvertently fail to object, would be made in bad faith. On the other hand, in the normal case proposals and acceptances should be not second-guessed on the basis of the "value" of the collateral involved. Disputes about valuation or even a clear excess of collateral value over the amount of obligations satisfied do not necessarily demonstrate the absence of good faith.

12. **Special Rules in Consumer Cases.** Subsection (e) imposes an obligation on the secured party to dispose of consumer goods under certain circumstances. Subsection (f) explains when a disposition that is required under subsection (e) is timely. An effective acceptance of collateral cannot occur if subsection (e) requires a disposition unless the debtor waives this requirement pursuant to Section 9–624(b). Moreover, a secured party who takes possession of collateral and unreasonably delays disposition violates subsection (e), if applicable, and may also violate Section 9–610 or other provisions of this Part. Subsection (e) eliminates as superfluous the express statutory reference to "conversion" found in former Section 9–505. Remedies available under oth-

er law, including conversion, remain available under this Article in appropriate cases. See Sections 1–103, 1–106.

Subsection (g) prohibits the secured party in consumer transactions from accepting collateral in partial satisfaction of the obligation it secures. If a secured party attempts an acceptance in partial satisfaction in a consumer transaction, the attempted acceptance is void.

§ 9–621. Notification of Proposal to Accept Collateral

(a) [Persons to which proposal to be sent.] A secured party that desires to accept collateral in full or partial satisfaction of the obligation it secures shall send its proposal to:

(1) any person from which the secured party has received, before the debtor consented to the acceptance, an authenticated notification of a claim of an interest in the collateral;

(2) any other secured party or lienholder that, 10 days before the debtor consented to the acceptance, held a security interest in or other lien on the collateral perfected by the filing of a financing statement that:

(A) identified the collateral;

(B) was indexed under the debtor's name as of that date; and

(C) was filed in the office or offices in which to file a financing statement against the debtor covering the collateral as of that date; and

(3) any other secured party that, 10 days before the debtor consented to the acceptance, held a security interest in the collateral perfected by compliance with a statute, regulation, or treaty described in Section 9–311(a).

(b) [Proposal to be sent to secondary obligor in partial satisfaction.] A secured party that desires to accept collateral in partial satisfaction of the obligation it secures shall send its proposal to any secondary obligor in addition to the persons described in subsection (a).

UNOFFICIAL COMMENTS

We have an explanation of section 9–621 on pages 403–408 infra.

OFFICIAL COMMENT

* * *

2. **Notification Requirement.** Subsection (a) specifies three classes of competing claimants to whom the secured party must send notification of its proposal: (i) those who notify the secured party that they claim an interest in the collateral, (ii) holders of certain security interests and liens who have filed against the debtor, and (iii) holders of certain security interests who have perfected by compliance with a statute (including a certificate-of-title statute), regulation, or treaty

described in Section 9–311(a). With regard to (ii), see Section 9–611, Comment 4. Subsection (b) also requires notification to any secondary obligor if the proposal is for acceptance in partial satisfaction.

Unlike Section 9–611, this section contains no "safe harbor," which excuses an enforcing secured party from notifying certain secured parties and other lienholders. This is because, unlike Section 9–610, which requires that a disposition of collateral be commercially reasonable, Section 9–620 permits the debtor and secured party to set the amount of credit the debtor will receive for the collateral subject only to the requirement of good faith. An effective acceptance discharges subordinate security interests and other subordinate liens. See Section 9–622. If collateral is subject to several liens securing debts much larger than the value of the collateral, the debtor may be disinclined to refrain from consenting to an acceptance by the holder of the senior security interest, even though, had the debtor objected and the senior disposed of the collateral under Section 9–610, the collateral may have yielded more than enough to satisfy the senior security interest (but not enough to satisfy all the liens). Accordingly, this section imposes upon the enforcing secured party the risk of the filing office's errors and delay. The holder of a security interest who is entitled to notification under this section but does not receive it has the right to recover under Section 9–625(b) any loss resulting from the enforcing secured party's noncompliance with this section.

§ 9–622. Effect of Acceptance of Collateral

(a) [Effect of acceptance.] A secured party's acceptance of collateral in full or partial satisfaction of the obligation it secures:

   (1) discharges the obligation to the extent consented to by the debtor;

   (2) transfers to the secured party all of a debtor's rights in the collateral;

   (3) discharges the security interest or agricultural lien that is the subject of the debtor's consent and any subordinate security interest or other subordinate lien; and

   (4) terminates any other subordinate interest.

(b) [Discharge of subordinate interest notwithstanding noncompliance.] A subordinate interest is discharged or terminated under subsection (a), even if the secured party fails to comply with this article.

UNOFFICIAL COMMENTS

We have an explanation of section 9–622 on pages 408–409 infra.

OFFICIAL COMMENT

* * *

2. **Effect of Acceptance.** Subsection (a) specifies the effect of an acceptance of collateral in full or partial satisfaction of the secured obligation. The acceptance to which it refers is an effective acceptance. If a purported acceptance is ineffective under Section 9–620, e.g., because the secured party receives a timely objection from a person entitled to notification, then neither this subsection nor subsection (b) applies. Paragraph (1) expresses the fundamental consequence of accepting collateral in full or partial sat-

isfaction of the secured obligation—the obligation is discharged to the extent consented to by the debtor. Unless otherwise agreed, the obligor remains liable for any deficiency. Paragraphs (2) through (4) indicate the effects of an acceptance on various property rights and interests. Paragraph (2) follows Section 9–617(a) in providing that the secured party acquires "all of a debtor's rights in the collateral." Under paragraph (3), the effect of strict foreclosure on holders of junior security interests and other liens is the same regardless of whether the collateral is accepted in full or partial satisfaction of the secured obligation: all junior encumbrances are discharged. Paragraph (4) provides for the termination of other subordinate interests.

Subsection (b) makes clear that subordinate interests are discharged under subsection (a) regardless of whether the secured party complies with this Article. Thus, subordinate interests are discharged regardless of whether a proposal was required to be sent or, if required, was sent. However, a secured party's failure to send a proposal or otherwise to comply with this Article may subject the secured party to liability under Section 9–625.

§ 9–623. Right to Redeem Collateral

(a) [Persons that may redeem.] A debtor, any secondary obligor, or any other secured party or lienholder may redeem collateral.

(b) [Requirements for redemption.] To redeem collateral, a person shall tender:

(1) fulfillment of all obligations secured by the collateral; and

(2) the reasonable expenses and attorney's fees described in Section 9–615(a)(1).

(c) [When redemption may occur.] A redemption may occur at any time before a secured party:

(1) has collected collateral under Section 9–607;

(2) has disposed of collateral or entered into a contract for its disposition under Section 9–610; or

(3) has accepted collateral in full or partial satisfaction of the obligation it secures under Section 9–622.

UNOFFICIAL COMMENTS

Any exam fact pattern with redemption issues is likely to involve one or both of the following questions: (1) how much do you have to pay to redeem (9–623(b)) and/or (2) when is it too late to redeem (section 9–623(c)).

NON–OBVIOUS DEFINITIONS

This section uses the term "debtor" and the term "secondary obligor" throughout. Not the term "obligor." Remember that under the section 9–102 definitions, the "debtor" can be a different person from the "obligor", and the "secondary obligor" is a different person from the "obligor."

§ 9–623   ART. 9   Unit 4

This section also uses the terms "redeem" and "redemption" without definitions. In essence, UCC redemption refers to a debtor or other secured party "buying back" repossessed collateral.

OTHER UCC SECTIONS TO LOOK TO WHEN YOU LOOK AT SECTION 9–623

Think about acceleration clauses in the security agreement when you think about default and paying "all obligations secured" in order to redeem under section 9–623(b)(1). Cf. Official Comment 2 to section 9–623. And when you think about acceleration, think about section 1–208/Revised 1–309.

If you professor also taught bankruptcy law, then you might need to compare the amount necessary to redeem under section 9–623 with the amount necessary for redemption under section 722 of the Bankruptcy Code.

Waiver of redemption rights is not permitted in consumer goods transactions. In other transactions, section 9–624 permits any waiver of redemption rights must occur after "default."

OFFICIAL COMMENT

* * *

2. Redemption Right. Under this section, as under former Section 9–506, the debtor or another secured party may redeem collateral as long as the secured party has not collected (Section 9–607), disposed of or contracted for the disposition of (Section 9–610), or accepted (Section 9–620) the collateral. Although this section generally follows former Section 9–506, it extends the right of redemption to holders of nonconsensual liens. To redeem the collateral a person must tender fulfillment of all obligations secured, plus certain expenses. If the entire balance of a secured obligation has been accelerated, it would be necessary to tender the entire balance. A tender of fulfillment obviously means more than a new promise to perform an existing promise. It requires payment in full of all monetary obligations then due and performance in full of all other obligations then matured. If unmatured secured obligations remain, the security interest continues to secure them (i.e., as if there had been no default).

3. Redemption of Remaining Collateral Following Partial Enforcement. Under Section 9–610 a secured party may make successive dispositions of portions of its collateral. These dispositions would not affect the debtor's, another secured party's, or a lienholder's right to redeem the remaining collateral.

4. Effect of "Repledging." Section 9–207 generally permits a secured party having possession or control of collateral to create a security interest in the collateral. As explained in the Comments to that section, the debtor's right (as opposed to its practical ability) to redeem collateral is not affected by, and does not affect, the priority of a security interest created by the debtor's secured party.

§ 9–624. Waiver

(a) [Waiver of disposition notification.] A debtor or secondary obligor may waive the right to notification of disposition of collateral under Section 9–611 only by an agreement to that effect entered into and authenticated after default.

(b) [Waiver of mandatory disposition.] A debtor may waive the right to require disposition of collateral under Section 9–620(e) only by an agreement to that effect entered into and authenticated after default.

(c) [Waiver of redemption right.] Except in a consumer-goods transaction, a debtor or secondary obligor may waive the right to redeem collateral under Section 9–623 only by an agreement to that effect entered into and authenticated after default.

OFFICIAL COMMENT

* * *

2. **Waiver.** This section is a limited exception to Section 9–602, which generally prohibits waiver by debtors and obligors. It makes no provision for waiver of the rule prohibiting a secured party from buying at its own private disposition. Transactions of this kind are equivalent to "strict foreclosures" and are governed by Sections 9–620, 9–621, and 9–622.

[SUBPART 2. NONCOMPLIANCE WITH ARTICLE]

§ 9–625. Remedies for Secured Party's Failure to Comply With Article

(a) [Judicial orders concerning noncompliance.] If it is established that a secured party is not proceeding in accordance with this article, a court may order or restrain collection, enforcement, or disposition of collateral on appropriate terms and conditions.

(b) [Damages for noncompliance.] Subject to subsections (c), (d), and (f), a person is liable for damages in the amount of any loss caused by a failure to comply with this article. Loss caused by a failure to comply may include loss resulting from the debtor's inability to obtain, or increased costs of, alternative financing.

(c) [Persons entitled to recover damages; statutory damages in consumer-goods transaction.] Except as otherwise provided in Section 9–628:

  (1) a person that, at the time of the failure, was a debtor, was an obligor, or held a security interest in or other lien on the collateral may recover damages under subsection (b) for its loss; and

  (2) if the collateral is consumer goods, a person that was a debtor or a secondary obligor at the time a secured party failed to comply with this part may recover for that failure in any event an amount not less than the credit service charge plus 10 percent of the principal amount of the obligation or the time-price differential plus 10 percent of the cash price.

(d) [Recovery when deficiency eliminated or reduced.] A debtor whose deficiency is eliminated under Section 9–626 may recover damages for the loss of any surplus. However, a debtor or secondary obligor whose deficiency is eliminated or reduced under Section 9–626 may not otherwise recover under subsection (b) for noncompliance with the provisions of this part relating to collection, enforcement, disposition, or acceptance.

(e) [Statutory damages: noncompliance with specified provisions.] In addition to any damages recoverable under subsection (b), the debtor, consumer obligor, or person named as a debtor in a filed record, as applicable, may recover $500 in each case from a person that:

- **(1)** fails to comply with Section 9–208;
- **(2)** fails to comply with Section 9–209;
- **(3)** files a record that the person is not entitled to file under Section 9–509(a);
- **(4)** fails to cause the secured party of record to file or send a termination statement as required by Section 9–513(a) or (c);
- **(5)** fails to comply with Section 9–616(b)(1) and whose failure is part of a pattern, or consistent with a practice, of noncompliance; or
- **(6)** fails to comply with Section 9–616(b)(2).

(f) [Statutory damages: noncompliance with Section 9–210.] A debtor or consumer obligor may recover damages under subsection (b) and, in addition, $500 in each case from a person that, without reasonable cause, fails to comply with a request under Section 9–210. A recipient of a request under Section 9–210 which never claimed an interest in the collateral or obligations that are the subject of a request under that section has a reasonable excuse for failure to comply with the request within the meaning of this subsection.

(g) [Limitation of security interest: noncompliance with Section 9–210.] If a secured party fails to comply with a request regarding a list of collateral or a statement of account under Section 9–210, the secured party may claim a security interest only as shown in the list or statement included in the request as against a person that is reasonably misled by the failure.

UNOFFICIAL COMMENTS

Section 9–625(a) provides for injunctive relief.

Section 9–625(b) provides for recovery of actual loss. with a minimum recovery under section 9–625(c)(2) if the collateral is consumer goods. Notice that while the Official Comment 4 uses the term "minimum damages", the title to section 9–625(c) uses the phrase "statutory damages." What is the relationship between section 9–625(b) and section 9–625(c)(2)? Can there be double recovery?

Section 9–625(d) deals with the relationship between section 9–625(b) and section 9–626. Not a double recovery.

Sections 9–625(e) and (f) provide for "supplemental damages" for violations of certain specified statutory requirements. See Official Comment 5 to 9–625.

OTHER SECTIONS YOU NEED TO LOOK TO WHEN YOU LOOK AT SECTION 9–625

You are looking at section 9–625 to see the "Remedies for Secured Party's Failure to Comply with Article". Section 9–626 has another such remedy.

And, section 9–617(b) has a non-remedy–undoing a sale.

Even if the disposition did not completely comply with all of the requirements of Article 9, the buyer is protected from undoing the sale.

OFFICIAL COMMENT

* * *

2. **Remedies for Noncompliance; Scope.** Subsections (a) and (b) provide the basic remedies afforded to those aggrieved by a secured party's failure to comply with this Article. Like all provisions that create liability, they are subject to Section 9–628, which should be read in conjunction with Section 9–605. The principal limitations under this Part on a secured party's right to enforce its security interest against collateral are the requirements that it proceed in good faith (Section 1–203), in a commercially reasonable manner (Sections 9–607 and 9–610), and, in most cases, with reasonable notification (Sections 9–611 through 9–614). Following former Section 9–507, under subsection (a) an aggrieved person may seek injunctive relief, and under subsection (b) the person may recover damages for losses caused by noncompliance. Unlike former Section 9–507, however, subsections (a) and (b) are not limited to noncompliance with provisions of this Part of Article 9. Rather, they apply to noncompliance with any provision of this Article. The change makes this section applicable to noncompliance with Sections 9–207 (duties of secured party in possession of collateral), 9–208 (duties of secured party having control over deposit account), 9–209 (duties of secured party if account debtor has been notified of an assignment), 9–210 (duty to comply with request for accounting, etc.), 9–509(a) (duty to refrain from filing unauthorized financing statement), and 9–513(a) or (c) (duty to provide termination statement). Subsection (a) also modifies the first sentence of former Section 9–507(1) by adding the references to "collection" and "enforcement." Subsection (c)(2), which gives a minimum damage recovery in consumer-goods transactions, applies only to noncompliance with the provisions of this Part.

3. **Damages for Noncompliance with This Article.** Subsection (b) sets forth the basic remedy for failure to com-

ply with the requirements of this Article: a damage recovery in the amount of loss caused by the noncompliance. Subsection (c) identifies who may recover under subsection (b). It affords a remedy to any aggrieved person who is a debtor or obligor. However, a principal obligor who is not a debtor may recover damages only for noncompliance with Section 9–616, inasmuch as none of the other rights and duties in this Article run in favor of such a principal obligor. Such a principal obligor could not suffer any loss or damage on account of noncompliance with rights or duties of which it is not a beneficiary. Subsection (c) also affords a remedy to an aggrieved person who holds a competing security interest or other lien, regardless of whether the aggrieved person is entitled to notification under Part 6. The remedy is available even to holders of senior security interests and other liens. The exercise of this remedy is subject to the normal rules of pleading and proof. A person who has delegated the duties of a secured party but who remains obligated to perform them is liable under this subsection. The last sentence of subsection (d) eliminates the possibility of double recovery or other over-compensation arising out of a reduction or elimination of a deficiency under Section 9–626, based on noncompliance with the provisions of this Part relating to collection, enforcement, disposition, or acceptance. Assuming no double recovery, a debtor whose deficiency is eliminated under Section 9–626 may pursue a claim for a surplus. Because Section 9–626 does not apply to consumer transactions, the statute is silent as to whether a double recovery or other over-compensation is possible in a consumer transaction.

Damages for violation of the requirements of this Article, including Section 9–609, are those reasonably calculated to put an eligible claimant in the position that it would have occupied had no violation occurred. See Section 1–106. Subsection (b) supports the recovery of actual damages for committing a breach of the peace in violation of Section 9–609, and principles of tort law supplement this subsection. See Section 1–103. However, to the extent that damages in tort compensate the debtor for the same loss dealt with by this Article, the debtor should be entitled to only one recovery.

4. **Minimum Damages in Consumer–Goods Transactions.** Subsection (c)(2) provides a minimum, statutory, damage recovery for a debtor and secondary obligor in a consumer-goods transaction. It is patterned on former Section 9–507(1) and is designed to ensure that every noncompliance with the requirements of Part 6 in a consumer-goods transaction results in liability, regardless of any injury that may have resulted. Subsection (c)(2) leaves the treatment of statutory damages as it was under former Article 9. A secured party is not liable for statutory damages under this subsection more than once with respect to any one secured obligation (see Section 9–628(e)), nor is a secured party liable under this subsection for failure to comply with Section 9–616 (see Section 9–628(d)).

Following former Section 9–507(1), this Article does not include a definition or explanation of the terms "credit service charge," "principal amount," "time-price differential," or "cash price," as used in subsection (c)(2). It leaves their construction and application to the court, taking into account the subsection's purpose of providing a minimum recovery in consumer-goods transactions.

5. **Supplemental Damages.** Subsections (e) and (f) provide damages that supplement the recovery, if any, under subsection (b). Subsection (e) imposes an additional $500 liability upon a person who fails to comply with the provisions specified in that subsection, and subsection (f) imposes like damages on a person who, without reasonable excuse, fails to comply with a request for an accounting or a request regarding a list of collateral or statement of account under Section 9–210. However, under subsection (f), a person has a reasonable excuse for the failure if the person never claimed an interest in the collateral or obligations that were the subject of the request.

6. **Estoppel.** Subsection (g) limits the extent to which a secured party who fails to comply with a request regarding a list

of collateral or statement of account may claim a security interest.

§ 9–626. Action in Which Deficiency or Surplus Is in Issue

(a) [Applicable rules if amount of deficiency or surplus in issue.] In an action arising from a transaction, other than a consumer transaction, in which the amount of a deficiency or surplus is in issue, the following rules apply:

> (1) A secured party need not prove compliance with the provisions of this part relating to collection, enforcement, disposition, or acceptance unless the debtor or a secondary obligor places the secured party's compliance in issue.
>
> (2) If the secured party's compliance is placed in issue, the secured party has the burden of establishing that the collection, enforcement, disposition, or acceptance was conducted in accordance with this part.
>
> (3) Except as otherwise provided in Section 9–628, if a secured party fails to prove that the collection, enforcement, disposition, or acceptance was conducted in accordance with the provisions of this part relating to collection, enforcement, disposition, or acceptance, the liability of a debtor or a secondary obligor for a deficiency is limited to an amount by which the sum of the secured obligation, expenses, and attorney's fees exceeds the greater of:
>
>> (A) the proceeds of the collection, enforcement, disposition, or acceptance; or
>>
>> (B) the amount of proceeds that would have been realized had the noncomplying secured party proceeded in accordance with the provisions of this part relating to collection, enforcement, disposition, or acceptance.
>
> (4) For purposes of paragraph (3)(B), the amount of proceeds that would have been realized is equal to the sum of the secured obligation, expenses, and attorney's fees unless the secured party proves that the amount is less than that sum.
>
> (5) If a deficiency or surplus is calculated under Section 9–615(f), the debtor or obligor has the burden of establishing that the amount of proceeds of the disposition is significantly below the range of prices that a complying disposition to a

person other than the secured party, a person related to the secured party, or a secondary obligor would have brought.

(b) [Non-consumer transactions; no inference.] The limitation of the rules in subsection (a) to transactions other than consumer transactions is intended to leave to the court the determination of the proper rules in consumer transactions. The court may not infer from that limitation the nature of the proper rule in consumer transactions and may continue to apply established approaches.

UNOFFICIAL COMMENTS

Most important thing to see in 9–626 is the phrase "other than a consumer transaction." So important that it appears both at the beginning in section 9–626(a) and the end in section 9–626(b). Section 9–626 does not apply to consumer transactions, and problems of "compliance with the provisions of this part" typically arise in consumer transactions.

As Official Comment 3 to section 9–626 explains, section 9–626 adopts a rebuttable presumption rule for commercial transactions that do not completely comply with part 6 of Article 9: the value of the collateral is presumed to have equaled the entire secured debt (thus eliminating any deficiency claim) unless the secured party is able to prove a lower collateral value.

OTHER UCC SECTIONS TO LOOK TO WHEN YOU LOOK AT SECTION 9–626

If the net proceeds from the secured party's disposition of the collateral is not enough to satisfy the secured debt, the obligor is liable for any deficiency, section 9–615(e).

Look at the relationship between section 9–625 and section 9–626. Primarily section 9–625(b). Notice also that "failure to comply with Article [9]" triggers section 9–625 while only [non]"compliance with the provisions of this part [Part 6 of Article 9]" triggers section 9–626.

OFFICIAL COMMENT

* * *

2. **Scope.** The basic damage remedy under Section 9–625(b) is subject to the special rules in this section for transactions other than consumer transactions. This section addresses situations in which the amount of a deficiency or surplus is in issue, i.e., situations in which the secured party has collected, enforced, disposed of, or accepted the collateral. It contains special rules applicable to a determination of the amount of a deficiency or surplus. Because this section affects a person's liability for a deficiency, it is subject to Section 9–628, which should be read in conjunction with Section 9–605. The rules in this section apply only to noncompliance in connection with the "collection, enforcement, disposition, or acceptance" under Part 6. For other types of noncompliance with Part 6, the general liability rule of Section 9–625(b)—recovery of ac-

tual damages—applies. Consider, for example, a repossession that does not comply with Section 9–609 for want of a default. The debtor's remedy is under Section 9–625(b). In a proper case, the secured party also may be liable for conversion under non-UCC law. If the secured party thereafter disposed of the collateral, however, it would violate Section 9–610 at that time, and this section would apply.

3. **Rebuttable Presumption Rule.** Subsection (a) establishes the rebuttable presumption rule for transactions other than consumer transactions. Under paragraph (1), the secured party need not prove compliance with the relevant provisions of this Part as part of its prima facie case. If, however, the debtor or a secondary obligor raises the issue (in accordance with the forum's rules of pleading and practice), then the secured party bears the burden of proving that the collection, enforcement, disposition, or acceptance complied. In the event the secured party is unable to meet this burden, then paragraph (3) explains how to calculate the deficiency. Under this rebuttable presumption rule, the debtor or obligor is to be credited with the greater of the actual proceeds of the disposition or the proceeds that would have been realized had the secured party complied with the relevant provisions. If a deficiency remains, then the secured party is entitled to recover it. The references to "the secured obligation, expenses, and attorney's fees" in paragraphs (3) and (4) embrace the application rules in Sections 9–608(a) and 9–615(a).

Unless the secured party proves that compliance with the relevant provisions would have yielded a smaller amount, under paragraph (4) the amount that a complying collection, enforcement, or disposition would have yielded is deemed to be equal to the amount of the secured obligation, together with expenses and attorney's fees. Thus, the secured party may not recover any deficiency unless it meets this burden.

4. **Consumer Transactions.** Although subsection (a) adopts a version of the rebuttable presumption rule for transactions other than consumer transactions, with certain exceptions Part 6 does not specify the effect of a secured party's noncompliance in consumer transactions. (The exceptions are the provisions for the recovery of damages in Section 9–625.) Subsection (b) provides that the limitation of subsection (a) to transactions other than consumer transactions is intended to leave to the court the determination of the proper rules in consumer transactions. It also instructs the court not to draw any inference from the limitation as to the proper rules for consumer transactions and leaves the court free to continue to apply established approaches to those transactions.

Courts construing former Section 9–507 disagreed about the consequences of a secured party's failure to comply with the requirements of former Part 5. Three general approaches emerged. Some courts have held that a noncomplying secured party may not recover a deficiency (the "absolute bar" rule). A few courts held that the debtor can offset against a claim to a deficiency all damages recoverable under former Section 9–507 resulting from the secured party's noncompliance (the "offset" rule). A plurality of courts considering the issue held that the noncomplying secured party is barred from recovering a deficiency unless it overcomes a rebuttable presumption that compliance with former Part 5 would have yielded an amount sufficient to satisfy the secured debt. In addition to the nonuniformity resulting from court decisions, some States enacted special rules governing the availability of deficiencies.

5. **Burden of Proof When Section 9–615(f) Applies.** In a non-consumer transaction, subsection (a)(5) imposes upon a debtor or obligor the burden of proving that the proceeds of a disposition are so low that, under Section 9–615(f), the actual proceeds should not serve as the basis upon which a deficiency or surplus is calculated. Were the burden placed on the secured party, then debtors might be encouraged to challenge the price received in every disposition to the secured party, a person related to the secured party, or a secondary obligor.

6. **Delay in Applying This Section.** There is an inevitable delay between the time a secured party engages in a non-complying collection, enforcement, disposition, or acceptance and the time of a subsequent judicial determination that the secured party did not comply with Part 6. During the interim, the secured party, believing that the secured obligation is larger than it ultimately is determined to be, may continue to enforce its security interest in collateral. If some or all of the secured indebtedness ultimately is discharged under this section, a reasonable application of this section would impose liability on the secured party for the amount of any excess, unwarranted recoveries but would not make the enforcement efforts wrongful.

§ 9–627. Determination of Whether Conduct Was Commercially Reasonable

(a) [Greater amount obtainable under other circumstances; no preclusion of commercial reasonableness.] The fact that a greater amount could have been obtained by a collection, enforcement, disposition, or acceptance at a different time or in a different method from that selected by the secured party is not of itself sufficient to preclude the secured party from establishing that the collection, enforcement, disposition, or acceptance was made in a commercially reasonable manner.

(b) [Dispositions that are commercially reasonable.] A disposition of collateral is made in a commercially reasonable manner if the disposition is made:

   (1) in the usual manner on any recognized market;

   (2) at the price current in any recognized market at the time of the disposition; or

   (3) otherwise in conformity with reasonable commercial practices among dealers in the type of property that was the subject of the disposition.

(c) [Approval by court or on behalf of creditors.] A collection, enforcement, disposition, or acceptance is commercially reasonable if it has been approved:

   (1) in a judicial proceeding;

   (2) by a bona fide creditors' committee;

   (3) by a representative of creditors; or

   (4) by an assignee for the benefit of creditors.

(d) [Approval under subsection (c) not necessary; absence of approval has no effect.] Approval under subsection (c) need not be obtained, and lack of approval does not mean that the collection, enforcement, disposition, or acceptance is not commercially reasonable.

UNOFFICIAL COMMENTS

Use this section when there is some question about whether the sale (disposition) was commercially reasonable., The section title uses the broader term "conduct" but the section deals with disposition issues.

And, if you have an exam fact pattern involving a secured party's sale of collateral, watch for information about (1) the reasonableness of the price received ("not of itself sufficient" section 9–627(a)); (2) the identity of the buyer (secured party? section 9–610(c) or "person related to" the "secured party"? section 9–615(f)) and (3) notice preceding the sale (sections 9–611 to 9–614).

NON–OBVIOUS DEFINITIONS

"Recognized market" is not defined in the UCC. The discussion of "recognized market" in Official Comment 4 to section 9–627 is helpful.

OFFICIAL COMMENT

* * *

2. Relationship of Price to Commercial Reasonableness. Some observers have found the notion contained in subsection (a) (derived from former Section 9–507(2)) (the fact that a better price could have been obtained does not establish lack of commercial reasonableness) to be inconsistent with that found in Section 9–610(b) (derived from former Section 9–504(3)) (every aspect of the disposition, including its terms, must be commercially reasonable). There is no such inconsistency. While not itself sufficient to establish a violation of this Part, a low price suggests that a court should scrutinize carefully all aspects of a disposition to ensure that each aspect was commercially reasonable.

The law long has grappled with the problem of dispositions of personal and real property which comply with applicable procedural requirements (e.g., advertising, notification to interested persons, etc.) but which yield a price that seems low. This Article addresses that issue in Section 9–615(f). That section applies only when the transferee is the secured party, a person related to the secured party, or a secondary obligor. It contains a special rule for calculating a deficiency or surplus in a complying disposition that yields a price that is "significantly below the range of proceeds that a complying disposition to a person other than the secured party, a person related to the secured party, or a secondary obligor would have brought."

3. Determination of Commercial Reasonableness; Advance Approval. It is important to make clear the conduct and procedures that are commercially reasonable and to provide a secured party with the means of obtaining, by court order or negotiation with a creditors' committee or a representative of creditors, advance approval of a proposed method of enforcement as commercially reasonable. This section contains rules that assist in that determination and provides for advance approval in appropriate situations. However, none of the specific methods of disposition specified in subsection (b) is required or exclusive.

4. "Recognized Market." As in Sections 9–610(c) and 9–611(d), the concept of a "recognized market" in subsections (b)(1) and (2) is quite limited; it applies only to markets in which there are standardized price quotations for property that is essentially fungible, such as stock exchanges.

§ 9–628. Nonliability and Limitation on Liability of Secured Party; Liability of Secondary Obligor

(a) [Limitation of liability of secured party for noncompliance with article.] Unless a secured party knows that a person is a debtor or obligor, knows the identity of the person, and knows how to communicate with the person:

> (1) the secured party is not liable to the person, or to a secured party or lienholder that has filed a financing statement against the person, for failure to comply with this article; and
>
> (2) the secured party's failure to comply with this article does not affect the liability of the person for a deficiency.

(b) [Limitation of liability based on status as secured party.] A secured party is not liable because of its status as secured party:

> (1) to a person that is a debtor or obligor, unless the secured party knows:
>
>> (A) that the person is a debtor or obligor;
>>
>> (B) the identity of the person; and
>>
>> (C) how to communicate with the person; or
>
> (2) to a secured party or lienholder that has filed a financing statement against a person, unless the secured party knows:
>
>> (A) that the person is a debtor; and
>>
>> (B) the identity of the person.

(c) [Limitation of liability if reasonable belief that transaction not a consumer-goods transaction or consumer transaction.] A secured party is not liable to any person, and a person's liability for a deficiency is not affected, because of any act or omission arising out of the secured party's reasonable belief that a transaction is not a consumer-goods transaction or a consumer transaction or that goods are not consumer goods, if the secured party's belief is based on its reasonable reliance on:

> (1) a debtor's representation concerning the purpose for which collateral was to be used, acquired, or held; or
>
> (2) an obligor's representation concerning the purpose for which a secured obligation was incurred.

(d) [Limitation of liability for statutory damages.] A secured party is not liable to any person under Section 9–625(c)(2) for its failure to comply with Section 9–616.

(e) [Limitation of multiple liability for statutory damages.] A secured party is not liable under Section 9–625(c)(2) more than once with respect to any one secured obligation.

OFFICIAL COMMENT

2. **Exculpatory Provisions.** Subsections (a), (b), and (c) contain exculpatory provisions that should be read in conjunction with Section 9–605. Without this group of provisions, a secured party could incur liability to unknown persons and under circumstances that would not allow the secured party to protect itself. The broadened definition of the term "debtor" underscores the need for these provisions.

If a secured party reasonably, but mistakenly, believes that a consumer transaction or consumer-goods transaction is a non-consumer transaction or non-consumer-goods transaction, and if the secured party's belief is based on its reasonable reliance on a representation of the type specified in subsection (c)(1) or (c)(2), then this Article should be applied as if the facts reasonably believed and the representation reasonably relied upon were true. For example, if a secured party reasonably believed that a transaction was a non-consumer transaction and its belief was based on reasonable reliance on the debtor's representation that the collateral secured an obligation incurred for business purposes, the secured party is not liable to any person, and the debtor's liability for a deficiency is not affected, because of any act or omission of the secured party which arises out of the reasonable belief. Of course, if the secured party's belief is not reasonable or, even if reasonable, is not based on reasonable reliance on the debtor's representation, this limitation on liability is inapplicable.

3. **Inapplicability of Statutory Damages to Section 9–616.** Subsection (d) excludes noncompliance with Section 9–616 entirely from the scope of statutory damage liability under Section 9–625(c)(2).

4. **Single Liability for Statutory Minimum Damages.** Subsection (e) ensures that a secured party will incur statutory damages only once in connection with any one secured obligation.

* * *

Unit 5

MORE EXTENDED STUDENT ARTICLE 9 COMMENTS

MORE ON 9–109 AND THE SALE OF RECEIVABLES

Article 9 incorporates the sale of receivables through the key defined terms for creating a security interest. And, expressly in section 9–109(a)(3). This approach increases the difficulty of interpreting and applying the specific provisions of Article 9 that govern the sales of receivables. It has also led to unintended errors in the drafting of Article 9. These difficulties derive from two specific defects in the drafting of Article 9.

First, Article 9 is a comprehensive statute that governs the creation, perfection, priority and enforcement of security interests in personal property to secure payment or performance of an obligation. Accordingly, Article 9 appropriately embodies a "lien" paradigm that rightly assumes that the "debtor" retains title to the personal property subject to a security interest and can therefore create more than one security interest in the personal property that it owns. Article 9 uses terminology that reflects this paradigm when it refers to the "attachment" of a security interest to "collateral," and the "subordination" and "priority" of security interests and the interests of lien creditors.

The sale of a receivables, however, does not fit this paradigm. The seller of a receivable retains no interest in the receivable sold, and it transfers ownership to the buyer. Hence, one does not normally think of a buyer's interest "attaching" to the sold receivable. Moreover, if a seller sells a receivable to a buyer that fails to perfect and later sells the same receivable to a second buyer that does perfect, the second sale does not merely "subordinate" the first buyer's interest, it totally destroys the first buyer's interest. In the language of the real estate recording acts, the first sale is "void."

Second, the terminology by which Article 9 incorporates the sale of receivables is misleading. The term "debtor" does not give the reader of Article 9 notice that the "debtor" is also a seller of receivables. Similarly, the terms "security interest," "secured party," "security agreement," or "collateral" do not give the reader of Article 9 notice that provisions using those terms also apply to a buyer's interest in the receivables, the buyer of receivables, a sale agreement, or receivables that have been sold.

Therefore, in interpreting and applying Article 9 in the context of a sale of receivables, the reader must first be aware that Article 9, entitled "Secured Transactions," also governs the sale of receivables and then must be more than ordinarily diligent by inserting in the relevant places the substance of the misleading definitions governing such sale.

MORE ON 9–203 AND ATTACHMENT

1. In general, a security interest under Article 9 is the personal property counterpart to a mortgage under real estate law. A security interest is a contract-based lien on personal property just like a mortgage is a contract-based lien on real property.

2. How do you get a security interest in the debtor's collateral? Answer: meet the requirements for attachment. The same question can be stated in a different manner: how does a creditor change its status from "unsecured" to "secured?" Answer: meet the requirements for attachment. Once attachment has occurred, a creditor can take advantage of all of the article 9 provisions that specify what a "secured party" can do.

3. Attachment occurs when ALL of the following three requirements have been met (in any order). Stated another way, a creditor does not have a security interest (*i.e.*, is not a "secured party") until ALL of the following three elements have been met:

   (i) Value has been given.

   (ii) The debtor has rights in the collateral.

   (iii) Security agreement.

4. Attachment deals with the relationship between the creditor and the debtor. By contrast, perfection and priority deal with the relationship between the creditor and the rest of the world (*e.g.*, other creditors, buyers). a security interest can be unperfected, yet still attached.

§ 9–203(b)(1) Comments

1. The issue is typically whether the secured party has given value.

2. Value includes all forms of consideration that you learned about in your first-year Contracts course (*e.g.*, promises to do something,

money), plus it includes past consideration. *See* § 1-201(44) (defining value); Rev. § 1-204 (same).

3. A promise can constitute value. Thus, value can be given even if no money has exchanged hands. When the creditor has neither made a promise nor loaned any money, however, there is a good chance that the value requirement has not been met.

4. Even though past consideration does not suffice as "consideration" under the common-law of contracts, past consideration can satisfy the value requirement under article 9.

5. To whom must value be given? Notice, that § 9-203(b)(1) only requires that "value [be] given." Thus, the value requirement may be satisfied if value is given to anyone, so long as the secured aprty gives value.

§ 9-203(b)(2) Comments

1. Not surprisingly, a debtor cannot grant a security interest in someone else's property. This explains the requirement that the debtor must have "rights in the collateral."

2. Although the "debtor" and the "obligor" are typically the same person, they do not have to be. *Compare* § 9-102(a)(28) (defining "debtor" in part as a person "having an interest ... in the collateral") *with* § 9-102(a)(59) (defining "obligor" in part as "a person that ... owes payment or other performance of the obligation"). Thus, if a mother agrees to offer her jewelry to a bank as collateral for a loan to her son, the mother is the "debtor" (because she owns the collateral) while the son is the "obligor" (because the loan was made to him).

§ 9-203(b)(3) Comments

1. A security agreement is simply a contract between the debtor and the creditor that "creates or provides for a security interest." *See* § 9-102(a)(73). Regardless of whether a security agreement is written or oral, therefore, there must be some language suggesting that the debtor is granting the creditor a security interest in the debtor's property.

2. In most transactions, the security agreement is written. *See* § 9-203(b)(3)(A). Note, however, that an oral security agreement is permissible if the creditor is in possession of the collateral. *See* § 9-203(b)(3)(B). Think about how unusual it is for the creditor to be in possession of the collateral. For example, if you buy a new car on credit, you (the debtor) want to be in possession of that car. While it is unusual for the creditor to be in possession of the collateral, it may nevertheless occur on law school exams.

3. In the typical transaction involving a written security agreement, the security agreement must be authenticated by the debtor and must contain a description of the collateral. *See* § 9–203(b)(3)(A). That description may include after-acquired property. *See* § 9–204 (discussing after-acquired property and future advances).

4. The authentication requirement is satisfied by the debtor's signature or by any symbol made by the debtor (*e.g.*, a smiley face, an "X") with the present intent "to identify the person and [to] adopt or accept" the agreement. *See* § 9–102(a)(7).

5. The description requirement is satisfied if the description "reasonably identifies" the collateral. *See* § 9–108(a). Reasonable identification includes describing the collateral by specific listing or category, or by using the article 9 "types" of collateral (*e.g.*, inventory, chattel paper, or other type of collateral defined in § 9–102). *See* § 9–102(b). *But see* § 9–102(e) (prohibiting descriptions by article 9 "type" in certain situations).

6. As mentioned, a security agreement is simply a contract between the debtor and the creditor. Thus, a court will interpret the language of a security agreement just as it would interpret the language of any contract. Courts will usually assume that the terms used by the parties were intended to have their article 9 meanings. For example, if the parties state that a security interest shall be granted in the debtor's "accounts," a court will typically assume that the parties meant to cover article 9 "accounts"—*i.e.*, accounts receivable, and not bank accounts. *See* § 9–102(a)(2) (defining "account"); § 9–102(a)(29) (defining "deposit account").

7. Keep in mind that a security agreement is only ONE of the THREE requirements needed to have a security interest (*i.e.*, only one of the three requirements needed for attachment). Thus, there can be a security agreement without having a security interest (if, for example, value has not yet been given and/or the debtor does not yet have rights in the collateral).

§ 9–203(f) Comments

1. A security agreement does not have to state that the secured creditor has a security interest in proceeds. A secured creditor is automatically provided with a security interest in identifiable proceeds. *See* §§ 9–203(f), 9–315(b)(2).

2. Proceeds, as defined by § 9–102(a)(64), includes "*whatever* is acquired upon the sale, lease, license, exchange, or other disposition of collateral," as well as "*whatever* is collected on ... collateral." Notice,

therefore, that the definition of proceeds is extremely broad. In effect, the concept of proceeds extends the definition of collateral by allowing a security interest to reach property "stemming" or "deriving" from the collateral, even though such items may not be explicitly described in the security agreement.

3. The definition of proceeds includes "whatever is acquired upon the ... disposition of *collateral*," and the definition of "collateral" includes "proceeds to which a security interest attaches." *See* § 9–102(a)(12)(A). Notice, therefore, that the definition of proceeds includes whatever is acquired upon the disposition of collateral AND whatever is acquired upon the disposition of proceeds. (Stated more informally, proceeds of proceeds are proceeds). For example, assume that a creditor has taken a security interest in inventory. The inventory is sold for cash. The cash is then used to buy a copier and a horse, and the horse is then swapped for a refrigerator. So long as the cash, copier, horse, and refrigerator are identifiable (*see* § 9–315(a)(2)), they are all proceeds of the creditor's collateral, and the creditor has a security interest in all of them. (Note: The security interest in the cash was likely lost as soon as the cash was used to purchase the copier and the horse. *See* § 9–332).

4. Proceeds are "identifiable" if the secured creditor can prove that the proceeds came from its collateral. Thus, in the example above, the creditor would only have a security interest in the refrigerator if it can prove (1) that the refrigerator came from the horse; (2) that the horse came from the cash; and (3) that the cash came from the original inventory collateral.

5. When proceeds are commingled with non-proceeds, identifiability can be lost. (Because a security interest extends only to *identifiable* proceeds, *see* §§ 9–203(f), 9–315(a)(2), the loss of identifiability means that the creditor does not have a security interest in the proceeds). For example, assume again that a creditor has taken a security interest in inventory. An item of inventory is sold for $2,000, and that $2,000 is deposited in the debtor's bank account. The debtor then writes numerous checks on the account. If the debtor had non-proceeds monies in the account (*e.g.*, monies from an inheritance) at the time the $2,000 of proceeds was deposited, those proceeds may have lost their identifiability. Why? Because the creditor will have difficulty proving that the money remaining in the account is its proceeds versus the debtor's inheritance money. Nevertheless, there are tracing rules, such as the lowest intermediate balance rule, that allow a creditor to establish that a portion of a commingled mass (such as commingled monies in a bank account) is identifiable. *See* § 9–315(b)(2) and OC 3.

MORE ON 9-204 AND FLOATING LIEN

1. A security agreement may cover "after-acquired property"—essentially property acquired by the debtor after the attachment of the security interest. If the secured creditor wants to have a security interest in after-acquired property, it usually needs to include an explicit after-acquired property clause in the security agreement (e.g., "Debtor grants a security interest to Creditor in Debtor's equipment, *now owned or later acquired* . . .").

2. Even if an after-acquired property clause is not included in the security agreement, a court may imply one in situations involving collateral that turns over rapidly (e.g., inventory, accounts). Implying an after-acquired property clause is based on the notion that a security agreement is a contract and that a court should consider the intent of the parties when attempting to determine if after-acquired property was meant to be covered by the security agreement. For example, assume that a debtor's inventory turns over and is replaced every thirty days. In these circumstances, does it make sense that a creditor would have taken a security interest only in inventory that the debtor owned at the time of attachment—inventory that will disappear in the next thirty days? Such an interpretation arguably makes little sense, as the creditor's security interest will reach nothing (other than identifiable proceeds) at the end of the thirty-day period. This suggests that the parties meant to cover after-acquired inventory, even if their security agreement simply described the collateral as "inventory" rather than the more explicit "inventory, now owned or later acquired."

3. Even though a court may imply an after-acquired property clause for collateral that turns over rapidly, the much safer course is to include an explicit after-acquired property clause in the security agreement.

4. To be effective, an explicit after-acquired property clause must be included in the security agreement. The inclusion of such a clause in the financing statement is unnecessary as well as ineffective. *See* § 9-204 OC 7.

§ 9-204(b) Comments

1. Notice that after-acquired property clauses are effective for consumer goods (non-accession consumer goods) only if the debtor acquires rights in the consumer goods within ten days after the secured creditor gives value. Watch out for this issue on an exam.

2. Similarly, notice that after-acquired property clauses are ineffective for commercial tort claims.

§ 9–204(c) Comments

1. A security agreement may provide that the described collateral secures not only the initial loan at issue, but also any subsequent loans that the creditor may make. Such a security agreement provision is known as a "future advance" clause.

2. For example, assume that Lisa took a security interest in Catherine's prized crystal collection to secure a $10,000 loan. Assume further that the security agreement contained a future advance clause. Two years later, Lisa loans Catherine another $5,000. The $10,000 initial loan, as well as the $5,000 subsequent loan, are both secured by the crystal collection.

3. If the security agreement did not contain a future advance clause in the prior example, only the $10,000 initial loan would be secured by the crystal collection. The $5,000 subsequent advance would be an unsecured loan (unless the parties executed another security agreement).

4. To be effective, a future advance clause must be included in the security agreement. The inclusion of such a clause in the financing statement is unnecessary as well as ineffective. See § 9–204 OC 7.

MORE ON 9–309 AND THE SALE OF RECEIVABLES

Sections 9–309(3) & (4) provide for the automatic perfection of a sale of a payment intangible and a promissory note. Section 9–312(a) provides that a security interest in an instrument, which includes a promissory note, may be perfected by filing.

There is, however, no express authorization for a buyer of a payment intangible to perfect a security interest by filing as well as by automatic perfection. Accordingly, Article 9 contains an ambiguity on whether a buyer of payment intangibles that buys payment intangibles over time may use the first-to-file-or-perfect rule of 9–322 to preserve priority against subsequent secured parties that take a collateral assignment of the debtor's payment intangibles, that is, a security interest to secure payment or performance of an obligation.

This issue is illustrated by the following example:

On Day 1, debtor signs a security/sale agreement to sell newly originated payment intangibles to SP–1/Buyer on a continuous basis. Debtor sells pool #1 of loans to SP–1/Buyer pursuant to the security/sale agreement. SP–1/Buyer files a financing statement covering all payment intangibles sold by debtor to SP–1/Buyer pursuant to the security/sale agreement. At this point, SP–1/Buyer has an automatically perfected first priority ownership interest in pool #1.

On Day 15, debtor obtains a loan from SP–2/Lender, signs a security agreement granting SP–2/Lender a security interest in all of debtor's payment intangibles now owned or thereafter acquired and files a financing statement covering all payment intangibles owned by debtor.

Between Day 16 and Day 30, debtor originates a second pool of payment intangibles, pool #2. SP–2/Lender's security interest attaches to each payment intangible as soon as debtor originates each payment intangible.

On Day 30, debtor sells pool #2 to SP–1/Buyer.

SP–1/Buyer's security/ownership interest in pool #2 is perfected on Day 30, after SP–2/Lender's security interest is perfected. If SP–1/Buyer has the benefit of the first to file or perfect rule, SP–1/Buyer would have priority in pool #2 on the basis of its filing on Day 1, before the filing of SP–2/Lender's financing statement on Day 15. On the other hand, filing is not necessary to perfect SP–1/Buyer's security/ownership interest, and therefore the earlier filing may not be a "filing" for purposes of Section 9–322(a)(1). If so, SP–1/Buyer's priority would date from the perfection of its interest in pool #2, Day 30, which is after the filing by SP–2/Lender. Despite the filing by SP–1/Buyer, if SP–1/Buyer cannot take advantage of the first to file or perfect rule, SP–2/Lender would have priority as the first to file or perfect.

This result would seem to be inconsistent with the policy of Article 9 expressed in Sections 9–204 and 9–322(a)(1) to permit one agreement and one financing statement to establish attachment, perfection and priority for after-acquired collateral and therefore obviate the need to check the financing statement records before making a future advance with the expectation of having perfection and priority in after acquired property.

MORE ON 9–315 AND "AUTHORIZED"

Section 9–315 allows a buyer to take free of the security interest, if the secured party "authorized" the sale of the collateral free of the security interest. Authorization may be express, or it may be implied. For example, the security agreement might expressly allow the debtor to sell the collateral free of the security interest in all circumstances, or it might allow such a sale only after the seller (that is, the debtor) conducts a credit check on the buyer. Implied authorization, on the other hand, could be inferred from the "course of dealings" (the secured party's conduct over several transactions) or the "course of performance" (the secured party's conduct in this particular transaction) (see § 1–303). This situation might arise in a situation where the security agreement says nothing about authorization, but the secured party has permitted the debtor to sell similar collateral on several occasions.

Generally, there will be authorization when the collateral is inventory-the secured party has an interest in the success of the debtor's business, and the debtor's business can only succeed if inventory is sold. But be careful not to confuse authorization with the protection afforded buyers in ordinary course of business.

Authorization under this section is one exception to the general priority rule in favor of secured parties; buyer in ordinary course of business status under section 9–320(a) is another. Very often, both exceptions will apply, but this is not always the case. For example, it is unlikely that one would be a buyer in ordinary course of business if purchasing equipment subject to a security interest from the debtor, but the buyer may nevertheless take free of the security interest if the sale was authorized under this section.

MORE ON 9–316 AND CHANGE IN LOCATION

Section 9–316(a) (1) A change in the location of the debtor or the collateral can cause the law governing perfection to change. (see sections 9–301, 9–305). In that event, the secured party will want to re-perfect its security interest according to the law of the new jurisdiction; (2) The secured party does not immediately lose perfection when there is such a change. This section tells you how long a creditor remains perfected after a change in the governing law. (3) If there is no transfer (change in debtor) and there is a change in the governing law, then perfection expires either when it would have expired under the local law of the original jurisdiction or four months after a change in the debtor's location to another jurisdiction, whichever is earlier, 9–316(a)(1)-(2); (4). If the debtor transfers the collateral and there is a change in the governing law, then the secured party remains perfected for one year after the transfer. The secured party must then re-perfect in the new jurisdiction within that one year in order to maintain its priority.

Section 9–316(b): If the secured party described in 9–316(a) fails to re-perfect in the new jurisdiction within the time prescribed, then it becomes unperfected and is deemed to have never been perfected as against a purchaser of the collateral for value.

MORE ON 9–317 AND PRIORITY
Section 9–317 General Comments.

Section 9–317 is another exception to the general rule provided in 9–201 and 9–315. If a buyer satisfies the requirements in this section he takes free of the security interest. However, for the buyer to prevail under this section the buyer must complete the process of buying (*i.e.*, give value and take possession, if possession is possible) before the security interest is perfected.

§ 9–317(b) Comments.

The requirements of section 9–317(b) are as follows: If a buyer (1) gives value and (2) receives delivery of the collateral (3) without knowledge of the security interest and (4) before the security interest is perfected, the buyer takes free.

Subpart (b) applies to buyers, but excludes "secured parties." By definition, most buyers of chattel paper and promissory notes are secured parties. See § 9–102(a)(72)(D). But some sales of receivables are excluded from the scope of Article 9. See § 9–109(d)(4)-(7). A buyer who takes chattel paper or promissory notes in one of these transactions-a buyer who acquires chattel paper when he buys the business from which the paper arose, for example-is not a secured party. Rather, he is just a buyer. As such, section 9–317 applies. On the other hand, where the sale of chattel paper is an Article 9 transaction, 9–317 does not apply; "rather, priority rules generally applicable to competing security interests apply." § 9–317, Official Comment 6 discusses the distinction in detail.

Note that this subsection applies to tangible types of collateral; for intangible collateral, see subpart (d).

§ 9–317(d) Comments.

Subpart (d) states essentially the same rule as (b), except that (d) deals with *intangible* types of collateral (i.e., collateral incapable of being physically possessed). Therefore, this subpart eliminates the requirement of delivery.

Again, this subpart does not apply to secured parties. So if you are dealing with a buyer of chattel paper or promissory notes, you need to determine if the buyer purchased the collateral in an Article 9 transaction. If the answer is yes, the buyer is a secured party, and 9–317 does not apply. If the answer is no-if the purchase is one of a type described in 9–109(d)(4)-(7)-then the buyer is not a secured party, and 9–317 *does* apply.

§ 9–317(e) Comments.

This subpart gives the secured party a 20–day "grace period" in which to file a financing statement if the secured party holds a purchase-money security interest in the collateral. Therefore, the secured party can either file before, or within 20 days after, the debtor receives delivery of the collateral, and the effectiveness of the filing "relates back" to the date of delivery. This can act as an exception to subpart (b). For example, on Day 1, the debtor takes delivery of goods that are subject to a purchase-money security interest. On Day 5, while the security interest is still unperfected, the debtor sells the goods to a buyer. On Day 19, the secured party files. As a result of the 20–day grace period, the secured party would have priority-even if the buyer had already satisfied the requirements of subpart (b).

Note, however, that subpart (e) defers to section 9–320, which applies "even if the security interest is perfected and the buyer knows of its existence"; so if you are dealing with a buyer in ordinary course of business, be sure to consult that section.

MORE ON 9–320 AND SALE OF COLLATERAL
Section 9–320 General Comments.

1) Remember, this section applies only to goods. Therefore, if you come across a hypothetical where a person is buying chattel paper (non-goods) from a dealer in chattel paper (i.e. someone who is a seller of chattel paper) this section would not apply. So, as a first step, be sure that the collateral in question is goods before applying this section.

9–320(a) Comments

1) Under section 9–320(a) a buyer in ordinary course of business takes free of a security interest, even if that security interested is perfected. Therefore, be on the lookout for scenarios that attempt to mislead you by having a perfected security interest in the goods.

2) This section only applies if the buyer is a 'buyer in ordinary course of business.' In determining whether a buyer is a buyer in ordinary course of business, you must focus on the seller and the seller's business. If a buyer buys goods from a seller who is not in the

business of selling such goods, the buyer would not qualify as a buyer in ordinary course of business. It may be helpful to consider the following examples: If the buyer buys a table from a furniture store the buyer is a buyer in ordinary course of business. However, if a buyer buys a used forklift from a furniture store the buyer is *not* a buyer in ordinary course of business even if the buyer runs a used forklift store; the furniture store does not ordinarily sell forklifts.

3) Also, note that the security interest must be created by the 'buyer's seller,' not someone else. Therefore, it is essential to determine who created the security interest before deciding whether the buyer takes free of the security interest. Section 9–320(a) will apply *only* if the security interest was created by the seller who sold him the goods.

4) In most situations, the goods in question will be inventory. If you are in the business of selling certain goods (a requirement for a "buyer in ordinary course of business"), by definition you hold those goods for sale ('inventory'). This accords with the expectations of someone with a security interest in the inventory; that party would benefit from the ultimate sale.

9–320(b) Comments

1) The section is commonly referred to as the yard sale exception. Under this section the sale *must* be a sale by one consumer to another consumer. Do not be fooled by a scenario that involves a consumer selling to a non-consumer. For example, if a consumer sold a table that was subject to a security interest at a yard sale to a representative of a used furniture store, the security interest would continue in the table.

2) A secured party with an automatically perfected purchase-money security interest can protect itself from this exception by filing a financing statement. In a sense, then, filing provides "super-perfection" as it accords more protection to the secured party than automatic perfection.

9–320(e) Comments

1) If the secured party has possession of the collateral, the buyer cannot take free of the security interest under either 9–320(a) or (b). Thus, perfection by possession sometimes provides greater protection than filing a financing statement or automatic perfection.

MORE ON 9–322 AND SP v. SP PRIORITY
§ 9–322(a)

The first thing you have to do when analyzing a secured party versus secured party priority dispute is to determine whether the situation involves two perfected security interests, one that is perfected and one that is not, or two unperfected security interests.

If only one party is perfected, look to subpart (a)(2). The rule is simple: the party who perfected has priority.

If both are unperfected, you should apply subpart (a)(3): the security interest that attached first has priority.

Subpart (a)(1), the "first to file or perfect" rule, *only* applies to two *perfected* security interests. The party with the earlier "priority date"-i.e., the secured party who filed or perfected first-has priority. When determining a secured party's priority date, be sure to look to whichever event, whether filing or perfection, happened first. Even if filing comes before the security interest attaches, the date of filing will be the priority date, assuming the secured party subsequently perfects.

Example: Suppose Bob Borrower applies to Larry Lender for a loan, offering his forklift as collateral. Larry wants time to investigate Bob's credit record. In the meantime, Larry files a financing statement covering the forklift. (Larry, of course, must have Bob's authorization to do so; *see* §§ 9–509(a), 9–502(d).) Bob is impatient, so while he is waiting for Larry, he applies to Fred Financer for a loan instead. Fred is not as diligent as Larry, and immediately makes the loan, taking all the necessary steps to obtain a perfected security interest in the forklift. If Larry now also lends to Bob, and Larry's security interest is perfected, it is Larry, not Bob, who will have priority. Even though Fred perfected first, Larry filed first.

This rule is somewhat qualified by the last phrase in subpart (a)(1): "if there is no period thereafter when there is neither filing nor perfection." By implication, if there is an intervening time when a secured party has neither filed nor perfected, that party loses his original priority date. As Official Comment 4 explains, " 'Filing' . refers to the filing of an effective financing statement." If Larry's financing statement had lapsed, for example (*see* § 9–515), and Bob filed or perfected before Larry corrected the problem, Bob would have priority.

Although this subsection states the basic rule of priority between two secured parties, it is subject to several exceptions. *See* Official Comment 2.

§ 9–322(b)

This subsection tells you how to apply the "first to file or perfect" rule when the collateral happens to be proceeds. The priority date that applies to the original collateral also applies to the proceeds of that collateral.

Suppose Larry lends $10,000 to Bob's Forklift Store, taking a security interest in all Bob's inventory. Larry files on Day 1. On Day 2, Larry sells a forklift for $4000 on unsecured credit. This account is proceeds of the original collateral, and by way of the "same office rule" (*see* § 9–315(d)(1)), Larry's security interest in the account will remain perfected. On Day 5, Larry decides he needs more cash, so he gets a second loan from Fred. Fred takes a security interest in all Larry's accounts. On Day 6, Fred perfects this security interest by filing. In the ensuing dispute over priority in the accounts, Larry will prevail. *See* Official Comment 6.

Be careful—if the security interest in proceeds is not perfected, this rule is inapplicable. Priority will instead be determined according to (a)(2) or (a)(3).

§ 9–322(c)

This subsection applies to secured parties who have priority not based on subsection (a)(1), but rather on one of the special rules for "non-filing" collateral (*e.g.*, chattel paper, instruments, and investment property). Priority under one of these rules extends to proceeds of that collateral, if the requirements of subsection (c)(2) are met. For example, a secured party obtaining priority via § 9–330 over an earlier security interest in chattel paper will also have priority in proceeds of the chattel paper, *if* (1) the security interest in proceeds is perfected; and (2) the proceeds are cash proceeds or chattel paper. In situations where the proceeds are themselves proceeds, the additional requirement of subsection (c)(2)(C) applies. *See* Official Comments 7, 8.

§ 9–322(f)

In addition to several other sections of Article 9 (*see* Official Comment 2 and subsection (g), below), other law may override the general rule of subsection (a). This subsection lists other provisions of the U.C.C. that may have this effect. For example, if a bank has a security interest in a check under § 4–210, the bank will prevail over another secured party, even if the other security interest is perfected.

MORE ON 9–334 AND FIXTURES

1. **Determining whether a fixture is involved.** State property law, not Article 9 determines whether a fixture is involved. Generally, a three-factor test is used to determine whether or not a fixture is created as a result of the attachment of personal property to a parcel of real property. The first factor is "Annexation." Annexation involves how securely the personal property is attached to the real property. The item must be

connected to the land, not just "sitting" on top. Therefore, if you can simply pick up the personal property and walk away with it, it is not a fixture. But note that permanent attachment is not a requirement. The fact that the property could be disconnected does not mean it cannot be a fixture.

The second factor is "Adaptation." Adaptation refers to the purpose of the real property involved, and how the personal property is used to facilitate the use and purpose of the real property.

The final factor, and perhaps the most important, is "Intent." In fact, the parties' intent may be proven using the first two factors. For example, a seemingly permanent annexation may indicate that the debtor intended the property to remain on the land as a fixture. Ask, "Did the debtor make any indication that the attached property would not be moved any time in the near future?" If so, then the property is likely a fixture. If not, it is still personal property and the fixture rules do not apply.

2. **The same basic priority principles apply to fixtures.** Despite the special language in the Code Sections regarding fixtures, the same priority rules and principles found throughout Article 9 are still applicable. The first party to perfect its interest (see Comment 5) in the fixture has priority over other interests. This basic rule applies unless a party obtains a purchase-money security interest in the fixture and perfects the interest within 20 days of the property obtaining fixture status. If the creditor perfects within this 20-day grace period, the purchase-money security interest prevails over all other interests. Here, one notable divergence exists in the priority rules relating to fixtures, involving construction lenders and their priority (See Note 4.)

3. **Readily removable collateral.** Another fixture-specific exception to the general priority rules exists for readily removable collateral. In some jurisdictions, if property is "readily removable" and, 1) A factory or office machine, 2) Equipment not primarily used or leased for use in the operation of the real property to which the goods are affixed, or 3) A replacement of domestic appliances that are consumer goods, a creditor may perfect their interest under Article 9 by any available method, without the necessity of a fixture filing. A creditor with an interest in readily removable collateral obtains priority over all other creditors, so long as the creditor perfects the security interest before the property is affixed to the real property. Examples of "readily removable" goods include items such as washing machines and photocopiers.

4. **Construction Lenders.** A major exception, and super-priority, that prevails over even a purchase-money security interest, is the securi-

ty interest obtained by a construction lender. When a fixture is involved, construction lenders may prevail over all other interests, so long as the property involved becomes a fixture before the construction is completed. If the property does not become a fixture before the completion of the construction, the basic rules of priority will apply.

However, exceptions to the construction lender priority may exist based on consent or a debtor's right of removal. Construction lenders may consent in writing to relinquish their security interest in the property, or to subordinate their interest to another interest. A construction lender may also agree in writing to allow the debtor to remove the fixtures from the real property. In this situation, the secured party will acquire priority over the construction lender's interest with respect to those particular fixtures.

5. **Fixture Filings vs. Perfection by "any means under Article 9".** To perfect and acquire priority in a fixture, a creditor must generally file a "fixture filing" in the county where the real property is located. The fixture filing must include the essential requirements of a financing statement, a statement that the filing must be in the real property records, a description of the real property, a description of the fixture, and the name of the owner if the debtor does not have a record interest in the real property.

In contrast, if an item is readily removable, or a creditor is a lien creditor, Article 9 permits the fixture secured party to perfect by "any means under Article 9." For example, a secured party could perfect its interest by filing a financing statement without the necessity of filing a fixture filing.

6. **Consumer Goods that become Fixtures.** Under § 9–309(1), purchase-money security interests in consumer goods are automatically perfected upon attachment. However, as the Comment #3 to the Section indicates, if a consumer good later becomes a fixture, the creditor may have to file a fixture filing to preserve the purchase-money priority in the good.

7. **Enforcement of an Interest in a Fixture.** Upon default, a secured party with a security interest in a fixture may either enforce their security interest under Article 9, or under applicable state real estate law. For example, under Article 9, the creditor may repossess the property, so long as a non-debtor owner is promptly reimbursed for any damage caused by the removal.

If applicable state real estate law allows, a secured party may join in a foreclosure action and enforce its interest through that proceeding.

Note, however, that if the creditor elects to use the state law remedy, then none of Article 9's enforcement provisions will apply.

MORE ON 9–335 AND ACCESSIONS

1. **Accessions vs. Fixtures.** Accessions are almost identical to fixtures. However, accessions result from an item's attachment (being connected) to other personal property (which Art. 9 calls the "other property"). Fixtures, on the other hand, result from an item's attachment (being connected) to real property. Accessions retain their identity despite their attachment to other personal property. This means that after attachment, it is still possible to remove the accession and have it exist independent of the other property.

2. **Priority.** (a) Attachment of Security Interest. When an accession is connected to the other goods, the combination is called the "whole" by Art. 9. Whether a security interest in the accession is transferred to the "whole" when the accession is connected to the other goods turns on the description in the security agreement that created the security interest in the accession. If the security agreement gives the secured party a security interest in things to which the accession is connected, then the security interest in the accession is transferred to the "whole".

(b) Priority Rules. Under § 9–335(c), unlike Old Article 9, accessions do not have different priority rules. Rather the Code's ordinary priority rules apply to accessions. For example, suppose Creditor–1 takes a security interest an engine that the debtor is going to put in his car. The car is already subject to the security interest of Creditor–2. If Creditor–1 has a purchase-money security interest in the engine, and perfects within 20 days of the debtor taking possession of the engine, then Creditor–1 will take priority in the engine over Creditor–2. But, in any other situation (ie—Creditor–1 did not have a purchase-money security interest; Creditor–1 did not perfect within 20 days) Creditor–2 will take priority based on the prior-perfected security interest in the whole car.

Now, suppose that after the debtor installs the engine in the car, the debtor sells the car. If Creditor–1 perfected its security interest in the engine before the sale, Creditor–1's security interest will remain effective against the purchaser of the car. But, if the buyer was a good faith purchaser for value, then the buyer will take the car free of Creditor–1's interest in the engine.

These examples illustrate that security interests in accessions are treated identically to other security interests in goods under Article 9 in terms of priority.

3. **Removal of Accessions.** Under § 9–335(f), the rule for removing accessions is almost identical to the removal rule regarding fixtures. When a creditor has a superior priority interest in accessions, upon default, they may remove their collateral/accession. Like a fixture removal, the creditor must reimburse the owner or other secured parties for any damage caused as a result of the removal.

MORE ON 9–601 AND RIGHTS ON DEFAULT

Part Six of Article 9 deals with default and the various ways in which secured parties, within certain limitations, can legally enforce security interests.

Comment to § 9–601(a) and (e)

§ 9–601(a) contains four requirements for the exercise of Article 9 remedies:

(1) Two express requirements:
   a. An event of default must have taken place.
   b. The injured party must be a Secured Party.
(2) Two "hidden" requirements:
   a. The Secured Party must proceed in Good Faith
   b. The Secured Party is bound by the unconscionability doctrine.

To determine whether a party is a Secured Party, see § 9–102(a)(72), as well as the relevant provisions of Part 2 of Article 9. To determine whether a contract (or any portion thereof) is unconscionable, see § 2–302. 2–302 is directly applicable if the secured transaction takes the form of a conditional sale, i.e., a sale of goods on credit in which the seller reserves a security interest. However, even if the secured transaction takes another form, the law relating to unconscionability may be applied because 1–103(b) makes the common law of contracts applicable to any transaction within the scope of the Uniform Commercial Code unless it is displaced.

The Concept of Default

The term "default" is not defined anywhere in Article 9 [See Comment 3 to § 9–601]. Therefore, an event of default is whatever the parties agree it is in the default clause of the security agreement. For example, failure to make timely payments, failure to maintain certain financial ratios [e.g., interest payments-to-revenue or debt-to-equity ratios], failure to insure the collateral properly, and failure to notify the secured party when certain events take place [e.g., change in business structure, name changes, moving the collateral to a different location] can all be defined as events of default. Some of these are events that may materially affect the risk of nonpayment by the debtor or the value of the collateral upon which the secured party relies. Others (e.g., failure to notify the secured party of a name change) are included as events of default in an effort to make sure that the secured party finds out about them in time to protect its interest (e.g., by filing an amendment to a financing statement, as required by 9–507(c)).

Insecurity Clauses, Good Faith, and Demand Instruments

Because no secured party can anticipate all the possible events that might affect his risk or provide a reason to foreclose on the collateral, "insecurity clauses" have become common features of security agreements. Such clauses are often included among the events of default in a default clause, but are sometimes freestanding. In either case, they are normally coupled with an acceleration clause, which permits the secured party to declare the entire balance of the relevant debt due, even if it was originally an installment obligation.

While insecurity clauses may be formulated in a variety of ways, they typically provide that the secured party may accelerate the debt and exercise Article 9 remedies when the secured party "deems itself insecure" or "has reasonable grounds for insecurity." In some cases, the express language of the clause permits the secured party to accelerate and resort to other remedies "at will." 1–309 expressly subjects the rights created by any such language to a good faith requirement. The acceleration option may only be exercised if the secured party in good faith believes that the prospect of payment or performance is impaired. This specific good faith requirement meshes with the more general obligation of good faith that 1–304 imposes on every contract or duty within the Uniform Commercial Code.

We know from § 1–201(b)(20) that good faith means "honesty in fact and the observance of reasonable commercial standards of fair dealing." Thus, good faith imposes two requirements on a secured party: (1) subjective honesty, and (2) objective commercial reasonableness [see Comment 20 to § 1–201].[1] If a secured party repossesses the

---

1. Some jurisdictions have not enacted the most recent revision of Article 1, and a few

collateral without satisfying the duty of good faith, or otherwise violates the duty of good faith in exercising its Article 9 remedies, it may be deemed to have committed a tort or a breach of contract, and/or it may lose its right to a deficiency judgment or some other remedy [See Comment 1 to § 1–304]. The statutory consequences of violation of the duty of good faith or violation of other Article 9 requirements are found in 9–625 and 9–626.

One fairly obvious way of violating the duty of good faith (and running afoul of 9–625 and 9–626) is to repossess and sell the collateral when the debtor is not in default. Many events of default (e.g., failure to pay an installment when due) are both simple and easily verifiable, and one might therefore assume that such a possibility is remote. However, the exercise of rights and remedies on the basis of an insecurity clause can occasionally create difficulties in this regard. More specifically, if a secured party accelerates and repossesses based on an insecurity clause but without sufficient factual basis, he runs the risk of a subsequent judicial determination that his decision to do so did not satisfy the "commercial reasonableness" component of the requirement of good faith. If the insecurity clause is improperly invoked, and there is no other basis for declaring the debtor in default, the exercise of remedies by the secured party is wrongful.

The foregoing unpleasant scenario can be avoided if the debtor's underlying obligation is a true demand instrument. Comment 1 to 1–309 explicitly removes such obligations from the scope of that section and the good faith requirement it contains. It is thus still possible to create "obligations whose very nature permits call at any time with or without reason." Even in the case of purported demand instruments, however, there are potential pitfalls. Occasionally, a secured party has coupled language in an agreement purporting to make a debt due "on demand" with a default clause enumerating events of default authorizing acceleration. Theoretically, the latter should be unnecessary in a true demand instrument. Such careless draftsmanship once again risks an adverse judicial construction that, notwithstanding the secured party's belief that he has created a demand instrument, he has actually created a contract under which remedies may only be exercised upon occurrence of one or more of the specified events of default.

Waiver of Default and Related Issues

A similar risk of a subsequent judicial determination of wrongful foreclosure faces a secured party who seeks to exercise his Article 9

have deliberately preserved the pre-revision Article 1 definition of good faith as "honesty in fact in the conduct or transaction concerned."

remedies after having tolerated past departures by the debtor from the strict letter of the underlying agreement. Acceptance of late payments is probably the most common example of such tolerance by a secured party. A secured party who has previously accepted late payments and then seeks to accelerate and repossess after a further instance of nonpayment may encounter at least two possible arguments by the debtor.

The first relies on the critical role that 1-303 assigns to course of dealing and course of performance in the interpretation of agreements. The secured party's acceptance of late payments under previous agreements enables the debtor to argue that a course of dealing shows that the due dates specified in the current agreement are mere targets, rather than absolutely fixed deadlines. The secured party's acceptance of late payments under the current agreement enables the debtor to argue that a course of performance establishes the same conclusion. The secured party is not without possible responses. He may argue, for example, that, under 1-303(e), the express terms of the agreement prevail over both course of dealing and course of performance. However, if the secured party loses on that issue, his exercise of Article 9 remedies is wrongful because the debtor is not in default under a proper interpretation of the relevant agreement.

The second possible debtor argument likewise focuses on the secured party's past conduct. However, instead of forming a basis for the interpretation of the agreement, the secured party's conduct is used as the basis for arguing that the agreement has been modified by conduct, that any default has been waived, or that the secured party is estopped by his conduct from relying on any default as the basis for exercising remedies. Such arguments are possible under Article 9 because 1-103(b) effectively incorporates the common law of contracts unless it is displaced. If the debtor's argument is successful, the effect is to make acceleration and repossession wrongful.

Once again, the secured party can take certain precautions to avoid such consequences. In some instances, the problem can be avoided by providing advance notice that, in the future, strict performance of the letter of the underlying agreement will be required. In effect, such notice may retract any past waiver. The most common precaution is perhaps the inclusion of a clause in the underlying loan or security agreement to the effect that tolerance of any event of default is not a waiver of any subsequent event of default.

Particularly in commercial cases, the use of such a clause minimizes the chances of success of any waiver argument. However, particularly in consumer cases, there are some instances in which courts have accepted waiver or estoppel arguments notwithstanding the presence of such clauses in the governing agreements. In Comment 3 to 9–601, the Drafters of the Code explicitly decline to resolve the resulting conflict of authority by legislation. The issue is left for further development by the courts.

The Secured Party's Options

If the express and "hidden" requirements are satisfied and the secured party has not expressly or impliedly waived its rights, then the secured party may:

(1) Pursue a non-judicial foreclosure,

(2) Reduce the claim to judgment, or

(3) Otherwise enforce the security interest by any available judicial procedure

Usually, a secured party will opt to exercise its remedy outside the judicial system if it can do so without breaching the peace, as 9–609(b) requires. Doing so has its advantages, including relatively quick resolution and reduced expense. It also has disadvantages, such as the fact that a secured party is limited to the collateral, or its value, unless it subsequently obtains and enforces a deficiency judgment. If the debtor is so uncooperative that a repossession cannot be accomplished without a breach of the peace, even a foreclosure under Article 9 might require judicial intervention, at least in the form of issuance of an appropriate writ.

If the collateral has deteriorated substantially in value, or if it is otherwise clear that pursuit of the debtor's non-exempt assets (other than the collateral) will ultimately be necessary, the secured party might seek to reduce its claim to judgment and pursue the other assets through post-judgment execution procedures. To do so, the secured party will normally need to (1) proceed to trial and judgment on its claim or, at least, obtain a summary judgment (unless it is lucky enough to obtain a default judgment), (2) obtain a writ authorizing the sheriff to seize the collateral and/or the debtor's other property, (3) give public notice of sale, (4) sell the property to the highest bidder, and (5) if the property sold is of sufficient value, give the debtor the excess of the sale price and expenses over the amount of the obligation.

The advantage of reducing the secured party's claim to judgment is that the secured party may pursue the debtor's non-exempt assets other than the collateral if the sale price of the collateral does not or would not fully satisfy the amount of the underlying debt. With respect to the property that is collateral, reducing the claim to judgment and using state levy and execution procedures to dispose of the collateral does not effect a forfeiture of the priority rights that 9–322 confers. The priority of any levy relates back to the earlier of filing or perfection, and thus is effectively subsumed under the "first to file or perfect" rule of 9–322. Additionally, the creditor is allowed to bid on the collateral at the auction [See § 9–601(f)].

While the right to purchase the collateral is also available to a secured party who, in lieu of reducing his claim to judgment, makes a collateral disposition by *public* sale under 9–610, it is not available to a secured party who makes a *private* 9–610 sale, except in the circumstances specified in 9–610(c)(2).

Comment to 9–601(c)

The secured party is not required to make an irrevocable election among the remedial alternatives available under 9–601(a). He may pursue one remedy and, if it proves unsuccessful or insufficient, pursue another. Moreover, 9–601(c) not only authorizes the sequential exercise of various remedies; it also expressly states that the secured party may exercise his remedial alternatives simultaneously.

This express authorization is subjected to two limitations by Comment 5 to 9–601. First, the secured party must act in good faith, which includes an obligation to act with commercial reasonableness. Second, the Drafters expressly defer to any non-UCC law that makes simultaneous pursuit of various remedies actionable abuse or harassment. The source of such non-UCC liability may be either a special protective statute or common law authority, including the law of torts.

MORE ON 9–607 AND WHAT SECURED PARTY CAN DO ON DEFAULT

1. **Main Issues to Keep in Mind:**
    (1) How many parties must the Secured Party deal with to enforce its Security interest?
    (2) Is there a "notification agreement"?
    (3) The five things the Secured Party can do under § 9–607(a)
    (4) Rival Interests, Cross-default and Priority
    (5) Does § 9–607(c) apply?

How a Secured Party proceeds in response to an event of default will depend on many factors. At the outset, the Secured Party will want to know how many parties it must engage in order to enforce its Security Interest.

For instance, if the Collateral is a piece of equipment used by the Debtor on its farm, and the Secured Party holds the only encumbrance on that piece of equipment, then the Secured Party will likely only have to engage the Debtor. However, if the Collateral is royalty payments made by a third-party to the Debtor, or a deposit account held by a deposit institution, then the Secured Party will likely have to engage other parties. The following example illustrates the latter more complicated type of case.

Assume Paul McCartney owns the copyright to *Let It Be* and agrees to license it to Sirius Radio for five years. Sirius, in turn, agrees to make periodic royalty payments to McCartney in exchange for its right to play the song, with the royalty amount dependent upon the number of times the song is actually played. McCartney later turns to Bank of America for a loan to finance an upcoming 18-month tour. Bank of America agrees to loan McCartney the money he needs and McCartney grants the Bank a security interest in "all Sirius Radio *Let It Be* royalty payments." Under the terms of the agreement, McCartney is to make periodic repayments on the loan. A year later, McCartney defaults on his agreement with Bank of America by missing a payment, and the Bank wants Sirius Radio to send it the royalty payments that would otherwise be due to McCartney.

§ 9–607 governs collection and enforcement by a Secured Party against the Debtor and other third parties associated with Collateral consisting of rights to payment. Such rights to payment may fall within various defined Code collateral types, including accounts (9–102(a)(2)), chattel paper (9–102(a)(11)), general intangibles (9–102(a)(42)), and instruments (9–102(a)(47)). As indicated in Comment 2 to 9–607, such rights to payment have certain advantages as collateral, including the relative ease with which they can be liquidated in favor the Secured Party and the possibility of liquidation without disruption of the Debtor's business.

§ 9–607 extends to the triangular relationship outlined above. Bank of America is the Secured Party, Paul McCartney is the Debtor, and Sirius Radio is known as an "Account Debtor." Notice that § 9–102(a)(3) tells us both who is and who is not an "Account Debtor." In the example above, Sirius Radio is an Account Debtor because it is obligated to pay royalties, an account under § 9–102(a)(2). (It is a "right to payment of a monetary obligation...(i) for property that has been or is to be...licensed....")

More mundane examples of relationships between Secured Parties, Debtors, and Account Debtors abound. For example, suppose a manufacturer of furniture sells tables and chairs to a number of retailers on 90 days open credit. If the manufacturer borrows money from Bank to finance its manufacturing operations and grants Bank a security interest in the payments due from the retailers, the Bank is the Secured Party, the manufacturer is the Debtor, and the retailers are all account debtors (because the payments due for goods sold on open credit are accounts under 9–102(a)(2)). If one of the retailers, Mom and Pop's Furniture, sells tables and chairs to its customers on credit and requires each of the customers to sign a conditional sale contract obligating the customer to pay in installments over time and reserving a security interest in the tables and chairs until the full balance is paid, each conditional sale contract is a piece of chattel paper. If Mom and Pop's Furniture finances its retail operations by borrowing from Commercial Finance Company and giving Commercial Finance Company a security interest in all the chattel paper generated by sales to Mom and Pop's customers, Commercial Finance Company is the Secured Party, Mom and Pop's Furniture is the Debtor, and Mom and Pop's individual customers are all Account Debtors.[2]

Often, the security agreement between the Secured Party and the Debtor contains a provision that requires the Account Debtor to forward payments directly to the Secured Party from the very beginning. This is typically known as a "notification agreement."

In the hypothetical outlined above, McCartney and Bank of America might have agreed from the start that Sirius would forward any royalty payments directly to Bank of America in addition to (or in lieu of) periodic repayments by McCartney to the Bank. If the agreement between the Secured Party and the Debtor is of this form, then there is very little left for § 9–607 to do. Absent this kind of advance express agreement, § 9–607 provides a mechanism by which the Secured Party can exercise its right under the Security Agreement by collecting this type of collateral once the Debtor has defaulted.

---

2. If the agreement between Mom and Pop's Furniture and its customers took a different form, the situation might be a little more complicated. If for example, Mom and Pop's had each customer sign a negotiable promissory note providing for installment payments as well as an accompanying security agreement reserving a security interest in the tables and chairs, each note and security agreement collectively constitutes chattel paper, but the customers are technically not Account Debtors under 9–102(a)(3) because the notes are negotiable instruments. This would not preclude direct collection of the notes by Commercial Finance company under 9–607, as 9–607 authorizes collection from "other person(s) obligated on collateral." However, certain provisions concerning, e.g., the defenses of account debtors (9–404) and the notification procedure for collection from account debtors (9–406) will not apply, and the questions those provisions answer for account debtors in the strict sense will generally be answered by Article 3. See Comment 5.h. to 9–102.

Even if a "notification agreement" does not exist, but default has occurred, § 9–607(a) allows the Secured Party to:

(1) Require an Account Debtor (or other person obligated on a right of payment) to make payments directly to the Secured Party,

(2) Take any proceeds of collections on the right to payment (see § 9–315) that would otherwise belong to the Debtor,

(3) Step into the Debtor's shoes and exercise any of his rights vis-à-vis the Account Debtor (or other person obligated to make payment),

(4) Take enough money from the Debtor's Deposit Account [see § 9–102(a)(29)] to satisfy the payment obligation, if the Secured Party holds a Security Interest in the Deposit Account perfected by control pursuant to § 9–104(a)(1),

(5) Instruct the bank where the Debtor maintains a Deposit Account to pay the balance of the Deposit Account, if the Secured Party holds a Security Interest perfected by control pursuant to § 9–104(a)(2) or (3).

As a Secured Party assesses what course of action to take, it may want to know what effect his actions will have on any relationships between the Debtor and other Secured Parties. For example, will his declaration of an event of default trigger a cross-default clause in an agreement between the Debtor and another Secured Party? McCartney, for example, may have made a previous (or subsequent) assignment or encumbrance of the Sirius *Let it Be* royalty payments in favor of another secured party. If the rival secured party has a well-drafted security agreement, McCartney's default to Bank of America will also be a default under the rival secured party's agreement, entitling the rival secured party to resort to 9–607. If so, who will have priority?

The answer may well turn on the order of filing or perfection under 9–322.[3] Questions of priority may undoubtedly require additional questions about the type of collateral involved. For example, if payments on the collateral have found their way to a Deposit Account and the Secured Party is not the bank where the Deposit Account is maintained, then the Secured Party will want to know if the bank at which the

---

3. The question of perfection might, in this somewhat unusual case, turn out to be a little more complicated than first appears. In the usual accounts receivable financing arrangement, one perfects a security interest in accounts by filing. See 9–310. Priority would thus normally be determined under 9–322 by the order of filing. However, if one makes the plausible assumption that McCartney has licensed a lot of songs and generated a lot of rights to royalty payments, it is conceivable that Bank of America could argue entitlement to automatic perfection under 9–309(2) ("an assignment of accounts...which does not... transfer a significant part of the assignor's outstanding accounts....")

account is maintained has a Security Interest in the Deposit Account [See § 9–327(3)] or a right of set-off [See 9–340]. For example, suppose Bank of America perfected its security interest in the Sirius Let It Be royalty payments by filing but required McCartney to segregate any payments received from Sirius in a dedicated proceeds account maintained by McCartney at Chase Bank. Once the payments from Sirius were received by McCartney and deposited in the Chase account, Bank of America's security interest would persist in the deposit account as proceeds under 9–315(a)(2) and would remain perfected automatically under 9–315(d)(2). However, if Chase Bank has loaned McCartney money secured by the Deposit Account, it is perfected by control under 9–104(a)(1) and prior to Bank of America under 9–327(1). Thus, 9–607 is primarily directed to the relationship between the Debtor, the Secured Party, and the Account Debtor(s) (or other persons obligated to make payment). It does not comprehensively resolve questions of priority with respect to the collateral or its proceeds.

A Secured Party may or may not have a right of recourse against the Debtor beyond the value of the collateral. § 9–607(c) requires a Secured Party to proceed in a "commercially reasonable manner," but only when Secured Party has recourse [See Comment 9 to § 9–607]. In the original example set forth above, McCartney borrowed money, promised to repay it (presumably with interest) over time, and granted a security interest in the royalty payments to secure that payment obligation. If he defaults, and if Bank of America successfully collects all the Sirius royalty payments due, Bank of America can pursue McCartney for a deficiency if those royalty payments ultimately prove insufficient to retire McCartney's loan balance. See 9–608(a)(4). If such recourse against McCartney is available, then 9–607(c) imposes a duty on Bank of America to act in a commercially reasonable fashion when exercising its rights of direct collection under 9–607(a).

If, for example, Sirius disputes the amount of royalties due or argues that it has a defense because of McCartney's unlawful interference with its exercise of the license, Bank of America may, in the course of 9–607(a) collection, compromise the claim. See Comment 9 to 9–607. But Bank of America must be commercially reasonable in compromising it, as the terms of the compromise will affect McCartney's deficiency liability. *Id*. Bank of America's failure to act in a commercially reasonable fashion could render it liable to McCartney under 9–625 or result in its loss of the right to a deficiency judgment under 9–626. This duty of commercial reasonableness may not be waived (9–602(3)), but the parties may agree to standards for its measurement if the standards are not manifestly unreasonable (9–603(a)).

On the other hand, at the outset, McCartney and Bank of America could have structured their transaction quite differently. They could have agreed that Bank of America would just buy the payment stream from the *Let it Be* license for a set price, with Bank of America just assuming the risk that the royalty payments might not ever rise to the level of the sale price. McCartney could use the sale proceeds to go on tour, knowing that if Bank of America ultimately lost money on the sale transaction, it was not his problem, in the sense that the Bank had no recourse against him for its loss. Under such circumstances, Bank of America's loss could not be shifted to McCartney, and there is no reason to impose a duty of commercial reasonableness on the Bank. Any folly on its part would increase its own loss, not McCartney's, and there is therefore no point in imposing a duty of commercial reasonableness.

The only complication is that a transaction may be characterized as a *sale* of rights to payment and yet give the buyer/Secured Party a right of recourse against the seller/Debtor if the rights to payment prove uncollectable in whole or in part. It is the fact of recourse, not the characterization of the transaction, that triggers the Secured Party's obligation of commercial reasonableness under 9–607(c).

Finally, keep in mind that § 9–607 does not require there be a specifically-defined event of default like the failure to make a payment when due used in the McCartney/Bank of America hypothetical. In other words, § 9–607 is available to a secured party who, in good faith [§ 1–201(b)(20)], deems itself insecure, whether insecurity is itself included as part of the definition of "default" in a default clause or whether insecurity provides a trigger for the exercise of Article 9 remedies even in the absence of a defined event of default.

2. **Related Issues.**

   a. **The Mechanics of Exercising Rights Under 9–607.**

If the obligor on a payment obligation subject to an Article 9 security interest fits within the definition of "account debtor" under 9–102(a)(3), the manner in which 9–607 collection rights may be invoked is effectively dictated by 9–406(a). That section permits an account debtor on an account, chattel paper, or a payment intangible to satisfy his payment obligation by paying the assignor (i.e., the Debtor) until receipt of an effective, authenticated notification to pay the assignee (i.e., the Secured Party). Thereafter, the account debtor may discharge his payment obligation only by paying the assignee (the Secured Party). Under 9–406(c), the account debtor is entitled, upon request, to reasonable proof of the assignment. The requisite notification of assignment may be authenticated by the assignor or assignee (i.e., the Debtor or the Secured Party).

Certain specific limitations on effectiveness of a notification are spelled out in 9–406(b). In the event the obligor on the payment obligation in question does not fit the definition of "account debtor," 9–406(a) is inapplicable. This will not necessarily preclude a secured party from direct collection under 9–607(a), but the method for engaging in direct collection is not supplied by 9–406. In many instances the governing law will be Article 3.

b. Defenses of Account Debtor or Other Obligor.

What happens if the person who owes payment claims to have a defense to the original obligation? For example, what if Bank of America notifies Sirius Radio to make the McCartney *Let It Be* royalty payments directly to the Bank, and Sirius contends that McCartney has interfered with its use of the license in ways that deprive him of the right to royalties?

Again, if the obligor qualifies as an "account debtor," Article 9 provides an answer, this time in 9–404. With some exceptions, 9–404 makes the Secured Party's rights subject to the Account Debtor's defenses against the Debtor arising out of the agreement or transaction that generated the payment obligation in the first place, as well as other claims or defenses that accrue in favor of the Account Debtor against the Debtor before receipt of the notification of assignment contemplated by 9–406. If the obligor does not fit within the technical definition of "account debtor," law other than 9–404 answers the question of what defenses he has. If, for example, chattel paper consists of a negotiable note (an "instrument" under 9–102(a)(47)) coupled with a security agreement, the maker of the note is not an account debtor. If the chattel paper is subject to a security interest, the defenses the maker may assert against the secured party are determined by Article 3.

c. Attempts to Limit Assignment.

What happens if a secured party claims a security interest in a payment obligation, but the Debtor (to whom the obligation is owed) and the Account Debtor (or other obligor) have purported to prohibit assignment of their underlying agreement (or make it a default constituting a defense) in a term of the agreement? Alternatively, what if they claim that the encumbrance in favor of the Secured Party violates some provision of law beyond their agreement? Article 9 supplies somewhat complicated answers to these questions in a patchwork of provisions, including 9–406(d)-(j) and 9–407–9–409. With some exceptions, Article 9 is unsympathetic to attempts to limit assignment or encumbrance of rights to payment

MORE ON 9–608 AND DEFAULT PROCEEDS

1. Main Issues.

Notice that § 9–607 tells us how a Secured Party may collect and enforce its rights under the Security Agreement, while § 9–608 tells us what the Secured Party can do with the proceeds. Thus, it is helpful to think of these two sections as Sonny and Cher, John and Yoko, Stockton and Malone, Kobe and Shaq, or Rice and Montana (i.e. you can't think of one without the other).[4]

Generally, § 9–608 is about relationships. A § 9–607 collection affects the relationship between a Secured Party and the Debtor as well as the relationship between the Secured Party and other Secured Parties. It may be helpful to think of § 9–608 as a Section that contains **FOUR** principal themes. First, when a § 9–607 collection results in cash proceeds, § 9–608(a)(1) provides a three-step hierarchal order of distribution that must be honored by the "triggering" Secured Party. Second, If the Collateral is subject to subordinate Security Interests, then § 9–608(a)(1)(C) and § 9–608(a)(2) govern the relationship between Secured Parties. Third, § 9–608(a)(3) governs the relationship between a Secured Party and the Debtor in the event the § 9–607 collection results in non-cash proceeds. Finally, § 9–608(a)(4) and § 9–608(b) address the issues of rights and responsibilities in the event of surplus or deficiency.

Theme #1: The Hierarchal Order of Distribution

Once a Secured Party makes a § 9–607 collection or enforcement that results in cash proceeds, § 9–608(a)(1) establishes a three-step hierarchal distribution that must be followed. First, the Secured Party may subtract reasonable collection fees and attorneys' fees. Attorneys' fees can only be subtracted (a) to the extent provided for by agreement, (b) not prohibited by law, and (c) so long as they are reasonable.[5] Second, after these expenses are subtracted, the Secured Party must subtract the value of its Security Interest (see Theme #4 below for a discussion about deficiencies). Third, any remaining cash proceeds

---

4. Of course, the example of Kobe and Shaq reminds us that even the closest of such pairings among humans may be fleeting. See, e.g., Simon and Garfunkel, Brad and Jen, Richard Burton and Liz Taylor, and the Donald and Ivana. The bond between 9–607 and 9–608 is, fortunately, more permanent.

5. Comment 10. to 9–607 holds out the possibility that "expenses of collection" might include an allocation of a portion of the Secured Party's overhead expenses, if the parties have so agreed. Whether such an agreement was permissible was not settled by previous versions of Article 9.

must be applied to satisfy subordinate Security Interests, if any, provided each junior Secured Party has made an appropriate demand on the triggering Secured Party.

Theme #2: Subordinate Security Interests

§ 9-608(a)(1)(C) and § 9-608(a)(2) set out the requirements imposed on junior Secured Parties if they wish to share in the distribution of proceeds of 9-607 collections. As an aside, notice that this Section does not expressly require the "triggering" Secured Party to notify the subordinate Security Interest holders that they may have a right to the balance of the cash proceeds. This stands in contrast to the rules governing disposition of other forms of collateral by sale under 9-610. With some exceptions, 9-611(c)(3)(B) and 9-612 require advance notice of disposition to rival secured parties who have perfected by filing. In any event, once a junior Secured Party learns that a § 9-607 collection has been or is about to be effectuated, it must notify the "triggering" Secured Party by sending it an "authenticated demand for proceeds before distribution of the proceeds is completed" [see § 9-608(a)(1)(C)]. Under § 9-608(a)(2), a Secured Party is not required to distribute any portion of the § 9-607 proceeds if it asks for, and never receives, proof of the junior Secured Party's subordinate Security Interest.

Theme #3: Non-cash Proceeds

If a § 9-607 collection yields non-cash proceeds, the "triggering" Secured Party is not obligated to to apply the non-cash proceeds to the underlying debt or pay them over to subordinate secured parties unless failing to do so would be commercially unreasonable. As clarified by Comment 4 to 9-608 and Comment 3 to 9-615, the principal effect of 9-608(a)(3) is to determine the timing of credit for non-cash proceeds and the propriety and manner of further disposition of non-cash proceeds. For example, suppose the Debtor granted the "triggering" Secured Party a Security Interest in accounts, including a specific account in the face amount of $100,000, and the § 9-607 collection resulted in that Account Debtor's transfer of an art collection ostensibly worth $150,000 to the "triggering" Secured Party. If the Secured Party nevertheless refuses to reduce the secured debt by any amount at any time, the Secured Party has presumably acted unreasonably in violation of 9-608(a)(3). But must he credit the Debtor *immediately* to avoid commercial unreasonableness? Comment 3 to 9-608 suggests the Secured Party need not immediately reduce the Debtor's obligation (or transfer any portion of the art collection to subordinate Secured Parties) if the prospect of realizing on the non-cash proceeds is uncertain. Given the uncertainties in valuing art, it would arguably be perfectly reasonable for the Secured Party to delay crediting the Debtor as a result of the art collection until it resold the art collection. Of course, the resale of the non-cash proceeds (the art collection) would itself be a disposition of collateral (presumably under 9–610 or 9–620) and would be subject to the relevant Article 9 requirements. Whether a "triggering" Secured Party's decision to apply or not apply the value of non-cash proceeds to a Debtor's obligation is commercially reasonable or unreasonable will be decided on a case-by-case basis [See Comment 4 to § 9–608]. The requirements of 9–608(a) with respect to non cash proceeds may not be waived or varied by agreement. [See 9–602(4).]

Theme #4: Rights and Responsibilities in the Event of a Deficiency or Surplus

When a Secured Party triggers a § 9–607 collection, it may wind up holding proceeds worth more or less than the balance left on the transaction that created its Security Interest. Notice that § 9–608(a)(4) uses two defined terms, Debtor [§ 9–102(a)(28)] and Obligor [§ 9–102(a)(59)]. The "Debtor" is normally the party who had sufficient rights in the collateral to grant a security interest in the collateral and who retains any residual interest in it. The "Obligor" is normally the party who owes payment of the monetary obligation. The Debtor and the Obligor need not be the same person or entity, although they normally are. In any event, a Secured Party is required to transfer any surplus from 9–607 collections back to the Debtor. If, on the other hand, the proceeds from collections on the Collateral do not fully satisfy the debt, the Obligor remains liable for the deficiency.

Four types of Collateral add a layer of complexity to the § 9–608 analysis: accounts, chattel paper, payment intangibles, and promissory notes. A borrower who owns any of these assets may use them as collateral by granting a security Interest in exchange for a loan. On the other hand, the borrower may instead sell any of these assets outright in exchange for a price . Whether the agreement between the borrower and the lender involves a security Interest in or a sale of any of these assets, the borrower/seller is a Debtor in the eyes of Article 9 [See § 9–102(a)(28)], and the sale or security interest is an Article 9 transaction [See 9–109(a)(3)]. The effect is that Article 9 attachment and perfection requirements are triggered by either form of transaction. However, the distinction between an outright sale and a loan coupled with a security interest remains important. If the agreement involves an extension of credit and a security Interest, then the § 9–608(a)(4) analysis discussed above applies. If, however, the agreement involves a sale of any of the four relevant types of Collateral, then § 9–608(b) applies. Under § 9–608(b), the Secured Party is entitled to retain any surplus and the

Obligor is not liable for any deficiency. The distinction between outright sales of, and security interests in, accounts, chattel paper, payment intangibles and promissory notes is important for other purposes as well, particularly in securitization transactions. However, the classification of any particular transaction is not settled by any specific provision of Article 9; issues of classification are left to the courts. See Comment 4 to 9–109.

2. Related Issues. Collections by Junior Secured Parties.

Notice that 9–608(a) only requires that the collecting Secured Party pay over proceeds to *subordinate* secured parties if the proceeds of collections exceed the sum of his collection expenses and secured debt. It does not expressly require payment of proceeds to a senior secured party. Indeed, Comment 5 to 9–607 confirms that a junior secured party may exercise 9–607 collection rights notwithstanding the existence of the senior security interest. But does the collecting (junior) Secured Party have priority in the proceeds over a secured party who was senior as to the original collateral? After all, if the senior secured party is diligent and demands, in advance of any collection activity, that the junior secured party refrain from collection activity and permit the senior party to collect on its collateral, the junior secured party would presumably violate the senior secured party's rights (and commit a conversion) by disregarding the demand. When, then, may a junior secured party make 9–607 collections and retain the proceeds? Comment 5 to 9–607 indicates that, in order to qualify for priority in the proceeds of collection, the junior secured party must qualify for priority as a transferee of money under 9–332(a), a holder in due course of an instrument under 3–305 and 9–331(a), or as a purchaser of an instrument under 9–330(d). The latter two provisions are particularly important in the common case of a junior secured party who receives 9–607 collections in the form of checks from account debtors. Both impose a "good faith" requirement on the collecting junior secured party, and good faith requires both honesty in fact and the observance of reasonable commercial standards of fair dealing. See 1–201(20). While the application of the standards of good faith in this context is quite fact-dependent, some guidance on the question (and the limited degree to which good faith requires inquiry or is violated by mere notice of a financing statement) is supplied by Comments 6 and 7 to 9–330 and Comment 5 to 9–331.

MORE ON 9–620 AND SECURED PARTY'S KEEPING COLLATERAL

As its title suggests, § 9–620 is a remedial statute available to a secured creditor seeking to take its collateral and apply it in satisfaction of the secured debt, subject to certain restrictions and conditions. The remedy is a statutory descendant of common law "accord and satisfaction" and is colloquially known as "strict foreclosure." It is an alternative to foreclosure by repossession and sale under 9–609—9–617. In certain types of cases, it has some advantages over disposition by public or private sale under 9–610. For example, taking the steps necessary to satisfy the commercial reasonableness requirement of 9–610(b) may add some cost to a public or private disposition under that section, and failure to take those steps and incur those costs might result in a forfeited deficiency under 9–626. If a deficiency is unlikely to be collectable anyway, it may make sense to accept the collateral in full satisfaction of the secured obligation (thereby giving up the worthless right to a deficiency claim) and save the increased costs of disposition. 9–620 has no commercial reasonableness requirement comparable to 9–610(b) or 9–607(c), although it is subject to a requirement of good faith. (See Comment 11 to 9–620.) Indeed, if the collateral is of a type that presents a particular risk of subsequent attack on grounds of commercial unreasonableness—e.g., highly specialized equipment that will be difficult to sell—it may be worth trading the prospect of a deficiency claim for insulation from subsequent attack.

Depending on the value of collateral and the agreement between debtor and secured creditor, the secured party's acceptance of the collateral may partially or completely satisfy the underlying debt. Although § 9–620 is a lengthy section, it may be helpful to think of it in the following manner:

(1) § 9–620(a) does two things: First, it lays out two requirements for either full or partial satisfaction of the underlying obligation. Second, it establishes special rules when dealing with consumer goods.

(2) § 9–620(b) tells us when a purported acceptance is ineffective.

(3) § 9–620(c) tells us what has to occur for the debtor to consent to the secured party's acceptance of the collateral.

(4) § 9–620(e) & (f) set out special requirements for disposition of the collateral by the secured party if the collateral is consumer goods.

§ 9–620(a): Conditions to Acceptance in Satisfaction

§ 9–620(a) is the starting point, whether the secured party accepts the collateral in full or partial satisfaction. By way of qualification, however, notice that § 9–620(g) provides that a secured party cannot accept collateral in *partial* satisfaction of the obligation if the transaction that led to its security interest is a consumer transaction [as defined in § 9–102(a)(26)]. In consumer cases, only acceptance in *full* satisfaction is allowed.

The First § 9–620(a) Requirement: Debtor's Consent Under § 9–620(c)

§ 9–620(a)(1) first requires the debtor's consent to the secured party's acceptance of collateral, whether the resulting satisfaction is to be full or partial. § 9–620(c) specifies the requirements for debtor consent. If the secured party purports to accept collateral in partial satisfaction of the underlying obligation, then the secured party must meet the requirements in § 9–620(c)(1) to obtain the debtor's consent. If, however, the debtor surrenders collateral in exchange for full satisfaction of the underlying obligation, then § 9–620(c)(2) specifies a second possible way to obtain the debtor's consent.

Under § 9–620(c)(1), if the secured party wishes to accept the collateral in partial satisfaction of the underlying debt, then § 9–620(c)(1) requires three things: (1) that the debtor agree to the secured party's terms of acceptance; (2) that such agreement be reflected in a record authenticated [§ 9–102(a)(7)] by the debtor; and (3) that the record in question be authenticated after default. Thus, a boilerplate consent in the original security agreement to acceptance on whatever terms the secured party later sees fit will not be recognized.

If, however, the secured party wishes to accept the collateral in full satisfaction of the secured debt, then consent can be obtained in either of two ways. First, the debtor consents if the § 9–620(c)(1) requirements (discussed immediately above) are satisfied. Alternatively, the secured creditor can obtain the debtor's "implied" consent by following the procedure set forth in 9–620(c)(2)(A)—(C). The procedure requires first, that, after the debtor's default, the secured party send the debtor a proposal for acceptance of the collateral. The proposal must provide for the secured party's acceptance of the collateral in full satisfaction of the secured obligation, and it may not contain any condition except a condition that collateral not in the possession of the secured party be preserved or maintained. Finally, the debtor must refrain from blocking the acceptance.

The debtor may effectively block the proposal for acceptance in full satisfaction by notifying the secured party of its objection in an authenticated writing. The secured party must *receive* the objection authenticated by the debtor within 20 days after the proposal of the secured party was *sent*. Thus, if the secured party sends a proposal on June 1, and the debtor sends an authentication notification of objection on June 19 that does not reach the secured party until June 23, the purported objection is untimely.

9–620 requires the secured party's proposal to be unconditional (with minor exceptions), but it says little else about the requirements for the content of the secured party's proposal for acceptance in full satisfaction. It thus appears to place few restrictions on the freedom of the parties to reach an accord and full satisfaction. Comment 11, however, contains a reminder that, like all enforcement mechanisms under Article 9, the procedure outlined in 9–620(c)(2)(A)—(C) is subject to the requirement of good faith imposed by 1–203 [now 1–304].

The obvious risk with which the Code Drafters were concerned was the risk that an opportunistic secured party might propose acceptance of collateral in full satisfaction of the secured obligation when the collateral value dramatically exceeded the amount of the secured obligation to be satisfied. Such use of 9–620 could deprive the debtor of a surplus to which he would have been entitled under 9–615(d) if disposition under 9–610 had been conducted or to which he would have been be entitled under 9–608(a)(4) if collection under 9–607 had been pursued. It could also result in the strictly foreclosing secured party's appropriation of value that might have been available for the satisfaction of subordinate secured parties.

Notice, however, that the example of bad faith the Drafters give is that of a secured party who sends a proposal to accept collateral in full satisfaction when the collateral is worth *ten times* the amount of the loan balance, hoping that an inattentive debtor will fail to reject it. The Drafters then urge the courts not to second guess the secured party's proposal merely because the value of the collateral is disputed, or even because there is a clear excess of collateral value over the balance of the secured obligation. The Drafters thus appear to be suggesting that the role of good faith should be confined to policing egregious cases of abuse. Otherwise, one principal advantage of strict foreclosure over other remedies—the freedom from the "commercial reasonableness" requirement of 9–610(b) or 9–607(c)—would be lost.

The Second § 9–620(a) Requirement: The Proposal is not Timely Rejected

§ 9–620(a)(2) gives certain parties the power to prevent the debtor and the secured party from agreeing to exchange the collateral for full or partial cancellation of the underlying obligation. Apart from the debtor and the secured party, the parties who may block a strict foreclosure include: (1) anyone entitled to receive the strict foreclosure proposal under § 9–621; and (2) any other person holding a subordinate interest in the collateral. The class of parties who may block a proposal by objection is thus potentially quite broad. Under 9–621(a), the strictly foreclosing secured party is supposed to send a notice of his proposal to anyone from whom he has received an authenticated notification of a claim of an interest in the collateral, as well as to any rival secured parties perfected (by specified deadlines) by filing or compliance with certificate of title or similar statutes. (For the consequences of the foreclosing secured party's failure to send the required notification of his proposal, see the Student Comments to 9–621). If the secured party complies with his duties under 9–621, any of the recipients of a 9–621 notification has an opportunity to object to the proposal. In addition, holders of subordinate interests in the collateral who become aware of the secured party's intention to effect a strict foreclosure have an opportunity to block it by objection, even if the secured party did not actually notify them of the proposal. A successful objection by a party entitled to make one effectively requires the secured party to resort to a disposition under other Code provisions.

Though § 9–620(a)(2) thus confers valuable powers upon individuals other than the debtor and the secured party, it also requires such individuals to reject the proposal within a specified number of days or period of time under § 9–620(d). Anyone who is sent a notification of a strict foreclosure proposal under § 9–621 must send an authenticated notification of objection to the secured party, and the secured party must receive it within 20 days after the secured party sent notice of the proposal. Notice, once again, that the 20–day period begins at the time the Secured Party *sends* notification of the proposal and is only satisfied by the Secured Party's *receipt* of notification of objection within the specified period. Subordinate interest holders or 9–621 claimants who have not been sent a notification of the proposal by the secured party may still object in an authenticated record in order to block the proposal under § 9–620(a)(2)(assuming they find out about it somehow). Objections from such interest holders must be received by the secured party within 20 days after the last notification of the proposal was sent to any other person. If the secured party failed to send the notice of proposal to anyone, then eligible interest holders are allowed to object to strict foreclosure provided any objection is received by the secured party before the debtor has consented to the plan under § 9–620(c).

§ 9–620(a) and Consumer Goods

A secured party that seeks to foreclose on consumer-goods-collateral must satisfy the same two requirements found in § 9–620(a)(1) and

(2) that any other secured party conducting a strict foreclosure must satisfy. However, § 9–620(a)(3) and (4) impose two special additional requirements pertaining to consumer-goods-collateral.

First under § 9–620(a)(3), if the collateral is consumer goods, then such goods cannot be in the debtor's possession when the debtor purports to consent under § 9–620(a)(1) and (c). Normally, this means the secured party will already have repossessed the goods.

Second, if a secured party is required to dispose of the goods under § 9–620(e), then the secured party cannot meet the § 9–620(a) requirements unless he also obtains a post-default, authenticated waiver of the debtor's right to a mandatory 9–610 disposition pursuant to 9–624(b). § 9–620(a)(4) specifically incorporates a secured party's affirmative duty to dispose of consumer goods under § 9–620(e). A secured party may accept consumer-goods-collateral in full satisfaction of the secured obligation, but only if § 9–620(e) does not require it to dispose of the collateral (or that requirement is effectively waived). § 9–620(e) requires a secured party in possession of consumer-goods-collateral to dispose of it under two circumstances. First, a secured party in possession of consumer-goods-collateral must dispose of it if the consumer debtor has paid at least 60% of the cash price in the case of a purchase-money security interest in consumer goods. Second, a secured party in possession of consumer-goods-collateral must dispose of it if the consumer debtor has paid at least 60% of the principal amount of the obligation in the case of a non-purchase-money security interest in consumer goods. Thus, if the debtor has paid the requisite amount, disposition under 9–610 and its attendant "commercial reasonableness" requirement is necessary. Presumably, this maximizes the chances that a consumer debtor who has paid enough to have some equity in the goods will not be deprived of it. If the debtor has paid less than the specified amounts (or waives 9–620(e)), acceptance of the collateral in full satisfaction (but not partial satisfaction) of the secured obligation is permitted.

If the secured party is required to dispose of the consumer-goods-collateral by § 9–620(e), then he must do so either within 90 days after taking possession of the collateral, or within any extension period agreed to by the debtor and all secondary obligors. Any extension of the 90–day period to which the debtor and all secondary obligors agree must be reflected in a record authenticated by all the parties *after* default. Thus, a boilerplate variation of the 9–620(f) time limit in the original security agreement will not be effective. Verbal agreements to an extension are likewise precluded.

Even if the secured party is required to dispose of the collateral under § 9–620(e), the debtor may nevertheless waive the requirement and thereby allow the secured party to conduct a strict foreclosure. However, 9–624(b) requires that such a waiver be reflected in an agreement authenticated after default. Neither an advance waiver in the original security agreement nor a verbal waiver is possible.

§ 9–620(b): Purported Acceptance Ineffective

To be effective, acceptance of collateral in exchange for full or partial satisfaction of the underlying obligation requires the consent of *both* the debtor and the secured party. The debtor's consent is required by 9–620(a) and (b)(2), and the manner of the debtor's consent is governed by 9–620(c), as explained above. The secured party's consent is required by 9–620(b)(1).

The secured party may consent in either of two ways. The secured party consents explicitly by authenticating a record to that effect. However, the secured party may also consent "implicitly" by sending a proper strict foreclosure proposal to the debtor. However, the Drafters, in Comment 5 to 9–620, express their disapproval of a line of authority under the previous version of Article 9 inferring a secured party's "implied" consent to strict foreclosure from mere retention of the collateral for a period of time a reviewing court found too long. A secured party who repossessed collateral and held it too long (as second-guessed by a court) before disposing of it thus ran the risk that the court would find its implied consent to a strict foreclosure and thereby wipe out any hope of a deficiency. Comment 5 expresses the Drafters' disapproval of such theories of "constructive strict foreclosure" and suggests that either explicit authenticated consent by the secured party or consent reflected by his proposal is mandatory for an effective strict foreclosure.

Summary

Think of § 9–620 as dealing with four possible combinations that involve four variables: (1) the parties agree that the secured party will accept non-consumer goods collateral in exchange for full satisfaction of the underlying obligation; (2) the parties agree that the secured party will accept non-consumer-goods collateral in exchange for partial satisfaction of the underlying obligation; (3) the parties agree that the secured party will accept consumer-goods-collateral in exchange for full satisfaction of the underlying obligation; and (4) the parties agree that the secured party will accept consumer-goods-collateral in exchange for partial satisfaction of the underlying obligation. Recall, however, that

§ 9–620(g) prohibits possibility (4) (i.e., exchange of consumer-goods-collateral for partial satisfaction of the underlying obligation). The following diagram may help bring it all together:

	Full Satisfaction	**Partial Satisfaction**
Non-consumer-goods-collateral	Step 1: § 9–620(a)(1) Step 2: § 9–620(c) (1) or (2) Step 3: no § 9–620(a)(2) or (c)(2)(C) notification received	Step 1: § 9–620(a)(1) Step 2: § 9–620(c)(1) only Step 3: no § 9–620(a)(2) notification received
Consumer-goods-collateral	Step 1: § 9–620(a)(1), but satisfy § 9–620(a)(3) Step 2: § 9–620(c)(1) or (2) Step 3: no 9–620(a)(2) or (c)(2)(C) notification received Step 4: Satisfy § 9–620(a)(4) by not having to dispose under § 9–620(e) & (f), or get debtor to waive the requirement post-default in an authenticated record	**Not permitted by § 9–620(g)**

MORE ON 9–621 DEFAULT NOTIFICATION

Introduction

Think of § 9–621 as a procedural requirement of notification imposed on a Secured Party—normally the senior Secured Party—when it agrees to accept Collateral in full or partial satisfaction of the debt (sometimes referred to as "strict foreclosure," especially in the case of acceptance in full satisfaction). § 9–621 requires the Secured Party to notify four types of claimants of its intention to accept the collateral:

(1) Claimants that make their interests in the Collateral known

(2) Secured Parties perfected by filing a Financing Statement

(3) Secured Parties perfected by compliance with § 9–311(a)

(4) Secondary Obligors, but only in the event of acceptance of the collateral in partial satisfaction of the secured obligation.

General Observations

The classes of claimants that must be sent a proposal for acceptance of collateral in full or partial satisfaction of the secured obligation are defined, in part, by the varying nature of their claims and, in part, by their varying degrees of temporal proximity to the debtor's consent to such acceptance:

First Type: Rival Claimants Who Have Made Their Interests Known.

First the Secured Party is required to notify all those rival claimants that have notified it of their interests in the Collateral at any time before the Debtor consents to the acceptance. Notice that the first class of claimants is not confined to rival *secured parties*. Anyone who claims an interest in the Collateral (e.g., an unpaid reclaiming seller under 2–507 or 2–702 or someone who claims to have bought the Collateral from the Debtor) is entitled to notification, provided he has submitted an authenticated notification of his claim to the Secured Party who seeks to accept the Collateral in full or partial satisfaction of the secured obligation. (See 9–102(a)(7) for the definition of "authenticate." Since "authentication" is something one does to a "record" (9–102(a)(69)), verbal notification of a claimed interest is not sufficient.) Notice further that the Secured Party must send a notification to the a rival claimant even if that rival claimant's authenticated notice of its interest in the Collateral reaches the Secured Party very shortly before the Debtor's consent to the acceptance. Thus, a rival claimant (secured party or otherwise) who learns of the negotiations between the Debtor and Secured Party for acceptance of the Collateral at the last minute may entitle itself to a notice of the proposal by authenticating and delivering a notice of its interest to the Secured Party.

The second and third type of claimants, specified in § 9–621(a)(2) & (3) do not have to notify the senior Secured Party of an interest in the Collateral. It is the senior Secured Party's responsibility to find and notify § 9–621(a)(2) & (3) claimants. Moreover, the claimants to whom 9–621(a)(2) and (3) require notification are confined to rival perfected secured parties. However, neither subsection is confined to *subordinate* secured parties. Any secured party, senior or subordinate, who meets the qualifications of 9–621(a)(2) or (3) must be notified.

Second Type: Secured Parties Perfected by Filing a Financing Statement.

The 1972 version of Article 9 only required the Secured Party to notify the type of claimants identified in § 9–621(a)(1), and then only if they were rival secured parties. The current version of Article 9 expands the class of secured parties entitled to notification of the proposal to accept the Collateral in full or partial satisfaction of the secured obligation. 9–621(a)(2) requires the Secured Party who proposes to accept the Collateral to send its proposal to rival secured parties who have perfected by filing. More specifically, 9–621(a)(2) creates a 10–day "look back" period. This ten-day period "looks back" from the date of the Debtor's acceptance of the proposal and requires submission of the proposal to all secured parties who were perfected by filing as of 10 days earlier. By way of illustration, if the Debtor consents to the Secured Party's acceptance of the Collateral in satisfaction of the secured obligation on April 11, the Secured Party must send the proposal to all secured parties who were perfected by filing as of April 1. The senior Secured Party is only required to send its proposal to any other Secured Parties whose Financing Statements (a) identify the Collateral, (b) were indexed under the Debtor's name, and (c) were filed in the proper office.

Third Type: Secured Parties Perfected as a Result of Complying with § 9–311(a).

Section 9–311 makes compliance with certain statutes, treaties, or regulations (most notably, certificate of title statutes) a complete substitute for filing as a method of perfecting a security interest. Filing is neither necessary nor effective to perfect a security interest to which such a statute, treaty or regulation applies, and compliance with the statute, treaty or regulation becomes the exclusive method of perfection. Under 9–621(a)(3), any secured party who has perfected by compliance with such a statute (e.g., by notation of its security interest on a motor vehicle certificate of title) must be notified of a proposal by another Secured Party to accept the Collateral in full or partial satisfaction of the latter Secured Party's debt. Section 9–621(a)(3) has a 10–day "look back" period analogous to that created by 9–621(a)(2) for secured parties who have perfected by filing. Thus, if the Debtor consents to acceptance of the Collateral in full or partial satisfaction of a secured obligation on April 11, any rival secured party perfected by compliance with 9–311(a) (e.g., by certificate of title notation) as of April 1 must be notified of the enforcing Secured Party's strict foreclosure proposal.

   a. *Opportunity for and Effect of Objection.*

If a strictly foreclosing Secured Party complies with 9–621 and sends the notifications required by 9–621 to the holders of rival interests in the Collateral, any recipient of such a notice may block the effectiveness of the proposal for acceptance of the collateral by sending a notification of objection that is received by the Secured Party within 20 days of the time the Secured Party's notification of the proposal was sent. See 9–620(a)(2)(A), (b)(2) and (d)(1). Indeed, even a rival secured party or other holder of a subordinate rival interest in the Collateral who has not been notified of the proposal by the strictly foreclosing Secured Party, but who finds out about it anyway, may block a strict foreclosure proposal by a notification of objection to the strictly foreclosing Secured Party within the relevant time limit specified in 9–620(d).

    b. *Failure to Notify a Party Covered by 9–621(a)*.

It is, of course, possible that a strictly foreclosing Secured Party might deliberately or inadvertently neglect to send a notification of its proposal to a party to whom 9–621(a) requires notice. Notice that § 9–622(b) implies that subordinate Security Interests, and other kinds of subordinate interests, will be discharged even if the senior Secured Party fails to notify any of the required § 9–621 claimants. The foreclosing Secured Party's failure to notify a 9–621(a) claimant may thus prevent that claimant from objecting and blocking the effectiveness of the acceptance of the collateral under 9–620(a) and (b)(2). If the rival claimant's interest is subordinate to that of the foreclosing Secured Party, the rival claimant's interest will nevertheless be discharged (if it is a security interest or agricultural lien) or terminated (if it is some other kind of subordinate interest). While this is true, it does not necessarily enable a strictly foreclosing Secured Party to profit from his own non-compliance. A senior Secured Party's failure to notify as required by 9–621(a) may trigger a right to damages in favor of the holder of a subordinate security interest or lien under § 9–625(b) and (c)(1). Thus, a subordinate secured party who should have been notified of the strictly foreclosing Secured Party's proposal, but was not, may later claim that, had he been notified, he could have blocked the proposal and forced a public disposition. He may then argue that the collateral value was high enough that a public disposition would have yielded a surplus for his benefit after the foreclosing Secured Party's claim was satisfied.

    c. *Senior Secured Parties*.

It is now possible to see why, normally, only a senior secured party has an incentive to resort to strict foreclosure under 9–620—9–622. If a junior secured party tries to accept collateral in satisfaction of a subordinate secured obligation, 9–621(a) will normally require that the junior secured party send a notification of his proposal to the senior secured party. The senior secured party may then easily block the proposal under 9–620(a)(2)(A) by notification of objection within the time specified by 9–620(d). If the junior secured party fails to send the required notification of the proposal to the senior secured party (deliberately or through neglect), the junior secured party gains very little. The negative implication of 9-622(b) is that a senior security interest is not discharged by the junior secured party's acceptance of the Collateral, and the senior secured party may presumably pursue the Collateral now in the hands of the junior secured party. If for some reason the Collateral can no longer be pursued (e.g., if it has depreciated or been destroyed) and the senior secured party cannot satisfy his claim otherwise, it is presumably open for him to claim damages against the junior secured party under § 9-625(b) and (c)(1) for the latter's failure to comply with Article 9.

d. *No Safe Harbor.*

Comment 2 to 9-621 points out one asymmetry between foreclosure by disposition under 9-610—9-617 and strict foreclosure under 9-620—9-622. In the case of foreclosure by disposition, 9-611(c)(3)(B) requires notification of a proposed disposition to rival secured parties perfected by filing, just as 9-621(a)(2) requires in the case of strict foreclosure. However, 9-611(d) sets out a procedure by which a party foreclosing by sale may request information from the filing office concerning secured parties perfected by filing. If the filing officer does not respond, or if he responds but errs by omission of one or more secured parties perfected by filing, the filing officer's neglect or error does not injure the foreclosing secured party, provided the latter sends a notification to all secured parties mentioned in any response by the filing officer. The foreclosing secured party, by resorting to the procedure, is deemed to have complied with 9-611(c)(3)(B) in spite of the filing officer error and the resulting literal non-compliance. There is no parallel provision excusing a strictly foreclosing secured party from literal compliance with 9-620(a)(2) because of filing officer neglect or omission. Thus, if a Secured Party who proposes to accept the Collateral in satisfaction of the secured obligation requests a UCC-1 search from the relevant filing office and receives a response omitting a rival secured party perfected by filing, the foreclosing Secured Party is not excused if he fails to send the rival secured party a notification of his proposal. While this may not prevent an effective acceptance or the discharge of the rival's security interest (if it is subordinate), it will nonetheless create potential damage exposure under 9-625(b).

Fourth Type: Secondary Obligors in the Event of Partial Satisfaction

§ 9-621(b) requires the Secured Party to send its proposal to a fourth type of claimant: Secondary Obligors [see § 9-102(a)(71)]. However, Secondary Obligors need only be notified if the Secured Party's acceptance of Collateral is in PARTIAL satisfaction of the obligation. This is in accord with common sense. An acceptance of Collateral in full satisfaction of the secured obligation creates no risk for a Secondary

Obligor. If the primary obligation is extinguished, no secondary liability is even possible. However, if the proposal is for retention of the Collateral in partial satisfaction of the secured obligation, the Secondary Obligor is potentially liable for whatever portion of the secured obligation is not discharged under 9–622(a)(1). If the foreclosing Secured Party somehow persuades the Debtor and/or primary obligor to consent to a proposal for acceptance in partial satisfaction that undervalues the Collateral and discharges too little of the secured obligation, the Secondary Obligor will be treated unfairly. It is thus only fair to provide the Secondary Obligor notice of a proposal to accept in partial satisfaction and the corresponding opportunity to block it by objection under 9–620(a)(2)(A) and (b)(2).

MORE ON 9–622 AND SECURED PARTY'S KEEPING COLLATERAL

§ 9–622 specifies the consequences of acceptance of Collateral in full or partial satisfaction of the obligation it secures. § 9–622 is divided into two parts. The first part, § 9–622(a), deals with the effect of acceptance of the Collateral upon the Debtor, Secured Party, and subordinate interests, including subordinate security interests. The second part, § 9–622(b), cures any act of noncompliance with Article 9, but only to the extent the noncompliance affects subordinate Security Interests or other subordinate interests.

The first part, § 9–622(a), is divided into four subparts. In reality, however, subpart (a)(3) has two components. Thus, it may helpful to think of § 9–622(a) as specifying five effects of a Secured Party's acceptance of Collateral. The first three effects involve the Secured Party and the Debtor, while the last two involve subordinate Security Interests and other subordinate interest holders.

First, the acceptance of Collateral discharges the secured obligation to the extent consented to by the Debtor. Section 9–622(a)(1) thus reaffirms the clear implications of 9–620(a)(1) and (b). The Debtor's consent is absolutely necessary to an effective acceptance of Collateral in full or partial satisfaction. Under 9–620(c), the Debtor's consent must be express in the case of partial satisfaction and may be express or implied (under the proposal and failure to object procedure) in the case of full satisfaction. The absence of effective Debtor consent makes any purported acceptance of Collateral ineffective and thereby renders 9–622 irrelevant. The same is true of any other event (e.g., objection by a secured party or any other party entitled to object under 9–620(a)) that prevents effective acceptance under 9–620(b). See Comment 2 to 9–622. Assuming an effective acceptance, however, the secured obligation is extinguished to the extent the Debtor has consented to its discharge. In the case of acceptance in partial satisfaction of the secured obligation, the Obligor (which is most often the Debtor itself) remains liable for any deficiency, absent an agreement providing otherwise.

Second, the acceptance of Collateral constitutes a transfer of all the Debtor's rights in the Collateral prior to transfer.

Third, since the Secured Party has now acquired all the rights the Debtor had in the Collateral, acceptance of the Collateral discharges the Security Interest (or agricultural lien) of the strictly foreclosing Secured Party.

Fourth, acceptance of the Collateral by the Secured Party constitutes a discharge of any subordinate Security Interests or other subordinate liens.

Fifth, the Secured Party's acceptance constitutes a termination of any other subordinate interests.

The second part of the Section, § 9–622(b), deems any subordinate Security Interest or other interest discharged or terminated in spite of any noncompliance with Article 9 on the part of the strictly foreclosing Secured Party. Notice that § 9–622 is only concerned with *subordinate* interests. The clear negative implication is that, if a senior secured party was entitled to notification under 9–621(a)(2) or (3) but the foreclosing Secured Party failed to send a notice of the proposal to him, the senior secured party's security interest is not discharged. This is one way in which noncompliance will continue to affect the Debtor–Secured Party relationship or the relationship among secured parties.

In addition, even if a strict foreclosure that fails to comply with Article 9 nonetheless discharges subordinate interests, the foreclosing Secured Party is not immunized from all liability. If a foreclosing Secured Party's failure to send a required notification or other non-compliance with Article 9 causes loss to the holder of a subordinate security interest or some other type of subordinate interest, the holder may have a damage action against the foreclosing Secured Party under 9–625(b).

MORE ON CONSIGNMENTS

1. **Policy Behind Article 9's Inclusion of Consignments.** Section 9–102(a)(20) expressly includes consignments within the scope of Article 9. A consignment involves the transfer of possession of a good to a merchant so the merchant may sell the good. At common law, there is no requirement that merchants file notice regarding their relationship

with the goods sold. This creates the same ostensible ownership and creditor reliance issues present in the non-possessory security interests in personal property that Article 9 was created to address. The consignee's creditors may unknowingly extend credit based on the consignee's possession of goods that he/she does not actually own. As a result, Article 9 now expressly includes certain consignment transactions within its scope, thus requiring the usual steps for perfection of a security interest.

However, as a result of the inclusion of consignments within Article 9's scope, some consignors may be caught off guard. For example, an artist who paints, makes jewelry or Christmas decorations at home to sell, will find her arrangements with the local gallery or hobby store subject to Art. 9 if paintings, jewelry or Christmas decorations have a value of more than $1000. Should a creditor of the gallery or hobby store repossess the inventory subject to its security interest, the paintings, jewelry and Christmas decorations would be part of the creditor's collateral, and if the artist has not complied with Art. 9, the artist will not be able to reclaim her artwork from the creditor after repossession and foreclosure.

2. **What Consignment Transactions does Article 9 apply to.** Only a limited number of consignment transactions fall under the scope of Article 9. Under § 9–102(a)(20), a merchant must be involved in the transaction. For example, if your brother is having a garage sale and you give him items to sell for you, this would not be considered a consignment under Article 9 because no merchant is involved and Article 9 would not be applicable.

Next, the goods must not be consumer goods immediately before delivery. A consignment of consumer goods is not included under Article 9. Therefore, if you take your old clothes to a recycled clothing store that sells used clothing on consignment, the transaction is not subject to Article 9 because your clothes were consumer goods in your hands. The final two requirements are that the goods must have a total value of $1000 or more at the time of delivery and the transaction cannot create a security interest that secures any obligation.

3. **Purchase Money Security Treatment of Consignments—Notice Requirements.** Consignments that fall within the definition in 9–102(a)(20) are treated as purchase-money security interests in inventory under § 9–324. Therefore, the priority rules for purchase-money security interests also apply to consignments. Note, however, that because of the treatment as inventory, there are additional requirements to obtain purchase-money status. First, the perfection of the security interest must

have occurred prior to the debtor/consignee taking possession of the goods. This is more restrictive requirement than the 20-day grace period normally allowed under Article 9 to obtain purchase-money priority. Next, the secured party/consignor must send an authenticated notice to any conflicting interest holder in the goods before the debtor gets the goods. The notice must state that the party has or expects to get a purchase-money interest in the goods and describe those goods. If the consignor does not take these steps, the consignor will not have a purchase-money priority as to the goods, and the general priority rules will apply.

4. **True Consignments.** A consignment whether "true" or otherwise is subject to Art. 9 if it falls within the definition of consignments in section 9-102(a)(20). Part 6 of Article 9 does not apply to a true consignment.

MORE ON LEASES

Article 9 applies to a lease that is a disguised sale. Generally, for both a debtor and a creditor, there are advantages to structuring a transaction as a lease (e.g. special tax treatment). But the downside of this arrangement is that the debtor ends up paying a lot of money under the lease with nothing to show for it (he hasn't built up any equity). The best of both worlds would be to lease the product and receive the tax breaks and other benefits, but have a credit arrangement where you get to keep the product at the end of the term.

The danger arises in the situation where you call something a lease and treat it as such, but in reality it is a secured transaction. If the lessor has not taken the necessary steps to perfect his security interest under Article 9, he will end up being unperfected and lose to other creditors.

In a bankruptcy situation, where a lease has been determined to be a secured transaction, a lessor will lose out to the bankruptcy trustee if he has not complied with Article 9, because he is now an unperfected secured critor and so an unsecured creditor section 544(a).

This is why it's essential that we are able to distinguish between a true lease and a disguised secured transaction.

Article 9 cares about transactions that, in substance, create a security interest. If Article 9 cares about the transaction, then the parties MUST go through the steps to create and protect their security interest. The key here is that we're looking to the substance of the transaction rather than the form. It does not matter if the transaction is called a lease, or even looks like a lease, if the transaction functions as a secured transaction, then the "lessor" must comply with the requirements set forth by Article 9 to secure his interest.

A true lease presumes that the lessor gets something back of value at the end of the lease term. If there is nothing of value to return to the lessor, then the lessee has consumed the product, which is equivalent to the lessee having bought the product. The transaction cannot be a lease, it must be classified as a secured transaction.

The simplest way in distinguishing between a true lease and a disguised secured transaction is to remember the predicate inquiry found in 1–203. The key to analyzing a lease is to ask whether the obligation to pay rent is for the entire term of the lease, whether the lessee has no right to terminate the lease prior to the expiration of the term.

The next step is to compare the term of the lease with the economic life of the product leased. When you lease something and the term is greater than or equal to the useful life of that product, there is nothing of value to return to the lessor at the end of the term. If the term exceeds the useful life, this is a secured transaction and the lessor must comply with Article 9.

We tend to think of nominal consideration as a small or little amount, but this is not the appropriate test. The UCC sets the test in determining if consideration is nominal or not based on the reasonably predictable fair market value. Nominal consideration is in effect no consideration, depending on the facts of the case.

For example, assume you have a 5–year lease with an option to buy Leased Good for $10,000 at the end of the lease term. To determine whether or not $10,000 is nominal consideration, we have to look to the reasonably predictable fair market value of the Leased Good in Year 5. If the fair market value of Leased Good in Year 5 is projected to be $1,000,000, then $10,000 is surely nominal consideration. Note that we are not concerned with what the actual fair market value of Leased Good is in Year 5, only the projected fair market value of Leased Good in Year 5 as determined at the beginning of the lease.

The code also only requires some reasonable basis for this projection. For example, if, in the lessor's experience, the Leased Good is worth only 25% of its original cost in Year 5, an option price equal to 25% of the original cost is not nominal, regardless of the actual market value of the Leased Good when Year 5 arrives. If the option price is challenged as nominal, you need only articulate this basis and your failure to comply with Article 9 will not be a problem.

If no consideration is required or the consideration to be paid is determined to be nominal, then essentially the transaction was a disguised sale and the purchase price of the product is paid during the term of the lease.

Another point in determining nominal consideration is the cost of compliance. If the cost of complying with the lease at the end of the term exceeds the cost of any option to buy or to renew the lease, the option price will be deemed nominal consideration.

Assume that your lease agreement includes an option to buy Leased Good for $1,000 at the end of the lease term and but if you choose not to exercise this option, you are required to return Leased Good to lessor. The cost of complying with this requirement is $5,000, which includes such things as packaging, shipping, and handling. Even if $1,000 is not determined to be nominal consideration using the reasonably predictable fair market value test, it will be deemed nominal consideration because it will cost you more to comply with the lease agreement than it will to exercise the option. Therefore, the lessor has insured that you will exercise the option rather than send the Leased Good back.

The mere fact that at some point the lessee has is an option to purchase (or to renew the lease) the good for nominal consideration does not transform the lease into a secured transaction. A secured transaction is created only when the nominal consideration option necessarily arises at the end of the current term of the lease.

Assume you have a 3-year lease on a snow cone machine. The agreement provides that at the end of the 3-year term, you have the option to buy the snow cone machine for fair market value or you can renew the lease for 3 years. If you choose to renew, you can buy the snow cone machine at the end of the second term for $1. Assuming the machine has utility beyond the second term, $1 would presumably be nominal consideration. The existence of the $1 option does not automatically transform the lease into a secured transaction. Only when we are in the term at the end of which the $1 option arises has the lease become a secured transaction.

Always keep in mind that above all else, whether a transaction is a lease or a security interest is determined by the facts of the case. Despite all of the factors provided in 1-203, the code ultimately establishes a totality of the circumstances test.

MORE ON SALES OF RECEIVABLES

Perhaps one of the simplest things to overlook when dealing with specific types of problems (such as those dealing with the sale of receivables) is the overall scheme and structure of analyzing Article 9 Problems. Because these problems range from very simple to very complex, a step-by-step analysis can be helpful to provide a basic structure to "ferret out" and organize the necessary pieces of information to reach the answer. For example, one way of organizing analyses and answers to Article 9 problems is to answer the following questions:

(1) Is it a secured transaction?

(2) What type of collateral is involved?

(3) Has the security interest attached?

(4) Has the security interest been perfected?

(5) If more than one person has a security interest in the property, who has priority?

Is it a secured transaction?

Section 9–109(a)(3) provides that the general scope of Article 9 includes transactions for "a sale of accounts, chattel paper, payment intangibles, or promissory notes." We must determine whether a security interest has been created. Section 1–201(a)(37), which provides the definition for "security interest," "includes any interest of ... a buyer of accounts, chattel paper, a payment intangible, or a promissory note in a transaction that is subject to Article 9." Thus, Article 9 covers *sales* of accounts, chattel paper, promissory notes, or payment intangibles, and the secured party must perfect his security interest in those transactions.

What type of collateral is involved? Is it a receivable?

The provisions of Article 9 governing the sale of receivables come into play when dealing with sales of accounts, chattel paper, payment intangibles, and promissory notes. (see 9–109). Each of these terms is a "term of art" and is defined by the UCC.

According to 9–102(a)(2), "account" ... "means a right to payment of a monetary obligation, whether or not earned by performance...." The definition of account then lists eight specific categories of accounts, including monetary obligations "for property that has been or is to be sold, leased, licensed, assigned, or otherwise disposed of"; "for services to be rendered"; and monetary obligations arising from the "use of a credit card."

"Chattel paper," as defined by 9–102(a)(11) "means a record or records that evidence both a monetary obligation and a security interest in specific goods. ... It does not include records that evidence a right to payment arising out of the use of a credit card." A common example of chattel paper would be a promissory note coupled with a security interest in specific property. Chattel paper must include both the monetary obligation *and* a security interest, and multiple documents can be read together to create chattel paper within the meaning of Article 9.

9–102(a)(61) defines "payment intangible" as "a general intangible under which the account debtor's principal obligation is a monetary obligation." A common example of a payment intangible is a participation agreement.

" 'Promissory note' means an instrument that evidences a promise to pay a monetary obligation, does not evidence an order to pay, and does not contain an acknowledgement by a bank that the bank has received for deposit a sum of money or funds." 9–102(a)(65). An "instrument" means a negotiable instrument or any other writing that evidences a right to payment of a monetary obligation, is not itself a security interest or lease, and is of a type that in ordinary course of business is transferred by delivery with any necessary indorsement or assignment." 9–102(a)(47).

Has the security interest been perfected?

Perfection under Article 9 protects the secured party's interest against third parties or other parties who may have an interest in the collateral. Generally, to perfect a security interest, a party must file a proper financing statement in the proper filing office. However, perfection for the sale of certain receivables may be automatic. Under 9–309, independent assignments of accounts or payment intangibles, sales of payment intangibles, and sales of promissory notes will be automatically perfected when they attach. However, *there is no automatic perfection for the sale of chattel paper.* Also, automatic perfection for the assignment of accounts is limited in application.

When perfection is not automatic, we start by looking at 9–312(b), which provides that a security interest instruments may be perfected by filing. Next, we look to 9–301 to begin our analysis. 9–301(1) provides that except as otherwise provided, the debtor's location governs perfection, the effect of perfection, and priority of security interests in collateral. A debtor, under Section 9–102(a)(28)(B), includes a "seller of accounts, chattel paper, payment intangibles, or promissory notes." Thus, the location of the debtor/seller of receivables governs perfection, the effect of perfection, and the priority of security interests created in the receivables because the receivables are the collateral.

Section 9–307 provides a guide for determining the location of a debtor. This section provides that individual debtors are located in the "individual's principle residence" (9–307(b)(1)), whereas debtors that are organizations (see definition of organization in 9–102) that have only one place of business will be located in that jurisdiction (9–307(b)(2)), and organizational debtors with more than one place of business will be located at their chief executive office (9–307(b)(3)). Once we have determined the location of debtor, we know which state's UCC applies. For example, if the debtor is a registered organization incorporated in Michigan, then Michigan UCC 9–301 would apply to the transaction. Further, once the security interest has been perfected under the appropriate law, then perfection will be continuous without a lapse in perfection according to 9–308(c).

Who has priority?

If more than one secured party has a perfected security interest in the collateral, the next step will be determining who has priority to see who will "win." According to 9–322(a)(1), conflicting perfected security interest rank according to the first to file *OR* the first to perfect.

Other Noteworthy Provisions

Under 9–318(a), the debtor will not retain a security interest in accounts that it has sold. BUT, under 9–318(b), for purposes of determining the rights of creditors, a debtor that has sold an account or chattel paper, while the buyer's security interest is unperfected, the debtor is deemed to have rights and title to the account or chattel paper identical to those the debtor sold.

Unit 6

BANKRUPTCY CODE

CHAPTER 3—CASE ADMINISTRATION

SUBCHAPTER IV—ADMINISTRATIVE POWERS

Sec.
361. Adequate Protection
362. Automatic Stay
363. Use, Sale, or Lease of Property
364. Obtaining Credit

CHAPTER 5—CREDITORS, THE DEBTOR, AND THE ESTATE

SUBCHAPTER I—CREDITORS AND CLAIMS

506. Determination of Secured Status

SUBCHAPTER II—DEBTOR'S DUTIES AND BENEFITS

522. Exemptions
524. Effect of Discharge

SUBCHAPTER III—THE ESTATE

544. Trustee as Lien Creditor and as Successor to Certain Creditors and Purchasers
547. Preferences
550. Fraudulent Transfers and Obligations
552. Postpetition Effect of Security Interest

CHAPTER 7—LIQUIDATION

SUBCHAPTER II—COLLECTION, LIQUIDATION, AND DISTRIBUTION OF THE ESTATE

722. Redemption

CHAPTER 13—ADJUSTMENT OF DEBTS OF AN INDIVIDUAL WITH REGULAR INCOME

SUBCHAPTER II—THE PLAN

1325. Confirmation of Plan

SUBCHAPTER IV—ADMINISTRATIVE POWERS

§ 361. Adequate protection

When adequate protection is required under section 362, 363, or 364 of this title of an interest of an entity in property, such adequate protection may be provided by—

    (1) requiring the trustee to make a cash payment or periodic cash payments to such entity, to the extent that the stay under section 362 of this title, use, sale, or lease under section 363 of this title, or any grant of a lien under section 364 of this title results in a decrease in the value of such entity's interest in such property;

    (2) providing to such entity an additional or replacement lien to the extent that such stay, use, sale, lease, or grant results in a decrease in the value of such entity's interest in such property; or

    (3) granting such other relief, other than entitling such entity to compensation allowable under section 503(b)(1) of this title as an administrative expense, as will result in the realization by such entity of the indubitable equivalent of such entity's interest in such property.

UNOFFICIAL COMMENTS

When you think "adequate protection", think secured parties and their property. More specifically, think a secured party and its collateral that secures its right to payment by the debtor. "Adequate protection" is about recognition and preservation of a secured party's collateral value. That is what the oblique references to "interest of an entity in property" mean.

Section 361 gives three examples of what "may be" "adequate protection" of such rights in collateral. The third such example, "indubitable equivalent", is obviously the most comprehensive (and the most likely to be involved in a law school exam question).

§ 362. Automatic stay

    (a) Except as provided in subsection (b) of this section, a [bankruptcy] petition filed * * * operates as a stay, applicable to all entities of—

    (1) the commencement or continuation, including the issuance or employment of process, of a judicial, administrative, or other action or proceeding against the debtor that was or could have been commenced before the commencement of the case under this title, or to recover a claim against the debtor that arose before the commencement of the case under this title;

(2) the enforcement, against the debtor or against property of the estate, of a judgment obtained before the commencement of the case under this title;

(3) any act to obtain possession of property of the estate or of property from the estate or to exercise control over property of the estate;

(4) any act to create, perfect, or enforce any lien against property of the estate;

(5) any act to create, perfect, or enforce against property of the debtor any lien to the extent that such lien secures a claim that arose before the commencement of the case under this title;

(6) any act to collect, assess, or recover a claim against the debtor that arose before the commencement of the case under this title;

(7) the setoff of any debt owing to the debtor that arose before the commencement of the case under this title against any claim against the debtor; and

* * *

(c) Except as provided in subsections (d), (e), (f), and (h) of this section—

(1) the stay of an act against property of the estate under subsection (a) of this section continues until such property is no longer property of the estate;

(2) the stay of any other act under subsection (a) of this section continues until the earliest of—

(A) the time the case is closed;

(B) the time the case is dismissed; or

(C) if the case is a case under chapter 7 of this title concerning an individual or a case under chapter 9, 11, 12, or 13 of this title, the time a discharge is granted or denied;

* * *

(d) On request of a party in interest and after notice and a hearing, the court shall grant relief from the stay provided under subsection (a) of this section, such as by terminating, annulling, modifying, or conditioning such stay—

(1) for cause, including the lack of adequate protection of an interest in property of such party in interest;

(2) with respect to a stay of an act against property under subsection (a) of this section, if—

(A) the debtor does not have an equity in such property; and

(B) such property is not necessary to an effective reorganization;

* * *

(g) In any hearing under subsection (d) or (e) of this section concerning relief from the stay of any act under subsection (a) of this section—

(1) the party requesting such relief has the burden of proof on the issue of the debtor's equity in property; and

(2) the party opposing such relief has the burden of proof on all other issues.

* * *

UNOFFICIAL COMMENTS

Subsection (a) answers the questions (1) when does the automatic stay become effective and (2) what is covered by the automatic stay. The best short answer I have heard to the second question was the statement by a creditor client: "What you are telling me is that anything that might be helpful in collecting from the debtor is covered by that stay."

Subsection (c) answers the question of when does the automatic stay end. In a business chapter 11 case, it may be years before any of the section 362(c) events that end the automatic stay occurs. Accordingly, it can be important—especially in such chapter 11 cases, to answer the question of what can a creditor do to obtain relief from the stay.

And subsection (d) answers that important question of what a creditor can do to obtain relief from the automatic stay. And, in using section 362(d) it is important that you understand that

— the word "request" in the Code is a motion under the Bankruptcy Rules;

— section 362(g) fixes the burden of proof in section 362(d) litigation;

— "cause" in section 362(d)(1) encompasses more than simply a lack of adequate protection of an interest in property and that "cause" is

— the only statutory basis for a holder of an unsecured claim to seek relief from the stay;

— relief from stay is often different from termination of the automatic stay.

§ 363. Use, sale, or lease of property

(a) In this section, "cash collateral" means cash, negotiable instruments, documents of title, securities, deposit accounts, or other cash equivalents whenever acquired in which the estate and an entity other than the estate have an interest and includes the proceeds, products, offspring, rents, or profits of property and the fees, charges, accounts or other payments for the use or occupancy of rooms and other public facilities in hotels, motels, or other lodging properties subject to a security interest as provided in section 552(b) of this title, whether existing before or after the commencement of a case under this title.

(b)(1) The trustee, after notice and a hearing, may use, sell, or lease, other than in the ordinary course of business, property of the estate, * * *

(c)(1) If the business of the debtor is authorized to be operated under section 721, 1108, 1203, 1204, or 1304 of this title and unless the court orders otherwise, the trustee may enter into transactions, including the sale or lease of property of the estate, in the ordinary course of business, without notice or a hearing, and may use property of the estate in the ordinary course of business without notice or a hearing.

(2) The trustee may not use, sell, or lease cash collateral under paragraph (1) of this subsection unless—

(A) each entity that has an interest in such cash collateral consents; or

(B) the court, after notice and a hearing, authorizes such use, sale, or lease in accordance with the provisions of this section. * * *

(4) Except as provided in paragraph (2) of this subsection, the trustee shall segregate and account for any cash collateral in the trustee's possession, custody, or control.

(d) The trustee may use, sell, or lease property under subsection (b) or (c) of this section only—

(1) in accordance with applicable nonbankruptcy law that governs the transfer of property by a corporation or trust that is not a moneyed, business, or commercial corporation or trust; and

(2) to the extent not inconsistent with any relief granted under subsection (c), (d), (e), or (f) of section 362.

(e) Notwithstanding any other provision of this section, at any time, on request of an entity that has an interest in property used, sold, or leased, or proposed to be used, sold, or leased, by the trustee, the court, with or without a hearing, shall prohibit or condition such use, sale, or lease as is necessary to provide adequate protection of such interest. This subsection also applies to property that is subject to any unexpired lease of personal property (to the exclusion of such property being subject to an order to grant relief from the stay under section 362).

(f) The trustee may sell property under subsection (b) or (c) of this section free and clear of any interest in such property of an entity other than the estate, only if—

(1) applicable nonbankruptcy law permits sale of such property free and clear of such interest;

(2) such entity consents;

(3) such interest is a lien and the price at which such property is to be sold is greater than the aggregate value of all liens on such property;

(4) such interest is in bona fide dispute; or

(5) such entity could be compelled, in a legal or equitable proceeding, to accept a money satisfaction of such interest.

* * *

(k) At a sale under subsection (b) of this section of property that is subject to a lien that secures an allowed claim, unless the court for cause orders otherwise the holder of such claim may bid at such sale, and, if the holder of such claim purchases such property, such holder may offset such claim against the purchase price of such property.

* * *

(p) In any hearing under this section—

(1) the trustee has the burden of proof on the issue of adequate protection; and

(2) the entity asserting an interest in property has the burden of proof on the issue of the validity, priority, or extent of such interest.

UNOFFICIAL COMMENTS

Everywhere the word "trustee" appears in section 363 think "debtor in possession" because (1) almost all 363 questions arise in chapter 11 cases, and (2) almost all chapter 11 cases have a debtor in possession—not a trustee, and (3) almost all statutory powers of trustees are also statutory powers of chapter 11 debtors in possession under section 1107(a).

Subsections (b) and (c) distinguish between doing stuff that is in the "ordinary course of business" and doing stuff that is not, without defining "ordinary course." Under subsection (b) "other than in the ordinary course" requires a "hearing" but does not indicate what the court wants to hear about at that hearing.

Subsection (c) further distinguishes between property that is cash collateral and property that is not. Section 363(c)(2)(B) requires a "hearing" but does not indicate what the courts wants to hear about at that hearing.

Generally, what the court wants to hear about at a hearing involving section 363 is whether the property interests of the creditor whose collateral is being used, sold, or leased is adequately protected. Re-read section 363(e). Also re-read section 363(p) on allocation of burdens of proof at such a hearing.

[And if that creditor has an Article 9 security interest and a floating lien, you will also need to read section 552 to understand cash collateral use and adequate protection. Section 552(a) limits the effectiveness in bankruptcy of an after-acquired property clause in a pre-petition credit agreement. This has the effect of enabling the debtor in possession to use assets acquired postpetition as adequate protection for using cash collateral.]

§ 364. Obtaining credit

(a) If the trustee is authorized to operate the business of the debtor under section 721, 1108, 1203, 1204, or 1304 of this title, unless the court orders otherwise, the trustee may obtain unsecured credit and incur unsecured debt in the ordinary course of business allowable under section 503(b)(1) of this title as an administrative expense.

(b) The court, after notice and a hearing, may authorize the trustee to obtain unsecured credit or to incur unsecured debt other than under subsection (a) of this section, allowable under section 503(b)(1) of this title as an administrative expense.

(c) If the trustee is unable to obtain unsecured credit allowable under section 503(b)(1) of this title as an administrative expense, the court, after notice and a hearing, may authorize the obtaining of credit or the incurring of debt—

(1) with priority over any or all administrative expenses of the kind specified in section 503(b) or 507(b) of this title;

(2) secured by a lien on property of the estate that is not otherwise subject to a lien; or

(3) secured by a junior lien on property of the estate that is subject to a lien.

(d)(1) The court, after notice and a hearing, may authorize the obtaining of credit or the incurring of debt secured by a senior or equal lien on property of the estate that is subject to a lien only if—

(A) the trustee is unable to obtain such credit otherwise; and

(B) there is adequate protection of the interest of the holder of the lien on the property of the estate on which such senior or equal lien is proposed to be granted.

(2) In any hearing under this subsection, the trustee has the burden of proof on the issue of adequate protection.

* * *

CHAPTER 5—CREDITORS, THE DEBTOR, AND THE ESTATE

SUBCHAPTER I—CREDITORS AND CLAIMS

§ 506. Determination of secured status

(a)(1) An allowed claim of a creditor secured by a lien on property in which the estate has an interest, or that is subject to setoff under section 553 of this title, is a secured claim to the extent of the value of such creditor's interest in the estate's interest in such property, or to the extent of the amount subject to setoff, as the case may be, and is an unsecured claim to the extent that the value of such creditor's interest or the amount so subject to setoff is less than the amount of such allowed claim. Such value shall be determined in light of the purpose of the valuation and of the proposed disposition or use of such property, and in conjunction with any hearing on such disposition or use or on a plan affecting such creditor's interest.

(2) If the debtor is an individual in a case under chapter 7 or 13, such value with respect to personal property securing an allowed claim shall be determined based on the replacement value of such property as of the date of the filing of the petition without deduction for costs of sale or marketing. With respect to property acquired for personal, family, or household purposes, replacement value shall mean the price a retail merchant would charge for property of that kind considering the age and condition of the property at the time value is determined.

(b) To the extent that an allowed secured claim is secured by property the value of which, after any recovery under subsection (c) of this section, is greater than the amount of such claim, there shall be allowed to the holder of such claim, interest on such claim, and any reasonable fees, costs, or charges provided for under the agreement or State statute under which such claim arose.

(c) The trustee may recover from property securing an allowed secured claim the reasonable, necessary costs and expenses of preserving, or disposing of, such property to the extent of any benefit to the holder of such claim, including the payment of all ad valorem property taxes with respect to the property.

* * *

UNOFFICIAL COMMENTS

If you understand section 506, you will understand that a single transaction evidenced by a single set of documents can result in two separate loans. Assume, for example, that S loans D 1000 and obtains a first mortgage on Blackacre. One deal, one note, one mortgage. Nonetheless, if Blackacre is valued at 700, then S has a 700 secured claim and a 300 unsecured claim.

Look at the first sentence of section 506(a)(1) to learn that the amount of the secured claim depends not solely on the amount that is owed but also on the "value" of the collateral.

Look to the second sentence of section 506(a)(1) [and in some instances to section 506(a)(2)] to determine how to determine the value of the collateral.

You will rarely need to look to section 506(b). More often in law school than in the "real world." It applies only in the "unreal" situation in which the value of a creditor's collateral is greater than the amount of the creditor's claim, i.e., where the creditor is over-secured.

§ 522. Exemptions

* * *

(f)(1) * * * the debtor may avoid the fixing of a lien on an interest of the debtor in property to the extent that such lien impairs an exemption to which the debtor would have been entitled under subsection (b) of this section, if such lien is—

* * *

(B) a nonpossessory, nonpurchase-money security interest in any—

(i) household furnishings, household goods, wearing apparel, appliances, books, animals, crops, musical instruments, or jewelry that are held primarily for the personal, family, or household use of the debtor or a dependent of the debtor;

(ii) implements, professional books, or tools, of the trade of the debtor or the trade of a dependent of the debtor; or

(iii) professionally prescribed health aids for the debtor or a dependent of the debtor.

* * *

(4)(A) Subject to subparagraph (B), for purposes of paragraph (1)(B), the term "household goods" means—

(i) clothing;

(ii) furniture;

(iii) appliances;

(iv) 1 radio;

(v) 1 television;

(vi) 1 VCR;

(vii) linens;

(viii) china;

(ix) crockery;

(x) kitchenware;

(xi) educational materials and educational equipment primarily for the use of minor dependent children of the debtor;

(xii) medical equipment and supplies;

(xiii) furniture exclusively for the use of minor children, or elderly or disabled dependents of the debtor;

(xiv) personal effects (including the toys and hobby equipment of minor dependent children and wedding rings) of the debtor and the dependents of the debtor; and

(xv) 1 personal computer and related equipment.

(B) The term "household goods" does not include—

(i) works of art (unless by or of the debtor, or any relative of the debtor);

(ii) electronic entertainment equipment with a fair market value of more than $550 in the aggregate (except 1 television, 1 radio, and 1 VCR);

(iii) items acquired as antiques with a fair market value of more than $550 in the aggregate;

(iv) jewelry with a fair market value of more than $550 in the aggregate (except wedding rings); and

(v) a computer (except as otherwise provided for in this section), motor vehicle (including a tractor or lawn tractor), boat, or a motorized recreational device, conveyance, vehicle, watercraft, or aircraft.

* * *

§ 524. Effect of discharge

(a) A discharge in a case under this title—

(1) voids any judgment at any time obtained, to the extent that such judgment is a determination of the personal liability of the debtor with respect to any debt discharged under section 727, 944, 1141, 1228, or 1328 of this title, whether or not discharge of such debt is waived;

(2) operates as an injunction against the commencement or continuation of an action, the employment of process, or an act, to collect, recover or offset any such debt as a personal liability of the debtor, whether or not discharge of such debt is waived; and

* * *

(c) An agreement between a holder of a claim and the debtor, the consideration for which, in whole or in part, is based on a debt that is dischargeable in a case under this title is enforceable only to any extent enforceable under applicable nonbankruptcy law, whether or not discharge of such debt is waived, only if—

(1) such agreement was made before the granting of the discharge under section 727, 1141, 1228, or 1328 of this title;

(2) the debtor received the disclosures described in subsection (k) at or before the time at which the debtor signed the agreement;

(3) such agreement has been filed with the court and, if applicable, accompanied by a declaration or an affidavit of the attorney that represented the debtor during the course of negotiating an agreement under this subsection, which states that—

(A) such agreement represents a fully informed and voluntary agreement by the debtor;

(B) such agreement does not impose an undue hardship on the debtor or a dependent of the debtor; and

(C) the attorney fully advised the debtor of the legal effect and consequences of—

(i) an agreement of the kind specified in this subsection; and

(ii) any default under such an agreement;

(4) the debtor has not rescinded such agreement at any time prior to discharge or within sixty days after such agreement is filed with the court, whichever occurs later, by giving notice of rescission to the holder of such claim;

(5) the provisions of subsection (d) of this section have been complied with; and

(6)(A) in a case concerning an individual who was not represented by an attorney during the course of negotiating an agreement under this subsection, the court approves such agreement as—

(i) not imposing an undue hardship on the debtor or a dependent of the debtor; and

(ii) in the best interest of the debtor.

(B) Subparagraph (A) shall not apply to the extent that such debt is a consumer debt secured by real property.

* * *

(B) of the legal effect and consequences of—

* * *

§ 544. Trustee as lien creditor and as successor to certain creditors and purchasers

(a) The trustee shall have, as of the commencement of the case, and without regard to any knowledge of the trustee or of any creditor, the rights and powers of, or may avoid any transfer of property of the debtor or any obligation incurred by the debtor that is voidable by—

(1) a creditor that extends credit to the debtor at the time of the commencement of the case, and that obtains, at such time and with respect to such credit, a judicial lien on all property on which a creditor on a simple contract could have obtained such a judicial lien, whether or not such a creditor exists;

(2) a creditor that extends credit to the debtor at the time of the commencement of the case, and obtains, at such time and with respect to such credit, an execution against the debtor that is returned unsatisfied at such time, whether or not such a creditor exists; or

(3) a bona fide purchaser of real property, other than fixtures, from the debtor, against whom applicable law permits such transfer to be perfected, that obtains the status of a bona fide purchaser and has perfected such transfer at the time of the commencement of the case, whether or not such a purchaser exists.

(b)(1) * * *, the trustee may avoid any transfer of an interest of the debtor in property or any obligation incurred by the debtor that is voidable under applicable law by a creditor holding an unsecured claim that is allowable under section 502 of this title or that is not allowable only under section 502(e) of this title.

* * *

UNOFFICIAL COMMENTS

The words "avoidance action" are commonly used to refer to section 544 (and sections 547 and 548) although those words do not appear in the Bankruptcy Code.

Section 544 is in many ways two very different statutes. Subsection (a) is used to deal with unrecorded transfers. Subsection (b) is used to deal with transfers that are recorded before bankruptcy but are not timely recorded and to deal with fraudulent transfers.

What both subsection (a) and subsection (b) have in common is that each gives the bankruptcy trustee rights and powers that a private creditor would have under nonbankruptcy law. In using section 544(a), you will most often also be using section 9–317 of the Uniform Commercial Code. In using section 544(b), you will most often be using a state fraudulent conveyance law based on the Uniform Fraudulent Transfer Act.

Subsection (a) is commonly referred to as the "strong arm clause" although those words do not appear in the Bankruptcy Code. The most common section 544(a) fact pattern is one in which (i) the debtor grants a security interest in personal property and (ii) there is no perfection (even though there is no mention of perfection in section 544(a)).

And subsection (b) is commonly used in connection with state fraudulent conveyance law (even though the words "fraudulent conveyance" do not appear in subsection (b)). The most common section 544(b) fact pattern is one in which (i) more than two years before the bankruptcy filing (ii) there was a transfer of the debtor's property that was a fraudulent conveyance under state law and (iii) at least one of the creditors with an allowable claim is a creditor protected by that state fraudulent conveyance law. While there is no mention of fraudulent conveyances in section 544(b), "applicable law" means law other than Bankruptcy Code and so includes state fraudulent conveyance law.

§ 547. Preferences

(a) In this section—

(1) "inventory" means personal property leased or furnished, held for sale or lease, or to be furnished under a contract for service, raw materials, work in process, or materials used or consumed in a business, including farm products such as crops or livestock, held for sale or lease;

(2) "new value" means money or money's worth in goods, services, or new credit, or release by a transferee of property previously transferred to such transferee in a transaction that is neither void nor voidable by the debtor or the trustee under any applicable law, including proceeds of such property, but does not include an obligation substituted for an existing obligation;

* * *

(b) Except as provided in subsections (c) and (i) of this section, the trustee may avoid any transfer of an interest of the debtor in property—

(1) to or for the benefit of a creditor;

(2) for or on account of an antecedent debt owed by the debtor before such transfer was made;

(3) made while the debtor was insolvent;

(4) made—

(A) on or within 90 days before the date of the filing of the petition; or

(B) between ninety days and one year before the date of the filing of the petition, if such creditor at the time of such transfer was an insider; and

(5) that enables such creditor to receive more than such creditor would receive if—

(A) the case were a case under chapter 7 of this title;

(B) the transfer had not been made; and

(C) such creditor received payment of such debt to the extent provided by the provisions of this title.

(c) The trustee may not avoid under this section a transfer—

(1) to the extent that such transfer was—

(A) intended by the debtor and the creditor to or for whose benefit such transfer was made to be a contemporaneous exchange for new value given to the debtor; and

(B) in fact a substantially contemporaneous exchange;

(2) to the extent that such transfer was in payment of a debt incurred by the debtor in the ordinary course of business or financial affairs of the debtor and the transferee, and such transfer was—

(A) made in the ordinary course of business or financial affairs of the debtor and the transferee; or

(B) made according to ordinary business terms;

(3) that creates a security interest in property acquired by the debtor—

(A) to the extent such security interest secures new value that was—

(i) given at or after the signing of a security agreement that contains a description of such property as collateral;

(ii) given by or on behalf of the secured party under such agreement;

(iii) given to enable the debtor to acquire such property; and

(iv) in fact used by the debtor to acquire such property; and

(B) that is perfected on or before 30 days after the debtor receives possession of such property;

(4) to or for the benefit of a creditor, to the extent that, after such transfer, such creditor gave new value to or for the benefit of the debtor—

(A) not secured by an otherwise unavoidable security interest; and

(B) on account of which new value the debtor did not make an otherwise unavoidable transfer to or for the benefit of such creditor;

(5) that creates a perfected security interest in inventory or a receivable or the proceeds of either, except to the extent that the aggregate of all such transfers to the transferee caused a reduction, as of the date of the filing of the petition and to the prejudice of other creditors holding unsecured claims, of any amount by which the debt secured by such security interest exceeded the value of all security interests for such debt on the later of—

(A)(i) with respect to a transfer to which subsection (b)(4)(A) of this section applies, 90 days before the date of the filing of the petition; or

(ii) with respect to a transfer to which subsection (b)(4)(B) of this section applies, one year before the date of the filing of the petition; or

(B) the date on which new value was first given under the security agreement creating such security interest;

* * *

(e)(1) For the purposes of this section—

(A) a transfer of real property other than fixtures, but including the interest of a seller or purchaser under a contract for the sale of real property, is perfected when a bona fide purchaser of such property from the debtor against whom applicable law permits such transfer to be perfected cannot acquire an interest that is superior to the interest of the transferee; and

(B) a transfer of a fixture or property other than real property is perfected when a creditor on a simple contract cannot acquire a judicial lien that is superior to the interest of the transferee.

(2) For the purposes of this section, except as provided in paragraph (3) of this subsection, a transfer is made—

(A) at the time such transfer takes effect between the transferor and the transferee, if such transfer is perfected at, or within 30 days after, such time, except as provided in subsection (c)(3)(B);

(B) at the time such transfer is perfected, if such transfer is perfected after such 30 days; or

(C) immediately before the date of the filing of the petition, if such transfer is not perfected at the later of—

(i) the commencement of the case; or

(ii) 30 days after such transfer takes effect between the transferor and the transferee.

(3) For the purposes of this section, a transfer is not made until the debtor has acquired rights in the property transferred.

(f) For the purposes of this section, the debtor is presumed to have been insolvent on and during the 90 days immediately preceding the date of the filing of the petition.

(g) For the purposes of this section, the trustee has the burden of proving the avoidability of a transfer under subsection (b) of this section, and the creditor or party in interest against whom recovery or avoidance is sought has the burden of proving the nonavoidability of a transfer under subsection (c) of this section.

* * *

(i) If the trustee avoids under subsection (b) a transfer made between 90 days and 1 year before the date of the filing of the petition, by the debtor to an entity that is not an insider for the benefit of a creditor that is an insider, such transfer shall be considered to be avoided under this section only with respect to the creditor that is an insider.

UNOFFICIAL COMMENTS

This is one of the most important provisions of the Bankruptcy Code. Especially for law students. Almost certain to be covered by your exam, if your prof covered bankruptcy.

The keys to understanding section 547 are (i) understanding the relationship among the various subsections and paragraphs of section 547 and (ii) understanding the purposes of the section.

Subsection (a) is definitional. Subsection (b) sets out the elements of (your teacher might say "requirements for") a preference. Five numbered elements. Notice that the conjunction in section 547(b) is "and". Need to have all five numbered elements.

Even more important, notice that there are two other requirements in section 547(b) before you even get to the numbered elements, two other requirements in the phrase "transfer of an interest of the debtor in property." First, there must be a "transfer", as that term is defined in section 101. Second, what is being transferred to the creditor must be the debtor's stuff. If D owes C 1000, and M. D's momma, pays C, and then 89 days later D files for bankruptcy, that payment by M of M's money to C is not a preference in D's bankruptcy case.

In doing section 547(b)(3), be sure and do section 547(f). And law professors love to ask questions that test your understanding of the relationship of 547(b)(3), 547(f) and 547(b)(4). Warning: only do section 547(f)—only assume insolvency—when you are doing section 547. Note the prefatory language in section 547(f): "For purposes of this section." See also 553(c).

In the main, section 547(b) is about a creditor's doing better than other creditors with similar legal status as a result of a transfer before bankruptcy. In essence, the primary purpose of section 547(b) is a retroactive application of the bankruptcy policy of equality of distribution.

Because of section 547(e), section 547 serves a second purpose. It provides a basis for avoiding a transfer that (i) must be recorded or otherwise perfected under state law, (ii) was recorded or otherwise perfected before a bankruptcy filing but (iii) was not timely recorded or perfected.

If, for example, on January 15, D borrows 1000 from C and at the time of the loan D grants C a security interest, no basis for a preference attack—no "antecedent debt" as required by section 547(b)(2). If you have the additional facts that C did not perfect the January 15 security interest until December 7 and bankruptcy was filed on December 12, then there would be a section 547(b) preference. Because of section 547(e), the security interest which was actually transferred to C on January 15 would be treated as a December 7th transfer for purposes of applying the various requirements of section 547(b).

Always do section 547(b) before you do (c). Only if you have a preference under (b), do you look for an exception under (c).

The parts of (c) that you will most often look at are section 547(c)(2) and section 547(c)(4).

In looking at (c)(2), pay special attention to the word "or" connecting 547(c)(2)(A) with (B). In looking at (c)(4), focus on the word "after."

§ 550. Liability of transferee of avoided transfer

(a) Except as otherwise provided in this section, to the extent that a transfer is avoided under section 544, 545, 547, 548, 549, 553(b), or 724(a) of this title, the trustee may recover, for the benefit of the estate, the property transferred, or, if the court so orders, the value of such property, from—

  (1) the initial transferee of such transfer or the entity for whose benefit such transfer was made; or

  (2) any immediate or mediate transferee of such initial transferee.

(b) The trustee may not recover under section [FN1] (a)(2) of this section from—

  (1) a transferee that takes for value, including satisfaction or securing of a present or antecedent debt, in good faith, and without knowledge of the voidability of the transfer avoided; or

  (2) any immediate or mediate good faith transferee of such transferee.

(c) If a transfer made between 90 days and one year before the filing of the petition—

  (1) is avoided under section 547(b) of this title; and

  (2) was made for the benefit of a creditor that at the time of such transfer was an insider;

the trustee may not recover under subsection (a) from a transferee that is not an insider.

(d) The trustee is entitled to only a single satisfaction under subsection (a) of this section.

(e)(1) A good faith transferee from whom the trustee may recover under subsection (a) of this section has a lien on the property recovered to secure the lesser of—

  (A) the cost, to such transferee, of any improvement made after the transfer, less the amount of any profit realized by or accruing to such transferee from such property; and

  (B) any increase in the value of such property as a result of such improvement, of the property transferred.

  (2) In this subsection, "improvement" includes—

(A) physical additions or changes to the property transferred;

(B) repairs to such property;

(C) payment of any tax on such property;

(D) payment of any debt secured by a lien on such property that is superior or equal to the rights of the trustee; and

(E) preservation of such property.

(f) An action or proceeding under this section may not be commenced after the earlier of—

(1) one year after the avoidance of the transfer on account of which recovery under this section is sought; or

(2) the time the case is closed or dismissed.

§ 552. Postpetition effect of security interest

(a) Except as provided in subsection (b) of this section, property acquired by the estate or by the debtor after the commencement of the case is not subject to any lien resulting from any security agreement entered into by the debtor before the commencement of the case.

(b)(1) Except as provided in sections 363, 506(c), 522, 544, 545, 547, and 548 of this title, if the debtor and an entity entered into a security agreement before the commencement of the case and if the security interest created by such security agreement extends to property of the debtor acquired before the commencement of the case and to proceeds, products, offspring, or profits of such property, then such security interest extends to such proceeds, products, offspring, or profits acquired by the estate after the commencement of the case to the extent provided by such security agreement and by applicable nonbankruptcy law, except to any extent that the court, after notice and a hearing and based on the equities of the case, orders otherwise.

(2) Except as provided in sections 363, 506(c), 522, 544, 545, 547, and 548 of this title, and notwithstanding section 546(b) of this title, if the debtor and an entity entered into a security agreement before the commencement of the case and if the security interest created by such security agreement extends to property of the debtor acquired before the commencement of the case and to amounts paid as rents of such property or the fees, charges, accounts, or other payments for the use or occupancy of rooms and other public facilities in hotels, motels, or other lodging properties, then such security interest extends to such rents and such fees, charges, accounts, or other payments acquired by the estate after

the commencement of the case to the extent provided in such security agreement, except to any extent that the court, after notice and a hearing and based on the equities of the case, orders otherwise.

UNOFFICIAL COMMENTS

This section makes sense only if you remember the basics of Article 9 of the Uniform Commercial Code. UCC section 9–204, permits a creditor to obtain a lien that "floats"—that encumbers not only stuff that the debtor now has but also stuff that the debtor might later acquire.

Section 552 limits the effect of such a floating lien in bankruptcy. Subsection (a) establishes the general rule that a security interest obtained before bankruptcy only encumbers stuff that the debtor has rights in before it filed for bankruptcy. Subsection (b) creates an exception for proceeds and the like.

To illustrate, on January 2, D obtains financing from S and grants S a security interest in its present and future inventory. D files for bankruptcy on January 15. Under section 552(a), S's lien would not reach inventory that D acquired after January 15th. Under section 552(b), S's lien would reach the cash and accounts receivable that result from post-January 15th sales of pre-January 15th inventory.

* * *

CHAPTER 7—LIQUIDATION

SUBCHAPTER II—COLLECTION, LIQUIDATION, AND DISTRIBUTION OF THE ESTATE

§ 722. Redemption

An individual debtor may, whether or not the debtor has waived the right to redeem under this section, redeem tangible personal property intended primarily for personal, family, or household use, from a lien securing a dischargeable consumer debt, if such property is exempted under section 522 of this title or has been abandoned under section 554 of this title, by paying the holder of such lien the amount of the allowed secured claim of such holder that is secured by such lien in full at the time of redemption.

UNOFFICIAL COMMENTS

Understanding section 722 requires an understanding of the limited effect of discharge. Discharge only affects the debtor's payment obligations, only protects a debtor from being compelled to pay discharged debts. Discharge does not protect a debtor from losing property encumbered by liens.

Section 722 permits certain debtors to keep encumbered property. There are basically two different section 722 questions: (1) when does it apply? (2) what does it require?

First, section 722 only applies if

— the debtor is "an individual debtor", and

— the encumbered property is "tangible personal property", not real property such as a house, and

— the encumbered property is "intended primarily for personal, family or household use", and

— the encumbered property is "exempted under section 522" or "abandoned under section 554", and

— the secured debt is "a dischargeable consumer debt".

Second, section 722 requires a payment

— the amount of which depends not on the amount that is owed but the by the amount of the allowed secured claim, an amount determined by section 506, and

— that must be made "in full at the time of redemption".

Section 722 redemption must be compared with section 524 reaffirmation. Reaffirmation but not redemption requires (1) an agreement between the debtor and the affected creditor and (2) court approval.

Section 722 should also be read together with section 506(a)(2) which tells you how to determine the amount of the secured claim which is the amount that must be paid under section 722.

(Notice the relationship between the second sentence of section 506(a)(2) which uses the phrase "property ACQUIRED for personal, family or household purposes" and section 722 which uses the similar but not identical language "INTENDED PRIMARILY for personal, family or household purposes")

Section 9–623 of the Uniform Commercial Code, provides a right of redemption that is similar to section 722 in concept but different in terms of when it applies and what it amount it requires be paid.

* * *

CHAPTER 13—ADJUSTMENT OF DEBTS OF AN INDIVIDUAL WITH REGULAR INCOME

SUBCHAPTER II—THE PLAN

§ 1325. Confirmation of plan

(a) Except as provided in subsection (b), the court shall confirm a plan if—

* * *

(5) with respect to each allowed secured claim provided for by the plan—

(A) the holder of such claim has accepted the plan; [or]

(B)(i) the plan provides that—

(I) the holder of such claim retain the lien securing such claim until the earlier of—

(aa) the payment of the underlying debt determined under nonbankruptcy law; or

(bb) discharge under section 1328; and

(II) if the case under this chapter is dismissed or converted without completion of the plan, such lien shall also be retained by such holder to the extent recognized by applicable nonbankruptcy law;

(ii) the value, as of the effective date of the plan, of property to be distributed under the plan on account of such claim is not less than the allowed amount of such claim; and

(iii) if—

(I) property to be distributed pursuant to this subsection is in the form of periodic payments, such payments shall be <u>in equal monthly amounts;</u> and

(II) the holder of the claim is secured by personal property, the amount of such payments shall not be less than an amount sufficient to provide to the holder of such claim adequate protection during the period of the plan; or

(C) the debtor surrenders the property securing such claim to such holder;

* * *

For purposes of paragraph (5), section 506 shall not apply to a claim described in that paragraph if the creditor has a purchase-money security interest securing the debt that is the subject of the claim, the debt was incurred within the 910–day[s] (sic) preceding the date of the filing of the petition, and the collateral for that debt consists of a motor vehicle (* * *) acquired for the personal use of the debtor, or if collateral for that debt consists of any other thing of value, if the debt was incurred during the 1–year period preceding that filing;

(b)(1) If the trustee or the holder of an allowed unsecured claim objects to the confirmation of the plan, then the court may not approve the plan unless, as of the effective date of the plan—

> **(A)** the value of the property to be distributed under the plan on account of such claim is not less than the amount of such claim; or

> **(B)** the plan provides that all of the debtor's projected disposable income to be received in the applicable commitment period beginning on the date that the first payment is due under the plan will be applied to make payments to unsecured creditors under the plan.

* * *

Unit 7

FEDERAL TAX LIEN ACT (TITLE 28)

FEDERAL TAX LIEN STATUTES INTERNAL REVENUE CODE

Sec.
6321. Lien for Taxes
6322. Period of Lien
6323. Validity and Priority

§ 6321. Lien for taxes

If any person liable to pay any tax neglects or refuses to pay the same after demand, the amount (including any interest, additional amount, addition to tax, or assessable penalty, together with any costs that may accrue in addition thereto) shall be a lien in favor of the United States upon all property and rights to property, whether real or personal, belonging to such person.

§ 6322. Period of lien

Unless another date is specifically fixed by law, the lien imposed by section 6321 shall arise at the time the assessment is made and shall continue until the liability for the amount so assessed (or a judgment against the taxpayer arising out of such liability) is satisfied or becomes unenforceable by reason of lapse of time.

§ 6323. Validity and priority against certain persons

(a) Purchasers, holders of security interests, mechanic's lienors, and judgment lien creditors.—The lien imposed by section 6321 shall not be valid as against any purchaser, holder of a security interest, mechanic's lienor, or judgment lien creditor until notice thereof which meets the requirements of subsection (f) has been filed by the Secretary.
* * *

(c) Protection for certain commercial transactions financing agreements, etc.—

(1) **In general.**—To the extent provided in this subsection, even though notice of a lien imposed by section 6321 has been filed, such lien shall not be valid with respect to a security interest which came into existence after tax lien filing but which—

(A) is in qualified property covered by the terms of a written agreement entered into before tax lien filing and constituting—

(i) a commercial transactions financing agreement,

(ii) a real property construction or improvement financing agreement, or

(iii) an obligatory disbursement agreement, and

(B) is protected under local law against a judgment lien arising, as of the time of tax lien filing, out of an unsecured obligation.

(2) **Commercial transactions financing agreement.**—For purposes of this subsection—

(A) **Definition.**—The term "commercial transactions financing agreement" means an agreement (entered into by a person in the course of his trade or business)—

(i) to make loans to the taxpayer to be secured by commercial financing security acquired by the taxpayer in the ordinary course of his trade or business, or

(ii) to purchase commercial financing security (other than inventory) acquired by the taxpayer in the ordinary course of his trade or business;

but such an agreement shall be treated as coming within the term only to the extent that such loan or purchase is made before the 46th day after the date of tax lien filing or (if earlier) before the lender or purchaser had actual notice or knowledge of such tax lien filing.

(B) **Limitation on qualified property.**—The term "qualified property", when used with respect to a commercial transactions financing agreement, includes only commercial financing security acquired by the taxpayer before the 46th day after the date of tax lien filing.

(C) **Commercial financing security defined.**—The term "commercial financing security" means (i) paper of a kind ordinarily arising in commercial transactions, (ii) accounts receivable, (iii) mortgages on real property, and (iv) inventory.

(D) Purchaser treated as acquiring security interest.—A person who satisfies subparagraph (A) by reason of clause (ii) thereof shall be treated as having acquired a security interest in commercial financing security.

(3) Real property construction or improvement financing agreement.—For purposes of this subsection—

(A) Definition.—The term "real property construction or improvement financing agreement" means an agreement to make cash disbursements to finance—

(i) the construction or improvement of real property,

(ii) a contract to construct or improve real property, or

(iii) the raising or harvesting of a farm crop or the raising of livestock or other animals.

For purposes of clause (iii), the furnishing of goods and services shall be treated as the disbursement of cash.

(B) Limitation on qualified property.—The term "qualified property", when used with respect to a real property construction or improvement financing agreement, includes only—

(i) in the case of subparagraph (A)(i), the real property with respect to which the construction or improvement has been or is to be made,

(ii) in the case of subparagraph (A)(ii), the proceeds of the contract described therein, and

(iii) in the case of subparagraph (A)(iii), property subject to the lien imposed by section 6321 at the time of tax lien filing and the crop or the livestock or other animals referred to in subparagraph (A)(iii).

(4) Obligatory disbursement agreement.—For purposes of this subsection—

(A) Definition.—The term "obligatory disbursement agreement" means an agreement (entered into by a person in the course of his trade or business) to make disbursements, but such an agreement shall be treated as coming within the term only to the extent of disbursements which are required to be made by reason of the intervention of the rights of a person other than the taxpayer.

(B) Limitation on qualified property.—The term "qualified property", when used with respect to an obligatory disbursement agreement, means property subject to the lien imposed by section 6321 at the time of tax lien filing and (to the extent that the acquisition is directly traceable to the disbursements referred to in subparagraph (A)) property acquired by the taxpayer after tax lien filing.

(C) Special rules for surety agreements.—Where the obligatory disbursement agreement is an agreement ensuring the performance of a contract between the taxpayer and another person—

(i) the term "qualified property" shall be treated as also including the proceeds of the contract the performance of which was ensured, and

(ii) if the contract the performance of which was ensured was a contract to construct or improve real property, to produce goods, or to furnish services, the term "qualified property" shall be treated as also including any tangible personal property used by the taxpayer in the performance of such ensured contract.

(d) 45-day period for making disbursements.—Even though notice of a lien imposed by section 6321 has been filed, such lien shall not be valid with respect to a security interest which came into existence after tax lien filing by reason of disbursements made before the 46th day after the date of tax lien filing, or (if earlier) before the person making such disbursements had actual notice or knowledge of tax lien filing, but only if such security interest—

(1) is in property (A) subject, at the time of tax lien filing, to the lien imposed by section 6321, and (B) covered by the terms of a written agreement entered into before tax lien filing, and

(2) is protected under local law against a judgment lien arising, as of the time of tax lien filing, out of an unsecured obligation.

* * *

(f) Place for filing notice; form.—

(1) Place for filing.—The notice referred to in subsection (a) shall be filed—

(A) Under State laws.—

(i) Real property.—In the case of real property, in one office within the State (or the county, or other governmental subdivision), as designated by the laws of such State, in which the property subject to the lien is situated; and

(ii) Personal property.—In the case of personal property, whether tangible or intangible, in one office within the State (or the county, or other governmental subdivision), as designated by the laws of such State, in which the property subject to the lien is situated, except that State law merely conforming to or reenacting Federal law establishing a national filing system does not constitute a second office for filing as designated by the laws of such State; or

(B) With clerk of district court.—In the office of the clerk of the United States district court for the judicial district in which the property subject to the lien is situated, whenever the State has not by law designated one office which meets the requirements of subparagraph (A); or

(C) With Recorder of Deeds of the District of Columbia.—In the office of the Recorder of Deeds of the District of Columbia, if the property subject to the lien is situated in the District of Columbia.

(2) Situs of property subject to lien.—For purposes of paragraphs (1) and (4), property shall be deemed to be situated—

(A) Real property.—In the case of real property, at its physical location; or

(B) Personal property.—In the case of personal property, whether tangible or intangible, at the residence of the taxpayer at the time the notice of lien is filed.

For purposes of paragraph (2)(B), the residence of a corporation or partnership shall be deemed to be the place at which the principal executive office of the business is located, and the residence of a taxpayer whose residence is without the United States shall be deemed to be in the District of Columbia.

(3) Form.—The form and content of the notice referred to in subsection (a) shall be prescribed by the Secretary. Such notice shall be valid notwithstanding any other provision of law regarding the form or content of a notice of lien.

(4) Indexing required with respect to certain real property.—In the case of real property, if—

(A) under the laws of the State in which the real property is located, a deed is not valid as against a purchaser of the property who (at the time of purchase) does not have actual notice or knowledge of the existence of such deed unless the fact of filing of such deed has been entered and recorded in a public index at the place of filing in such a manner that a reasonable inspection of the index will reveal the existence of the deed, and

(B) there is maintained (at the applicable office under paragraph (1)) an adequate system for the public indexing of Federal tax liens,

then the notice of lien referred to in subsection (a) shall not be treated as meeting the filing requirements under paragraph (1) unless the fact of filing is entered and recorded in the index referred to in subparagraph (B) in such a manner that a reasonable inspection of the index will reveal the existence of the lien.

(5) National filing systems.—The filing of a notice of lien shall be governed solely by this title and shall not be subject to any other Federal law establishing a place or places for the filing of liens or encumbrances under a national filing system.

* * *

(h) Definitions.—For purposes of this section and section 6324—

(1) Security interest.—The term "security interest" means any interest in property acquired by contract for the purpose of securing payment or performance of an obligation or indemnifying against loss or liability. A security interest exists at any time (A) if, at such time, the property is in existence and the interest has become protected under local law against a subsequent judgment lien arising out of an unsecured obligation, and (B) to the extent that, at such time, the holder has parted with money or money's worth.

(2) Mechanic's lienor.—The term "mechanic's lienor" means any person who under local law has a lien on real property (or on the proceeds of a contract relating to real property) for services, labor, or materials furnished in connection with the construction or improvement of such property. For purposes of the preceding sentence, a person has a lien on the earliest date such lien becomes valid under local law against subsequent purchasers without actual notice, but not before he begins to furnish the services, labor, or materials.

* * *

(5) Tax lien filing.—The term "tax lien filing" means the filing of notice (referred to in subsection (a)) of the lien imposed by section 6321.

(6) Purchaser.—The term "purchaser" means a person who, for adequate and full consideration in money or money's worth, acquires an interest (other than a lien or security interest) in property which is valid under local law against subsequent purchasers without actual notice. In applying the preceding sentence for purposes of subsection (a) of this section, and for purposes of section 6324—

(A) a lease of property,

(B) a written executory contract to purchase or lease property,

(C) an option to purchase or lease property or any interest therein, or

(D) an option to renew or extend a lease of property,

which is not a lien or security interest shall be treated as an interest in property.

* * *

Unit 8

UNIFORM FRAUDULENT TRANSFER ACT*

Sec.
1. Definitions
2. Insolvency
3. Value
4. Transfers Fraudulent as to Present and Future Creditors
5. Transfers Fraudulent as to Present Creditors
6. When Transfer is Made or Obligation is Incurred
7. Remedies of Creditors
8. Defenses, Liability, and Protection of Transferee
9. Extinguishment of [Claim for Relief] [Cause of Action]
10. Supplementary Provisions
11. Uniformity of Application and Construction
12. *Short Title*
13. *Repeal*

§ 1. Definitions

As used in this [Act]:

(1) "Affiliate" means:

(i) a person who directly or indirectly owns, controls, or holds with power to vote, 20 percent or more of the outstanding voting securities of the debtor, other than a person who holds the securities,

(A) as a fiduciary or agent without sole discretionary power to vote the securities; or

(B) solely to secure a debt, if the person has not exercised the power to vote;

(ii) a corporation 20 percent or more of whose outstanding voting securities are directly or indirectly owned, controlled, or

---

* Reproduced by permission of the National Conference of Commissioners on Uniform State Laws.

held with power to vote, by the debtor or a person who directly or indirectly owns, controls, or holds, with power to vote, 20 percent or more of the outstanding voting securities of the debtor, other than a person who holds the securities,

(A) as a fiduciary or agent without sole power to vote the securities; or

(B) solely to secure a debt, if the person has not in fact exercised the power to vote;

(iii) a person whose business is operated by the debtor under a lease or other agreement, or a person substantially all of whose assets are controlled by the debtor; or

(iv) a person who operates the debtor's business under a lease or other agreement or controls substantially all of the debtor's assets.

(2) "Asset" means property of a debtor, but the term does not include:

(i) property to the extent it is encumbered by a valid lien;

(ii) property to the extent it is generally exempt under nonbankruptcy law; or

(iii) an interest in property held in tenancy by the entireties to the extent it is not subject to process by a creditor holding a claim against only one tenant.

(3) "Claim" means a right to payment, whether or not the right is reduced to judgment, liquidated, unliquidated, fixed, contingent, matured, unmatured, disputed, undisputed, legal, equitable, secured, or unsecured.

(4) "Creditor" means a person who has a claim.

(5) "Debt" means liability on a claim.

(6) "Debtor" means a person who is liable on a claim.

(7) "Insider" includes:

(i) if the debtor is an individual,

(A) a relative of the debtor or of a general partner of the debtor;

(B) a partnership in which the debtor is a general partner;

(C) a general partner in a partnership described in clause (B); or

(D) a corporation of which the debtor is a director, officer, or person in control;

(ii) if the debtor is a corporation,

(A) a director of the debtor;

(B) an officer of the debtor;

(C) a person in control of the debtor;

(D) a partnership in which the debtor is a general partner;

(E) a general partner in a partnership described in clause (D); or

(F) a relative of a general partner, director, officer, or person in control of the debtor;

(iii) if the debtor is a partnership,

(A) a general partner in the debtor;

(B) a relative of a general partner in, a general partner of, or a person in control of the debtor;

(C) another partnership in which the debtor is a general partner;

(D) a general partner in a partnership described in clause (C); or

(E) a person in control of the debtor;

(iv) an affiliate, or an insider of an affiliate as if the affiliate were the debtor; and

(v) a managing agent of the debtor.

(8) "Lien" means a charge against or an interest in property to secure payment of a debt or performance of an obligation, and includes a security interest created by agreement, a judicial lien obtained by legal or equitable process or proceedings, a common-law lien, or a statutory lien.

(9) "Person" means an individual, partnership, corporation, association, organization, government or governmental subdivision or agency, business trust, estate, trust, or any other legal or commercial entity.

(10) "Property" means anything that may be the subject of ownership.

(11) "Relative" means an individual related by consanguinity within the third degree as determined by the common law, a spouse,

or an individual related to a spouse within the third degree as so determined, and includes an individual in an adoptive relationship within the third degree.

(12) "Transfer" means every mode, direct or indirect, absolute or conditional, voluntary or involuntary, of disposing of or parting with an asset or an interest in an asset, and includes payment of money, release, lease, and creation of a lien or other encumbrance.

(13) "Valid lien" means a lien that is effective against the holder of a judicial lien subsequently obtained by legal or equitable process or proceedings.

§ 2. Insolvency

(a) A debtor is insolvent if the sum of the debtor's debts is greater than all of the debtor's assets at a fair valuation.

(b) A debtor who is generally not paying his [or her] debts as they become due is presumed to be insolvent.

(c) A partnership is insolvent under subsection (a) if the sum of the partnership's debts is greater than the aggregate, at a fair valuation, of all of the partnership's assets and the sum of the excess of the value of each general partner's nonpartnership assets over the partner's nonpartnership debts.

(d) Assets under this section do not include property that has been transferred, concealed, or removed with intent to hinder, delay, or defraud creditors or that has been transferred in a manner making the transfer voidable under this [Act].

(e) Debts under this section do not include an obligation to the extent it is secured by a valid lien on property of the debtor not included as an asset.

§ 3. Value

(a) Value is given for a transfer or an obligation if, in exchange for the transfer or obligation, property is transferred or an antecedent debt is secured or satisfied, but value does not include an unperformed promise made otherwise than in the ordinary course of the promisor's business to furnish support to the debtor or another person.

(b) For the purposes of Sections 4(a)(2) and 5, a person gives a reasonably equivalent value if the person acquires an interest of the debtor in an asset pursuant to a regularly conducted, noncollusive foreclosure sale or execution of a power of sale for the acquisition or disposition of the interest of the debtor upon default under a mortgage, deed of trust, or security agreement.

(c) A transfer is made for present value if the exchange between the debtor and the transferee is intended by them to be contemporaneous and is in fact substantially contemporaneous.

§ 4. Transfers Fraudulent as to Present and Future Creditors

(a) A transfer made or obligation incurred by a debtor is fraudulent as to a creditor, whether the creditor's claim arose before or after the transfer was made or the obligation was incurred, if the debtor made the transfer or incurred the obligation:

(1) with actual intent to hinder, delay, or defraud any creditor of the debtor; or

(2) without receiving a reasonably equivalent value in exchange for the transfer or obligation, and the debtor:

(i) was engaged or was about to engage in a business or a transaction for which the remaining assets of the debtor were unreasonably small in relation to the business or transaction; or

(ii) intended to incur, or believed or reasonably should have believed that he [or she] would incur, debts beyond his [or her] ability to pay as they became due.

(b) In determining actual intent under subsection (a)(1), consideration may be given, among other factors, to whether:

(1) the transfer or obligation was to an insider;

(2) the debtor retained possession or control of the property transferred after the transfer;

(3) the transfer or obligation was disclosed or concealed;

(4) before the transfer was made or obligation was incurred, the debtor had been sued or threatened with suit;

(5) the transfer was of substantially all the debtor's assets;

(6) the debtor absconded;

(7) the debtor removed or concealed assets;

(8) the value of the consideration received by the debtor was reasonably equivalent to the value of the asset transferred or the amount of the obligation incurred;

(9) the debtor was insolvent or became insolvent shortly after the transfer was made or the obligation was incurred;

(10) the transfer occurred shortly before or shortly after a substantial debt was incurred; and

(11) the debtor transferred the essential assets of the business to a lienor who transferred the assets to an insider of the debtor.

§ 5. Transfers Fraudulent as to Present Creditors

(a) A transfer made or obligation incurred by a debtor is fraudulent as to a creditor whose claim arose before the transfer was made or the obligation was incurred if the debtor made the transfer or incurred the obligation without receiving a reasonably equivalent value in exchange for the transfer or obligation and the debtor was insolvent at that time or the debtor became insolvent as a result of the transfer or obligation.

(b) A transfer made by a debtor is fraudulent as to a creditor whose claim arose before the transfer was made if the transfer was made to an insider for an antecedent debt, the debtor was insolvent at that time, and the insider had reasonable cause to believe that the debtor was insolvent.

§ 6. When Transfer is Made or Obligation is Incurred

For the purposes of this [Act]:

(1) a transfer is made:

(i) with respect to an asset that is real property other than a fixture, but including the interest of a seller or purchaser under a contract for the sale of the asset, when the transfer is so far perfected that a good-faith purchaser of the asset from the debtor against whom applicable law permits the transfer to be perfected cannot acquire an interest in the asset that is superior to the interest of the transferee; and

(ii) with respect to an asset that is not real property or that is a fixture, when the transfer is so far perfected that a creditor on a simple contract cannot acquire a judicial lien otherwise than under this [Act] that is superior to the interest of the transferee;

(2) if applicable law permits the transfer to be perfected as provided in paragraph (1) and the transfer is not so perfected before the commencement of an action for relief under this [Act], the transfer is deemed made immediately before the commencement of the action;

(3) if applicable law does not permit the transfer to be perfected as provided in paragraph (1), the transfer is made when it becomes effective between the debtor and the transferee;

(4) a transfer is not made until the debtor has acquired rights in the asset transferred;

(5) an obligation is incurred:

(i) if oral, when it becomes effective between the parties; or

(ii) if evidenced by a writing, when the writing executed by the obligor is delivered to or for the benefit of the obligee.

§ 7. Remedies of Creditors

(a) In an action for relief against a transfer or obligation under this [Act], a creditor, subject to the limitations in Section 8, may obtain:

(1) avoidance of the transfer or obligation to the extent necessary to satisfy the creditor's claim;

[(2) an attachment or other provisional remedy against the asset transferred or other property of the transferee in accordance with the procedure prescribed by [ ];]

(3) subject to applicable principles of equity and in accordance with applicable rules of civil procedure,

(i) an injunction against further disposition by the debtor or a transferee, or both, of the asset transferred or of other property;

(ii) appointment of a receiver to take charge of the asset transferred or of other property of the transferee; or

(iii) any other relief the circumstances may require.

(b) If a creditor has obtained a judgment on a claim against the debtor, the creditor, if the court so orders, may levy execution on the asset transferred or its proceeds.

§ 8. Defenses, Liability, and Protection of Transferee

(a) A transfer or obligation is not voidable under Section 4(a)(1) against a person who took in good faith and for a reasonably equivalent value or against any subsequent transferee or obligee.

(b) Except as otherwise provided in this section, to the extent a transfer is voidable in an action by a creditor under Section 7(a)(1), the creditor may recover judgment for the value of the asset transferred, as adjusted under subsection (c), or the amount necessary to satisfy the creditor's claim, whichever is less. The judgment may be entered against:

(1) the first transferee of the asset or the person for whose benefit the transfer was made; or

(2) any subsequent transferee other than a good faith transferee who took for value or from any subsequent transferee.

(c) If the judgment under subsection (b) is based upon the value of the asset transferred, the judgment must be for an amount equal to the value of the asset at the time of the transfer, subject to adjustment as the equities may require.

(d) Notwithstanding voidability of a transfer or an obligation under this [Act], a good-faith transferee or obligee is entitled, to the extent of the value given the debtor for the transfer or obligation, to

(1) a lien on or a right to retain any interest in the asset transferred;

(2) enforcement of any obligation incurred; or

(3) a reduction in the amount of the liability on the judgment.

(e) A transfer is not voidable under Section 4(a)(2) or Section 5 if the transfer results from:

(1) termination of a lease upon default by the debtor when the termination is pursuant to the lease and applicable law; or

(2) enforcement of a security interest in compliance with Article 9 of the Uniform Commercial Code.

(f) A transfer is not voidable under Section 5(b):

(1) to the extent the insider gave new value to or for the benefit of the debtor after the transfer was made unless the new value was secured by a valid lien;

(2) if made in the ordinary course of business or financial affairs of the debtor and the insider; or

(3) if made pursuant to a good-faith effort to rehabilitate the debtor and the transfer secured present value given for that purpose as well as an antecedent debt of the debtor.

§ 9. Extinguishment of [Claim for Relief] [Cause of Action]

A [claim for relief] [cause of action] with respect to a fraudulent transfer or obligation under this [Act] is extinguished unless action is brought:

(a) under Section 4(a)(1), within 4 years after the transfer was made or the obligation was incurred or, if later, within one year after the transfer or obligation was or could reasonably have been discovered by the claimant;

(b) under Section 4(a)(2) or 5(a), within 4 years after the transfer was made or the obligation was incurred; or

(c) under Section 5(b), within one year after the transfer was made or the obligation was incurred.

* * *

§ 10. Supplementary Provisions

Unless displaced by the provisions of this [Act], the principles of law and equity, including the law merchant and the law relating to principal and agent, estoppel, laches, fraud, misrepresentation, duress, coercion, mistake, insolvency, or other validating or invalidating cause, supplement its provisions.

§ 11. Uniformity of Application and Construction

This [Act] shall be applied and construed to effectuate its general purpose to make uniform the law with respect to the subject of this [Act] among states enacting it.

* * *

Unit 9

UNIFORM CERTIFICATE OF TITLE ACT *

Sec.
1. Short Title
2. Definitions
3. Supplemental Principles of Law and Equity
4. Law Governing Vehicle Covered by Certificate of Title or Certificate of Origin
5. Exclusions
6. Vehicle Identification Number, Make, and Model Year
7. Execution of Certificate of Origin
8. Cancellation and Replacement of Certificate of Origin
9. Application for Certificate Of Title
10. Creation and Cancellation of Certificate of Title
11. Contents of Certificate of Title
12. Effect of Possession of Certificate of Title or Certificate of Origin; Judicial Process
13. Other Information
14. Maintenance of And Access to Files
15. Delivery of Certificate of Title
16. Transfer
17. Notice of Transfer Without Application
18. Power to Transfer
19. Other Transferees of Vehicle Covered by Certificate of Title
20. Effect of Omission or Incorrect Information
21. Transfer by Secured Party's Transfer Statement
22. Transfer by Operation of Law
23. Application For Transfer of Ownership or Termination of Security-Interest Statement Without Certificate of Title or Certificate of Origin
24. Replacement Certificate of Title
25. Effectiveness of Security-Interest Statement
26. Perfection of Security Interest
27. Termination Statement
28. Duties and Operation of Filing Office
29. Uniformity of Application and Construction
30. Electronic Signatures in Global and National Commerce Act

* Reproduced by permission of the National Conference of Commissioners on Uniform State Laws.

Sec.
31. Savings Clause
32. Repeals
33. Effective Date

---

§ 1. Short Title

This [act] may be cited as the Uniform Certificate of Title Act.

§ 2. Definitions

(a) In this [act]:

(1) "Buyer" means a person that buys or contracts to buy goods.

(2) "Buyer in ordinary course of business" means a person that buys goods in good faith, without knowledge that the sale violates the rights of another person in the goods, and in ordinary course from a person, other than a pawnbroker, in the business of selling goods of that kind. A person buys goods in ordinary course if the sale comports with the usual or customary practices in the kind of business in which the seller is engaged or with the seller's own usual or customary practices. A buyer in ordinary course of business may buy for cash, by exchange of other property, or on secured or unsecured credit, and may acquire goods under a pre-existing contract for sale. Only a buyer that takes possession of the goods or has a right to recover the goods from the seller under [Uniform Commercial Code Article 2] may be a buyer in ordinary course of business. The term does not include a person that acquires goods in a transfer in bulk or as security for or in total or partial satisfaction of a money debt. A buyer in ordinary course of business does not lose that status solely because a certificate of title was not executed to the buyer.

(3) "Cancel", with respect to a certificate of title or a certificate of origin, means to make the certificate ineffective.

(4) "Certificate of origin" means a record created by a manufacturer or importer as the manufacturer's or importer's proof of identity of a vehicle.

(5) "Certificate of title", except in the phrases "certificate of title created by a governmental agency of any state" and "certificate of title created by a governmental agency of any jurisdiction", means a record, created by the office and designated as a certificate of title by it, that is evidence of ownership of a vehicle.

(6) "Create" means to bring a record into existence by making or authorizing the record.

(7) "Deliver" means voluntarily to give possession of a record or to transmit it, by any reasonable means, properly addressed and with the cost of delivery provided.

(8) "Electronic" means relating to technology having electrical, digital, magnetic, wireless, optical, electromagnetic, or similar capabilities.

(9) "Electronic certificate of origin" means a certificate of origin consisting of information that is stored solely in an electronic medium and is retrievable in perceivable form.

(10) "Electronic certificate of title" means a certificate of title consisting of information that is stored solely in an electronic medium and is retrievable in perceivable form.

(11) "Execute" means to sign and deliver a record on, attached to, accompanying, or logically associated with a certificate of title or certificate of origin to transfer ownership of the vehicle covered by the certificate.

(12) "Good faith" means honesty in fact and the observance of reasonable commercial standards of fair dealing.

(13) "Importer" means a person authorized by a manufacturer to bring into and distribute in the United States new vehicles manufactured outside the United States.

(14) "Lessee in ordinary course of business" means a person that leases goods in good faith, without knowledge that the lease violates the rights of another person, and in ordinary course of business from a person, other than a pawnbroker, in the business of selling or leasing goods of that kind. A person leases in ordinary course if the lease to the person comports with the usual or customary practices in the kind of business in which the lessor is engaged or with the lessor's own usual and customary practices. A lessee in ordinary course of business may lease for cash, by exchange of other property, or on secured or unsecured credit, and may acquire goods or a certificate of title covering goods under a preexisting lease contract. Only a lessee that takes possession of the goods or has a right to recover the goods from the lessor under [Uniform Commercial Code Article 2A] may be a lessee in ordinary course of business. A person that acquires goods in bulk or as security for or in total or partial satisfaction of a money debt is not a lessee in ordinary course of business.

(15) "Lien creditor" means:

(A) a creditor that has acquired a lien on the property involved by attachment, levy, or the like;

(B) an assignee for the benefit of creditors from the time of assignment;

(C) a trustee in bankruptcy from the date of the filing of the petition; or

(D) a receiver in equity from the time of appointment.

(16) "Manufacturer" means a person that manufactures, fabricates, assembles, or completes new vehicles.

(17) "Office" means [insert name of relevant department or agency that creates certificates of title in enacting state].

(18) "Owner" means a person that has legal title to a vehicle.

(19) "Owner of record" means the owner of a vehicle as indicated in the files of the office.

(20) "Person" means an individual, corporation, business trust, estate, trust, partnership, limited liability company, association, joint venture, federally recognized Indian Tribe, public corporation, government, or governmental subdivision, agency, or instrumentality, or any other legal or commercial entity.

(21) "Purchase" means to take by sale, lease, mortgage, pledge, consensual lien, security interest, gift, or any other voluntary transaction that creates an interest in a vehicle.

(22) "Purchaser" means a person that takes by purchase.

(23) "Record" means information that is inscribed on a tangible medium or that is stored in an electronic or other medium and is retrievable in perceivable form.

(24) "Secured party" means:

(A) a person in whose favor a security interest is created or provided for under a security agreement, whether or not any obligation to be secured is outstanding;

(B) a person that is a consignor under [Uniform Commercial Code Article 9];

(C) a person to which accounts, chattel paper, payment intangibles, or promissory notes have been sold;

(D) a trustee, indenture trustee, agent, collateral agent, or other representative in whose favor a security interest is created or provided for; or

(E) a person that holds a security interest arising under [Uniform Commercial Code Section 2–401, 2–505, 2–711(3), or 2A–508(5)].

(25) "Secured party of record" means the secured party whose name is provided as the name of the secured party or a representative of the secured party in a security-interest statement that has been received by the office or, if more than one are indicated, the first indicated in the files of the office.

(26) "Security interest" means an interest in a vehicle which secures payment or performance of an obligation. The term includes any interest of a consignor in a vehicle in a transaction that is subject to [Uniform Commercial Code Article 9]. The term does not include the special property interest of a buyer of a vehicle on identification of that vehicle to a contract for sale under [Uniform Commercial Code Section 2–401], but a buyer may also acquire a security interest by complying with [Uniform Commercial Code Article 9]. Except as otherwise provided in [Uniform Commercial Code Section 2–505], the right of a seller or lessor of a vehicle under [Uniform Commercial Code Article 2 or 2A] to retain or acquire possession of the vehicle is not a security interest, but a seller or lessor may also acquire a security interest by complying with [Uniform Commercial Code Article 9]. The retention or reservation of title by a seller of a vehicle notwithstanding shipment or delivery to the buyer under [Uniform Commercial Code Section 2–401] is limited in effect to a reservation of a security interest. Whether a transaction in the form of a lease creates a security interest is determined by law other than this [act].

(27) "Security-interest statement" means a record created by a secured party which indicates a security interest.

(28) "Sign" means, with present intent to authenticate or adopt a record, to:

(A) make or adopt a tangible symbol; or

(B) attach to or logically associate with the record an electronic sound, symbol, or process.

(29) "State" means a state of the United States, the District of Columbia, Puerto Rico, the United States Virgin Islands, a federally

recognized Indian tribe, or any territory or insular possession subject to the jurisdiction of the United States.

(30) "Termination statement" means a record created by a secured party pursuant to Section 27 which:

(A) identifies the security-interest statement to which it relates; and

(B) indicates that it is a termination statement or that the identified security-interest statement is not effective.

(31) "Title brand" means a designation of previous damage, use, or condition that [this [act] or] law other than this [act] requires to be indicated on a certificate of title or a certificate of origin created by a governmental agency of any jurisdiction.

(32) "Transfer" means to convey, voluntarily or involuntarily, an interest in a vehicle.

(33) "Transferee" means a person that takes by transfer.

(34) "Vehicle" means goods that are any type of motorized, wheeled device of a type in, upon, or by which an individual or property is customarily transported on a road or highway, or a commercial, recreational, travel, or other trailer customarily transported on a road or highway. The term does not include:

(A) an item of specialized mobile equipment not designed primarily for transportation of individuals or property on a road or highway;

(B) an implement of husbandry; [or]

(C) a wheelchair or similar device designed for use by an individual having a physical impairment[; or

(D) a manufactured home].

Legislative note: *The enacting state should compare this definition of "Vehicle" with existing state law to determine if adjustments are needed to conform to other law, as this term may appear in other statutes and affect the scope and application of those statutes.*

(35) "Written certificate of origin" means a certificate of origin consisting of information inscribed on a tangible medium.

(36) "Written certificate of title" means a certificate of title consisting of information inscribed on a tangible medium.

(b) The following definitions and terms also apply to this [act]:

(1) "Agreement", [UCC Section 1–201(b)(3)].

(2) "Collateral", [UCC Section 9–102(a)(12)].

(3) "Debtor", [UCC Section 9–102(a)(28)].

(4) "Lease", [UCC Section 2A–103(a)(j)].

(5) "Lessee", [UCC Section 2A–103(1)(n)].

(6) "Lessor", [UCC Section 2A–103(a)(p)].

(7) "Manufactured home", [UCC Section 9–102(a)(53)].

(8) "Merchant", [UCC Section 2–104(1)].

(9) "Notice; Knowledge", [UCC Section 1–202].

(10) "Representative", [UCC Section 1–201(b)(33)].

(11) "Sale", [UCC Section 2–106(1)].

(12) "Security agreement", [UCC Section 9–102(a)(73)].

(13) "Seller", [UCC Section 2–103(1)(o)].

(14) "Send", [UCC Section 1–201(b)(36)].

(15) "Value", [UCC Section 1–204].

Legislative Note: *If a state has not enacted the 2002 uniform text of Uniform Commercial Code Articles 1, 2, and 2A, the references to Articles 1, 2, and 2A, section numbers should be adjusted as needed to reflect state law.*

§ 3. Supplemental Principles of Law and Equity

Unless displaced by this act, the principles of law and equity supplement its provisions.

§ 4. Law Governing Vehicle Covered by Certificate of Title or Certificate of Origin

(a) In this section, "certificate of title" means a certificate of title created by a governmental agency of any state.

(b) The local law of the state under whose certificate of title a vehicle is covered governs all issues relating to the certificate of title, from the time the vehicle becomes covered by the certificate of title until the vehicle ceases to be covered by the certificate of title, even if no other relationship exists between the state and the vehicle or its owner.

(c) A vehicle becomes covered by a certificate of title created in this State when an application for a certificate of title and the fee are received by the office in accordance with this act. A vehicle becomes covered by a certificate of title in another state when an application for a certificate of title and the fee are received in that state pursuant to the law of that state.

(d) A vehicle ceases to be covered by a certificate of title at the earlier of the time the certificate of title ceases to be effective under the law of the state pursuant to which it was created or the time the vehicle becomes covered subsequently by another certificate of title.

(e) If a vehicle is not covered by a certificate of title but a certificate of origin has been created for the vehicle:

(1) if the parties to the certificate of origin have chosen the law of a jurisdiction, the law of that jurisdiction applies to the certificate of origin, even if there is no other relationship between that jurisdiction and the vehicle or its owner; and

(2) in the absence of an agreement effective under paragraph (1), the rights and obligations of the parties are determined by the law that would apply under this state's choice-of-law principles.

§ 5. Exclusions

Unless the vehicle is covered by a certificate of title, this act does not apply to a vehicle owned by the United States, a state, or a foreign government, or a political subdivision of any of them.

§ 6. Vehicle Identification Number, Make, and Model Year

For a vehicle covered by a certificate of title, the office shall indicate in its files the vehicle identification number, make, and model year, if any, assigned by its chassis manufacturer or importer. If a vehicle identification number, make, or model year has not been assigned, the office shall assign a vehicle identification number, make, or model year and indicate the assignment in its files.

§ 7. Execution of Certificate of Origin

(a) If a manufacturer or importer creates or is authorized or required to create a certificate of origin for a vehicle, upon transfer of ownership of the vehicle, the manufacturer or importer shall execute a certificate of origin to the transferee or deliver a signed certificate of origin to the office. Each succeeding transferor shall execute to the next transferee or sign and deliver to the office all certificates of origin covering the vehicle which are known to the transferor.

(b) If a certificate of title created by a governmental agency of any jurisdiction is not delivered to the buyer and a written certificate of origin or equivalent evidence of ownership is required by the office to obtain a certificate of title, a buyer may require that the buyer's transferor execute to the buyer a written certificate of origin or provide equivalent evidence of ownership sufficient to satisfy the requirements of the office.

§ 8. Cancellation and Replacement of Certificate of Origin

(a) If a written certificate of origin is created to replace an electronic certificate of origin, the electronic certificate of origin is canceled and replaced by the written certificate of origin.

(b) If an electronic certificate of origin is created to replace a written certificate of origin, the written certificate of origin must be canceled.

§ 9. Application for Certificate of Title

(a) Except as otherwise provided in Sections 21 and 22, only the owner of a vehicle may apply for a certificate of title covering the vehicle.

(b) An application for a certificate of title must be signed by the applicant and contain:

(1) the applicant's name, street address, and, if different, address for receiving first class mail delivered by the United States Postal Service;

(2) the vehicle identification number;

(3) a description of the vehicle including, as required by the office, the make, model, model year, and body type;

(4) an indication of all security interests in the vehicle known to the applicant and, if the application includes a direction to terminate a security-interest statement, the information required for sufficiency of a security-interest statement under Section 25(a) and the secured party's name and address for receiving communications;

(5) any title brand known to the applicant and, if known, the jurisdiction whose governmental agency created the title brand;

(6) if law other than this act requires that an odometer reading be provided by the transferor upon transfer of ownership of the vehicle, a signed record disclosing the vehicle's odometer reading; and

(7) if the application is made in connection with a transfer of ownership, the transferor's name, physical address and, if different, address for receiving first class mail delivered by the United States Postal Service, the sales price if any, and the date of the transfer.

(c) In addition to the information required in subsection (b), an application for a certificate of title may contain electronic communication addresses of the owner and the transferor.

(d) Except as otherwise provided in Section 21, 22, or 23, if an application for a certificate of title includes an indication of a transfer of ownership, the application must be accompanied by all existing certificates of origin and any certificate of title created by a governmental agency of any jurisdiction covering the vehicle, which have been executed to the applicant or are known to the applicant. Except as otherwise provided in Section 23, if an application includes a direction to terminate a security-interest statement, the application must be accompanied by a termination statement.

(e) Except as otherwise provided in Section 24, if an application for a certificate of title does not include an indication of a transfer of ownership or a direction to terminate a security-interest statement, the application must be accompanied by all existing certificates of origin and any certificate of title created by a governmental agency of any jurisdiction covering the vehicle, which are known to the applicant and evidencing the applicant as owner of the vehicle.

(f) If the applicant does not know of any existing certificate of origin or certificate of title created by a governmental agency of any jurisdiction covering the vehicle, the applicant shall include in the application for a certificate of title all existing records and other information of the vehicle's ownership known to the applicant. Information submitted under this subsection is part of the application for the certificate of title and must be indicated in the files of the office.

(g) The office may require that an application for a certificate of title or a security-interest statement be accompanied by payment of all taxes and fees payable by the applicant under the law of this state in connection with the acquisition or use of a vehicle or evidence of payment of the tax or fee.

§ 10. Creation and Cancellation of Certificate of Title

(a) Unless an application for a certificate of title is rejected under subsection (c), the office shall create a certificate of title upon receipt of an application that complies with Section 9 and payment of all taxes and fees.

(b) Upon request of the secured party of record, the office shall create a written certificate of title or, if the office is authorized to do so, an electronic certificate of title. If no security interest is indicated in the files of the office, the owner of record may have the office create a written certificate of title or, if the office is authorized to do so, an electronic certificate of title. If no request is made by an owner of record or secured party, the office may create a written certificate of title or, if authorized to do so, an electronic certificate of title.

(c) The office may reject an application for a certificate of title only if:

(1) the application does not comply with Section 9;

(2) there is a reasonable basis for concluding that the application is fraudulent or would facilitate a fraudulent or illegal act; or

(3) the application does not comply with law of this state other than this act.

(d) If the office has created a certificate of title, it may cancel the certificate of title only if it could have rejected the application under subsection (c) or is required to cancel the certificate of title under another provision of this act. [The office shall provide an opportunity for a hearing at which the applicant and any other interested party may present evidence in support of or opposition to the cancellation. The office shall serve the notice of the opportunity in person or send it by first class mail delivered by the United States Postal Service to the applicant, the owner of record, and all secured parties indicated in the files of the office. If the applicant or any other interested party requests a hearing not later than [10] days after receiving the notice, the office shall hold the hearing not later than [20] days after receiving the request].

§ 11. Contents of Certificate of Title

(a) A certificate of title must contain:

(1) the date the certificate of title was created;

(2) except as otherwise provided in Section 26(b), the name and address of any secured party of record and an indication of whether there are additional security interests indicated in the files of the office or on a record created by a governmental agency of any jurisdiction and submitted to the office;

(3) all title brands covering the vehicle, including brands previously indicated on a certificate of origin or certificate of title created by a governmental agency of any jurisdiction, which are known to the office; and

(4) any other information required by Section 9(b), except the applicant's address.

(b) An indication of a title brand on a certificate of title may consist of an abbreviation, but not a symbol, and must identify the jurisdiction that created the title brand or the jurisdiction that created a certificate of title created by a governmental agency of any jurisdiction that indicated the title brand. If the meaning of a title brand is not easily ascertainable or cannot be accommodated on the certificate of title, the certificate of title may state: "Previously branded in [insert the particular jurisdiction that created the title brand or whose certificate of title previously indicated the title brand]."

(c) If a vehicle was previously registered in a jurisdiction other than a state, the office shall indicate on the certificate of title that the vehicle was registered in that jurisdiction.

(d) A certificate of title must contain a form that the owner may sign in order to execute the certificate.

§ 12. Effect of Possession of Certificate of Title or Certificate of Origin; Judicial Process

A certificate of title created by a governmental agency of any jurisdiction or a certificate of origin does not by itself provide a means to obtain possession of a vehicle. Garnishment, attachment, levy, replevin, or other judicial process against the certificate of title or a certificate of origin is not effective to determine possessory rights with respect to the vehicle. However, this act does not prohibit enforcement of a security interest in, levy on, or foreclosure of a statutory or common-law lien on a vehicle under law of this state other than this act. The absence of an indication of a statutory or common-law lien on a certificate of title does not invalidate the lien.

§ 13. Other Information

(a) The office may accept a submission of information relating to a vehicle for indication in the files of the office, even if the requirements for a certificate of title, an application for a certificate of title, a security-interest statement, or a termination statement have not been met.

(b) A submission of information under this section, to the extent practicable, must include the information required by Section 9(b) for an application for a certificate of title.

(c) The office may require the submission of information relating to a vehicle required for payment of taxes and fees for issuance or renewal of registration.

(d) The office may require a person submitting information under this section to provide a bond in a form and amount determined by the office. A bond must provide for indemnification of any secured party or other interested party against any expense, loss, or damage resulting from indication of the information in the files of the office.

(e) A submission of information under this section and its indication in the files of the office is not a certificate of title, an application for a certificate of title, a security-interest statement, or a termination statement and does not provide a basis for transferring or determining ownership of a vehicle or the effectiveness of a security-interest statement.

§ 14. Maintenance of and Access to Files

(a) For each record relating to a certificate of title submitted to the office, the office shall:

(1) ascertain or assign the vehicle identification number, make, and model year of the vehicle to which the record relates pursuant to Section 6;

(2) indicate in the files of the office the vehicle identification number, make, and model year of the vehicle to which the record relates and the information in the record, including the date [and time] the record was delivered to the office;

(3) maintain the file for public inspection subject to subsection (d); and

(4) index the files of the office so as to be accessible as required by subsection (b).

(b) The office shall indicate in the files of the office the information contained in all certificates of title created under this act. The files of the office must be accessible by the vehicle identification number for the vehicle covered by the certificate and any other indexing method used by the office.

(c) To the extent known to the office, the files of the office maintained under this section relating to a vehicle must indicate all title brands and the name or names of any secured party and claimant to ownership of the vehicle and include stolen-property reports and security-interest statements.

[(d) Except as otherwise provided by law of this state other than this act, the information required under Section 11 is a public record. Whether other information in the files of the office is made available to the public is governed by law of this state other than this act.]

Legislative Note: *A state with separate public records laws governing disclosure of personal information should cross-reference those laws at subsection (d). A state without such a law to govern these files should enact the optional language at subsection (d) to distinguish between private and public information.*

§ 15. Delivery of Certificate of Title

(a) Upon creation of a certificate of title, the office shall promptly deliver a written certificate of title, or a record evidencing an electronic certificate of title, to any secured party of record at the address shown on the security-interest statement submitted by the secured party of record. Unless previously provided to the owner of record, the office shall promptly deliver a record evidencing the certificate of title to the owner of record at the address indicated in the files of the office. If no secured party is indicated in the files of the office, the written certificate of title or record evidencing the electronic certificate of title must be delivered to the owner of record. A record evidencing an electronic certificate of title may be delivered to a mailing address or, if indicated in the files of the office, an electronic communication address.

(b) Within a reasonable time not to exceed [15] business days after receipt of a request that a written certificate of title be created and delivered pursuant to subsection (a), the office shall create the certificate and deliver it to the person making the request.

(c) If a written certificate of title is created, any electronic certificate of title is canceled and replaced by the written certificate of title. The cancellation must be indicated in the files of the office with an indication of the date [and time] of cancellation.

(d) Before an electronic certificate of title is created, any certificate of title must be surrendered. If an electronic certificate of title is created, any existing written certificate of title that has been surrendered to the office must be destroyed or otherwise canceled, with an indication in the files of the office of the date [and time] of destruction or other cancellation. If the written certificate of title being canceled is not destroyed, the cancellation must be indicated on the face of the written certificate of title.

§ 16. Transfer

(a) Upon sale of a vehicle covered by a certificate of title, a person authorized to execute the certificate of title, as promptly as practicable and in compliance with this act and law of this state other than this act, shall execute the certificate to the buyer or deliver to the office a signed certificate of title or a record evidencing execution of an electronic certificate of title to the buyer. The buyer of a vehicle covered by a certificate of title has a specifically enforceable right to require the seller to execute the certificate of title to the buyer or deliver to the office a signed certificate of title or other record evidencing the transfer.

(b) Execution of a certificate of title created by a governmental agency of any jurisdiction satisfies subsection (a).

(c) As between the parties to a transfer and their assignees and successors, a transfer of ownership is not rendered ineffective by a failure to execute a certificate of title or certificate of origin as provided in this section. However, except as otherwise provided in Section 18 (b) and (c), 19, 21, or 22, a transfer of ownership without execution of a certificate of title or certificate of origin is not effective as to other persons claiming an interest in the vehicle.

(d) Before an agreement to transfer ownership by an electronic certificate of title is made or any consideration for the transfer is paid, and before a record evidencing the transfer is executed to the transferee or delivered by the transferor to the office, the transferor shall deliver to the transferee a signed record containing the information required by Section 9(b), and the transferee shall deliver to the transferor a signed record acknowledging receipt of the information. The transferee has a specifically enforceable right to receive this information before any consideration is paid. The record delivered to the office must indicate that these requirements have been met.

(e) After execution of the certificate of title and delivery of possession of the vehicle to the transferee, the transferor is not liable as owner for any damages resulting from operation of the vehicle thereafter even if the transferee fails to apply for a new certificate of title reflecting the transfer.

§ 17. Notice of Transfer Without Application

A transferee or transferor, in accordance with standards and procedures established by the office, may deliver a signed record to the office giving notice of the transfer, to indicate its ownership or lack of ownership, without filing an application for a certificate of title. The record may indicate the transfer of ownership between the transferor and transferee. The record is not a certificate of title and is not effective as to other persons claiming an interest in the vehicle. The delivery to the office of the record containing the notice does not relieve any party of any obligation under Section 9 or 16.

§ 18. Power to Transfer

(a) A purchaser of a vehicle has the protections afforded by [Uniform Commercial Code Sections 2–403(1), 2A–304(1), and 2A–305(1)].

(b) A buyer in ordinary course of business or lessee in ordinary course of business of a vehicle has the protections afforded by [Uniform Commercial Code Sections 2–403(2), 2A–304(2), and 2A–305(2)], even if the certificate of title is not executed to the buyer or lessee.

(c) A purchase of a leasehold interest is subject to [Uniform Commercial Code Section 2A–303].

(d) Except as otherwise provided in Section 16, the rights of other purchasers of vehicles and of lien creditors are governed by [Uniform Commercial Code Articles 2, 2A, [6,] 7, and 9].

§ 19. Other Transferees of Vehicle Covered by Certificate of Title

(a) Except as otherwise provided in this section or Section 18(b), a transferee of ownership takes subject to:

(1) a security interest in the vehicle indicated on a certificate of title; and

(2) if the certificate of title contains a statement that the vehicle is or may be subject to security interests not indicated on the certificate of title, a security interest not so indicated.

(b) If, while a security interest in a vehicle is perfected by any method under the law of any jurisdiction, the office creates a certificate of title that does not indicate the vehicle is subject to the security interest or contain a statement that it may be subject to security interests not indicated on the certificate, a buyer of the vehicle, other than a person in the business of selling or leasing goods of that kind, takes free of the security interest if the buyer:

(1) gives value in good faith, receives possession of the vehicle, and obtains execution of the certificate of title; and

(2) does not have knowledge of the security interest in the vehicle.

(c) A buyer in ordinary course of business takes free of a security interest in the vehicle, including a security interest indicated on a certificate of title, created by the buyer's seller, even if the security interest is perfected, the buyer knows of its existence, and the certificate of title was not executed to the buyer. A lessee in ordinary course of business takes its leasehold interest free of a security interest in the vehicle, including a security interest indicated on a certificate of title, created by the lessee's lessor, even if the security interest is perfected, the lessee knows of its existence, and the certificate of title was not executed to the lessee. This subsection does not affect a security interest in a vehicle in the possession of the secured party under [Uniform Commercial Code Article 9].

(d) If, while a security interest in a vehicle is perfected by any method under the law of any jurisdiction, the office creates a certificate of title that does not indicate that the vehicle is subject to the security interest or contain a statement that it may be subject to security interests not indicated on the certificate of title, the security interest is subordinate to a conflicting security interest in the vehicle which is perfected after creation of the certificate of title and without the conflicting secured party's knowledge of the security interest.

(e) A security interest is indicated on an electronic certificate of title if it is indicated in the record of the certificate of title maintained by the office.

§ 20. Effect of Omission or Incorrect Information

(a) Except as otherwise provided in this section, a certificate of title, certificate of origin, security-interest statement, or other record required or authorized by this act is effective even if it contains incorrect information or does not contain required information.

(b) In addition to any rights provided under Section 18 or 19, if a certificate of title, certificate of origin, security-interest statement, or other record required or authorized by this act is seriously misleading because it contains incorrect information or omits required information, a purchaser of the vehicle to which the record relates takes free of any interest that would have been indicated in the record if the correct or omitted information had been indicated, to the extent that the purchaser gives value in reasonable reliance on the incorrect information or the absence of the omitted information.

(c) Except as otherwise provided in subsection (d) or Section 25(c), a description of a vehicle, including the vehicle identification number, in a certificate of title, certificate of origin, security-interest statement, or other record required or authorized by this act which otherwise satisfies this act is not seriously misleading, even if not specific and accurate, if the description reasonably identifies the vehicle.

(d) With respect to a security interest or other interest indicated in the files of the office and not indicated on a written certificate of title, a failure to indicate the information specifically or accurately is not seriously misleading if a search of the files of the office using the correct vehicle identification number or other required information, using the office's standard search logic, if any, would disclose the security interest or other interest.

§ 21. Transfer by Secured Party's Transfer Statement

(a) In this section, "secured party's transfer statement" means a record signed by the secured party of record stating:

(1) that the owner of record has defaulted on an obligation to the secured party of record;

(2) that the secured party of record is exercising or has exercised post-default remedies with respect to the vehicle;

(3) that, by reason of the exercise, the secured party of record has the right to transfer the rights of the owner of record;

(4) the name and last known mailing address of:

(A) the owner of record;

(B) the secured party of record; and

(C) any other purchaser;

(5) any other information required by Section 9(b); and

(6) that the certificate of title is an electronic certificate of title, or that the secured party does not have possession of the written certificate of title created in the name of the owner of record, or that the secured party is delivering the written certificate of title to the office with the secured party's transfer statement.

(b) Completion and delivery to the office of a secured party's transfer statement, and payment of all applicable taxes and fees, entitles the secured party to the creation of a certificate of title showing the secured party of record or other purchaser as the owner of record. Unless the secured party's transfer statement is rejected by the office for a reason set forth in Section 10(c), the office shall:

(1) accept the secured party's transfer statement;

(2) amend the files of the office to reflect the transfer;

(3) cancel the certificate of title created in the name of the owner of record listed in the secured party's transfer statement, whether or not the certificate of title has been delivered to the office;

(4) create a new certificate of title indicating the secured party of record or other purchaser as the vehicle's owner of record; and

(5) deliver the new certificate of title pursuant to Section 15.

(c) The creation of a certificate of title under subsection (b) is not of itself a disposition of the vehicle and does not of itself relieve the secured party of its duties under [Uniform Commercial Code Article 9].

§ 22. Transfer by Operation of Law

(a) In this section:

(1) "By operation of law" means pursuant to a law or judicial order affecting ownership of a vehicle:

(A) on account of death, divorce or other family law proceeding, merger, consolidation, dissolution, or bankruptcy;

(B) through the exercise of the rights of a lien creditor or a person having a statutory or common law lien or other nonconsensual lien; or

(C) through other legal process.

(2) "Transfer-by-law statement" means a record signed by a transferee stating that, by operation of law, the transferee has acquired or has the right to acquire the ownership interest of the owner of record and containing:

(A) the name and mailing address of the owner of record and the transferee and the other information required by Section 9(b);

(B) documentation sufficient to establish the transferee's interest or right to acquire the ownership interest of the owner of record; and

(C) a statement that:

(i) the certificate of title is an electronic certificate of title;

(ii) the transferee does not have possession of the written certificate of title created in the name of the owner of record; or

(iii) the transferee is delivering the written certificate of title to the office with the transfer-by-law statement.

(b) If a transfer-by-law statement is delivered to the office with all taxes and fees and documentation satisfactory to the office as to the transferee's ownership interest or right to acquire the ownership interest of the owner of record, unless it is rejected by the office for a reason set forth in Section 10(c), the office shall:

(1) accept delivery of the transfer-by-law statement;

(2) promptly send notice to the owner of record and to all persons indicated in the files of the office as having an interest, including a security interest, in the vehicle that a transfer-by-law statement has been delivered to the office;

(3) amend the files of the office to reflect the transfer;

(4) cancel the certificate of title created in the name of the owner of record indicated in the transfer-by-law statement, whether or not the certificate has been delivered to the office;

(5) create a new certificate of title, indicating the transferee as owner of record; and

(6) deliver the new certificate of title.

(c) This section does not apply to a transfer of an interest in a vehicle by a secured party under [Uniform Commercial Code Article 9] or Section 21.

§ 23. Application for Transfer of Ownership or Termination of Security-Interest Statement Without Certificate of Title or Certificate of Origin

(a) Except as otherwise provided in Section 21 or 22, upon receiving an application that includes an indication of a transfer of ownership or a direction to terminate a security-interest statement but is not accompanied by submission of a signed certificate of title or certificate of origin or, as applicable, a termination statement pursuant to Section 27, the office may create a certificate of title or terminate the security-interest statement under this section only if:

(1) all other requirements under Sections 9 and 10 are met;

(2) the applicant has provided an affidavit stating facts that indicate the applicant is entitled to a transfer of ownership or termination of the effectiveness of a security-interest statement;

(3) at least 45 days before the office creates the certificate of title, the office has sent notice of the application to all persons having an interest in the vehicle as indicated in the files of the office and no objection from any of those persons has been received by the office; and

(4) the applicant submits any other information required by the office to evidence the applicant's ownership or right to termination of the security-interest statement, and the office has no credible information indicating theft, fraud, or any undisclosed or unsatisfied security interest, lien, or other claim to an interest in the vehicle.

(b) Unless the office determines, by any reasonable method, that the value of the vehicle is less than [$3,000], before creating a certificate of title, the office may require an applicant under subsection (a) to post a bond or provide an equivalent source of indemnity or security. The bond, indemnity, or other security must be in a form prescribed by the office and provide for indemnification of any owner, purchaser, or other claimant for any expense, loss, delay, or damage, including reasonable attorney's fees and costs but not consequential damages, resulting from creation of a certificate of title or termination of a security-interest statement, but may not exceed twice the value of the vehicle as determined by the office.

Legislative Note: *The enacting state should consider the appropriate amount to insert in subsection (b) as the benchmark to determine which vehicles are not subject to the requirement for a bond. Such a requirement is not cost effective for low-value vehicles. The determination should weigh the need for a cost-effective remedy against the risk that applications without a bond pose in terms of potential fraud.*

(c) If the office has not received a claim for indemnity within one year after creation of the certificate of title under subsection (a), upon request in a form and manner specified by the office, the office shall release any bond, indemnity, or other security.

(d) The office may indicate in a certificate of title created under subsection (a) that the certificate of title was created without submission of a signed certificate of title or termination statement. If no credible information indicating theft, fraud, or any undisclosed or unsatisfied security interest, lien, or other claim to an interest in the vehicle has been delivered to the office within one year after creation of the certificate of title, upon request in a form and manner specified by the office, the office shall remove the indication from the certificate of title.

§ 24. Replacement Certificate of Title

(a) If a written certificate of title is lost, stolen, mutilated, destroyed, or otherwise becomes unavailable or illegible, the secured party of record or, if there is no secured party indicated in the files of the office, the owner of record may apply for and, by furnishing information satisfactory to the office, obtain a replacement certificate of title in the name of the owner of record.

(b) An application for a replacement certificate of title must be submitted in a record signed by the applicant and, except as otherwise permitted by the office, must comply with Section 9.

(c) Unless it has been lost, stolen, or destroyed or is otherwise unavailable, the existing written certificate of title must be submitted to the office with an application for a replacement certificate of title.

(d) A replacement certificate of title created by the office must comply with Section 11 and indicate on the face of the certificate of title that it is a replacement certificate of title.

(e) If a person receiving a replacement certificate of title subsequently obtains possession of the original written certificate of title, the person shall promptly destroy the original written certificate of title.

§ 25. Effectiveness of Security-Interest Statement

(a) A security-interest statement is sufficient if it includes the name of the debtor, the name of the secured party or a representative of the secured party, and a description of the vehicle and it is delivered by a person authorized to file an initial financing statement covering the vehicle pursuant to [Uniform Commercial Code Section 9–509]. A description of the vehicle is sufficient if it reasonably identifies the vehicle and is not seriously misleading under Section 20.

(b) A security-interest statement that is sufficient under subsection (a) is effective upon receipt by the office.

(c) Subject to subsections (e) and (f), a security-interest statement is not received if the office rejects the statement pursuant to subsection (e). The office may reject a security-interest statement only in the manner specified in subsection (e) and only if:

(1) the record is not delivered by a means authorized by the office;

(2) an amount equal to or greater than the required filing fee is not tendered with the statement or, if the office elects to notify the secured party of the filing fee deficiency, within seven days after the notification has been given;

(3) the record does not include the name and mailing address of a debtor and a secured party or a representative of a secured party;

(4) the record does not contain the vehicle identification number; or

(5) the office cannot identify a file of the office, certificate of title, or application for a certificate of title to which the security-interest statement relates.

(d) The office shall maintain files of the office showing the date of receipt of each security-interest statement that is not rejected and shall make this information available on request.

(e) To reject a security-interest statement, the office must send notice of rejection to the person that delivered the statement, indicating the reasons for the rejection and the date the statement would have been received had the office not rejected it.

(f) If the office does not send notice of rejection under subsection (e), the security-interest statement is received as of the time it was delivered to the office. Confirmation by the office that the security-interest statement has been entered in the files of the office is conclusive proof that receipt has occurred.

(g) If a security-interest statement sufficient under subsection (a) is tendered with the filing fee and the office sends a notice of rejection without indicating a reason set forth in subsection (c), the security-interest statement is effective as of the business day on which the statement was tendered to the office except as against a purchaser of the vehicle which gives value in reasonable reliance upon the absence of the security-interest statement from the files of the office.

(h) Failure of the office to index a security-interest statement correctly or to indicate the security interest on the certificate of title does not affect the receipt of the security-interest statement.

§ 26. Perfection of Security Interest

(a) Except as otherwise provided in subsection (b), (d), or (e), a security interest in a vehicle may be perfected only by a security-interest statement that is effective under Section 25. The security interest is perfected upon the later of receipt of the security-interest statement under Section 25 or attachment of the security interest under [Uniform Commercial Code Section 9–203].

(b) If the office creates a certificate of title naming a lessor, consignor, bailor, or secured party as owner and the interest of the person named as owner is a security interest, the certificate of title serves as a security-interest statement that provides the name of the person as secured party. If the interest of the person named as owner in an application for a certificate of title delivered to the office in accordance with Section 9 is a security interest, the application is a security-interest statement that provides the name of the person as secured party. The naming of the person as owner on the application or certificate of title is not of itself a factor in determining whether the interest is a security interest.

(c) If a secured party assigns a perfected security interest in a vehicle, the receipt by the office of a security-interest statement providing the name of the transferee or its representative as secured party is not required in order to continue the perfected status of the security interest against creditors of and transferees from the original debtor. However, a purchaser of a vehicle subject to a security interest which obtains a release from the secured party indicated in the files of the office or on the certificate of title takes free of the security interest and of the rights of a transferee if the transfer is not indicated in the files of the office and on the certificate of title.

(d) This section does not apply to a security interest in a vehicle created by a person during any period in which the vehicle is inventory held for sale or lease by the person or is leased by the person as lessor if the person is in the business of selling goods of that kind.

(e) A secured party may perfect a security interest by taking possession of a vehicle only pursuant to [Uniform Commercial Code Sections 9–313(b) and 9–316(d)].

§ 27. Termination Statement

(a) A secured party indicated in the files of the office as having a security interest in a vehicle shall deliver to the office and, upon the debtor's request, to the debtor, a signed termination statement if:

(1) there is no obligation secured by the vehicle subject to the security interest and no commitment to make an advance, incur an obligation, or otherwise give value secured by the vehicle; or

(2) the debtor did not authorize the filing of the security-interest statement.

(b) A secured party indicated in the files of the office as having a security interest in a vehicle shall deliver a signed termination statement to the debtor or the office upon the earlier of:

(1) [30] days after there is no obligation secured by the vehicle subject to the security-interest statement and no commitment to make an advance, incur an obligation, or otherwise give value secured by the vehicle; or

(2) [14] days after the secured party receives a signed demand from an owner and there is no obligation secured by the vehicle subject to the security interest and no commitment to make an advance, incur an obligation, or otherwise give value secured by the vehicle.

(c) If a written certificate of title has been created and delivered to a secured party and a termination statement is required under subsection (a), the secured party, within the time provided in subsection (b), shall deliver the written certificate of title to the debtor or the office with the termination statement. If the written certificate is lost, stolen, mutilated, or destroyed or is otherwise unavailable or illegible, the secured party shall deliver with the termination statement, within the time provided in subsection (b), an application for a replacement certificate of title meeting the requirements of Section 24.

(d) Upon the delivery of a termination statement to the office pursuant to this section, the security-interest statement and any indication of the security interest on the certificate of title to which the termination statement relates ceases to be effective. The files of the office must indicate the date [and time] of delivery of the termination statement to the office.

Legislative note: *The optional, bracketed language in subsection (b) allows a State to determine whether to require the office to maintain information in its files indicating the time of delivery for each termination statement. This determination may be affected by the procedural, staffing, and technical capabilities of the office.*

(e) A secured party is liable for damages in the amount of any loss caused by its failure to comply with this section and for the reasonable cost of an application for a certificate of title under Section 9 or 24.

§ 28. Duties and Operation of Filing Office

(a) The files of the office must indicate the information provided in security-interest statements and termination statements received by the office under Section 25 or 27 for at least [10] years after termination of the security-interest statement under Section 27. The information must be accessible by the vehicle identification number for the vehicle and any other indexing methods provided by the office.

(b) The office shall send to a person that submits a record to the office, or submits information that is accepted by the office, and requests an acknowledgment of the filing or submission, an acknowledgment showing the vehicle identification number of the vehicle to which the record or submission relates, the information in the filed record or submission, and the date [and time] the record was received or the submission accepted. A request under this section must contain the vehicle identification number and be delivered by means authorized by the office.

(c) The office shall send or otherwise make available in a record the following information to any person that requests it:

(1) whether the files of the office indicate, as of a date [and time] specified by the office, but not a date earlier than [three] business days before the office received the request, any certificate of title, security-interest statement, or termination statement that relates to a vehicle identified by a vehicle identification number designated in the request; and

(2) the name of the owner of record and the effective date of all security-interest statements and termination statements indicated in the files of the office.

Legislative note: Optional, bracketed language in subsection (c)(1) allows a State to determine whether to require the office to specify a time as of which its response to a request for information relating to a security-interest statement, termination statement, or and request for information is effective. Additional bracketed language enables the State to determine an appropriate limitation on the discretion of the office to determine the effective date of its response. The procedural, staffing, and technical capabilities of the office may affect these determinations.

(d) In responding to a request under this section, the office may communicate the requested information in any medium. However, if requested, the office shall send the requested information in a record that is self-authenticating under [cite applicable rule of evidence].

(e) The office shall comply with this section at the time and in the manner prescribed by the rules of the office but shall respond to requests under this section not later than [two] business days after the office receives the request.

§ 29. Uniformity of Application and Construction

In applying and construing this uniform act, consideration must be given to the need to promote uniformity of the law with respect to its subject matter among states that enact it.

§ 30. Electronic Signatures in Global and National Commerce Act

This act modifies, limits, and supersedes the federal Electronic Signatures in Global and National Commerce Act (15 U.S.C. Section 7001, et seq.) but does not modify, limit, or supersede Section 101(c) of that act (15 U.S.C. Section 7001(c)) or authorize electronic delivery of any of the notices described in Section 103(b) of that act (15 U.S.C. Section 7003(b)).

§ 31. Savings Clause

(a) Except as otherwise provided in this section, this act applies to any transaction, certificate of title, or record involving a vehicle, even if the transaction, certificate of title, or record was entered into or created before the effective date of this act.

(b) A transaction, certificate of title, or record that was validly entered into or created before the effective date of this act and would be subject to this act if it had been entered into or created on or after the effective date of this act, and the rights, duties, and interests flowing from the transaction, certificate of title, or record remains valid after the effective date of this act.

(c) This act does not affect an action or proceeding commenced before the effective date of this act.

(d) A security interest that is enforceable immediately before the effective date of this act and would have priority over the rights of a person that becomes a lien creditor at that time is a perfected security interest under this act.

(e) This act does not affect the priority of a security interest in a vehicle if immediately before the effective date of this act the security interest is enforceable and perfected, and that priority is established.

§ 32. Repeals

The following acts and parts of acts are repealed:

[add legislative note]

§ 33. Effective Date

This act takes effect....

†